AMNESTY
INTERNATIONAL
REPORT
1999

This report
covers the period
January to December
1998

Amnesty International is a worldwide voluntary activist movement working towards the observance of all human rights as enshrined in the Universal Declaration of Human Rights and other international standards. It does so by promoting human rights generally as well as taking action against specific abuses of human rights.

Amnesty International seeks to promote the observance of the full range of human rights, which it considers to be indivisible and interdependent, through campaigning and public awareness activities, as well as through human rights education and pushing for ratification and implementation of human rights treaties.

Amnesty International takes action against some of the gravest violations by governments of people's civil and political rights. The focus of its campaigning against human rights violations is to:

- *free all prisoners of conscience.* These are people detained for their political, religious or other conscientiously held beliefs or because of their ethnic origin, sex, colour, language, national or social origin, economic status, birth or other status – who have not used or advocated violence;
- *ensure fair and prompt trials for all political prisoners;*
- *abolish the death penalty, torture and other ill-treatment of prisoners;*
- *end political killings and "disappearances".*

Amnesty International also seeks to support the protection of human rights by other activities, including its work with the United Nations and regional intergovernmental organizations, and its work for refugees, on international military, security and police relations, and on economic and cultural relations.

Amnesty International calls on armed political groups to respect human rights and to halt abuses such as the detention of prisoners of conscience, hostage-taking, torture and unlawful killings.

Amnesty International is independent of any government, political persuasion or religious creed. It does not support or oppose any government or political system, nor does it support or oppose the views of the victims whose rights it seeks to protect. It is concerned solely with the impartial protection of human rights.

Amnesty International seeks to disclose the reality about human rights violations anywhere in the world and to respond quickly and persistently. The organization systematically and impartially researches the facts about individual cases and patterns of human rights abuses. The findings are publicized and members, supporters and staff around the world mobilize public pressure on governments and others with influence to stop the abuses. Activities range from public demonstrations to letter-writing, from human rights education to fundraising concerts, from targeted appeals on a single individual to global campaigns on a specific issue, from approaches to local authorities to presentations at intergovernmental organizations.

Amnesty International is an international human rights movement with more than a million members and supporters in over 140 countries and territories. There are more than 7,500 Amnesty International groups, including local groups, youth or student groups and professional groups, in more than 90 countries and territories throughout the world. To ensure the organization's impartiality and objectivity, Amnesty International members work on specific cases of human rights violations in countries other than their own.

Amnesty International is a democratic, self-governing movement. It is funded largely by its worldwide membership and by donations from the public. No funds are sought or accepted from governments for Amnesty International's work in documenting and campaigning against human rights violations.

AMNESTY INTERNATIONAL REPORT

1999

Amnesty International USA
322 Eighth Avenue
New York, NY 10001
http://www.amnesty.org

First published 1999
by Amnesty International Publications,
1 Easton Street, London WC1X 8DJ, United Kingdom

© Copyright Amnesty International Publications 1999

ISBN: 1 887204 17 2
AI Index: POL 10/01/99
Original language: English

Typesetting and page make-up by:
Accent on Type, 30/31 Great Sutton Street, London EC1V 0NA, United Kingdom

Printed by:
John D. Lucas Printing Co., Baltimore, MD

Cover design:
John Finn, Artworkers

Cover image:
"Death Penalty", donated to Amnesty International by the artist, George Mallelieu

Library of Congress Catalog Number: 99-63294

This report documents Amnesty International's work and its concerns throughout the world during 1998. The absence of an entry in this report on a particular country or territory does not imply that no human rights violations of concern to Amnesty International have taken place there during the year. Nor is the length of a country entry any basis for a comparison of the extent and depth of Amnesty International's concerns in a country. Regional maps have been included in this report to indicate the location of countries and territories cited in the text and for that purpose only. It is not possible on the small scale used to show precise political boundaries. The maps should not be taken as indicating any view on the status of disputed territory. Amnesty International takes no position on territorial questions. Disputed boundaries and cease-fire lines are shown, where possible, by broken lines. Areas whose disputed status is a matter of unresolved concern before the relevant bodies of the United Nations have been indicated by striping only on the maps of the country which has *de facto* control of the area.

CONTENTS

CONTENTS

CONTENTS

APPENDICES

INTRODUCTION

The death penalty: an affront to our humanity

> 'I cannot believe that to defend life and punish the person that kills, the State should in its turn kill. The death penalty is as inhuman as the crime which motivates it.'
> President Eduardo Frei of Chile

Saba Tekle's life ended in terror. She was outside her apartment in Virginia, USA, when a young man she had never met, Dwayne Allen Wright, ordered her at gunpoint to remove her clothes. She began to undress, then tried to flee. Moments later she was dead, shot in the back at close range. She was 33 years old, an Ethiopian who was working in the USA to raise enough money to send for her three children, aged 14, 12 and five, who were still in Ethiopia. All of her family, including her sister who heard her being killed, were devastated. Nine years later her murderer was led to an execution chamber and given a lethal injection. For supporters of the death penalty, justice had been served and the execution was a fitting conclusion to a brutal murder.

Closer examination of the case, however, shows that the "fitting conclusion" of the execution was itself a brutal murder. Dwayne

Charlie and Charles Williams protesting against the death penalty in Houston, USA, in 1998

Wright grew up in extreme poverty in a deprived neighbourhood in Washington DC. From the day he was born he was surrounded by violence – drug-related crime, routine shoot-outs, murder. When he was four, his father was imprisoned, so he was left with his mother who was mentally ill and often without work. When he was 10, his half-brother, whom he worshipped, was murdered. After this, Dwayne developed serious emotional problems. He did poorly at school. He was sent to juvenile detention facilities and to hospital, where he was treated for "major depression with psychotic episodes". His mental capacity was assessed as "borderline retarded", his speech as "retarded". Doctors found signs of organic brain damage.

A month after he turned 17 he went on a two-day violent crime spree, which culminated in the murder of Saba Tekle. He was caught the next day and immediately confessed. Society had failed him throughout his short life. And that same society condemned him to death.

The "fitting conclusion" to his crime demanded by the state took place in Virginia on 14 October 1998. In general, when someone is to be executed by lethal injection in the USA, they know their final moments are approaching when guards unlock the overnight death row cell. The prisoner's clothes are removed. Heart monitoring equipment designed by doctors to save lives, not destroy them, is attached to the prisoner's chest. The prisoner is then given special clothing to wear before being led into the execution chamber, surrounded by officials rather than their friends or family, who are kept under guard in a separate room. The prisoner is strapped to a gurney across the chest, the legs and arms, so they cannot move. A health professional hidden behind a screen verifies that the heart monitoring equipment is working. One or two drips are inserted into a vein. Usually, a few minutes before the poison flows, everyone leaves the chamber, leaving the prisoner alone.

A journalist described what he and relatives saw from the viewing room when Dwayne Wright was executed. The intravenous line wiggled a bit indicating that the first syringe had been inserted, bringing in a chemical that induces unconsciousness. A second wiggle indicated the arrival of a chemical to stop the breathing. "His chest and stomach heaved deeply, again, again, again, again. Then it stopped. A third wiggle from the intravenous tube brought the final dose into the lethal cocktail, a chemical to stop his heart." A few minutes later, Dwayne was declared dead.

How this "fitting conclusion" helped to heal the devastation of Saba Tekle's family is hard to comprehend. What is certain is that real concern about her relatives should have focused on providing material and moral support to help them deal with their tragic loss.

The story of Saba Tekle and Dwayne Wright shows that killing is always abhorrent. The murder of Saba was brutal, shocking and devastating for her family. The state murder of Dwayne was

Superintendent of Hattieville Rehabilitation Centre, Belize, shows how the rope will be used for an execution

brutal, shocking and devastating for his family. Both types of killing have a brutalizing effect on society. Both are wrong.

No solution to crime

Some governments argue that the death penalty is necessary in societies scarred by violent crime. The ultimate punishment is needed, they say, to deter others from committing similar crimes, and to address the feelings of victims of crime and their relatives by offering commensurate retribution.

Such governments are simply abdicating their responsibilities. They should concentrate on eradicating crime by improving policing and addressing the causes of crime. The quick fix "solution" of the death penalty does no more to deter crime than other punishments while doing much to increase the climate of violence. Governments could offer victims of crime and their families financial and other forms of support so their shattered lives can be rebuilt. Instead, some governments bow to popular pressure and focus on retribution, stoking up a climate of vengeance and brutality. Governments could introduce reforms to eradicate poverty, slums and despair. Instead, some governments rely on ill-equipped criminal justice systems to deal with the consequences of despair in the only way they can – by meting out ever harsher punishments.

Recent experience in Kenya has shown that the death penalty does not help to deter crime and can be used to cover up government reluctance to tackle police corruption and poverty. Kiraitu Murungi, a member of parliament, stated in 1994 during a debate on the death penalty that, "We have more violent robberies in the 1990s than in 1975 when we introduced capital punishment for

4

violent robbery. If anything, robbery has increased despite our having capital punishment on our books." By 1998 more than 1,400 people had been sentenced to death for a range of crimes by a Kenyan justice system notorious for its widespread corruption. Many people in Kenya, including Peter Kimanthi, a police spokesman, have admitted that poverty and unemployment cause crime. Yet rather than tackling problems in the police and justice

> **'Every person shall have the right to life. If not, the killer unwittingly achieves a final and perverse moral victory by making the state a killer too, thus reducing social abhorrence at the conscious extinction of human beings.'**
>
> Justice Sachs, South African Constitutional Court, 1995

system or addressing social deprivation, the Kenyan authorities continue to rely on mandatory death sentences for serious crimes, including robbery, often imposed after grossly unfair trials.

Society should not condone the premeditated killing of defenceless people, whatever they have done. If it does, it condemns us all to live in a world where brutality is officially sanctioned, where murderers set the moral tone and where state officials are authorized to shoot, hang, poison or electrocute women and men in cold blood.

The cruelty of executions

The death penalty is not an abstract concept. It involves inflicting severe trauma and injury on a human body to the point where life is extinguished. It means the overpowering of basic human instincts – the will to survive and the desire to help fellow human beings who are in pain. It is a repulsive act which no one should be asked to perform or witness, and which no one should have the power to authorize.

All execution methods are gruesome, and all methods of execution can go wrong. The idea that lethal injection is somehow a "humane" way of killing is nonsense. The condemned still have to suffer the terror of waiting for their preordained moment of death, and the method of killing is not always the clinical and painless process claimed by its proponents. Many such executions have resulted in prolonged deaths, including Guatemala's first execution by lethal injection in February 1998. Manuel Martínez Coronado, an impoverished peasant farmer of indigenous descent, took 18 minutes to die, despite assurances by the authorities that the execution would be painless and "over in 30 seconds". After the execution had begun, there was a power cut, so the lethal injection machine switched off and the chemicals stopped flowing. Witnesses in the observation room also reported that the executioners had trouble finding a vein into which to insert the needle. Human Rights Procurator Julio Arango said: "I think we all have the obligation to tell what happened: his arms

A firing squad in Escuintla City, Guatemala, in September 1996 opens fire on two prisoners, one of whom, Pedro Castillo, does not die...

A soldier walks up to Pedro Castillo and fires at his head at point-blank range, finally killing him. Outrage following the live broadcast on television of the botched execution forces Guatemala's Congress to change the method of execution to lethal injection...

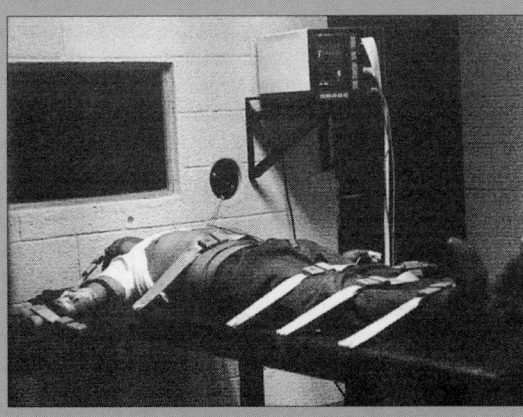

Guatemala's first lethal injection execution, in February 1998, of Manuel Martínez Coronado, is botched. Problems finding a vein for the needle leads to heavy bleeding, and a power cut switches off the flow of lethal chemicals. It takes 18 minutes before Manuel Martínez dies.

Silas Munyagishali was one of 21 men and one woman publicly executed in April by firing squad in Rwanda. He was sentenced to death after an unfair trial in which several defence witnesses were threatened. His arrest may have been politically motivated.

were bleeding heavily." The execution was broadcast live: audiences could hear Manuel Martínez Coronado's three children and their mother sobbing in the observation room as the execution took place.

This execution was an attempt by the authorities to sanitize the method of inducing death. The previous executions, Guatemala's first for 13 years, were carried out in 1996 by firing squad. One of the prisoners was not killed by the first volley of bullets. He may even have heard the order for another shot to be fired at his head to kill him. Public outrage in Guatemala and abroad forced the authorities to end the use of firing squads. A more appropriate response would have been to end the use of capital punishment altogether.

In the USA, several states still use the electric chair. One of the most recent such executions took place in Florida in 1997. Pedro Medino, a Cuban refugee with a history of mental illness, was strapped to a chair that was built in 1924. The chair malfunctioned and the black leather face mask shielding Pedro's terrified face burst into orange and blue flames, filling the death chamber with dense smoke. The power was kept on until he died.

In Afghanistan in 1998 at least five men, convicted of sodomy by Islamic *Shari'a* courts, were placed next to walls and then buried under the rubble as the walls were broken over them. Two of the men did not die until the next day in hospital. One man survived. In the same country people can also be executed by being stoned or hanged from cranes, or by having their throats slit.

These are particularly disturbing examples of executions. But the fact is that once states believe they have the right to execute prisoners, they end up endorsing practices which are akin to torture, whatever method they choose.

Torture is universally condemned and outlawed, including by those who advocate the death penalty. Yet an execution is an extreme, purposeful, physical and mental assault on a person already rendered helpless by the state – the essential elements of torture. If hanging someone by the arms or legs until they scream out in pain is condemned as torture, how should we describe hanging someone by the neck until they are dead? If giving 100 volts of electricity to sensitive parts of the body in order to extract a confession is condemned as torture, how should we describe the administration of 2,000 volts in order to inflict death? If carrying out mock executions is condemned as torture, how should we describe the mental anguish of people who are given years to contemplate being poisoned by lethal injection at the hands of the state?

The truth is that the intervention of a legal process to allow such cruelty does not make it any less painful. The fact that the death penalty is imposed in the name of justice does not mitigate the suffering and humiliation.

In some parts of the world there has been a move towards making executions more public. It is a disturbing trend: it indicates that some governments are losing the sense of shame about what they are doing, and that in some countries people are becoming inured to brutality and death.

A public execution in Tabarjah, Lebanon, May 1998

8

International bodies have condemned public executions. In 1996 the United Nations (UN) Human Rights Committee stated that public executions are "incompatible with human dignity". Yet in various parts of the world, governments allow – even invite – the public to witness executions. In Saudi Arabia, executions are routinely carried out in public. In the case of migrant workers, relatives may not even know that an execution is happening, yet the general public is there to watch the final moments of their loved ones. Elsewhere, public executions are a recent development. In Rwanda, for instance, 21 men and a woman were executed by firing squad on 24 April 1998 for participating in the genocide of 1994. The executions were staged in front of large crowds which included scores of children.

An unjust justice

The death penalty is always an unjust method of justice. It is applied unfairly – death row cells are filled with people from impoverished and ethnic minority backgrounds, those least able to defend themselves in court. Millionaires are rarely found among them. The death penalty is applied arbitrarily, depending on such random factors as the competence of lawyers, plea bargaining or pardons granted to mark the birthdays of rulers. Whether someone lives or dies can be a lottery. And the death penalty always carries the risk of ending the lives of people innocent of any crime, either because it is used as a political tool to silence government opponents for good, or because of inevitable miscarriages of justice.

Amnesty International's major campaign against human rights violations in the USA in 1998 highlighted the way race continues to play a major part in the application of the death penalty in the country. The race of the victim and that of the defendant seem to play a significant role in determining whether or not someone is sentenced to death. The number of black and white people who are murdered in the USA is almost equal, yet 82 per cent of prisoners executed since 1977 were convicted of the murder of a white person. Black people make up just 12 per cent of the country's population, but 42 per cent of those on death row. Nationwide studies have consistently found that other factors, such as the severity of the crime and the background of the defendant, cannot explain such disparities.

In countries where the death penalty is mandatory for murder, such as Trinidad and Tobago, courts cannot take into account any mitigating factors, including the particular discrimination and violence faced by women. In September 1998 the UN Special Rapporteur on extrajudicial, summary or arbitrary executions appealed to Trinidad and Tobago not to execute Indravani Pamela Ramjattan, who was sentenced to death for the murder of her abusive common-law husband in 1995. Indravani Pamela Ramjattan had suffered years of violent abuse at his hands. Days before the murder, she ran away. Her husband tracked her down and brought her back to his home where for days he reportedly beat her viciously and repeatedly threatened to kill her. Indravani Pamela Ramjattan was sentenced to death along with two men who came to rescue her. The Special Rapporteur expressed her concern that the abuse and extreme violence suffered by Indravani Pamela Ramjattan – including beatings, threats to shoot her and repeated rapes – had not been considered by the investigating authorities or the courts to constitute mitigating circumstances. The Special Rapporteur stated that the death penalty was too harsh a punishment for crimes committed in such situations. Indravani Pamela Ramjattan remained in prison under sentence of death at the end of the year.

Many governments still use the death penalty to terrorize their opponents. In 1998, three years after the execution in Nigeria of Ken Saro-Wiwa and eight other Ogoni for political reasons provoked widespread condemnation, people still faced political trials for capital offences. In April former Deputy Head of State General Oladipo Diya and five others were sentenced to death after secret and grossly unfair trials. The sentences were commuted later in the year after the Head of State died.

In Iran, Ruhollah Rawhani, a member of the Baha'i religious minority, was executed in July 1998. He had been arrested with two other men and convicted of being involved in the conversion of a Muslim woman to the Baha'i faith, even though she stated that she had been raised as a Baha'i by her parents. His two co-defendants – Sirus Dhabihi-Muqaddam and Hedayatollah Kashifi-Najafabadi – remained in danger of execution at the end of 1998.

Every year tireless campaigns by relatives and friends of those condemned to death expose miscarriages of justice, some of which succeed after it is too late to save the life of their loved one.

> **'I have full sympathy for the families of the victims of murder and other crimes but I do not accept that one death justifies another.'**
> Mary Robinson, UN High Commissioner for Human Rights, following the execution of Karla Faye Tucker in the USA, February 1998

In the United Kingdom (UK) in 1998 alone, the courts overturned two convictions which had led to executions in the 1950s, before the death penalty was abolished. In February the Court of Appeal in London quashed the conviction of Mahmood Hussein Mattan, a Somali seaman who had been hanged for murder in Cardiff, Wales, 46 years earlier. The appeal judge in the case, Lord Justice G.H. Rose, said during his ruling that capital punishment was not a "prudent culmination for a criminal justice system which is human and therefore fallible". For more than 40 years relatives of Derek Bentley, a 19-year-old epileptic with a mental age of 11, fought to prove that he was innocent of the crime for which he was hanged in 1952. The campaign, which suffered numerous defeats and humiliation at the hands of the courts, was led by Derek

Bentley's sister Iris, who died in 1997 still demanding justice for her family which had been so devastated by the execution. When Derek Bentley's conviction was finally quashed in July 1998, the only surviving member of his family was his niece.

Such cases highlight an essential fault of the death penalty – that it is irrevocable. Mistakes cannot be rectified, death cannot be reversed. Yet mistakes are inevitable in all systems of justice, however scrupulous the process and however honest the participants.

A further problem is that around the world it is not just that inadvertent mistakes are made or that a few corrupt police officers pervert the course of justice. Often, international standards to ensure fair trial are routinely flouted in capital cases.

Prisoners facing death sentences are often represented by inexperienced lawyers, by lawyers appointed for political reasons by the state, or even by no lawyer at all. Defendants may not understand the charges or evidence against them, particularly if the proceedings are in a language they do not know. Sometimes they are denied the right to appeal to a court of higher jurisdiction or to petition for clemency. Some prisoners are tried before special courts lacking elementary safeguards. As a result, many prisoners each year are condemned to death after unfair trials, some of which are a travesty of justice.

Maqsood Ahmed was executed in February 1998 in Pakistan. He had been arrested in May 1989 and sentenced to death for shooting a man during a robbery. The execution went ahead despite the fact that two other men had confessed to the murder and that the Superintendent of Police had stated that Maqsood Ahmed was in police custody at the time of the murder. His lawyer called the execution a "murder of justice".

In October 1998, 24 soldiers were executed in Sierra Leone, a week after they were convicted of offences related to a military coup in May 1997. The soldiers were tried by court martial and had no right of appeal against their convictions and sentences to a higher jurisdiction.

Narrowing the scope of the death penalty

Fortunately, the world is increasingly rejecting the legitimacy of the death penalty. One indication is the growing consensus that the death penalty should not apply to certain types of people, such as juvenile offenders, the elderly and the mentally ill. There is support for these exemptions even in countries where the public and state officials favour the use of the death penalty.

The exclusion of juvenile offenders – those under 18 years old at the time of the offence – is now so widely accepted in law and practice that it is approaching the status of a norm of customary international law. The International Covenant on Civil and Political Rights (ICCPR – Article 6(5)) and other major human rights instruments prohibit sentencing juvenile offenders to death. More recently, the same prohibition was set out in the UN Convention

Maria Bentley-Dingwall, the niece of Derek Bentley (inset), celebrates outside the court in London, UK, which finally quashed his conviction 46 years after he was executed

© Hex

© Russell Boyce/Reuters

on the Rights of the Child, which has been ratified by all UN member states except Somalia and the USA. The very few states that do put to death juvenile offenders provoke widespread condemnation.

Since 1990 Amnesty International has documented 18 executions of juvenile offenders worldwide, carried out in six countries – Iran, Nigeria, Pakistan, Saudi Arabia, the USA and Yemen. Nine of these were carried out in the USA, the only country known to have executed juvenile offenders in 1998. Two of these cases highlight the particularly disturbing nature of executions of young offenders (see page12).

International standards also hold that the mentally ill should be excluded from the death penalty. UN Safeguards approved in 1984 by the Economic and Social Council (ECOSOC) guaranteeing protection of the rights of those facing the death penalty ("ECOSOC Safeguards") state that executions shall not be carried out on "persons who have become insane". In 1989 ECOSOC recommended that UN member states should eliminate the death penalty "for persons suffering from mental retardation or extremely limited mental competence, whether at the stage of sentence or execution". Sadly, these exclusions have been ignored in some countries, including the USA (see page12).

International standards have established that in countries which have yet to abolish it, the death penalty should be used only for the most serious crimes. The "ECOSOC Safeguards" state that the scope of these crimes "should not go beyond intentional crimes with lethal or other extremely grave consequences". In a few countries,

'I want people to know I have repented for what I have done, and if I could do something, anything, to change what has been, I would... I am very ashamed to die this way.'
Joseph Cannon

'I'm going to a better place. I hope the victim's family will forgive me, because I didn't mean to hurt or kill no one.'
Robert Carter

Opponents of the death penalty in front of the US embassy in Rome, Italy, protest against the planned execution of Joseph Cannon

Joseph John Cannon and Robert Anthony Carter were executed in Texas within 27 days of each other for crimes committed when they were 17 years old. Both their childhoods were marked by serious abuse and deprivation. Both suffered from brain damage and limited intelligence. When they were put to death in 1998, many years after their crimes, the hopes raised by their efforts towards rehabilitation were extinguished. Joseph Cannon was led to the lethal injection chamber on 22 April. The first attempt to kill him failed when the needle "blew out of his arm" as the lethal solution began to flow. His mother collapsed and all the observers were led away while the needle was reinserted. Robert Carter was executed on 18 May: the jury which sentenced him to die was unaware that he had been severely abused as a child and was brain damaged.

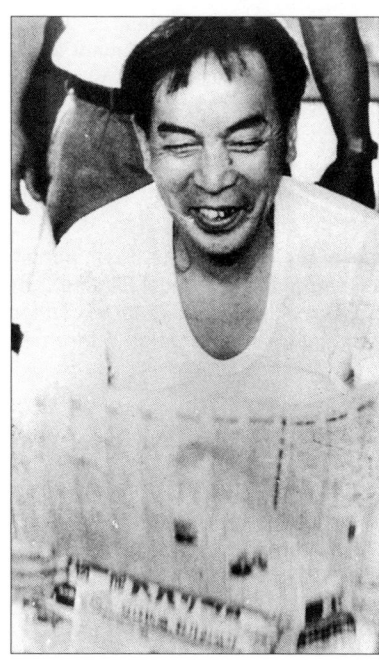

Sakae Menda, acquitted in 1983 after spending 34 years under sentence of death in Japan. Since his acquittal he has campaigned against the death penalty.

however, people face execution for a wide range of offences which pose no threat to life, including crimes against property and peaceful political activities. In China, for example, the death penalty continues to be applied for a wide variety of violent and non-violent crimes, including tax fraud, counterfeiting, embezzlement and corruption. In June 1998 Luo Feng, a manager in the Beijing Xiwang Computer Company, was sentenced to death for embezzlement, accepting bribes and using company funds to "play the stock market", despite an apparent lack of coherent evidence.

In Myanmar, six political prisoners – Ko Thein, Naing Aung, Thant Zaw Swe, Myint Han, Khin Hlaing and Let Yar Htun – were sentenced to death in 1998. Two of them are members of the non-violent National League for Democracy, led by Nobel Peace Prize winner Daw Aung San Suu Kyi. Myanmar's military government claimed that four of the six were members of the All Burma Students' Democratic Front (ABSDF), an opposition group established in exile predominantly by former students who fled Myanmar after the 1988 pro-democracy movement was suppressed by the military. The six men were among a group of 39 people arrested in connection with an alleged anti-government "plot". The ABSDF stated that none of the 39 people arrested was given legal representation during their trial at a special court inside Insein Prison.

Campaigning against the death penalty

Among those campaigning against the death penalty are some of the very people that capital punishment is supposed to help –

14

victims of crime and their relatives. In the face of increasing evidence that capital punishment does not act as a deterrent against crime more effectively than other forms of punishment, proponents of the death penalty have increasingly claimed that it is needed to help the process of recovery of murder victims' families. It is true that some relatives of murder victims do find consolation in such retribution. But many others do not. Some relatives

> 'Before, my views on the death penalty and executions were just the same as any typical Filipino... they [criminals] deserve to die. But all of my views on executions changed when I was given the chance to watch a forum hosted by the Philippine Journey of Hope.'
> A student at Siena College, the Philippines

have reported that the execution of the murderer makes it more difficult to come to terms with their loss.

In the USA, for example, a small but growing number of relatives of murder victims are speaking out against the death penalty, saying that it offers no solution to their personal tragedies. In 1998 a delegation from the US group Journey of Hope... From Violence to Healing went to the Philippines to raise awareness of the arguments against the death penalty at a time when the Philippine government was considering ending the moratorium on executions. The trip was organized by a coalition of local non-governmental organizations, including the Free Legal Assistance Group and Amnesty International's Philippine Section. The delegation visited prisoners on death row and their families, gave numerous media interviews, took part in live radio and television debates, met religious and other officials, and held lively discussions with anti-crime groups which advocate the death penalty. Many people who had favoured the death penalty said they felt compelled to change their minds after coming into contact with the delegation. Unfortunately, at the end of the year the government announced

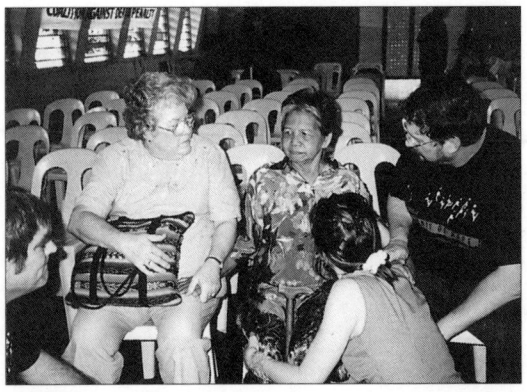

A delegation from the US group, Journey of Hope... From Violence to Healing, who visited the Philippines in 1998 to campaign against a proposed resumption of executions in the country, consoles the mother of Leo Echegaray, who was under sentence of death

that executions would resume in the Philippines in early 1999. More than 800 people were under sentence of death in the country.

Countless other human rights defenders and other activists also campaign against the death penalty, by promoting the arguments against the punishment and by appealing on behalf of people under sentence of death or in imminent danger of execution, calling for clemency, pardon, commutation or retrial. Each year such appeals result in the threat of execution being lifted.

For example, in India it was learned during 1998 that the death sentences against Gantela Vijayavardhana Rao and Satuluri Chalapathi Rao had been commuted to life imprisonment by the President of India. Amnesty International had joined local non-governmental organizations in appealing on the men's behalf since they were sentenced to death in September 1995 for murder committed in 1993. In Pakistan, Roop Lal, who had been held in a death cell in solitary confinement for 25 years in Sahiwal Central Jail, had his death sentence commuted to life imprisonment. In Belarus the Supreme Court upheld F. Verega's appeal and commuted the death sentence imposed on him in June 1997 for murder to 15 years' imprisonment. In the United Arab Emirates it was reported that the Dubai Supreme Court had referred the cases of Rabi' Ghassan Taraf and Ryan Dominic Mahoney back to the appeals court for a retrial. The two men had been convicted of drugs-related charges and sentenced to death in November 1997.

The efforts of campaigners have not only saved lives. They have also contributed to a moral and political climate in many countries which has resulted in the permanent abolition of the death penalty.

The march towards worldwide abolition
Every year more countries abolish the death penalty. Recently, the pace of abolition has been especially remarkable.

STOPPING EXECUTIONS WORLDWIDE

Each year the vast majority of executions worldwide are carried out in a tiny handful of countries. In 1998 more than 80 per cent of all known executions took place in China, the Democratic Republic of the Congo (DRC), the USA and Iran. In China, 1,067 people were known to have been executed, although the true figure was believed to be much higher. More than 100 executions were carried out in the DRC. Sixty-eight people were executed in the USA. In Iran, 66 executions were reported, but the total was believed to have been higher. In addition, hundreds of executions were reported in Iraq, although Amnesty International was unable to confirm most of the reports.

If these five countries heeded the UN call for a moratorium on executions, most executions in the world would immediately stop and other retentionist countries would find themselves under intense pressure to follow suit. These countries should be shamed into action against the death penalty so the world can be freed from the shame of executions.

16

In 1899, on the eve of the 20th century, only three states had permanently abolished the death penalty for all crimes – Costa Rica, San Marino and Venezuela. When the Universal Declaration of Human Rights was adopted in 1948, the number stood at eight. By the end of 1978 it had risen to 19. During the past 20 years the number has almost tripled. In 1998 the trend continued, with Azerbaijan, Bulgaria, Canada, Estonia and Lithuania abolishing the death penalty for all crimes. In addition, the Russian Minister of Justice stated that the Russian Federation would abolish the death penalty by April 1999.

By the end of 1998, 67 countries had abolished the death penalty for all offences and 14 for all but exceptional offences, such as wartime crimes. At least 24 countries which retained the death penalty in law were considered abolitionist in practice, in that they had not executed anyone for at least 10 years or had made an international commitment not to carry out executions. Some countries reduced the scope of the death penalty. For example, in Tajikistan the number of crimes carrying a possible death sentence was reduced in 1998 from 44 to 15.

International treaties to abolish the death penalty altogether continue to attract new states parties. During 1998, Belgium, Costa Rica, Liechtenstein and Nepal became parties to the Second Optional Protocol to the ICCPR, aiming at the abolition of the death penalty, bringing the number of states parties to 35. Belgium, Estonia and Greece ratified Protocol No. 6 to the European Convention for the Protection of Human Rights and Fundamental Freedoms (European Convention on Human Rights) concerning the abolition of the death penalty, bringing the number of states parties to 30. Costa Rica and Ecuador ratified the Protocol to the American Convention on Human Rights to Abolish the Death Penalty, bringing the number of states parties to six. A number of other countries had signed one or another of the protocols, indicating their intention to become parties at a later date.

In April the UN Commission on Human Rights adopted resolution 1998/8 calling on all states that maintain the punishment "to establish a moratorium on executions, with a view to completely abolishing the death penalty". The resolution was co-sponsored by 66 states, a marked increase over the 47 states which co-sponsored a similar resolution at the Commission on Human Rights in 1997. In response, 51 other states circulated a statement at the UN Economic and Social Council dissociating themselves from the resolution.

While over 90 countries can still be said to retain and use the death penalty, the number of countries which actually execute prisoners in any one year is much smaller. During 1998, at least 1,625 prisoners were executed in 37 countries and 3,899 people were sentenced to death in 78 countries. These figures include only cases known to Amnesty International; the true figures are certainly higher. As in previous years, a small number of countries accounted for the great majority of executions.

ROUTE TO ABOLITION

Events in Azerbaijan, which abolished the death penalty in 1998, show how abolition can be achieved.

October 1993	Heidar Aliyev is elected President and a *de facto* moratorium on executions is imposed. However, death sentences continue to be handed down – at least 144 people are sentenced to death between 1993 and 1998.
October 1994	The death penalty is abolished for women.
November 1995	A new Constitution is adopted which retains the death penalty as "an exceptional measure of punishment until its complete abolition... only for especially serious crimes against the state, and against the life and health of an individual".
May 1996	The death penalty is abolished for men over 65 years old. The number of offences punishable by death is reduced from 33 to 12.
August 1997	The Chairman of the Supreme Court publicly expresses his support for the abolition of the death penalty.
January 1998	President Aliyev announces: "I believe that strengthening the struggle against crime in itself will reduce the number of criminal actions. At the same time humanization of our policy and punishment will also create among the people a healthy attitude towards violations and crimes."
February 1998	Parliament agrees by 104 votes to three to adopt the President's proposal to abolish the death penalty. The death penalty is abolished.

A few countries took steps to expand the scope of the death penalty or to speed up or resume executions. In January 1998 Jamaica's withdrawal from the (first) Optional Protocol to the ICCPR came into effect. This unprecedented step, which the Jamaican government took in order to speed up executions, has deprived anyone who believes that their human rights guaranteed under the ICCPR have been violated by the Jamaican authorities of the right to petition the UN Human Rights Committee. In August Trinidad and Tobago's withdrawal from the (first) Optional Protocol to the ICCPR came into effect along with its reaccession to it with a reservation that attempts to prevent anyone under sentence

18

Prison officers attach the execution notices of Trevor Fisher and Richard Woods at the Fox Hill Prison in Nassau, Bahamas. The two men were hanged in October.

of death from petitioning the UN Human Rights Committee. In November the parliament in Guyana voted to take a similar course of action.

In the Bahamas Trevor Fisher and Richard Woods were executed while their petitions to the Inter-American Commission on Human Rights (IACHR) were still pending. The IACHR had told the Bahamian government that it would issue its conclusions on the petitions within two weeks and asked the government to suspend the two men's death sentences at least until it had issued its decisions. The European Union made a similar request. However, the government ignored the requests and the two men were hanged in October. More than 190 people were on death row at the end of the year in the 13 English-speaking Caribbean countries and territories which retain the death penalty.

In Yemen, a presidential decree calling for the death penalty to be imposed on "anyone who leads a band of kidnappers or bandits or who loots public or private property" and their "partners in crime" was published in August and came into immediate effect. Execution in Yemen is by firing squad. In Gaza the Palestinian Authority carried out its first executions in 1998: two brothers were executed in August by firing squad after a military court sentenced them to death for murder committed two days previously following a summary and unjust trial.

In Japan, three men were executed about three weeks after the UN Human Rights Committee called on Japan to take measures towards abolishing the death penalty. This was the second time in five years that Japan had responded in this way to the UN Human

Rights Committee's recommendations in light of Japan's periodic report. In Taiwan, the trend of an increasing number of executions continued: in 1998 at least 32 people were known to have been executed. Egypt and the DRC also saw an increasing number of executions during the year.

Despite such developments, growing international opposition to the death penalty was symbolized in 1998 with the adoption in July of the Statute of the International Criminal Court. After much debate, it was decided to exclude the death penalty as punishment for what are arguably the most heinous crimes of all – genocide, other crimes against humanity and war crimes. The clear implication is that if the death penalty should not be used for the worst possible crimes, then it should not be used for lesser crimes. In other words, it should never be used.

Worldwide abolition now

Amnesty International, along with other abolitionist organizations, is calling for a permanent end to all executions in the year 2000. We believe this is both justified and achievable.

Our confidence is based on two trends that are reflected in this annual survey of human rights worldwide. The first is the inexorable momentum towards worldwide abolition of the death penalty, reflected in the UN Commission on Human Rights' call for a moratorium. The second is the growing number of people around the world who are campaigning for human rights.

More than 12 million people around the world have promised to do everything in their power to uphold the rights spelled out in the Universal Declaration of Human Rights (UDHR), including the right to life, showing the overwhelming support for fundamental human rights. Amnesty International's campaign to celebrate the 50 years of the UDHR has gained the support of ordinary people in all regions as well as of many government officials, police officers and others in positions of power.

An end to executions is an essential part of the struggle for human rights and it can be realized. Every state has the power not to carry out executions. The argument that the death penalty is needed to deter crime has been discredited by the consistent lack of scientific evidence that it acts as a deterrent more effectively than other punishments. Moreover, the death penalty negates the internationally accepted goal of rehabilitating offenders. In short, there is no penological justification for the death penalty which outweighs the human rights grounds for abolishing it.

It can take courage to call for abolition of the death penalty. Politicians may face enormous pressure from members of the public who are clamouring for action on crime. Human rights activists may face abuse for seeming to ignore the suffering of victims of crime. But the prize is worth fighting for. The death penalty not only violates fundamental human rights, it also carries the official message that killing is an appropriate response to killing. It brutalizes, it contributes to desensitizing the public to violence and it can engender an increasing toleration of other human rights abuses.

Public acceptance of abolition can be won. The way people think and behave changes over time, often after long battles and heated debates. Injustices that were the norm in earlier centuries are outlawed today. Injustices that were reluctantly accepted as inevitable by our forebears have been fought against by their descendants and overcome. Museums display thumbscrews and racks, guillotines and garrottes – instruments of torture and death once commonly in use but now serving as reminders of a cruel and distant past. Our aim is to relegate electric chairs, nooses, the guns of firing squads and lethal injections to museums, where future generations will wonder how any society could ever have sanctioned their use.

It is not by chance that for the past two decades an average of two countries a year have abolished the death penalty. Such reforms have come about because human rights defenders, lawyers, members of parliament and a vast range of grassroots activists have worked to stop executions. Sooner or later the world's governments will accept that executing people in cold blood violates fundamental human rights and serves no legitimate penal purpose. So why wait? What better way to herald a new age for humanity than for all governments to abandon the death penalty for ever?

Campaigning for universal human rights

> 'This is a day when the people have spoken, and they have spoken as one. This is a day when they have put our conscience on notice.'
>
> UN Secretary-General Kofi Annan, receiving millions of pledges to support the Universal Declaration of Human Rights, December 1998

Thirteen million people in 124 countries promised to do everything in their power to "ensure that the rights contained in the Universal Declaration of Human Rights become a reality around the world" as part of Amnesty International's year-long mass educational drive. Their personal pledges were handed over to the Secretary-General of the UN, Kofi Annan, at the Palais de Chaillot in Paris, France – the historic public building in which the UN had adopted the Universal Declaration 50 years earlier, on 10 December 1948.

On a purpose-built stage more than a million pledges were displayed – it proved impossible to feature all the pledges in the form of "the world's biggest book" because the floor simply was not strong enough to take their weight. At the same time, in a globally coordinated event, Amnesty International representatives handed over pledges to UN officials in more than 20 countries.

Pierre Sané (*left*), Amnesty International's Secretary General, hands over millions of pledges of support for the Universal Declaration of Human Rights to the UN Secretary-General, Kofi Annan.

"These pledges, signed by so many people from all walks of life in so many countries not only show powerful global support for the Universal Declaration, but a demand to governments that they live up to the promise they made when adopting it – a world without cruelty and injustice," said Pierre Sané, Secretary General of Amnesty International.

Nobel Laureate and leader of the Burmese opposition Daw Aung San Suu Kyi had been the first person to sign the pledge at the start of the campaign in December 1997. She was followed by UN High Commissioner for Human Rights Mary Robinson and politicians including Yasser Arafat, Tony Blair, Rafael Caldera, Jacques Chirac, Bill Clinton, Kim Dae-jung, Václav Havel, Yoweri Museveni, Lech Walesa, Ezer Weizmann and Abderrahmane Youssoufi; human rights defenders including the Mothers of the Plaza de Mayo from Argentina, Danielle Mitterrand and Graça Machel; religious leaders including His Holiness the Dalai Lama and Archbishop Desmond Tutu; entertainers including U2, Annie Lennox, Mick Jagger, Courtney Love, Nour Sharif, Harrison Ford and Julia Roberts; and sports personalities such as Muhammad Ali, Brian Lara and the national football teams of South Africa, France and the Netherlands.

Alongside the well-known names, millions of ordinary people – teachers, schoolchildren, trade unionists, police and army officers – signed the pledge either in one of the 35,000 books distributed worldwide by Amnesty International or electronically through several specially created web sites. One million people, almost one third of the total population of Ireland signed, and more than 600,000 pledges were obtained in Tanzania. One million signatures were gathered from all parts of Morocco.

Every Amnesty International section took part in the campaign; there is no room here to describe even a small proportion of their imaginative and innovative activities. In Ramallah, under the control of the Palestinian Authority, Palestinian Amnesty International members took part in a cultural festival in August; in Turkey, trees were planted in a central area of Istanbul in remembrance of the "disappeared" and as a living reminder of the importance of the right to life. In Morocco members held a human rights film festival in Casablanca in June.

The Body Shop was one of several commercial companies to join forces with Amnesty International in the campaign. In an initiative called "Make Your Mark", customers at Body Shop stores in 34 countries contributed three million thumbprints to the campaign pledge, which were turned into portraits of human rights defenders. In the Netherlands, the television company AVRO worked with the Dutch Section of Amnesty International to collect more than three million signatures. Another television company, MTV, collected signatures from entertainers who visited its broadcasting studios around the world and *Al Jazira*, Qatar's satellite television station, promoted the campaign in the Middle East.

In Mongolia, members of the police and army sign pledges to support the Universal Declaration of Human Rights at a human rights training workshop organized by Amnesty International members

This landmark campaign aimed not only to publicize the relevance of the Universal Declaration, but also to forge a stronger and more dynamic human rights movement. The protection of human rights defenders was therefore a key campaign goal. Twenty-eight individual appeal cases were circulated. Conditions improved for many of them and two were released from jail during the year – Dr Beko Ransome-Kuti from Nigeria and Akhtam Nu'aysa from Syria. Countless letters, faxes and e-mails were sent to government leaders, local officials and prison governors demanding an end to persecution, harassment and ill-treatment of the defenders.

More than 350 human rights defenders from over 100 countries were brought together in an unprecedented four-day Human Rights Defenders Summit held in Paris in December. At its final session on 10 December, the Summit adopted the "Paris Declaration", which challenges governments to bring their actions into line with their speeches commemorating the Universal Declaration.

Organized by four non-governmental organizations (NGOs) – Amnesty International, the *Fédération Internationale des Ligues des Droits de l'Homme* (International Federation of Human Rights Leagues), *France Libertés* and *ATD Quart-Monde* – this largest ever working summit of human rights defenders built on regional conferences that had been held in Colombia, Côte d'Ivoire, South

Africa, Tanzania, Zimbabwe and Morocco, and prompted an extraordinarily fertile exchange of experiences and ideas. Practical suggestions on dealing with issues such as impunity, extreme poverty, children, armed conflict and racism were exchanged between men and women from all regions, from organizations large and small, national and local, broadly based or tightly focused, united only by their dedication to defending the rights of others.

Participants included Nobel Prize winners the Dalai Lama, José Ramos Horta and Rigoberta Menchú, internationally renowned defenders such as the Chinese dissident Wei Jingsheng and activists in the US civil rights struggle such as Angela Davis. A minute of silence was observed in honour of the many human rights defenders unable to come to Paris, those imprisoned or killed for their work. The silence was broken by a video message from Daw Aung Sun Suu Kyi, under house arrest in Myanmar. Another defender unable to attend was Aref Mohamed Aref, whose passport was confiscated at the airport in Djibouti before he could board a plane for Paris. Hafez Abu Sa'ada, Secretary General of the Egyptian Organization for Human Rights was able to attend, but only after international protests had secured his release from prison. He had been arrested on 1 December because of his human rights work.

The defenders said that their presence in Paris was a recognition of what had been achieved in the human rights struggle over the last 50 years, but deplored the fact that they have become targets and victims of repression which makes it harder for them to operate.

The Paris Declaration was read out by Salima Ghezali, editor of a banned Algerian newspaper, who is also a tireless defender of the victims of the continuing tragedy in her country. It strongly reaffirmed the indivisibility of human rights and attacked economic and social insecurity which leads to extreme poverty and exclusion.

During the Summit came news that one of the obstacles to the extradition of former Chilean President Augusto Pinochet from the United Kingdom (UK) had been cleared. The UK Home Secretary had ordered that the application for Augusto Pinochet's extradition to stand trial for human rights crimes committed during his time in power should proceed. The announcement was greeted by the hundreds of defenders at the Summit with excitement and tears of joy. Huddled around the Chilean delegates and Fabiola Letelier, sister of one of the victims, the defenders celebrated what should open a new era in the fight against impunity.

Making a difference: 'I am alive and free'

Global campaigning initiatives by Amnesty International's members and supporters go hand in hand with activists' tireless work on behalf of the individual victims of human rights violations. Their efforts make a difference. "I cannot tell you how wonderful it feels to be free again," wrote journalist Chris Anyanwu from

Nigeria after her release in June. "It is impossible to paint an accurate picture of the actions and reactions as I sat in that tiny cell, the floor carpeted with cards and envelopes. It was deeply touching, greatly encouraging and strengthening."

Kim Song-man, a South Korean released from prison in August, said: "Thank you. I am alive and free. I was in prison for 13 years and on death row for two years. I didn't know whether or not I would die. Sometimes it was exhausting and sometimes lonely, but Amnesty International's work consoled and encouraged me."

These two were among 20 prisoners who were freed during 1998 whose cases had been featured in the *Amnesty International News* monthly "Worldwide Appeals" – selected from the more than 5,000 cases currently being worked on by Amnesty International members. Individuals and groups around the world used the information in the "Worldwide Appeals" to send letters, faxes and e-mails on behalf of those unable to speak for themselves.

Another such prisoner was Fray Antonio Puigjané, the one remaining prisoner of conscience in Argentina, who was listening to the radio in his cell at the end of May 1998 when he suddenly heard it give out the chant: "Free Fray Antonio Puigjané! Free Fray Antonio Puigjané!" The radio station was transmitting live from Madrid, Spain, where scores of Amnesty International members had gathered around the Argentine embassy, shouting and demonstrating for his release. In June, on the day before his 70th birthday, Fray Antonio Puigjané was released from jail and transferred to a convent where he remains under house arrest.

"We will not stop now, even if they shoot us, until we know where our children are." Mothers of the "disappeared" in Algeria visiting Amnesty International's International Secretariat talk about their campaign to find out what has happened to their missing relatives.

Amnesty International delegates and section directors visiting Israel and areas under the control of the Palestinian Authority at the end of April were privileged to join in the excitement and joy of Palestinians released from administrative detention. They joined in a celebration in Ramallah which united the former detainees, their families and Palestinian and Israeli NGOs who had worked on their behalf. However, more than 120 people remained in administrative detention, and Amnesty International members committed themselves to continuing the struggle for their release and an end to the system of administrative detention.

Imagination, coordination and determination were the hallmarks of a campaign to win the release of Mariana Cetiner, a prisoner of conscience in Romania sentenced to three years' imprisonment because of her homosexuality. Amnesty International's gay, lesbian, bisexual and transgender network, together with local groups, wrote letters, organized demonstrations outside Romanian embassies around the world and generated a huge amount of publicity. "Love is a basic human right" read banners held by members of Amnesty International Argentina. In Australia, Amnesty International members held a vigil outside Melbourne Town Hall and presented a one-metre-high letter to the public for signatures seeking Mariana's release. Amnesty International Sweden created a web page about the case. Mariana Cetiner was released in March, and, with the help of a German group which had worked for her release, travelled to Germany for treatment at a centre for the victims of torture, following the abuses she had suffered in prison.

Many of these prisoners were the subject of Action Files, long-term human rights campaigning assignments given to local Amnesty International groups. A single group or a few groups in different countries work for the release of a prisoner of conscience, or for a victim of torture, or on any other concern within Amnesty International's mandate. In a further development of this mechanism, groups in several countries are forging links with a children's centre in Bosnia-Herzegovina, run by a Bosnian NGO called *Zemljia Djece*, Land of the Children. Working with children displaced from Srebrenica and now resettled in the Tuzla region, the centre provides the only opportunity for these young people to expand their horizons, to develop new skills, or simply to enjoy themselves in a supportive environment.

Action Files may last for many years, often until the case is resolved. There are currently more than 1,500 active Action Files, which together with shorter term Regional Action Network actions, name more than 4,000 victims of human rights violations.

While many Amnesty International activists work on long-term cases which may require sustained efforts over a number of years, participants in the Urgent Action network respond to an immediate risk. Urgent Actions are initiated whenever speedy action is required to protect anyone, anywhere in the world, from abuse of the human rights covered in Amnesty International's mandate.

Thousands of activists send urgent messages from every corner of the globe in response to such emergencies. During 1998, 425 such actions were launched.

In many cases, positive outcomes were achieved. For example, in November 1998 a Somali asylum-seeker was due to be deported from Australia back to Somalia, where he would be at risk of grave human rights abuses. The day before his scheduled deportation, Amnesty International issued an Urgent Action. Appeals flooded in by e-mail and fax as government and security officials took him to a plane in a restraining belt and forced him to board a flight to Mogadishu. During a stopover in Perth, he was given a last-minute reprieve and permission to stay in Australia temporarily, following interventions not only by Amnesty International but also the UN Committee against Torture, Australian members of parliament and an Australian transport union, which took action to prevent the man's connecting flight leaving Perth.

USA campaign: Rights for All

The USA has long seen itself as the champion of the rights and freedoms of the individual. But for many the USA has failed to deliver the promise of rights for all. Across the USA people have been injured and killed by police using excessive force or deliberately brutal treatment. In many prisons and jails inmates have been tortured or ill-treated. Asylum-seekers are detained indefinitely in conditions that are sometimes inhuman and degrading. More than 500 people have been executed since 1997, some for crimes committed when they were less than 18 years old.

Human rights are universal and indivisible; all human rights should be enjoyed by everyone, whatever their position in society, their racial or ethnic origin, their sexual orientation or their level of income. This fundamental and unshakeable belief led to

Members of Amnesty International UK, in London, call for Augusto Pinochet, former President of Chile, not to be granted immunity from prosecution for human rights crimes.

the launch of Amnesty International's year-long campaign against human rights violations in the USA.

The "USA: Rights for All" campaign presented a major challenge to the movement. It sought to puncture the widespread complacency on domestic human rights issues in a country which prides itself on its democracy, individual freedom and its political and legal equality; it had to build collaboration between Amnesty International members in the USA and around the world with the thousands of other organizations in the country promoting a broad range of human rights issues; and it sought to effect some positive improvements in the human rights situation.

Amnesty International sections around the world took on the challenge. They gained widespread press coverage, both in newspapers and on radio and television. "I'd like to share our happiness with the media coverage we had this day ... it is really unbelievable how interested the media is in a campaign on the USA", reported a Dutch section member. In Pakistan, there was coverage in languages including Urdu and Sindhi. In Finland – where a group built a "jailed Statue of Liberty" to publicize the campaign – the largest daily newspaper published front-page articles two days running. Sections organized visits to their own government officials and to US embassies to press their case. Several sections reported that US embassy officials had been unusually willing to talk to them – in Japan, for example, the US embassy contacted the section asking for a meeting to discuss Amnesty International's work.

Media coverage on television and radio in the USA, as well as in the vast array of US national and local newspapers and journals, was excellent, with many publicizing the powerful stories told by human rights victims. For example, former prisoner Warnice Robinson described how she had to give birth to her baby daughter in shackles, and how the experience had degraded her.

An early success in the efforts to prevent such inhumane treatment came in November, when Detroit City Council passed a resolution calling on the State of Michigan to ban the use of restraints on pregnant women before and during labour:

> "We call upon the State of Michigan to provide for the swift punishment of prison officials and personnel who violate the human rights of women in Michigan state prisons. We call upon the State of Michigan to end the practice of closing Michigan prisons to investigators such as Amnesty International and other international and domestic NGOs..."

This landmark resolution followed a public Legislative Hearing to debate human rights violations of women and children in Michigan prisons called by Congressman John Conyers Jr at which Amnesty International was invited to present its concerns. Other panellists included a former inmate who has now become a professional social worker and advocate for incarcerated women; attorneys working on behalf of women in prison; and key members

Members of Amnesty International's Greek Section demonstrating outside the US embassy in Athens as part of the "USA: Rights for All" campaign

of Detroit's City Council. The meeting was well attended by members of the public and was filmed for television.

In early December it emerged that the Illinois Department of Corrections had changed their policy so that, in future, no restraints would be used on pregnant women in transit or in the hospital. One of Amnesty International's contacts in Chicago said: "It seems as if the pressure from Amnesty and local groups has been effective. Chipping away, bit by bit."

A ban on the shackling of pregnant prisoners is one of the campaign's specific goals. Others include increasing the accountability of the police by setting up effective oversight and monitoring mechanisms; establishing enforceable standards for the treatment of prisoners, including steps to prevent sexual abuse of women and a ban on the use of electro-stun belts; an end to the execution of juvenile offenders and the mentally impaired (as a step towards abolition of the death penalty); stopping the inappropriate detention of asylum-seekers in jails; ratifying, in full, international human rights treaties; and adopting a code of conduct to prevent US arms and equipment being used to commit abuses elsewhere in the world.

The campaign against human rights violations by the US authorities was an integral part of Amnesty International's efforts to mobilize support for the rights enshrined in the Universal Declaration. The USA is an immensely powerful nation with a key role to play in promoting human rights throughout the world. It has a responsibility to take a lead by living up to its human rights promises; promises to be found in the USA's own laws and in international human rights standards.

A worldwide campaign

One day before the launch of a campaign against unfair trials in the Middle East, Ahmed Qatamesh, the longest serving-administrative detainee held by Israel, was released. He had been detained since 1992 and held without charge or trial since a judge ordered his release in 1993. His case had been featured in the campaign, which aimed to show the human dimension to unfair trial issues, to stimulate public debate, and to encourage governments in the Middle East and North Africa to respect the right to fair trial.

Amnesty International members around the world addressed public officials in all the countries of the Middle East and North Africa, calling on them to ratify international human rights treaties and to implement in law and practice the minimum standards for fair trial that these treaties set out. Throughout the region political prisoners, including prisoners of conscience, languish in prison or await execution, on spurious convictions or after sham trials. Miscarriages of justice can happen in any judicial system, but are inevitable in any country where the authority and independence of the judiciary are systematically undermined through government interference or the introduction of laws that circumvent the normal judicial process.

Strife-torn Burundi is often neglected in the international news media, and receives much less attention than its neighbours, Rwanda and the Democratic Republic of the Congo. In June Amnesty International members stepped up their long-term work on Burundi by launching a worldwide effort to inform the international community, to gain reforms in the judicial system, to help prevent further executions, both judicial and extrajudicial, and to assist in the protection of refugees.

Other concerted campaigning actions during the year addressed human rights violations in countries including Cambodia, several Caribbean states bringing back the death penalty, Croatia, Mozambique, Myanmar, Romania, Rwanda and Turkey.

Themes and issues

In the run-up to international women's day in March, Amnesty International launched a campaign calling on governments to mark the 50th anniversary of the Universal Declaration of Human Rights by integrating human rights practices which fully recognize women's rights into the mainstream of their work. Despite their long struggle for human rights, women continue to suffer from second class status both in their own countries and at the UN. Women's rights have been explicitly recognized as human rights in international human rights treaties such as the UN Convention on the Elimination of All Forms of Discrimination against Women, and by intergovernmental conferences such as the UN World Conference on Human Rights held in Vienna in 1993 and the UN World Conference on Women held in Beijing in 1995. Yet the UN has not always included a gender perspective

© Antonio Sesta

Thousands of people lie down in the road outside the Coliseum in Rome, Italy, to put pressure on delegates negotiating the statute for the International Criminal Court. Amnesty International members around the world have campaigned for the establishment of a just, fair and independent court to try the most heinous crimes in the world.

in human rights reporting and gender expertise in field visits and operations.

Amnesty International urged governments to give high priority to promoting and protecting women's human rights by ratifying and implementing human rights treaties relating to women, fully integrating work on women's rights with human rights work, stopping discrimination against women, training police and military personnel on gender issues, and protecting women from gender-based violence. Amnesty International also called on the UN to bring women's human rights from the margins into the mainstream.

In countries from Australia to Tanzania, Amnesty International members organized to promote women's human rights, often linked to the 50th anniversary campaign. In Nepal, a training course on gender awareness was run, in Nigeria members produced a board game on women's rights. In many countries, concerts and conferences were organized to communicate the women's rights message. Other vehicles were exhibitions of women's art, films by and about women, plays, street theatre and songs. Many of these activities were carried out in collaboration with women's groups and other NGOs. Amnesty International members, especially in West and East Africa, also continued their work to eradicate female genital mutilation, a practice which blights the lives of millions of women and girls.

In May the campaign to promote the Universal Declaration gained another dimension with the launch of an intensive effort to work with trade unions at local and national level. Joint initiatives were planned to publicize the right of everyone to enjoy the basic freedom to organize unions. Amnesty International members expressed their solidarity and backing for trade unions as defenders of human rights, and secured valuable support within the trade unions for Amnesty International's work. As well as the more usual appeal leaflets on behalf of trade unionists in prison or at risk, "tattoos" – multicoloured images that transfer to the skin and last for days – made an appearance, bearing the message "Labour Rights = Human Rights".

The development of understanding of children's rights has been one of the achievements of the human rights movement over the past decades. Integrating work on children's rights has been a challenge for Amnesty International, and progress in this field continues.

A worldwide effort to improve the treatment of children who come into contact with the law was launched in November. While international standards provide that decisions in cases involving children should be based on the best interests of the child, in practice justice systems the world over are violating the basic human rights of youngsters. Children are tortured and ill-treated in police custody. They are held in prisons in inhuman and degrading conditions. They are denied due process which should guarantee them fair trials. They are given sentences which disregard the key principles of juvenile justice – rehabilitation and the primacy of the well-being of the child.

One focus of the juvenile justice action, linked with the USA campaign, was the treatment of juveniles in the USA. The USA is one of only two countries in the world which has not ratified the UN Convention on the Rights of the Child. In 24 US states, laws permit juvenile offenders to be sentenced to death and executed. In at least 33 states, children who are tried and convicted as adults may be imprisoned with adult inmates.

Amnesty International's members also mounted a special campaign in April to highlight the plight of children in South Asia. South Asia's children face a litany of human rights abuse at the hands of the state and armed opposition groups; as sex workers, bonded labourers and in brothels.

Launch of the *Amnesty International Report 1998* by the Ghanaian Section in Kumasi, Ghana.

All the governments in South Asia have made a commitment to uphold the UN Convention on the Rights of the Child, yet children continue to be ill- treated in the custody of the state as it administers juvenile justice, are left unprotected in the family and community and suffer the consequences of living in the midst of armed conflict. All over the South Asia region, children often work in dangerous and unhealthy environments and are deprived of rights such as health, education and recreation. They find themselves trapped in a cycle of poverty, growing up illiterate, unskilled and prone to involvement in crime.

The human rights organization called on the international community – governments, international agencies, businesses and ordinary people – to raise human rights concerns with regional governments and to support defenders of children's rights within the region.

Business, arms and human rights

Amnesty International continued to develop its campaigning work with companies during 1998. Secretary General Pierre Sané launched Amnesty International's "Human Rights Principles for Companies" at the World Economic Forum in Davos, Switzerland, in January. The Principles summarize companies' responsibilities for human rights, based on international law. They call on companies to respect human rights in their own operations, and to use their influence with governments to promote human rights in the countries in which they operate.

Following the launch, Amnesty International campaigned at national and international level to raise companies' awareness of human rights. At business conferences, and in bilateral meetings with multinational companies, Amnesty International called on companies to develop codes of conduct incorporating international human rights standards, and to implement policies and procedures to monitor compliance.

New Amnesty International Business Groups were launched in Australia, Denmark, France, Italy and Switzerland to build support for human rights in national business communities. Amnesty International Business Groups in Australia, Belgium and the UK organized public seminars on human rights and business. The Director of Amnesty International Australia visited Thailand in October to address an international symposium on "Human Rights and Business Ethics". In November Amnesty International Netherlands published a joint report on "Multinational Enterprises and Human Rights" with the NGO *Pax Christi*. At the international level, Amnesty International's Secretary General promoted the organization's commitment to human rights in business through speeches to business leaders in Stavanger, Norway and Berne, Switzerland.

Amnesty International researchers continued to receive reports of companies' involvement in human rights violations in several countries. Following a UK press article in October about the security operations of multinational oil companies in Colombia, Amnesty International issued a press release calling on the oil companies to condemn human rights violations and to promote human rights standards in Colombia.

A growing number of Amnesty International groups and sections work on military, security and police (MSP) relations – opposing transfers of MSP equipment, training or personnel to countries where they are likely to facilitate human rights violations or breaches of humanitarian law. Such campaigns increase the pressure on those directly responsible for human rights violations and highlight the responsibility of supplier governments. During the year MSP activists campaigned on a range of transfers, including the shipment of sub-machine guns, armoured personnel carriers and surveillance equipment to Indonesia; light weapons, military training and assistance to the Great Lakes region; and MSP goods and services to Turkey, including electro-shock devices, attack helicopters and small arms production expertise.

Much of Amnesty International's work on MSP has involved lobbying for the development and implementation of stringent controls on MSP transfers at the national, regional and international level. In June 1998, the European Union (EU) adopted the Code of Conduct on Arms Exports, following concerted campaigning by NGOs including Amnesty International. The Code includes respect for human rights as a criterion for deciding whether to grant an export licence and requires EU countries to inform each other when they refuse such licences. If one country wants to grant a licence which has been denied by another within the previous three years, it has first to consult the state which issued the denial. Despite its loopholes, the Code represents an important advance. Initiatives by Amnesty International and other NGOs in the USA resulted in a proposed US Code of Conduct on Arms Transfers, which was passed by the US House of Representatives, but had not yet been adopted by the full Congress by the end of the year. However, a major advance in US controls has been the "Leahy Amendment", which prohibits US aid from being given to units of foreign security forces which have been implicated in gross human rights violations. In October 1998 the amendment was successfully used to stop the US government financing the transfer of armoured personnel carriers to units of the Turkish Anti-Terror Police.

The crisis in Kosovo

For more than a decade, Amnesty International has been warning of the growing human rights crisis in Kosovo province in the Federal Republic of Yugoslavia, where ethnic Albanians have been daily victims, particularly through the years when the world's attention was on the conflicts in Croatia and Bosnia. In 1998 these warnings were tragically borne out, as Serbian police and military operations, although ostensibly directed at the armed opposition

Kosovo Liberation Army, led to hundreds of civilian deaths, apparently a result of extrajudicial executions or indiscriminate attacks. Villages in Kosovo were burned to the ground and more than 250,000 displaced people and refugees were forced to flee or crowded into inadequate shelters. The vast majority of the victims in Kosovo were ethnic Albanians, but Serbs also suffered human rights abuses at the hands of armed ethnic Albanians.

Amnesty International mobilized its membership to make a special effort in the face of the human rights crisis in Kosovo. Amnesty International members and supporters around the world wore black for Kosovo on 19 September to generate public concern at the continuing human rights tragedy in Kosovo province. The program of events included vigils, demonstrations, public meetings and other activities in towns and cities worldwide.

Amnesty International's "Day of Action" was also a display of solidarity for the Serbian organization, Women in Black, which has been in the forefront of the peace movement in the Federal Republic of Yugoslavia.

Amnesty International appealed to the international community to introduce immediate, effective, independent human rights monitoring in the province and to provide durable protection for those displaced by the conflict. The organization repeated its call to the Yugoslav authorities to order a halt to indiscriminate attacks, to investigate human rights violations thoroughly and to prosecute the perpetrators, and to guarantee the safety and wellbeing of ethnic Albanian detainees. Amnesty International also called on the Kosovo Liberation Army to respect fundamental standards of international humanitarian law.

Human rights education

Teachers today are confronted by some of the greatest challenges they have ever had to face. They will shape the attitudes and values of the 21st century.

One of Amnesty International's objectives is to make all people of all ages aware of the basic rights and responsibilities that each individual possesses and, in the long term, to build a "culture of prevention" of human rights abuses. In 1998, the year of the 50th anniversary of the Universal Declaration, Amnesty International members around the world continued the campaign for incorporation of human rights in all educational curricula, by lobbying governments and by designing and developing a variety of human rights education programs.

Siniko – Towards a Human Rights Culture in Africa is the title of a manual for teaching human rights in Africa, which was produced by Amnesty International in December 1998 to mark the 50th anniversary. *"Siniko"* is a word in the African languages of Bambara, Mandingo and Dioula which loosely translates as "things that we want for a future generation" or "to have a better tomorrow". Human rights education is aimed at the development of the skills, knowledge and attitudes that people need to work towards a world free of human rights violations. It is in the hope of a better tomorrow that we choose to teach about human rights.

In June, as part of the implementation of Amnesty International's Human Rights Education Strategy for Africa, a training workshop was organized in Dakar, Senegal. Delegates from Côte d'Ivoire, Senegal and Togo took part in the workshop which focused on curriculum development. The objective was to train the delegates to enable them to participate effectively in curriculum reform processes aimed at the incorporation of human rights. This was the first in a series of four human rights education workshops to be organized in West Africa.

The Irish Section of Amnesty International published a human rights education resource manual as part of their celebrations of the 50th anniversary. The book, *The Rights Stuff*, explores the UN Convention on the Rights of the Child, in order to develop young people's understanding of the rights contained in the Convention and how these rights relate to their everyday lives.

In October the first ever meeting of the organization's human rights education coordinators from countries of Eastern and Central Europe was held in Bratislava, Slovakia. Participants included representatives from Croatia, Czech Republic, Moldova, Poland, Slovakia, Slovenia and Ukraine. They agreed to formulate a joint regional strategy.

Amnesty International Ukraine developed and implemented an extensive program of teacher training run by educators based in three different cities in 1998. The experience gained resulted in the production of a manual entitled *Human Rights, classroom activities for forms 2 and 3 of primary schools*. In the Czech Republic Amnesty International developed a multi-faceted program of human rights education and human rights awareness raising. A series of training workshops for secondary schools based on the *First Steps* human rights education manual was launched in November 1998. In Poland, Amnesty members planned the launch of a human rights education program which will make use of the opportunities offered by the current reform of state education. The program involves the dissemination of Amnesty International's Polish language human rights materials to schools, introducing teachers to new teaching methods appropriate to human rights education and lobbying the government to incorporate human rights in the school curriculum.

In August, as part of their activities to mark the 50th anniversary of the Universal Declaration, Amnesty International's members in Morocco staged the first national human rights forum for children and young people, in cooperation with youth NGOs. Hundreds of children, as well youth workers and prominent figures in civil society and the government, attended the forum. They discussed children's rights and the origins of the Universal Declaration. During the year Amnesty International Morocco also organized a three-day workshop for 30 teacher trainers. The organization's members in Tunisia produced a comprehensive

©AI

Children learning about human rights through activities organized by Amnesty International Argentina

human rights education manual aimed at secondary school students in early 1998. Despite repeated interventions, however, the Tunisian authorities refused to allow the manual to be printed and distributed.

In Asia, Amnesty International members from Taiwan attended their first human rights education conference, where they made contact with the Taipei Teachers College. An agreement was reached to produce a teaching plan and human rights teaching materials. In Thailand a workshop to train trainers was organized, as a result of which a network has been developed among participants. Members in Thailand also devised an art competition to design posters on human rights themes in the Thai language.

In June over 30 teachers from across Guyana took part in a three-day music workshop. The training was designed to show teachers how they can work with students using music as a means of conveying human rights themes and messages. The workshop was a joint initiative of Amnesty International and the Guyana Human Rights Association, and was sponsored by the Guyanese Ministry of Education. Further workshops are planned for other arts-related areas such as drama, drawing and poster-making.

Amnesty International's human rights education coordinators from Latin America met in Peru in March for a workshop and discussion meeting. Agreement was reached to design a human rights education strategy for the region. Amnesty International members from Peru also held workshops during the year with the aim of training human rights education "multipliers", who will pass on to others the knowledge and skills they gained during the training. The participants were teachers and others connected to the education system. Talks have also been held with government officials in Peru in an effort to encourage the development of human rights teaching, and to include Amnesty International books and materials as official textbooks.

Amnesty International Uruguay organized several seminars and workshops during 1998 on the theme of diversity with students of secondary schools and universities. In Mexico, in cooperation with Amnesty International's Spanish language translation unit, the section published a manual for teachers entitled *La Zanahoria.*

Throughout the year Amnesty International Argentina held workshops and seminars for teachers, lawyers and members of the government. They also published a book of children's stories with human rights themes. To celebrate the 50th anniversary, their members, together with the Red Cross and UNHCR, gave awards to children for producing stories and pictures about human rights. As many as 1,500 youngsters participated in the different workshops and events.

From South Africa to Brazil, Spain to Venezuela, Amnesty International sections across the world continued in 1998 to develop their programs and materials for training police and law enforcement officials in human rights. Publications in this field produced during the year include *10 Basic Human Rights Standards for Law Enforcement Officials, A 12 Point Guide for Good Practice in the Training and Education for Human Rights of Government Officials* and a *Fair Trials Manual.*

Hundreds of thousands of people worldwide have been touched by Amnesty International's human rights education activities and programs. In Argentinians alone, more than 2,000 teachers have been trained in the teaching of human rights – through them an estimated 51,500 young Argentinians have developed a greater knowledge and understanding of human rights. In Peru and Brazil, thousands of people – including Brazilian police officers – have received human rights training. During 1998 the Ghanaian Section ran a series of workshops in teacher training colleges attended by more than 900 student teachers and set up human rights clubs in 20 secondary schools across the country. These clubs aim to develop a new generation of human rights activists in Ghana.

Education in human rights is itself a fundamental human right and also a responsibility. Article 26 of the Universal Declaration states that everyone has the right to education, and that education should strengthen respect for human rights. Through their human rights education work, Amnesty International members are doing what they can to fulfil this part of the Universal Declaration. If people do not know their rights, they cannot defend or fight for them. Human rights education teaches both **about** and **for** human rights. The goal is to help people understand human rights, value human rights, and to take responsibility for respecting, defending and promoting their human rights as well as the rights of others.

Refugee protection under attack

States in all corners of the globe continue to flout their obligations under refugee law. Refugees continue to have their most basic rights violated; they are at risk of *refoulement* (forcible return to a country where they risk grave human rights abuses), arbitrary detention, and even violence in the country of asylum. Rather than discussing how to strengthen the embattled system of refugee protection, states appear to be debating how to weaken it further.

Secret moves to undermine protection

The 1951 Convention relating to the Status of Refugees (Refugee Convention), the international basis of refugee protection, came under renewed attack during the year. According to a confidential strategy paper by the Austrian government, the Refugee Convention is an outdated instrument and should be replaced by a "new approach" towards refugee protection; one which moves away from the current rights-based system. The new approach should be "more politically oriented"; an approach where protection is not

Afghan refugees, Nasir Bagh refugee village, Pakistan. Fighting has continued to ravage Afghanistan and human rights abuses remain widespread.

seen as a "subjective individual right, but rather as a political offer on the part of the host country". The government of Austria's "Strategy Paper on Immigration and Asylum Policy" was submitted in confidence to the K4 Committee[1] of the European Union (EU) in July 1998. The paper was leaked and widely reported in the press.

The Strategy Paper makes little if any distinction between refugee flows and other migratory movements, stating for example that the Refugee Convention "is not at all geared to ... coping with illegal immigration from many crisis regions, especially in the Third World". The paper proposes an international system of concentric circles spreading out from the inner core of Schengen states.[2] Economic aid to countries in the outer circles would be linked to their "fulfilment of their obligations" to ensure that migration (including, apparently, the movement of refugees) is curtailed.

The Austrian government withdrew the paper after other EU governments expressed concern and submitted a revised version to the K4 in late September. However, the issuing of this paper and its confidential nature are troubling developments. Amnesty International believes that it is unacceptable that such debates are taking place behind closed doors, without the public scrutiny needed to ensure that states live up to their obligations towards refugees and asylum-seekers.

The process of drafting the Conclusions of the Executive Committee (Excom)[3] of the UN High Commissioner for Refugees (UNHCR) is another example of the lack of transparency in the refugee protection regime. UNHCR is the international agency charged with ensuring the protection of refugees, and Excom Conclusions on specific refugee issues are vitally important to refugee protection worldwide. However, draft Conclusions are debated by governments behind closed doors. Despite the crucial role of non-governmental organizations (NGOs) in refugee protection and assistance, there is no formal mechanism for NGOs to observe the consultations where governments reach consensus on the text of the Conclusions, much less to participate in the debate. Indeed, when Excom established its Standing Committee, which meets three or four times between plenary sessions of Excom, there was initially a debate over whether NGOs would be able to attend as observers. Together with others, Amnesty International lobbied governments during 1997 to allow NGO access, and a decision was eventually taken to allow NGOs observer status, on a temporary basis. By the end of the year, it was still not clear whether NGOs would be allowed permanent access.

Detention: deterring asylum-seekers

The detention of refugees and asylum-seekers is currently under debate on the international stage. International standards set out explicit provisions regarding the detention of refugees and asylum-seekers, forbidding detention except in specifically defined circumstances.[4] Conditions must be humane, and refugees and asylum-seekers should not be held with criminal prisoners. In

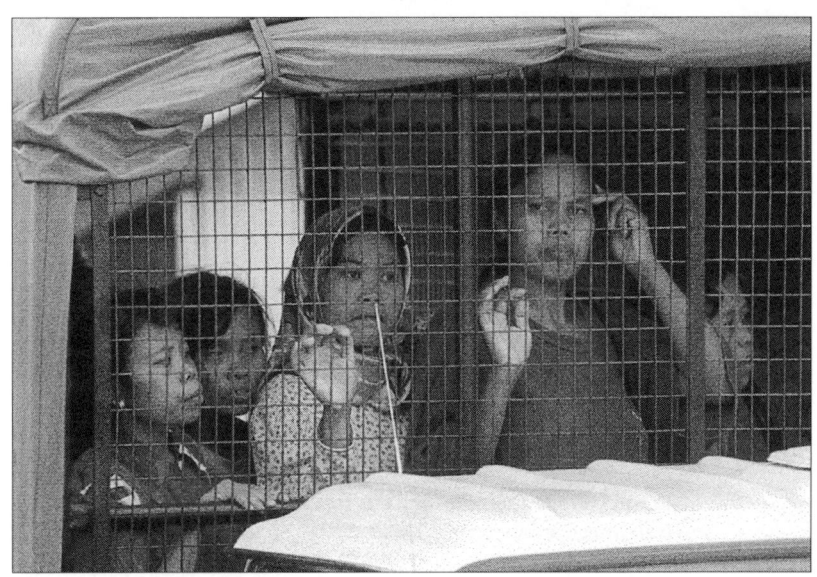

Semenyih detention camp, Malaysia, where conditions of detention for asylum-seekers and other detainees have caused grave concern

addition, international standards which regulate all forms of detention apply equally to the detention of refugees and asylum-seekers, in particular standards regarding the lawfulness of detention.

During the drafting of Excom's General Conclusion on International Protection in October 1998, these principles came under sustained pressure. In particular, a number of influential states reportedly argued against maintaining the principle that refugees should not be detained together with criminal prisoners. In the end, the principle was included, but only after a long and arduous debate.

A number of countries detain asylum-seekers in contravention of international standards, often in harsh conditions and for long periods. Detention is being used as another measure to limit refugees' ability to seek and enjoy the international protection they deserve.

In Japan, asylum-seekers who attempt to enter the country without documentation are as a general rule detained, and often face criminal charges of illegal entry. Li Xumei, a pregnant Chinese asylum-seeker fleeing from China's one child family planning policy, arrived in Japan without documentation in February 1998. She was detained and charged with illegal entry. She filed a claim for refugee status in April and, in July, after more than five months' detention, she was released on humanitarian grounds. Her asylum claim was rejected and she lodged an appeal.

The government of Tanzania has recently introduced new legislation which includes broad provisions for detention. Under the Refugees Act 1998, asylum-seekers or refugees who act "in a manner prejudicial to peace and good order or relations between the Government of Tanzania and any other Government" may be detained for up to three months. At the time of writing, the draft law had not been promulgated by the President.

In the USA undocumented asylum-seekers are generally detained until final resolution of their case; a process which can take months or even years. Many are detained with criminal prisoners, often in harsh conditions; many are subjected to frequent strip searches, and are shackled or handcuffed when taken to hearings outside the detention facility. A refugee who had been detained in harsh conditions for 14 months before being granted asylum stated, "Everyone says America is the place for human rights. I thought maybe I had arrived in the wrong country."

Asylum-seekers in the US are often transferred with little or no notice from one facility to another. Little effort is made to keep asylum-seekers close to their families or legal counsel, or to notify these people that the asylum-seeker has been moved. Yudaya Nanyonga, a 20-year-old asylum-seeker from Uganda, was transferred without explanation to York County Prison, Pennsylvania, in June 1998, after being detained in another state for over six months. Once at York, Yudaya Nanyonga was told that she was to be held in the maximum security section of the prison. When she became distraught, prison officials stripped her, shackled her with arms and legs outstretched, and injected her with sedatives.

Conditions of detention remain a grave concern in Immigration Detention Centres in Malaysia, with persistent reports of overcrowding and inadequate food. One family of asylum-seekers with two adults and four young children held in Semenyih Detention Centre was allowed just two litres of drinking water a day. Ill-treatment is also reportedly common, with reports of guards beating detainees and sexually abusing female detainees. Some detainees suffering treatable diseases have reportedly died from lack of medical attention. The Malaysian authorities continue to deny UNHCR and other outside observers access to these detention centres.

Asylum-seekers have been held in airport transit lounges with clearly inadequate facilities. Rahime Bekaj, her three daughters and two young sons, lived in the transit lounge of Budapest airport, Hungary, for 11 days in September 1998. They had fled from the province of Kosovo in the Federal Republic of Yugoslavia. During this time, they had nowhere to sleep and received no blankets, no food, and no information regarding their status. They could only afford to buy one meal a day at the airport restaurant. Rahime Bekaj told Amnesty International, "I can't believe that in a country where there is no war, people are treated like this." After intervention by Amnesty International and by UNHCR, the Bekaj family were transferred from the transit zone to a different facility, and the Hungarian authorities formally apologized.

Asylum-seekers in detention are frequently denied access to outside assistance, and decisions on detention are often made

Yudaya Nanyonga, a Ugandan seeking asylum in the USA. When she became distraught at learning she was to be moved to a maximum security unit, she was stripped, shackled, and injected with sedatives.

without effective judicial oversight. In Australia, asylum-seekers who arrive without documentation are detained in almost complete isolation from the outside world, and are not told how to claim asylum or obtain legal advice. Detention is mandatory, and Australian courts have no jurisdiction to release detained asylum-seekers. The Human Rights Committee[5] stated in the case of *A v. Australia* that this policy amounted to arbitrary detention. The Australian government rejected the Committee's views, and reiterated its position in a statement to Excom in October 1998. The United Kingdom (UK) is another country where there is no effective judicial oversight of detention in asylum cases. Amnesty International submitted concerns regarding the detention of asylum-seekers in the UK to the UN Working Group on Arbitrary Detention in September.

Refoulement: forcible return to danger

Thambirajah Kamalathasan, a Sri Lankan Tamil, was one of 192 Sri Lankan asylum-seekers on board a boat intercepted in the territorial waters of Senegal in February 1998. They were reportedly not given any meaningful opportunity to claim asylum, and were returned to Sri Lanka three days later, where they were immediately detained. They were released after several weeks, but Thambirajah Kamalathasan was detained once again in July and was reportedly tortured in a police station for several days.

This is just one of many examples of *refoulement* which Amnesty International witnessed over the past year. States continued in 1998 to violate this most fundamental principle of refugee protection.

All too often, refugees are lumped together with economic migrants and branded "illegals". In early 1998 the Malaysian authorities rounded up tens of thousands of undocumented foreign labourers into detention centres pending deportation. Among them were an unknown number of refugees and asylum-seekers. Detainees are denied access to UNHCR. Many are from the province of Aceh in Indonesia, where serious human rights violations continued into 1998: 545 Acehnese forcibly returned to Aceh from Malaysia in March were detained incommunicado for weeks in an Indonesian military detention centre known for torture and ill-treatment.

In Thailand, even refugees recognized by UNHCR are often detained by the authorities as "illegal immigrants" and subjected to *refoulement*. The Thai authorities sometimes target particular groups; in May 1998, the authorities raided the human rights office of a Myanmar (Burmese) opposition group. Fourteen people were arrested, including recognized refugees. Three days later they were forced across the Myanmar border.

Lack of physical protection
Nyan Lin, an ethnic Karen refugee from Myanmar, was reportedly beaten to death by soldiers in Thailand in March 1998, just because he had returned to the refugee camp after curfew. His case illustrates the dangers many refugees face in countries of asylum. Refugees are one of the most vulnerable groups in any host country, and in many states their rights continue to be violated.

Armed groups from Sierra Leone have crossed the border into Guinea, terrorizing Sierra Leonean refugees and continuing their campaign of atrocities against civilians – "Operation no living thing". In September 1998 an armed group attacked a refugee camp at the village of Tomandu. At least seven refugee women were killed. Witnesses said that the armed group raided local food stores, killing everyone nearby. Other refugees were forced to carry stolen goods back across the border into Sierra Leone.

Refugees continued to be targeted for extrajudicial execution by government forces in the Democratic Republic of the Congo. Approximately 54 Rwandese refugees and at least 100 Congolese civilians were killed at close range by government forces in the province of South-Kivu in late March and early April. The Congolese civilians were reportedly targeted because they had allowed the refugees to live in their village.

In many countries, refugees were at risk for exercising their human rights. In Zimbabwe, approximately 25 refugees and asylum-

Rwandese refugees in the Democratic Republic of the Congo

seekers demonstrated over conditions and procedural delays by staging a sit-in protest within the UNHCR compound in Harare in June 1998. The Zimbabwean authorities reportedly used a disproportionate level of force in dispersing this demonstration, and many refugees (including a four-year-old child) were injured when they were beaten by police using batons.

The internally displaced

The internally displaced are in a similar situation to refugees. Indeed, as the conflict in Kosovo shows, for many people, internal displacement is the first step to fleeing across an international border and becoming a refugee. Close scrutiny is needed of any assistance provided to the internally displaced, so that they are not in practice prevented from seeking safety in a different part of the country, or from crossing an international border and seeking asylum elsewhere.

UNHCR provides assistance to the internally displaced only in situations where it receives a specific mandate from the UN General Assembly. Some argue that this role compromises UNHCR's refugee protection mandate, in that UNHCR is required to provide protection within the country of origin even if that may result in people being discouraged, or even prevented, from fleeing abroad. Regardless of the merits of this argument, this debate is an indication of the difficulties that UNHCR faces in fulfilling its primary role, that of ensuring protection for refugees.

Independent scrutiny of compliance with the Refugee Convention

States in all parts of the world continue to flout their obligations under international refugee law. The international community must ensure that states are held accountable for implementing their international obligations towards refugees and asylum-seekers. To do this, a rigorous system of monitoring and public reporting is required.

Most major human rights treaties, such as the International Covenant on Civil and Political Rights and the Convention against Torture and Other Cruel, Inhuman or Degrading Treatment or Punishment, establish an independent body to monitor application of the treaty. State parties are obliged to submit periodic reports on the implementation of the treaty to the monitoring body, which reviews these reports, often along with other information supplied by NGOs. Treaty bodies may also adopt general comments to guide states on the implementation of specific treaty provisions. These monitoring functions, which play a key role in the protection of human rights, are performed in public, with states called to account in an open process.

There are clear criteria for effective monitoring of states' obligations. First and foremost, the monitoring body must be independent; it must be free to operate without political pressure from governments. Monitoring must be open to public scrutiny, with a meaningful opportunity for NGOs to provide input. A monitoring body must be able to review compliance with legal standards, and make recommendations for improvement, in public.

One body which might appear able to perform this monitoring function is UNHCR.[6] However, Amnesty International is concerned that UNHCR, at least as it currently operates, would not be able to monitor state parties' compliance with the Refugee Convention effectively. UNHCR is an intergovernmental agency, with a governing body of states. Not all member states of Excom are even party to the Refugee Convention, despite its crucial role in setting UNHCR policy and international standards on refugee protection. The process of drafting Excom Conclusions is far from open and transparent, and is certainly not independent of the political considerations of member states.

On a day-to-day basis, UNHCR can be vulnerable to political pressure, and is not always able to voice its concerns publicly. UNHCR is a large operational agency, with offices and operations in countries worldwide, and its access to a country depends on the consent of the government. Some governments have reportedly made UNHCR's presence conditional on it not criticizing that country's refugee policies. UNHCR therefore often faces a fundamental dilemma. Should it speak out and risk reprisals against its staff or being expelled, preventing it from accomplishing anything on the ground? Or should it keep quiet and do its best to contain abuses on the ground, at the cost of not alerting the international community? This would be an impossible situation for a monitoring body.

The funding structure of UNHCR can also make it susceptible to political pressure, in particular from large donor governments. UNHCR is funded almost entirely from voluntary contributions from states, forcing it to rely on a few, affluent countries. Many of

The family of this child fled the fighting in Kosovo and was detained by border guards in Hungary.

the funds are "earmarked" for specific projects, increasing UNHCR's vulnerability to the political agendas of states.[7]

The following example is an illustration of how governments may be able to exert undue influence on UNHCR. In response to an increase in the arrival of asylum-seekers from Iraq, the EU adopted a Joint Action Plan in early 1998 outlining a number of restrictive measures. UNHCR submitted to the K4 Committee in April 1998 the document "Action Plan on the influx of Iraqi asylum-seekers; UNHCR Observations". This document provides UNHCR's views on the availability of protection for Iraqi asylum-seekers in numerous countries in the Middle East and in Central and Eastern Europe, and also outlines UNHCR's views on an "internal flight alternative", (a safe area within the country of origin), in northern Iraq.

The document was submitted in confidence to the K4 Committee, but was subsequently leaked. Amnesty International urged UNHCR to issue it publicly, to enable refugee advocates to cite it and to promote debate on the important issue of an "internal flight alternative". However, UNHCR stated that it was unable to do so. Indeed, in another confidential communication to the K4 Committee, UNHCR had requested EU governments to refrain from citing the "Observations" document as a source. In its document, UNHCR concludes that the situation in northern Iraq has stabilized and that therefore "an internal flight alternative may be applied in certain cases". This conclusion appears to contradict an opinion issued publicly by UNHCR less than a month earlier, where UNHCR stated that for Iraqi asylum-seekers, internal flight was "not a realistic alternative".[8] Amnesty International is concerned about apparently conflicting opinions given by UNHCR, one in public, and the other in confidence with a group of governments. In addition, the assessment that the situation in northern Iraq had stabilized sufficiently did not accord with Amnesty International's view at the time. Worryingly, at least one EU state, Denmark, has rejected the claims of several Kurdish Iraqi asylum-seekers on the basis of UNHCR's confidential assessment.[9]

Ultimately, protecting refugees is the responsibility of states; the international community must ensure effective monitoring of states' compliance with their obligations. The body which performs this function cannot be in any way compromised; it must be able to function independently of political pressure, must operate in a transparent way, and must be able to hold states accountable publicly for failures to fulfil their obligations towards refugees and asylum-seekers. If states cannot guarantee this in all aspects of UNHCR's work, then the time has come to establish a different body to perform the monitoring function for the Refugee Convention. This function is urgently needed and cannot be compromised by political considerations; the rights of refugees must always be respected.

1 A committee made up of high-ranking civil servants of EU member states, the K4 Committee discusses policy matters, including those pertaining to immigration and asylum.
2 European states which are party to the Schengen Agreement, which aims to eliminate border control between EU member states.
3 Excom is an intergovernmental body made up of 53 governments. Excom, which oversees the work of UNHCR, meets once a year in Geneva and adopts Conclusions on specific issues relating to refugee protection. Conclusions are not legally binding as such; however, they serve as authoritative interpretations of the Refugee Convention and represent the views of the international community on refugee matters.
4 Excom Conclusion 44 states that detention may be resorted to only when it is necessary, and even then "only on grounds prescribed by law to verify identity; to determine the elements on which the claim to refugee status or asylum is based; to deal with cases where refugees or asylum-seekers have destroyed their travel or identity documents or have used fraudulent documents in order to mislead the authorities of the State in which they intend to claim asylum; or to protect national security or public order."
5 The Human Rights Committee is a treaty body of experts which monitors the implementation of the International Covenant on Civil and Political Rights (ICCPR).
6 Under its Statute, UNHCR is mandated to "[supervise] the application" of the Refugee Convention. Article 35 of the Refugee Convention requires state parties to "co-operate with the [UNHCR] in the exercise of its functions", and "in particular facilitate its duty of supervising the application" of the Convention. Article 35 also requires state parties to report to UNHCR, providing information regarding the implementation of the Convention.
7 At the 1998 Excom, UNHCR announced that it was requesting donor states to reduce the proportion of earmarked funds in their contributions.
8 "Update on Regional Developments in Europe", 2 April 1998, EC/48/SC/CRP.9, para. 5, submitted to the April 1998 meeting of the Excom Standing Committee.
9 At the end of the year there were indications that the Danish Refugee Appeals Board would suspend consideration of refugee claims from northern Iraq, pending further information from UNHCR.

International organizations – rhetoric and reality

Introduction

Intergovernmental organizations such as the UN are the sum of their member states. Decisions reflect the will of governments. With few exceptions, governments act on the basis of their perceived economic, political or security interests, often at the expense of their human rights treaty obligations. Yet governments undertake these obligations freely, and governments must be held to account for their actions in their own country and on the international stage.

This chapter reviews some of Amnesty International's efforts to further human rights work at the UN and within regional intergovernmental organizations during 1998, the 50th anniversary of the Universal Declaration of Human Rights.

Intergovernmental organizations play an important role in the protection and promotion of human rights worldwide. New international human rights standards are elaborated and adopted by governments; fact-finding procedures and technical programs to enhance human rights are established and entrusted to independent experts; human rights observers are sent to countries to

In a historic conference in Rome, Italy, delegates from 120 nations adopted the Statute of the International Criminal Court, July 1998.

50

monitor and report on the human rights situation; and other initiatives are developed and implemented to protect and promote human rights.

Intergovernmental organizations can have a significant influence on specific country situations. However, they often avoid their responsibilities. For example, in 1998 the UN Commission on Human Rights failed yet again to take any action to protect the victims of human rights abuses in Algeria, despite a human rights crisis which has claimed over 80,000 lives since 1992. Algeria's strategic importance and its close cultural or economic ties with other influential states took precedence over the lives of Algerians.

The need for international justice

When those who have committed the most heinous crimes escape justice, an ominous message is sent to society: perpetrators need not be afraid. Amnesty International's experience around the world over 40 years indicates that impunity is the single most important factor leading to continued human rights violations. Where abuses have not been properly investigated; where those responsible have not been brought to account for their crimes; where the truth has not been revealed because the rule of law has

> **'It is my fervent hope that by [31 December 2000] a large majority of United Nations member states will have signed and ratified [the Statute of the International Criminal Court], so that the Court will have unquestioned authority and the widest possible jurisdiction.'**
> UN Secretary-General Kofi Annan, July 1998

broken down or because of a lack of political will, a self-perpetuating cycle of violence has all too often arisen. Events in the former Yugoslavia and the Great Lakes region of Africa are but two tragic examples. In countries emerging from armed conflict and embarking on reconstruction and reconciliation, the need for justice is overwhelming. It was this need that led 120 governments to adopt the Statute of the International Criminal Court (ICC) in Rome, Italy, on 17 July 1998. The ICC is intended to have jurisdiction over the worst crimes in the world: genocide, other crimes against humanity and war crimes.

Only seven governments voted against adopting the ICC Statute, including the USA, and 21 abstained. This success came only four years after Amnesty International members worldwide began campaigning for the establishment of a just, fair and independent ICC. Their efforts were reinforced by 800 other nongovernmental organizations (NGOs), members of the worldwide NGO Coalition for an International Criminal Court, which Amnesty International helped to found in 1994. Amnesty International has published a variety of documents to assist governments and

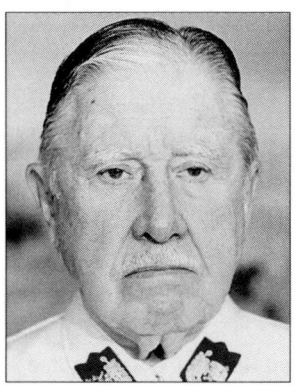

At the end of the year Augusto Pinochet, former President of Chile, was awaiting a legal decision on whether he could be extradited from the United Kingdom (UK) to Spain to face prosecution for crimes against humanity.

NGOs, such as the five-part series, *The international criminal court: Making the right choices*, and to mobilize the general public, such as *International justice now! Time for an effective international criminal court*.

Most of the principles which Amnesty International regards as fundamental were incorporated in the ICC Statute. The definition of crimes against humanity includes systematic or widespread "disappearances"; that of war crimes includes the conscription of children under the age of 15; that of genocide is the same as in the Convention for the Prevention and Punishment of the Crime of Genocide. The ICC can try those accused of violating humanitarian law in internal armed conflicts, the most common type of armed conflict today. An independent Prosecutor can begin investigating and prosecuting crimes based on information from victims or their families and other sources without waiting for the UN Security Council or states to act.

The ICC Statute helps to ensure justice for women by giving the ICC power to try cases of rape or other sexual abuse as war crimes and, when committed on a widespread or systematic basis, as crimes against humanity. The Judges, Prosecutor and staff of the ICC must receive training in the investigation and prosecution of gender-based crimes.

The ICC Statute provides extensive guarantees of the right to fair trial, including some, such as an express right to silence, which are stronger than in existing international human rights instruments. The Statute excludes the death penalty as a punishment for the gravest crimes under international law, reinforcing the momentum towards abolition. In an important advance in international law, the ICC can award reparations to victims, including restitution, compensation and rehabilitation, and states parties have to enforce those awards.

However, the Statute fails to give the ICC the same universal jurisdiction which all states have today over these horrendous crimes, re-emphasizing the continued primary role of states in achieving justice. The Prosecutor is heavily dependent on national authorities in conducting investigations. The UN Security Council can require the ICC to delay an investigation or prosecution for successive one-year periods. When states ratify the Statute, they can declare that for seven years they will not accept the ICC's power to try war crimes on their territory or committed by their own nationals.

By the end of the year, the Statute – which requires 60 ratifications to enter into force – had been signed by 71 states, but no states had yet ratified it. Amnesty International and hundreds of other NGOs are campaigning for prompt ratification of the Statute so that the ICC can start delivering justice. As part of this effort,

> 'Had Hitler managed to flee to the United Kingdom after the Second World War, under English law he could still be "strolling around in Hyde Park" and no-one would be able to touch him provided he had not contravened the law of the land.'
>
> Peter Burns, Chairman of the UN Committee against Torture, commenting on the UK High Court decision that Augusto Pinochet enjoyed immunity from prosecution as a former Head of State, November 1998

Amnesty International is pressing states to enact the necessary legislation providing for full cooperation with the ICC and giving national courts universal jurisdiction over the crimes listed in the ICC Statute.

International justice for crimes against humanity became headline news around the world when Augusto Pinochet, former President of Chile, was arrested in the United Kingdom (UK) in October after an extradition request from Spain. The fate of the former President, under whose military government thousands of people were tortured, killed or "disappeared", focused unprecedented attention on the issue. At the end of the year, legal proceedings were pending to determine whether or not he should be extradited from the UK to Spain, Belgium, France or Switzerland.

International Criminal Tribunals
Amnesty International issued a document in April appraising both the achievements and shortcomings of the International Criminal Tribunal for Rwanda (ICTR). Despite being beset by problems arising from lack of cooperation from states and shortages of human and financial resources, the ICTR has taken into custody some of the most senior officials of the former Rwandese government accused of genocide and other crimes against humanity, such as former Prime Minister Jean Kambanda, who was sentenced to life imprisonment. By the end of the year, the ICTR had completed hearings in its third trial. In the first-ever judgment by an international court for the crime of genocide, in September the ICTR convicted Jean-Paul Akayesu, a former city mayor, of genocide and crimes against humanity. The judgment was also

Jean-Paul Akayesu listens to court proceedings at the International Criminal Tribunal for Rwanda, in September. He was found guilty of genocide and crimes against humanity, including rape and sexual violence.

unprecedented in recognizing that rape and sexual violence constitute genocide if committed with the specific intent of destroying, in whole or in part, a particular, targeted group. Amnesty International acknowledged the progress made and recommended that the ICTR adhere strictly both to its own Rules of Procedure and Evidence and to internationally recognized standards protecting the right to a fair trial.

> 'The Office of the High Commissioner for Human Rights is encouraged to learn that the International Criminal Tribunal for Rwanda has just handed down the first verdict on the crime of genocide. This is indeed a powerful symbol that individuals cannot commit such horrendous crimes with impunity.'
> Mary Robinson, UN High Commissioner for Human Rights, September 1998

In December the International Criminal Tribunal for the former Yugoslavia convicted Anto Furundzija, a former local commander of a Croatian military police unit, of war crimes. The Tribunal found that aiding and abetting in outrages upon personal dignity, including rape, constitutes a war crime.

Politics over principles

The UN Commission on Human Rights

The 1998 session of the UN Commission on Human Rights exemplified a diplomatic policy of "constructive engagement" in which human rights principles were sacrificed in the interests of compromise. Member states of the Commission continued to be preoccupied with reaching consensus and obtaining the cooperation of the perpetrating state, rather than addressing the human rights situation in the country concerned. For example, Amnesty International called on the Commission to adopt a resolution on Indonesia, but this was traded for a far weaker statement by the Commission's Chairman. Governments who openly worked for the weaker text included those of Australia and of the European Union (EU).

Despite the Algerian government's outright refusal to cooperate with the Commission, and despite continuing reports of killings in Algeria during the Commission's six-week session, the EU, the USA and Canada eventually admitted to lacking the necessary determination to take any action. Amnesty International, Human Rights Watch, *Reporters sans frontières*, and the International Federation of Human Rights organized a meeting on Algeria in parallel with the Commission, to prompt governments into action. However, calls for the despatch of an international team to investigate the situation and the plight of the Algerian victims were not seriously considered. In addition, the Algerian government went back on its initial promise to allow visits by the Special Rapporteurs on torture and on extrajudicial, summary and arbitrary executions. The human rights situation in Algeria represents a direct challenge to the authority and competence of the Commission.

At the same session of the Commission, Amnesty International urged governments to tackle gross human rights violations in Cambodia, Colombia, Kenya, Saudi Arabia and Turkey. The organization expressed dismay at the Commission's decision to drop scrutiny of Saudi Arabia's record from its confidential "1503 procedure" and deplored the conspicuous absence of any scrutiny of China's human rights record. Before the start of the session, the EU had made public its decision not to table a resolution on China. Amnesty International condemned this decision and pointed out that it had more to do with policy splits among EU governments and trade deals than with any significant improvement in China's human rights record.

Despite the Commission's failures, a number of its independent experts made significant contributions to human rights protection and promotion during the year. For instance, the report of the UN Special Rapporteur on the independence of judges and lawyers, who undertook a fact-finding mission to the UK, highlighted the lack of safeguards for suspects arrested under emergency legislation in Northern Ireland, and made a number of recommendations to ensure respect for the rule of law and human rights.

The Commission adopted a landmark resolution calling for a moratorium on the death penalty "with a view to completely abolishing" it. Encouragingly, the resolution was sponsored by 65 states, 15 more than the 1997 resolution. The USA was among a minority of retentionist states which voted against the resolution. The very high number of co-sponsors would not have been achieved without NGO efforts in lobbying governments.

Amnesty International urged the Commission and its member states to pay more attention to the human rights abuses which often force people to flee their homes and become refugees. Amnesty International deplored measures taken by some states which violate fundamental principles of refugee protection. These included ignoring the prohibition of forcible return (*refoulement*) of individuals at risk of human rights abuses and adopting unduly restrictive interpretations of the definition of who is a refugee, in particular failing to recognize gender-based persecution and persecution by individuals and groups other than the state.

Standard-setting

International human rights standards provide the benchmarks against which states' actions at the national and international level can be measured. Human rights codification and the creation of new avenues of redress for victims is a continuing process. Amnesty International's work on standard-setting involves campaigning and lobbying by its worldwide membership, as well as participation in meetings of intergovernmental organizations, to seek the strongest possible mechanisms to protect human rights.

Despite the adoption of the ICC Statute and progress on the protection of human rights defenders (see below), the drafting of new international standards was beset with problems. Drafting groups frequently became hostage to the negotiating position of a few states and often faced the stark choice of accepting the minimum common denominator or abandoning the drafting exercise altogether.

The USA played a negative role in the proceedings of the Commission on Human Rights Working Group drafting an optional protocol (on the involvement of children in armed conflict) to the Convention on the Rights of the Child. This protocol aims to raise the minimum age for recruitment of children into armed forces and their participation in hostilities from 15 to 18 years. At the

> **'It is immoral that adults should want children to fight their wars for them... There is simply no excuse, no acceptable argument for arming children.'**
> Archbishop Desmond M. Tutu

Working Group meeting in February, the USA continued to refuse to accept a broad consensus on a minimum age of 18 years for participation in hostilities. While it was not alone, no other state was prepared to block the overwhelming majority of states from all regions of the world. The stalemate caused by the USA is ironic given that the protocol is optional and can only be ratified by states which are parties to the Convention on the Rights of the Child, which the USA is not.

In response, Amnesty International and five other international NGOs – Human Rights Watch, International Federation *Terre des Hommes*, the International Save the Children Alliance, the Jesuit

The Coalition to Stop the Use of Child Soldiers was launched in June 1998 by Amnesty International and five other non-governmental organizations.

Refugee Service and the Quaker UN Office (Geneva) – launched the Coalition to Stop the Use of Child Soldiers. The Coalition established links with the International Red Cross and Red Crescent Movement, and UN bodies and agencies, including the Office of the UN High Commissioner for Human Rights, the Special Representative of the UN Secretary-General for Children and Armed Conflict, the UN High Commissioner for Refugees and the UN Children's Fund (UNICEF). The Coalition submitted to the Working Group a provisional draft optional protocol to the Convention on the Rights of the Child on the involvement of children in armed conflict.

While governments in the Working Group were deadlocked on the issue, in October the UN Secretary-General established a new policy for the minimum age of UN peacekeepers. Civilian police and military observers on UN peacekeeping operations are to be at least 25 years old, and "troops in national contingents should preferably be 21 years, but not less than 18."

The outcome of the October session of the Commission's Working Group drafting an optional protocol to the Convention against Torture and Other Cruel, Inhuman or Degrading Treatment or Punishment was equally disappointing. This protocol aims to create a global inspection system for places of detention as a way of preventing torture and ill-treatment. The Working Group has been meeting since 1992. However, a small group of states opposed to a strong protocol played an obstructive role by making drafting suggestions aimed at limiting the scope of this instrument. They eventually managed to block not only final adoption of all substantive articles discussed during the session, but also the Working Group's report, casting doubt on the future of this drafting exercise.

Amnesty International also worked for the adoption of an optional protocol to the Convention on the Elimination of All Forms of Discrimination against Women. This protocol aims to create a mechanism whereby the Committee on the Elimination of Discrimination against Women – the body monitoring the implementation of the Convention by states parties – will be empowered to receive individual complaints about violations of the Convention by states which are party to the protocol, and to investigate systematic or serious violations of the Convention. Although some progress was achieved, key contentious issues, including the basis on which individuals or groups could bring complaints, remained unresolved. Advocacy and campaigning initiatives undertaken by NGOs were instrumental in ensuring support for a strong protocol.

One welcome development in standard-setting was the adoption in August by the UN Sub-Commission on Prevention of Discrimination and Protection of Minorities of the "draft international convention on the protection of all persons from enforced disappearance". The transmission of this draft convention to the Commission on Human Rights is a major step forward for Amnesty International and other NGOs which had worked on the draft for four years. Such a convention would codify "disappearance" as a treaty crime, reinforcing the inclusion of enforced disappearances as a crime against humanity within the jurisdiction of the ICC, and provide victims and their families with an additional avenue of redress. The draft also provides effective ways to challenge the legality of detention and obtain release if that detention is unlawful. However, vigilance in years to come will be necessary to ensure that its provisions are not weakened by governments as the draft proceeds through the UN system.

UN treaty bodies and human rights monitoring

UN treaty bodies hold governments directly accountable for compliance with their obligations under international human rights treaties. As in previous years, consideration of states' reports by treaty bodies in 1998 highlighted the repeated failure of some governments to comply with their treaty obligations, and to implement recommendations previously made by the treaty bodies.

Amnesty International presented information on the human rights situations in countries reporting to the UN Committee against Torture, which monitors compliance with the Convention against Torture, and the Human Rights Committee, which monitors compliance with the International Covenant on Civil and Political Rights (ICCPR). The countries included Algeria, Belgium, Croatia, Egypt, France, Germany, Guatemala, Italy, Israel, Japan, Peru, Sri Lanka, Tunisia and the UK. The organization provided information on Azerbaijan and the Republic of Korea to the Committee on the Elimination of Discrimination against Women. It also submitted information about its work to eradicate female genital mutilation to these treaty bodies and to the Committee on the Rights of the Child.

Amnesty International submitted further information on Egypt to the Committee against Torture. The Committee had taken the rare step in 1996 of issuing a public statement that torture was

58

widespread and systematic in Egypt (see *Amnesty International Report 1997*) and had made recommendations in both 1994 and 1996 to combat this practice. In May 1998 the Committee asked the Egyptian government not only to submit its report promptly but also to respond to this additional information.

The Committee against Torture considered the second periodic report of Israel. Amnesty International provided information on the continued use of interrogation methods which the Committee had found, in 1997, to constitute torture (see *Amnesty International Report 1998*). The Committee repeated its call to the Israeli government to immediately stop the use of torture and ill-treatment during interrogation and recommended that the practice of administrative detention in the Occupied Territories should be reviewed.

Amnesty International raised concerns about the implementation of the ICCPR in Japan. The Human Rights Committee stated that conditions of detention, including those for death row inmates, amounted to cruel, inhuman or degrading treatment. It called for restrictions on the application of the death penalty and registered concern about allegations of violence and sexual harassment of people detained pending immigration procedures.

UN thematic mechanisms

Expert working groups and special rapporteurs appointed by the Commission on Human Rights to work on different themes are known as UN thematic mechanisms.

The UN Working Group on Arbitrary Detention stated in May that the deprivation of liberty of 22 Lebanese nationals by Israel was arbitrary. It asked the Israeli government to remedy the situation and to bring its legislation into conformity with the Universal Declaration of Human Rights and other international standards accepted by that state. Amnesty International had submitted information about these detainees; some had been detained beyond the expiry of their sentences and two had been denied access to the International Committee of the Red Cross for more than nine years.

Amnesty International, the Asian Federation Against Involuntary Disappearances (AFAD) and *La Federación Latinoamericana de Asociaciones de Familiares de Detenidos-Desaparecidos* (FEDEFAM), the Federation of Latin American Families of the Disappeared, met members of the UN Working Group on Enforced or Involuntary Disappearances in September to discuss its working methods and states' obligations under the UN Declaration on the Protection of All Persons from Enforced Disappearance.

Amnesty International welcomed the appeal in October of the UN Special Rapporteur on extrajudicial, summary or arbitrary executions to the government of Trinidad and Tobago not to execute Indravani Pamela Ramjattan, a woman sentenced to death in connection with the killing of her abusive common-law husband. The Special Rapporteur expressed concern that domestic violence had not been taken into account as a mitigating circumstance at trial.

At the end of the year, the case was pending before the UK-based Judicial Committee of the Privy Council (Trinidad and Tobago's highest court of appeal) and the Inter-American Commission on Human Rights.

Following a decision at the 1998 Commission on Human Rights, Amnesty International submitted proposals to enhance the effectiveness and efficiency of the Commission's country and thematic mechanisms. Amnesty International urged that the review process lead to strengthening existing country or thematic rapporteurs and working groups; securing their independence and providing them with adequate resources; taking measures to enhance their impact; and improving their integration within the UN system.

The UN Secretariat

In October Amnesty International's Secretary General, Pierre Sané, met the newly appointed UN Deputy Secretary-General, Louise Fréchette. The meeting assessed progress in implementing a "cross-cutting" approach to human rights, making them integral to all other areas of the work of the UN, as set out in the reform package endorsed by the UN General Assembly in December 1997. Pierre Sané also met heads of UN agencies and departments, including the Coordinator for Humanitarian Affairs, the UN Development Program and UNICEF.

Amnesty International urged that integration of human rights within the UN system proceed promptly and that human rights information be fed into decision-making at all levels. If the UN system is to move towards a more rights-based approach, human rights issues have to be brought to bear within the UN's political bodies. Human rights information produced by the UN's own human rights machinery and others must be examined when these bodies take decisions.

However, the UN Security Council continued to ignore the crucial importance of human rights when considering country situations, hampering its ability to maintain international peace and security. For instance, when presented with the findings of the UN Secretary-General's Investigative Team in the Democratic Republic of the Congo that crimes against humanity and possibly genocide had been committed, the UN Security Council chose to rely on the very officials accused of having instigated massacres to bring perpetrators to justice.

Recognizing the human rights dimension of a crisis can have a major impact on its containment, resolution and aftermath. During the year, Amnesty International continued to lobby members of the UN Security Council to consider human rights when taking decisions on Afghanistan, Angola, the Great Lakes region in Africa, the Federal Republic of Yugoslavia and Sierra Leone. When the UN Security Council established the UN Observer Mission in Sierra Leone in July, Amnesty International called on the Security Council and other UN member states to ensure the provision of effective human rights monitoring and reporting.

The UN Economic and Social Council

In July the UN Economic and Social Council (ECOSOC) discussed the review and follow-up to the Vienna Declaration and Programme of Action, the final document of the 1993 UN World Conference on Human Rights. Amnesty International emphasized that the development of joint work plans between the UN Division for the Advancement of Women and the UN High Commissioner for Human Rights was a pragmatic step towards integrating a gender perspective into the mainstream of the UN's work. Amnesty International called on all parts of the UN system to follow this example and urged them, whenever possible, to provide the UN human rights machinery with data which differentiates between women and men. Amnesty International also noted the human rights impact of international financial institutions, and urged ECOSOC to do its utmost to ensure that both the UN system and the International Monetary Fund (IMF) and World Bank assess their policies' and programs' impact on human rights.

The UN General Assembly

Despite governments' rhetoric at the 1998 session of the UN General Assembly, few states contributed to the report of the UN High Commissioner for Human Rights on the follow-up to the 1993 UN World Conference on Human Rights in Vienna. It was business as usual, with many countries citing sovereignty, territorial integrity and cultural relativism to justify their stance on human rights, such as refusing to grant access to UN human rights experts. States continued to undermine treaties and limit their obligations by introducing reservations, although in Vienna states had been encouraged to limit the use of such reservations. Also, governments adopted weak resolutions such as those on the Democratic Republic of the Congo; the former Yugoslavia, including Kosovo; Iran; the ICC; and the Vienna Declaration and Programme of Action.

Amnesty International welcomed the adoption by the UN General Assembly of the Declaration on the Right and Responsibility of Individuals, Groups and Organs of Society to Promote and Protect Universally Recognized Human Rights and Fundamental Freedoms (Declaration on Human Rights Defenders). However, the Vienna Declaration and Programme of Action had recommended its speedy adoption in 1993, and the Declaration finally adopted after 13 years' work represents the bare minimum for the protection of human rights defenders. To achieve enhanced protection of human rights defenders, states' implementation of the Declaration must be monitored by the Commission on Human Rights through the establishment of an appropriate mechanism.

UN High Commissioner for Human Rights

In September Mary Robinson celebrated her first year in office as UN High Commissioner for Human Rights. During her tenure, the Bureau of the UN Commission on Human Rights reviewed its mechanisms and a special task force within her Office cooperated closely with the Bureau. The year also saw the High Commissioner facing challenges to her role. For example, in April the High Commissioner appealed to the government of Rwanda to reconsider its decision to publicly execute a number of people convicted of genocide crimes. She stated that the executions would violate internationally recognized fair trial guarantees and, therefore, the universal right to life, and would damage the process of national reconciliation. Despite appeals by the High Commissioner and the African Commission on Human and Peoples' Rights (see below), the executions went ahead. In May the government of Rwanda suspended the activities of the UN Human Rights Field Operation in the country, pending discussions on its future role. The Field Operation was withdrawn in July when the High Commissioner and the government of Rwanda could not agree on a new mandate, mainly because of the Rwandese government's refusal to allow continued monitoring of the human rights situation.

The High Commissioner expressed concern about the announced withdrawal by the Democratic People's Republic of Korea from the ICCPR and Jamaica's decision to withdraw from the (first) Optional Protocol to the ICCPR. However, during the year, Jamaica's withdrawal from the (first) Optional Protocol came into effect. In addition, both Guyana and Trinidad and Tobago withdrew from the (first) Optional Protocol to the ICCPR, although Trinidad and Tobago immediately reacceded, with a reservation precluding the Human Rights Committee from considering cases from individuals under sentence of death. Trinidad and Tobago also informed the Organization of American States that it was taking the unprecedented step of withdrawing as a state party from the American Convention on Human Rights. Amnesty International deplored the fact that as a result of these actions avenues of international redress for individuals have been cut off.

The High Commissioner has committed herself to speaking out on behalf of all human rights victims and to redressing the imbalance between civil and political rights on the one hand and economic, social and cultural rights on the other. However, the ability of her Office to implement this approach has been severely hampered by financial constraints. It remains to be seen whether the "constructive engagement" approach, which led to her signing agreements with a number of governments, will lead to enhanced respect for human rights in those countries.

Regional work
Throughout the year, Amnesty International continued to campaign for integration of human rights concerns in decision-making in regional intergovernmental organizations.

Africa
The UN Secretary-General identified human rights abuses as one of the roots of conflict in a report on durable peace and sustainable development in Africa, issued in April. He stressed that

respect for human rights and the rule of law are necessary to ensure long-term peace and stability. The report was submitted not only to the UN Security Council and General Assembly, but also to other bodies with responsibilities in Africa, including, for the first time, the IMF and World Bank.

African governments bear responsibility at the regional level as members of the Organization of African Unity (OAU). Amnesty International welcomed the OAU's initiative to convene its first-ever Ministerial Conference on human rights. In view of the planned and subsequently postponed OAU human rights conference, Amnesty International issued a document in which it reaffirmed the responsibility of the OAU to address human rights issues and made recommendations on its role in human rights protection and promotion. The adoption of human rights treaties and the creation of an African Court on Human and Peoples' Rights – as provided for by the Protocol adopted by the OAU Assembly in July – are important steps, but the OAU should exert pressure on governments to ensure implementation of their obligations under international law. This includes ratifying the African Charter on the Rights and Welfare of the Child which was adopted in 1990 and has yet to enter into force.

All OAU member states but one (Eritrea) have ratified the African Charter on Human and Peoples' Rights (the African Charter) and accepted scrutiny of their human rights record by the African Commission on Human and Peoples' Rights (the African Commission). In August Amnesty International made a number of recommendations to the African Commission on improving its working methods and practices so as to contribute more effectively to the enhancement of human rights across the continent. During the year Amnesty International urged the African Commission to hold governments accountable for violations of the African Charter, including in Chad, the Great Lakes region and Senegal. Following appeals from Amnesty International delegates attending the 23rd session of the African Commission in the Gambia, the African Commission expressed concern about imminent executions in Rwanda and asked its Special Rapporteur on extrajudicial executions to appeal to the Rwandese authorities to stop the executions. Welcoming the appointment of the Special Rapporteur on women's human rights in Africa, Amnesty International called on the African Commission to make combating the practice of female genital mutilation a specific part of her mandate.

The Americas

In the context of the Organization of American States (OAS), Amnesty International's work during the year focused on challenges to the international system of human rights protection by a number of Caribbean countries.

In February the organization presented a memorandum to the Inter-American Commission on Human Rights (IACHR) concerning attempts by Jamaica and Trinidad and Tobago to introduce time limits on the consideration of petitions from death-row prisoners by the Human Rights Committee and the IACHR. Amnesty International maintained that national authorities cannot invoke domestic legislation in order to evade their obligations under international law. Amnesty International participated in the General Assembly of the OAS in Venezuela in June. It issued an Open Letter on the death penalty, impunity for human rights violations, human rights defenders and strengthening the protection and promotion of human rights within the Inter-American system. In addition, the organization expressed concern about the unprecedented denunciation by Trinidad and Tobago of the American Convention on Human Rights. Together with a number of regional and national NGOs, it issued a joint statement on human rights in the region.

Amnesty International addressed the Inter-American Court on Human Rights (Inter-American Court) in June. It argued that the right of access to consular authorities for foreign nationals facing a possible death penalty was part of the internationally recognized right to a fair trial.

Amnesty International also worked on individual cases, including that of Consuelo Benavides, a "disappeared" Ecuadorian citizen who had been arbitrarily detained, tortured and killed by the armed forces with the complicity of top civilian and military officials. During the year, the Ecuadorian authorities reached a settlement with the IACHR and the Benavides family, which the IACHR is to monitor. The authorities paid compensation to the victim's family and committed themselves to bringing all those responsible to justice.

Amnesty International wrote to the IACHR about Trevor Fisher, a Bahamian citizen under sentence of death. The Judicial Committee of the Privy Council issued a decision stating that Trevor Fisher's execution while his case was pending before the IACHR would not violate the Bahamian Constitution or principles of public law. Trevor Fisher and Richard Woods were then hanged, despite requests by the IACHR to protect their lives at least pending the IACHR's decision on their cases.

Asia

In the months leading up to the second Asia Europe Meeting (ASEM), held in London, UK, in April, Amnesty International's members in European and Asian countries worked to ensure that human rights concerns found a place on the meeting's agenda and in the cooperation and exchange programs developing under ASEM's auspices. Amnesty International delegates participated in various ASEM initiatives, including an NGO people's forum and an intergovernmental seminar in Sweden on the rule of law.

In April, as part of its campaign on children's rights in South Asia (see **Amnesty International in Action**), Amnesty International sought not only to engage South Asian governments and

64

their donors, but also the South Asian Association for Regional Co-operation (SAARC), which in 2001 will launch the SAARC Decade for the Rights of the Child.

In July Amnesty International undertook a major lobbying action around the Association of South-East Asian Nations (ASEAN) Regional Forum, as well as ASEAN ministerial conferences and other dialogues held in Manila, the Philippines. Amnesty International's concerns in Indonesia, East Timor, Myanmar and Cambodia were a major focus of this action. There was unprecedented debate among ASEAN governments this year about human rights issues in the face of Asia's economic crisis, renewed conflict in Cambodia and the continuing political impasse in Myanmar. Some governments, such as that of Thailand, argued that ASEAN members should move beyond their traditional doctrine of "non-interference" towards greater "constructive intervention" in each other's affairs. ASEAN ministers also affirmed ongoing work by a special ASEAN working group towards the development of a regional human rights mechanism.

In September Amnesty International delegates participated in the third regional meeting of the Asia-Pacific Forum of National Human Rights Institutions in Jakarta, Indonesia. Amnesty International has attached high priority to engaging with the various national human rights commissions in the region, both on country and regional human rights issues. The Jakarta forum made strong statements about the human rights impact of the economic crisis, child sexual exploitation and women's rights, and decided to establish an advisory council of jurists to help develop human rights jurisprudence in the region.

Throughout the year, Amnesty International pursued work with the various working groups, business councils and other bodies developed by Asia-Pacific Economic Co-operation (APEC). Amnesty International launched an action on the human rights impact of the economic crisis at the time of the APEC summit in Kuala Lumpur, Malaysia, in November.

Europe

Intergovernmental organizations failed throughout 1998 to consider human rights as a vital component of efforts to find a solution to the crisis in Kosovo province in the Federal Republic of Yugoslavia, despite the loss of civilian lives and the forced displacement of more than 250,000 people. Amnesty International repeatedly called on the UN Secretary-General to present information about human rights abuses in Kosovo as an integral part of his reports to the UN Security Council. In September the UN Security Council adopted a resolution calling for the withdrawal from Kosovo of security units used for civilian repression, and emphasized its concern about violations of human rights and international humanitarian law. A month later, the UN Security Council endorsed the establishment by the Organization for Security and Co-operation in Europe (OSCE) of the Kosovo Verification Mission

An ethnic Albanian in Kosovo tries to identify the bodies of his relatives. The human rights crisis in Kosovo has led to countless deaths and the forced displacement of hundreds of thousands of people.

and entrusted it with monitoring compliance by the Federal Republic of Yugoslavia with the Security Council's September resolution.

However, the Kosovo Verification Mission's mandate barely addressed the need to monitor the human rights situation and bring to justice those responsible for human rights abuses. The agreement between the Federal Republic of Yugoslavia and the OSCE merely provides that the Verification Mission would receive information from the government about possible human rights violations, without even mentioning other sources such as victims or NGOs. In addition, the mandate did not require the Verification Mission to protect or provide reparations to the internally displaced and refugees. In November, at an OSCE meeting in Warsaw, Poland, Amnesty International, Human Rights Watch, the International Helsinki Federation, the Norwegian Helsinki Committee, the Conference of European Churches and the Minority Rights Group urged participating states of the OSCE to place human rights protection and promotion at the top of the Kosovo Verification Mission's operational program.

At the same OSCE meeting, Amnesty International raised its concerns about human rights violations in the USA in a special meeting for government and NGO representatives.

Amnesty International welcomed the Council of Europe's initiative to create a position of Commissioner for Human Rights as an opportunity to consider the strengths and weaknesses in the Council's human rights protection and promotion arsenal. In October Amnesty International recommended that the Commissioner's mandate should focus on a capacity to react

66

rapidly to crises, and on strengthening the implementation of commitments undertaken by member states.

Amnesty International welcomed the establishment in November of a single expanded European Court of Human Rights, under Protocol 11 to the European Convention for the Protection of Human Rights and Fundamental Freedoms. This replaced the previous two-tier system, where complaints were heard first by the European Commission of Human Rights and then by the Court, and should provide quicker access to justice. Amnesty International also participated in the Council of Europe's Specialists' Group on Conscientious Objection to Military Service. The Group was convened by the Steering Committee for Human Rights to assist member states to comply with Council of Europe standards. In June Amnesty International and other NGOs participated in an open meeting with the Steering Committee and urged it to strengthen the draft protocol to the European Convention on the rights of detainees.

COUNTRY ENTRIES

AFGHANISTAN

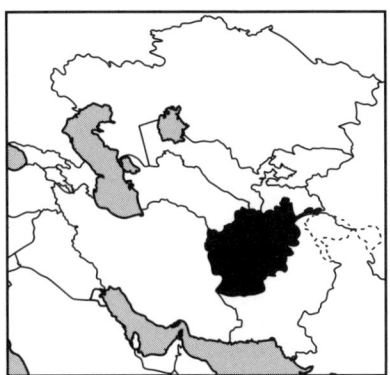

Tens of thousands of women effectively remained prisoners in their homes under *Taleban* edicts. Several thousand civilians, including possible prisoners of conscience, were taken prisoner. Almost all the detainees were reportedly tortured or ill-treated. Thousands of people were deliberately and systematically killed; thousands of others remained missing. Scores of civilians were killed in direct or indiscriminate attacks by all warring factions on the civilian population in residential areas. At least eight floggings, 14 amputations and 10 executions were announced, but the actual numbers were believed to be higher.

Heavy fighting continued throughout the year between the *Taleban*, led by Mullah Mohammad Omar, and the opposition United Front. Many localities changed hands several times. Neighbouring countries reportedly continued to supply weapons to their favoured warring factions. Despite renewed UN efforts, the prospects for peace remained remote.

The limitations on access for independent monitors to various parts of the country made information on human rights abuses difficult to gather and verify.

In April the UN Commission on Human Rights condemned the widespread human rights abuses in Afghanistan, expressing deep concern about abuses against women and girls. In November the UN Security Council approved the establishment within the UN Special Mission to Afghanistan of a unit to monitor and deter human rights abuses.

On 8 August *Taleban* forces captured the northern city of Mazar-e Sharif. On 13 September they took over the province of Bamyan. Panjshir and some areas northeast of Kabul, the capital, remained under the control of Commander Ahmad Shah Masood.

On 20 August the USA carried out an air strike in Afghanistan on military camps allegedly linked to bomb attacks on the US embassies in Kenya and Tanzania. In September Iran massed thousands of troops on the border with Afghanistan as tension grew over the killing of Iranian nationals in Mazar-e Sharif.

Hundreds of thousands of people in the northern and central regions fled their homes after the arrival of the *Taleban*. Many later returned, although some became refugees in neighbouring countries. Severe restrictions by the *Taleban* prevented UN agencies and non-governmental organizations (NGOs) from providing immediate humanitarian assistance to destitute families. Access to many women in need, especially widows, was further curtailed when expatriate Muslim women staff of international aid agencies were banned from travelling inside Afghanistan unless accompanied by a close male relative. Pressure on humanitarian NGOs to move their offices to a designated area despite serious security concerns forced them to leave the country pending assurances of security and unrestricted access to people in need.

Fear of "punishment" under *Taleban* edicts prevented tens of thousands of women from seeking education and employment or leaving home without a close male relative – effectively making them prisoners in their homes on account of their gender. Many of those accused of defying the edicts were taken to detention centres where they were humiliated or beaten by officials of the Department for the Promotion of Virtue and Prevention of Vice (DPVPV). On 17 June the DPVPV ordered the closure of all "home schools" (schools held discreetly in individuals' houses defying the ban on girls' education) and suspension of community-based vocational training programs for women in Kabul, further restricting women's movement. Scores of Hazara young women were taken by the *Taleban* as *kaniz* (servants) to be married off to *Taleban* militia deployed at war fronts.

70

More than a dozen male teachers were reportedly arrested for teaching children at home schools. Hundreds of men were reportedly detained for days or weeks and were ill-treated for defying *Taleban* edicts. They included men not attending congregational prayers, those trimming facial hair, taxi drivers carrying women passengers, and tailors making women's clothes.

In May the *Taleban* announced that "communists" would be detected and if found to be "committing heinous deeds and crimes against the people, they would be heavily punished". This raised fears that Pashtun nationalists opposing *Taleban* policies, particularly some members of the former *Khalq* (People), a communist party, might be targeted for human rights abuses.

Non-Pashtun Afghans were barred from moving about the country freely. Many were detained solely on the basis of their ethnicity. In July alone, hundreds of people travelling to Pakistan were stopped in the Jalalabad area by *Taleban* guards who took away Tajik, Hazara, Uzbek and Panjsheri men and boys as young as 12. Some of the detainees were classified as "important" and sent to Kandahar, where thousands of such prisoners were reportedly held. Some men were released on payment of a ransom. Women, children and the elderly of non-Pashtun families were sent to camps near Jalalabad with no material support.

Several thousand civilians, including posssible prisoners of conscience, were reportedly detained on suspicion of opposing the *Taleban*. The majority were detained in August after the *Taleban* entered Mazar-e Sharif and were interrogated to identify their ethnic identity. The vast majority of those detained were non-Pashtuns, particularly Hazaras. In October the *Taleban* reportedly took prisoner dozens of civilians, targeting educated people, in the Tajik-populated city of Taloqan immediately before it was recaptured by opposition forces.

Scores of people were reportedly arrested in October mainly in Jalalabad, apparently for their peaceful opposition to the continuing war in the country.

Others arrested included locally recruited staff of international organizations and at least three Afghan staff members of the UN who were reportedly held without charge. The whereabouts of thousands of people detained particularly in the second part of the year remained unknown.

Almost all prisoners detained on suspicion of opposing the *Taleban* were reported to have been tortured or ill-treated. A chemist arrested in October was reportedly beaten so badly that he needed a blood transfusion. In August more than 100 people were reportedly suffocated to death inside metal containers in which the *Taleban* transferred prisoners from Mazar-e Sharif to Shebarghan.

Amid reports of ill-treatment and killing of prisoners, *Radio Voice of Shari'a* quoted *Taleban* leader Mullah Mohammad Omar as saying, "Whoever resorts to killing the prisoners or the war-wounded shall be tried in the Islamic court. Nobody is allowed to kill prisoners unless there is a threat."

Thousands of people were killed deliberately and arbitrarily by different warring factions. In July Nazar Mohammad, a deputy leader of *Da Solh Ghorzan* (Peace Movement), an Afghan organization, was shot dead by two gunmen on a motorbike in Quetta, Pakistan. An Afghan warring faction was believed to be responsible. Mohammad Nazir Habibi and Mohammad Hashim Basharyar, two Afghans working with UN aid agencies in Jalalabad, were abducted on 13 July. Their bodies were found several days later. In September UN officials said the *Taleban* had failed to provide credible reports on the UN personnel's murders, despite repeated requests.

Taleban guards deliberately and systematically killed thousands of ethnic Hazara civilians in the days following their military takeover of Mazar-e Sharif in August. The vast majority were living in the Zara'at, Saidabad and Elm Arab areas of the city. They were killed in their homes or on the streets, or executed in locations between Mazar-e Sharif and Hairatan. Women, children and the elderly were shot while trying to flee the city. At least one group of prisoners was executed in front of villagers near the city of Hairatan. About 70 men were reportedly executed by having their throats slit in Mazar-e Sharif.

Ten Iranian diplomats and one journalist were killed when *Taleban* guards entered the Iranian consulate in Mazar-e Sharif in August.

On 21 August a clearly marked UN vehicle carrying UN Special Mission to

Afghanistan (UNSMA) officials was approached by a vehicle bearing official *Taleban* markings. A gunman jumped out of the *Taleban* vehicle and began shooting at the UN officials. Lieutenant Colonel Carmine Calo died the next day from his wounds. *Taleban* authorities reportedly arrested two suspects, allegedly of Pakistan origin. They had reportedly not been tried by the end of the year. There were several other reports of assault by *Taleban* officials on the staff of the UN and aid agencies.

Direct or indiscriminate attacks by all warring factions on the civilian population in residential areas reportedly killed scores of people. Over 1,000 civilians were reportedly victims of landmines.

Executions or other cruel, inhuman or degrading punishments were believed to be widespread, but were not always reported by the authorities. Of those announced, eight people were flogged, including a woman accused of adultery who was given 100 lashes at the Kabul Sports Stadium in February in front of some 30,000 spectators.

There were at least 14 reports of public amputations carried out by doctors from the Ministry of Public Health, usually in football stadiums in front of thousands of spectators, some of whom said they had been forced to attend.

At least 10 public executions were reported. They included five men convicted of "sodomy" and sentenced to death by being crushed by a wall. Several of the executions were carried out by the victims' families.

In a report published in April, *Children in South Asia*, Amnesty International called on all armed groups in Afghanistan to respect the human rights of children. In September Amnesty International called for an international body to be set up to investigate the massacres in Mazar-e Sharif in order to identify the perpetrators and recommend ways of bringing them to justice. It warned that tens of thousands of ethnic Hazara civilians in Bamyan province were at risk of being massacred by advancing *Taleban* forces. There was no formal response by the *Taleban* or other factions in 1998.

ALBANIA

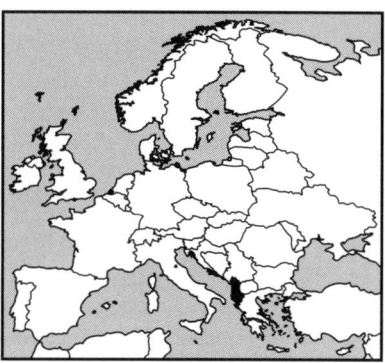

Six officials of the former administration were detained on charges of "genocide" and faced procedures that fell short of international fair trial standards. There were allegations of ill-treatment by police. Prison conditions amounting to cruel, inhuman or degrading treatment were reported. There were allegations of extra-judicial executions. At least four men were sentenced to death.

The public order situation improved, although lawlessness prevailed in many parts of the country. There were a number of assassinations and attempted assassinations of political activists.

A political crisis began in August with the arrest of six officials of the former administration led by the Democratic Party (DP). The crisis deepened in September when a prominent DP member, Azem Hajdari, was assassinated. In response, DP leader and former President, Sali Berisha, led protests of DP supporters in the capital Tirana claiming that the government was responsible for the killing. Armed DP supporters briefly took control of government offices and the state television station. The same month Prime Minister Fatos Nano of the Socialist Party (SP) resigned as a result of the crisis and was replaced by another SP member, Pandeli Majko. In November a new constitution was approved in a referendum.

Six former officials were arrested in September, including former ministers and police commanders who held office under the DP-led government which ended in 1997. The arrest warrants reportedly cited charges of violating the country's

72

"genocide" law by "ordering the use of chemical weapons", arming civilians and taking and giving orders which violated the Constitution. These related to the authorities' response to the countrywide unrest which started in early 1997 (see *Amnesty International Report 1998*). The men were reportedly denied access to their lawyers during the initial stages of the detention, which may have prejudiced the preparation of their defence. At the end of the year, five of the men remained in custody.

There were allegations of ill-treatment by police. For example, Gjergj Deda, a former police chief in Shkodra, was reportedly beaten severely after he was detained in February. In some cases the victims were active supporters of opposition parties, most frequently the DP. In February Fran Voci, reportedly a DP supporter, was detained by special police forces in Shkodra on suspicion of involvement in an armed attack on the town's main police station. About four days later, his family visited him in the Tirana Prison hospital and found that he had been beaten severely. Fran Voci subsequently stated that during police interrogation he had been hit continuously about the face and had his head knocked against a wall to make him sign a confession.

Prison conditions which amounted to cruel, inhuman or degrading treatment were reported. Adem Bendaj, who was sentenced to death in April for murder, was reportedly held for at least five months with his hands and feet in chains and an iron helmet over his head. Other prisoners under sentence of death were reported to have been treated in a similar manner.

Extrajudicial executions were reported, but were difficult to document. In January, for example, police in Fier allegedly took Agron Pasha from hospital and killed him in a village outside the town.

At least three men other than Adem Bendaj were sentenced to death during the year. No executions were reported to have been carried out since 1995. One report indicated that there were more than 20 men under sentence of death.

In December Amnesty International wrote to the authorities expressing its concern about the alleged extrajudicial execution of Agron Pasha and reported cases of ill-treatment or torture. It also expressed concern about reports of prison conditions which amounted to cruel, inhuman or degrading treatment.

ALGERIA

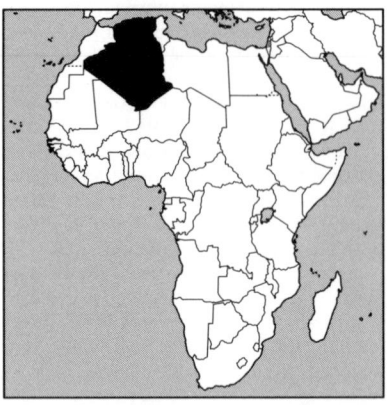

Thousands of civilians were killed; some were extrajudicially executed by security forces or by militias armed by the state, others were deliberately and arbitrarily killed by armed groups which define themselves as "Islamic groups". Thousands of people, including possible prisoners of conscience, were detained; many were released without charge and hundreds were charged under the "anti-terrorist" law. Hundreds of people arrested in previous years were sentenced to prison terms after unfair trials. Hundreds of people remained detained without trial. Torture and ill-treatment by security forces remained widespread, especially during secret detention but also in prisons. Torture, including rape, by armed groups also continued. Dozens of people "disappeared" after arrest by security forces. Thousands of people who "disappeared" in previous years remained unaccounted for. Scores of people were abducted by armed groups. Hundreds of people were sentenced to death, the vast majority *in absentia*. Hundreds of others remained under sentence of death. No judicial executions were carried out.

In September President Liamine Zeroual announced that he would step down in February 1999, 21 months before the end of his term, and that presidential elections would be held. General Mohamed

Betchine, President Zeroual's adviser, and Minister of Justice Mohamed 'Adami resigned in October after allegations of their involvement in corruption and human rights abuses appeared in the press. Prime Minister Ahmed Ouyahia resigned in December and was replaced by Smai'l Hamdani.

Prime Minister Ouyahia told the National Assembly in February that more than 5,000 militias armed by the state, redefined Groupes de légitime défense, Legitimate Defence Groups, and also known as "patriotes" ("patriots"), had been set up. On the same occasion he stated that the total number of civilians and members of the security forces killed from 1992 to 1997 was 26,536. No figure was given for the number of people killed by security forces in military operations or other situations. It was the first time the government had given an official death toll. Other sources put the total number of dead for the same period at between 65,000 and 100,000.

The state of emergency imposed in 1992 (see previous Amnesty International Reports) remained in force.

The UN Special Rapporteurs on torture and on extrajudicial, summary or arbitrary executions were refused access to Algeria throughout the year. The government rejected calls by the UN High Commissioner for Human Rights, the European Union, the G8 and others for the Special Rapporteurs to be allowed to visit the country to investigate human rights issues. It also rejected an attempt by the UN Secretary-General to discuss the situation. Amnesty International and other international human rights organizations were refused access to the country throughout the year.

In July the UN Human Rights Committee examined Algeria's second periodic report on its implementation of the International Covenant on Civil and Political Rights, which had been overdue since 1995. The Committee expressed grave concern at the situation in Algeria and called on the government to take effective measures to prevent massacres and attacks against the civilian population; conduct investigations to determine who the offenders are and to bring them to justice; make inquiries into the conduct of the security forces in all cases of massacres; investigate all allegations of torture and prosecute officials involved in torture;

record all reported cases of "disappearances" and assist families to trace the "disappeared"; and ensure that nobody is arrested or detained outside the law and that complaints about such arrest or detention be given immediate attention.

A UN panel composed of six international political figures and headed by former Portuguese President Mario Soares visited Algeria in July/August. It subsequently called on the government to hold the law enforcement, security and self-defence forces to strict standards of accountability; work resolutely to change the attitude in the judiciary, police, army and the institutions responsible for upholding human rights; and give expeditious attention to complaints of arbitrary detention, extrajudicial executions and "disappearances".

The unilateral truce declared in October 1997 by the Armée islamique du salut (AIS), Islamic Salvation Army – the armed wing of the outlawed Front islamique du salut (FIS), Islamic Salvation Front – remained in place. AIS groups reportedly cooperated with army and security forces units to combat the Groupe islamique armé (GIA), Armed Islamic Group, and other such armed groups in various parts of the country.

The level of violence remained high throughout the year, but appeared to be lower than in 1997. Responsibility for human rights abuses could often not be established because security forces, militias armed by the state and armed groups defining themselves as "Islamic groups" often adopted similar patterns of conduct and because there were no investigations. Restrictions on access to the country for international media and human rights organizations, and restrictions imposed on the local media severely curtailed reporting of human rights abuses.

Hundreds of people were killed in military operations against GIA groups carried out by the army, other security forces, and militias armed by the state. It was not possible in most cases to obtain details concerning the number of those killed, their identity or the exact circumstances in which they were killed. It was routinely reported by officials and the media that entire groups attacked by the security forces had been killed and no prisoners taken. There were allegations that many of those killed had been extrajudicially

74

executed after they were captured. In March Riadh Boutekdjeret, a 21-year-old student, was reportedly shot in the back by a member of the security forces in the el-Biar district in Algiers, the capital, and died soon after. No inquiry was known to have been carried out.

No investigations were known to have been carried out into the alleged extrajudicial execution of Rachid Medjahed in 1997 (see *Amnesty International Report 1998*). A representative of the Algerian government told the UN Human Rights Committee in July that Rachid Medjahed had been shot by security forces in January, whereas the government had previously maintained that he had been shot in February.

Reports of extrajudicial executions and other grave abuses by militias armed by the state continued to be widespread. Two militia chiefs who were also mayors of Relizane and Jdiouia for the *Rassemblement national démocratique*, National Democratic Rally, the largest party in the government, were arrested in April. They were accused of widespread human rights abuses, including numerous murders, torture, abductions and racketeering, committed since 1995. However, they were released on bail within days and had not been brought to trial by the end of the year. The authorities announced in February that more than 120 members of the security forces and militias had been brought to justice for human rights abuses committed in previous years, including murder, rape and abduction. However, the authorities refused to provide further information.

Armed groups which define themselves as "Islamic groups" deliberately and arbitrarily killed hundreds of civilians and non-combatants. Some women abducted by these groups were reportedly raped before being killed. The singer Ma'toub Lounes was shot dead by an armed group in June as he was driving near Tizi Ouzou in Kabilia. His wife and two sisters-in-law were injured in the attack.

In January up to 200 men, women and children were killed by an armed group near Relizane, in the west of the country, in the largest massacre reported during the year. Some of the victims were families of AIS members. Security forces only came to the scene the following day, after the attackers had fled. By the end of the year no one was known to have been brought to

justice for this massacre or for the massacres of hundreds of civilians in Rais and Bentalha in 1997 (see *Amnesty International Report 1998*).

Scores of civilians died in bomb attacks by armed groups, who targeted markets, cafés and other public places in different parts of the country.

Thousands of people, among them possible prisoners of conscience, were detained during the year. Many were released without charge having spent periods ranging from a few days to a few months in secret detention. Hundreds were charged under the "anti-terrorist" law. Hundreds of others detained in previous years were sentenced to prison terms after unfair trials or continued to be detained awaiting trial. Allegations of torture during often prolonged secret detention were routinely disregarded by the courts, as were defence lawyers' requests to call witnesses. In January, 37 detainees and one prison guard were tried in connection with a mutiny in Serkadji Prison in which at least 96 detainees and five prison guards were killed (see *Amnesty International Report 1996*). The defendants were accused of attempting to escape, destruction of property and holding hostages. The guard was also accused of participation in murder. The court did not seek to establish the causes and circumstances of the deaths of the detainees, and defence lawyers were not allowed to call key witnesses. The prison guard was sentenced to death, 21 detainees were sentenced to between two and 10 years' imprisonment and 16 were acquitted. Among those acquitted and released was Nadir Hammoudi, who had been detained since 1992 (see previous *Amnesty International Reports*).

In December the Supreme Court quashed the conviction against human rights lawyer and prisoner of conscience Rachid Mesli, who had been sentenced to three years' imprisonment in 1997 (see *Amnesty International Report 1998*). He was refused bail and remained in detention awaiting retrial at the end of the year.

Torture and ill-treatment remained widespread, especially during secret detention after arrest. For example, Mohamed Boukhlaf was arrested in August with his wife, baby daughter and 10-year-old nephew and was reportedly tortured in the gendarmerie station in Bab Djedid in Algiers. He said that he was raped and sexually abused, had teeth pulled out and was threatened that his wife would be raped. His wife, child and nephew were released after 11 days. He remained detained on charges of links with armed groups. No investigations were known to have been carried out into his complaint of torture or into any other torture complaint in 1998 or previous years.

The maximum 12-day limit for incommunicado detention was routinely breached by security forces who often held suspects in secret detention for weeks or months. A 70-year-old Imam from Constantine was released in April after 11 months in secret detention. During this entire period his family was unable to obtain any information on his whereabouts from the authorities who consistently denied his arrest.

Dozens of other people "disappeared" after arrest by security forces and were believed to be held in secret detention. For example, Mohamed Cheridji, a father of four, "disappeared" after he was arrested at his home in Baraki in January in front of his family. Thousands of others who "disappeared" in previous years remained unaccounted for. 'Aziz Bou'abdallah, 'Allaoua Ziou, Djamaleddine Fahassi, Mohamed Rosli, Brahim Cherrada, Mohamed Chergui, Yamine 'Ali Kebaili and 13 others who "disappeared" after arrest between 1993 and 1997 remained unaccounted for (see previous *Amnesty International Reports*).

In August hundreds of relatives of people who had "disappeared" began to hold weekly demonstrations outside the office of the official human rights body, the ONDH, and other government buildings. In response the Ministry of the Interior opened offices in the capital and elsewhere to receive the families' complaints and promised to investigate the cases. At the same time both the government and the ONDH continued to deny that most of the "disappeared" had ever been arrested, and claimed that others had been killed by the security forces in combat or while attempting to escape, or had been killed by "terrorist" groups. Some of the "disappeared" were alleged to have died as a result of torture or to have been extrajudicially executed after arrest. No independent investigations were known to have been carried out into the "disappearances" by the end of the year.

'Ali Belhadj, a FIS leader arrested in 1991 and sentenced to 12 years' imprisonment in 1992, who had "disappeared" in mid-1995, was allowed to be visited by his family for the first time since then in September in Blida Military Prison (see *Amnesty International Report 1998*).

Hundreds of people were sentenced to death, most of them *in absentia*. Hundreds of others remained under sentence of death. The moratorium on executions remained in force.

In March and April Amnesty International and three other organizations, the International Federation of Human Rights, Human Rights Watch and *Reporters sans frontières*, called on the UN Commission on Human Rights to appoint a Special Rapporteur on Algeria and to set up an international investigation into the human rights situation in the country. However, the Commission failed to take any concrete action (see **International Organizations**).

Throughout the year Amnesty International called on the authorities to take concrete measures to stop and prevent human rights abuses by its security forces, by militias armed by the state and by armed groups; investigate all incidents of human rights abuses; and ensure that the perpetrators are brought to justice.

ANGOLA

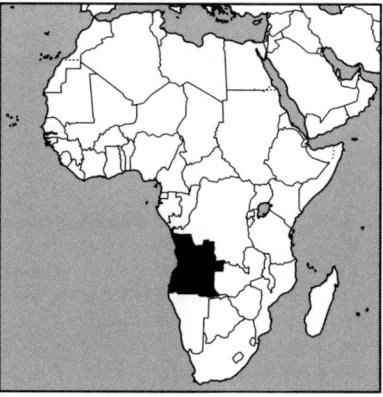

Suspected government critics and supporters of armed groups were detained for varying periods. Some suspected armed government opponents "disappeared". There were scores of reported

76

extrajudicial executions by government security forces. The *União Nacional para a Independência Total de Angola* (UNITA), National Union for the Total Independence of Angola, abducted and deliberately and arbitrarily killed unarmed civilians. An armed opposition group held hostages.

Tension mounted as completion of the 1994 peace agreement between the government of President José Eduardo dos Santos and UNITA, led by Jonas Savimbi, increasingly gave way to armed confrontation.

Under pressure from the UN Observer Mission in Angola (MONUA), UNITA announced in March that it had demobilized all its forces. As a result, UNITA was legalized as a political party, although 70 UNITA deputies had already taken seats in the National Assembly in April 1997 (see *Amnesty International Report 1998*). UNITA appointees took up posts in provincial government and as ambassadors.

UNITA continued to hold territory. It retained an estimated 30,000 troops and continued to receive supplies by air. In July, after UNITA failed to allow the extension of government authority to key areas, including its strongholds in Andulo and Bailundo, the UN imposed further sanctions (see *Amnesty International Report 1998*). The government demanded that UNITA disarm its troops and hand over the remaining territory by September. When UNITA failed to comply, the government and parliament suspended UNITA representatives from their posts. All but two officials and parliamentary deputies were reinstated after some suspended officials renounced the leadership of Jonas Savimbi and formed the UNITA Renewal Committee. In November most of the UNITA deputies declared they were committed to peace and formed a separate Platform of Understanding.

The government recognized the Renewal Committee as its counterpart in the peace agreement. It was supported in this action by southern African governments. Contact between the government and Jonas Savimbi ceased and the government refused security clearance to allow the UN Secretary-General's Special Representative for Angola to meet Jonas Savimbi at his headquarters. The Special Representative had replaced the former head of MONUA, who was killed in an air crash in June.

Armed attacks increased from March. Some appeared to be acts of banditry, but many appeared to be politically motivated. Clashes between government and UNITA forces intensified, particularly in the north, the diamond mining areas in the northeast and the central highlands. They resulted in the deaths of hundreds and displacement of thousands of civilians. An attack on the Bula diamond mine in July left about 100 dead; the government and UNITA blamed each other for the attack. Several UN staff and members of international aid organizations were killed or injured, mostly by unidentified groups, although some attacks were attributed to UNITA. In December a UN aircraft carrying 14 people was shot down near Huambo. The same month fighting escalated and was particularly intense in the provinces of Bié, Malange and Huambo. Government aircraft attacked UNITA's headquarters in the central highlands, and heavily armed UNITA forces surrounded and shelled Kuito in Bié province and Malange city in Malange province. Hundreds of civilians were killed, many in indiscriminate shelling, and more than 200,000 were displaced.

Events in the Democratic Republic of the Congo (DRC) continued to affect Angola and several hundred Angolan troops remained in the Republic of the Congo (see *Amnesty International Report 1998*). After conflict broke out in the DRC in August, the government sent an estimated 7,000 troops to assist DRC President Laurent-Désiré Kabila. Some of these troops were withdrawn late in the year. The authorities also aimed to prevent UNITA and separatist rebels in Cabinda, an Angolan enclave between the DRC and the Republic of the Congo, from using the DRC and the Republic of the Congo as rear bases. Troops were deployed throughout Cabinda where government forces faced armed factions of the *Frente para a Libertação do Enclave de Cabinda* (FLEC), Cabinda Enclave Liberation Front. UNITA allegedly cooperated with opposition groups fighting the DRC government.

Both the government and UNITA forcibly conscripted civilians. In November the National Assembly approved a resolution for the enrolment of young men approaching military age (20 years). However, there were frequent reports of illegal conscription drives in which young men, including minors, were rounded up. Some were believed to have been incorporated into illegal civil defence units. The authorities failed to complete the disarming of civilians as required under the peace agreement.

The deteriorating security situation and economic difficulties affected most Angolans. By the end of the year the number of internally displaced persons had reached an estimated 1.4 million. The level of violent crime remained high. Little progress was made in equipping the judiciary and training the police to protect and enforce human rights (see *Amnesty International Report 1998*).

The MONUA Human Rights Division (see *Amnesty International Report 1998*) recruited new staff. Its officers and UN Civilian Police investigated human rights abuses, visited prisons and promoted awareness of human rights. MONUA repeatedly stressed the need for police to receive training in human rights standards for law enforcement officials.

Hundreds of people were reportedly arrested for political reasons. Most were suspected UNITA supporters, demobilized soldiers or members of UNITA local committees detained in areas recently returned to state administration. Many were reportedly beaten at the time of arrest. It was usually impossible to obtain further details about those detained.

Afonso Justino Waco, a Protestant cleric and a non-violent advocate of Cabinda's independence, was detained in Cabinda city in August. In a radio interview he had spoken of troop movements towards the border with the DRC and was accused of defaming the government. He was released five days later, the day after the government first confirmed that it had sent troops to the DRC.

There were frequent reports of people "disappearing" in custody in areas formerly held by UNITA. Police arrested nine demobilized UNITA soldiers, including former Colonel Jose Maria Kapinala, in Mumbué, Bié province, in late December 1997 or early January and said that they were taking them to Menongue, Kuando Kubango province. UN officials subsequently made inquiries but found no trace of the nine men. Two other UNITA supporters, Luis Chiponde and Joaquim Chimbali, were arrested in Kawewe in June and taken to Chitembo, Kuando Kubango province, where they apparently "disappeared".

Pedro Zacarias Lelo and Vicente Armando were arrested in September in the vicinity of Cabinda city, apparently on suspicion that they were members of a FLEC faction. They were said to have been initially taken to a military police centre. In November witnesses stated that their vehicle was parked in a military camp and that a body, with clothing similar to that last worn by Pedro Zacarias Lelo, was seen in a nearby area sewn with landmines.

Real or suspected opponents of the government received threats, including death threats. Journalists, a trade unionist and UNITA members who refused to join the Renewal Committee received threats by mail, telephone or in person. There was an apparent attempt in October on the life of a UNITA deputy, Abel Chivukuvuku, who had not joined the Renewal Committee. Two UNITA deputies were briefly arrested in connection with the incident, but no one had been brought to justice by the end of the year.

A Roman Catholic priest expressed concern in a sermon in September that some former FLEC members had pointed out suspected FLEC supporters to the authorities. The Provincial Delegate of the Interior Ministry wrote in a letter that the priest's attitude encouraged civil disobedience and declined any responsibility for what might happen if the priest did not change his behaviour.

There were allegations of extrajudicial executions of criminal suspects and of people who disobeyed police orders. Hundreds of suspected armed opponents, particularly UNITA members, were reported to have been extrajudicially executed, but in most cases it was impossible to clarify or corroborate the reports. In none of the following reported cases of torture and killings were those responsible known to have been brought to justice.

António Mavungo, a catering worker, was reportedly beaten to death by a police officer in Cacongo, Cabinda, in March after a dispute over a water container. When António Mavungo stooped to pick up the container the officer reportedly hit him on the back of the head with the butt of his gun. The officer and a colleague subsequently fled in a stolen car. The Cacongo police commander promptly ordered the arrest of the two officers, but there was no report of anyone being detained or charged in connection with the

78

killing. In November a 12-year-old girl was reportedly raped by two police officers in Quibala district, Kwanza Sul province, in daylight in view of other children.

There was apparently no investigation into the deaths of at least six people in raids which followed the shooting of a police officer in the Sambizanga suburb of Luanda in April. Local people said the perpetrators were police officers. Some said they had heard the perpetrators claim that they aimed to avenge the officer's death. Those killed included Domingos da Costa and Moisés Daniel. Moisés Daniel was arrested in his bedroom. The family later found his body, riddled with bullets, in a street.

At least three young men were reported to have been killed in a police operation in Cazenga suburb, Luanda, in July. Family members of two of the dead told journalists that they had witnessed the killings. The relatives of a third victim, Clementino Cardoso, said that after police led him away they heard the shots that killed him.

At least five people were reportedly extrajudicially executed during an operation by military police in Kikolo, Luanda province. Some witnesses suggested that the operation was one of several unauthorized conscription drives reported in July. Others claimed that the victims were UNITA supporters or suspected criminals.

A Protestant cleric, Manuel Milongo, was killed in what may have been an extrajudicial execution in Quibala district, Kwanza Sul province, in August. Several Protestant clerics had fled from villages in the area on hearing that local officials suspected that they were UNITA supporters. Manuel Milongo, who had not fled, was reportedly killed a few days later by a group of men carrying machetes and guns.

In late September and early October police and soldiers in Negage, Uige province, reportedly arrested several UNITA supporters or demobilized soldiers and killed at least two of them. The body of one, Monteiro Cambenge, was found in the street the day after the arrests.

Four youths, at least one of whom appeared to be a minor, died in a police post in Luanda in November. The cause of the deaths was reportedly registered as asphyxiation. According to reports, the youths had been held in a hot, overcrowded cell full of human excrement. An autopsy carried out on one of the bodies reportedly found a cranial fracture, broken ribs and arm, and marks on the back and legs indicating that he had been beaten severely. The police said they were conducting an inquiry, but did not publish the results before the end of the year. There were also reports that police interrogated members of non-governmental organizations working on the case with the apparent intention of dissuading them from criticizing the police.

Both UNITA and FLEC factions carried out human rights abuses. UNITA reportedly abducted hundreds of civilians, including children, and raped women. In March UNITA reportedly abducted 16 police officers in Kuando Kubango province, then disarmed and killed 14 of them. Traditional leaders suspected of supporting the government were also targeted. UNITA forces reportedly stabbed and beat six traditional leaders to death in June in Kissanga, Malange province. At least 60 people were killed in Luremo, Lunda Norte province, in August in an attack attributed to UNITA. Some of the victims appeared to have been deliberately killed. The body of a man had his arms tied behind his back and a woman had been stabbed and then shot. In October UNITA troops in Catabola, Bié province, reportedly murdered two traditional leaders who had refused to give them food. Several people were said to have died after being shut in a house which was then set alight in Kimbilimba, Kwanza Sul province, in August.

One of the FLEC factions held hostages. Nine Angolan and two Portuguese road workers were abducted in April. In June the Portuguese and one Angolan were released, but the fate of the other Angolans remained unclarified. A Malaysian forestry worker, Omar Bin Norola, who had been held since February 1997, was released. Marcelin Alime, a Philippine national arrested with him, reportedly died in custody of an illness. Supporters of another FLEC faction reportedly killed teacher Mateus Gomes at his school in June, then decapitated his body. Mateus Gomes had reportedly refused to teach their children.

Amnesty International expressed concern about extrajudicial executions and other politically motivated killings. It sought information about reports of death threats against perceived political opponents. In April Amnesty International published a report, *Angola: Extrajudicial executions and torture in Cabinda*. The Interior Ministry provided a copy of its report into the deaths in custody of 10 UNITA members in Malange in 1997 (see *Amnesty International Report 1998*), but did not address fully the organization's concerns about the lack of independence of the commission of inquiry or the omission of essential information such as the precise causes of death. The Ministry also responded to the organization's request for information about the arrest and alleged torture of Afonso Justino Waco, saying that Afonso Justino Waco had been legally detained and charged with defaming the government and that he had not been tortured.

ARGENTINA

One prisoner of conscience remained under house arrest. There were reports of torture by police; victims included minors. Killings in circumstances suggesting possible extrajudicial executions continued to be reported. Threats against human rights defenders continued. There was little progress in clarifying past human rights violations, but a number of investigations were initiated.

In March the National Congress repealed the Full Stop and Due Obedience Laws, passed by the civilian government in 1986 and 1987 respectively. These laws granted immunity from prosecution to members of the security forces involved in human rights violations committed during the period of military government between 1976 and 1983, and prevented the victims of these violations and their relatives from

seeking legal redress, although cases of "disappeared" children were excluded (see *Amnesty International Reports 1986* and *1987*). The repeal of the laws was interpreted by some members of the judiciary as not being effective retroactively.

In August the Inter-American Court of Human Rights set the amount of reparations and costs to be paid by the State of Argentina to relatives of Adolfo Garrido and Raul Baigorria who "disappeared" in 1990 after being detained by members of the Mendoza Provincial Police. The Court also ruled that the State of Argentina must investigate the facts surrounding the "disappearance" of the two men and bring to trial those found responsible and anyone who had covered up or participated in the "disappearances".

The Argentine authorities remained obstructive and unwilling to cooperate with Spanish court proceedings relating to past human rights violations (see *Amnesty International Reports 1997* and *1998*).

In January former navy officer Alfredo Astiz was put under military arrest for 60 days after publicly admitting that he had participated in operations by units of the *Escuela de Mecánica de la Armada* (ESMA), Navy Mechanics School, during the period of military rule. The ESMA had been responsible for the abduction, "disappearance" and murder of people considered "enemies" of the military government. A few days after his arrest, Alfredo Astiz was expelled from the Navy and stripped of his rank by the Navy High Command. He was subsequently released. In April he was called to give testimony before a federal judge in relation to investigations into illegal adoptions of "disappeared" children of detainees held at the ESMA.

Three former senior officers were arrested during the year on charges relating to cases of "disappeared" children. The children had either been abducted with their parents or been born in secret detention centres during the period of military government; some had been adopted by members of the security forces. In June, 72-year-old Jorge Rafael Videla, a former army commander and President of the military junta between 1976 and 1981, was arrested in connection with the illegal adoptions of five children whose parents "disappeared" between 1976 and 1978 and who had been abducted by the security forces. The investigation was subsequently

80

extended to 10 cases. In July he was released from prison and placed under house arrest. In November, 73-year-old Emilio Massera, a former admiral and member of the first military junta, was arrested in connection with kidnappings involving the cases of 17 "disappeared" children. He too was transferred from prison to house arrest. In December, 71-year-old former Navy Commander Rubén Franco was arrested also in connection with the kidnapping of children. The investigations had not concluded by the end of the year.

In June prisoner of conscience Fray Antonio Puigjané, who had been arrested in 1989 (see Amnesty International Reports 1997 and 1998), was released from prison and transferred to a Franciscan convent on the eve of his 70th birthday. His transfer followed a judicial ruling made under a discretionary procedure which allows prisoners aged over 70 to complete their sentences outside prison. At the end of the year he continued to serve a 20-year sentence under house arrest.

Recommendations made in December 1997 by the Inter-American Commission on Human Rights regarding the cases of members of the Movimiento Todos por la Patria, All for the Fatherland Movement (see Amnesty International Reports 1990 to 1993 and 1998), were not implemented.

There were reports that detainees and street children were tortured by police. Several victims did not file formal complaints for fear of reprisals. Killings in circumstances suggesting possible extrajudicial executions continued to be reported. When investigations were initiated into allegations of human rights abuses, progress was slow. According to the nongovernmental human rights organization Servicio Paz y Justicia, Service Peace and Justice, street children and minors were arbitrarily detained and attacked by police officers in Buenos Aires. Among the victims was Diego Martín Arbia, a minor, who was arrested by members of the federal police in January and taken to the División Roca police station where he was beaten by two police officers while handcuffed, and doused in petrol. When the handcuffs were taken off and he was placed in a cell, a lighted match was thrown into the cell. He was left in the cell until the following day. Diego Martín Arbia needed medical treatment for burns on his neck, ears and head.

During the year the Coordinadora Contra la Represión Policial e Institucional (CORREPI), Association against Police and Institutional Repression, recorded more than 40 cases of killings by police, known as "gatillo fácil" ("trigger-happy") killings (see Amnesty International Reports 1996 and 1998). For example, in May Diego Pavón, a minor, was in the street outside his house playing, when a police officer shot him dead at point-blank range. According to reports, the police officer had threatened Diego Pavón, who was to give testimony against the police officer's brother who was charged in connection with the killing of another youth. Witnesses to Diego Pavón's killing were reportedly reluctant to give evidence for fear of reprisals. The investigation was closed for lack of evidence.

Human rights defenders were threatened and attacked. In July a threatening message was left on the answering machine of Sergio Smietniansky, a lawyer working with CORREPI to support relatives of the victims of police repression. In November Esteban Cuya, a Peruvian delegate from the Coalición contra la Impunidad, Coalition Against Impunity – a German human rights organization which campaigns for German courts to bring to justice those responsible for human rights violations against German nationals during the period of military government in Argentina – was attacked in Buenos Aires. Unidentified men gagged him with a wet towel and threatened him with death. An official complaint was filed, but no information was available on the progress of the investigation by the end of the year.

In May Amnesty International published a report, Argentina and Chile: The international community's responsibility regarding crimes against humanity – trials in Spain for crimes against humanity under military regimes in Argentina and Chile. In May Amnesty International delegates met provincial and federal authorities to present Argentina: "Occupational hazards"? Attacks, threats and harassment against journalists". The delegates raised the organization's concerns about human rights violations committed by police officers and death threats and attacks against journalists and human rights defenders. The delegates called for the unconditional release of Fray Antonio Puigjané. They also called for the annulment of legislation which obstructs the investigation of past human rights violations and the bringing of those found responsible to justice.

ARMENIA

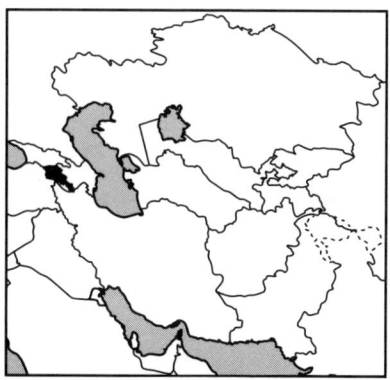

At least seven prisoners of conscience were imprisoned for refusing on grounds of conscience to perform compulsory military service. Allegations of ill-treatment in detention continued to be reported. At least 25 men were under sentence of death. No executions took place.

President Levon Ter-Petrosyan resigned in February, following disagreements about policy regarding the disputed Karabakh region in neighbouring Azerbaijan. Shortly afterwards, the opposition Armenian Revolutionary Federation was able to resume legal activity and several of the political prisoners convicted in the so-called Dro and Ovanessian trials (see *Amnesty International Report 1998*) were released.

Robert Kocharian was elected President in March. The following month he appointed former prisoner of conscience Paruir Hairikian as chairman of a new presidential Human Rights Commission, which in June proposed establishing the office of ombudsperson in Armenia.

In October the UN Human Rights Committee reviewed Armenia's first periodic report under the International Covenant on Civil and Political Rights (ICCPR). The Committee expressed concern about, among other things, allegations of torture and ill-treatment by law enforcement officials; poor prison conditions; and discrimination

against women in public and private employment and their under-representation in the conduct of public affairs.

The Committee also expressed its regret at the lack of legal provision for an alternative service to compulsory military conscription for conscientious objectors, deploring the fact that some had been conscripted by force and that there had been instances of reprisal against their family members.

The Committee also noted that the independence of the judiciary was not fully guaranteed, and that several provisions of the Armenian Constitution were not compatible with the ICCPR.

Recommendations by the Committee included the establishment of a special independent body to investigate complaints of torture and ill-treatment by law enforcement personnel; the implementation of the UN Standard Minimum Rules for the Treatment of Prisoners; the commutation of all death sentences; and the adoption of specific preventive and punitive measures with respect to all forms of violence against women, including rape.

The Committee also recommended human rights training for the legal profession and the judiciary, and urged Armenia to disseminate widely its initial report and the Committee's concluding observations.

The draft new criminal code, which, among other things, would have decriminalized consenting homosexual acts between adult males, had not become law by the end of the year. The number of prosecutions for such acts during the year was not known, but the Prosecutor General's office reported in May that there had been 21 criminal prosecutions since 1993 (including four in 1997 and seven in 1996).

Conscientious objectors to compulsory military service continued to be imprisoned, in the absence of any civilian alternative. Some were charged with refusing their call-up papers, while others faced potentially more severe sentences under the military criminal code after they were forcibly conscripted. At least one was serving his second term for refusing military service.

Some were reportedly beaten because of their religious beliefs. Karen Voskanian, for example, was taken to Mashtots conscription point in March. He was allegedly beaten after declaring that he was a Jehovah's Witness and unable to perform military service on religious grounds. He was then forcibly conscripted into a military unit in Gyumri. In June he refused to take the military oath of allegiance and was charged with evading military service. In September Karen Voskanian was sentenced to three years' imprisonment.

Brutal hazing in the army was also widely reported, often allegedly with the consent or active participation of officers. In September, two soldiers and five officers were sentenced to up to 10 years' imprisonment in connection with the case of Private Mkrtich Ohanian, who in February shot dead six comrades and then killed himself. The prosecution described how Private Ohanian had opened fire as a result of systematic abuse and violence at the hands of the men he killed, and that commanding officers were aware of what was going on but took no action.

At least 25 men were on death row at the end of the year, pending adoption of the new criminal code which would replace the death penalty with a maximum sentence of life imprisonment. The code had passed its first reading in parliament in April 1997, and in October 1998 Armenia's representatives told the UN Human Rights Committee that the code would come into force on 1 January 1999. No presidential commutations were reported. No executions took place.

Amnesty International urged the authorities to release immediately and unconditionally all those imprisoned solely for refusing military service on grounds of conscience, and to enact legislation creating an alternative civilian service of non-punitive length, together with a fair procedure in law for implementing it.

Amnesty International also called for the immediate and unconditional release of anyone imprisoned for consensual homosexual relations between adult males and for a halt to further prosecutions for such acts; for the repeal of Article 116 (part one) of the Criminal Code, which criminalizes such acts; and for the equalization of ages of consent for homosexual and heterosexual relations.

The organization urged that reports of ill-treatment be investigated impartially and comprehensively, with the results made public and those responsible brought to justice.

Amnesty International consistently called for the death penalty to be abol-

ished, and urged President Kocharian to commute all death sentences, in view of parliament's stated aim of abolition in law.

AUSTRALIA

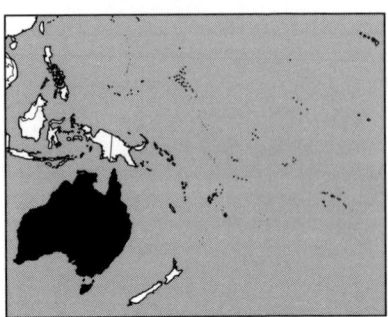

Asylum-seekers continued to be subjected to mandatory detention. Children, in particular Aboriginal children, were arrested and detained in circumstances amounting in some cases to cruel, inhuman or degrading treatment. Prisoners were ill-treated and at least 92 deaths in custody or during police operations were reported.

The Liberal-National Party coalition of Prime Minister John Howard was re-elected in October. The issue of social and economic equality for Aborigines and Australians in rural areas dominated much of public and parliamentary debate. The government, the opposition and community groups campaigned against a new political party, One Nation, which attacked the UN human rights system, immigration from Asia and policies to address Aboriginal disadvantage.

In September the UN Committee on the Elimination of Racial Discrimination asked the government to explain how its policies and a new law restricting Aboriginal rights were compatible with Australia's obligations under international human rights treaties.

After the Prime Minister threatened to dissolve both houses of parliament for twice rejecting controversial legislation on Aboriginal traditional rights, parliament passed a compromise law in July. The law seeks to secure the economic interests of farmers and miners by limiting Aboriginal rights to negotiate their traditional use of government land.

In June parliament repealed electoral legislation which had led to the imprisonment of a prisoner of conscience during previous federal elections (see *Amnesty International Report 1997*).

In September a parliamentary committee reported that children, particularly Aboriginal children, were arbitrarily detained under mandatory sentencing laws which prevented courts from taking into account a child's age, personal circumstances and the severity of the offence, in violation of the UN Convention on the Rights of the Child. The report's recommendations included the creation of a national Office for Children and a review of laws "to ensure that children and young people cannot receive longer [prison] sentences than adults for any particular offence". Few steps had been taken to implement these recommendations by the end of the year. Official studies indicated that race appeared to be a determining factor in the imprisonment or sentencing of juveniles. In May a report by the Judicial Commission of New South Wales found that Aboriginal and Pacific Islander children were much more frequently sentenced to imprisonment or harsh penalties than comparable white offenders.

In May the national Human Rights and Equal Opportunity Commission (HREOC) published a report on the mandatory detention of people who arrived in the country without proper travel documents, including asylum-seekers. HREOC found that extended detention violated international human rights standards (see *Amnesty International Report 1998*). The government dismissed the report's main findings and reportedly accused the Human Rights Commissioner of "refusing to reflect the government's legal advice" on its international human rights obligations. The government stated that problems were being addressed through steps including the privatization of detention security services and the refurbishment of Sydney's immigration detention centre, but had made no formal response to the report by the end of the year.

In November the UN Committee against Torture intervened to halt the deportation of Sadiq Shek Elmi, a Somali asylum-seeker, to Somalia, where he risked torture or extrajudicial execution. The Australian government's decision to allow Sadiq Shek Elmi to remain in the country followed appeals by Amnesty International which triggered protests and trade union action to prevent Sadiq Shek Elmi's plane leaving Australia. However, he was transferred to Port Hedland detention centre, some 4,000 kilometres from his lawyers and friends in Melbourne. The government warned Amnesty International that there would be "serious consequences" if the organization continued to use Sadiq Shek Elmi's name publicly; the authorities had sought a court order prohibiting publication of his name or "any information which might identify" him. The court order was overturned in December.

New juvenile justice policies resulted in the detention of minors, particularly Aboriginal children, in circumstances which in some cases constituted cruel, inhuman or degrading treatment. Juvenile criminal suspects from the age of 11 were routinely detained for short periods in police cells for adults or in juvenile detention centres far from their homes. A 13-year-old girl from the Northern Territory was repeatedly detained for a series of minor offences for a total of about six weeks, mostly in local police cells for adults and a detention centre some 1,500 kilometres from her home, impeding contact with her family. Kwementye Ross, a 16-year-old Aborigine arrested in March for "protective custody" on suspicion of drunkenness, died in hospital after hanging himself from the bars of his police cell door in Alice Springs. Police failed to check his condition or the video monitoring his cell for about 40 minutes after he was placed in a police cell for adult women. Police had also failed to contact his family or local youth, legal and welfare institutions when arresting him, but had taken him directly to the police station where they left him in a cage on the back of the police van for 35 minutes. By the end of the year, no police officer had been charged with a criminal or disciplinary offence for his treatment.

Five prisoners and five police officers were injured in March after clashes between police and some 15 prisoners, mostly Aborigines and Maoris, at the Melbourne Custody Centre. Police officers working as prison guards repeatedly hit already subdued prisoners with batons after two officers were allegedly assaulted by prisoners. The injured prisoners were charged with rioting and affray, assaulting

84

an officer and other charges, some of which were dropped when they confessed to having attacked police officers. None of the officers involved were charged or suspended from duty, but some faced possible "criminal interviews" by police internal investigators on the amount of force used. The incident was linked to intermittent overcrowding in the windowless underground prison where prisoners awaiting trial were held for up to three weeks, allegedly sharing cells with convicted prisoners for up to 20 hours a day.

In July Amnesty International received more than 50 reports of alleged ill-treatment and use of excessive force by Northern Territory police during the arrest of several non-Aboriginal young people engaged in non-violent protests against a new uranium mine on Aboriginal land. Up to 108 female and male protesters were held together overnight in a single small police cell. An Ombudsman investigation into these events had not been completed by the end of the year.

At least 92 people died in custody or during police operations, 16 of them Aborigines. The rate and circumstances of deaths in custody led to several inquiries, with some cases raising concerns about ill-treatment, inhuman prison conditions and lack of care.

For example, in January 18-year-old Neil Holt died in Canning Vale Prison near Perth after reportedly being forcibly restrained by guards who placed a mask over his head and chained his hands and feet together. The Western Australia Ombudsman subsequently began an inquiry into rising prisoner death rates, which had not been completed by the end of the year.

There were new developments in cases from previous years. In June a coroner's inquest found no explanation as to why Victorino Bongay Vivas' decomposed and decapitated body had not been discovered inside Western Australia's Wooroloo Prison for more than six weeks after he went missing in July 1996, reportedly leaving a suicide note.

Compensation of 60,000 Australian dollars (US$38,000) was awarded to the son of Janet Beetson who died in June 1994 of a heart condition at Mulawa Prison, New South Wales, after a court found that neglect in medical care had contributed to her death.

In June, two police officers were charged with assault following a Criminal Justice Commission inquiry into the brutal beating during arrest of several young Aborigines in Ipswich in March 1997 (see *Amnesty International Report 1998*).

In March an Amnesty International report, *Australia: Silence on human rights – government responds to "Stolen Children" inquiry*, urged the federal government to acknowledge as human rights violations the removal on racial grounds of thousands of indigenous children from their families under past government policies and to provide redress for victims (see *Amnesty International Report 1998*).

Also in March an Amnesty International delegate visited detention facilities and met government and prison officials, prisoners, lawyers and representatives of community organizations.

In June Amnesty International issued *Western Australia Government should act on prisoner deaths*, which recommended improvements in prisoner supervision and prison health care.

In October Amnesty International wrote to the Victorian authorities expressing concern about prison conditions at the Melbourne Custody Centre.

By the end of the year, Amnesty International had received a reply from Victoria police, which gave details of a violent clash between officers and prisoners in March, but had not received a response to a separate letter to the Minister for Police.

In a letter to Amnesty International in September, the Department of Immigration argued that Australia's policy on the detention of asylum-seekers did not contravene international law.

In November Amnesty International urged the Northern Territory government to ensure that children did not suffer discrimination in the justice system and were only detained as a last resort and then held separately from adults, in circumstances which allowed them to maintain contact with their families. In December Amnesty International received a letter from the Chief Minister of the Northern Territory which criticized the wording of a case study used by Amnesty International but failed to address any of the juvenile justice issues raised by the organization.

AZERBAIJAN

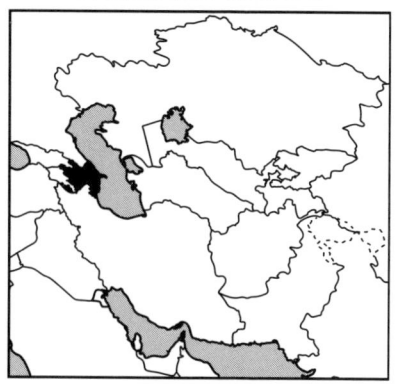

At least five possible prisoners of conscience were reportedly held solely on grounds of their ethnic origin. There were numerous reports of torture and ill-treatment in detention. All death sentences were commuted and the death penalty was abolished for all crimes.

In February parliament adopted overwhelmingly a bill, proposed the previous month by President Heydar Aliyev, which abolished the death penalty completely from the criminal code.

Also in February President Aliyev issued a decree "On measures to ensure human rights and the rights and freedoms of citizens", which contained a range of proposals to parliament on promoting and protecting human rights. This was followed in June by a "State program for the defence of human rights", which included the intention to: ratify the first and Second Optional Protocols to the International Covenant on Civil and Political Rights by the end of the year; improve conditions in pre-trial and penal institutions; and establish the institution of an ombudsperson. In December parliament voted to ratify the Second Optional Protocol, but by the end of the year there had been no decision on the first and no ombudsperson appointed.

The cease-fire of May 1994 held in the disputed Karabakh region (see Amnesty International Report 1998), and mediation for a political resolution continued.

There were further allegations that ethnic Armenian civilians were held as hostages solely on grounds of their ethnic origin. They were possible prisoners of conscience. The Azerbaijani authorities in the past stated that ethnic Armenians suspected of, for example, complicity in acts of political violence were taken to a special holding centre in the town of Gobustan and detained while their identity and reasons for travelling in Azerbaijan were confirmed. However, there were reports that ethnic Armenians were still being held although no evidence of criminal activity had been found and no criminal charges had been laid against them. They included Artur Papayan, who was said to have been seized in January 1997, when aged 17, while walking in Armenia's border district of Taushsky (see Amnesty International Report 1998). Zhora Oganesyan was said to have been seized by persons unknown in Sadakhlo in Georgia in July 1997 after he had left his home in Armenia during a period of mental illness. He was handed over to the Azerbaijani authorities at some point, and was still held in Gobustan until the second half of the year.

New cases were also reported. Armine Kurdoyan was said to have been detained at Baku airport in February after arriving from Moscow on a flight which she believed would make only a transit stop in Azerbaijan. Artur Papayan, Zhora Oganesyan and Armine Kurdoyan were reportedly released in prisoner exchanges in the second half of the year.

There were numerous allegations of torture and ill-treatment. Most of them related to pre-trial detention. Allegations were also made in connection with convicted prisoners, police conduct at demonstrations, and during brutal hazing (bullying and humiliating) of new recruits by or with the tacit consent of senior soldiers and officers. Although the majority of allegations related to male detainees, in some cases their wives and other female relatives were reportedly threatened with rape or other abuses as a way of exerting pressure on prisoners to confess. Unofficial sources said that proceedings in alleged ill-treatment cases were either not instituted or, if opened, rarely resulted in prosecution or imprisonment.

Lawyer Namik Aliyev, for example, alleged that both he and his client Zeybulla Abdulkerimov were assaulted in March by officers at police station No. 29 in the Yasamalsky District of Baku. Namik Aliyev reported that he met his client briefly at the station, at which point he

86

had no visible signs of injury. When the lawyer returned later the same day, he noticed that Zeybulla Abdulkerimov had a fresh bruise on his face. Namik Aliyev said that he demanded that his client be given a medical examination, but that instead he was himself verbally abused and beaten by two police officers. The beating was said to have taken place in front of his client, employees of the police station and other people who were in the police station at the time. Namik Aliyev was then searched, placed in a cell and taken an hour later to a hospital to be tested for alcohol. He alleged he was returned to a cell before being released later that evening after his father and colleagues intervened. A doctor who examined Namik Aliyev after his release reportedly found contusions to his head and buttocks. Two police officers were reported to have been charged in connection with the incident, but no trial was known to have taken place by the end of the year.

In at least four instances, law enforcement officials did stand trial charged with ill-treatment of detainees and other offences. Mahammad Agahanov was tried at the beginning of the year on charges of murder and bribe-taking. The case concerned the death in custody in July 1997 of Samir Zulfugarov after he was allegedly beaten severely by officers from an anti-drug unit in Baku (see *Amnesty International Report 1998*). Samir Zulfugarov's father alleged that Mahammad Agahanov and another officer had demanded money for his son's release, which he paid after seeing his injured son in custody. Mahammad Agahanov was acquitted on both counts after testifying that the death occurred at another police station.

Three other police officers received long prison sentences after being convicted of physically assaulting in 1994 Jamal Aliyev, a detainee who subsequently died in custody. In another case, a prison guard was given a conditional prison sentence for assaulting a convicted prisoner, who suffered a broken rib.

In May a former police officer, Adyl Ismaylov, was sentenced to three years' imprisonment for, among other things, raping the mother of a detainee. Baku City Court heard that Adyl Ismaylov, then head of the investigation department of Baku City Police Administration, had noticed the woman while interrogating her son in

June 1996. According to the court, Adyl Ismaylov had asked her to accompany him to his office, where he raped her.

After the death penalty was abolished in February, 128 men on death row at that time had their sentences commuted to terms of imprisonment. Conditions on death row had been said to be severely overcrowded: in some cells prisoners had to take turns to sleep. By April, 102 former death row inmates had been moved to a different prison. Those remaining included several political prisoners who claimed their transfer to better conditions had been delayed as a punishment.

Amnesty International sought further information on possible prisoners of conscience and urged the release of anyone held without charge as a hostage or solely because of their ethnic origin.

The organization urged that all allegations of ill-treatment and torture by law enforcement officials be investigated promptly and impartially, with the findings made public and the perpetrators brought to justice.

Amnesty International welcomed the abolition of the death penalty in February and the subsequent commutation of all death sentences.

BAHAMAS

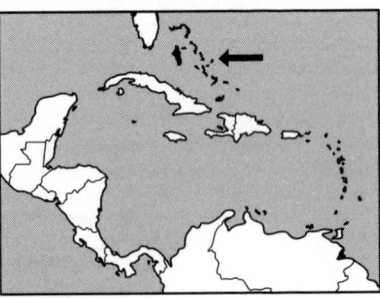

Two people were hanged. Five men who were scheduled to be executed were granted reprieves. About 20 people remained under sentence of death at the end of the year. Asylum-seekers were among hundreds of Cubans forcibly repatriated to Cuba.

Trevor Fisher, sentenced to death in March 1994, and Richard Woods, sentenced to death in January 1995, were hanged in October. The two men were executed despite requests from the Inter-American Commission on Human Rights (IACHR) that the executions be suspended at least until the IACHR had issued its decisions on whether their rights guaranteed under the American Declaration of the Rights and Duties of Man had been violated. The government of Prime Minister Hubert Alexander Ingraham rejected these requests even though, on the eve of the executions, the IACHR informed the government that it expected to deliver its decisions within two weeks. The executions were scheduled following a ruling by the Judicial Committee of the Privy Council (JCPC) in the United Kingdom, the Bahamas' highest appeal court, that executing Trevor Fisher while his case was pending before the IACHR would not violate the Constitution of the Bahamas or domestic law.

Four men – Roger Chad Goodman and Anatole McQuay, sentenced to death in 1996, and Sean Poitier and Alexander Williams, sentenced to death in 1993 – were scheduled to be executed in January. Philip Joshua Rahming, who was sentenced to death in 1997, was scheduled to be executed in December. All received reprieves as a result of additional proceedings initiated on their behalf. All five had appeals pending either before the IACHR or the JCPC at the end of the year.

In January, 17 people who had each spent at least five years on death row had their death sentences commuted in accordance with previous JCPC decisions which restrict the length of time a condemned person can be held on death row prior to execution (see previous *Amnesty International Reports*). About 20 other people remained under sentence of death at the end of the year.

In July the Court of Appeal granted a new trial to Cecil Musgrove, who had been sentenced in 1997 to six lashes of the cane and 10 years' imprisonment with hard labour after a trial at which he did not have a defence lawyer (see *Amnesty International Report 1998*). Following a retrial in October, he was convicted and sentenced to 15 years' imprisonment and ordered to undergo psychiatric treatment. Corporal punishment was not part of the new sentence.

In June the Bahamas modified a 1994 agreement with Cuba providing for the more expeditious repatriation of Cubans arriving in the Bahamas without prior authorization. Under this agreement, which contains no reference to the Bahamas' obligations under the UN Convention relating to the Status of Refugees or its 1967 Protocol, the government agreed to provide Cuban authorities with details of all "Cuban illegal emigrants who arrive in its territory" within a maximum of 72 hours of their arrival and to repatriate them within 15 days. At least 190 Cubans had been repatriated from the Bahamas by August, some reportedly without access to full refugee determination procedures or to the UN High Commissioner for Refugees.

In August, in response to a petition filed jointly by two international non-governmental organizations – the Center for Equality and Justice in International Law and the Forced Migration Projects of the Open Society Institute (the Projects) – the IACHR requested that the government suspend deportation of 120 Cubans. The petition alleged that Cubans were not being afforded necessary facilities or a full and fair procedure to determine whether they were in need of international protection. The authorities continued to repatriate Cubans, including people who had sought asylum, over the course of the year.

Throughout the year Amnesty International urged the authorities not to carry out executions. In October Amnesty International expressed deep regret at the executions of Trevor Fisher and Richard Woods. The organization expressed concern that by hanging them while their cases were pending with the IACHR, the government had irrevocably denied them effective international protection. Amnesty International urged the government to abolish the death penalty and, as a preliminary step, to propose and support the enactment of legislation which would create alternative non-capital punishments for murder.

Amnesty International wrote to the government in June seeking assurances that all foreign nationals arriving in the Bahamas seeking asylum would be given meaningful access to full and fair procedures to determine whether they were in need of international protection, in accordance with international standards.

In September Amnesty International and the Projects expressed concern that the procedures in place and the time limits contained in the agreement between the governments of Cuba and the Bahamas

88

rendered a full and fair determination of a claim for protection improbable. The organizations urged the government to take steps to ensure that all asylum-seekers were treated in accordance with international standards.

BAHRAIN

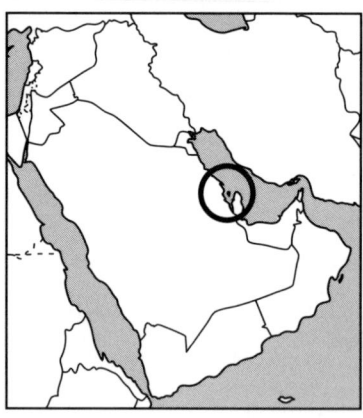

Hundreds of people were reported to have been arrested during the year for suspected anti-government activities or in connection with anti-government protests. Hundreds of others arrested in previous years remained held without charge or trial; they included eight religious and political leaders, all prisoners of conscience, who were arrested in 1996, as well as possible prisoners of conscience. Sixteen people charged with arson and possession of "unlawful leaflets" were sentenced to prison terms after an unfair trial. Torture and ill-treatment continued to be reported. One person died in custody reportedly following torture. Three people remained under sentence of death. At least three Bahraini nationals were banned from entering the country.

Anti-government protests continued during the year reportedly on a lesser scale than in previous years (see *Amnesty International Reports 1995* to *1998*). The protests called for the reinstatement of the National Assembly, which was dissolved by the Amir, Shaikh 'Issa bin Salman Al Khalifa, in 1975; the restoration of the country's 1973 Constitution; and the release of political prisoners. Security forces carried out arrests of suspected political opponents, especially in Shi'a Muslim areas such as al-Sanabis, al-Nu'aim, al-Daih and Sitra. A number of arson attacks, often targeting commercial buildings, were reported.

In March the Ministry of Labour and Social Affairs issued an order to dissolve the elected executive committee of the Bar Society. The dissolution was reported to have been connected with seminars about economic and social developments in Bahrain organized by the Bar Society.

Also in March Bahrain acceded, with some limiting reservations, to the UN Convention against Torture and Other Cruel, Inhuman or Degrading Treatment or Punishment. However, by the end of the year the government had reportedly agreed to remove the reservations and to allow the UN Working Group on Arbitrary Detention to visit the country.

Hundreds of people were said to have been arrested during the year for suspected anti-government activities or in connection with anti-government protests, including arson attacks. Arrests reportedly took place at homes during the night or at dawn, at workplaces, or following anti-government protests. Many of those held were released without charge after days or weeks of incommunicado detention; the rest were still held without charge or trial at the end of the year. Scores of young women and men, as well as children, were reportedly among those arrested, some of whom were said to have been beaten before being released without charge.

Other people were arrested during 1998 and held incommunicado before being released without charge. In February Muhammad 'Ali Muhammad al-'Ikri, aged 17, was arrested while visiting his mother's home in Jidd Hafs, apparently in connection with a previous arrest and conviction (see *Amnesty International Report 1996*). He was held incommunicado until his release without charge in March. He was then rearrested in November for unknown reasons and remained held without charge at the end of the year. Rabab 'Abd al-Nabi 'Abd al-Wahab Rabi' and her father 'Abd al-Nabi were arrested in March at their house in Sitra, held incommunicado and released without charge in April. The reason for their arrest remained unclear at the end of the year. In May 'Abd al-Hussain 'Ali al-Sayegh, aged 66 and ill, was arrested in

Madinat 'Issa and released without charge after five days of incommunicado detention. The reason for his arrest was not known but was said to be connected with his son Yassir, who was arrested in December 1996, accused of possessing "illegal pamphlets" and allegedly subjected to various forms of torture. The son was held until May 1997, after which he travelled to the United Kingdom where he described to the press how he had been tortured.

In November, five women – Salwa Hassan Haidar, Hanan Salman Haidar, Maryam Sa'id al-'Aradi, Mona Salman Haidar and Laila Mahdi al-Bazaz – were among a number of people arrested at their homes in al-Daih village near the capital al-Manama. The authorities reportedly suspected them of hiding weapons. Salwa Hassan Haidar and Hanan Salman Haidar remained held incommunicado until their release on 30 December; the other three women were released without charge after a few days in custody.

Hundreds of people, including prisoners of conscience, arrested in previous years remained held without charge or trial at the end of the year. Among the prisoners of conscience were Shaikh 'Abd al-Amir al-Jamri and 'Abd al-Wahab Hussain 'Ali who, with six other prisoners of conscience, remained held since their arrest in January 1996 (see *Amnesty International Report 1997*). Sayyid Jalal Sayyid 'Alawi Sayyid Sharaf, who was arrested in March 1997 reportedly on suspicion of transmitting information about the internal situation in Bahrain to people abroad, reportedly received a one-year prison sentence and was released in November 1998 (see *Amnesty International Report 1998*).

Muhammad Jamil 'Abd al-Amir al-Jamri, son of Shaikh 'Abd al-Amir al-Jamri (see above), was released in September on completion of his prison sentence. He had been arrested in September 1988 on charges of membership of an unauthorized organization and other offences, and sentenced in 1990 to 10 years' imprisonment (see previous *Amnesty International Reports*).

Four young women – Ahlam al-Sayyid Mahdi Hassan al-Sitri, Amal Ahmad Rabi', Maryam Ahmad 'Ali Bilway and Laila 'Abd al-Nabi Rabi' (see *Amnesty International Report 1998*) – appeared before the State Security Court in April and received three-month suspended prison sentences reportedly for taking part in anti-government demonstrations in March 1997.

In June, 16 people were sentenced after an unfair trial by the State Security Court to prison terms ranging from one to four years on charges of arson and possession of "unlawful leaflets". The 16 had been arrested in 1996. Thirteen other defendants were acquitted. Among those sentenced were Ibrahim Yusuf 'Abd al-Rasul Hamadi and Muhammad 'Abd al-Karim 'Ali Jawad who received prison terms of four and three years respectively.

Torture and ill-treatment of detainees and suspected political opponents continued to be reported, mainly during the first days after arrest in order to extract information. Reported methods of torture and ill-treatment included severe beating with electric cables on the back and on the soles of the feet; suspension by the limbs; victims being blindfolded and forced to stand for hours with their hands tied behind their back; and solitary confinement. In general, family visits were allowed only after a few weeks of incommunicado detention. The five women arrested in al-Daih village (see above) were all reportedly tortured or ill-treated. Salwa Hassan Haidar was said to have been beaten on the soles of the feet and suspended by her limbs.

One detainee died in circumstances suggesting that torture contributed to his death. In July Nuh Khalil 'Abdullah al-Nuh was arrested apparently in good health at his shop in al-Nu'aim, a district of al-Manama. Two days later his body was handed over to his family for burial bearing marks suggesting that he had been tortured. The authorities were reported to have promised an investigation into the death but by the end of the year no investigation was known to have been carried out.

There was no further news of three prisoners – 'Ali Ahmad 'Abdullah al-'Usfur, Yusuf Hussain 'Abd al-Baqi and Ahmad Khalil Ibrahim al-Kattab – who were sentenced to death by the State Security Court in July 1996 on charges of carrying out a fire-bomb attack in Sitra (see *Amnesty International Reports 1997* and *1998*).

At least three Bahraini nationals, who had spent time living abroad, were banned from entering the country. In July

Qusay Shaikh 'Ali Mohsin al-'Uraibi and 'Abd al-Amir al-Isqafi were reportedly held at the airport and then forcibly exiled to the United Arab Emirates and Syria respectively. In December 'Abd al-Majid Muhsin Muhammad al-'Usfar, his Saudi Arabian wife and their five children were held at the airport for four days and then forcibly returned to Denmark.

Amnesty International appealed to the government to release prisoners of conscience, investigate reports of torture and ill-treatment of detainees, and provide details of all those detained without charge or trial. It also expressed concern at the dissolution of the executive committee of the Bar Society.

In April Amnesty International submitted information about its continuing concerns in Bahrain for UN review under a procedure established by Economic and Social Council Resolutions 728F/1503 for confidential consideration of communications about human rights violations.

In November Amnesty International wrote to the authorities and proposed to send delegates to Bahrain to discuss human rights protection and promotion with government officials and others. No response had been received by the end of the year.

In response to a letter sent in April, Amnesty International received in September a letter from the authorities stating that information received by the organization about a number of cases was "distorted, incomplete and inaccurate", and that Bahrain had been the target of a "sustained campaign of violence and terrorism organized and funded from abroad". The authorities pointed out that reports concerning the arrests of Rabab 'Abd al-Nabi 'Abd al-Wahab Rabi', 'Abd al-Nabi 'Abd al-Wahab Rabi' and Muhammad 'Ali Muhammad al-'Ikri (see above) were unfounded and that no one of these names was known to have been arrested during the year. The letter added that Ahlam al-Sayyid Mahdi Hassan al-Sitri, Amal Ahmad Rabi', Maryam Ahmad 'Ali Bilway and Laila 'Abd al-Nabi Rabi' (see above) were charged, tried and convicted in accordance with the law. It confirmed the sentences against three of the women but, contrary to reports received by Amnesty International, indicated that Laila 'Abd al-Nabi Rabi' had been acquitted of all charges. The authorities stated that arrest, detention and trial procedures were all conducted in accordance with Bahraini laws and international standards. However, the government failed to allay Amnesty International's continuing concerns about human rights violations in the country.

BANGLADESH

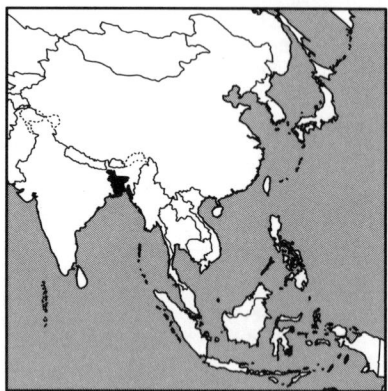

Scores of political activists were detained without charge or trial under the Special Powers Act (SPA). Torture, including rape, in custody was widespread and led to at least one death. At least 24 people were sentenced to death. No executions were reported.

In March the Awami League government of Prime Minister Sheikh Hasina reached an agreement with the main opposition Bangladesh Nationalist Party (BNP) to end its six-month boycott of parliament. The government agreed to review criminal charges pending against BNP activists. Supporters of the ruling and opposition parties clashed frequently during the year in strikes and demonstrations that were often violent.

In the Chittagong Hill Tracts (CHT), steps were taken to implement the peace accord reached by the government and tribal representatives. Throughout February members of the armed opposition group *Shanti Bahini* (Peace Force) surrendered their weapons in exchange for an amnesty and rehabilitation. In May parliament passed legislation for the establishment of a regional council granting more political autonomy to the area. By the end of the year the last of some 50,000 refugees living in camps in India had been repatriated to the CHT.

The trial of those accused of killing former President Sheikh Mujibur Rahman and his close relatives in a military coup in 1975 concluded in November. Fifteen people were convicted and sentenced to death by firing squad. Four appealed against the judgment, but their petitions had not been heard by the end of the year. In September, three senior BNP politicians were arrested in connection with the killing of four national leaders inside Dhaka Central Jail in November 1975. In October they were charged in connection with the killings, along with 20 others, including Major Khairuzzaman who had been held for over two years without charge or trial (see *Amnesty International Report 1998*).

No further steps were taken by the government towards the establishment of a national human rights commission after a draft bill was made public in December 1997.

In October Bangladesh acceded to international human rights instruments, including the Convention against Torture and Other Cruel, Inhuman or Degrading Treatment or Punishment, and the International Covenant on Economic, Social and Cultural Rights.

The SPA, which allows detention without charge or trial for an indefinite period, continued to be used to detain scores of political activists, often during demonstrations. Most were released after several days or weeks. Several people were reportedly arrested at the instigation of politically influential individuals on false charges. In January, for example, three men were arrested following an altercation with the son of a government minister in a street in Dhaka, the capital. The minister's son threatened to punish the three men and they were later arrested at their homes by police accompanied by relatives of the minister's son. While in custody the officer in charge of the police station reportedly allowed the elder brother of the government minister's son and two other armed men to enter the room where the three men were detained and beat them. In February the three men were released after the Home Minister withdrew the SPA detention order and dropped the charges.

In September the writer Taslima Nasrin returned to Bangladesh after four years of self-imposed exile. Charges of hurting "religious sentiments" brought against her in 1994 (see previous *Amnesty International Reports*) remained pending. However, calls for her arrest by Islamists were ignored by the authorities. In November she was granted bail after appearing in court. No further legal developments in her case were reported.

Torture in police custody remained widespread. In July a student, Shamim Reza Rubel, was allegedly beaten to death in police custody five hours after being arrested at his home in Dhaka. According to the autopsy report he suffered a brain haemorrhage. Following an investigation by the Criminal Investigation Department, 13 policemen and a local Awami League leader were charged in connection with his death. A judicial inquiry into the case confirmed that Shamim Reza Rubel's death was not accidental, although the full findings of the commission were not made public by the end of the year.

At least three cases of rape in custody by the security forces were reported, in addition to the rape of a 10-year-old girl by an off-duty policeman in April in Dhaka. In one case, a policeman and another man were arrested for the attempted rape of a 15-year-old girl on the premises of the Chief Metropolitan Magistrate's Court in Dhaka in May. They were later released on bail. There were no reports of any police officer being tried or convicted of rape during the year. The government's appeal against the court decision to acquit four police officers accused of raping Shima Chowdhury in 1996 had not been heard by the end of the year (see *Amnesty International Reports 1997* and *1998*).

At least 23 men and one woman were sentenced to death for murder. No executions were reported.

Throughout the year Amnesty International expressed concern about torture in police custody and urged the government to take steps to eradicate the practice. In April Amnesty International published a report on children in South Asia appealing to all South Asian governments, including Bangladesh, to take concrete steps to protect children both in custody and in the community and to fully implement the provisions of the UN Convention on the Rights of the Child, which Bangladesh ratified in 1990. The organization called on the government to ensure the safety of the writer Taslima Nasrin who was subject to renewed threats from Islamists after she returned to the country. It also urged that the charges against her be dropped.

BELARUS

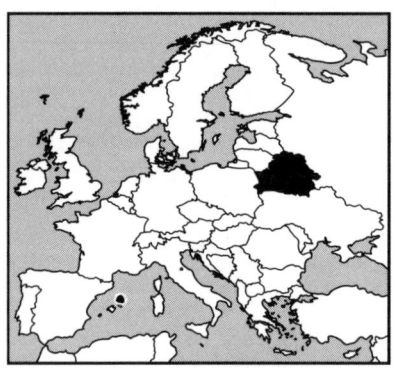

Hundreds of peaceful demonstrators were detained, including prisoners of conscience. Many were severely beaten by police. At least 84 people were reportedly under sentence of death and 33 people were reportedly executed.

President Alyaksandr Lukashenka continued to exercise total control over most aspects of government. The main law enforcement bodies – the Committee for State Security (KGB) and Ministry of Internal Affairs (MVD) – were both answerable to the President.

Political unrest, in the form of protests and demonstrations, increased during the year. Police responded with violence, forcibly breaking up peaceful opposition demonstrations.

Military service remained compulsory; there are no provisions for conscientious objection in the Constitution.

Prisoners of conscience were among hundreds of protesters arrested after peaceful protests. On 22 March up to 50 men and women were arrested and beaten by police following a peaceful demonstration in the capital, Minsk, to mark the 80th anniversary of the independence of Belorussia (the former name of Belarus). Among those detained were journalists and members of the opposition Belorussian Popular Front (BNF), including Boris Khamaida and Vladimir Pleshchenka. A 15-year-old boy, Pavel Rakhmanov, was also arrested. Seven

people were convicted of shouting censored slogans and insulting the President, but were not given custodial sentences. Five members of a local human rights group, the Belarusian Helsinki Committee, were briefly detained.

On 2 April a large anti-government demonstration was forcibly broken up by police who arrested more than 50 protesters. Vyacheslav Sivchyk, secretary of the BNF, was arrested and reportedly beaten severely by police. The next day he was sentenced to 10 days' imprisonment under the Administrative Code of Belarus. Pavel Severinets, leader of the BNF's Youth Front, was arrested and faced up to five years' imprisonment on charges of "instigating mass disorder", "organization or participation in group actions violating the public order" and "hooliganism". Both men were prisoners of conscience.

Four other prisoners of conscience were arrested during the 2 April protest and charged with similar offences. Alyaksandr Kashenya and Ivan Abadovsky reportedly received sentences of 10 and 15 days' imprisonment respectively. Leonid Vasyuchenko and Dmitriy Vaskovich were reportedly held after arrest. Dmitriy Vaskovich was allegedly beaten in custody to force him to implicate Pavel Severinets and other detainees in criminal acts during the protest. More than 50 other people, about one third of them reportedly minors, were detained for several hours and in some cases overnight. Some were convicted on 3 April of charges relating to their participation in an unauthorized demonstration. They were released after the court ruled either to fine them or to issue them with a warning.

Two other prisoners of conscience, 19-year-old Aleksey Shidlovsky and 16-year-old Vadim Labkovich, both members of the BNF's Youth Front, stood trial in February on charges of "malicious hooliganism" under Article 201(2) of the Belarusian Criminal Code and "abuse of state symbols" under Article 186. They had been detained since August 1997 for allegedly writing anti-presidential and anti-government graffiti on the walls of public buildings, and for allegedly replacing the national flag of Belarus on the town administration building with the banned red and white flag which is a symbol of the opposition and of the BNF. On 24 February the Minsk Regional Court sentenced

Vadim Labkovich to a suspended prison term of 18 months and Aleksey Shidlovsky to 18 months' imprisonment in a strict regime colony. There were reports that Aleksey Shidlovsky was severely beaten by prison guards in the pre-trial detention centre (SIZO) in the town of Zhodino and had to spend a month in the prison medical ward.

Following a peaceful demonstration on 25 April to commemorate the 1986 Chernobyl nuclear disaster, police reportedly arrested up to 40 demonstrators and allegedly beat some of them in detention (see below).

Human rights lawyers and advocates were persecuted by the authorities. Vera Stremkovskaya, a human rights lawyer, was called to meetings with officials at the Ministry of Justice, and at both the Belarusian and the Minsk City Collegium of Advocates, in an attempt to put pressure on her and to initiate a process to disbar her. It appeared that the persecution and harassment of Vera Stremkovskaya were politically motivated.

The government officials also accused Vera Stremkovskaya of revealing case information about three of her clients – Andrey Klimov, Vasiliy Starovoitov and Vladimir Kudzinnov – which they alleged constituted a violation of lawyers' ethics. The clients, all businessmen and former members of parliament of the 13 Supreme Soviet, dissolved by President Lukashenka, were imprisoned on charges of bribery. It was alleged that the real reason for their imprisonment was that they had publicly criticized the President's policies. They were prisoners of conscience. In September there were reports that Vladimir Kudzinnov had been ill-treated in Minsk colony UZH 15/1.

On 8 June lawyer Alyaksey Filipchanka reportedly set himself on fire outside the Novopolotsk City Court building to protest against violations of human rights and the judicial process in Belarus. He died in August.

Restrictions on freedom of expression continued to lead to trials of prisoners of conscience. In January Pavel Sheremet and Dmitry Zavadsky, Russian television journalists, were sentenced to suspended prison terms of two and one and a half years respectively (see *Amnesty International Report 1998*). They were convicted of conspiracy and illegally crossing the state border. Pavel Sheremet was also convicted of "exceeding his professional powers as a journalist resulting in damage to the public interest".

Many opposition supporters were beaten by police during arrest and in pre-trial detention. Vyacheslav Sivchyk was reported to have been severely beaten by police on 2 April. He needed hospital treatment for concussion. Fourteen-year-old Anton Taras, arrested at the April rally commemorating the Chernobyl disaster, was allegedly forced by police to put on a gas mask he had worn symbolically during the rally. They then stopped the air supply until he began to suffocate, a torture method known as "elephant". No investigations were known to have been carried out into allegations of torture or ill-treatment.

The death penalty continued to be used extensively. However, information about the death penalty was hard to obtain as it is classed as a state secret. President Lukashenka reportedly stated in January that 30 people had been executed in 1997. At least 84 people were reportedly under sentence of death. The Deputy Procurator General of Belarus was reported to have said that 33 people were executed between January and August.

Prisoners facing imminent execution included five prisoners held in SIZO No. 1 in Minsk: Ivan Fomin, Sergey Protiraev, Igor Sklyarenko, Mikhail Glushenok and Sergey Zababurin. Ivan Fomin and Mikhail Glushenok were reportedly tortured and forced to sign confessions. Four of them were thought to have received unfair trials. According to reports, prisoners under sentence of death in SIZO No. 1 in Minsk were regularly ill-treated, including by being beaten with a wooden hammer. The death sentence on F. Verega was commuted to 15 years' imprisonment by the Supreme Court in January.

Amnesty International called for the immediate and unconditional release of all prisoners of conscience, including any demonstrators detained solely for peacefully exercising their right to freedom of assembly. It urged prompt and impartial investigations into allegations of ill-treatment and for anyone responsible to be brought to justice.

The organization called on the authorities to stop the apparent practice of censuring and silencing human rights lawyers by

94

taking away their licences, including the attempts to disbar Vera Stremkovskaya. Amnesty International called on the authorities to reinstate all human rights lawyers, including Nadezhda Dudareva and Gary Pogonyailo, who had previously been disbarred solely because of their human rights activities.

Amnesty International urged the government to abolish the death penalty and to declare a moratorium on executions. It called on the President to grant clemency to all those under sentence of death.

BELGIUM

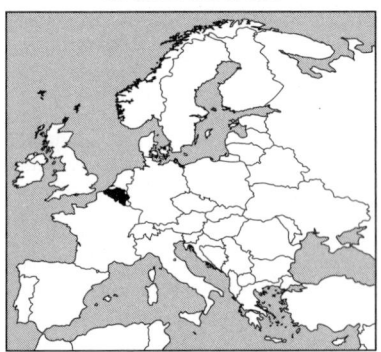

Criminal proceedings were under way against members of the Belgian armed forces accused of torture, ill-treatment and unlawful killing of Somalis in 1993, during a UN peace-keeping operation. There were reports of ill-treatment by law enforcement officers: they concerned criminal suspects, and asylum-seekers being forcibly deported. The death of a foreign national underlined the dangers of a method of restraint used during such deportations.

In December Belgium ratified the Second Optional Protocol to the International Covenant on Civil and Political Rights, aiming at the abolition of the death penalty, and Protocol No. 6 to the European Convention for the Protection of Human Rights and Fundamental Freedoms concerning the abolition of the death penalty.

In June the European Committee for the Prevention of Torture and Inhuman or Degrading Treatment or Punishment published the findings of its September 1997 visit of inspection to 22 places of detention. The Committee reported allegations

that guards in one of four prisons visited had ill-treated several prisoners in 1997 and said it had heard "a number of allegations of physical ill-treatment" made against police and gendarmes by both Belgian and foreign nationals, some of them minors. It said it was "very concerned" by the treatment of detainees by law enforcement officers. The ill-treatment alleged consisted generally of kicks, punches and baton blows, inflicted at the time of arrest and during transfer to and inside police and gendarmerie stations. The Committee said it had also received allegations of ill-treatment – "such as blows and excessive recourse to physical means of restraint" – concerning foreign nationals being forcibly expelled from the country: the majority involved people being escorted onto planes at Brussels-National Airport by gendarmes.

The Committee underlined that only the minimum amount of restraint necessary to reach the required objective should be employed in forcible deportations. It also called on the authorities to demonstrate greater vigilance regarding the treatment of detainees and made a series of recommendations aimed at preventing ill-treatment by law enforcement officers. The Committee expressed serious concern that no progress had been made regarding the introduction of certain fundamental safeguards against ill-treatment in police custody which it had recommended following its first visit of inspection in 1993. These included recognition of the right of access to a lawyer from the beginning of the custody period; systematic and prompt provision to detainees of a document setting out all their rights, and the drawing up of a code of conduct for interrogations.

In October the Permanent Monitoring Committee of Police Services, a body examining the functioning of all Belgian law enforcement agencies, submitted its fourth annual report to parliament and the government. It reiterated a number of concerns raised in its previous reports. These included the Committee's concern that it continued to receive numerous allegations of unprovoked physical assault and use of excessive force by law enforcement officers, that such behaviour was "very rarely" punished by either the administrative or judicial authorities, that officers commonly justified use of violence by accusing alleged victims of resisting arrest and that the internal hierarchy was seemingly satisfied with such explanations.

In November, following its examination of Belgium's third periodic report on its implementation of the International Covenant on Civil and Political Rights, the UN Human Rights Committee expressed "grave concern" about "reports of widespread police brutality" and regret at "the lack of transparency in the conduct of investigations on the part of police authorities and the difficulty in obtaining access to this information". It also expressed concern that criminal suspects had no right of access to a lawyer and a medical visit from the moment of arrest and said that they should also be informed promptly of their rights, in a language they understood.

The Committee stated that "Procedures used in the repatriation of some asylum-seekers and in particular the method of placing a cushion on the face of an individual in order to overcome resistance entails a risk to life." It said that the death of a Nigerian national in September, after the use of such techniques (see below), illustrated "the need to re-examine the whole procedure of forcible deportations". The Committee asked for "written information on the results of the investigations as well as of any criminal or disciplinary proceedings" and recommended that "all security forces concerned in effecting deportations should receive special training".

It also expressed concern about the behaviour of Belgian soldiers in Somalia in 1993 and noted that, in response to its questioning, the government's representatives had stated that 270 files had been opened "for purposes of investigation". However, the Committee expressed regret that it had "not received further information on the result of the investigations and adjudication of cases" and requested the government to submit such information.

There were developments in several judicial proceedings opened in 1997 concerning alleged human rights violations committed by Belgian soldiers in Somalia (see *Amnesty International Report 1998*). These included a first instance military court's acquittal in March of a sergeant accused of assault and battery with threats, and of violating legislation prohibiting certain racist acts, in connection with the alleged forcible feeding of a Muslim Somali child with pork and salted water until he vomited. The court reportedly sentenced the sergeant to one month's suspended imprisonment for tying a Somali child to a military vehicle and then giving the order for the vehicle to move off, and to a further two months' suspended imprisonment for incitement to debauchery after he procured and offered a teenage Somali girl as a "present" at the birthday party of a paratrooper in his charge. The girl was then allegedly forced to perform a "strip show" and to have sexual relations with two paratroopers.

In May, following appeals lodged against the verdict, a military court found the sergeant guilty of all the above offences. It reportedly sentenced him to a total of 12 months' imprisonment, six of them suspended, together with a payment of 15,000 Belgian francs (US$400) in damages, deprivation of civil rights for a period of five years, and exclusion from the army. The outcome of an appeal which the sergeant lodged with a higher court was apparently still awaited at the end of the year.

There were a number of allegations that some foreign nationals being forcibly deported were physically assaulted and subjected to dangerous restraint techniques by gendarmes.

Semira Adamu, a Nigerian national, died in September within hours of an attempt to deport her forcibly from Brussels-National Airport. She had physically resisted five previous attempts to deport her following the rejection of her asylum application. It was alleged that gendarmes who escorted her onto a plane subjected her to verbal abuse and that one of them pressed a cushion against her face. Within days of her death the Ministry of the Interior stated that she was handcuffed and shackled during the deportation operation and that for a "certain", unspecified length of time a gendarme used the so-called "cushion technique", a method of restraint authorized by the Belgian authorities, that allows gendarmes to press a cushion against the mouth, but not the nose, of a recalcitrant deportee, to prevent biting and shouting. When Semira Adamu lost consciousness, medical assistance was immediately sought and she was transferred to hospital where she died later that day. An initial autopsy indicated that she died of asphyxia. It subsequently emerged that two other foreign nationals had died following use of the "cushion technique" in previous years.

96

The Brussels Public Prosecutor's office immediately ordered a judicial investigation into the circumstances and cause of Semira Adamu's collapse and death and two gendarmes were placed under formal investigation in connection with a possible charge of manslaughter. In December the Public Prosecutor's office stated that a third officer had been placed under investigation on the same charge and that a second autopsy and various forensic tests had confirmed that Semira Adamu had died of asphyxia. A disciplinary investigation was opened but then suspended pending the outcome of the judicial investigation. The Minister of the Interior resigned following the revelation, within days of the death, that one of the escorting gendarmes had sanctions imposed on him in January for ill-treating a detained asylum-seeker.

In October the government announced an "evaluation" of asylum procedures. The measures included a ban on the use of the "cushion technique" pending the outcome of an analysis of methods of restraint during forcible deportations, to be carried out by a newly created independent commission; and additional training for gendarmes involved in forcible deportations.

In September Amnesty International wrote to the authorities expressing concern at the death of Semira Adamu and the use of the "cushion technique" and seeking precise details on its application. The organization asked to be informed of the eventual outcome of the judicial inquiry and of any further criminal or disciplinary proceedings arising from it. It also urged the government to conduct a full and impartial investigation into alleged ill-treatment by gendarmes during forcible deportations, together with a full review of restraint techniques to subdue recalcitrant deportees and of the training of officers required to deal with such deportees.

In October the new Minister of the Interior assured Amnesty International of the government's "sincere intent to collaborate" with the organization regarding the case of Semira Adamu in particular, and "Belgian forced repatriation policy in general". In December the Minister supplied information in response to some of the requests made in Amnesty International's letter of September, and explained that this was an initial response.

In June Amnesty International asked the Minister of Defence for his cooperation in supplying the organization with copies of several court verdicts issued in 1998 relating to alleged human rights violations committed by members of the Belgian armed forces in Somalia. The organization also recalled the information on various investigations and judicial proceedings which it had sought in a letter sent to the Minister in July 1997 but to which it had received no response (see *Amnesty International Report 1998*). Amnesty International reiterated its wish to receive the information, including news of progress in proceedings relating to photographs showing a sergeant-major urinating on the inanimate body of a Somali man and the alleged death of a Somali child locked inside a metal container, without food or drink. Amnesty International also asked whether those carrying out official investigations into the allegations of human rights violations made during 1997 had travelled to Somalia to carry out on-site investigations and to collect testimony from witnesses.

In June the Minister wrote to Amnesty International expressing regret that it had received no response to its July 1997 letter. He stated that he was unable to supply copies of verdicts of the military courts and recommended that the organization seek them and information about any investigations and testimony collected in Somalia from the Chief Military Prosecutor. The Minister supplied copies of a report concerning army reforms and outlined steps being taken towards introducing them relating, in particular, to speedier and more effective disciplinary proceedings and sanctions; and changes to army recruitment and selection, as well as training.

Amnesty International wrote to the Chief Military Prosecutor in August and he subsequently supplied various court verdicts issued in 1995 and a copy of a court verdict issued in 1997 relating to the case of a Somali boy swung over an open fire by paratroopers (see *Amnesty International Report 1998*). However, he did not supply the other information requested by the organization.

In October Amnesty International submitted information about a number of its concerns in Belgium to the UN Human Rights Committee.

BELIZE

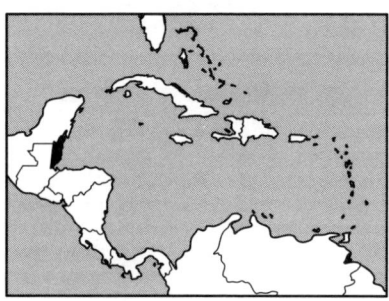

There were further reports of ill-treatment by police. Eight prisoners remained under sentence of death. No death sentences were issued and no executions were carried out during the year.

Said Musa of the People's United Party was elected Prime Minister in general elections in August.

There were further reports of ill-treatment in detention centres and at the time of arrest by police. According to reports, Orvin Myvette, a soldier in the Belize Defence Force, was repeatedly beaten by law enforcement officials while held for questioning at the Orange Walk police station in September. Orvin Myvette's lawyer reportedly lodged a complaint and was told by the police that the case would be investigated. In October the Attorney General told Amnesty International that an inquiry into the incident would soon be completed and that the results would be forwarded to the organization. By the end of the year no further information on the case had been received.

No further information was received regarding the investigation into the beating of John Joy Hernandez in September 1997 (see *Amnesty International Report 1998*).

Conditions at Hattieville Rehabilitation Centre, the main penal institution, fell short of international standards. There were reports of poor sanitation due to overcrowding, inadequate water and toilet facilities, and lack of exercise.

Eight men were under sentence of death at the end of the year. No death sentences were passed and no executions took place.

In April, in its first judgment on the constitutionality of the death penalty, the Supreme Court dismissed the constitutional motion made on behalf of death row prisoners Pasqual Bull, Herman Mejía and Nicolás Antonio Guevara (see *Amnesty International Report 1998*). The judge rejected the motion, which claimed that hanging the men would amount to cruel and inhuman punishment, on the grounds that the death penalty is sanctioned by the Belize Constitution and therefore cannot be called cruel or inhuman. The judge also rejected the argument that conditions at the Hattieville Rehabilitation Centre constituted inhuman and degrading treatment and that execution after prolonged detention in such conditions would again contravene the Constitution.

In March Pasqual Bull's murder conviction was reduced to manslaughter by the Judicial Committee of the Privy Council (JCPC) in the United Kingdom, the final court of appeal for Belize, and his sentence was subsequently commuted to 25 years' imprisonment by the Supreme Court. An appeal by Herman Mejía and Nicolás Guevara against the Supreme Court decision was scheduled to be heard by the Court of Appeal in February 1999.

A petition for leave to file a constitutional appeal on behalf of Wilfred Lauriano (see *Amnesty International Report 1998*) was adjourned pending the outcome of the appeal of Herman Mejía and Nicolás Guevara. A further criminal petition was lodged with the JCPC on Wilfred Lauriano's behalf on the basis of new evidence. In December the JCPC concluded that the petition required further investigation and granted special leave to refer the case back to the Court of Appeal, which was scheduled to hear the case in February 1999.

A constitutional appeal on behalf of Adolph Harris before the Court of Appeal and the final appeal to the JCPC on behalf of Dean Tillett (see *Amnesty International Report 1998*) were still pending at the end of the year.

In April the JCPC quashed the conviction of Marco Tulio Ibañez (see *Amnesty International Report 1998*) and remitted the case to the Court of Appeal to consider whether to order a retrial.

Appeals on behalf of Norman Shaw and Cleon Smith were believed to be pending at the end of the year (see *Amnesty International Report 1998*).

Amnesty International expressed concern about the renewed reports of ill-

98

treatment by police and called on the authorities to investigate the beating of John Joy Hernandez and Orvin Myvette and to bring those responsible to justice. The organization also expressed concern about the prison conditions in Hattieville Rehabilitation Centre. It again urged the government to accede to the Second Optional Protocol to the International Covenant on Civil and Political Rights, aiming at the abolition of the death penalty, and to submit its second report to the UN Committee against Torture, which was due in 1992. The organization continued to call for the abolition of the death penalty.

BENIN

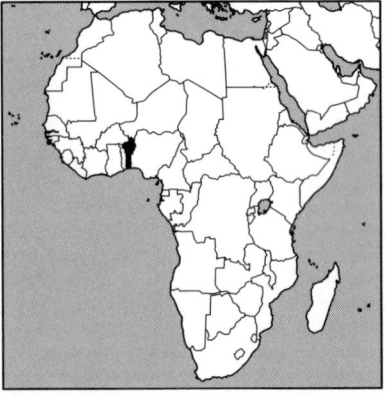

At least two people killed by the security forces appeared to have been extrajudicially executed. Fourteen people were sentenced to death. There were no executions during the year.

In January Florent Adoko, who had been arrested on suspicion of robbery, was shot dead in his cell by a guard in the main police station of Cotonou. There were reports that other detainees were killed on the same day in the same police station. In May the security forces broke up a peaceful demonstration in Gbendo, near Abomey, killing Adjakiejè Alexandre. No investigations had been opened into these cases by the end of the year.

In August, during a national celebration, a journalist, Robert Amengan, was assaulted by members of the security forces. He was handcuffed with his hands behind his back and was released after several hours' detention.

Six people were sentenced to death *in absentia* in July, and eight others were sentenced to death in October after being convicted of armed robbery and murder. No executions were carried out: the last judicial execution in Benin took place in 1986.

BHUTAN

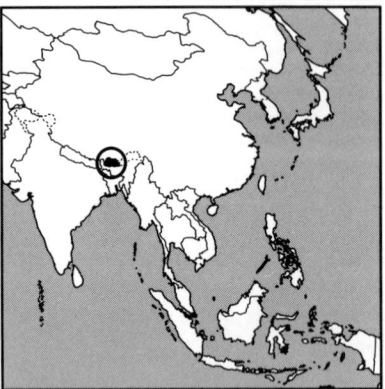

A prisoner of conscience held since 1989 continued to serve a life sentence. At least 30 possible prisoners of conscience were detained. Some 120 political prisoners were sentenced to up to 15 years' imprisonment. Many of those detained were reportedly tortured or ill-treated.

The 76th National Assembly voted in June to approve an edict by King Jigme Singye Wangchuck transferring executive powers to a six-member cabinet to be elected every five years.

The Druk National Congress (DNC) and the United Front for Democracy (UFD), two political organizations in exile in Nepal, continued their campaigning activities throughout the year, demanding a democratic system of government and greater respect for human rights in Bhutan.

Meetings of officials from Bhutan and Nepal were held in Thimphu in May, October and November aimed at reviving talks between the two governments on the fate of more than 90,000 mostly Nepali-speaking people from southern Bhutan living in refugee camps in eastern Nepal (see previous *Amnesty International Reports*).

In August a statement by the Chairman of the UN Sub-Commission on Prevention of Discrimination and Protection of Minorities encouraged the governments of

Bhutan and Nepal to set up an impartial verification process for the people in the refugee camps in Nepal and to make more effective and urgent efforts to negotiate their return.

In January, 219 civil servants and employees of government corporations were compulsorily retired as a result of a resolution adopted by the National Assembly in 1997. This was interpreted to be a discriminatory practice aimed at Nepali-speaking people from southern Bhutan, many of whom were relatives of people living in the refugee camps in eastern Nepal. At least 23 school students, aged between seven and 21, whose relatives had been arrested for supporting the pro-democracy movement, were expelled from school in eastern Bhutan.

Tek Nath Rizal, a prisoner of conscience, spent his ninth year in prison (see *Amnesty International Report 1994*).

At least 30 possible prisoners of conscience were detained, most on suspicion of being members or supporters of the DNC. They were detained under the National Security Act (NSA) 1992.

Rongthong Kunley Dorji, leader of the DNC and the UFD, was released on bail in India, while awaiting the outcome of extradition proceedings to Bhutan (see *Amnesty International Report 1998*).

As of early December, 120 political prisoners arrested during 1997 in the east (see *Amnesty International Report 1998*) had been tried under the NSA and sentenced to up to 15 years' imprisonment. Among them were Thinley Oezer, a senior monk of the Nyingmapa tradition of Mahayana Buddhism, and several other monks and religious teachers. Thinley Oezer was sentenced to eight years' imprisonment. His trial may have fallen short of international fair trial standards.

Many of those detained on suspicion of being DNC sympathizers were reportedly tortured or ill-treated. Methods included *chepuwa*, a form of torture where the thighs are compressed between two objects such as bamboo sticks, and severe beatings. Needup Phuntsho, a 19-year-old pupil who had been expelled from school in March, was reportedly tortured by members of the Royal Bhutan Police following his arrest in Thimphu in July.

Amnesty International continued to appeal for the immediate and unconditional release of Tek Nath Rizal; for political

prisoners to be released unless promptly charged with a recognizably criminal offence; and for fair trials for all political prisoners. The organization also appealed for an end to torture and ill-treatment.

In November an Amnesty International delegation visited the country and met the King and Chairman of the Council of Ministers and Minister of Foreign Affairs, Lyonpo Jigme Thinley, to discuss the organization's concerns and make recommendations for the protection of human rights. The delegates visited Mongar and Tashigang districts in the east and Sarbhang district in the south.

BOLIVIA

Scores of trade unionists and peasant leaders were detained for short periods and reportedly ill-treated. At least 13 deaths were reported, possibly caused by excessive use of force by the security forces. Military conscripts were reportedly ill-treated and at least two died in disputed circumstances. Human rights defenders continued to be threatened and attacked.

The government's decision to mobilize the army to assist the *Unidad Móvil de Patrullaje Rural* (UMOPAR), Mobile Rural Patrol Unit, in eradicating coca-leaf crops in El Chapare, Cochabamba Department, intensified the long-running conflict in the area. At least 15 people were killed, including two policemen, and dozens were injured during confrontations between the security forces and peasants. The army closed off some areas of El Chapare, preventing journalists and non-governmental human rights organizations from gaining access to the area.

100

In December the Ombudsman announced the publication of her report on human rights violations in El Chapare.

In April coca-leaf growers joined the general strike called by the *Central Obrera Boliviana*, Confederation of Bolivian Workers. Strike demands included a call for the authorities to abide by the agreement they had signed with coca-leaf producers in October 1997. Mass demonstrations and roadblocks staged by coca-leaf growers in the towns of Shinahota, Entre Ríos and Villa Tunari in El Chapare area, were broken up by members of UMOPAR and the army. Scores of peasants were arrested and several were allegedly beaten. At least five civilians died and over 60 people required hospital treatment for their injuries.

According to reports, members of UMOPAR and the army fired indiscriminately into crowds in the town of Shinahota and threw tear-gas canisters into a local school. At least five people were treated for bullet wounds. Among those reportedly killed in Shinahota were Bernardo Huancara, who died of bullet wounds to the head, and Agapito Checa, who was reportedly beaten to death. In a separate incident in the Entre Ríos-Ichoa area, the security forces were accused of causing the death of Remigildo Cori, who died from a bullet wound in the thorax, and one-year-old Raúl Díaz Camacho, who died from tear-gas inhalation.

Members of the security forces reportedly raided houses searching for trade union leaders and ill-treated several women in the town of Villa 14 de Septiembre. For example, 17-year-old Verónica Daza Lafuente, leader of the Alto Mariscal Union, needed medical treatment for facial wounds and Dominga Marín Sandoval and Elena Ortíz, both members of a peasant union, were beaten about the head with gun butts. No independent investigation was known to have been initiated into the deaths or into the complaints of ill-treatment by the security forces.

Among those arrested in the town of Ivirgarzama were Marcelo Portillo, Modesto Condori and David Herrera, all trade union leaders, and Felix Sánchez, a national deputy for the United Left. The four men had been trying to initiate a dialogue with the security forces. Felix Sánchez was released shortly after his arrest. The trade union leaders were on provisional liberty at the end of the year.

According to reports, conscripts were ill-treated and at least two died in disputed circumstances. Luis Quispe Balderrama, who was performing his military service at the IV Army Division in Charagua, Camiri District, died in February. Initially his family was informed that he had died of sunstroke. However, the autopsy report indicated that his death was the result of a severe beating on the head. In July Marcelo Rubén Flores, who was serving with the Padilla 20 Infantry Battalion in Tarija, was paralysed after allegedly being beaten about the neck by a superior officer. Investigations initiated into these incidents had not been concluded by the end of the year.

Human rights defenders continued to be harassed, threatened and assaulted. In April Verónica Ramos and José Luis Mamani, both members of the non-governmental *Asamblea Permanente de Derechos Humanos* (APDH), Permanent Human Rights Assembly, in Cochabamba came under attack from the authorities for documenting and publicizing human rights violations in El Chapare. According to reports, the Minister of Government accused them of "instigating violence" in the area.

In July Father Hugo Ortíz, a Catholic priest and President of the APDH in Caranavi, La Paz Department, was beaten by members of UMOPAR as he was travelling to attend a diocesan meeting. Later the same month Father Gines Mateo Rocamora, chaplain of the Chonchocoro prison in La Paz, had his identity documents confiscated by prison guards and was taken to see Luis Garcia Meza, a former President and former general, who was serving a 30-year prison sentence for several offences, including human rights violations. The prison guards stood by while Luis Garcia Meza threatened and insulted the priest. No investigation was initiated into the attack on Father Hugo Ortíz. A police investigation into the complaint of Father Rocamora had not been completed by the end of the year.

Investigations into the killings in the north of Potosí Department in 1996 (see *Amnesty International Reports 1997* and *1998*) made no progress and no information was forthcoming on the review of the rules for the use of force by the security forces, which had been recommended in a 1997 report on the killings by the Inter-American Commission on Human Rights of the Organization of American States. The Commission had also recommended, *inter alia*, an appropriate investigation to determine the responsibility of individual officers for the killings and sanctions for the military and police agents involved.

Amnesty International appealed to the authorities to investigate all reports of human rights violations in El Chapare and to bring those responsible to justice. The organization asked the authorities to issue clear instructions to members of the security forces to respect relevant codes of conduct and international standards and to grant assistance to non-governmental organizations in the gathering of information on the human rights situation in the country. Amnesty International expressed concern about attacks and threats against human rights defenders and about the failure of the authorities to bring to justice those involved in the abduction and torture of Waldo Albarracín in 1997 (see *Amnesty International Report 1998*). The authorities replied denying the accusations of human rights violations in El Chapare and claiming that investigations had been initiated into reported incidents. However, local non-governmental human rights organizations claimed that investigations were stalled.

BOSNIA-HERZEGOVINA

Scores of war crimes suspects remained at large. Continuing violence and administrative obstacles prevented refugees and displaced people from returning to their homes. The situation was exacerbated by the repatriation policies of some states hosting refugees from Bosnia-Herzegovina. Several people were arbitrarily detained on account of their nationality. Political prisoners were held in illegal detention facilities and given unfair trials. Scores of detainees were ill-treated by police. More than 19,000 people remained unaccounted for; many were believed to have "disappeared". The death penalty was abolished in the Federation of Bosnia-Herzegovina (Federation).

During the year, some 6,000 refugees fleeing the armed conflict in Kosovo province (see **Yugoslavia, Federal Republic of,** entry) were given "temporary admission" in accordance with procedures adopted in September by the Bosnia-Herzegovina Council of Ministers. Most had fled to the Federation.

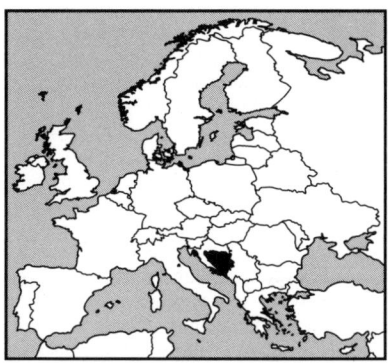

Intergovernmental organizations and their High Representative, Carlos Westendorp, continued to oversee implementation of the 1995 General Framework Agreement for Peace (the peace agreement). The UN Mission in Bosnia and Herzegovina, including the International Police Task Force (IPTF), and the Organization for Security and Co-operation in Europe (OSCE) continued to maintain significant field missions engaged in human rights monitoring and investigation.

The Human Rights Ombudsperson and Human Rights Chamber, national human rights institutions established under the peace agreement, issued a number of binding decisions. However, the authorities in the Republika Srpska (RS) – the Bosnian Serb entity – and those in the Federation – the Bosniac (Bosnian Muslim) and Bosnian Croat entity – often failed to comply with the recommendations of intergovernmental organizations and national human rights institutions. The High Representative imposed binding decisions in some instances because the parties themselves failed to reach agreement or cooperate.

In 1997 intergovernmental organizations had decided to make 1998 the year of "minority return", referring to extra efforts to facilitate the return of refugees or displaced people to the communities from which they had fled or been expelled during the 1992-1995 armed conflict, and

102

where they would be in a minority. Visits to home communities increased, including to towns which had been the scenes of some of the worst human rights violations during the war, such as Foča (RS), Srebrenica (RS) and Ahmići (Federation). However, "minority returns" were hindered by continuing human rights abuses and administrative obstacles.

General elections in September, organized and monitored by the OSCE, were won by nationalist parties. Elections for the three-member presidency were won by Alija Izetbegović, the Bosniac member; Ante Jelavić, the Bosnian Croat member; and Živko Radišić, the Bosnian Serb member, who replaced Alija Izetbegović as Chairman. Nikola Poplašen was elected President of the RS. Ejup Ganić was re-elected President of the Federation for another year by the newly elected federal parliament in December.

Scores of war crime suspects remained at large, although 11 people charged with crimes against humanity or war crimes were taken into custody. Six people indicted by the International Criminal Tribunal for the former Yugoslavia (Tribunal) were arrested by members of the multinational Stabilization Force (SFOR) and five suspects surrendered voluntarily. By the end of the year, 22 people were in the Tribunal's custody on or awaiting trial and six people were awaiting the outcome of appeals. One detainee, Milan Kovačević, died in August, apparently of a heart attack. In November, two Bosniacs, Hazim Delić and Esad Landžo, and one Bosnian Croat, Zdravko Mučić, were found guilty of grave breaches of the Geneva Conventions and violations of the laws or customs of war and sentenced to 20, 15 and seven years' imprisonment, respectively. A fourth Bosniac indicted with them, Zejnil Delalić, was acquitted. In December another Bosnian Croat, Anto Furundžija, was found guilty of violations of the laws or customs of war and sentenced to 10 years' imprisonment. In March Dražen Erdemović, who had been sentenced to 10 years' imprisonment in 1997 (see *Amnesty International Report 1998*), had his sentence reduced on appeal to five years' imprisonment.

In May the Tribunal Prosecutor withdrew charges against 14 suspects, to focus her resources on people holding higher levels of responsibility or those personally responsible for exceptionally brutal or otherwise extremely serious offences. The Prosecutor emphasized that the withdrawal was not for lack of evidence and that she expected national courts to pursue the prosecutions. However, by the end of the year, no attempts had been made by either RS or Federation courts to initiate such prosecutions. Twenty-seven people publicly indicted by the Tribunal for crimes committed in Bosnia-Herzegovina remained at large. All but four were indicted for crimes committed by those loyal to the Bosnian Serb leadership.

Members of national minorities were the most frequent targets of human rights abuses. Many violations were committed in the context of "minority returns" (see above). At the end of the year, approximately 1.2 million people remained refugees or internally displaced. Most had been victims of mass expulsions carried out by warring parties trying to create communities of a single nationality. Official failure to take effective action against violent attacks on members of national minorities prevented safe and dignified "minority returns". Administrative obstacles, such as difficulty in gaining access to housing, also hindered the return of refugees and displaced people to their homes. The houses of members of national minorities were deliberately destroyed to prevent the return of their pre-war occupants. In many cases, the houses were destroyed when repairs were nearing completion or when the owners' return was imminent. In the Bosnian-Croat-controlled municipalities of Drvar and Stolac (Federation), which were particularly obstructive to the return of pre-war residents, there were reports of around 80 and possibly as many as 100 such cases, respectively. With very few exceptions, local authorities did little to find those responsible or bring them to justice.

Returnees were also attacked; the authorities failed to ensure their protection. A cycle of retaliatory attacks was sparked by the killing of Vojislav Trninić and Mileva Trninić, an elderly Bosnian Serb couple who returned in early April to their pre-war home village near Bosnian-Croat-controlled Drvar (Federation). The following week, protests in Derventa (RS) by an angry crowd of Bosnian Serb displaced people, some of them from Drvar, prevented hundreds of Bosnian Croat refugees from Croatia from attending a religious service at the Roman Catholic church; six Bosnian Croats were injured. The following day, hundreds of Bosnian Croats in Drvar rioted. Fourteen people were injured in the Drvar demonstrations, including the Bosnian Serb mayor of the town, Mile Marčeta, who was assaulted by the crowd, hit by stones hurled by the rioters and had a bottle broken over his head. At least one police officer took part in the demonstrations. Other police officers were present, but did not effectively intervene to prevent the violence. Dozens of homes were damaged or destroyed. By the end of the year no one had been brought to account for the killings.

Returning refugees and displaced people also met violence in isolated incidents. In April in Velika Bukovica village near Travnik (Federation), a Bosniac-controlled town, two Bosnian Croats who were preparing to return were seriously injured by an explosion as they entered a house. In May an elderly Bosnian Serb woman was reportedly beaten after a crowd of 150 Bosniacs carrying rocks and sticks had gathered to protest against the visit of more than 50 Bosnian Serbs to Ključ (Federation). According to reports, Hamdija Vehtić, a Bosniac who had returned to Bijeljina (RS) from Germany, was ill-treated by police in September. He was unable to file a complaint because, as a result of discrimination by the RS authorities, he did not have identification documents. In October a Bosniac was killed and two others were injured in attacks after approximately 50 Bosniacs returned to the Bosnian Croat town of Tasovići (Federation).

The repatriation policies of some countries hosting refugees from Bosnia-Herzegovina contributed to the perpetuation of the effects of mass expulsion by forcing refugees to repatriate even though they were unable to return to their pre-war homes. For example, Germany deported more than 2,000 people to Bosnia-Herzegovina throughout the year. The repatriation of an additional 88,000 people was not wholly voluntary as the refugees did not have a real option to stay in the host country. Most refugees came from areas where their nationality had become a minority and they frequently had no alternative but to settle in other areas in the houses of other displaced people, thus preventing those people from returning to their homes. For example, in May the municipalities of Gradačac (Federation) and Modriča (RS) agreed to proceed with the bilateral return of Bosniac and Bosnian Serb displaced people from one town to the other. However, several thousand Bosniacs from Modriča repatriated from Germany during the year had settled in Gradačac in the houses of Bosnian Serb displaced people. As a result, the Bosnian Serb displaced people were not able to return to Gradačac, and Bosniacs were not able to return to Modriča.

Politicians and others in both entities used slander laws to silence journalists who exposed government corruption, including at least one possible prisoner of conscience. In October Mirjana Mičić was given a five-month suspended sentence for exposing financial gains made by elected officials in Zvornik (RS). In the RS, draft evaders and deserters continued to be excluded from amnesty laws. At least two men were reported to have been given suspended prison sentences for draft evasion.

Several political prisoners were detained without trial or charge in both entities. In February the Human Rights Chamber reported that Federation authorities accepted that the procedure of February 1996 (known as "Rules of the Road"), whereby no one was to be detained on war crimes charges until their case had been reviewed by the Tribunal Prosecutor (see *Amnesty International Report 1998*), was obligatory. However, several people were arrested in violation of the procedure, including Robert Rebac, a Bosnian Croat arrested by Bosnian Serb police while visiting Ljubinje (RS) in August. He was released after 28 days following international protest. Financial compensation was awarded to a number of individuals who had been arrested in violation of this agreement in 1996 and 1997, including some who may have been prisoners of conscience. In August, 14 prisoners were found in a factory in Pale (RS), an illegal detention centre. They were being investigated in connection with the murder of a Bosnian Serb police officer. After five days seven of them were transferred to Kula prison; the remaining detainees were released four days later. Only in December were six of them charged with the murder of Srdjan Knežević (see below).

In January the "Zvornik Seven" (see *Amnesty International Report 1998*) were granted a retrial by the Bijeljina district

104 court. Court sessions opened in May, after having been adjourned for four months. In December, four of the men were convicted of the murder of four Bosnian Serbs and a Bosniac and sentenced to up to 20 years' imprisonment. The retrial was criticized by international observers for repeating the procedural irregularities of the original trial.

The trials continued of at least 18 suspects indicted on nationally defined war crimes charges; most were unfair. For example, in October Ibrahim Djedović was found guilty on nationally defined war crimes charges and sentenced to 10 years' imprisonment, despite monitors' reports that there was insufficient evidence to establish guilt beyond a reasonable doubt. There were also serious procedural irregularities during the trial. For example, Ibrahim Djedović was denied access to legal counsel during the first five months of his detention; he was prevented from summoning defence witnesses; and the indictment was substantially altered the day before closing arguments were to be heard.

Scores of people were ill-treated by the police, including the 14 suspects arrested and illegally detained in Pale (see above). In February a Bosnian Serb suspected of the January 1993 murder of Deputy Prime Minister Hakija Turajlić was ill-treated during arrest by Bosnian Federation police and in pre-trial detention. In August Hasan Šabić, an opposition political candidate, was ill-treated after being summoned for a traffic violation in Travnik (Federation). In a number of cases, prosecutions of police officers for ill-treatment were initiated after IPTF intervention.

More than 19,000 people missing since the end of the armed conflict remained unaccounted for; many were believed to have "disappeared". Exhumations of mass graves continued to be the main source of information about their fate. In March an agreement by the parties to allow exhumations to take place in their territory without reciprocal exhumations taking place in areas under the control of the other side, ended a deadlock over the issue. By the end of the year more than 2,000 bodies had been exhumed both by the Tribunal and national authorities, of which more than half had been identified.

Srdjan Knežević, assistant to the head of the RS State Security Service in Pale (RS), was shot dead in August when returning home. An investigation was launched into possible state complicity in his death, as he was known to have been a follower of rival Bosnian Serb political factions to those dominating Pale. One investigating officer was removed by the IPTF Commissioner after he was found to have ill-treated suspects during the investigation.

In June the Human Rights Chamber ordered that the death sentences on two prisoners in the Federation – Borislav Herak (see *Amnesty International Report 1994*) and Nail Rizvanović – be commuted. In November the death penalty was effectively abolished in the Federation when a new Criminal Code came into effect which replaced it with extended prison terms.

Amnesty International addressed the authorities on a number of concerns throughout the year. In February the organization issued *Bosnia-Herzegovina: All the way home, safe "minority returns" as a just remedy and for a secure future*, updated in April, urging the authorities to protect members of minorities from violent attacks. The organization additionally called on countries hosting refugees from Bosnia-Herzegovina not to repatriate, or promote the repatriation of, any refugees who were unable to return in safety to their pre-war homes. The organization also continued to call on states contributing to SFOR to live up to their obligations to seek out and arrest individuals indicted by the Tribunal.

BRAZIL

Torture and ill-treatment by police were reported to be widespread. Conditions of detention amounted to cruel, inhuman or degrading treatment. Hundreds of people were killed by police and death squads linked to the security forces in circumstances suggesting extrajudicial executions. Human rights defenders were threatened, harassed and attacked. Most of those responsible for human rights violations continued to benefit from impunity. Land reform activists faced criminal charges which appeared to be politically motivated.

President Fernando Henrique Cardoso was re-elected for a second four-year term in October. Legislative bills introduced by the government which could potentially reduce impunity for human rights violations were still under discussion (see *Amnesty International Report 1998*).

In April the Inter-American Commission on Human Rights criticized Brazil's failure to protect João Canuto, a rural trade unionist killed in Pará state in 1985 following a number of death threats, and its slowness in bringing those responsible to justice. In December Brazil announced its acceptance of the jurisdiction of the Inter-American Court of Human Rights.

There were widespread reports of torture in civil police stations and of ill-treatment in prisons and juvenile detention centres where conditions were often cruel, inhuman or degrading. Remand and convicted prisoners in the civil police precincts in Espírito Santo and Minas Gerais alleged that they were routinely beaten and subjected to methods of torture including the "parrot's perch" (suspension by the legs and arms from a metal bar), near-asphyxiation and electric shocks. In February a civil police special unit entered the Depatri police station in São Paulo and allegedly beat, tortured and shot at some 200 of the 356 prisoners. In January and February prisoners held in the "*masmorra*" ("dungeon") wing of the *Casa de Detenção* prison in São Paulo state were allegedly beaten with iron bars and wooden clubs by guards.

Severe overcrowding and poor sanitary conditions in most prisons and police jails resulted in the spread of infectious diseases such as tuberculosis. Medical care for detainees, including those with terminal illness or severe disability, was gener-

ally inadequate or non-existent. A number of state authorities denied local and international human rights organizations access to prisons and police stations. Conditions in Muniz Sodré prison in Rio de Janeiro remained extremely overcrowded following the transfer there of 362 juvenile offenders in December 1997.

Unlawful police killings of civilians in Rio de Janeiro state continued to rise (see *Amnesty International Reports 1997* and *1998*); according to the Civil Police, between January and September police reportedly killed 511 civilians. In São Paulo state civil and military police reportedly killed 525 civilians during the year, an increase on previous years.

In August, four military police officers in Salvador, capital of Bahia state, reportedly attempted to kill two transvestites who were forced to strip and enter the sea; one drowned. By the end of the year the police officers had been dismissed and were awaiting trial in a civilian prison, but their commanding officer, who was under investigation, remained on active service.

In February Samuel dos Santos and Antônio Marcos da Rocha were shot dead by military police officers in Curitiba, Paraná state. The two young evangelical Christians "disappeared" while praying outside at night. Their bodies were dumped in a reservoir three days later. One police officer had been arrested in connection with the killings by the end of the year. Few of the civil and military police officers believed to be responsible for extrajudicial executions of unarmed civilians, including minors, in Paraná in previous years have been brought to justice or suspended from active duty.

There were continued reports of violent attacks on indigenous communities, landless peasants, and their leaders in the context of land disputes. In May Francisco de Assis Araújo (known as "Chicão"), a leader and advocate for the land rights of the Xucuru people in Pernambuco state, was killed. He had received numerous death threats in previous years because of his campaigning activities. For example, in 1992 his name had appeared on a death list along with those of 20 other indigenous leaders. An investigation into the killing was launched by federal police, but the outcome was not known at the end of the year. Most of those responsible for killings in the context of land disputes

106

continued to benefit from the prevailing climate of impunity.

In March Valentim Silva Serra (known as "Doutor"), and Onalício Barros (known as "Fusquinha"), two local leaders of the Landless Rural Workers' Movement (MST), were killed by gunmen in the context of a land dispute in southern Pará state. By the end of the year, nine estate owners had been charged with homicide. Eleven military police officers, nine of whom were accused of involvement in the Eldorado de Carajás massacre of landless peasants in the same region (see below), were charged with seeking to pervert the course of justice. However, they had not been removed from active duty by the end of the year.

Death squads, composed of off-duty police officers, continued to act with impunity in a number of states. In January in Mato Grosso do Sul, 10-year-old Carlos Cezar Fernandes was abducted, possibly sexually assaulted, and murdered. His death may have been a reprisal killing because his mother had implicated local police officers and politicians in her brother's murder in September 1997. A police investigation into the child's murder was only initiated after the Ministry of Justice intervened. Two men were arrested and confessed that they had been contracted by local military police officers to carry out the killing. They also admitted murdering another 12-year-old boy whom they mistook for Carlos Cezar Fernandes.

Human rights defenders were harassed, threatened and attacked. In September gunmen attempted to kill Frei Rodrigo de Castro Amédée Péret Humberto, a Roman Catholic Franciscan monk and coordinator of a diocesan pastoral organization in Minas Gerais state, when he and four other land activists went to mediate in a dispute between landless peasants and local landowners. The authorities had failed to investigate previous attacks on Frei Rodrigo or to disarm local landowners. They had also failed to investigate reports that in previous incidents military police officers had cooperated with armed militias formed by local landowners in Santa Vitória.

In April members of the Rio de Janeiro-based group *Grupo Tortura Nunca Mais*, Torture No More, received a number of anonymous death threats and suffered other forms of intimidation. The threats followed the group's public campaign against the promotion of an army doctor alleged to have participated in torture under the military government which held power between 1964 and 1985.

The military police officers involved in the shooting of Vágner Marcos da Silva in August 1997 in Rio de Janeiro remained on active service; one was promoted and another was recommended for a "bravery award" (see *Amnesty International Report 1998*). In January Vágner Marcos da Silva, who survived the shooting despite severe injuries, was charged with drug dealing and attempted homicide of the police. He was denied adequate medical treatment and there were grave concerns about his deteriorating health. By the end of the year no investigation had been opened into the police officers' actions and Vágner Marcos da Silva remained in prison awaiting trial.

In August the fifth and final defendant, a former military police officer, was tried in relation to the 1993 Candelária massacre in Rio de Janeiro in which seven street children and one youth were killed (see *Amnesty International Reports 1993, 1997* and *1998*). The officer was found guilty of all eight homicides and sentenced to a total of 204 years' imprisonment.

In November the third trial was held in Rio de Janeiro in connection with the 1993 Vigário Geral massacre in which 21 people were killed (see *Amnesty International Reports 1994, 1997* and *1998*). Ten former military police officers were acquitted. An appeal lodged by the prosecution was pending at the end of the year. The two former military police officers who had already been convicted in the case became eligible for a retrial after the Supreme Court reduced their sentences on a technicality. The retrial had not taken place by the end of the year. The other 36 officers charged in connection with this case were still awaiting trial at the end of the year.

Thirteen Rondônia state military police officers were indicted in April for the killing of 10 peasants in Corumbiara in August 1995 (see *Amnesty International Report 1996*) and were awaiting trial by a civilian court at the end of the year.

No date was set for the trial of 153 Pará state military police officers collectively charged with killing 19 landless peasants in Eldorado de Carajás in April 1996 (see *Amnesty International Report 1997*). A decision by the courts on whether the trial should be transferred to the state capital of Belém do Pará was pending at the end of the year. Prosecutors argued that if the trial was held in Curionópolis, where the massacre took place, witnesses would be in danger because the military police officers accused of the killings were still on active service.

In February the government reached a "friendly settlement" with the Inter-American Commission on Human Rights over the deaths of 18 prisoners who died of asphyxiation in the 42nd Police Precinct in São Paulo in 1989. They were among 51 prisoners who were beaten and forced into a small cell with no ventilation (see *Amnesty International Report 1990*). No one had been brought to justice in connection with the deaths. In order to avoid a report critical of the Brazilian authorities, the federal government acknowledged responsibility and the state authorities agreed to compensate the victims' relatives.

In March courts ruled that 85 of the 122 military police officers allegedly involved in the massacre of 111 prisoners in the *Casa de Detenção* prison in São Paulo in 1992 (see *Amnesty International Report 1993*) should be charged and tried before a civilian court. In April the federal government acknowledged responsibility for the massacre. However, the Colonel in charge of the operation enjoyed parliamentary immunity from prosecution as a state deputy.

In October a former military police officer was sentenced to 65 years' imprisonment for unlawfully shooting dead one unarmed civilian, Mario José Josino, and attempting to kill three others in Diadema, São Paulo state in March 1997 (see *Amnesty International Report 1998*). The civilian trial of nine other military police officers in connection with the shootings was continuing at the end of the year.

Land reform activists, including trade unionists, rural workers and members of the clergy, continued to be held under preventive detention orders and to have politically motivated criminal charges brought against them. In most cases charges appeared to be prompted solely by their non-violent activities in favour of land reform. Dutch development worker Winifridus Overbeeck was arrested in March by the Espírito Santo Federal Police under the 1980 National Security law, accused of "interfering in internal political affairs". He was threatened with deportation for his alleged involvement in a demarcation dispute between the Tupiniquim-Guarani indigenous groups in Aracruz and a local company. An Italian priest, Luis Pescarmona, was threatened with expulsion for allegedly "forming a criminal gang and inciting workers to armed struggle" in Paraíba state. He had also received death threats and been the subject of a number of politically motivated police investigations, criminal charges and court cases in previous years.

Throughout the year Amnesty International called for investigations into human rights violations, including harassment of, and attacks on, human rights defenders; excessive use of force by police in the context of land disputes; and torture and ill-treatment by police.

The organization sent an observer to the trials relating to the Vigário Geral and Candelária massacres. Amnesty International representatives also met federal, state and municipal authorities during their visits to the country.

In January the organization published *Brazil: Corumbiara and Eldorado de Carajás – rural violence, police brutality and impunity*, criticizing the inadequacy of police investigations into massacres carried out by police officers, either while they were on duty or when operating as members of death squads, and the slowness in bringing those responsible to justice.

In April the organization published a report, *Brazil: Human rights defenders – protecting human rights for everyone*, which highlighted the risks faced by those seeking to protect the human rights of many marginalized sectors of society. The report *Brazil: Indigenous leaders marked for death – the killing of Francisco de Assis Araújo*, published in June, expressed Amnesty International's concern at the murder and urged the authorities to bring those responsible to justice.

BULGARIA

One conscientious objector to military service was imprisoned and considered to be a prisoner of conscience. There were numerous reports of torture and ill-treatment by law enforcement officials: many of the victims were Roma. At least nine

108

people were shot and killed by police officers in disputed circumstances; dozens of others were injured. At least three people were sentenced to death. The death penalty was abolished.

In February it was reported that President Petar Stoyanov would propose abolition of the death penalty to the Advisory Council on National Security. In October the Legal Committee of the National Assembly recommended that the death penalty should be abolished for all offences in the revision of the Penal Code. In December the National Assembly abolished the death penalty, replacing it with life imprisonment without the possibility of commutation.

When in April the Legal Committee of the National Assembly rejected a proposal for a moratorium on the imprisonment of journalists convicted of insult and libel, Vice-President Todor Kavaldjiev stated that he would grant such journalists pardons. Fifty-four members of the National Assembly signed a petition to the Constitutional Court calling for the abolition of insult and libel as criminal offences. However, the Court ruled in July that criminal prohibition of libel and insult was not unconstitutional.

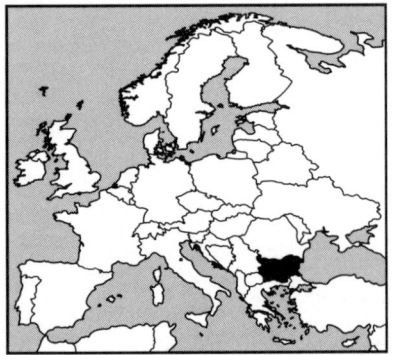

In September the Parliamentary Assembly of the Council of Europe decided to continue monitoring Bulgaria's honouring of obligations and commitments. Two Council of Europe rapporteurs who visited Bulgaria in June expressed concern about police violence – particularly against members of religious communities, Roma and street children – and about unacceptable conditions in two institutions for convicted juveniles.

In October the National Assembly adopted the Law on Alternative Service.

Certain provisions, including the length of alternative service which was envisaged to be twice as long as military service, were at variance with internationally recognized principles.

Prosecutions of conscientious objectors to military service continued. In April Krassimir Nikolov Savov was sentenced by Plovdiv Municipal Court to one year's imprisonment for evading military service. His conviction was confirmed by the District Court and the Plovdiv Appellate Court. In December he was imprisoned in Plovdiv prison to serve his sentence.

Many journalists were charged with insult and libel throughout the year. In October Karolina Kraeva, a journalist from Vratsa charged with libelling the local chief of police (see *Amnesty International Report 1998*), was sentenced to two years and four months' imprisonment. She was at liberty pending an appeal at the end of the year.

In July Mitko Shtirkov, who had been sentenced to four months' suspended imprisonment for defaming a local prosecutor (see *Amnesty International Reports 1997* and *1998*), was acquitted by the Superior Court of Cassation.

There were numerous reports of torture and ill-treatment by police officers. As in previous years, the authorities failed to investigate such reports promptly and impartially or to take adequate measures to address the problem of police torture and ill-treatment. In May this was acknowledged by the Chief Prosecutor and the Director of the National Investigation Service who stated that "serious violations of laws, of rights and freedoms of citizens are ever more frequent in the practice of the Ministry of the Interior". In a letter addressed to the President, the Prime Minister and chairs of parliamentary groups in the National Assembly, they described in detail five cases of police beatings and other abuses. Evgeni Ignatov, Nikolai Nikolov and Aleksandar Karaichev were detained in Sofia in January on suspicion of theft. The letter stated that "in the course of 'questioning' in the Fifth Regional Police Directorate physical force was illegally used in order to extract confessions". The three men were held for three days without ever being presented with an arrest warrant, "leading to the conclusion that their detention had been illegal". In another case, two suspects

detained in February in Sofia were severely beaten by officers who took from
them, without a receipt, a substantial sum
of money, a gold bracelet and a watch.

According to the Director of the National Investigation Service, 97 people detained in 1997 and 38 people detained
between January and mid-March 1998,
were subjected to police violence before
being admitted to the detention facilities
of the investigation services. The injuries
described ranged from serious fractures or
gunshot injuries, to lesions, contusions
and weals of varying extent and severity.
For example, Anatoli I. H., detained in
February in Smolyan, reportedly suffered
extensive bruising and complained of having been subjected to prolonged use of
electric shock batons. He was hospitalized
after suffering a heart attack.

In March the Deputy Chief Prosecutor
and the Prosecutor of the Armed Forces
reported on the status of more than 70 preliminary inquiries conducted by military
prosecutors into alleged "offences against
the person" by police officers. These inquiries had reportedly not been completed
because of lack of cooperation from the
Ministry of the Interior. For example, the
Sofia Military Prosecutor had still not
been able to complete an inquiry initiated
in 1993 into a shooting by two officers
which resulted in the death of one person
and grave injury to two others. In the first
four months of 1998, military prosecutors,
who are responsible for investigating alleged offences by police officers, reportedly initiated inquiries into nine cases,
including a death in custody as a result of
beating and three deaths by shooting.

Many victims of torture and ill-
treatment were Roma. For example, in
March in Krivodol, following a fight between a Romani man and a police officer,
approximately 15 police officers reportedly
entered the Romani neighbourhood and repeatedly fired their guns in the air and beat
people indiscriminately. At least 10 Roma
reportedly suffered injuries. In July approximately 80 police officers wearing helmets
and shields raided 15 houses in the
Romani neighbourhood of the village of
Mechka, in the Pleven region. They reportedly beat more than 30 men, women and
children indiscriminately with truncheons.
At least 15 people were injured; the oldest
victim was aged 67 and the youngest was
11. Although the motives for the raid were

not clear, one report stated that on the
same afternoon a Romani woman had
struck a police officer in a dispute.

At least nine unarmed people were
killed by police officers in disputed circumstances. Dozens of people were injured in other police shootings reported
throughout the year. For example, in January, in Sofia, Tsvetan Kovachev, a 17-year-
old Rom, was shot in the head by police
officers, reportedly while he was running
away from them with a man suspected of
having killed a taxi driver. Tsvetan Kovachev died in hospital the same day. An
investigation was initiated, but by the end
of the year no information was available
as to whether the officers involved had
been suspended from duty.

In August Hristo Tanev, who was in
pre-trial detention, was shot and killed by
a guard as he reportedly attempted to escape unarmed from the Pleven penitentiary by climbing over a fence. Another
detainee who was with Hristo Tanev was
apprehended 200 metres from the fence.

In October, two men were sentenced to
death for murder by the Pazardjik county
court. One man was sentenced to death for
murder by the Varna county court in November. After the abolition of the death
penalty in December, Vice-President Todor
Kavaldjiev reportedly stated that he would
pardon all those under sentence of death.

In February Amnesty International
called on the National Assembly to ensure
that the draft law on alternative service
conformed to internationally recognized
principles on conscientious objection. The
organization expressed concern that some
provisions under debate might allow the
government to deny the right to alternative service to people belonging to un-
recognized religious communities or to
individuals who developed a conscientious objection to carrying arms even
though their religious community was not
opposed to military service.

Throughout the year Amnesty International called on the authorities to revise
the Law on the Ministry of the Interior,
which regulates the use of firearms by law
enforcement officers and does not conform to the UN Basic Principles on the Use
of Force and Firearms by Law Enforcement Officials, and to investigate new incidents of police shootings in disputed
circumstances, described in a report
published in December.

In August the organization published *Bulgaria: New cases of ill-treatment of Roma* and urged the authorities to promptly and impartially investigate the incidents described. In December Amnesty International called for the release of Krassimir Nikolov Savov and urged President Stoyanov to initiate a judicial review of the Law on Alternative Service.

Amnesty International received replies from the Minister of the Interior and the Minister of Justice concerning four deaths in custody in suspicious circumstances in 1997. The organization was informed that a police officer had been sentenced to 16 years' imprisonment for murdering Stefan Traikov. Four police officers had been charged with murdering Mincho Simeonov Sartmachev. However, no one had been charged with the beating of another detainee, who was allegedly tortured at the same time as Mincho Simeonov Sartmachev. An investigation into the death of Valentin Nedev, who had reportedly died from tuberculosis five days after his release from custody, was in progress; the Minister of the Interior claimed that six days before his release he had been medically examined and given a clean bill of health. According to the Minister of Justice, a preliminary investigation into the death of Georgi Byandov (see *Amnesty International Report 1998*) was suspended because the police officers who participated in his arrest "had been disguised (masked)", and could not be identified. Police authorities in Burgas as well as the director of the National Police Service for Combating Organized Crime reportedly failed to respond to the investigator's repeated requests for information about the officers' identity.

In April a report was received from the Ministry of Foreign Affairs concerning investigations into shooting incidents raised by the organization in its report published in October 1997 (see *Amnesty International Report 1998*). In one case the military prosecutor decided not to charge the police officer responsible for the shooting, concluding that "the injuries suffered [a bullet injury in the left leg] were less significant than the damage caused [theft of a bicycle], and if the slight bodily injury was inflicted on an incidental bystander it was caused unintentionally." Similarly no one had been charged with the killing of two unarmed soldiers of Romani origin –

Kancho Angelov and Kiril Petkov – by military police who attempted to apprehend them after they went absent without permission from their unit in July 1996 (see *Amnesty International Report 1997*).

BURKINA FASO

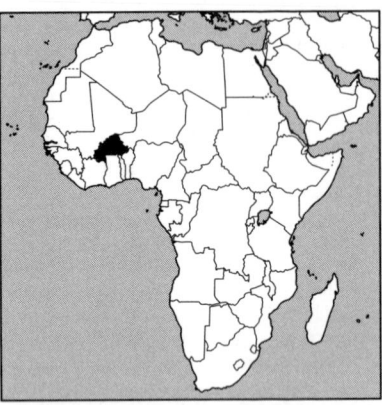

Two detainees died apparently as a result of torture or ill-treatment. Criminal suspects were reported to have been extrajudicially executed. A prominent journalist and government critic died with three other people in suspicious circumstances. Those responsible for past human rights violations were still not brought to justice.

In November President Blaise Compaoré was elected for a second seven-year term, defeating two other candidates. Nine opposition political parties had called for a boycott of the election on the grounds that the National Independent Electoral Commission inaugurated in July was not fully independent and autonomous. International observers concluded that the election had been fair. Opposition political parties, however, claimed that there had been fraud and irregularities.

Two detainees died in custody, apparently as a result of torture or ill-treatment. Ragnanguénéwindé David Ouédraogo, the chauffeur of François Compaoré, presidential adviser and brother of the President, was arrested with two other employees on 5 December 1997 in the capital, Ouagadougou, apparently accused of having stolen a large amount of money from their employer. They were arrested by soldiers and held incommunicado at the *Conseil de l'Entente* premises, headquarters of the presidential security forces. They were reportedly tortured in an attempt to extract confessions. David Ouédraogo died some time before mid-January. His family was not informed at the time of his death. The two other detainees were also reported to have suffered serious injuries as a result of torture. They were subsequently transferred to a prison in Ouagadougou, the *Maison d'arrêt et de correction de Ouagadougou*. Prominent members of opposition political parties condemned the death of David Ouédraogo and called on the President to clarify the circumstances of the death. David Ouédraogo's family also submitted a complaint to the judicial authorities.

David Guira, a mechanic, died after being held at the police headquarters in the district of Wemtenga, Ouagadougou. He had been arrested on 9 March, accused of theft, and held incommunicado. Although a detainee may only be held by law for 72 hours before being brought before a judicial authority to be either charged or released, the release of David Guira was not authorized until 17 March. His family were summoned to collect him the following day; they found him lying on the ground, unable to stand, with injuries to his head and body. David Guira, who had apparently been in good health before his arrest, died on 19 March.

Reports were received of extrajudicial executions of criminal suspects during a campaign against crime in 1997 and 1998. In Fada N'Gourma, Gourma Province, several captured armed robbers were reported to have been extrajudicially executed in 1997 by the security forces, including the police and gendarmerie. On 30 May 1997, for example, eight people were reported to have been summarily executed by the gendarmerie. In some cases the bodies were publicly displayed, apparently as a deterrent. Similar extrajudicial executions were reported during 1998 in other areas of the country, including in the region of Diébougou, Bougouriba Province. During the night of 5/6 September, up to 11 criminal suspects were reported to have been summarily shot by police after being arrested at diamond mining sites in AVV Village 2-Walala, Guéguéré Department. Some of the bodies were left by the roadside; others were buried where they had been shot.

On 13 December Norbert Zongo, a critic of the government and editor-in-chief of the independent weekly *L'Indépendant*, died with three other people, including his brother and his chauffeur, on the road to Sapouy, about 100 kilometres from Ouagadougou, in circumstances that were unclear. Norbert Zongo had persistently pursued the case of the death in custody of David Ouédraogo. His badly burned body was found with those of two other passengers in a vehicle; the fourth body was found beside the vehicle. There appeared to be no evidence that the vehicle had been involved in a road accident. There was widespread outrage at the death of Norbert Zongo and the government announced that an inquiry into his death would be opened. Dozens of people were held briefly after being arrested during demonstrations protesting against the death of Norbert Zongo.

There was still no official investigation into the death of a soldier who was killed in late December 1996 (see *Amnesty International Reports 1997* and *1998*). The findings of official investigations into apparent extrajudicial executions in 1995 of seven men from Kaya Navio, Nahouri Province, and into the killing of two school pupils during a demonstration in 1995 at Garango, Boulgou Province, were still not made public (see *Amnesty International Reports 1996* to *1998*).

In April a non-governmental organization, the *Mouvement burkinabè des droits de l'homme et des peuples* (MBDHP), Burkinabè Movement for Human and Peoples' Rights, submitted a complaint to the African Commission on Human and Peoples' Rights about the government's failure to investigate and establish accountability for these and other past human rights violations. The cases included the deaths in custody of a university teacher in late 1989 and a student in May 1990 (see *Amnesty International Report 1991*). In October the government agreed to negotiate with the MBDHP measures needed to resolve the various cases raised in the complaint.

In early April Amnesty International wrote to the government requesting clarification of the circumstances of the two deaths of detainees and urging full, independent inquiries in order to bring anyone found responsible to justice. Amnesty International also called for effective measures to be taken to protect all prisoners

112

and detainees from torture and ill-treatment and for the government to ratify the UN Convention against Torture and other Cruel, Inhuman or Degrading Treatment or Punishment. The director of the President's office replied, saying that judicial inquiries were being undertaken into the deaths and that ratification of the Convention was being considered by the government and National Assembly.

In December Amnesty International called for the investigation into the deaths of Norbert Zongo and the three others who died with him to be prompt and impartial, and, if the investigation concluded that the deaths were not accidental, for those responsible to be brought to justice. It expressed concern that official investigations into previous cases of deaths either in custody or in suspicious circumstances had not been concluded, their results had not been made public, and no one had been brought to justice. In response, the government provided details of the composition and terms of reference of the independent commission of inquiry into the deaths of Norbert Zongo and the three others.

BURUNDI

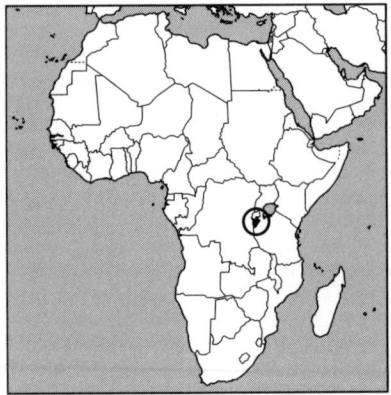

Hundreds of unarmed civilians were killed by the security forces and by armed opposition groups. Scores of extrajudicial executions were carried out shortly after arrest. At least 9,000 people, the majority of whom were accused of participating in politically motivated violence or armed opposition groups, remained in prolonged detention without trial. They included

several political opponents of the government. Hundreds of people were tried for their alleged part in politically motivated violence and a number of other political trials took place. Most of the trials did not meet international standards of fairness. Torture continued to be widely used in police and military custody. Conditions of detention were harsh and amounted to cruel, inhuman or degrading treatment. Scores of "disappearances" were also reported, often in military custody. At least 53 people were sentenced to death after unfair trials. No executions took place. Hundreds of thousands of internally displaced people remained in camps where they were at risk of human rights abuses. Armed opposition groups were also responsible for other human rights abuses, including rape and other forms of torture.

The *Forces pour la défense de la démocratie* (FDD), Forces for the Defence of Democracy, the armed wing of the Hutu-dominated *Conseil National pour la défense de la démocratie* (CNDD), National Council for the Defence of Democracy, and the armed wings of other Hutu opposition parties, continued their insurgency against the government. An armed opposition group allied to a Tutsi opposition party, the *Parti pour le redressement national* (PARENA), National Recovery Party, was also reported to be active, although PARENA officially denied any links to the *Front national pour la libération du Burundi* (FNLB), National Front for the Liberation of Burundi.

Negotiations aimed at finding a solution to the political crisis continued in Tanzania. In June a cease-fire agreement was signed, but it had not been implemented by the end of the year. Internal divisions within political parties and armed opposition groups, including a public split within the CNDD, complicated the process. Negotiations also took place in Burundi between the government and political opposition parties, resulting in a new transitional government, which included members of opposition parties, and a transitional constitution. Major Pierre Buyoya remained Head of State.

In August war broke out in the neighbouring Democratic Republic of the Congo (DRC). Although the Burundian government denied involvement in the conflict and offered to help in any mediation, Burundian soldiers were reportedly involved in the capture of Uvira and other towns by the Congolese armed opposition group, the *Rassemblement congolais pour la démocratie* (RCD), Congolese Rally for Democracy, and offered other support to Rwandese and Ugandan soldiers also involved in the conflict on the side of the RCD.

A new law allowing greater government control of the activities of national and international non-governmental organizations was passed. A draft law on repressing and preventing the crime of genocide was tabled for discussion by the Council of Ministers during the year, but by the end of the year had not been promulgated. Provisions of the draft violated several international human rights treaties which Burundi had ratified, including the UN Conventions on the Prevention and Punishment of the Crime of Genocide, on the Non-Applicability of Statutory Limitations to War Crimes and Crimes against Humanity, and on the Rights of the Child, and the International Covenant on Civil and Political Rights.

The conflict continued to render some areas inaccessible, making verification of information on alleged abuses difficult to obtain. In August restrictions were placed on the access of human rights groups and others to detainees and prisoners. These appeared to have been lifted by the end of the year.

Large-scale killings of unarmed civilians continued throughout the year. There were numerous reports of killings from the southern provinces of Makamba and Bururi, and from the province of Rural Bujumbura. Most killings by government soldiers appeared to take place in reprisal for insurgent activity. Hundreds of civilians were killed by government soldiers who accused them of failing to provide information on armed opposition groups, or of having in some way protected or colluded with them.

In early January up to 100 people were reportedly killed in Kizuka zone, Rumonge commune, Bururi province in reprisal for an attack by the FDD in which at least two soldiers were allegedly killed. Soldiers reportedly shot at fleeing unarmed civilians before systematically searching the houses and surrounding area for people who may have been hiding, and extrajudicially executing them. Justine Niyukulu and her seven-month-old child were among those extrajudicially executed.

On 3 November soldiers killed at least 165 people in Rutovo and Busenge collines, Mutambu commune, some 30 kilometres from the capital, Bujumbura. Some sources put the figure much higher. The victims were reportedly shot or bayoneted to death as they followed instructions to regroup around Busenge military post. Government and military sources initially claimed to be unaware of the massacre. However, on 10 November the Ministry of Defence issued a public statement acknowledging that around 30 people had been killed by members of the armed forces during a military operation against the *Forces nationales pour la libération* (FNL), National Liberation Forces, the armed wing of the *Parti pour la libération du peuple hutu* (PALIPEHUTU), Party for the Liberation of the Hutu People, and the FDD, and stated that an investigation would be launched. Three soldiers were reported to have been arrested.

Scores of people were extrajudicially executed after being arrested, often on the basis of unsubstantiated allegations of collaboration with armed groups. Spéciose Butore, Didace Bukoru, Jean Ndabagamye, Karidou Mugabonihera and Anaclet Bambara were reportedly extrajudicially executed in July, several days after their arrest, while held in a police lock-up in Mutaho commune, Gitega province. They had been accused of collaborating with armed opposition groups.

At least 9,000 people, mainly Hutu, were held in prolonged detention without trial, the majority on charges of participating in the massacres, primarily of members of the Tutsi ethnic group, which followed the assassination of President Melchior Ndadaye in October 1993, or of involvement in other political violence. Approximately 80 per cent of all detainees were held without trial, many had been detained for several years.

Senior members or alleged supporters of PARENA and *Solidarité jeunesse pour la défense des droits des minorités* (SOJEDEM), Youth Solidarity for the Defence of Minorities, arrested in March 1997, continued to be held without trial on charges of endangering state security (see *Amnesty International Report 1998*). In March a military court ruled that it was not competent to try the case, and released one of the defendants, former President Jean-Baptiste Bagaza, from house arrest

114

and allowed him to leave the country. The case was returned on appeal to military jurisdiction but no hearings had taken place by the end of the year. Pacelli Ndikumana, the lawyer of some of the defendants, was arrested in November on charges of endangering state security and remained in detention without trial at the end of the year. A number of other supposed PARENA supporters were arrested during the year on charges of endangering state security and having links with the FNLB.

Michel Nziguheba, a journalist, was released. He had been sentenced to five years' imprisonment in 1997 after a trial which appeared not to have met international standards for fair trial (see *Amnesty International Report 1998*).

Hundreds of political trials continued during the year. Those on trial included opponents of the government, people accused of participating in the 1993 massacres, people accused of collaborating with or belonging to Hutu-dominated armed opposition groups, and those accused of the assassination of President Ndadaye.

Trials of people accused of participating in the 1993 massacres continued to fall far short of international standards for fair trial, despite increased representation by lawyers. Statements allegedly made under duress were accepted in court and not all defendants had lawyers.

The trial by the Supreme Court of 79 people accused of assassinating President Ndadaye continued slowly. One defendant, François Ngeze, claimed to have been threatened in an attempt to intimidate him from testifying truthfully in the trial. In March Colonel Lambert Sibomana was killed in a car accident, shortly after making a statement in court incriminating members of the government and senior members of the *Union pour le progrès national*, Union for National Progress, in the assassination. No verdict had been reached by the end of the year.

In February the trial of 23 people charged in connection with a series of landmine explosions in Bujumbura concluded (see *Amnesty International Report 1998*). The trial failed to meet international fair trial standards. Allegations that some defendants had been tortured, and had made incriminating statements under duress were not investigated. Seven men

were sentenced to death, two *in absentia*. Two defendants, including the Reverend Jean-Pierre Mandende, who had reportedly been tortured, were acquitted. The cases against the 11 people, including Léonard Nyangoma and other senior members of the CNDD, who were being tried *in absentia* were referred to the Supreme Court for further investigation. No further investigations were known to have taken place by the end of the year.

In October Jean Minani was acquitted of all charges relating to the killing of Lieutenant Colonel Lucien Sakubu (see *Amnesty International Report 1996*). The witness for the prosecution retracted her 1995 statement incriminating Jean Minani in the murder, claiming that she had been threatened and forced to make the statement. Jean Minani had admitted to the killing while under torture at the *Brigade spéciale de recherche* (BSR), Special Investigation Unit, in Bujumbura. His lawyer argued in court that this statement should not be admissible as it was made under duress. Jean Minani had been awaiting trial since being charged in March 1995.

Torture continued to be widely used in police and military custody, despite official denials by the government. Detainees accused of links with armed opposition groups were particularly vulnerable to torture. Three detainees were arrested in August in Bujumbura on suspicion of collaborating with the CNDD. Two required hospital treatment after being ill-treated at the military barracks of the Third Intervention Battalion in Kamenge, Bujumbura. The third, Serge Bizimana, was transferred to the BSR in September where he remained at the end of the year.

Conditions of detention, which often amounted to cruel, inhuman or degrading treatment or punishment, were harsh and, in some cases, life-threatening. The majority of prisons were severely overcrowded. More than 200 people died in detention in Ngozi Prison between January and April as a result of prison conditions. More than 2,400 prisoners were held in Ngozi Prison, which was built to house only 400 inmates. Prisoners under sentence of death in Mpimba Central Prison in Bujumbura were held under particularly harsh conditions.

Scores of "disappearances" were reported, often after arrest by soldiers. Many of these reports were impossible to confirm because the authorities denied relatives access to detainees or refused to disclose places of detention, or because they occurred in areas which were not accessible because of the continuing conflict. In response to continued concern about the "disappearance" of Etienne Mvuykere shortly after his arrest in November 1997, the government stated that he was no longer at the military camp where he had been detained and must, therefore, have been released. No investigation had been initiated into his "disappearance". No further information was available about Paul Sirahenda who "disappeared" in August 1997 (see *Amnesty International Report 1998*).

At least 53 people were sentenced to death after unfair trials. At least 260 people were under sentence of death by the end of the year. The majority had been sentenced in connection with the massacres of October and November 1993. At least 73 people were awaiting presidential clemency, including Gaëtan Bwampaye who was sentenced to death after a grossly unfair trial in 1997. No executions took place.

Approximately 600,000 people were reported to be internally displaced in Burundi and approximately 300,000 Burundian refugees remained in neighbouring countries. In April Burundian security forces assisted in Congolese military operations to forcibly return Burundian refugees from eastern DRC. Hundreds of refugees returned from Rwanda; many appeared to have been coerced into returning.

Hundreds of thousands of internally displaced Hutus were held in "regroupment" camps where their freedom of movement was severely restricted (see *Amnesty International Report 1998*). Camps for the displaced, mostly inhabited by Tutsi civilians, were attacked on several occasions by Hutu-dominated armed opposition groups.

Thousands of Congolese refugees arrived from August onwards. In October, five Congolese refugees closely associated with a former governor of South-Kivu in the DRC, who had himself fled the DRC earlier in the year, were arrested by Burundian security forces in Bujumbura and forcibly repatriated days later. They were handed over to the RCD. They were reportedly released after several days in custody.

115

Armed opposition groups were responsible for killing scores of unarmed civilians. At least 50 people were reportedly killed by armed opposition groups in October in an attack on a camp for the displaced in Bubanza and in an attack near Bujumbura. Both attacks were attributed to the FNL. Many killings appeared to be of alleged or potential government informants, or in reprisal for alleged collaboration with government authorities. Armed opposition groups were also reportedly responsible for forcible recruitment, including of children, and rape, as well as other criminal acts including looting and extortion.

In March Amnesty International submitted a memorandum to the government outlining its concerns and recommendations in relation to the draft law on repressing and preventing the crime of genocide. Amnesty International delegates visited Burundi to collect information about human rights abuses and to discuss human rights concerns and held talks with government officials in April and May. Amnesty International observers attended a number of hearings in trials of defendants accused of participating in massacres and other political violence. A further memorandum on the right to a full appeal was also presented to the government in November.

Amnesty International published *Burundi: Justice on trial* in July and *Burundi: Insurgency and counter-insurgency perpetuate human rights abuses* in November. In its public statements in response to these reports the government failed to address most of the substantive issues raised and rejected some of the organization's findings.

CAMBODIA

Scores of demonstrators were arrested during a government crack-down in September; most were prisoners of conscience. At least 11 other prisoners of conscience and possible prisoners of conscience were arrested during the year. Five people, including one who had been extrajudicially executed in 1997, were unfairly tried *in absentia* and sentenced to long prison terms. Torture in police custody and prison conditions amounting to ill-treatment were widespread. Dozens of

people remained unaccounted for following the September crack-down. Dozens of people were extrajudicially executed. An armed opposition group committed human rights abuses, including deliberate and arbitrary killings.

Intensive diplomatic efforts to normalize the political situation following the July 1997 coup (see *Amnesty International Report 1998*) continued. Government troops and forces loyal to ousted First Prime Minister Prince Norodom Ranariddh declared a cease-fire in February, following the acceptance of a Japanese-brokered peace plan. The so-called "four pillars initiative" allowed exiled politicians to return home to participate in the July elections, but lacked any measures for human rights protection. By the end of March Prince Ranariddh and many other exiled politicians had returned to Cambodia.

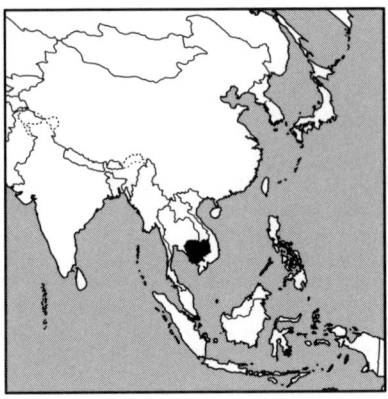

General elections in July resulted in a declared victory for the Cambodian People's Party (CPP). Prince Ranariddh's FUNCINPEC party came second and the Sam Rainsy Party (SRP) third. FUNCINPEC, the SRP and other smaller parties disputed the results and alleged widespread fraud. Mass demonstrations in the capital, Phnom Penh, were violently dispersed by the security forces. Talks initiated by King Norodom Sihanouk led to the formation of a CPP-FUNCINPEC government in November. The agreement will require substantial constitutional changes. The government imposed a travel ban on newly elected National Assembly members until after the swearing-in ceremony in September. Many left the country immediately afterwards in fear for their safety.

The Supreme Council of Magistracy and the Constitutional Council were finally convened, but were widely regarded as politically biased in favour of the CPP, as was the National Election Committee in charge of organizing the July elections.

In January the UN High Commissioner for Human Rights visited Cambodia and held talks with CPP Second Prime Minister Hun Sen. Agreement was reached on the continued presence in Cambodia of the Office of the High Commissioner for Human Rights for a further two years. The UN Special Representative on the situation of human rights in Cambodia submitted reports to the UN Commission on Human Rights in April and the UN General Assembly in November, condemning continuing government abuses and the ongoing impunity for human rights violators, including the leaders of the Khmer Rouge; both the Committee and the General Assembly adopted strong resolutions expressing grave concern about the ongoing government abuses and impunity. Cambodia's vacant seat at the UN was occupied by the representative of the new government.

Factionalism within the remnants of the Khmer Rouge political movement and armed forces continued during the first months of the year (see *Amnesty International Report 1998*), as did international efforts to bring to justice those responsible for serious human rights violations between 1975 and 1979. Former leader Pol Pot died in April. By the end of the year, most of the Khmer Rouge had defected to the government armed forces, which accepted all defectors, regardless of their alleged involvement in human rights abuses. In December Khieu Samphan and Nuon Chea, two senior members of the 1975 to 1979 Khmer Rouge government, defected to the government side. Prime Minister Hun Sen brought them to Phnom Penh for a visit and gave them government protection. In November a group of experts appointed following the UN General Assembly resolution in 1997 (see *Amnesty International Report 1998*) visited Cambodia to examine evidence about serious human rights violations in the country while the Khmer Rouge was in power.

Scores of people, possibly hundreds, were detained by the security forces in September following the violent crushing of opposition demonstrations. Most were arrested for the peaceful expression of their political views. Some were released after short periods in detention, but the fate and whereabouts of dozens of people remained unknown at the end of the year. The demonstrations began in August, led by Prince Ranariddh and Sam Rainsy, and attracted thousands of supporters. The vast majority of the demonstrations were peaceful, but in early September, four ethnic Vietnamese traders were beaten to death by angry mobs in the capital following a food poisoning outbreak. Some of those involved may also have attended the political demonstrations. Between 7 and 15 September, police and military police in Phnom Penh attacked demonstrators with electro-shock batons, filthy pressurized water and live ammunition, killing at least three people and injuring dozens of others, including Buddhist monks. Human rights workers discovered up to 25 bodies floating in the river or buried in shallow graves following the crack-down. Most showed signs of torture and apparent extrajudicial execution. The authorities denied that any of the bodies were linked to the violent crushing of the demonstrations. Human rights workers were subjected to death threats.

Seven prisoners of conscience were illegally detained throughout January in Koh Kong province. Two women FUNCINPEC members were arrested without a warrant by the Deputy Commander of the Provincial Military Forces. Both were held incommunicado and ill-treated at the Provincial Military Headquarters until intervention by the UN Special Representative for Human Rights in Cambodia secured their release, along with that of five other FUNCINPEC supporters.

Lim Pheng was arrested in June after shots were fired at the signpost for an SRP office located in his mother's house in Kampong Cham province. Although he had nothing to do with the shooting, he was unfairly tried and sentenced to one year's imprisonment for "illegal possession of weapons". Lim Pheng's arrest, trial and sentencing appeared to be motivated by his affiliation with the SRP; he was a possible prisoner of conscience.

Danh Teav, a FUNCINPEC employee at the Ministry of the Interior, and his wife, Ly Rosamy, an SRP election candidate, were arrested in July. She was released, but Danh Teav was held in incommunicado detention for 36 hours before Amnesty International delegates located him at the Municipal Court. He had been so badly beaten by the Phnom Penh Criminal Police that he could not stand without help (see below). The police had tried to make him confess to crimes including involvement in the attempted murder of a pro-government newspaper editor earlier in the year. After a brief court appearance, Danh Teav was returned to incommunicado detention for a further seven days and repeatedly denied access to a doctor despite his injuries. He was released without out charge in October.

Kem Sokha, President of the 1993-1998 Parliamentary Commission on Human Rights and the Reception of Complaints, lost his seat in the July elections and went into hiding in late September, after then Second Prime Minister Hun Sen stated that he could face arrest for his part in the opposition protests after the election. Two summonses were issued for Kem Sokha to answer questions on different charges, including "damage to public property", "incitement leading to the commission of a crime", and "incitement not leading to the commission of a crime". Anti-Vietnamese rhetoric was a feature of many speeches during the demonstrations, but Kem Sokha intervened to stop demonstrators vandalising the Viet Nam-Cambodian Friendship Memorial. In December Kem Sokha appeared in court to answer questions. If arrested he would be a prisoner of conscience.

In December Kim San and Meas Minear, employees of a local human rights group, were arrested without warrants in Sihanoukville, following public rioting after toxic waste was found near the city. The two men were charged with robbery and damage to property; no trial had taken place by the end of the year. Both men were prisoners of conscience.

Prisoner of conscience Srun Vong Vannak was released in a royal amnesty in September. The amnesty did not overturn his conviction (see *Amnesty International Report 1998*).

In March the Military Court held two trials *in absentia* of Prince Norodom Ranariddh and his close associates General Nhek Bun Chhay, Serei Kosal, Thach Soung and the late Chao Sambath who was extrajudicially executed in July 1997 (see *Amnesty International Report 1998*). The trials were grossly unfair; no defence

118

lawyers were present and court judgments bore little relation to the evidence presented. All five were found guilty of a number of crimes, including illegal importation of weapons and internal security offences, and sentenced to long prison terms. King Norodom Sihanouk granted a royal pardon to his son Prince Ranariddh, in accordance with the Japanese-brokered peace plan, thus allowing him to return home and take part in the elections. Pardons were granted to his co-defendants with the formation of the new government.

There were no impartial investigations or arrests in connection with the numerous human rights violations committed by the security forces in previous years, including scores of extrajudicial executions since the 1997 coup. A former member of the Khmer Rouge wanted in connection with the killings of three Western hostages in 1994 (see *Amnesty International Report 1995*) was arrested in August. He had not been tried by the end of the year.

Torture and ill-treatment by police were widespread. In April police beat demonstrators who had gathered in support of Prince Ranariddh. A UN human rights worker was beaten later that day by people including uniformed police in Phnom Penh. In July Amnesty International found five people handcuffed together with Danh Teav (see above) at the Phnom Penh Municipal Court. They had been beaten in police custody, were covered in cuts and bruises and had blood on their clothes. The handcuffs were so tight that their wrists were badly cut. They had no legal representation in court and did not know the charges against them.

Conditions in prisons were harsh. Lack of food contributed to serious health problems for inmates in most provincial prisons. Prolonged shackling of prisoners was reported in at least one provincial prison.

The fate and whereabouts of dozens of people missing after the crack-down on opposition demonstrators in September remained unknown at the end of the year. Eyewitnesses reported hundreds of arrests, but the authorities acknowledged only 22.

Dozens of extrajudicial executions were reported throughout the year. In February the wife, son and another relative of Captain Bun Sovanna were arrested in Banteay Meanchey province by government soldiers. The three were marched a short distance from their house and shot dead. Bun Sovanna had defected from his post in the Royal Cambodian Armed Forces to join the resistance loyal to Prince Ranariddh in July 1997. No investigation was carried out into the killings.

In March, during the first of the trials of Prince Ranariddh and his associates, Brigadier-General Thach Kim Sang, a senior FUNCINPEC official at the Ministry of the Interior, was killed in Phnom Penh. Before the 1997 coup, Thach Kim Sang was a close associate of General Nhek Bun Chhay. Thach Kim Sang feared for his life and had stopped going to his office. He was shot dead by two men dressed in police uniforms as he drove to a meeting with senior CPP officials. No investigation was carried out and no one was brought to justice.

In September, two opposition demonstrators were taken to the outskirts of Phnom Penh by plainclothes policemen and shot dead. Local people witnessed the killings. Only one body could be identified, the other had been shot so many times that his face was unrecognizable. Police claimed the two were "robbers fleeing the scene of a crime".

Khmer Rouge armed forces committed human rights abuses during the year, including deliberate and arbitrary killings. Khmer Rouge forces claimed responsibility for an attack on a fishing village in Kampong Chhnang province in April, in which 22 civilians were killed, including 12 ethnic Vietnamese. Khmer Rouge forces were also responsible for two attacks near Anlong Veng in July in which at least five people died, including civilians.

In March Amnesty International published a report, *Kingdom of Cambodia: Human rights at stake*, detailing political killings and intimidation since October 1997. At the UN Commission on Human Rights the organization called on member states to adopt a strong resolution on Cambodia, following the political violence during 1997. In August Second Prime Minister Hun Sen ordered all forces loyal to the CPP to stop harassing and intimidating opposition party activists, but in general there was no concrete response from the government to Amnesty International apart from public criticism of the organization's work.

During the demonstrations following the elections, Amnesty International called for restraint on all sides, and appealed to political leaders not to incite human rights abuses by using anti-Vietnamese rhetoric in their speeches. In September the organization published a report, *Kingdom of Cambodia: Demonstrations crushed with excessive use of force*, following the violent crack-down on opposition supporters in Phnom Penh. Throughout the year, Amnesty International criticized the government's harassment of human rights workers, including those working for the Cambodia Office of the UN High Commissioner for Human Rights, some of whom were subjected to death threats.

CAMEROON

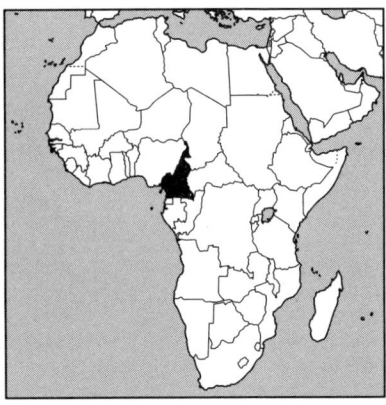

Several prisoners of conscience, including journalists and members of opposition political parties, were detained. Some 50 political prisoners were held without charge or trial throughout the year. Torture and ill-treatment remained routine and at least two prisoners died as a result. Harsh prison conditions amounted to cruel, inhuman or degrading treatment. Scores of people were reported to have been extrajudicially executed in the north of the country in an operation to combat armed robbery. Death sentences continued to be passed.

Attempts at dialogue between the government of President Paul Biya and the main opposition political party, the Social Democratic Front (SDF), failed. The government continued to reject the SDF's demands for an amendment to the Constitution which would provide for an independent electoral commission to

oversee future elections. International observers who monitored the 1997 legislative elections had recommended the creation of an independent electoral commission. The failure to set up such a commission had led the SDF and three other opposition parties to boycott the 1997 presidential election.

As in previous years, journalists writing for independent newspapers were convicted of criminal offences and imprisoned. Pius Njawé, director of *Le Messager*, arrested in December 1997 following an article which questioned President Biya's state of health, was convicted in January of disseminating false news and sentenced to two years' imprisonment and a fine. He was imprisoned at the Central Prison, New Bell, in Douala. In April the Court of Appeal reduced the fine and the prison term to one year and the Supreme Court upheld this sentence in September. There were many calls both within Cameroon and abroad for Pius Njawé's release. He was released in October, before completion of his sentence, after being granted a presidential pardon.

A member of a committee campaigning for Pius Njawé's release, the *Comité pour la libération de Pius Njawé*, who was part of a delegation of the committee planning to travel to Europe, was arrested at Douala airport in March and detained for two days.

Michel Michaut Moussala, editor of *Aurore Plus*, was convicted of defamation in January, in a separate case but at the same trial as Pius Njawé, and sentenced to six months' imprisonment and a fine. The charges related to an article which accused a member of the National Assembly of the ruling *Rassemblement démocratique du peuple camerounais*, Cameroon People's Democratic Movement (CPDM), of corruption and other offences. Although an arrest warrant was issued following the trial, he was not imprisoned until September when he was also accused of evading arrest because he had not presented himself to the prison authorities after his conviction. These new charges were, however, subsequently dismissed. He remained imprisoned in New Bell prison at the end of the year.

Among several other journalists imprisoned during the year was Patrick Tchouwa, director of *Le Jeune Détective*, who was arrested by police in July following an article which implicated a government minister and member of the National Assembly in misappropriation of government funds. He was convicted and given an eight-month suspended sentence in November, and was subsequently released. In November Christopher Ezieh of *The Herald* was arrested and detained briefly in Kumba after an article reported that the Governor of South-West Province had ordered a significant salary reduction for civil servants.

Members of opposition political parties were also detained. Two prominent SDF members were arrested in late August and early September in an apparent attempt to discredit the SDF. Ferdinand Asapngu, vice-chairman of Kumba Electoral District in South-West Province, and John Kumase Ndanga, chairman of Bonaberi Electoral District in Douala, were accused of planning armed attacks, although there was no evidence to substantiate these allegations. They were both released without charge in mid-September. Other SDF officials were also harassed and intimidated. In June armed gendarmes went to the house of the SDF chairman of Kribi Electoral District, South Province, to arrest him but were deterred by neighbours. When the gendarmes returned later, they physically assaulted his wife.

In northern Cameroon, traditional rulers, often prominent members of the ruling CPDM, and acting with the tacit approval of the authorities, continued to be responsible for the illegal detention and ill-treatment of political opponents, in particular members of the opposition *Union nationale pour la démocratie et le progrès* (UNDP), National Union for Democracy and Progress.

Nana Koulagna, a former UNDP member of the National Assembly, remained held throughout the year. He had been arrested in May 1997, shortly before the legislative elections, when a UNDP delegation was attacked by the private militia of the traditional ruler (*lamido*) of Rey Bouba in North Province; five people died in the confrontation. Nana Koulagna and 15 others were arrested, apparently accused of murder, and held at the Central Prison in Garoua; no member of the private militia was arrested (see *Amnesty International Report 1998*). None was charged and all but Nana Koulagna and six others were subsequently released. Although the judi-

cial authorities in Garoua ordered Nana Koulagna's release, he remained held under an order issued by the Senior Divisional Officer under legislation passed in December 1990 which provides for indefinite administrative detention. In October Nana Koulagna and six others were charged by a military tribunal with murder, looting, arson, illegal possession of arms and other offences. Their trial was expected in early 1999. The fact that a civilian court ruled that Nana Koulagna should be released, that charges were subsequently brought by a military tribunal, and that there appeared to be no evidence against him of individual responsibility for any criminal offence, suggested that he was held for purely political reasons.

A former government minister and his close associate, who had been sentenced to lengthy prison terms in 1997 after an unfair trial, remained imprisoned. Titus Edzoa, who had resigned as Minister of Health and stated his intention to contest the presidential election, and Michel Thierry Atangana Abega, his presidential campaign manager, were convicted of corruption and misappropriation of public funds in October 1997 and sentenced to 15 years' imprisonment. Their trial proceeded despite defence lawyers withdrawing in protest against being informed of the trial only 24 hours in advance (see *Amnesty International Report 1998*). Their appeal against conviction and sentence had not been heard by the end of 1998.

Some 50 prisoners who were arrested following attacks by armed groups in several towns in North-West Province in March 1997 remained in detention without charge or trial throughout the year (see *Amnesty International Report 1998*). Although 14 others were released without charge during the year, arrests of suspects continued, including two gendarmes who were arrested in August. The authorities attributed the attacks to a group supporting independence for Cameroon's two English-speaking provinces, North-West and South-West Provinces, and those arrested included members of the Southern Cameroons National Council (SCNC) and an affiliated organization, the Southern Cameroons Youth League (SCYL). Most of the prisoners were held at the Central Prison in Yaoundé, known as Nkondengui prison; others were held at the Principal Prison in Mfou.

Five other SCNC members who had been arrested in previous years in connection with a referendum on independence (see *Amnesty International Reports 1996* to *1998*) remained held without charge throughout the year.

Many among the group of prisoners held in connection with the events in North-West Province in 1997 were reported to be seriously ill either as a result of torture and ill-treatment or lack of medical care. Ebenezer Akwanga, President of the SCYL, was reported to have been admitted to hospital suffering paralysis of his lower limbs and impaired vision as a result of torture. Another prisoner reported to be critically ill, Lawrence Fai, died in late August after finally being admitted to hospital, bringing to at least nine the number of those arrested following the violence in North-West Province in 1997 who had died in detention.

Torture and ill-treatment of prisoners and detainees remained routine. In January Hamadou Mana (known as Agnana), a prisoner at the Central Prison in Maroua, Far-North Province, died from a severe head injury after being beaten by prison guards following an escape attempt. Another prisoner had died in similar circumstances at the prison in 1997 (see *Amnesty International Report 1998*). No action was known to have been taken by the authorities against those responsible in either case.

In at least two cases, however, those who had tortured and ill-treated detainees were prosecuted. Two police officers who were found responsible for the death of a young man in police custody in Yaoundé in November 1997 were sentenced to 10 years and six years' imprisonment respectively in June, under legislation passed in January 1997 which prohibited torture and made causing injury or death as a result of torture punishable by up to life imprisonment. They were also ordered to pay compensation to the man's family. Police officers responsible for a second death in custody in November 1997 were acquitted (see *Amnesty International Report 1998*).

Pius Njawé's wife, Jeanne Ongbatik, was physically assaulted by prison guards on several different occasions when she attempted to visit her husband and in January she had a stillborn child. A complaint submitted by Pius Njawé about his wife's ill-treatment was not pursued by the authorities.

Prison conditions remained extremely harsh throughout Cameroon, with severe overcrowding, inadequate or non-existent sanitary facilities and seriously deficient health care and nutrition. For example, Pius Njawé was held in a cell with some 100 other prisoners, all accused or convicted of criminal offences, at New Bell prison and violence frequently broke out in the cell. According to reports, in an attempt to isolate Pius Njawé, the prison authorities punished a number of prisoners who associated with him. Although Pius Njawé was allowed to see a specialist in hospital in May, the prison governor refused to allow him to attend subsequent appointments despite recommendations from the prison doctor.

Scores of people were reported to have been extrajudicially executed by the security forces in North and Far-North Provinces during an operation by security forces to combat a serious and long-standing problem of armed robbery. Several hundred people were estimated to have been killed by armed robbers in the area in recent years. A special unit of the army and gendarmerie was formed in March to tackle insecurity in the region. Captured armed robbers, who included Chadian nationals, and those suspected of armed robbery, were summarily executed or "disappeared" after their arrest. There were also reports that people denounced as armed robbers in personal settling of scores were among those extrajudicially executed. The security forces were reported to have taken suspects from their homes at night, killed them and abandoned their bodies. A non-governmental human rights organization, the *Mouvement pour la défense des droits de l'homme et des libertés*, Movement for the Defence of Human Rights and Liberties, compiled information about 12 extrajudicial executions in March and more than 40 in June. These summary killings continued throughout the rest of the year. In October a photographer, Alioum Aminou, was arrested in Maroua, apparently because he had distributed photographs of victims of extrajudicial executions. His whereabouts remained unknown at the end of the year. Extrajudicial executions were also reported to have taken place in North Province.

122

Several people were reported to have been killed or injured in incidents where the security forces appeared to have used excessive force. In July a trader was shot and killed by a police officer in Douala during a search for stolen goods. In August a street trader was shot dead by a police officer at a market in Yaoundé after he refused to pay money in exchange for being allowed to sell in the market. In late December a student was shot and killed in Bafoussam, West Province, by a police officer who was pursuing him after a fight had broken out between the two men. The authorities were reported to have started an investigation into the death and to have arrested two suspects.

Death sentences continued to be passed. Three men, one of whom subsequently died in detention, were sentenced to death after being convicted of murder by a court in Bafoussam in September.

Twelve refugees from Equatorial Guinea arrested in September 1997 remained in detention throughout the year while efforts were made by the UN High Commissioner for Refugees to resettle them in a third country. Eight Chadians, including three members of a former Chadian armed opposition group who had been arrested in November 1997, were released without charge in July and allowed to return voluntarily to Chad. All had been at risk of grave human rights violations if forcibly returned to their own countries (see *Amnesty International Report 1998*).

Amnesty International repeatedly called for the release of prisoners of conscience and for other political detainees either to be charged and tried or to be released. The organization called for safeguards to protect all detainees from torture and ill-treatment, for independent investigations into deaths in custody, and for those responsible to be brought to justice. Amnesty International also called on the international community to scrutinize human rights in Cameroon and to press Cameroon to adhere to its human rights commitments.

In April Amnesty International repeated calls not to forcibly return detained nationals from Equatorial Guinea.

In December Amnesty International published a report, *Cameroon: Extrajudicial executions in North and Far-North Provinces*, which called for an investigation into these killings in order to bring those responsible to justice and for urgent measures to be taken to prevent further killings.

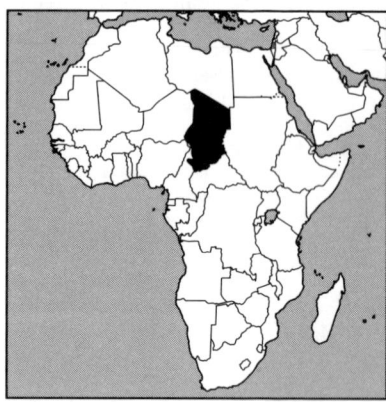

CHAD

Hundreds of people were extrajudicially executed by the security forces; many were tortured before being killed. Dozens of political prisoners, including prisoners of conscience, were held without trial or received unfair trials. Torture and ill-treatment were routine. Prison conditions were harsh; at least one person died in custody. Armed opposition groups were responsible for numerous human rights abuses, including deliberate and arbitrary killings and hostage-taking.

President Idriss Déby's government continued to face armed opposition in the northern and eastern parts of the country from the *Front national du Tchad rénové* (FNTR), Renewed National Front of Chad; the *Mouvement pour la démocratie et le développement*, Movement for Democracy and Development; and the *Armée nationale tchadienne en dissidence*, Dissident Chadian National Army; and, in the south of the country, from the *Forces armées pour la République fédérale* (FARF), Armed Forces for the Federal Republic. There were violent clashes between the security forces and armed opposition groups, particularly in the Logone districts.

In May a second peace accord between the government and the FARF officially ended the armed conflict in the south of the country. As with the previous accord,

123

it provided for an amnesty for all members of the FARF and for the integration of its members into the army (see *Amnesty International Report 1998*).

In April the UN Commission on Human Rights again decided not to transfer consideration of the human rights situation in Chad from the confidential 1503 procedure into the public procedure. In June the European Parliament passed a resolution urging the Chadian authorities to release prisoner of conscience Ngarléjy Yorongar Le Moïban (see below). It also urged the European Council, the European Commission and the member states of the European Union to put pressure on the Chadian government to respect human rights and the rule of law throughout the country, and to suspend military activities in the southern region following the massacre of at least one hundred unarmed civilians in March (see below).

Hundreds of people were extrajudicially executed by the security forces; many were tortured before being killed (see below). Although there was strong evidence that the security forces were responsible, the authorities did not take any action to bring the officers who ordered the massacres to justice. At least 20 people, including women and children, were killed by soldiers in February and March in the Doba region. Soldiers reportedly visited the region several times over a two-day period, shooting and killing unarmed civilians, including village chiefs, and burning down houses, in reprisal for the abduction of four Frenchmen by an armed opposition group (see below).

In March at least 100 people were reportedly killed in a series of massacres by the security forces. As many as 25 people were killed in the villages of Dobara and Lara on 1 March. On 11 March village chiefs and others were summoned to a meeting with the deputy prefect of Benoye, supposedly to discuss taxation. Instead of being received by the local authorities, the village chiefs were arrested by the security forces, who then reportedly shot and killed them and six others by the Logone River. Among them were Gaston Mbaïney and Bemadji Cheflengar, village chiefs from Goré and Ngara Ndoh villages. Three days later soldiers surrounded the village of Talade, where they reportedly tied up 25 people and killed them.

Dozens of political prisoners, including prisoners of conscience, were held without trial or received unfair trials. Critics of the government, including opposition politicians, journalists and human rights activists, were at serious risk of human rights violations, including death threats and ill-treatment. Some were sentenced to prison terms and heavy fines.

Firmin Nengomnang, a prisoner of conscience held without charge or trial since December 1997 and a member of the *Ligue tchadienne des droits de l'homme*, Chadian Human Rights League, was released by the Moundou tribunal in January. A week later he was given a two-year suspended sentence and a heavy fine by the same tribunal. The charges related to an article he had published which criticized the Moundou Commissioner of Police (see *Amnesty International Report 1998*). An appeal against the sentence was pending at the end of the year.

In February Oulatar Begoto and Dieudonné Djonabaye, respectively director and editor-in-chief of the independent newspaper *N'Djaména Hebdo*, were each given two-year suspended sentences for defamation of the President. The charges related to an article in the newspaper accusing the President of being partisan. Later the same month Dieudonné Djonabaye was detained for several hours and reportedly severely beaten by members of the security forces in a Chadian military barracks.

At least 12 people were arrested in February after four French nationals were taken hostage in the Sarh region by an armed opposition group. All those arrested were reportedly tortured or ill-treated. One of them, Dr Demane Nana, who had been undergoing medical treatment when arrested, died in detention in April. All the detainees came from the Sarh region, an area supposedly loyal to Dr Nahor, leader of an armed opposition group. Some were provisionally released, but at the end of the year four of them – Kono Guoi Nahor Dagal, Adallah Daba, Nadjara Kama and Lagoum Moussa – were still held without charge in Ndjaména. They were possible prisoners of conscience.

In July prisoner of conscience Ngarléjy Yorongar Le Moïban, a member of the National Assembly and a prominent opposition politician, was sentenced to three years' imprisonment and a large fine for

124

defamation of President Déby and of the President of the National Assembly, Wadal Abdelkader Kamougué. The sentence was confirmed in December by the N'Djaména Appeal Court. Ngarléjy Yorongar Le Moïban's parliamentary immunity had been lifted by his peers in May. The charges related to an interview given in July 1997 in which Ngarléjy Yorongar Le Moïban had accused Wadal Abdelkader Kamougué of accepting money from a French oil company to finance his 1996 election campaign. The two journalists who conducted the interview – Sy Koumbo Singa Gali and Polycarpe Togamissi – were arrested and charged with complicity in the defamation. In June they were convicted and given two-year suspended sentences and ordered to pay large fines before being provisionally released. In December the N'Djaména Appeal Court reduced their sentences to one year and halved their fines. There were serious procedural irregularities in the trials of all three. For example, in the trial of Ngarléjy Yorongar Le Moïban, lawyers for the defence were denied access to the case files until immediately before the hearing at N'Djaména High Court. Ngarléjy Yorongar Le Moïban was given a sentence one year longer than the maximum allowed by Chadian law for defamation, and the fines paid by the two journalists were twice the maximum allowed by law for complicity in defamation.

Following the massacres in March of more than 100 people in the Logone districts by the security forces, the *Collectif des associations de défense des droits de l'homme et des syndicats*, Collective of Associations for the Defence of Human Rights and Trade Unions, in Moundou called for a two-day, city-wide *opération ville morte* (general strike and "stay-away"). Fears for the safety of human rights activists, including Dobian Assingar and Julien Beassemda, two human rights defenders, intensified following the success of the *opération ville morte*. The deputy secretary at the Ministry of the Interior accused the organizations involved in the *opération ville morte* of calling for insurrection. The government subsequently banned all activities by Chadian human rights organizations and their offices were occupied by members of the security forces. The ban prevented a press conference, organized by local human rights or-

ganizations to highlight the deterioration in the human rights situation, from taking place.

In August, five people were released from prolonged detention without charge or trial. Those released included Souleymane Abdallah, the founder member of Alternative 94, a Chadian organization for political debate (see *Amnesty International Report 1998*); and Altebey Nadjiban, director of a private school in Nguéli, N'Djaména district. Also in August, four children, who were prisoners of conscience, were released. They included 14-year-old Guelngar Olivier and 13-year-old Djimtoloum Joël, who had been arrested in April and accused of collaborating with the enemy.

In October Souleymane Abdallah was rearrested along with another member of Alternative 94, Facho Ballam, a veterinary surgeon. Both were released without charge a few days later.

It was unclear whether the 10 or more political prisoners, including possible prisoners of conscience, arrested in previous years remained in detention without charge or trial or had voluntarily enlisted in the army. The authorities claimed that they had been integrated into the national army, in accordance with the provisions of the 1997 peace accord between the government and the FARF. However, there was no evidence that the detainees were linked to the FARF in any way and there were fears that they may have been forcibly conscripted into the army (see *Amnesty International Report 1998*).

Torture and ill-treatment by the security forces were frequently reported. Most of those extrajudicially executed in the Logone regions and in Doba in February and in March (see above) were believed to have been tortured. Most were reportedly subjected to the *arbatachar* method where the victim's arms and legs are tied behind the back, causing extreme pain and leading to open wounds and gangrene in some cases.

Prison conditions remained harsh and amounted to cruel, inhuman or degrading treatment. One prisoner died in custody in N'Djaména prison, apparently as a result of lack of medical care.

There was no information about the fate or whereabouts of those who "disappeared" in previous years (see *Amnesty International Report 1998*).

Armed opposition groups committed grave human rights abuses. In February a new armed opposition group, headed by Dr Nahor, was responsible for the abduction of four Frenchmen in the Doba region. The four were freed five days later by members of the Chadian security forces. In March a group of eight French and Italian tourists was taken hostage by the FNTR in the Tibesti, northern Chad. Seven of the hostages were released the following day, but the eighth was kept for five days. The FARF also killed unarmed civilians in February and March in the Logone districts.

An Amnesty International observer attended some of the proceedings in the trials of Ngarléjy Yorongar Le Moïban and the two journalists in May, and met members of the judiciary as well as members of human rights organizations.

Amnesty International called for prisoner of conscience Ngarléjy Yorongar Le Moïban to be immediately and unconditionally released and allowed access to medical care.

The organization urged the authorities to investigate human rights violations, including massacres by the security forces, and to bring those responsible to justice. Amnesty International also expressed concern about human rights abuses against human rights defenders and violations of the right to freedom of expression.

CHILE

New legal proceedings on past human rights violations were initiated in Chile and abroad. Scores of human rights de-

fenders received death threats. Detainees were reportedly ill-treated and tortured by the security forces; one person allegedly died as a result. There were reports of excessive use of force by the police. One death sentence was passed and subsequently commuted.

In March the Inter-American Commission on Human Rights (IACHR) recommended the repeal of the 1978 Amnesty Law (see *Amnesty International Report 1998*) after concluding, for the third time, that it was "incompatible with the provisions of the American Convention on Human Rights". The IACHR also concluded that the dismissal of past "disappearance" cases by courts applying the Amnesty Law, "not only aggravated the situation of impunity, but also doubtlessly violated the right to justice".

In July new legislation was passed on the detention of suspects which introduced, among other measures, sanctions of up to 10 years' imprisonment for the crime of torture (see *Amnesty International Report 1998*). The crimes of vagrancy and begging were removed from the penal code.

In September Chile signed the Rome Statute of the International Criminal Court.

In January, two criminal complaints were filed against the Head of the Army, General Augusto Pinochet Ugarte, for human rights violations committed between 1973 and 1990, during his military government. In March General Pinochet stepped down as Head of the Army and became a senator for life according to provisions of the Constitution passed under his government.

In October former General Pinochet was arrested in London, the United Kingdom (UK), at the request of a Spanish judge (see **Spain** entry) on charges of gross human rights violations, including crimes against humanity, committed during his government.

The Chilean authorities argued that he had diplomatic and parliamentary immunity and rejected the legal procedures against him on the grounds that the judicial system in Chile was able to investigate and judge alleged crimes committed in its territory. Requests for extradition of former General Pinochet were filed by the Spanish, French, Swiss and Belgian governments. By the end of the year, 17

126

criminal complaints filed against former General Pinochet for past human rights violations were under investigation by the Court of Appeals in Santiago. In November the Supreme Court rejected the government's petition for the appointment of a special supreme court judge to investigate the complaints.

At the end of October the UK High Court ruled that former General Pinochet had immunity from prosecution as a former head of state. An appeal against this decision was filed before the House of Lords, which in November reversed the High Court judgment. A request for former General Pinochet's extradition to Spain was filed before the UK authorities, on charges of crimes against humanity committed against over 3,000 victims during his military government. The crimes included genocide, widespread and systematic torture, and "disappearances". At the beginning of December the UK Home Secretary authorized the extradition proceedings to continue. Later the same month, following a challenge to the composition of the judicial panel, on the basis of links between one of the Law Lords and Amnesty International Charity Limited, the initial ruling was set aside; a new panel of the House of Lords was scheduled to reconsider the case in early 1999. Former General Pinochet remained under police guard in the UK at the end of the year while the legal proceedings continued.

Following the arrest of former General Pinochet in October, scores of human rights defenders and relatives of victims of past human rights violations were subjected to death threats and harassment. Among those who received anonymous death threats were José Balmes; former political prisoners, including Hector Reinaldo Pavelic, a journalist, and four members of the San Martín family; and members of the Communist Party, including Gladys Marín, its Secretary General. In December staff members of the *Corporación de Promoción y defensa de los Derechos del Pueblo*, Committee for the Promotion and Defence of the Rights of the People, were threatened, allegedly by the *Frente Nacionalista Patria y Libertad*, Country and Freedom National Front, a right-wing group that used to operate during the early years of the military government.

There were reports that detainees were tortured by *Carabineros* (uniformed police). In January the brothers Luis and Orlando Vásquez Ramirez were reportedly arrested at their home in Santiago, beaten and threatened with death by *Carabineros*. They were transferred to the *Sección de Investigaciones Policiales* (SIP), Police Investigations Unit, where Luis Vásquez Ramirez was allegedly handcuffed and hung from an iron bar while Orlando Vásquez Ramirez was subjected to electric shocks on the anus and lips.

One detainee died, allegedly as a result of torture. Raúl Palma Salgado, a taxi driver, was arrested in January by *Carabineros* and taken to the SIP. A few hours later he was transferred to hospital where he died as a result of respiratory failure. According to the autopsy, he had facial bruises and a fractured spine. Four members of the SIP were reportedly discharged from the police service in connection with the death of Raúl Palma Salgado, and legal proceedings were initiated in the Sixth Military Court. Luis Vásquez Ramirez was reportedly detained at the same place as Raúl Palma Salgado and was a witness in the case. Investigations into the case had not concluded by the end of the year.

In September marches in Santiago to mark the 25th anniversary of the military coup led by General Pinochet were met with large-scale repression by *Carabineros*. Hundreds of demonstrators were arrested. Some were allegedly ill-treated in custody. Several demonstrators were injured and two people were killed in disputed circumstances. Claudia Alejandra Benaiges was reportedly shot in the back in La Pincoya district, Santiago. A group of *Carabineros* reportedly approached her as she lay on the ground, but did not help her. Neighbours called the emergency services and she was taken to a medical centre, but died before arrival. Complaints were lodged and investigations were reportedly initiated into the incidents, but had not been completed by the end of the year.

In April Juan Zenón Soto Campos was sentenced to death by the Third Penal Court in Concepción for the kidnapping, rape and murder of a five-year-old girl in June 1996. In December the Second Chamber of the Supreme Court commuted the death sentence to life imprisonment.

In December the Military Court confirmed the life sentences of three political prisoners and acquitted two others (see *Amnesty International Reports 1996* and

1997). The five men, who had faced possible death sentences, were the subject of further proceedings on separate charges at the end of the year.

Amnesty International raised concerns with the authorities about reports of torture and ill-treatment by *Carabineros* and the death of Raúl Palma Salgado. The organization also expressed concern at reports of excessive use of force by the security forces and death threats against human rights defenders and relatives of victims of past human rights violations. It called for a thorough and independent investigation into all reported cases of human rights violations and for effective protection for those subjected to threats. The organization also expressed concern at the imposition of death sentences.

In May an Amnesty International delegation visited Chile and met senior officials, including some at ministerial level, to present the organization's concerns. The delegates called for cooperation with the Spanish legal proceedings, the annulment of the 1978 Amnesty Law, and the abolition of the death penalty. In October the Ministry of Foreign Affairs wrote to Amnesty International providing details already known on the measures taken by successive civilian governments to clarify past human rights violations.

Amnesty International published several reports on human rights violations, including crimes against humanity, committed during the military government of former General Pinochet. They included *Argentina and Chile: The international community's responsibility regarding crimes against humanity – trials in Spain for crimes against humanity under military regimes in Argentina and Chile*, which examined the responsibility of states under international law to bring those accused of systematic or widespread torture and other crimes against humanity to justice before national courts.

CHINA
(INCLUDING THE HONG KONG SPECIAL ADMINISTRATIVE REGION)

Hundreds, possibly thousands, of activists and suspected opponents of the government were detained during the year. Thousands of political prisoners jailed in previous years remained imprisoned, many of them prisoners of conscience. Some had been sentenced after unfair trials, others were still held without charge or trial. Political trials continued to fall short of international fair trial standards. Torture and ill-treatment remained endemic, in some cases resulting in death. The death penalty continued to be used extensively.

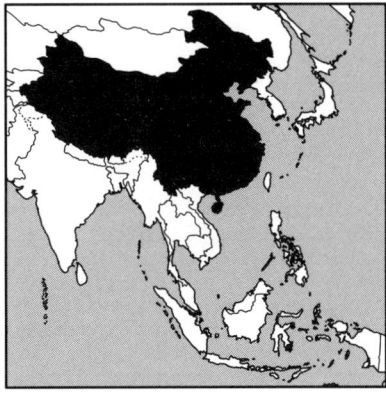

In March Zhu Rongji was appointed Prime Minister by the National People's Congress (NPC), China's parliament. Economic reforms intensified, resulting in increased unemployment, labour disputes and repression of worker rights activists.

The report on the 1997 visit to China by the UN Working Group on Arbitrary Detention, published in March, recommended changes to national security legislation in line with international standards. Two landmark visits to China – by the US President, Bill Clinton, and by the UN High Commissioner for Human Rights, Mary Robinson – highlighted the authorities' growing but limited willingness to discuss human rights, as well as continuing violations. In October China signed the International Covenant on Civil and Political Rights.

Despite such moves, repression of dissent continued, culminating in December in the trial of high profile dissidents. New regulations on the registration of "social groups" and on publishing were introduced in October and December, increasing restrictions on freedom of expression and association.

A crack-down on suspected Uighur nationalists and independent Muslim religious leaders continued in the Xinjiang

128

Uighur Autonomous Region (XUAR – see *Amnesty International Report 1998*). While violent clashes between small groups of Uighur nationalists and the security forces were reported, hundreds of people were arbitrarily detained merely for their suspected nationalist sympathies or for engaging in peaceful religious activities. Thousands of political prisoners were reportedly imprisoned in the region; many were tortured. At least 14 Uighur political prisoners accused of having used violence were executed.

Arbitrary arrests continued across the XUAR, particularly in the city of Gulja (Yining) and surrounding villages, where ethnic protests took place in 1997 (see *Amnesty International Report 1998*). Abdet Pettar, a medical surgeon at Gulja's military hospital, was reportedly arrested in early July and accused of having treated "nationalist separatists". He was still held without charge in a military prison at the end of the year. Three other Uighurs – Tursun Mehmet and Alimjan, both teachers, and Abdushukur, a local government official – were arrested later in July in Gulja for allegedly helping "separatists". They were still held without charge at the end of the year.

A crack-down on Tibetan nationalists and Buddhists continued in the Tibet Autonomous Region. At least 10 prisoners were reported to have died – one was reportedly shot dead – following a protest at Drapchi prison in early May at the time European Union representatives visited the prison. Many prisoners who had taken part in the protest were beaten and placed in solitary confinement. Ngawang Sungrab, a monk from Drepung monastery, and Gyaltsen Choephel, a layman from Lhasa, were beaten so severely that they needed hospital treatment. The authorities later admitted that "minor disturbances" had occurred at the prison in early May, but denied that any prisoners had died as a result. On 7 June four imprisoned nuns, Choekyi Wangmo, Tashi Lhamo, Dekyi Yangzom and Khedron Yonten, who had been placed in solitary confinement in May, reportedly died in Drapchi prison. Prison officials said they had committed suicide, but did not explain how they had all done so on the same day while held in solitary confinement.

Hundreds of other people were detained for political reasons, many of them prisoners of conscience. Four poets, Wu Ruohai, Ma Zhe, Ma Qiang and Xiong Jingren, were detained in January in Guiyang, Guizhou province, as they were planning to launch an independent literary magazine. Ma Qiang and Wu Ruohai were released after a few weeks, but the other two remained in secret detention. In November Ma Zhe was reportedly sentenced to seven years' imprisonment for "subversion". Li Yi, a businessman from Guiyang and friend of the poets, and Wu Ruojie, a rock singer and brother of one of the poets, were also detained and accused of "divulging state secrets" for reporting the arrests of the poets to foreign journalists and people outside China. They were sentenced without charge or trial to three years of "re-education through labour". Neither was a known dissident.

Worker rights activists were arbitrarily detained in the context of growing labour unrest. Some arrests followed demonstrations by workers, notably in Sichuan province. Others were of people who had called for reforms. Li Qingxi, a laid-off worker from the Datong coal mine in Shanxi province, was arrested in January when he posted publicly a statement calling for independent trade unions. He was sentenced in March without charge or trial to one year of "re-education through labour", reportedly to be served "at home". Zhang Shanguang, a labour rights activist from Hunan province, was detained in July after trying to set up a group to help laid-off workers. He was sentenced in December to 10 years' imprisonment, accused of having "illegally provided information to overseas hostile organizations and individuals", reportedly for speaking about farmers' protests in his province in a *Radio Free Asia* interview.

Widespread arrests were made during politically sensitive periods. Many people were detained in February and March before and during the annual session of the NPC, particularly those who addressed open letters to the NPC calling for reforms. A further wave of arrests took place in May in the weeks leading up to the ninth anniversary of the 4 June 1989 crack-down on pro-democracy activists.

In July, 10 pro-democracy activists were detained in Hangzhou city, Zhejiang province, after trying to register the Chinese Democratic Party (CDP). This was the first known attempt to register an alternative political party in China since 1949. Most of the 10 were released within hours or placed under house arrest. Wang Youcai, a founder of the CDP, was held for several weeks before being released. He was re-arrested in late November during a new crack-down on people associated with the CDP, which led to the detention or arrest of at least 30 people.

Wang Youcai and two other high profile dissidents, Qin Yongmin and Xu Wenli, were tried in December in different cities and sentenced to prison terms of 11, 12 and 13 years respectively on charges of "plotting to subvert the state power". Other dissidents who had been detained earlier in the year were also sentenced to terms of imprisonment or "re-education through labour".

Detention, ill-treatment and harassment of members of unapproved Christian groups continued. Most of some 200 Roman Catholics who were detained in late 1997 in Linchuan city, Jiangxi province, were held for between one and three months and released only after paying a fine. The arrests were apparently aimed at stopping them celebrating mass outside officially recognized churches. Detention of Roman Catholics continued in other provinces. For example, Julius Jia Zhiguo, Bishop of Zhengding, Hebei province, was detained in June, having been warned he would be "taken away" during President Clinton's visit to China.

In August information came to light about the detention of 16 leaders of a Christian group in Xingyang county, Henan province, who earlier in the year had been given terms of two or three years' detention in a labour camp and were reportedly beaten repeatedly in detention. In October, 11 house church leaders were detained in Wugang county, Henan province, and reportedly tortured at Fangcheng prison. Arrests of house church members subsequently continued in the province with those detained being made to pay heavy fines to secure release.

Thousands of political prisoners detained without trial or convicted after unfair trials in previous years remained in jail, including many prisoners of conscience. At least 2,000 convicted political prisoners were serving sentences for "counter-revolutionary" offences. The government made no move to review these cases, even though such offences had been abolished in law in 1997 (see *Amnesty International Report 1998*). More than 200,000 people continued to be administratively detained without charge or trial in labour camps for "re-education through labour".

A few prisoners of conscience were released on parole, although some continued to be subjected to police surveillance and harassment, and others were forced into exile. Wang Dan, for example, a student activist imprisoned twice since 1989, was released on medical parole in March but sent into effective exile in the USA.

Political trials continued to fall far short of international fair trial standards, with verdicts and sentences usually decided by the authorities before trial, and appeal hearings usually a formality. Turgun Tay, a Uighur businessman from Gulja, was reportedly sentenced to 10 years' imprisonment in April for involvement in "illegal" religious activities. His trial, by the Yining Intermediate People's Court, was reportedly held in secret, with no relatives or lawyer present. A series of unfair trials of pro-democracy activists took place in various provinces. Defendants were denied adequate time and facilities to defend themselves. In October, for example, Chen Zengxiang, a bookseller and veteran pro-democracy activist from Qingdao, Shandong province, was reportedly tried in secret and sentenced to seven years' imprisonment for "seeking to subvert the State power". Detained since May for investigation of his links to exiled dissidents, he was reportedly denied access to a lawyer on the grounds that his case involved "national security".

Torture and ill-treatment of detainees and prisoners held in detention centres, prisons and labour camps remained widespread, sometimes resulting in death. Prison conditions were often harsh, with inadequate food and medical care, and many prisoners suffered serious illness as a result.

Many cases of torture were reported by unofficial sources. Three men, Zhou Guiyi, Xiao Beizhou and Yu Li, were beaten to death by police in Hubei's Xinzhou county between April 1997 and February 1998. The families of the three men received compensation, but no action was taken to bring those responsible to justice. Abdul Helil, a Uighur detained in the XUAR for leading a demonstration in

130

Gulja in February 1997, was reportedly tortured after arrest to force him to confess to "crimes" and denounce friends. In mid-1998, he was reportedly held in the prison of the 4th Division of the Xinjiang Production and Construction Corps, a military-run institution, where he continued to be ill-treated. Zhu Shengwen, the Vice-Mayor of Harbin, Heilongjiang province, alleged he was tortured to force him to confess to corruption. He said he was punched, had his arms twisted and wrenched, and was repeatedly given electric shocks with an electric baton. In April he was sentenced to life imprisonment. No investigation into his allegation of torture was known to have been carried out. In October Li Jiayong, a member of the New Testament Church in Shandong province, reportedly died in police custody. The police reportedly claimed he had committed suicide by jumping out of a window, but private sources believed he had died as a result of torture. He had been detained and badly beaten twice before. There was no independent inquiry into his death.

Local media also reported cases of torture and ill-treatment. In March a newspaper revealed that police in Guangdong province had kept a farmer chained inside a two-square-metre iron cage for five years as punishment for attacking an officer. The day after the newspaper report, the man was set free. The Guangdong authorities subsequently set up a commission to investigate the incident. In June, for the first time in China, an official publication published figures for the number of people who had been tortured to death in custody in previous years: 126 people had died in such circumstances in 1993 and 115 in 1994.

The death penalty continued to be used extensively. The Criminal Law, revised in 1997 (see *Amnesty International Report 1998*), integrated offences made liable to the death penalty under regulations adopted since the 1980s, such as fraud and tax evasion, bringing the number of offences punishable by death to about 60. In September the Supreme People's Court announced that there had been a large reduction in the number of executions because of the 1997 legal revisions, but the government failed to publish statistics to prove this. The limited records available to Amnesty International at the end of the year showed that at least 1,657 people

were sentenced to death and 1,067 executed in 1998; the true figures were believed to be far higher.

In January, 89 people were executed in Beijing alone, purportedly to ensure "law and order" during the Lunar New Year. Others sentenced to death included Ma Yulan, a woman convicted in November of "organizing prostitution" – a capital crime since 1991.

During the year Amnesty International published several reports, including: in February, *People's Republic of China: Summary of Amnesty International's Concerns*; in June, *People's Republic of China: Nine Years after Tiananmen, Still a "Counter-Revolutionary Riot"?* and *China: Detention and Harassment of Dissidents and Others Between January and June 1998*; and in September, *People's Republic of China: The Death Penalty in 1997*.

On several occasions Amnesty International presented its human rights concerns to government representatives during meetings in various countries.

Hong Kong
Special Administrative Region (HKSAR)

Elections for a new legislature (Legco) to replace the Provisional Legislative Council (PLC) proceeded as planned in May, although on the basis of a greatly reduced franchise and curtailed powers for legislators (see *Amnesty International Report 1998*). Controversy over interpretation of key articles of Hong Kong's post-1997 Constitution, the Basic Law, continued throughout the year, raising questions about the extent of Hong Kong's autonomy. Controversial legal amendments passed by the PLC included an interpretive amendment whereby all ordinances which previously did not bind the "Crown" will not bind the "State", with the "State" now defined to include subordinate organs of central government such as the *Xinhua News Agency*. The amendment was widely criticized for undermining the new constitutional order expressed in Article 22 of the Basic Law and for providing potential immunity from Hong Kong laws for a range of official organizations whose precise role in Hong Kong remained unclear.

In December Hong Kong citizens Cheung Tze-keung, Chin Hon-sau and Chan Chi-hou were executed and 13 others were imprisoned in Guangdong, mainland China, for cross-border crimes and crimes committed in Hong Kong, even though Hong Kong law does not provide for the death penalty. The handling of the case appeared to undermine Hong Kong's judicial autonomy under the "one country two systems" principle. The HKSAR government and the Guangdong court cited the Chinese criminal code under which crimes "plotted, planned and prepared" on the mainland can be tried there even if committed elsewhere. However, little reliable evidence was reportedly presented at the trial to prove the crimes were planned on the mainland. Heavily criticized for misinterpreting the Basic Law and failing to assert jurisdiction over the case, the HKSAR government argued that it did not press for the defendants to be returned to Hong Kong because it did not have enough evidence to prosecute in Hong Kong and had no formal agreement with the rest of China on the return of criminal suspects. It promised to negotiate urgently such an agreement.

In November the International Labour Organisation (ILO) Committee on Freedom of Association determined that the PLC's repeal of amendments to labour laws, passed shortly before the handover, was a breach of ILO Convention No. 87 and a step backwards in implementing Convention No. 98 on freedom of association (see *Amnesty International Report 1998*).

The Secretary for Justice announced in June that it was not necessary to enact legislation on national security offences, as required under Article 23 of the Basic Law, during the first two-year session of Legco.

Peaceful demonstrations continued throughout the year. In May Lee Kin-yun and Ng Kung-siu were conditionally released after being convicted of desecrating two miniature national and regional flags in January in an incident that posed no threat to public order. It was the first conviction under post-handover laws which place restrictions on non-violent expression of protest. In June, in relation to a separate incident, the Independent Police Complaints Council upheld a demonstrator's complaint, ruling that the police abused their power when they played loud music to drown out protesters' speeches in July 1997.

In May, four police officers were sentenced to between four and six months' imprisonment for torturing a suspect. The four were accused of attempting to force Yiu So-man to admit to possessing heroin by stuffing a shoe in his mouth, pouring water into his nose and ears until he fainted, and threatening to throw him off a balcony.

In August a police officer with a history of mental health problems was convicted of manslaughter for shooting and killing detainee Chan Kwok-keung in Aberdeen police station in 1997 (see *Amnesty International Report 1998*). Police pledged to enhance measures to identify unfit officers. Legislators argued that the implementation of long-delayed safeguards for detainees might have prevented the incident.

Several prison officers and 21 prisoners were injured during a brawl between prisoners in Ma Poping prison on 27 July. More than 70 prisoners complained about violence used by officers during the disturbance when two Justices of the Peace (JPs) made an unannounced visit to the prison. Assault charges brought against several officers were still outstanding. During the year the government began a review of the JP prison inspection system and the Ombudsman criticized prison officers' overuse of their powers to isolate prisoners indefinitely.

In January the HKSAR government announced that it would abolish the "port of first asylum policy" for Vietnamese nationals so that all such people who arrive without proper documentation would in future face repatriation in the same way as other undocumented arrivals. At the end of the year nearly 1,000 refugees remained in Hong Kong with little prospect of resettlement overseas. Of these, 278 who had initially fled Viet Nam to China before seeking asylum in Hong Kong continued a court challenge to the government's plans to remove them to mainland China. A further 500 ethnic Chinese from Viet Nam who had been refused refugee status remained in limbo as the Vietnamese government refuse to accept them for repatriation.

In April Amnesty International submitted comments on the government's draft outline report on implementation of the International Covenant on Civil and Political Rights. In June Amnesty International published a report, *Hong Kong: No Room For Complacency*, describing developments since the handover in July 1997. In October and in December Amnesty

132 International made urgent representations on the case of Cheung Tze-keung and others, seeking a review of the case and commutation of the death sentences.

COLOMBIA

More than 1,000 civilians were killed by the security forces or paramilitary groups operating with their support or acquiescence. Many victims were tortured before being killed. At least 150 people "disappeared". Human rights activists were threatened and attacked; at least six were killed. "Death squad"-style killings continued in urban areas. Several army officers were charged in connection with human rights violations; many others continued to evade accountability. Armed opposition groups were responsible for numerous human rights abuses, including deliberate and arbitrary killings and the taking of hundreds of hostages.

Conservative Party candidate Andrés Pastrana Arango was elected President and assumed office in August. He immediately announced his willingness to negotiate with armed opposition groups to end decades of armed conflict. During the presidential campaign both principal armed opposition groups – the *Fuerzas Armadas Revolucionarias de Colombia* (FARC), Revolutionary Armed Forces of Colombia, and the *Ejército de Liberación Nacional* (ELN), National Liberation Army – expressed their willingness to enter into talks with the incoming government.

In October Congress gave preliminary approval to a draft bill designed to incorporate the crimes of forced disappearance, genocide and massacre into the Penal Code. A previous bill had failed to pass a second hearing (see *Amnesty International Report 1998*). Congress again failed to pass a draft bill to reform the Military Penal Code which had received preliminary approval in December 1997 (see *Amnesty International Report 1998*). The government announced a national human rights action program which included steps to combat impunity and to protect human rights defenders.

During a visit to Colombia in October, the UN High Commissioner for Human Rights reiterated the UN's concern about the human rights situation and, while welcoming the possibility of peace talks, clarified that international standards exclude the possibility of amnesties or pardons for crimes against humanity.

In July the ELN signed an agreement with representatives of "civil society", committing the organization to initiating a peace process. In addition, the ELN agreed to end certain practices which violated international humanitarian law and reaffirmed its acceptance of recommendations made by Amnesty International, including the ending of deliberate and arbitrary killings of non-combatants. A meeting in October between government representatives and the ELN command decided to hold a series of "national conventions" in 1999 to discuss issues including human rights, justice and impunity, as a prelude to formal peace talks.

In December the government concluded the temporary demilitarization of five municipalities in the south-central departments of Meta and Caquetá, thereby fulfilling a condition imposed by the FARC as a prerequisite to formal talks in the designated area. Talks were scheduled to begin in January 1999.

Despite agreements in principle to hold peace talks, no cease-fire was agreed and the armed conflict continued to escalate in many areas of the country. Over 1,000 people were killed during military confrontations, including scores of civilians. The army and police suffered a series of major defeats during attacks principally by the FARC or combined FARC and ELN forces. By the end of the year, the FARC were holding over 300 captured army and police personnel.

Paramilitary forces, declared illegal in 1989, continued their offensive which was increasingly characterized by attacks against civilians in areas of guerrilla presence. Regions particularly affected included the departments of Putumayo, Santander, Bolívar, Cesar, Chocó and Meta. Victims were frequently tortured before being shot dead or were decapitated and dismembered. At least 300,000 people were internally displaced by the conflict.

In May a unit attached to the national paramilitary organization *Autodefensas Unidas de Colombia* (AUC), United Self-Defence Groups of Colombia, attacked the village of Puerto Alvira, municipality of Mapiripán, Meta department. At least 18 civilians, including a six-year-old girl, were shot, stabbed and burned to death. A further eight "disappeared". Although the government had received numerous warnings of an impending attack against Puerto Alvira the authorities failed to take action to prevent the attack or to protect the inhabitants. In July 1997 up to 30 civilians had been killed by the AUC in a similar attack on Mapiripán (see *Amnesty International Report 1998*).

In July, 7,000 civilians from southern Bolívar department in the central Magdalena Medio region fled a major paramilitary offensive in the area and converged on the town of Barrancabermeja, Santander department. They returned to their communities in October after reaching a number of agreements with the government. President Pastrana personally signed the accords guaranteeing the safety of the returnees through the deployment of a special armed forces' unit to combat paramilitary groups, and emergency assistance to displaced families. The government failed to comply with these commitments and paramilitary groups renewed their attacks against the communities of returnees, targeting particularly community leaders. Compelling evidence emerged of close cooperation and complicity between regular armed forces and paramilitary groups in the region.

At least 150 people "disappeared" after capture by paramilitary groups. In May AUC forces raided several poor neighbourhoods of Barrancabermeja. Eleven people were killed outright in the attack and 25 "disappeared". Paramilitary leaders publicly admitted responsibility for the attack and claimed to have executed the captives. They also reportedly informed national authorities where the bodies of the

"disappeared" could be found. The government, however, failed to take action to secure the captives' release or recover their bodies and their whereabouts remained unknown at the end of the year. Evidence emerged of complicity of members of the Colombian security forces in the attack. In August an army corporal was arrested and charged with participating in the massacre, and in December the Procurator General opened formal disciplinary proceedings against eight members of the security forces, including the regional police commander. They were charged with dereliction of duty for failing to respond to pleas from witnesses to the attack to pursue the assailants or attempt to rescue the captives.

Responsibility in many hundreds of presumed politically motivated killings was difficult to establish. During the year more than 200 civilians were killed in Putumayo department – a long-time FARC stronghold – as paramilitary forces attempted to gain control of the region. Roman Catholic priest Alcides Jiménez Chicanganá was shot dead in September by two unidentified men as he celebrated mass in the church of Puerto Caicedo, Putumayo department. Earlier that day he had led a peace march. Father Alcides had received a number of death threats from both the FARC and paramilitary groups because of his work for peace. No organization accepted responsibility for the killing.

Investigations into links between the armed forces and paramilitary groups increasingly implicated senior army commanders. In August the Attorney General announced that General Fernando Millán, then commander of the 5th Brigade, was under investigation. Evidence emerged that, in association with regional paramilitary commanders, General Millán had set up a civilian vigilante association, known as *Convivir*, in Lebrija, Santander department, which was responsible for a series of killings in 1996. In October the case was passed to the military justice system, in breach of the 1997 Constitutional Court ruling that excluded serious human rights violations from military jurisdiction (see *Amnesty International Report 1998*). In October, while still under investigation, General Millán was promoted to head the army's intelligence operations.

Distinctions between legalized *Convivir* groups and illegal paramilitary groups

134

were further blurred in August when 300 *Convivir* groups renounced their government licences but continued to operate illegally. Thirty-nine *Convivir* groups publicly announced their intention of joining the AUC paramilitary forces. The move came in response to an attempt by the government to impose weapons restrictions and other controls on the *Convivir*.

Human rights defenders continued to be intimidated and attacked; at least six were murdered. Dr Jesús María Valle Jaramillo, president of the *Comité Permanente por la Defensa de los Derechos Humanos*, (CPDH), Permanent Committee for the Defence of Human Rights, was shot dead in his office in Medellín, Antioquia department, in February. Dr Valle Jaramillo was the fourth president of the CPDH to be killed in 10 years. Five people were arrested and charged in connection with the killing. Paramilitary leader Carlos Castaño Gil was charged *in absentia* with ordering the murder. He was also charged in connection with the killings of human rights and environmental activists Carlos Mario Calderón and Elsa Alvarado in May 1997 (see *Amnesty International Report 1998*). No progress was made, however, in enforcing numerous arrest warrants against him.

Internationally renowned lawyer Dr José Eduardo Umaña Mendoza was shot dead in his office in the capital, Bogotá, in April. Shortly before his death, he had informed judicial officials that an attempt on his life was being prepared by the army's intelligence department, the XX Brigade, and judicial police. For more than 20 years Dr Umaña Mendoza had represented political prisoners, trade unionists and relatives of the "disappeared" and had investigated and denounced numerous cases of serious human rights violations. Six people were arrested in connection with his murder.

Judicial officials investigating human rights abuses were also increasingly threatened, intimidated and attacked. Officials of the Human Rights Unit of the Attorney General's office responsible for investigating crimes attributed to members of the armed and security forces, paramilitary groups and guerrilla organizations were particularly vulnerable to attack.

Journalists, political activists and trade union leaders were among those targeted.

Jorge Ortega García, Vice-President of the *Central Unitaria de Trabajadores* (CUT), Trade Union Congress, was shot dead in October in Bogotá. The killing coincided with a strike of public sector workers, led by the CUT. Jorge Ortega had received numerous death threats. Despite repeated requests, he had not been provided with adequate protection by the authorities. A key witness to the killing was murdered in November.

The killing of so-called "disposables" – homosexuals, prostitutes, petty criminals and vagrants – by police-backed "death squads" and urban militias linked to armed opposition groups continued. In September in the northern city of Cúcuta, assailants threw a grenade into a group of sleeping homeless people, killing two and injuring six. In June formal disciplinary proceedings were opened against two police officers and two agents charged with participating in a "death squad" which killed up to 35 people in Yarumal, Antioquia department, between 1993 and 1994.

In July outgoing President Ernesto Samper Pizano formally accepted state responsibility for a series of massacres carried out by army and police personnel and paramilitary organizations, including the killing of eight children in Villatina, Medellín, Antioquia department, in 1992; the killing of 20 members of the Paéz indigenous community in El Nilo, Cauca department, in 1991; and the massacre of 17 peasant farmers in Los Uvos, Cauca department, in 1991. Although judicial investigations established the identity of armed forces and police personnel implicated in the massacres, no one had been brought to justice by the end of the year.

In October the Attorney General's office ordered the arrest of retired Colonel Bernardo Ruiz Silva, former commander of the XX Brigade, in connection with the murder of leading conservative politician Alvaro Gómez Hurtado in November 1995 (see previous *Amnesty International Reports*). The XX Brigade was formally disbanded in August following repeated allegations that it was operating "death squads". Colonel Ruiz Silva remained a fugitive from justice at the end of the year.

Official statements suggested that over 400 people were arrested during the year on charges of paramilitary activity. The renowned paramilitary leader Victor

Carranza was arrested in February accused of sponsoring illegal paramilitary organizations in the eastern plains region and Boyacá department. Little progress was made, however, in enforcing numerous arrest warrants against national paramilitary leaders such as Carlos Castaño Gil (see above), who continued to be protected by members of the Colombian armed forces.

Investigations by the Attorney General's office into human rights abuses attributed to armed opposition groups made progress. In November an alleged member of the FARC's 51st Front was arrested and charged in connection with the attack on a judicial commission in Usme, Cundinamarca department, in November 1991, in which six judicial officials and three national police were killed.

Armed opposition groups were responsible for numerous human rights abuses, including deliberate and arbitrary killings and indiscriminate attacks in which many civilians died.

Over 70 civilians burned to death and scores were seriously injured when the ELN dynamited Colombia's largest oil pipeline in October causing a fire which engulfed the village of Machuca, Antioquia department. The ELN subsequently accepted responsibility for the attack which it described as a "grave error" and promised to punish those responsible and compensate the victims.

Ten civilians died and over 30 were injured during a FARC attack on the towns of San Francisco and Cocorná, Antioquia department, in November.

The FARC and the ELN were also responsible for numerous deliberate and arbitrary killings of people they accused of collaboration with the security forces or paramilitary organizations.

Despite commitments made by the ELN to reduce kidnapping and claims by FARC commanders that they were holding no civilians, they and other armed opposition groups kidnapped at least 800 people. Victims included mayors and local and national politicians, journalists, health workers and judicial officials.

In August the ELN kidnapped prominent Liberal Party Senator Carlos Espinosa Facciolince. He was released in September with a message for the government from ELN commanders outlining their demands for assistance for the internally displaced.

Mayors and other local officials were also frequently threatened or kidnapped in order to coerce them into adopting pro-guerrilla policies or to subject them to "popular trials" for alleged corrupt practices. Many other people, including employees of multinational companies, landowners and businessmen, were kidnapped and held hostage against payment of ransom money. Most were eventually released. However, others were killed during escape or rescue attempts, or when ransom demands were not met.

Amnesty International raised its concerns about Colombia at the UN Commission on Human Rights. Some of these concerns were addressed in a statement by the Chairman of the Commission which expressed concern about the gravity and scale of human rights violations and breaches of international humanitarian law and, *inter alia*, urged the government to take steps to end impunity and to take effective action to prevent internal displacement. The Commission welcomed the agreement with the Colombian government to extend the mandate of the office of the UN High Commissioner for Human Rights in Colombia until April 1999.

Throughout the year Amnesty International consistently called on the authorities to investigate and bring to an end human rights violations by government forces and paramilitary groups acting with their support or acquiescence. In May the organization wrote to the President expressing its grave concern about the systematic persecution of human rights defenders and calling on the government to urgently adopt measures to ensure their protection and to bring those responsible to justice.

Amnesty International delegates visited Colombia on four occasions. In a meeting with Vice-President Gustavo Bell in November, the organization expressed its deep concern about the continuing widespread and systematic human rights violations and urged the government to urgently adopt measures to disband paramilitary groups and to end impunity.

Amnesty International condemned abuses committed by armed opposition groups and called for the release of hostages. The organization urged all parties to the conflict to observe basic humanitarian standards.

CONGO
(DEMOCRATIC REPUBLIC OF THE)

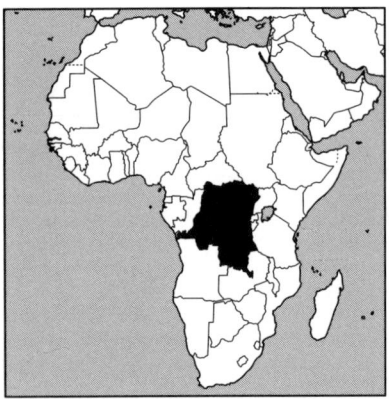

Thousands of people were extrajudicially executed. Hundreds of human rights defenders and suspected opponents of the government were detained; many were prisoners of conscience. Torture and ill-treatment were widespread. Unfair trials of political prisoners continued. Scores of people were sentenced to death. More than 100 were executed after unfair trials and two were executed without trial. The authorities forcibly returned refugees to countries where they were at risk of human rights violations. Armed opposition groups committed grave human rights abuses, including deliberate and arbitrary killings.

Armed conflict continued throughout the year in eastern Democratic Republic of the Congo (DRC) and in August flared into full-scale war. Before August the fighting was between government forces and armed opposition groups collectively known as *mayi-mayi*, most of whom had been part of the coalition that overthrew former President Mobutu Sese Seko in 1997 (see *Amnesty International Report 1998*). Relations between President Laurent-Désiré Kabila and his former political allies in the *Alliance des forces démocratiques pour la libération du Congo* (AFDL), Alliance of Democratic Forces for the Liberation of Congo, deteriorated and on 27 July he ordered all Rwandese and other foreign troops out of the DRC. On 2 August his opponents began an armed campaign to overthrow him and most *mayi-mayi* members joined his supporters.

The new opposition alliance known as the *Rassemblement congolais pour la démocratie* (RCD), Congolese Rally for Democracy, formed in August, contained disaffected DRC government soldiers, many of whom were members of the Tutsi ethnic group, and was backed by troops from Burundi, Rwanda and Uganda. In October a second armed group known as the *Mouvement de libération du Congo* (MLC), Movement for the Liberation of Congo, joined the fighting in northern DRC. By December the RCD controlled much of eastern DRC. In August other governments – notably Angola, Chad, Namibia and Zimbabwe – provided military support to President Kabila, preventing the capture of the capital Kinshasa by the armed opposition.

There were numerous unsuccessful attempts by the UN, the Organization of African Unity, the Southern African Development Community, the Non-Aligned Movement and various African governments to help bring the parties to the conflict to negotiate an end to the hostilities.

Throughout the year the Constitution remained suspended and political party activity outside the AFDL was banned. A commission appointed by the government in October 1997 submitted a draft Constitution to President Kabila in March. The commission recommended that more than 200 politicians be banned from standing for presidential elections scheduled for mid-1999. In September President Kabila appointed a new commission chaired by the Minister of Justice to propose modifications to the draft Constitution. The commission submitted its report in October.

In April the government outlawed the *Association zaïroise pour la défense des droits de l'homme*, Zairian Association for the Defence of Human Rights, and denied legal registration to many other human rights organizations.

The same month the UN Secretary-General withdrew his team investigating massacres and other human rights abuses committed in the DRC between 1993 and 1997, because of the repeated obstructions of the investigation by the DRC government. In June the team submitted a report confirming that combatants, including those loyal to President Kabila and Rwandese government troops, had committed atrocities. The team recommended further investigation by an independent body to identify those responsible. The UN Security Council ignored this recommendation and instead asked the governments of the DRC and Rwanda to investigate the crimes and bring the perpetrators to justice. The governments failed to report as requested by the UN Security Council.

In November the Minister of Justice dismissed 315 magistrates accused of corruption, incompetence, dereliction of duty and immorality. They were not given an opportunity to challenge the accusations against them.

Thousands of people were extra-judicially executed by government troops during the year. Most of the reported killings occurred in the east, particularly in North- and South-Kivu provinces.

Early in the year hundreds of civilians in and around the town of Butembo in North-Kivu province were reported to have been killed by members of the DRC's newly formed army, the *Forces armées congolaises* (FAC), Congolese Armed Forces, allegedly supported by Ugandan and Rwandese government forces. For example, between 20 and 23 February they reportedly killed as many as 300 unarmed civilians accused of supporting the *mayi-mayi*. Following further *mayi-mayi* attacks in early April, government forces surrounded the area and killed up to 600 men. Further north in Beni, around 40 civilians accused of collaborating with the *mayi-mayi* were said to have been extra-judicially executed by government forces between 2 and 6 April.

In late March and early April, about 54 Rwandese refugees and at least 100 DRC civilians were reported to have been extra-judicially executed by the FAC in Shabunda, South-Kivu province. The victims reportedly included Wandjo, chief of Lwamba locality, and his assistants (known as Camile and Cléophace).

When allies who overthrew former President Mobutu split into two hostile groups in August, FAC forces extrajudicially executed fellow soldiers and unarmed civilians accused of supporting the RCD, many of them solely on the basis of their Tutsi origin. In August FAC soldiers loyal to President Kabila extrajudicially executed at least 150 civilians in Kisangani before the town was captured by the RCD. In August and September, as DRC officials and media incited violence against Tutsi and people of Rwandese origin, hundreds of civilians and captured combatants were reportedly killed by civilians supporting the FAC in Kinshasa and other parts of the country.

Hundreds of people were detained, many of whom were prisoners of conscience. They included political party activists, community leaders, human rights defenders, journalists and people of Rwandese and Tutsi origin.

Political activists were detained for flouting the ban on opposition political party activity. Joseph Olengha Nkoy, leader of the *Forces novatrices pour l'union et la solidarité*, Innovative Forces for Union and Solidarity, was arrested in January and charged with endangering the security of the state. In May the Military Order Court sentenced him to 15 years' imprisonment. He was a prisoner of conscience.

Etienne Tshisekedi, leader of the *Union pour la démocratie et le progrès social* (UDPS), Union for Democracy and Social Progress, was arrested in Kinshasa in February and banished without charge to Kabeya-Kamwanga village, Kasai-Oriental province, where soldiers were deployed to prevent him from leaving. The restriction was lifted in June. Many UDPS members were prisoners of conscience, including approximately 40 who were arrested in July for supporting Etienne Tshisekedi. A further 13 were arrested by soldiers on 9 July, including Firmin Nkama and Shabana who were severely beaten. Around 30 others, including eight of Etienne Tshisekedi's bodyguards, were arrested by police five days later. Nearly all of them were released without charge by the end of July.

In the east, local community leaders were detained after criticizing human rights violations. They were prisoners of conscience. Among them were at least 10 prominent figures in South-Kivu, including traditional chiefs, university lecturers and opposition party leaders, who were arrested in January and detained for up to two and a half months. Désiré Rugemanizi, chief of Kabare, was reported to have been severely ill-treated by members of the *Agence nationale de renseignements* (ANR), National Intelligence Agency, in Bukavu before his release in February. Three prominent community leaders from Uvira, South-Kivu province, were arrested in July after leading a delegation to the provincial governor to discuss the political situation. They were said to have been repeatedly beaten and held in appalling conditions for criticizing the authorities. They were released without charge after several weeks in custody.

Human rights activists were detained; many were tortured or ill-treated. In March Floribert Chebeya Bahizire, President of *La Voix des sans-voix*, Voice of the Voiceless, was beaten at his home by armed men, some in army uniform. Paul Nsapu and Sabin Banza, leaders of the *Ligue des électeurs*, Electorate's League, were arrested in April on their return from a meeting at the Belgian Embassy in Kinshasa and held by the ANR. They were prisoners of conscience. Both were released in August without charge. Oswald Hakorimana, a human rights activist in North-Kivu, was severely beaten in March by soldiers who accused him of documenting massacres of civilians.

Church leaders were also targeted. For example, Théodore Ngoye Ilunga wa Nsenga, a Protestant pastor who had been arrested in December 1997, was charged in February with endangering the security of the state and insulting the Head of State. He was held in the Penitentiary and Reeducation Centre, formerly known as Makala prison, until his release without trial in September. He was a prisoner of conscience.

Other prisoners of conscience included trade unionists detained for peacefully demanding labour rights. For example, three leaders of the postal workers' union, including its Secretary General, Makiona Benga, were arrested in March after preparing to strike in protest at non-payment of salaries. They were released without charge in April.

Prisoners of conscience also included journalists who were ill-treated, their newspapers seized and radio stations silenced by the authorities. For example, Albert Bonsange Yema, editor-in-chief of *L'Alarme*, was arrested in February after his newspaper criticized the arrest of Joseph Olengha Nkoy (see above). He was found guilty of endangering the security of the state by the State Security Court and sentenced in June to one year's imprisonment and remained in detention throughout the year. His diabetes worsened, apparently as a result of harsh prison conditions.

From August onwards, hundreds of Tutsi civilians, people of Rwandese origin, DRC nationals married to Rwandese, and people suspected of sympathizing with the rebellion were arrested without warrant by the security forces. The authorities claimed that Tutsi civilians were being held in "preventive" detention to protect them from lynch mobs. Visits by humanitarian organizations to detention centres in Kinshasa revealed that just over 100 civilians were being held there. Hundreds more were held in Lubumbashi and other parts of Katanga province. Many more were reported to have been arrested. It was feared that many others had been killed by government forces soon after their arrest.

Torture and ill-treatment were widespread. Early in the year women dressed in mini-skirts, trousers or leggings were arrested and tortured or ill-treated by FAC soldiers. Many were beaten at the time of arrest, then raped and otherwise tortured in unofficial or security force detention centres. About 30 members of the UDPS, including Jovo Bossongo and Honoré Kabeya, were reportedly tortured, including with electric batons, after their arrest in January. Female relatives of political activists were also arrested and tortured.

Trials before the Military Order Court, set up in August 1997 to try cases of undisciplined soldiers, contravened international standards of fairness. Those tried included civilians accused of political offences. In January Matthieu Ka Bila Kalele, a university lecturer, and Jean-François Kabanda, a freelance journalist, were convicted of spreading rumours and sentenced to two years' imprisonment, following publication of an article opposing the influence in the DRC of Rwanda and the USA. They were still held at the end of the year.

The Military Order Court also sentenced dozens of soldiers and civilians to death. Most had no access to legal counsel and no right of appeal to a higher court. President Kabila had powers to commute sentences imposed by the Court, but only the death sentence imposed on a 15-year-old child soldier, Malume Mudherwa, convicted of murder in March, was known to have been commuted by the President.

More than 100 people sentenced to death by the Military Order Court were executed. Two soldiers, one accused of rape and the other of shooting and injuring a fellow soldier, were executed in March without trial in Kamanyola barracks near Bukavu on the orders of a military commander.

At least 200 refugees from Burundi and around 140 from Rwanda were forcibly returned in April by the DRC authorities to their countries where they were at risk of serious human rights violations.

Armed opposition groups and their allies, including Burundian, Rwandese and Ugandan government forces, were reported to have committed grave human rights abuses, including the deliberate and arbitrary killing of hundreds of unarmed civilians. Members of the RCD summarily executed government soldiers at Kavumu, near Bukavu, in August. The same month RCD combatants and Rwandese soldiers reportedly killed 37 people, including Stanislas Wabulakombe, a Roman Catholic priest, and three nuns at Kasika Roman Catholic parish and as many as 850 other unarmed civilians in surrounding villages. Between August and December, RCD forces and their allies reportedly killed hundreds of civilians around Uvira. They were also reported to have abducted or imprisoned scores of civilians and raped many of the women detained.

Throughout the year Amnesty International called on all parties to the conflict to respect human rights and international humanitarian law. The organization published several reports on the DRC, including *Civil Liberties denied* in February; *A year of dashed hopes* in May; and *A long-standing crisis spinning out of control* in September. In *War against unarmed civilians*, published in November, Amnesty International called on all parties to the conflict, governments in the region and beyond, and intergovernmental organizations to institute mechanisms to prevent an escalation of atrocities.

CONGO
(REPUBLIC OF THE)

Several dozen suspected opponents of the government, including possible prisoners of conscience, were detained without charge or trial. Hundreds of unarmed civilians and captured combatants were

extrajudicially executed by government forces and allied militia. Some detainees were tortured and virtually all were held in conditions that amounted to cruel, inhuman or degrading treatment. Dozens of deaths in custody were reported. Dozens of people "disappeared" in the custody of government forces. Armed opposition groups committed human rights abuses, including deliberate and arbitrary killings of civilians.

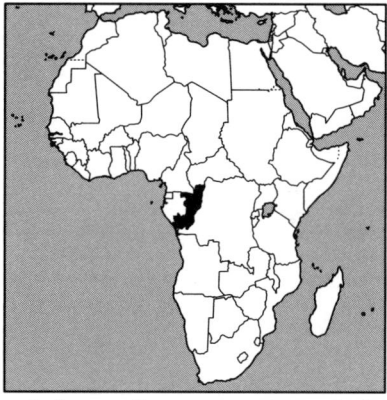

In January the government organized a national forum which approved a transitional constitution known as the *Acte fondamental* (Fundamental Act). This replaced the 1992 constitution which had been abrogated when President Denis Sassou Nguesso came to power in October 1997. In its preamble, the Fundamental Act reaffirmed the commitment of the Congolese people to democratic and human rights principles as defined by the Universal Declaration of Human Rights and by the African Charter on Human and Peoples' Rights. The forum also elected the *Conseil national de transition*, a 75-person transitional parliament. The transitional period was slated to last for as much as three years, followed by presidential and legislative elections.

The forum concluded that former President Pascal Lissouba, who was overthrown in October 1997, and his allies had committed grave human rights violations, including acts of genocide, and recommended to the government that those responsible be brought to justice. In June the government published a report containing allegations of human rights violations by former President Lissouba's government and supporters. Serious

140

human rights abuses, including many deliberate and arbitrary killings, "disappearances" and torture, committed by government forces and allied militia under President Nguesso, did not feature in the report. The government started a process of enacting a law to punish the crime of genocide and other violations of human rights attributed to former President Lissouba's government and its allies, and another law setting up a court to try the perpetrators. In October a court indicted 100 people, including former President Lissouba, with offences ranging from killings and torture to fraud and theft. In November the government issued an international warrant for the arrest of former President Lissouba.

A spate of clashes between armed opposition groups, and President Nguesso's forces, which included militia not formally integrated into the regular security forces, occurred during the year. Among the armed opposition groups were the "Ninjas", loyal to former Prime Minister Bernard Kolelas, and the "Cocoyes", loyal to former President Lissouba. Government forces included members of the Congolese National Police and armed forces, as well as members of President Nguesso's former militia, the "Cobras". Government forces were supported by troops of the governments of Angola and Chad. After a lull early in the year, fighting between armed opposition groups and government forces intensified in Brazzaville and the Pool region from late August onwards. At the end of December President Nguesso announced that hundreds of people had been killed. Most of the victims were unarmed civilians, many of whom were extrajudicially executed by government forces during reprisal attacks or counter-insurgency operations. By the end of the year, at least 40,000 people had fled to the neighbouring Democratic Republic of the Congo and tens of thousands more had been internally displaced.

People accused of supporting former President Lissouba were detained without charge or trial. They included Henri-Marcellin Dzouma-Nguelet, a former official in the Ministry of Finance, who was arrested in February and held in the southwestern town of Pointe-Noire. He and Colonel Michel Ebaka, a former regional administrator of Cuvette region, were detained by the *Direction de la surveillance du territoire* (DST) security service in Pointe-Noire. They were not charged with any specific offence, although government officials claimed that they had committed crimes during the civil war in late 1997. In July the two men were allowed to visit their families during the day, but spent the nights at the Pointe-Noire headquarters of the DST. They were still held without charge at the end of the year.

Some civilian political detainees were held without charge. They included Jacques Moanda Mpassi, a former government minister. He had been arrested in November 1997, apparently as he tried to board a flight out of the country, and held in Pointe-Noire. He was released in April. Although he was not charged with any specific offence, the authorities claimed that he had attempted to use his brother's passport to leave the country and said that he would eventually be formally charged with fraud. Two former members of the Constitutional Council were arrested in November, accused of complicity in crimes against humanity because they voted in June 1997 to extend former President Lissouba's presidential mandate. They were Nestor Makoundzi-Wolo and the President of the Brazzaville Bar Association, Hervé-Ambroïse Malonga. They appeared to be prisoners of conscience.

Albert Moungoundo, who was detained in 1997 (see *Amnesty International Report 1998*), was released without trial. However, later in the year, the authorities claimed that he would be tried at a future date on fraud charges.

About 30 military officers arrested in late 1997 and early 1998 remained in custody without charge at the end of the year. Most of them were held at the Military Academy near the capital, Brazzaville. Those held included army colonels Oscar Ewolo, Eugène Mavoungou and Benjamin Loubaki. They were accused of supporting former President Lissouba. Although the authorities reportedly claimed that they would be tried in connection with crimes committed by former President Lissouba's government, none of them had been charged with any specific offence by the end of the year. They appeared to be held solely because they failed to support President Nguesso during the war which culminated in his coming to power. It was unclear whether they had been involved in human rights abuses.

Hundreds of unarmed civilians and captured combatants were extrajudicially executed by government forces and allied militia. Most were killed during counter-insurgency operations after attacks by armed opposition groups on members of the security forces or on civilians. For example, as many as 300 unarmed civilians were reportedly killed in Mouyounzi between April and June by government agents, including members of the "Cobras" militia, after members of the "Cocoyes" armed opposition group killed a policeman and a local government administrator. In October government forces, together with allied Angolan and Chadian government forces, reportedly killed hundreds more civilians during an offensive against the "Ninja" armed opposition group in the Pool region. Despite widespread reports of violence, including the burning of hundreds of homes, the authorities failed to investigate the killings or take any action against the perpetrators.

Dozens of people accused of armed robbery were killed by members of the security forces enforcing what appeared to be a shoot-to-kill policy. For example, two men accused of trying to rob passengers in a taxi were shot dead at Tié-Tié near Pointe-Noire. One of them was killed instantly and the other, who survived the initial shooting, was found and killed in a nearby hospital. As many as 43 alleged armed robbers in Brazzaville were arrested and shot dead by the police at Itatolo cemetery. They included 78-year-old Jean Ndinga, who was reportedly killed when the police failed to find his son who was being sought for armed robbery.

There were reports of rape by government and Angolan soldiers. For example, in late July several Angolan soldiers beat and raped a woman near their military barracks in a suburb of Pointe-Noire.

Many detainees were beaten at the time of their arrest or in custody. Most detainees, particularly in Brazzaville, were held in overcrowded cells with virtually no ventilation; some reportedly died from thirst and starvation, as well as from lack of medical care.

Dozens of detainees who "disappeared" in the custody of the police, particularly in Brazzaville, were feared dead. For example, as many as 17 detainees "disappeared" after they were removed from the Brazzaville central police station in April.

Armed opposition groups deliberately and arbitrarily killed civilians they believed to be government supporters. Members of the "Ninja" armed group killed unarmed civilians who refused to support them, particularly before and during clashes with government forces. In September members of the "Ninja" armed group killed a journalist and several other people who were travelling with a government minister.

Amnesty International condemned human rights abuses by government forces and by armed opposition groups. In a letter to President Nguesso in March and during a visit to the country in July, Amnesty International urged the authorities to set up an independent and impartial inquiry into human rights abuses that occurred in the recent past and to ensure that the perpetrators were brought to justice. In December the organization called on President Nguesso and leaders of armed groups to give clear public instructions to their forces not to commit human rights abuses, and urged the government to prevent the shelling of civilian targets.

141

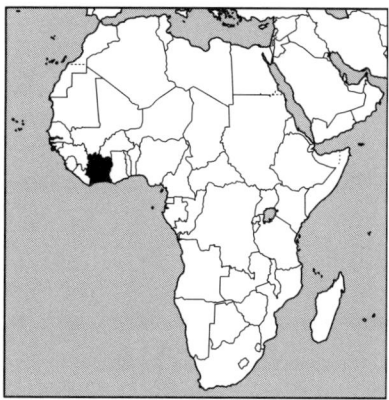

CÔTE D'IVOIRE

Some 30 opposition party supporters arrested in 1995, including possible prisoners of conscience, were detained throughout the year. At least 19 Liberian nationals continued to be held without charge or trial. Several people were killed by the security forces in circumstances suggesting excessive use of force.

In September opposition parties protested publicly against several constitutional

142 changes including the extension of the presidential term from five to seven years, and an amendment allowing an incumbent President to extend his term of office indefinitely, should conditions not be suitable for the organization of presidential elections.

Some 30 opposition party supporters, including possible prisoners of conscience, sentenced in connection with political unrest that followed presidential elections in October 1995, remained in detention throughout the year (see *Amnesty International Reports 1996* to *1998*). All were released after an amnesty was approved by the National Assembly at the end of December.

At least 19 Liberian nationals, who had been held without trial since 1995, continued to be detained in the penal camp in Bouaké. None had been formally charged, but it was believed that some may have been arrested on suspicion of involvement with armed attacks from Liberia. The detainees had no access to a lawyer. Several were sick and at least three had reportedly died in custody as a result of the harsh prison conditions, inadequate food and lack of access to medical treatment.

Several people were killed by the security forces in circumstances suggesting excessive use of force. In February a policeman shot dead a passenger in a car that did not stop at traffic lights. No inquiry was opened into the case. In May Elele Sombo Magès, a 17-year-old student, was killed by a member of the security forces in a school in Anyama, 10 kilometres north of Abidjan, during clashes between students and the police at the school. One policeman was arrested and sentenced to 10 years' imprisonment for the killing.

CROATIA

Some critics of the government were prosecuted on criminal charges. Tens of thousands of Croatian Serbs remained exiled: many were prevented from returning because of administrative obstacles; others feared for their safety if they returned. Dozens of houses of Croatian Serbs, possibly more, were deliberately destroyed for political reasons. Political prisoners faced unfair trial procedures. Police ill-treated

detainees and at least one person died as a result. Although hundreds of cases of "disappearance" were resolved, the fate of more than 2,000 people who went missing or had "disappeared" in previous years remained unclear. There was little progress in resolving hundreds of cases of ethnically motivated killings committed in 1995.

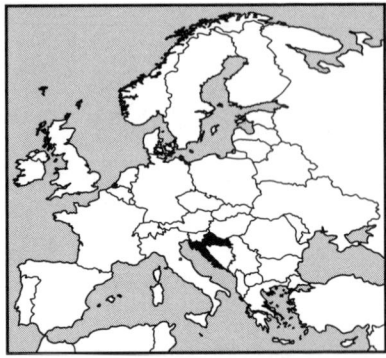

In January the mandate of the UN Transitional Authority in Eastern Slavonia, Baranja and Sirmium (UNTAES) ended and the region returned to the full control of the Croatian authorities. Although the peaceful transition of the region from rebel Croatian Serb control was hailed as a success, international monitors who remained continued to report ethnically motivated incidents of violence. A UN Police Support Group was mandated to monitor the civilian police in the Danube region following the UN's withdrawal. Violent attacks continued against Croatian Serbs and were reported to have increased in Eastern Slavonia following the withdrawal of UNTAES. In July a mixed Serb-Hungarian couple was murdered in Topolje village near Beli Manastir in the Baranja region. Local police immediately arrested a suspect, a former Croatian soldier, who confessed. He had reportedly threatened the couple with violence previously and they had told the police, although no steps were taken to offer them additional protection. As the suspect was deemed mentally unstable, the opening of his trial was postponed pending his psychiatric investigation. The UN Police Support Group's mandate was terminated in October; it was replaced by international civilian police monitors supported by the Organization for Security and Co-operation in Europe (OSCE) mission.

In April a plan for the return of refugees and displaced persons was severely criticized by the international community because it was vague and imposed unjustified conditions on Croatian Serbs who wanted to return. A plan which met the demands of the international community, particularly the missions of the OSCE and the UN High Commissioner for Refugees (UNHCR), was passed by parliament in June. However, implementation of the plan was slow, mainly owing to lack of political will to remove local administrative obstacles. According to government statistics, by the end of the year some 2,000 Croatian Serbs had returned to the country under the plan, in addition to several thousand Croatian Serbs who reportedly returned unofficially and whose number was impossible to confirm independently. According to the same statistics, more than 22,000 Croatian displaced persons were able to return to their pre-war homes. Some 20,000 Bosnian Croats remained as refugees in Croatia; many of them occupied the pre-war homes of Croatian Serbs. In addition, several hundred Croats from Kosovo province in the Federal Republic of Yugoslavia (FRY) settled in Croatia by similarly moving into Serb-owned property. The authorities did little to find them alternative accommodation.

The trial ended of Croatian Serb Slavko Dokmanović at the International Criminal Tribunal for the former Yugoslavia (the Tribunal) after he was found dead in his cell in June. The death, an apparent suicide, happened eight days before the verdict was expected. He had faced charges related to the killing of approximately 260 people taken from Vukovar hospital by Yugoslav National Army (JNA) forces in 1991 and had been arrested with the support of UNTAES personnel in 1997 (see *Amnesty International Report 1998*). Four other men indicted by the Tribunal for crimes committed in Croatia remained at large and were believed to be in the FRY or Bosnia-Herzegovina. In December the Tribunal's prosecutor requested the FRY to defer to its competence proceedings instigated against three of these suspects.

In September members of the European Committee for the Prevention of Torture and Inhuman or Degrading Treatment or Punishment visited Croatia. In November the UN Committee against Torture considered Croatia's second periodic report on its implementation of the UN Convention against Torture and Other Cruel, Inhuman or Degrading Treatment or Punishment. The Committee raised concern relating to several cases about which it had been briefed by Amnesty International. In particular, it asked the authorities about the status of the case of Šefik Mujkić, who died following torture by the secret police in 1995. Two police officers were found guilty of extracting a statement from him and causing serious bodily harm in May 1996, but both were released pending a retrial ordered by the Supreme Court (see below). The Committee also requested Croatia to respond in full to allegations made by Amnesty International and other organizations that human rights violations, including torture, committed by Croatian security forces in 1995 had not been adequately investigated and that in most cases no one had been brought to account for them.

Croatian Serbs and critics of the government were the most frequently targeted for a range of human rights violations. Journalists and other critics of the government were prosecuted on criminal charges. The trial of Viktor Ivančić and Marinko Čulić, editor and journalist of the independent weekly *Feral Tribune* (see *Amnesty International Report 1998*), ended with their acquittal in December. Victor Ivančić and Petar Dorić, another *Feral Tribune* journalist, also came under investigation for "slandering" President Franjo Tudjman because of an article published in March. If they were imprisoned, Amnesty International would consider them prisoners of conscience. In all these cases, the state prosecutor received the President's endorsement to pursue the charges.

Other journalists were prosecuted on criminal charges. For example, Davor Butković, former editor of the independent weekly *Globus*, and journalist Vlado Vurušić were found guilty of "spreading false information" and given suspended prison sentences for reporting that an individual indicted by the Tribunal, who at the time was at large, was seen at residences owned by the Ministry of Defence in 1996. Others had reported the individual's presence there, but were not charged. In hundreds of other civil cases, libel and slander legislation was used to silence government critics.

144

Dozens of houses, possibly more, were destroyed for political reasons. For example, explosives were deliberately detonated in the weekend house of a man in Karlobag in March after he and two others had made public their willingness to testify before the Tribunal about violations of humanitarian law by Croatian forces during the war. In most cases, however, houses were destroyed to prevent Croatian Serbs from returning to them. For example, the house of Mirko Mrkalj and his family in Donji Sjeničak was destroyed by an arson attack in early April, just one month after the family had visited it to plan their return. No one was known to have been brought to account for these criminal acts.

Despite agreements by the authorities to facilitate return, tens of thousands of Croatian Serbs in the FRY or Bosnia-Herzegovina who had announced their wish to return to Croatia were unable to do so. In addition to house destruction, other acts of arson appeared to be intimidatory and intended to prevent the return of the owners. The Croatian Helsinki Committee for Human Rights reported more than 100 such cases of arson in the first quarter of the year alone. Continued impunity for past abuses and the government's failure to guarantee safety contributed to Croatian Serb mistrust of the authorities; at least 7,000 Croatian Serbs left Croatia as a result. For example, official condoning of continued harassment and ill-treatment prompted Jovo Dabić and Ljuba Dabić to leave Croatia in May. Jovo Dabić had been repeatedly attacked in his village near Hrvatska Kostajnica, including by rioting Bosnian Croat refugees in May 1997 when police allegedly stood by while he was beaten (see *Amnesty International Report 1998*). In September the UN Police Support Group reported increasing numbers of ethnically motivated violent incidents, including shootings, explosions, assault and vandalism. It also reported a growing unwillingness by some police officers to take action in such cases.

Several trials for political prisoners fell short of international standards for fairness. Some political prisoners were held in pre-trial detention illegally. Radenko Radojčić, for example, was released in October after the court reconsidered its original objection to his release (fear of the prisoner absconding), stating that it now believed that it was unlikely that he would abscond, particularly in view of his poor health. Scores of other Croatian Serbs facing nationally defined war crimes charges remained imprisoned. In February the Supreme Court ruled in favour of an appeal by Mirko Graorac, who had been sentenced after an unfair trial in 1996 to 20 years' imprisonment followed by expulsion from the country for committing war crimes against a civilian population and war crimes against prisoners of war. The Supreme Court dismissed almost all elements of the defence appeal, most importantly that the conviction had been based almost entirely on circumstantial and uncorroborated evidence and that the defendant had not been allowed to call witnesses. However, it ruled in favour of the appeal on grounds that it was necessary to re-examine the Croatian Army soldiers whose original testimony on behalf of the prosecutor implicated Croatia in the war in Bosnia-Herzegovina.

Ill-treatment by the police continued to be reported. The authorities acted quickly in the case of Riccardo Cetina, an Italian tourist who died from injuries inflicted by police after an alleged traffic offence. The authorities stated that this was the first case of its kind, despite several earlier reports of ill-treatment in police custody. No date was set for the retrial of two secret police officers charged with "extracting a statement" from and "inflicting serious bodily harm" on Šefik Mujkić, a Croatian resident of Bosniac nationality who died after being tortured in September 1995. In other cases where victims needed hospital treatment as a result of police ill-treatment, it was not known whether action was taken against the perpetrators.

Exhumations helped clarify the fate of hundreds of people who went missing and "disappeared" in previous years. The authorities exhumed 938 bodies from graves in Vukovar between April and June, of which more than half were identified. The exhumations were conducted as a result of information provided by the FRY authorities as part of continuing efforts to resolve the thousands of cases of missing persons from Croatia, many of whom "disappeared" in the custody of the JNA in 1991 (see *Amnesty International Report 1992*, **Yugoslavia** entry). Although most of the exhumed victims had died during the struggle for control of the town, some showed signs that they may have been extrajudicially executed or otherwise unlawfully killed, according to Croatian investigators. For example, the remains of Dragutin Šavorić were identified; he was last seen during a prisoner exchange in 1991, but was reportedly separated from the other prisoners by JNA forces. According to the Croatian authorities, his corpse had two bullet wounds to the head and one to the right foot. Little progress, however, was made in resolving the cases of more than 700 Croatian Serbs who went missing during the armed conflict, many of whom may have "disappeared".

There was little progress in criminal investigations and prosecutions in cases of human rights violations, including hundreds of ethnically motivated killings, committed during the 1995 security forces' offensives Operations Flash and Storm. The Justice Ministry stated that the statistics it had provided about these killings were meaningless, and it continued to refuse to provide information about individual cases, including some which had been well documented and publicized. International organizations had discovered and documented the bodies of more than 200 victims, and government statistics from 1995 had indicated that more than 450 civilians had been killed during the offensives.

Amnesty International raised with the authorities a variety of human rights concerns. Attacks on human rights defenders were featured throughout the year as part of Amnesty International's campaign to mark the 50th anniversary of the Universal Declaration of Human Rights.

In August the organization published a document, *Croatia: Impunity for killings after Storm*, and launched an action to provide information about specific killings to the appropriate judicial bodies. Amnesty International recommended that the authorities take steps to ascertain whether any attempt was made to cover up crimes committed during and after Operations Flash and Storm.

In November the organization informed the UN Committee against Torture about some of its concerns.

In December Amnesty International published *Croatia: Mirko Graorac, Short-changing justice – war crimes trials in former Yugoslavia*.

CUBA

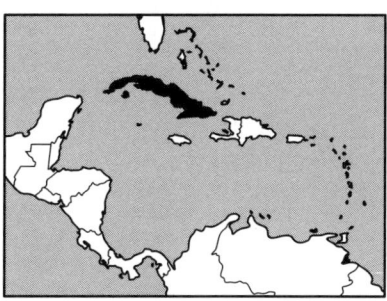

At least 150 political prisoners, including 30 prisoners of conscience, were released, many on condition that they leave the country. At least 350 others remained imprisoned, including some 100 prisoners of conscience. Many political dissidents were detained for short periods or harassed. There were frequent reports of ill-treatment. Prison conditions sometimes constituted cruel, inhuman or degrading treatment. At least 10 unarmed civilians were shot dead by law enforcement officials who used lethal force unjustifiably. There were at least five executions. New death sentences were passed and several men remained under sentence of death at the end of the year.

In April Cuba escaped censure at the UN Commission on Human Rights for the first time in seven years, when a US-sponsored resolution was defeated. In October the UN General Assembly overwhelmingly demanded an end to the US embargo against Cuba for the seventh year running.

In August the UN Committee on the Elimination of Racial Discrimination considered Cuba's 10th, 11th and 12th periodic reports. It recognized that "Cuba had experienced serious economic difficulties as a result of the embargo." It also expressed appreciation of Cuba's commitment to "eliminate all manifestations of racial discrimination" and recommended that particular attention be paid to "the training of law enforcement officials in the protection of human rights."

A visit to Cuba by Pope John Paul II in January was followed by the release of nearly 300 prisoners, including more than 100 political prisoners, 19 of whom were prisoners of conscience. Thirteen prisoners of conscience were unconditionally

146

released in February, including Héctor Palacio Ruiz (see *Amnesty International Report 1998*). The other six prisoners of conscience were released in April and May on condition that they went into exile in Canada. Following the Pope's visit, suppression of political dissent continued, but was generally less severe than the previous year. In November, two prisoners of conscience charged with "enemy propaganda" – Jesús Chamber Ramírez (see *Amnesty International Report 1994*), imprisoned since 1992, and Dr Desi Mendoza Rivero (see *Amnesty International Report 1998*), imprisoned since 1997 – were released from prison "for humanitarian reasons" because of ill health, on condition that they leave the country.

Radamés García de la Vega, Vice-President of *Jóvenes por la Democracia*, Young People for Democracy, who was serving an 18-month sentence of "correctional work with internment" for "disrespect", was released in February, eight months before his sentence expired. Nestor Rodríguez Lobaina, President of *Jóvenes por la Democracia*, was released in October after completing an 18-month sentence for "disrespect" and "resisting authority" (see *Amnesty International Reports 1997* and *1998*). However, Nestor Rodríguez was detained again for a week in December after protesting at the government's refusal to let him leave the country to attend a conference in France marking the 50th anniversary of the Universal Declaration of Human Rights. On his release, he was ordered to go to Baracoa, Guantánamo province, and forbidden from going to Havana, the capital.

Six members of the unofficial *Partido Pro Derechos Humanos en Cuba* (PPDHC), Party for Human Rights in Cuba, arrested in Santa Clara in October 1997 (see *Amnesty International Report 1998*) remained in detention at the end of the year. They had been detained after starting a fast in protest at the arrest of fellow PPDHC member Daula Carpio Mata. Four of those remaining in detention were serving sentences varying from 16 to 18 months' imprisonment or "correctional work with internment". The other two – Lilian Meneses Martínez and Ileana Peñalver Duque – were being held in Guamajal Women's Prison, despite the fact that they had been sentenced to 18 months' "correctional work without internment".

It was estimated that at least 350 political prisoners who had been convicted of state security offences, many after unfair trials, remained imprisoned at the end of the year, including at least 60 prisoners of conscience and possible prisoners of conscience. However, the exact figure was not known because of the absence of official data and the continuing severe restrictions on human rights monitoring.

Several members of unofficial groups working in the field of civil and political rights, journalists working for independent press agencies, and human rights activists, were detained for short periods; most were released without charge. Many were subjected to other forms of intimidation, including being refused permission to leave the country with the right to return, and *actos de repudio* (acts of repudiation) organized by government officials, which involved being verbally abused and sometimes physically assaulted by government supporters. For example, following the arrest of Manuel Antonio González Castellanos, a reporter for the independent press agency *Cuba Press*, in Holguín in October, his family wrote anti-government slogans on the walls and doors of their home. The next day their home was reportedly surrounded by several hundred people who were shouting threats and abuse. Government agents then forced open the door and beat two members of the family – Yoani and Leonardo Varona González – and a visitor, Roberto Rodríguez Rodríguez. Yoani Varona and Roberto Rodríguez were released, but Manuel González and Leonardo Varona remained detained at the end of the year. All four were reportedly charged with "disrespect".

In September at least eight dissidents were arrested in a crack-down on anti-government activism. Most had taken part in a demonstration outside the court where the trial of Reinaldo Alfaro García (see below) was taking place. All were released without charge within a few days. Two of the detainees – Dr Oscar Elías Biscet and Rolando Muñoz Yllobre, President and Vice-President respectively of the *Fundación Lawton de Derechos Humanos*, Lawton Human Rights Foundation – were detained several times during the year.

Lázaro Constantín Durán, one of those detained for demonstrating on the day of Reinaldo Alfaro's trial, was arrested again on 10 December and beaten. On 17 December he was sentenced to three years' imprisonment for "dangerousness". On the eve and day of Lázaro Constantín's trial about a dozen people were detained, possibly to prevent them from attending the trial. All were released within a couple of days.

In November several people were detained outside the court where the trial of Mario Julio Viera González, Director of the independent press agency *Cuba Verdad* (Cuba Truth), was to take place. He was accused of "slander" to the head of the legal department of the Ministry of Foreign Affairs because of an article he wrote implying that the government was hypocritical in stating that the proposed international criminal court should be independent and impartial. All the detainees were released without charge, but the trial of Mario Julio Viera González had not taken place by the end of the year.

At least 30 political prisoners, including prisoners of conscience, were brought to trial; most had been detained in previous years. Prisoner of conscience Cecilio Monteagudo Sánchez, a member of the unofficial *Partido Solidaridad Democrática*, Democratic Solidarity Party, who was detained in September 1997, was convicted of "enemy propaganda" and sentenced to four years' imprisonment in February. The charges related to a leaflet he had written, which was never printed, calling on people not to vote in the October 1997 local elections. Journalist Juan Carlos Recio Martínez, who was tried in the same case, was convicted of "other acts against state security" and sentenced to one year's "correctional work without internment". He was convicted on the grounds that he knew of the existence of Cecilio Monteagudo's leaflet, but did not inform the authorities.

In April Julio Cesar Coizeau Rizo, who had been detained in October 1997, was sentenced to three years' imprisonment for "disrespect", reportedly because he had written anti-government graffiti on public walls.

In August Reinaldo Alfaro García, a political activist detained in May 1997, was sentenced to three years' imprisonment for "spreading false news against international peace". The charge reportedly related to a statement he had made in 1995 to a US-based radio station in which

he reported that a military officer had gone missing and later died and that a woman had told him that she had been tortured. At Reinaldo Alfaro's trial, which took place at the Havana People's Provincial Court, the alleged torture victim and the mother of the military officer both appeared as witnesses and denied the allegations. However, there were reports that the alleged torture victim who appeared in court was not the same woman who had made the torture allegation to Reinaldo Alfaro. In addition, several witnesses were not allowed to testify.

In September, four members of a dissident study group arrested in July 1997 after criticizing a document disseminated for the Fifth Congress of the *Partido Comunista de Cuba*, Cuban Communist Party (see *Amnesty International Report 1998*), were formally charged with "other acts against state security" in relation to the crime of "sedition". Their trial had not taken place by the end of the year.

Trials in political cases again fell far short of international standards of fairness. Defendants in cases heard by municipal courts, often only hours or days after arrest, sometimes had no legal representation. Detainees held under investigation on state security charges often had very limited access to lawyers while in pre-trial detention at police stations or at State Security headquarters and were sometimes subjected to psychological pressure, such as solitary confinement, long intense interrogations, threats and insults.

Several prisoners were beaten by police at the time of arrest or by prison guards in detention centres. In April prisoner of conscience Bernardo Arévalo Padrón was beaten in Cienfuegos Provincial Prison, Ariza, reportedly because it was mistakenly believed that he had distributed anti-government propaganda within the prison. According to reports, he was badly bruised and suffered memory loss as a result of the beatings.

Prison conditions continued to be poor and in some cases constituted cruel, inhuman or degrading treatment. There were allegations that prisoners were subjected to threats, discrimination on political grounds and verbal abuse. During the year, two prisoners – Jesús Chamber Ramírez and Jorge Luis García Pérez (known as "Antúnez") (see *Amnesty International Reports 1994* and *1998*) – were

148

held in isolation cells where the lighting, ventilation and hygiene were said to be very poor. Some prisons were said to have a high incidence of disease as a result of poor sanitation and nutrition and a scarcity of water. The effects of the US embargo on the availability of medicines and equipment contributed to the problem. However, there were reports that medical attention and food were often deliberately withheld as a punishment.

At least 10 unarmed people died after being shot by the police who used lethal force unjustifiably. In May Yusel Ochoterena López died in Havana, reportedly after police officers entered his home and shot him, mistaking him for a fugitive who was apparently in the area. A police investigation was reportedly held but no one was brought to justice.

At least five people were executed during the year. Among them were Emilio Betancourt Bonne and Jorge Luis Sánchez Guilarte, who were executed in May. An appeal by Humberto Real Suárez (see *Amnesty International Reports 1997* and *1998*), who had been sentenced to death in 1996, was still pending before the People's Supreme Court at the end of the year. Several new death sentences were issued and several men remained on death row at the end of the year.

Throughout the year Amnesty International appealed for the release of all prisoners of conscience and urged that those facing trial for politically motivated offences be granted full judicial guarantees in accordance with international standards. Appeals were also sent on behalf of prisoners in need of medical attention. The organization called for all prisoners to be provided with nutrition, medical care and sanitation in keeping with the standards of the general population and for independent and impartial investigations into allegations of ill-treatment. No replies were received from the authorities.

CYPRUS

There were allegations of ill-treatment by law enforcement officers.

In May the House of Representatives (parliament) amended Article 171 of the Penal Code. Because of its very restrictive definition of privacy, the amended article could still lead to imprisonment of up to five years for consensual sexual relations between male adults in private. The new provisions are also discriminatory. The age of consent for sexual activity between men is 18 while the age of consent for sexual activity between heterosexuals is 16; and the restrictive definition of privacy applies only to sexual activity between men. The wide scope of the newly adopted Article 174(A), which provides for a one-year prison sentence for "indecent behaviour or invitation or provocation or advertisement aimed at performing unnatural acts between males", could lead to the imprisonment of people solely for exercising their right to freedom of expression and to freedom of assembly and association.

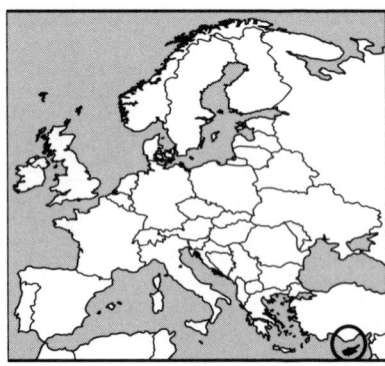

There were allegations of ill-treatment. In June, 113 people from Africa and the Middle East rescued from a fishing trawler drifting off the coast of Cyprus were remanded under police guard in an hotel in Limassol pending a decision on their asylum applications. In August, 30 asylum-seekers, most of them Africans, were transferred from the hotel to the cells of the former Police Headquarters in Larnaca pending deportation. At least four of them alleged they were beaten by police officers while a police inspector was watching. As a result of the beatings the asylum-seekers sustained various injuries; they were initially denied access to hospital. One asylum-seeker alleged that as he opened the door of his hotel room, he was kicked in his genitals, and that five police officers then came into his room, beat and kicked him for up to 15 minutes. As a result of the beatings he sustained injuries to his eye, which required stitches, and jaw. He alleged that a week later he was brought before the police inspector who had accompanied the police officers responsible for his ill-treatment at the hotel, and threatened with further beating if he refused to sign a statement denying that the ill-treatment had occurred. Thirty of the 113 asylum-seekers were deported to their country of origin between July and October.

In October, when 48 of the 113 asylum-seekers were held in Larnaca detention centre pending deportation, officers from MMAD (rapid intervention police force) units threw tear gas to force the asylum-seekers out of their cells into the yard and forced them to lie face down on the ground, in an effort to carry out the deportation order. Television footage showed police officers kicking and stamping on the asylum-seekers and hitting them with truncheons. About 10 of the asylum-seekers were reportedly transferred to hospital as a result of the beatings and respiratory difficulties caused by tear gas. An inquiry was subsequently set up.

In June Amnesty International called on the government to revise Article 171, paragraphs 1 and 3, of the Penal Code to equalize the age of consent for homosexual and heterosexual relations, and to revise Article 174(A).

In July Amnesty International urged the authorities to ensure that all asylum-seekers would be given access to a full and satisfactory asylum procedure and that they would not be returned to countries where they might face human rights violations. No answer was received by the end of the year.

CZECH REPUBLIC

Reports were received of ill-treatment by police officers.

In January Václav Havel was re-elected President for a second five-year term. Following general elections in June, Miloš Zeman, leader of the Czech Social Democratic Party, was appointed Prime Minister.

In March the UN Committee on the Elimination of Racial Discrimination considered the initial and second reports of the Czech Republic. In its conclusions the Committee expressed concern about the six-fold increase in racially motivated

crimes between 1994 and 1996, and about reports that the authorities have not been "sufficiently active in effectively countering racial violence against members of minority groups". In view of the reported cases of harassment and of excessive use of force by the police against minority groups, especially against members of the Romani community (see *Amnesty International Report 1996*), the Committee called for improved training of law enforcement officials in the provisions of the International Convention on the Elimination of All Forms of Racial Discrimination.

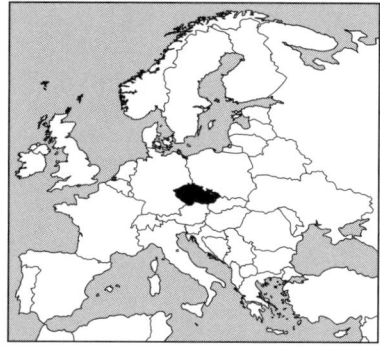

In May police officers reportedly beat dozens of people following a demonstration through the centre of the capital, Prague, by around 3,000 people supporting environmental and left-wing youth groups. Demonstrators and passers by were among the victims. The police action, which was in response to a number of violent incidents, began as the demonstrators were dispersing. Some of the demonstrators, including many who were reportedly not involved in any violence, were trapped by police vehicles in Vodičkova Street where around 100 police officers reportedly beat them with truncheons and kicked them.

Police officers forced about 50 young people suspected of participating in the demonstration to lie on the pavement or to stand against a wall and reportedly kicked and hit them with truncheons. They were then taken into the basement of the police headquarters building in Bartolomějská Street, where many of the detainees were reportedly kicked and beaten by police officers. Some were forced to kneel facing a wall with their hands held above their heads. They were reportedly put into small cells and denied

150

access to toilets. According to reports they were not permitted to contact a lawyer or inform a relative or a third party of their whereabouts. During the night the detainees were driven in groups of 10 to the police hospital *Na Míčánkách*, where many were ill-treated before and after medical examinations, which were reportedly aimed solely at establishing whether the detainees were under the influence of drugs or alcohol. They were then returned to Bartolomějská Street police station and interrogated. Twenty-seven of the detainees were under investigation for hooliganism, assault of a public official and destruction of property, but according to reports investigations of 18 detainees were subsequently closed for lack of evidence. One detainee was still in pre-trial detention at the end of the year. Nine of the detainees were held for three weeks; the others were released. The Ministry of the Interior stated that the conduct of the police officers involved had been legal and that force had only been used to restrain detained suspects.

In July Amnesty International urged Otokar Motejl, the Minister of Justice, to ensure that the investigation into the reported ill-treatment of detainees on Vodičkova Street, in Bartolomějská Street police station, and at the police hospital was conducted promptly and impartially. Amnesty International also urged the Czech authorities to provide information about investigations into two similar incidents of reported police ill-treatment in 1996 and 1997.

DJIBOUTI

Scores of critics of the government were arrested. Eighteen political prisoners received unfair trials. There were reports of torture.

During 1998 there was fighting between government forces and an armed faction of the *Front pour la restauration de l'unité et de la démocratie* (FRUD), Front for the Restoration of Unity and Democracy. Government soldiers reportedly mistreated Afar civilians suspected of supporting the rebels.

In December Djibouti acceded to the UN Convention on the Elimination of All Forms of Discrimination against Women.

Government critics, including trade unionists and members of opposition parties, were detained or harassed by the police and security services. Aref Mohamed Aref, a human rights lawyer, had his passport confiscated to prevent him attending the Paris Human Rights Defenders' Summit organized by Amnesty International and other international human rights organizations in December. In March scores of striking health workers were detained for a few days; they were released without charge. In May Ahmed Omar and Abubaker Ahmed Awled, journalists on the newspaper of the opposition *Parti de renouveau démocratique*, Party of Democratic Revival, were arrested. They were subsequently sentenced to three months' imprisonment and a fine, and their newspaper was banned.

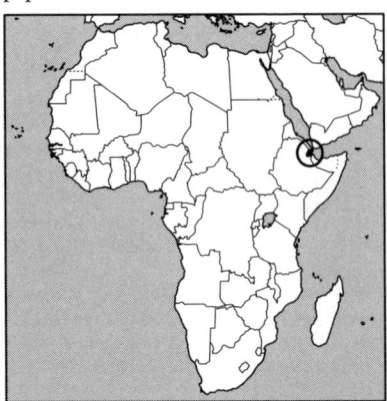

In September, 18 people charged with political offences received unfair trials; several said that they had been tortured to extract false confessions which were accepted as evidence in court. They included 16 soldiers arrested in August and charged with plotting a coup, and two leaders of the *Groupement pour la démocratie et de la République* (GDR), Group for Democracy and the Republic – Ahmed Boulaleh Barreh and Moumin Bahdon Farah, both former prisoners of conscience (see *Amnesty International Report 1998*). All were convicted of inciting civil disobedience and sentenced to suspended prison terms ranging from six to 12 months.

Ten relatives and associates of former prisoner of conscience Ismail Guedi Hared, former Director of the President's cabinet, were arrested in November and charged with armed conspiracy. Some were allegedly tortured. Their trial had not started by the end of the year.

Two FRUD members deported from Ethiopia in May were detained and charged with armed conspiracy. Over 30 other FRUD members, including 14 deported from Ethiopia in 1997, remained held awaiting trial on charges of armed conspiracy. One of those deported in 1997, Aicha Dabale Ahmed, was released in March after giving birth and allowed to go abroad for medical treatment (see *Amnesty International Report 1998*).

Six Ethiopian Oromos, including Ali Omar, a community leader and a recognized refugee, were handed over to the Ethiopian authorities in January and reportedly detained.

Prison conditions were harsh. In June political prisoners in Gabode prison went on hunger strike for several days in protest against the denial of adequate medical treatment. Ethiopian refugee women were reportedly raped in police stations during round-ups of suspected illegal immigrants.

Amnesty International called on the government of President Hassan Gouled Aptidon to release prisoners of conscience and ensure fair trials for political detainees. It also called for detainees to be treated humanely.

DOMINICAN REPUBLIC

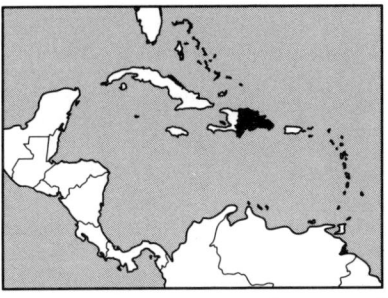

There were further reports of torture and ill-treatment of Haitian immigrants. One person who "disappeared" in 1994 remained unaccounted for. At least six people were shot dead and many others wounded allegedly by police using lethal force unlawfully.

In January the authorities announced the possible creation of an internal affairs department to investigate human rights violations by the police. The Senate discussed the creation of a Human Rights Procurator to investigate violations and an Ombudsman's office to receive citizens' complaints about human rights violations. None of these initiatives had been implemented by the end of the year.

The opposition Dominican Revolutionary Party won the legislative elections held in May.

In September President Leonel Fernández Reyna dismissed the Head of the National Drugs Control Office, reportedly for carrying out and permitting human rights violations against detainees. Several hundred policemen were also dismissed for serious misconduct. However, it was not clear how many were accused of human rights violations.

Some 700 people were detained for short periods during the year, mainly during protests and strikes about various economic and social issues.

There were further reports of torture, including rape, and ill-treatment of Haitian immigrants by Dominican soldiers during round-ups for deportation. In August immigration officials and soldiers reportedly raped several women, including a 14-year-old girl, at a sugar-cane work camp. In November, in two separate incidents, two Haitians were shot dead by Dominican soldiers as they tried to escape deportation. Thousands of Haitian immigrants were repatriated throughout the year, including some living in the country legally. Haitians were often deported without their residence papers being verified, in contravention of their rights.

No investigation was known to have been opened into the alleged torture and ill-treatment of Danilo de la Cruz and Kennedy Vargas in November 1997 (see *Amnesty International Report 1998*).

Several military and police officers, including the then Secretary of State for the Armed Forces, were briefly detained for questioning in connection with the "disappearance" in May 1994 of Narciso González. The judicial investigation had not concluded by the end of the year (see previous *Amnesty International Reports*).

At least six people were killed and many others injured by the security forces in circumstances in which excessive force

152

appeared to have been employed, mainly in the context of demonstrations or in disputed circumstances. In March, 17-year-old Gabriel Corporán Reyes was reportedly shot in the back by police during a protest in Villa Mella, Santo Domingo. He died shortly after arriving at a clinic. In July Franklin Fabián, a student of the Autonomous University of Santo Domingo, was reportedly shot dead by police officers during a student demonstration. According to reports, he was putting away his stall where he had been selling goods at the time. Three police officers accused of killing Franklin Fabián were reportedly tried by a police tribunal, but the outcome was not known. In August a priest, José Tineo Núñez, was shot dead by police while he waited in front of the offices of the *Misioneros del Sagrado Corazón*, Missionaries of the Sacred Heart, in Santo Domingo. Witnesses claimed that the policeman opened fire without identifying himself to the victim or making any attempt to arrest him. A police investigation reportedly concluded that the police had acted with negligence and carelessness. The officers implicated in the shooting were awaiting trial by court martial at the end of the year.

There was no further information about the killing by police of Manuel Mancebo and Ilex Actoin in 1997 (see *Amnesty International Report 1998*).

In November the trial began of six former military officers accused of killing journalist Orlando Martínez Howley in 1975 after he criticized the then President, Joaquín Balaguer. All had been imprisoned for almost a year, apart from one former member of the armed forces who was arrested in New York, USA, in November. President Fernández Reyna authorized the Attorney General to request his extradition to face charges. The judicial investigation, which had called more than 100 witnesses, including Joaquín Balaguer, had not been concluded by the end of the year.

Amnesty International continued to call for a thorough and independent investigation into the "disappearance" of Narciso González. The organization also urged the authorities to conduct full and impartial investigations into several cases of people shot dead by police and into allegations of torture and ill-treatment of Haitians.

ECUADOR

Torture and ill-treatment by members of the security forces continued to be reported. At least one person was shot dead in circumstances suggesting an extrajudicial execution. Although the authorities accepted full responsibility for two prominent cases in which three victims were tortured, "disappeared" and killed in the 1980s, the vast majority of human rights cases documented in previous years remained unresolved.

In August Jamil Mahuad Witt took office as President. In his inaugural speech he promised to respect human rights. The promise followed Congress' adoption in March of a National Plan for Human Rights. Clashes in November between the security forces and demonstrators protesting at the new government's economic measures left two civilians dead.

A new Constitution which came into effect in August asserted, as a "fundamental principle", that one of the "primary responsibilities of the State is to ensure that human rights are applied". Ecuador's new Constitution includes a number of human rights guarantees, including the right to life and personal integrity. It prohibits torture and cruel, inhuman and degrading treatment or punishment. It also states that those responsible for crimes of genocide, torture, enforced disappearance, abduction or homicide may not benefit from an amnesty or be pardoned and that international treaties, including those designed to protect human rights, once approved by the National Congress and published in the Official Gazette, are deemed to be part of domestic law. The death penalty remained abolished.

In July, following its examination of Ecuador's fourth periodic report, the UN Human Rights Committee expressed concern about the human rights situation in the country, including delays in bringing imprisoned criminal suspects to trial. In a move designed to resolve this particular issue, the new Constitution made provision for judges to order the immediate release of all prisoners who had not been convicted and who had been detained for more than a year, without prejudicing the continuation of criminal proceedings against them. By the end of the year, of at least 2,100 prisoners reportedly entitled to the provision, some 600 had been released.

In October, following examination of Ecuador's initial report, the UN Committee on the Rights of the Child expressed concern about disparities between international provision for the protection of children's rights and domestic practices, including the failure by the authorities to only deprive children of their liberty "as a measure of last resort".

In April Ecuador ratified the Protocol to the American Convention on Human Rights to Abolish the Death Penalty.

Reports of torture and ill-treatment by members of the security forces continued. In January a young indigenous girl alleged that she had been raped by several marines at a riverside naval base in Puerto de Francisco de Orellana, Napo province. Despite threats to her life if she reported the matter, the girl informed the local police. However, the marines refused to cooperate with the police investigation. By the end of the year those responsible had apparently not been brought to justice. In late November, Saúl Filormo Cañar Pauta, a prominent trade union leader, was abducted in Quito, the capital, by eight men travelling in vehicles of a type reportedly used by the military. His body, bearing injuries consistent with his having been tortured, was found in December on a rubbish dump near the town of Latacunga.

In September the Constitutional Court issued a ruling which effectively meant that the case involving the death in police custody of Aníbal Aguas in 1997 should remain under the jurisdiction of a police court (see *Amnesty International Report 1998*). By the end of the year, a judge attached to the police court had yet to consider a prosecutor's recommendation that the case be closed.

At least one person was shot dead in circumstances suggesting an extrajudicial execution. In June, four policemen in Buena Fe, Milagro, El Oro province, entered a brothel and, according to witnesses, arrested Leonardo Pita García, took him to a nearby spot and shot him dead. The commander of District IV of the National Police acknowledged that Leonardo Pita had been shot by a policeman, and an officer implicated in the killing was detained. The case was referred to the jurisdiction of a police rather than an independent court.

The authorities accepted full responsibility for two prominent cases of gross human rights violations in the 1980s. In June Ecuador recognized before the Inter-American Commission on Human Rights that its agents were responsible for the "arrest, illegal detention, torture and murder" of Consuelo Benavides in December 1985 (see previous *Amnesty International Reports*). Ecuador awarded compensation to her parents and agreed to take the necessary measures to bring all those responsible for Consuelo Benavides' death to justice. Also in June, the Inter-American Court of Human Rights noted Ecuador's "recognition of its international responsibility" for the fate of Consuelo Benavides and asked the government to continue investigations with a view to bringing those responsible to justice.

In May the government admitted responsibility for the "disappearance", torture and killing, in January 1988, of the brothers Carlos Santiago and Pedro Andrés Restrepo (see *Amnesty International Reports 1992* to *1996*). The government awarded compensation to the family and agreed to take measures to locate the brothers' remains and bring all those responsible to justice.

Scores of other human rights cases documented in previous years remained unresolved. These included allegations about the "disappearance" of five men and the extrajudicial execution of a further six in 1997 (see *Amnesty International Report 1998*), and of hundreds of cases of torture, "disappearance", and extrajudicial executions brought to the attention of two human rights commissions, established in 1996 by the executive and legislature respectively, which failed to publish their findings (see *Amnesty International Reports 1997* and *1998*).

153

154

In February the organization published *Amnesty International's concerns in Ecuador*. The report addressed concerns about the torture and ill-treatment of detainees and prisoners in the custody of the National Police, the military and the prison authorities; deaths resulting from the use of firearms by the security forces; "disappearances"; and the practice of institutionalized impunity. The organization concluded that the protection of human rights in Ecuador was in need of an urgent and thorough review and recommended that the authorities bring legislative, administrative, and judicial measures into line with international and regional human rights standards.

In May Amnesty International wrote to the Minister of Government and Police requesting that the necessary steps be taken to ensure those members of the security forces accused of human rights violations, including the death in police custody of Aníbal Aguas, be investigated and brought to justice before the ordinary courts. In December the organization recommended that the authorities conduct a full and independent investigation into the death of trade union leader Saúl Cañar Pauta.

EGYPT

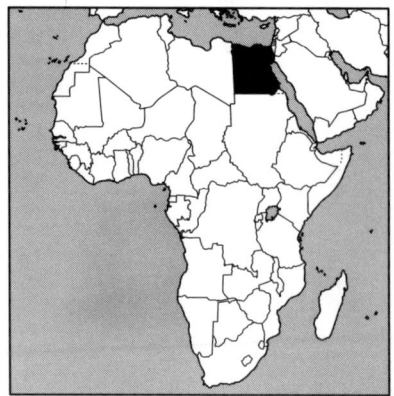

Twelve prisoners of conscience sentenced in previous years remained held. Thousands of suspected members or sympathizers of banned Islamist groups, including possible prisoners of conscience, were held without charge or trial; others were serving sentences imposed after grossly unfair trials before military courts. Torture and ill-treatment of detainees continued to be systematic; at least two people died reportedly as a result of torture. Prison conditions amounted to cruel, inhuman or degrading treatment. At least 73 people were sentenced to death and at least 48 people were executed. Armed opposition groups deliberately killed at least nine civilians.

Clashes between the security forces and armed Islamist groups were much less frequent than in previous years, resulting in a sharp reduction in the number of people killed by both sides and less frequent mass arrests by the security forces.

A state of emergency declared in 1981 (see previous *Amnesty International Reports*) remained in force.

In May the UN Committee against Torture requested from Egypt a "timely submission of the country's third periodic report" and called for a report on how the recommendations made by the Committee in May 1996 had been put into effect (see *Amnesty International Reports 1997* and *1998*).

A draft law to replace Law 32 of 1964 regulating non-governmental organizations was still being finalized at the end of the year.

Five prisoners of conscience, each serving a five-year prison term, remained in Mazra'at Tora Prison at the end of the year. They were among 53 prisoners of conscience tried and sentenced for membership of the banned Muslim Brothers organization in 1995 by the Supreme Military Court in Cairo (see *Amnesty International Reports 1996* to *1998*). The rest were released during the year after completing their sentences. Seven prisoners of conscience sentenced to three years' imprisonment for membership of the Muslim Brothers by the Supreme Military Court in August 1996 (see *Amnesty International Report 1997*) also continued to be held in Mazra'at Tora Prison.

In December Hafez Abu Sa'ada, Secretary General of the Egyptian Organization for Human Rights (EOHR), was arrested and detained for six days before being released on bail in connection with investigations concerning publications and funding of the EOHR.

Possible prisoners of conscience were among scores of people detained during the year. In February 'Abd al-Rahman

Lutfi, a farmer and secretary of the opposition Labour Party in Mallawi, Upper Egypt, was arrested, together with lawyer 'Ala' al-Din Higazi. They were initially held in a police station in Mallawi. 'Ala' al-Din Higazi was released a week later, but 'Abd al-Rahman Lutfi was transferred to al-Wadi al-Gadid Prison in the desert in the southwest of Egypt. He remained held without charge or trial until 11 May, when he was released after staging a hunger strike to protest against his detention. In March, 29 members of a sect (who believed Egypt would suffer massive floods but that they would be rescued because of their beliefs) were arrested in a flat in Cairo. Seven women were released the same day, but the other members, including the leader Baha' al-Din Ahmad Hussain al-'Aqqad, remained held without charge or trial until their release in May. More than 100 alleged members of the Muslim Brothers were arrested in separate incidents and many were detained for several months. At the end of the year at least 42 were still held in detention.

Although thousands of administrative detainees were released during the year, thousands of suspected members or sympathizers of banned Islamist groups, including possible prisoners of conscience, were still held without charge or trial under emergency legislation following their arrest in previous years. Among them were dozens of lawyers (see *Amnesty International Reports 1997* and *1998*). Others had been acquitted by military or (Emergency) Supreme State Security courts but remained in detention. 'Abd al-Mun'im Gamal al-Din 'Abd al-Mun'im, acquitted in 1993 (see previous *Amnesty International Reports*), remained held at the end of the year. In May he started a hunger strike to protest against his almost five-year illegal detention in al-Wadi al-Gadid Prison. He had already been suffering from poor health, including kidney problems and asthma, as a result of appalling prison conditions. When relatives visited him on 2 June he had to be carried by two prison guards to the visiting area, and could neither speak nor move. In July he ended his hunger strike and was transferred to Tora Penitentiary hospital. His health was said to have improved by the end of the year. Three lawyers, al-Shazli 'Obeid al-Saghier, Radhwan al-Tuni and Mostafa al-Sayyid (see *Amnesty Interna-*

tional Report 1998), remained held at the end of the year despite their acquittal by the Supreme Military Court on 1 February. A fourth, Khalaf 'Abd al-Ra'uf, was sentenced by the same court in the same case to five years' imprisonment.

At the beginning of the year several trials of alleged members of armed Islamist groups before military and (Emergency) Supreme State Security courts, which started in 1997 or previously, were completed. Proceedings before military courts continued to be grossly unfair (see previous *Amnesty International Reports*). For example, on 1 February the Supreme Military Court in Cairo gave its verdict in the case of 65 alleged members of *al-Gama'a al-Islamiya*, Islamic Group. The trial had begun in November 1997 and defendants were charged with, among other things, membership of an illegal secret organization, plotting to kill government officials and a civilian judge, possession of weapons, and forging documents. Two men, Gamal Mohammad Mostafa Abu Rawwash, a medical doctor, and Taha 'Abd al-Razeq 'Abd al-Maqsud, a student, were sentenced to death and in November were executed. One man was sentenced to life imprisonment with hard labour and 30 other defendants received prison terms ranging from 15 years with hard labour to three years. Thirty-two were acquitted. Defendants were denied adequate time to prepare their defence and had no right of appeal to a higher court. Before trial, they were held in prolonged incommunicado detention and many were reportedly tortured to extract confessions.

Torture of political prisoners continued to be systematic in the headquarters of the SSI in Lazoghly Square in Cairo, SSI branches elsewhere in the country, police stations and sometimes in prisons. The government continued to fail to implement the 1996 recommendations of the UN Committee against Torture. The most common torture methods reported were electric shocks, beatings, suspension by the wrists or ankles, burning with cigarettes, and various forms of psychological torture, including death threats and threats of rape or sexual abuse of the detainee or female relatives. In October the Alexandria Criminal Court decided to refer 13 police officers to the public prosecutor to investigate their involvement in torturing Muhammad Badr al-Din Isma'il in 1996.

156

In January Mohammad Hussein Mohammad Ibrahim Sallam, an Egyptian Muslim who had converted to Christianity a number of years previously, was arrested at Cairo Airport and detained for four days in the Giza branch of the SSI. He was allegedly punched and kicked while blindfolded, and threatened with rape. He was also threatened with being forced to divorce his wife, a United Kingdom national. He had been detained without trial from October 1990 to July 1991 and reportedly tortured because of his conversion to Christianity (see *Amnesty International Reports 1991* and *1992*).

In April Wahid Ahmad 'Abdallah died reportedly as a result of torture in the SSI building in Belqas, north of Cairo. He was reportedly whipped and beaten for several hours, had his fingernails pulled out and was given electric shocks, including to his genitals, ears and tongue. His body was taken by members of the security forces to his family. However, the family took the body back to the SSI building and requested an official report of the incident. An investigation was said to have been carried out by the office of the local prosecutor in Belqas, but no findings were released by the end of the year. In August Samir Shahhata Ramadhan died in Nezbet al-Nefla police station reportedly after he was tortured for several hours.

In August and September security forces reportedly tortured at least 20 villagers, including children, in the course of a murder investigation in the predominantly Coptic Christian village of al-Kushh, Upper Egypt. Several of the victims filed a complaint with the authorities.

Thousands of detainees continued to be held in prisons where conditions amounted to cruel, inhuman or degrading treatment. Political detainees and prisoners in several prisons were reportedly denied adequate medical care which led to several deaths. For example, in September Mahmoud Nour al-Din Sulayman, the head of the armed political group *Thawrat Misr* (Egypt's Revolution), who had been jailed since 1987 in connection with a series of anti-Israeli attacks, died in Tora Penitentiary hospital. He had been suffering for some years from kidney and liver problems and was reportedly denied specialized medical treatment outside the prison hospital. Scores of Islamists in administrative detention were reportedly suffering from various illnesses, including tuberculosis, skin diseases and paralysis, which were common because of lack of hygiene and medical care, overcrowding and poor quality food.

Several people who reportedly "disappeared" after arrest in previous years remained unaccounted for. No new information came to light regarding the "disappearance" of Nabil Mohammad 'Ali Hassan al-Battugi and Sayyid 'Ali Ibrahim (see *Amnesty International Report 1998*).

The death penalty was widely used during the year. At least 73 people were sentenced to death. Two of them were civilians sentenced in February by the Supreme Military Court after a grossly unfair trial and executed in November, and three others, including one *in absentia*, were sentenced by (Emergency) Supreme State Security Courts, which allow no appeal. At least 58 men and eight women were sentenced to death for murder by criminal courts. One man was sentenced to death for kidnapping and raping a woman and another for drug trafficking.

At least seven women and 41 men were executed. Four of them were executed by hanging in Cairo's Isti'naf Prison in February. They had been sentenced to death by the Supreme Military Court in Cairo in September 1997 in a case involving 97 alleged members of *al-Gama'a al-Islamiya* (see *Amnesty International Report 1998*). One man who had been sentenced to death by the Supreme Military Court in October 1997 was executed in November. Death sentences passed by military courts are subject only to review by the Military Appeals Bureau, a body composed of military judges which is not a court, and ratification by the President. To Amnesty International's knowledge all death sentences passed by military courts since 1992 have been confirmed by the Bureau and ratified by the President.

Armed political groups committed grave human rights abuses, including deliberate and arbitrary killings of civilians. At least nine unarmed civilians were killed during the year by armed men believed to be members of *al-Gama'a al-Islamiya*. In August, for example, three Coptic Christian brothers were shot dead outside their house in Samalut in Minya Governorate by three gunmen who were believed to be members of *al-Gama'a al-Islamiya*.

Dr Nasr Hamed Abu-Zeid remained under threat of death from *al-Gihad*, Holy Struggle (see previous *Amnesty International Reports*). He and his wife, Dr Ibtihal Younis, continued to live abroad fearing for their safety if they returned home.

Amnesty International appealed to the authorities to release immediately and unconditionally prisoners of conscience and criticized the long-term detention without charge or trial of political detainees. The organization called for political prisoners to be given fair trials and for an end to trials of civilians before military courts. It also called for the immediate implementation of safeguards to stop torture and ill-treatment of detainees and for executions to be halted.

In September Amnesty International published a report, *Egypt: Human rights abuses by armed groups*, which detailed abuses, including deliberate killings of civilians, committed in recent years by the two main armed political groups in the country, *al-Gama'a al-Islamiya* and *al-Gihad*.

EL SALVADOR

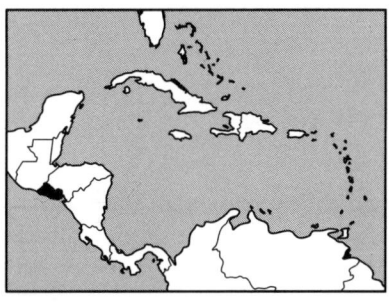

Several people reportedly died as a result of torture by members of security forces. Members of the judiciary involved in investigating human rights violations continued to receive death threats.

In April the Constitutional Division of the Supreme Court of Justice declared admissible an appeal, submitted in December 1997 by a private citizen, to declare unconstitutional the General Amnesty Law for the Consolidation of Peace. The law, which was approved by the government in March 1993, provided protection from prosecution for all those responsible for carrying out or covering up human rights abuses during the civil war, including judicial officials (see *Amnesty International Report 1994*). The Supreme Court had not issued a decision by the end of the year.

The term of office of Dr Victoria Marina Velásquez de Avilés, National Human Rights Procurator, ended in March. However, her successor, Eduardo Peñate Polanco, was not appointed until July after protracted discussions in the Legislative Assembly and deep disagreements on the appointment.

The Penal Code and Procedural Penal Code finally came into force in April; they had been expected to become operative in January but the Supreme Court of Justice, the Ministry of Justice and the Attorney General's office had requested a delay in late 1997 which was approved by the Legislative Assembly in January. Further reforms to the codes were pending at the end of the year.

In July President Armando Calderón Sol called on the Legislative Assembly to ratify the motion approved in October 1996 by the previous Assembly to reinstate the death penalty for rape, kidnapping and aggravated homicide. The Legislative Assembly had not responded to the call by the end of the year.

Several people died in custody reportedly as a result of torture by police. For example, Juan Carlos Presa Henríquez was arrested by members of the Metropolitan Police Force of Santa Ana at a fair celebrating the local patron saint's feast day in July. He was allegedly beaten in the vehicle while being transferred to the police station, and suffered multiple injuries, especially to the head, which caused his death. Twelve police agents were arrested, but in October the Third Magistrates Court in Santa Ana decided that there was sufficient evidence to prosecute only one agent for murder. A second agent was charged with a lesser offence. The trials of both agents were pending at the end of the year.

In September there were reports of the emergence of a new clandestine vigilante group calling itself *"Chicos Buenos"* ("Good Guys"). There was concern that the group's activities were reminiscent of previous groups, such as the *Sombra Negra* (Black Shadow), which functioned as "death squads" and were responsible for "social cleansing" in the mid-1990s;

158

some of those groups had been connected to the security forces. The "*Chicos Buenos*" issued public statements making death threats against alleged criminals and were suspected of being responsible for the deaths of five people found with their throats slit in early September in Santa Ana. By the end of the year, the authorities had reportedly neither commented on nor investigated the alleged involvement of this group in the murders.

Death threats against and harassment of members of the judiciary led Alirio Ernesto Orantes, a judge in Santiago Nonualco, Department of La Paz, to leave El Salvador in September. He had been involved in initial inquiries into the murder of a journalist in 1997. In the course of his work he had carried out searches of premises belonging to the *Policía Nacional Civil* (PNC), National Civil Police. He was subsequently subjected to threatening telephone calls, surveillance by the PNC, and harassment at his home. Another judge acting in the same case allegedly also received threats.

In October further judicial proceedings began against those accused of the killing in 1996 of Francisco Antonio Manzanares Monjaraz, a member of the *Frente Farabundo Martí de Liberación Nacional*, Farabundo Marti National Liberation Front (see *Amnesty International Reports 1997* and *1998*). The defendants were four members of the *División de Investigación*, Criminal Investigation Division, of the PNC. The final stage of the case was scheduled to take place in 1999.

Amnesty International called on members of the Legislative Assembly not to ratify the reinstatement of the death penalty.

EQUATORIAL GUINEA

Scores of members of the Bubi ethnic minority were arrested; many appeared to be prisoners of conscience. Fifteen were sentenced to death and some 70 others to between six and 26 years' imprisonment after grossly unfair trials. Peaceful political opponents of the government were detained without charge or trial and at least three were sentenced to prison terms. There were many reports of torture and ill-treatment. Prison conditions were harsh.

In April the UN Commission on Human Rights examined the report of the UN Special Rapporteur on Equatorial Guinea who had visited the country one month earlier. The Commission called on the government to implement the recommendations made by the Special Rapporteur, including those designed to put an end to arbitrary arrests and torture.

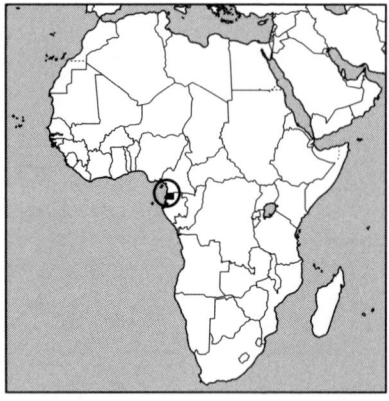

In January a group of Bubis, members of the indigenous ethnic group of Bioko Island, launched several attacks on military barracks in which three soldiers and several civilians were killed.

In a series of reprisal attacks on Bubi villages, hundreds of people were detained by the security forces and tortured (see below). Many appeared to be detained solely on account of their ethnic origin and appeared to be prisoners of conscience.

In May more than 110 people accused of involvement in the attacks on the barracks were tried in a five-day summary military trial that fell far short of international standards for fair trial. Fifteen people were sentenced to death, four *in absentia*, and some 70 others received sentences ranging from six to 26 years' imprisonment. The others were acquitted. In September President Teodoro Obiang Nguema Mbasogo commuted the 15 death sentences to life imprisonment.

Prisoner of conscience José Oló Obono, a lawyer who publicly denounced during the May trial the torture of detainees, was arrested at home in July. In September he was sentenced to five months' imprisonment for insulting the government, despite the fact that the prosecutor had withdrawn the accusations because of lack of evidence. José Oló Obono appeared to have been convicted solely because of his stance during the May trial.

Peaceful political opponents of the government were detained for short periods and tortured or ill-treated, apparently in order to force them to pay heavy fines or to join the ruling *Partido Democrático de Guinea Ecuatorial*, Democratic Party of Equatorial Guinea. Most appeared to be prisoners of conscience.

Two members of the *Fuerza Demócrata Republicana*, Republican Democratic Force, an opposition party which had not been legalized, continued to be held at the end of the year. They appeared to be prisoners of conscience. In August Felipe Ondó Obiang and Guillermo Nguema Ela were sentenced to two years and six months' imprisonment on charges such as making false accusations against the government. Both had been arrested in Gabon in November 1997 and transferred the same day to Malabo, the capital of Equatorial Guinea, in President Obiang's presidential plane (see *Amnesty International Report 1998*).

Many of the Bubis arrested after the attack on the military barracks were tortured in order to extract confessions. According to reports, some were forced to make statements while they were suspended between two tables with a metal bar between their bent elbows and knees. Others were interrogated while they were hung from the ceiling with their hands and feet bound together. Some were also tortured at the time of their arrest in reprisal for the attacks. Many were beaten with rifles, kicked and punched and some had part of their ears severed with razor blades and bayonets. Bubi women were also publicly humiliated in the courtyard of the police station in Malabo. Some were forced to swim naked in the mud in front of other detainees and others were sexually abused. At least six detainees died reportedly after torture.

The eleven prisoners under sentence of death who were in custody were kept in appalling conditions. They were not allowed to speak to anyone and could only leave their cells for a few minutes each day. For weeks they were in serious danger of dehydration and starvation as they were not allowed to receive food from their family and prison food was inadequate. On the day they were sentenced, a firing squad was already waiting to shoot them on a beach near the prison and their graves had been prepared. At the very last minute, the President suspended the executions. After the commutation of their death sentences, they continued to be held in incommunicado detention in harsh conditions.

Several other detainees were suffering ill health as a result of harsh prison conditions. In July Martin Puye, one of the leaders of the *Movimiento para la Autodeterminación de la Isla de Bioko*, Movement of the Self-determination of Bioko Island, died as a result of inadequate medical care. The prison authorities were reportedly reluctant to allow other detainees to be treated in hospital.

In May an Amnesty International delegation observed the trial of those alleged to have attacked the military bases. The delegation concluded that the trial did not meet international standards for fair trial. Amnesty International appealed for the commutation of the death sentences and called on the authorities to make immediate and substantial improvements to the conditions in which all the prisoners were being held. The organization urged the authorities to ensure detainees had enough food and water and access to professional medical treatment when needed.

ERITREA

Scores of political prisoners were reportedly detained without charge or trial. A prisoner of conscience was released. Some 120 officials in the former Ethiopian administration convicted of human rights violations were serving prison sentences imposed after unfair trials. There were allegations that some Ethiopian citizens were detained and ill-treated. The fate of several people who "disappeared" in previous years remained unresolved. Some civilians were reportedly killed unlawfully by both government forces and an armed opposition group.

In May war broke out between Eritrea and Ethiopia after Eritrean troops occupied an area claimed by Eritrea. Eritrean air strikes against Ethiopia in June killed 48 people, including children, in a school and in other civilian areas in Mekelle and Adigrat towns in Ethiopia's Tigray region.

160

An Ethiopian air attack on Asmara airport killed one person. Further air strikes by both sides were quickly suspended and there was little further fighting until November, when shelling resumed in contested border areas where Eritrea had mobilized troops and national service conscripts. Several hundred soldiers on each side were reportedly killed during fighting in June and a large number of others taken prisoner. More than 40,000 men, women and children of Eritrean origin, most of them Ethiopian citizens, were deported from Ethiopia to Eritrea in harsh conditions (see **Ethiopia** entry).

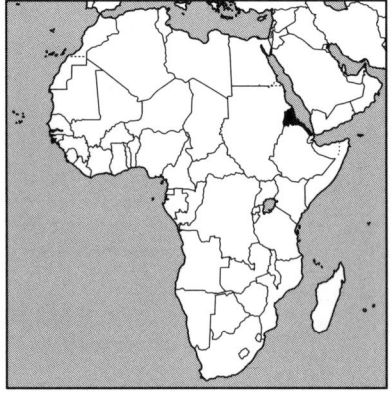

In September the Eritrean government allowed the International Committee of the Red Cross (ICRC) to open an office in Eritrea. The government released 70 prisoners of war and returned them to Ethiopia, but had not allowed the ICRC access to remaining prisoners of war by the end of the year. Over 100,000 civilians were displaced in the border areas. International mediation in the conflict, led by the Organization of African Unity, a UN Special Envoy and US government envoys, was still continuing at the end of the year.

The government of President Issayas Afewerki and the ruling People's Front for Democracy and Justice, the only permitted party, faced armed opposition within the country from the Eritrean Islamic *Jihad* Movement, which was renamed the Islamic Salvation Movement during the year, and from the Eritrean Liberation Front faction led by Abdallah Idris. Both groups were based in Sudan.

In November Eritrea handed back to Yemen the Red Sea Hanish islands, which it had occupied in 1995, after accepting the findings of an international arbitration tribunal.

By the end of the year Eritrea was the only African country not to have ratified the African Charter on Human and Peoples' Rights.

Prisoner of conscience Ruth Simon, an Eritrean journalist detained without charge or trial since April 1997, was released in December (see *Amnesty International Report 1998*).

Scores of suspected supporters of armed opposition groups, including some who had been arrested in previous years, were allegedly detained without charge or trial and held in secret places of detention, although these reports were difficult to confirm.

Some 120 officials of the previous Ethiopian administration detained since Eritrea gained independence in 1991, remained in prison. They were serving prison sentences imposed for crimes against humanity after secret trials which fell short of international standards. They were tried without legal representation and were denied the right to appeal against their convictions or sentences.

There were allegations that the Eritrean authorities arbitrarily detained, ill-treated and forcibly deported tens of thousands of Ethiopian citizens. The allegations could not be substantiated, but at least 22,000 Ethiopians returned to Ethiopia, most after losing their jobs or becoming destitute as a result of the hostilities. However, there appeared to have been some cases of arbitrary detention and ill-treatment during the first few weeks of the conflict, and some leaders of the Ethiopian community in Assab were reportedly still held without charge or trial at the end of the year.

The fate or whereabouts of several political opponents of the government who "disappeared" in previous years remained unknown (see previous *Amnesty International Reports*).

Some civilians were allegedly killed unlawfully by both government forces and members of the Eritrean Islamic *Jihad* Movement.

Following the outbreak of war with Ethiopia in May, Amnesty International appealed to the Eritrean government to respect the Geneva Conventions, not to target civilians, and to allow the ICRC access to prisoners of war. It also investigated the allegations of arrests, ill-treatment and deportation of Ethiopian nationals. At the end of the year an Amnesty International delegation was preparing to visit Eritrea to examine human rights issues in the conflict with Ethiopia.

Amnesty International called for all detained political opponents to be promptly and fairly tried and for Ruth Simon to be freed. The organization also repeated its calls for an independent inquiry into "disappearances" of political prisoners in 1991 and 1992 and raised concerns about allegations of mass arrests, ill-treatment and deportation of Ethiopian nationals.

ETHIOPIA

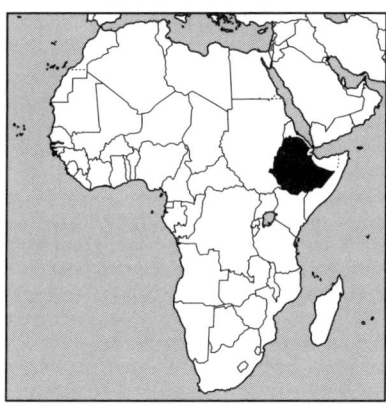

Thousands of critics and suspected opponents of the government were arrested, including prisoners of conscience. Some were tried, but most were detained without charge or trial. They included 1,200 people of Eritrean origin. More than 40,000 other Eritreans were briefly detained and then deported to Eritrea. More than 10,000 political prisoners arrested in earlier years remained in detention, most without charge or trial. The trial for genocide of 46 former government leaders continued for a fourth year, while more than 2,000 other former government and party officials, most held since 1991, appeared in court for the first time. Reports of torture continued. Eritrean deportees were ill-treated. Prison conditions were harsh. "Disappearances" and extrajudicial executions continued to be reported. Several death sentences were imposed. One execution took place – the first since 1991.

War broke out between Ethiopia and **161** Eritrea on 6 May over a border dispute. Air strikes by both sides were suspended after Eritrean air attacks in June killed 48 people, including children, in a school and in other civilian areas of Mekelle and Adigrat towns in Tigray in northern Ethiopia. An Ethiopian air attack on Eritrea's Asmara airport killed one person. Several hundred soldiers on each side were reportedly killed in June. Many others taken prisoner were reportedly allowed access to the International Committee of the Red Cross. Towards the end of the year there was renewed shelling around the contested areas and near Adigrat town. More than 200,000 civilians were displaced in northern border areas. International mediation in the conflict, led by the Organization of African Unity (OAU), a UN Special Envoy and US government envoys, had not achieved a peace agreement by the end of the year. More than 40,000 Eritreans, most of whom were Ethiopian citizens, were deported to Eritrea. Thousands of Ethiopian citizens in Eritrea lost their jobs as a result of the hostilities and had to return destitute to Ethiopia (see **Eritrea** entry).

The internal armed conflict between the government of Prime Minister Meles Zenawi and the Oromo Liberation Front (OLF) continued in the Oromo region; in the Somali region and at least three other regions there was armed opposition from the Ogaden National Liberation Front (ONLF) and the Ethiopian Unity Front. There were major intercommunal disturbances in July in the south between the Gedeo and Oromo-Guji peoples; 3,000 people were reportedly killed.

In early May Ethiopia called an international conference to consider the establishment of a national human rights commission and an ombudsman's office. The conference, attended by many international experts as well as hundreds of Ethiopian government officials, affirmed the need for the commission to be independent and impartial. Laws to establish it were still being drafted at the end of the year.

In June Ethiopia acceded to the African Charter on Human and Peoples' Rights.

Thousands of critics and opponents of the government were arrested, including prisoners of conscience. Some 20 journalists were arrested under the 1993 Press

162

Law and held without trial for publishing articles critical of the government. In January Anteneh Merid and Taye Belachew were among four journalists and six staff members of the newspaper *Tobia* who were arrested after *Tobia* published a security plan for UN staff in Addis Ababa. The government alleged they were inciting violence and detained them without charge for seven months. Kifle Mulat, an official of the Ethiopian Free Press Journalists Association, was arrested in February after publishing a list of detained journalists and held without charge for two months. Alemayehu Kifle of the newspaper *Zegabi* was arrested in May after publishing an article criticizing harsh prison conditions and held for several months. By the end of the year 17 journalists remained in prison, including seven who had been arrested in 1997 but who had not yet been tried.

There were further arrests in January of members of the Oromo ethnic group (or "nationality"). Several were among 31 people charged with armed conspiracy and involvement with the OLF. The 31 included seven members of the Human Rights League and two journalists detained in late 1997, who were prisoners of conscience (see *Amnesty International Report 1998*). Scores more Oromos were arrested in February in Addis Ababa and other towns, including folk-singers Mohamed Sheka and Muktar Usman, students, civil servants and journalists. Most were released without charge after a few weeks. However, 34 Oromos arrested in March, including Gizaw Irana, a doctor, and Zawditu Deressa, a nurse, were charged with armed conspiracy and brought into the trial of the 31. At the end of the year, the trial of the new total of 65 defendants was still at the preliminary stage. Many other people suspected of having links with the OLF were arrested, all of whom were detained without charge or trial.

Six Oromo refugees deported from Djibouti in January were arrested when they were handed over to Ethiopian police. Ali Omar, a refugee community leader, was released in mid-1998; others, including Sheikh Mussa Hassan Abdi, were believed to be still detained without charge or trial at the end of the year. These hand-overs were part of a security arrangement between Ethiopia and Djibouti, which in

May led to Ethiopia handing over two Djibouti opposition members to the Djibouti authorities who arrested them and charged them with armed conspiracy (see **Djibouti** entry).

In January, 1,500 Sudanese refugees were arrested in Addis Ababa and forcibly sent to rural refugee camps. One was shot dead by police during non-violent resistance to the move.

In June Ethiopia began mass arrests and deportations to Eritrea of men, women and children of full or part Eritrean origin, most of whom had been born in Ethiopia or had worked there as citizens prior to Eritrea achieving independence from Ethiopia in 1991. More than 40 UN and OAU staff, as well as Eritreans of foreign nationality and people of mixed Ethiopian/Eritrean parentage, were also deported, and Eritreans abroad had their Ethiopian citizenship withdrawn. Among the first to be deported was 87-year-old Gebre-Tensai Tedla. Ethiopia claimed that they were no longer Ethiopian citizens and said that they were a threat to national security. They and their families were deported to Eritrea without any formal or judicial process or opportunity to challenge their deportations. They were not allowed to take their property with them. By the end of the year more than 40,000 people had been deported in harsh conditions. Large numbers of Eritreans were also detained on suspicion of espionage. Some 1,200, mostly young men, were detained without charge or trial in the remote Bilate military camp near Awasa at the end of the year. Eighty-five Eritrean students on an exchange scheme studying at Addis Ababa University were detained, of whom 38 remained in detention without charge or trial at the end of the year.

Three officials of the independent Ethiopian Teachers Association (ETA), Shimelis Zewde, Abate Angore and Aworke Mulugeta, were arrested in Addis Ababa in September and held for almost a month without charge, in a further attempt by the government to close down the ETA for criticizing government policies.

Scores of ethnic Somalis suspected of involvement with armed opposition groups, such as the ONLF, were arrested in the Somali region throughout the year and detained without charge or trial. They included several members of the Ogaden

Women's Democratic Association, including Korad Ahmed Suhal, who were arrested in January on suspicion of being ONLF members. They remained in detention at the end of the year. Yusuf Hirsi Olow, an ONLF member deported from Djibouti in 1996 (see previous *Amnesty International Reports*), died in prison. He had reportedly been denied medical treatment after he was tortured.

Some political prisoners detained in previous years were released without being put on trial. They included Mengesha Dogoma, a politician from the south held since 1992, Mohamoud Muhumed Hashi of the Ogaden Welfare Society detained in 1996, and at least five journalists held since 1997.

More than 10,000 political detainees held since 1996 or earlier on account of their opposition to the government, some possibly prisoners of conscience, remained in detention. Few of them had been charged or tried.

Four long-running political trials continued with numerous lengthy adjournments. In the trials of 32 people, including Asrat Woldeyes, a prominent doctor and chairperson of the All-Amhara People's Organization, and of six people, including Taye Woldesemayat, an academic and ETA chairperson (see *Amnesty International Reports 1997* and *1998*) more witnesses testified that the defendants had been tortured to make false statements but the judges refused to open investigations into these claims. Asrat Woldeyes, imprisoned since 1994, was allowed to go abroad in December for urgent medical treatment. There were further repeated adjournments of the trials of six remaining defendants in the Anwar mosque case of 1995 and of 65 remaining defendants in a trial of OLF fighters held since 1992 (see *Amnesty International Report 1998*). Other defendants had been provisionally released.

In the ongoing trial of 46 members of the former military government (the *Dergue*) for genocide and other offences, which began in 1994, the prosecution presented a further 150 witnesses, bringing the total number to 550 so far. Preliminary proceedings were opened against some of the 2,246 other officials detained; most had been held since 1991.

Torture of political prisoners continued to be reported. The police deportations of more than 40,000 Eritrean men, women and children amounted to ill-treatment. Families were split up with men deported first and their wives and children deported separately later. They were held in harsh conditions before being forced to board buses under armed guard for a three-day journey with little water or food and no treatment for the sick. They were then dumped at the border with Eritrea and forced to walk long distances to reach safety.

Prison conditions were harsh and medical treatment was often delayed or denied. Abay Haile, editor of the newspaper *Agere*, who had been held without trial for two years, died in prison in February after inadequate medical treatment. Asrat Woldeyes (see above) was belatedly admitted to hospital in January after a mild stroke in prison. His health deteriorated seriously in December and he was finally allowed to go abroad for medical treatment not available in Ethiopia.

There were renewed reports of "disappearances" of suspected government opponents who were believed to be held in secret detention centres where they were at risk of torture or extrajudicial execution. Those reported as having "disappeared" in previous years were feared to have been extrajudicially executed.

Extrajudicial executions of suspected supporters of various armed opposition movements were reported, especially in the conflict zones. One prominent non-violent government opponent, Tesfaye Tadesse, a lawyer and publisher, was killed in Addis Ababa in June, allegedly by members of the security forces.

One execution was carried out – the first since the overthrow of the *Dergue* in 1991. Jamal Yasin Mohamed, an Eritrean businessman, was executed in June in Addis Ababa's Central Prison after losing an appeal against his conviction for the murder of an army general in 1977. Several people were sentenced to death during the year, adding to scores of prisoners who had been sentenced to death in previous years.

Amnesty International pressed for the release of prisoners of conscience, and for political prisoners to be tried in accordance with international standards of fair trial. It expressed concern at the slowness of the trials of former *Dergue* government officials. The organization criticized the deportations of Eritreans and campaigned against torture and ill-treatment, "disappearances" and extrajudicial executions. It expressed regret at Ethiopia's first execution since 1991, which seemed to have been politically motivated.

In its April report, *Ethiopia: Journalists in prison – press freedom under attack*, Amnesty International criticized the Press Law and the continuing detention and unfair trial of journalists. In May it published an open letter to participants at the conference on the formation of a national human rights commission and an ombudsman's office, calling for these to be empowered to conduct independent and impartial investigations into human rights violations. Amnesty International was denied an invitation to the human rights commission conference and its researcher on Ethiopia continued to be excluded from the country.

When war with Eritrea broke out in May, Amnesty International appealed to the Ethiopian government to respect the Geneva Conventions and not target civilians. Amnesty International representatives visited Ethiopia in October to examine human rights issues arising from the conflict with Eritrea. In December the organization wrote to the government expressing deep concern at the mass deportation of Eritreans and the ill-treatment of deportees.

FINLAND

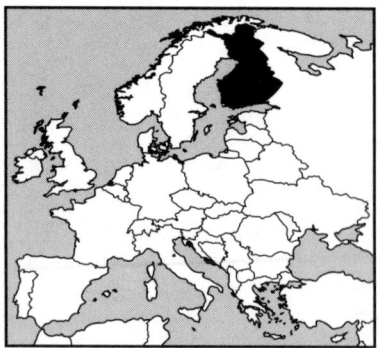

A new law governing alternative civilian service for conscientious objectors came into force which could lead to the imprisonment of prisoners of conscience.

In April the UN Human Rights Committee considered Finland's fourth periodic report on its implementation of the International Covenant on Civil and Political Rights. The Committee welcomed reforms of Finnish criminal procedure which, *inter alia*, ensure more prompt court appearance and trial, but expressed concern that a person charged with certain offences could be tried *in absentia* and sentenced to up to three months' imprisonment. The Committee recommended a review of these procedures.

The Committee was also concerned that asylum-seekers and foreign nationals with irregular status were held in prisons and police detention facilities during investigations into their status. The Committee regretted discrimination against Roma and expressed concern that Jehovah's Witnesses were granted preferential treatment as compared to other conscientious objectors to military service.

In July the new Military Service Act, passed by Parliament in December 1997, came into force. The Act altered the length of military service from 240, 285 and 330 days to 180, 270 and 362 days respectively, depending on rank, type of service and length of contract. The length of alternative civilian service for conscientious objectors to military service remained 395 days, more than double the 180 days served by approximately 50 per cent of army conscripts under the new legislation. This length was accepted by parliament in legislation adopted in December.

Throughout the year Amnesty International urged the government to reduce the length of alternative civilian service so that it was not punitive and did not breach international principles on conscientious objection. Amnesty International stated that it would consider anyone imprisoned for refusing to carry out civilian alternative service of a length considered punitive to be a prisoner of conscience and would call for their immediate release.

In December the government wrote to Amnesty International arguing that the longer period of alternative service was justified because "the leave and leisure time of conscripts serving the shortest period were reduced substantially" and that they would also have to perform between 40 and 100 days' reservist service.

FRANCE

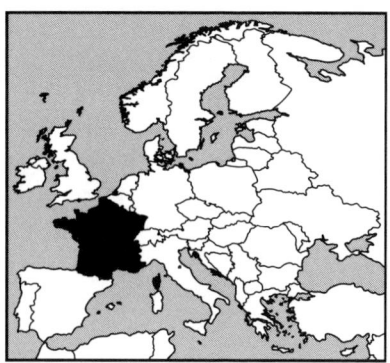

Some political refugees continued to be subject to administrative detention measures. Criminal proceedings were under way against conscientious objectors to the national service laws. A trial of 138 people breached international norms. Reports were received of ill-treatment and excessive use of force by law enforcement officers, and of ill-treatment by prison guards. Some people held for several years under a provisional detention regime were reportedly subjected to prolonged isolation. Criminal proceedings continued against police officers and gendarmes involved in ill-treatment and fatal shootings.

In January, shortly after fatal shootings by police officers of unarmed civilians, a draft law was introduced to create the *Conseil supérieur de la déontologie et de la sécurité* (CSDS) to oversee the working and implementation of codes of practice governing the different police forces and the gendarmerie. The Minister of Justice presented a series of draft laws aiming at a radical overhaul of the justice system. These included measures to confer a greater degree of independence on public prosecutors and to reinforce the principle of presumption of innocence. In May a new law on rights of entry and residence of foreign nationals and on the right of asylum came into force. It was widely criticized as too restrictive, particularly as regards access to asylum procedures.

An agreement on the future status of New Caledonia was signed in May by Prime Minister Lionel Jospin and leaders of the main parties in New Caledonia. The Nouméa agreement established a gradual transfer of power from the French state to the Pacific territory and was endorsed by a November referendum.

The European Committee for the Prevention of Torture and Inhuman or Degrading Treatment or Punishment published a report in May on a visit conducted in 1996 to detention centres in Paris, Marseille and Montpellier. It expressed concern about ill-treatment of suspects immediately after arrest and in police custody and described conditions in parts of Paris-La Santé prison as "inhuman and degrading".

In May the UN Committee against Torture examined France's second periodic report on its implementation of the UN Convention against Torture and Other Cruel, Inhuman or Degrading Treatment or Punishment. The Committee was "seriously" concerned that the police were handing people over to officials of countries where there was a substantial likelihood they would be at risk of torture. It also expressed concern about a number of allegations of ill-treatment of suspects by police forces and the gendarmerie during arrest and interrogation. It recommended that the authorities give "the greatest possible attention" to allegations of violence and ill-treatment by law enforcement officers and to ensuring that judicial inquiries were impartial and punishment appropriate. It stressed that the authorities should also ensure that judicial inquiries into every reasonable allegation of torture and ill-treatment were prompt and systematic.

Measures of administrative detention (*assignation à résidence*) were used against some political refugees. In April Salah Ben Hédi Ben Hassen Karker, a Tunisian political refugee who had been detained under an order of *assignation à résidence* for four years but who faced no criminal charges in France (see *Amnesty International Report 1998*), left Digne, where he was being confined, to see his family in Paris. He was arrested while taking his daughter to school and sentenced to a six-month suspended prison term by the Correctional Court of Pontoise, Val d'Oise, for infringing the detention order. In May the UN Committee against Torture raised the case of Salah Karker's long detention without trial with the French government.

Criminal proceedings were pursued against conscientious objectors failing to

166

conform to the national service laws, but the majority of objectors remained at liberty. A law enacted in 1997 providing for the total suspension of compulsory national service by 2002 (see *Amnesty International Report 1998*) meant that only male citizens born before 1979 remained liable for call-up. There was still no provision for conscientious objection developed during military service and the alternative civilian service available to recognized conscientious objectors remained, at 20 months, twice the length of ordinary military service. Refusal to perform military or alternative service remained punishable by terms of imprisonment.

The right to a fair trial was denied to 138 people in a mass trial that opened in September in a gymnasium for prison staff close to the remand prison of Fleury-Mérogis, Essonne. The defendants, detained during mass arrests in 1994 and 1995, were accused of belonging to support networks for Algerian armed opposition groups and charged with "criminal association... with a terrorist enterprise". Twenty-five were still in custody at the opening of the trial before the 11th Correctional Court of Paris. Another 34 had been released for lack of evidence after spending several weeks or months in provisional detention. A small minority of defendants was accused of trafficking in, or possession of, weapons. Most denied any connection with "terrorist" groups; none was charged with any specific act of violence. On the first day of the trial, about 50 of the defence lawyers refused to continue to appear before the court. Their request for a dismissal of the proceedings and retrial was supported by the Bar Council of Paris and the legal-aid lawyers it represented. The request was based on, among other things, the belief that the large number of defendants, the consequent huge size and expense of the 50,000-page case file, and the restrictions placed on access to the whole case file and on the period of time during which it was available for study, made a proper defence of their individual clients impossible. Judgment was reserved until January 1999.

Reports of ill-treatment by law enforcement officers, and of ill-treatment by prison guards continued to be received. In many cases the victims were of non-European ethnic origin. In January there were reports that eight detainees of North African origin, including three minors, had been severely beaten by seven guards at the prison of Grasse, Alpes-Maritimes, on New Year's Eve. Medical examinations reportedly confirmed the detainees' allegations. Administrative and judicial inquiries were opened and the prison guards were provisionally detained. They were subsequently charged with committing violent acts while in positions of authority, suspended from work, and forbidden from approaching the prison to meet victims or witnesses.

There were a number of allegations of ill-treatment of asylum-seekers and undocumented foreign nationals, some of whom were returned to countries where they faced persecution. In September, three Sri Lankans – Narendran Yogeswaran, Nadarajah Vijeyalalitha and Mylvaganan Arunan – claimed they were kicked, punched, handcuffed and muzzled with tape by French police while being forcibly expelled from France. Nadarajah Vijeyalalitha claimed that the tape was removed from her mouth after an hour, but when she cried out a pillow was pressed over her face and the tape replaced. She said she fainted from pain. An inquiry was initiated but the outcome was not known at the end of the year.

Some prisoners were reportedly held in prolonged isolation. In November Ilich Ramírez Sánchez (known as "Carlos"), who was held in the remand prison of Paris-La Santé, went on hunger strike in protest at his total isolation, allegedly since his arrest in 1994. He had been sentenced to life imprisonment for murder in 1997, but remained under investigation in connection with other alleged crimes. Joëlle Aubron and Nathalie Ménigon – two members of the group *Action directe* (Direct Action) (see *Amnesty International Report 1989*) who were still being provisionally detained at Fleury-Mérogis prison despite having been definitively sentenced to life imprisonment in 1994 – were also reportedly subjected to strict and prolonged isolation. Nathalie Ménigon was reported to be suffering from severe depression and to have suffered a heart attack.

There were new reports of excessive use of force by gendarmes and police officers. In March about 60 Chinese "boat people", who had taken refuge in New

Caledonia in November 1997 and were being held in a military hangar at Tontouta airport in Nouméa, staged a two-day rooftop protest against their imminent expulsion to China. Among them were young children and a baby. The protest came to an end when gendarmes attempted to dislodge them using tear gas, to which the refugees reportedly responded by throwing stones and other projectiles. The gendarmes then opened fire with rubber bullets. Nine refugees were taken to the Gaston Bourret hospital in Nouméa. Two, whose injuries were life-threatening, required intensive surgery. Several hours later the French government suspended deportation of the boat people and ordered their release from the hangar.

In August administrative and judicial inquiries were opened after Eric Benfatima was shot dead in Tarbes, Hautes-Pyrénées, by an off-duty officer of the *Brigade Anticriminalité*, Anti-crime Brigade. Eric Benfatima reportedly approached the officer, who was not in uniform, and asked him for a cigarette. The officer replied that begging was banned in Tarbes. Following an argument, the officer allegedly chased him into an alley and shot him three or four times with a revolver. The officer was provisionally detained and charged with murder.

In December, 17-year-old Habib Ould Mohamed was shot and fatally wounded in disputed circumstances in Toulouse by a police officer who suspected him and his friend of attempted car theft. Habib Mohamed, who was unarmed, managed to stagger away, but was not pursued. His body was later found by a passer-by. The officers on the patrol did not report firing their weapons when they returned to their station, as required by law, and the acting Minister of the Interior stated that "fundamental rules were not respected". It was also unclear why the officers had failed to follow or provide assistance to Habib Mohamed after the shooting. The police sergeant who fired the fatal shot was placed under investigation for manslaughter. Habib Mohamed's death and the subsequent release from detention, under judicial control, of the police sergeant involved provoked a wave of riots in Toulouse.

Judicial inquiries continued into cases of ill-treatment and fatal shootings by gendarmes and police officers in previous years. In April the criminal chamber of the Court of Cassation rejected an appeal by the police officer who shot and killed Todor Bogdanoviç, a Romani child, in 1995. The decision upheld the December 1997 finding of an Aix-en-Provence appeal court that there was sufficient doubt that the officer's action had fulfilled the criteria for "legitimate defence" to justify sending the case for trial before the Court of Assizes of Alpes-Maritimes (see *Amnesty International Reports 1996* and *1998*). The trial opened in December. The prosecutor, who concurred that the officer had fired at the car from behind and had therefore not acted in "legitimate defence", asked the jury to consider only a nominal prison sentence, accompanied by suspension. The Court of Assizes acquitted the officer.

In July the Grenoble Court of Appeal overturned the November 1997 decision of the Correctional Court of Valence to acquit the gendarme who shot dead Franck Moret in 1993 (see *Amnesty International Report 1998*). Sentencing the officer to an 18-month suspended prison term, a small sum of compensation and court costs, the Court held that although the gendarme was entitled under French law to shoot to stop the car, the fatal shot had been fired in a "particularly imprudent and clumsy way from the viewpoint of height and direction". The officer's appeal was pending at the end of the year.

In March the Ministry of the Interior wrote to Amnesty International, confirming the length of time Salah Karker had been detained and the reason for the *assignation à résidence*, but stating that his material conditions were "perfectly satisfactory" and there was no reason to review the situation. The Ministry did not respond to Amnesty International's concerns that Salah Karker had never been charged with a criminal offence in France and had never been given an effective opportunity to be heard by a judicial authority.

In March Amnesty International wrote to the Minister of Justice to request information about the progress of inquiries into the assault by prison staff on inmates at Grasse prison. In November Amnesty International requested information from the Minister of Justice about the alleged prolonged isolation of Ilich Ramírez Sánchez, Joëlle Aubron and Nathalie Ménigon and expressed its belief that prolonged isolation can have a detrimental effect on the physical and mental health of prisoners, in some cases amounting to cruel, inhuman or degrading treatment or punishment. In December Amnesty International wrote to the Minister of Justice to express its concern that the trial of 138 alleged members of Algerian support networks breached international norms governing fair trial. The organization raised the issues of "equality of arms" between defence and prosecution and the length of provisional detention. No replies had been received to any of these letters by the end of the year.

In May Amnesty International submitted to the UN Committee against Torture, and to the French government, a report entitled *France: Excessive force – a summary of Amnesty International's concerns about shootings and ill-treatment*. This described a number of individual cases and underlined the problem of effective impunity in the way they were handled by the courts. It also found that the use of rubber bullets against the Chinese "boat people" in New Caledonia had been disproportionate and excessive.

In December Amnesty International sent an observer to the trial of the police officer who shot dead Todor Bogdanoviç in 1995. The observer stated that the trial resembled the "chronicle of acquittal foretold". The President of the court did not show strict impartiality and the extent of bias displayed by the state prosecutor in support of the defence case was a cause for concern.

The organization sought information from the authorities about the progress of investigations into incidents of shootings, killings and ill-treatment.

Amnesty International continued to express concern that, because of its punitive length, civilian service did not provide an acceptable alternative to military service and that there was still no provision for conscientious objection developed during military service.

GAMBIA

At least 20 prisoners of conscience were held for short periods. At least three prisoners were reportedly tortured. Three military prisoners were sentenced to death. There were no investigations into past human rights violations.

Decrees introduced by Colonel (retired) Yahya Jammeh before the return to civilian rule in 1997 remained in force. One decree banned politicians active in government before the 1994 military coup from political activity, and another granted total immunity from prosecution to those who held power during the period of military rule. The latter decree was invoked to reject a compensation claim by Lamin Waa Juwara, a leading member of the opposition United Democratic Party (UDP), for illegal detention and mental torture (see *Amnesty International Reports 1996* to *1998*). An appeal against the court's verdict was pending at the end of the year. In October, two military detainees were released. They had been held without trial since a failed coup attempt in November 1994. They appeared to be the last detainees who had been arrested during the period of military rule.

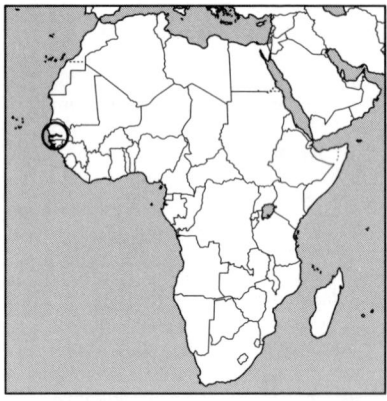

Attacks on freedom of expression and association continued throughout the year. Journalists were tried or detained for short periods (see below) and some journalists from other West African countries were deported or threatened with deportation. All foreign nationals were barred by immigration officials from entering the offices of the *Daily Observer* newspaper in April and May.

In an important ruling in March, the High Court concluded that denying the UDP the right to hold meetings was unconstitutional and discriminatory. However, one month later a UDP rally was disrupted by armed police. A set of sensitization meetings had been approved but, as they had not been completed, the police apparently denied the UDP permission to hold the rally. In May the first UDP national congress went ahead despite the arrest in Brikama of several UDP sympathizers and the brief detention of the party's leader (see below). In July Lamin Waa Juwara was prevented from attending a UDP workshop in Mansakonko by supporters of the ruling Alliance for Patriotic Reorientation and Construction. The government initially attempted to distance itself from the incident, but subsequently explained that the workshop had been intercepted because of evidence that Lamin Waa Juwara was planning an uprising.

At least 20 prisoners of conscience were held for short periods. In May at least 10 prisoners of conscience, including UDP members and the Imam of Brikama, Alhaji Karamo Touray, were arrested in or around Brikama and held incommunicado at the headquarters of the National Intelligence Agency (NIA). They were publicly accused by the Minister of the Interior of destroying a mosque. This allegation referred to attempts to destroy a wall around part of the mosque reportedly built by a youth group – seen as pro-government – to try and prevent the Imam speaking about political issues there. Ousainu Darboe, Secretary General of the UDP, was also held for questioning for several hours. A week later the detainees appeared in court and were charged with conspiracy to commit riot and damage to a building. At least one, Lamin Waa Juwara, had reportedly been tortured in custody. Medical evidence suggested that he still had bruises, several large scars on his torso, a markedly deformed finger and an infected swollen leg some three weeks after his arrest. The government continued to deny the allegations. In June all 10 were granted bail by the Supreme Court. The trial of four of them was continuing at the end of the year.

In February Boubacar Gaye and Ebrima Sillah, of the radio station *Citizen FM*, were arrested, apparently in connection with broadcasts about the NIA and its role in broadcasting information in local languages from the written media. The following day *Citizen FM* was shut down for what the authorities called "irresponsible journalism" and failing to renew its licence. The two men were held for three days, released on bail and then detained again briefly. In late August the court ruled that *Citizen FM* would remain closed and fined the two men for "operating a radio station without licence". An appeal was pending at the end of the year.

In April, seven staff members of the *Daily Observer* newspaper were arrested and detained briefly by the immigration authorities. They were all foreign nationals and were reportedly warned against working for the newspaper. In June a Nigerian freelance journalist with the *Daily Observer*, Sule Musa, was detained and deported from the Gambia.

In August the editor of the *Daily Observer* and Demba Jawo, a reporter and President of the Gambia Press Union, were arrested and held for two days. Their arrests followed the publication of an article, which the government claimed threatened security, about a wall which collapsed at President Yahya Jammeh's residence, revealing military equipment.

Three of those arrested in July 1997 at the time of an armed attack on Kartong military post (see *Amnesty International Report 1998*) were sentenced to death by the High Court. They pleaded not guilty to the charges against them, although one did state that they were intending to steal arms and sell them to Senegal, but not to overthrow the government. At least two of the accused men claimed that they had been tortured. The prosecution produced a so-called independent witness to refute these allegations, but the accused claimed never to have seen the witness previously. No independent investigation into the allegations of torture was carried out. An appeal was pending at the end of the year.

There were no investigations into suspected extrajudicial executions or into allegations of torture and ill-treatment in previous years (see previous *Amnesty International Reports*).

In May Amnesty International asked the government to clarify the reasons for the arrests of the Imam and others in Brikama and to end their incommunicado detention. No response was received.

GEORGIA

Defendants in a major political trial alleged that they had been tortured. There were numerous other reports of torture and ill-treatment in detention. In the disputed region of Abkhazia at least six prisoners of conscience were reportedly held

170

for refusing conscription. Tens of ethnic Georgian civilians were alleged to have been arbitrarily detained, and several others to have been deliberately and arbitrarily killed, by Abkhazian security forces. Around 12 people were under sentence of death in Abkhazia. Some 200,000 ethnic Georgians displaced by the conflict continued to face obstacles to their return.

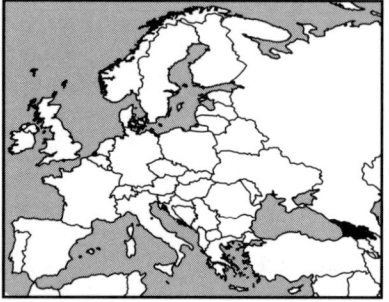

Supporters of former President Zviad Gamsakhurdia were said to have been behind a failed assassination attempt on President Eduard Shevardnadze in February and a short-lived army revolt in October.

May saw the worst fighting in the Gali district of the disputed region of Abkhazia since the end of the war in 1994. Scores of people were reportedly killed and some 30,000 ethnic Georgians fled their homes amid reports that civilians had been attacked by Abkhazian militia or armed Abkhazians operating without the explicit endorsement of the *de facto* Abkhazian authorities but with apparent impunity. Georgian partisan groups continued to claim responsibility for attacks, sometimes fatal, on Abkhazian targets. The Georgian government denied that such groups operated with its tacit support. Members of the peace-keeping force of the Commonwealth of Independent States and of the UN Observer Mission in Georgia were also attacked.

A law establishing a civilian alternative to compulsory military service came into force in January, but had not been implemented by the end of the year.

Allegations of torture emerged during a major political trial when defendants, many of whom had been held since 1995, began giving evidence after the start of proceedings in December 1997. Thirteen of the 15 men on trial for a range of offences, including involvement in an assassination attempt on President Shevardnadze in 1995, alleged that they had been beaten or otherwise ill-treated in pre-trial detention to force confessions. Gocha Gelashvili testified that he had suffered two broken ribs and a broken right arm, naming a former Interior Minister and a Tbilisi police chief as being among those who had tortured him. A court-ordered forensic medical examination of five defendants was carried out at the beginning of the year. Although it recorded certain injuries, including Gocha Gelashvili's fractured arm, it claimed it was unable to confirm the circumstances surrounding the injuries owing, among other things, to the passage of time since the injuries were said to have been sustained. All 15 defendants were convicted when the trial ended in November and received sentences ranging from 38 months' to 15 years' imprisonment.

Numerous other allegations of torture and ill-treatment were made. In March a senior local official reportedly refused to let police intervene as an angry crowd beat a man to death in the western town of Tsalendijikha. Sergo Kvaratskhelia had reportedly been accused of defiling a grave and stealing money and drugs buried with the deceased. He was severely beaten by those who thought him responsible and spent three days in hospital before being abducted by an angry crowd. The local police called for reinforcements, but the head of the district administration allegedly refused to let them intervene as the crowd beat Sergo Kvaratskhelia to death. The heads of the district and regional police forces were also said to have been present. Four people, none of whom were officials said to have been involved, were arrested in connection with the death.

There were allegations of torture and ill-treatment in police custody. In January Gogi Shiukashvili was detained in the Gldani district of the capital, Tbilisi, on suspicion of stealing vehicle wheels. He alleged that he was beaten initially without explanation and then in an attempt to make him say that another person detained was his brother. Gogi Shiukashvili was then transferred to Tbilisi City Police Administration. He alleged that he was then severely beaten with truncheons over a period of 15 days, until he confessed. He was subsequently transferred to investigation prison No. 1 in Tbilisi. He stated that for the first two weeks there he was virtually unable to move because of the beatings, which left him with a broken nose and severe headaches, as witnessed by 18 cellmates.

An arrest warrant was outstanding for a police officer in hiding alleged to have raped a young woman at Marnueli police station in September 1997 (see *Amnesty International Report 1998*). However, unofficial sources reported that investigations into reports of police ill-treatment rarely resulted in prosecution or imprisonment. It emerged that Gela Kavtelishvili, a senior police officer sentenced to four years' imprisonment in May 1997 on charges that included using electric shocks on suspects (see *Amnesty International Report 1998*), had not been imprisoned at that time. He had been at liberty pending various appeals, and had been arrested in October.

In Abkhazia there was no civilian alternative to compulsory military service. At least six prisoners of conscience were reportedly imprisoned for refusing conscription or completion of military service on grounds of conscience. Five, all Jehovah's Witnesses, were detained in April and released in June, although the cases against them continued. The sixth, Adgura Ashuba, was said to have deserted from the Abkhazian armed forces and then, having become a Jehovah's Witness, refused to complete his military service on religious grounds. He was arrested in March and sentenced in May to five years' imprisonment for desertion.

Allegations of arbitrary detention continued, mainly of ethnic Georgians returning to the tense Gali district of Abkhazia. They frequently complained that they were detained after document checks and only released after paying what the Abkhazians regarded as fines, but which the returnees regarded as bribes. There were reportedly no judicial proceedings or receipts. In other incidents in the district, civilians were reportedly held hostage for ransom. In July, for example, eight Abkhazian soldiers were said to have seized four ethnic Georgians – Guram Beselia, Eter Khuperia, Rezo Kvaraia and Oler Sakheishvili – and a Russian from the village of Orsantia in the Zugdidi district, on the Georgian side of the Inguri river border. They were reportedly taken to the village of Otobaia on the Abkhazian-held side of the Inguri river and held hostage for ransom. Oler Sakheishvili was reportedly killed and his body sent back with the other men when the money was handed over.

Detention without charge or trial was also alleged by Jehovah's Witnesses in Abkhazia, often accompanied by verbal and physical abuse by Abkhazian police, in conjunction with the break-up of their meetings, or house searches without a warrant. In March Arsen Topchyan, who had arrived from the Russian Federation to visit his parents in the village of Alakhadzy in Abkhazia, was reportedly detained without charge for three days by State Security officers and severely beaten in a cell in the city of Gagra. His parents reportedly obtained his release after paying the large sum of money demanded.

Abkhazia retained the death penalty, although the *de facto* moratorium on executions, in place since 1993, continued. In May officials reported that there were 12 people awaiting execution, including one woman convicted of murder. At least one prisoner was pardoned during the year. Ethnic Georgian Ruzgen Gogokhiya, who had been sentenced to death in 1995 for "terrorist acts" against civilians (see *Amnesty International Report 1996*), was reportedly handed over to Georgian government representatives in July.

Allegations of deliberate and arbitrary killings of ethnic Georgians by Abkhazian forces continued. In June, six residents of Chuburkhinji who had returned to tend their crops were reportedly led at gunpoint by Abkhazian forces to the Inguri river, forced into the water, then fired on. Two men named as Dzandzava and Ubilava were reportedly killed; three others were wounded.

Many of the estimated 200,000 ethnic Georgians displaced by the conflict in Abkhazia continued to face obstacles to their return, apparently on grounds of their ethnicity. After the May fighting, some 1,400 homes were reportedly set on fire, in what was described as widespread and systematic destruction of civilian housing in the Gali district. Houses and villages were also said to have been systematically looted before being burned. As most residents affected fled the swift onset of fighting with few personal effects, the loss of their possessions and crops further hampered their return. In July the UN

172

Security Council demanded that the *de facto* Abkhazian authorities allow the unconditional and immediate return of all those displaced since the resumption of hostilities in May, and condemned "the deliberate destruction of houses by Abkhaz forces, with the apparent motive of expelling people from their home areas".

Amnesty International continued to call for a judicial review of all political cases in which confessions had reportedly been obtained under duress, and for a full, prompt and impartial investigation into all allegations of torture and ill-treatment in custody, with the results made public and the perpetrators brought to justice.

Amnesty International urged the *de facto* Abkhazian authorities to release immediately and unconditionally all those imprisoned solely for refusing military service on grounds of conscience, and to enact legislation creating an alternative civilian service of non-punitive length together with a fair procedure in law for implementing it.

The organization urged the *de facto* Abkhazian authorities to ensure the safety of all residents, regardless of their ethnic origin, by, among other things, ensuring that no one was detained outside legitimate administrative and criminal proceedings, and by instigating prompt, impartial and comprehensive investigations into all instances in which Abkhazian forces were alleged to have deliberately and arbitrarily killed civilians. Amnesty International also urged the *de facto* authorities to take appropriate and timely measures to ensure the voluntary return of refugees and displaced persons under conditions in which their safety, and the safety of those already returned, could be guaranteed.

GERMANY

There were further allegations of ill-treatment of detainees, many of whom were asylum-seekers, by police officers.

A general election in September resulted in a new government headed by Gerhard Schroeder, who replaced Helmut Kohl as Chancellor.

In May the UN Committee against Torture met to consider Germany's second periodic report on its compliance with the UN Convention against Torture and Other Cruel, Inhuman or Degrading Treatment or Punishment. The Committee said that it was concerned at the large number of reports of ill-treatment, mostly in the context of arrest, and at the conclusion of an officially commissioned report that police abuse of foreign nationals was "more than 'just a few isolated cases'." It was also concerned at the "existence of certain open-ended legal provisions permitting under certain circumstances the discretionary but significant reduction of the legal guarantees of those detained by the police, such as provisions permitting the police in certain cases to refuse permission to someone detained at a police station to notify a relative of his arrest". The Committee expressed particular concern at the "apparently low rate of prosecution and conviction in the alleged incidents of ill-treatment by the police, especially of people of foreign descent." The Committee recommended, among other things, that complaints mechanisms be improved; that disciplinary and judicial measures against offending police officers be "significantly strengthened", in particular by permitting victims to participate in criminal prosecutions and improving procedures for civil damages; and that legislation be amended to ensure that in all cases evidence obtained by use of torture was not admissible in court. It also recommended that police and other officials receive compulsory training in human rights, and in conflict management with particular reference to ethnic minorities, and that Germany continue its efforts to ensure that all detainees were given a form outlining their rights in a language they understood at the outset of their custody.

There were further allegations of police ill-treatment of foreign nationals, particularly asylum-seekers, and members of ethnic minorities. A number of asylum-seekers made allegations about police ill-treatment during attempted deportations at Düsseldorf Airport. Khebil L. alleged that he was hit three or four times at the airport and again later on in an office. Frank E., an asylum-seeker from Rwanda, alleged that he was beaten in February or March when he refused to enter the plane. He described his mouth being "disfigured", and his eyes being "covered by blood". In April Ebezina C. reported that a police officer punched and kicked him,

AMNESTY INTERNATIONAL REPORT 1999

and subjected him to verbal abuse. An investigation into the allegations had not been completed by the end of the year.

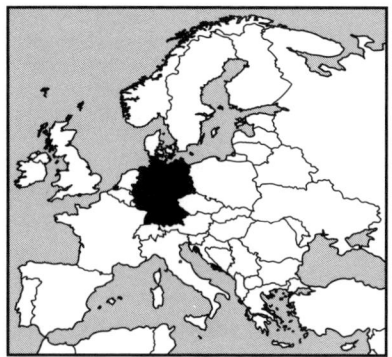

Abdul A. alleged that he was beaten and verbally abused by Bremen police officers in February. He said he was stopped by plainclothes police officers, one of whom pointed a handgun at him, and asked for his identity papers. He was then reportedly verbally abused, kicked and punched before being taken to a nearby police station where he was made to undress and detained in a cell for two hours. Later the same day his doctor certified the following injuries: contusions of both wrists, laceration of the left wrist, bruising in the region of the thorax and ribs, bruising of the face, right knee and thigh, and a sprain of the left shoulder. Several days after lodging a complaint with the Bremen police and prosecuting authorities, Abdul A. was informed that he was under investigation for threatening and insulting officers and for resisting them during the performance of their duty.

In February the retrial took place of the three police officers accused of assaulting Habib J. in 1992 (see *Amnesty International Reports 1994* to *1997*). The officers had been found guilty in 1994, but their convictions had been overturned on appeal in 1995. In July 1996 the Berlin Higher Regional Court had ordered a retrial of the three officers, arguing that the appeal court's findings had been "contradictory and full of holes". In its decision in February, the Court concluded that, although Habib J.'s credibility as a witness was not in doubt, the length of time that had elapsed since the incident had led to lapses of memory on his part and on the part of the other witnesses and

the accused officers, and to contradictions in the evidence presented by all the parties. The Court was unable to establish which version of events was correct and therefore upheld the officers' appeal against their original conviction.

In June an appeal by Algerian asylum-seeker Nasr B. for a judicial review of the prosecuting authorities' decision to reject his complaint of ill-treatment (see *Amnesty International Report 1998*) was rejected by the Supreme Court.

In May Dortmund Regional Court overturned the conviction of a police officer for assaulting Ahmet Delibas, a Turkish national (see *Amnesty International Reports 1997* and *1998*). Ahmet Delibas alleged that police officers had repeatedly punched him in the face in the back of a police car in 1995; medical evidence showed that he had suffered serious injuries to his face. He was subsequently accused of having assaulted one of the officers. In May 1997 one officer was found guilty of negligent assault; a second officer and Ahmet Delibas himself were acquitted. In overturning the lower court's decision, Dortmund Regional Court ruled that the injuries to Ahmet Delibas' face could have occurred when the officer struck him in self-defence after Ahmet Delibas had kicked him in the face at the time of the arrest. Although the officer was found to have hit Ahmet Delibas at least three more times in the upper body and head while the detainee's hands were cuffed behind his back in the police car, the Court ruled that the force which the officer used in order to break the detainee's resistance was justified. Ahmet Delibas was given a six-month suspended sentence for causing the officer serious bodily harm.

In May the authorities rejected Homayoun Ghaleh's complaint of ill-treatment by the police, despite medical evidence substantiating his claim that a Dortmund police officer had hit him on the head with a service radio. An investigation into the complaint filed by the officer involved against Homayoun Ghaleh was discontinued in May (see *Amnesty International Report 1998*).

In May, three Brandenburg police officers were convicted on 12 separate counts of ill-treating Vietnamese detainees in their custody in 1993 and 1994 (see *Amnesty International Reports 1995* and

174

1998). The officers received prison sentences of 10 to 24 months, suspended for three years. According to the findings of Frankfurt an der Oder Regional Court, the officers had punched and kicked detainees and subjected them to humiliating and degrading treatment – in some cases by forcing them to undress before assaulting them. A fourth officer was found guilty of failing to intervene and was fined. In pronouncing judgment, the chairman of Frankfurt an der Oder Regional Court criticized police witnesses for lying in order to protect their colleagues. At least two Vietnamese witnesses had been deported to Vietnam before the trial started. Attempts to bring them back to testify were abandoned after the Federal Ministry of the Interior expressed concern that the two men might use their return to claim asylum.

In September the Federal High Court overturned the 1996 conviction of two police officers for physically coercing and negligently causing actual bodily harm to journalist Oliver Ness while he was reporting on a demonstration in May 1994 (see *Amnesty International Reports 1995 to 1997*). In delivering its decision, the Federal High Court drew attention to the "enormous" delay on the part of the Public Prosecutor's Office, as a result of which the case was not brought to the High Court for two years.

Amnesty International expressed concern to the authorities about allegations of ill-treatment, urging that they be promptly and impartially investigated. The organization also expressed concern about investigations into allegations of ill-treatment in previous years.

In April Amnesty International urged the Berlin authorities to reopen the investigation into Nasr B.'s allegations and to ensure that the prosecuting authorities investigated the case thoroughly, in conformity with international standards.

In May Amnesty International reminded the government of its responsibility for ensuring that deportations of asylum-seekers were carried out in a manner which respected the human rights of the individual being deported. These include the right not to be tortured or ill-treated. Amnesty International called for prompt and impartial investigations into the actions of the officers involved in the deportation attempts that it had documented, and for a full, impartial and independent inquiry into the role and accountability of the Federal Border Police at Düsseldorf Airport. In August the Federal Ministry of the Interior informed Amnesty International that the matter was currently the subject of investigation by a public prosecutor, but that to date there were no indications of ill-treatment by the Federal Border Police.

In December Amnesty International wrote to the authorities seeking further information about aspects of the case of the two police officers whose convictions in the case of Oliver Ness had been overturned.

GHANA

At least eight possible prisoners of conscience remained imprisoned throughout the year. Two journalists were briefly imprisoned by the courts in connection with a civil libel case involving the Head of State's wife.

Protests at the imprisonment in July of two journalists, Kweku Baako and Haruna Atta (see below), highlighted the use of both contempt and criminal libel laws to imprison newspaper editors. Two criminal libel trials proceeded. One was of Ebenezer Quarcoo, former editor of the *Free Press* newspaper, and Tommy Thompson, publisher of the *Free Press* and former prisoner of conscience, who died in September; in 1995 they had been arrested, charged and released after a few days to await trial. The second trial was of Ebenezer Quarcoo, Tommy Thompson and Kofi Coomson, editor-in-chief of the

Ghanaian Chronicle newspaper; they had been arrested in 1996, charged and released on bail after about 10 days. The criminal libel laws provide for up to 10 years' imprisonment for false reporting likely to injure the reputation of the government.

In July the Supreme Court ruled that the Commission for Human Rights and Administrative Justice (CHRAJ) had jurisdiction to investigate government actions before the 1992 Constitution came into force and in cases where statutes of limitations had prevented investigations by the courts. In 1997 the government had sought to stop the CHRAJ from ordering redress in cases of arbitrary dismissal prior to the restoration of civilian rule in 1993.

The Supreme Court also ruled in July that the CHRAJ's powers to review government confiscations of property before the 1992 Constitution came into force did not extend to confiscations authorized by special courts set up by military decree. Such courts, outside the normal judicial system and not independent of government control, included Special Courts set up by the Armed Forces Revolutionary Council in 1979 and Public Tribunals set up by the Provisional National Defence Council in 1982, both military governments led by Flight-Lieutenant (now President) J.J. Rawlings following coups in 1979 and 1981.

The Supreme Court had still given no date for hearing an application made by the CHRAJ in early 1996 to investigate allegations that the government was involved in the killing of five demonstrators by armed government supporters in Accra in May 1995 (see *Amnesty International Report 1998*).

At least eight possible prisoners of conscience arrested in previous years remained imprisoned throughout 1998. Karim Salifu Adam, a member of the opposition New Patriotic Party, was sent for retrial in July 1997 because no judgment had been reached in his treason trial before one of the judges died, although all the evidence had been heard. In February 1998 the Supreme Court rejected a defence application against a retrial. His allegations that he was tortured while in incommunicado and illegal detention after his arrest in May 1994 were not thoroughly and impartially investigated (see previous *Amnesty International Reports*).

No judgment was given in the treason trial which began in 1997 of five possible prisoners of conscience – Sylvester Addai-Dwomoh, Kwame Alexander Ofei, Kwame Ofori-Appiah, Emmanuel Kofi Osei and John Kwadwo Owusu-Boakye (see previous *Amnesty International Reports*). Some of the defendants alleged that they had been beaten and ill-treated to coerce them into making incriminating statements. The High Court trying the case ruled such statements admissible despite evidence, from prosecution witnesses as well as from some of the defendants, that soldiers who later testified for the state and defendants had been beaten following their arrest.

On 23 July the Court of Appeal sentenced two newspaper editors to one month's imprisonment and fined each publisher 10 million cedis (about US$4,350) for contempt of court in connection with a civil libel case brought by the Head of State's wife, Nana Konadu Agyemang-Rawlings. It overturned an earlier High Court ruling that Kweku Baako of *The Guide* and Haruna Atta of *The Statesman* were not in contempt of court. They were alleged to have ignored an earlier court injunction, brought in connection with the civil libel case, not to make any further libellous statement about the complainant. The Chief Justice refused to grant a stay or hear an appeal against the contempt conviction on the grounds that all the other Supreme Court judges had started their three-month holidays.

At least two political prisoners remained in prison; they had been sentenced to death for treason in the mid-1980s after trials by special courts which failed to conform with international standards for fair trial. Former Captain Adjei Edward Ampofo was tried *in absentia* by Public Tribunal in 1983 and former Sergeant Oduro Frimpong was tried *in camera* by Public Tribunal in 1985. Their death sentences were commuted in 1997.

No prisoners were known to have been sentenced to death or executed during the year.

In October an Amnesty International delegation visited Ghana to investigate issues of concern to the organization.

GREECE

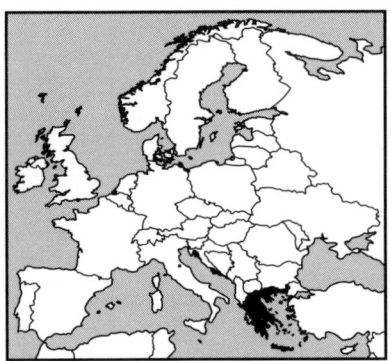

Around 80 conscientious objectors to military service on religious grounds continued to serve prison sentences. All were prisoners of conscience. Legal proceedings continued in the cases of 10 people prosecuted for peacefully exercising their rights to freedom of expression or religion. There were further allegations of ill-treatment and excessive use of force by law enforcement officers.

Law 2510/97 on conscription entered into force in January. Although this law allows for a civilian alternative to military service for the first time, some of its provisions, such as the punitive length of the alternative civilian service, fall short of international standards and recommendations (see *Amnesty International Report 1998*). About 80 conscientious objectors, who had been convicted before the law entered into force, continued to serve prison sentences. All had been released by the end of the year.

In September Parliament adopted the Law on Universal Defence. Under this legislation everyone aged between 18 and 60 not serving in the armed forces is required to complete up to four days' service a year in universal defence units. Pregnant women and mothers with children under the age of 12 are exempt. Although defence units perform a range of functions, units in border areas may be armed in certain circumstances, such as "in cases of war, mobilization or tension or for the purpose of scheduled exercises in peace time". Failure to report for service is punishable by one month's imprisonment and a repeat offence carries a three-month prison sentence.

In September Greece ratified Protocol No 6. to the European Convention for the Protection of Human Rights and Fundamental Freedoms concerning the abolition of the death penalty.

Legal proceedings continued against 10 people prosecuted for peacefully exercising their right to freedom of expression or religion. For example, in February Mehmet Emin Aga was sentenced to a total of 14 months' imprisonment by Lamia Appeal Court for "usurping the function of a Minister of a known religion in Greece". He had been elected by his community as Mufti of Xanthi. However, the Court found that by signing various messages as the "Mufti of Xanthi" he had "deliberately carried out duties which by their nature apply exclusively to the legitimate Mufti, E. Sinikoglou". Mehmet Emin Aga exercised his legal right to request that his prison sentence be converted into a fine, which was granted. In December he was sentenced to a further seven months' imprisonment for the same offence.

Vasilis Romas, Costas Tasopoulos, Petros Vasiliadis and Pavlos Voskopoulos, all members of the ethnic Macedonian minority *Ourania Toxo* (Rainbow) party, were acquitted in September (see *Amnesty International Reports 1997* and *1998*). They had been charged with "causing and inciting mutual hatred among citizens" for displaying a sign bearing the words "Florina Committee" in both Greek and Macedonian in September 1995.

The trial of Traianos Pasois, another member of the Rainbow party, began in March before the Florina Police Court. He was charged with "spreading false information and rumours which could provoke fear and anxiety amongst citizens" for reportedly having crossed the border into Greece from the Former Yugoslav Republic of Macedonia in 1996 carrying two wall calendars which "disputed the Greek character of Macedonia, aiming at its dismemberment, secession and annexation by a neighbouring state then enemy of Greece". He was acquitted in November.

Six members of the *Organosi gia tin Anasingrotisi tou Kommunistikou Kommatos Elladas*, Organization for the Reconstruction of the Communist Party, convicted in 1992 of incitement and illegally posting bills, were acquitted on appeal (see previous *Amnesty International Reports*).

During the year there were further allegations of police ill-treatment, including of members of ethnic minorities.

In May Lazaros Bekos and Lefteris Kotropoulos, two Roma aged 17 and 18 respectively, alleged that they were beaten by police officers during their arrest and interrogation at Mesolongi police station. Lazaros Bekos alleged that a police officer hit him on the back of the head with a gun, pushed him to the ground and stepped on him. He alleged that while in Mesolongi police station he was hit with truncheons and that during his interrogation a police officer put an iron bar under his throat and threatened to choke him if he refused to speak. When he pushed the police officer back, he was beaten on the back with the iron bar and kicked in the neck. Lefteris Kotropoulos also alleged that he was refused permission to telephone his mother to inform her of his whereabouts. A preliminary inquiry into the allegations was ordered by the Ministry of Public Order, but there were fears that pressure was put on the two youths to withdraw their complaint.

There were reports of severe overcrowding in the Drapetsona detention centre in Piraeus. Detainees also reportedly suffered from poor conditions including lack of adequate exercise; insufficient natural daylight; inadequate sanitary facilities; severely limited access to medical treatment; and restricted visits. In August, 12 detainees from outside the European Union (EU), who had either completed their sentences or had never been charged with any offence, alleged that they had been detained for long periods in these conditions pending deportation to their countries of origin.

There were reports of excessive use of force by law enforcement officers. In April Angelos Celal, a Rom, was fatally shot by police near Partheni, Thessaloniki. According to his two friends who survived the shooting, the three men had stopped their car to smoke hashish near a barn where policemen were hidden, deployed on an unrelated affair. As the three men ran back to their car, one of the police officers fired at them. Angelos Celal started to drive the car away, but was shot dead. The two survivors of the shooting claim none of the three men carried a weapon. An investigation into the circumstances surrounding Angelos Celal's death was initiated by the Ministry of Public Order in August. The Prosecutor's office said that three police officers had been charged with offences including manslaughter, attempted murder and illegally carrying and using weapons.

Throughout the year Amnesty International wrote to the authorities raising its concerns about restrictions on the right to freedom of expression. In April the Prime Minister's Office replied stating that the Greek authorities were particularly careful in the enforcement of restrictions to the right to freedom of expression and that these were imposed only in extreme circumstances.

In June Amnesty International expressed concern about the shortcomings of the draft Law on Universal Defence, which does not recognize the right to conscientious objection. In July the organization expressed concern about the practical application of Law 2510/97 after 16 conscientious objectors who had applied for alternative service complained about punitive conditions. No reply had been received by the end of the year.

Throughout the year Amnesty International sought information from the authorities about the progress of investigations into incidents of shootings and ill-treatment by police officers. In August Amnesty International wrote to the authorities requesting detailed information concerning the legal grounds for the continued detention of the 12 non-EU nationals and urging the authorities to take all necessary steps to ensure that conditions in Drapetsona detention centre were improved. No reply had been received by the end of the year.

GUATEMALA

Scores of people were killed in circumstances suggesting they may have been extrajudicially executed, although identification of the perpetrators was often virtually impossible. One prisoner of conscience was held. One prisoner was executed; 37 others were under sentence of death. Threats and harassment continued at a high level. There was little progress in bringing to justice those responsible for past human rights violations. Human rights abuses by the *Unidad Revolucionaria Nacional Guatemalteca* (URNG),

178 Guatemalan National Revolutionary Unity, a political party and former armed opposition group, during the civil conflict remained unclarified.

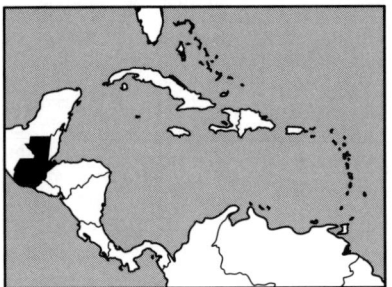

Implementation of the wide-ranging agreements included in the December 1996 Final Peace Accord, which formally ended Guatemala's long-term civil conflict (see *Amnesty International Reports 1997* and *1998*) proceeded slowly. Local human rights monitors expressed disappointment at what they saw as a diminished emphasis on human rights monitoring by the UN Verification Mission for Guatemala (MINUGUA), while government officials criticized MINUGUA for interference in matters outside its mandate. In September the UN extended MINUGUA's mandate to the end of the year 2000.

The Inter-American Commission on Human Rights (IACHR) made its first post-Peace Accord visit to the country in August.

The Historical Clarification Commission (CEH), established under the Peace Accord to clarify "human rights violations and acts of violence... linked to the period of armed conflict", extended its deliberations and was expected to report in January 1999.

In its report following its meeting in May the UN Committee against Torture expressed particular concern at the repeated instances of threats and intimidation directed at those involved in the judicial process and found that persistent inadequacies in the judiciary, the Public Ministry and the police remained major contributory factors to continued impunity in the country.

In the context of rising crime levels, widespread lynchings were reported. In some cases the army, police or other officials were alleged to have initiated the abuses. There were reports of so-called "social cleansing", when indigents, street children or other "undesirables" were reportedly harassed, attacked or murdered by armed individuals or groups. In July, for example, the bodies of two street youths were found in Zone 1 of Guatemala City. One had been slashed to death with machetes by unidentified assailants in the presence of witnesses. The other died of multiple knife wounds, after a similar attack.

Bishop Juan José Gerardi, Bishop of Guatemala and Coordinator of the Human Rights Office of the Archbishop of Guatemala (ODHA), was battered to death by unidentified assailants in April in Guatemala City as he returned home. His murder came just two days after he had presided over the public presentation of the Roman Catholic Church's interdiocesan Recuperation of the Historical Memory Project (REMHI). Bishop Gerardi had been a driving force behind REMHI, which synthesized testimonies collected over three years on the tens of thousands of extrajudicial executions and "disappearances" suffered by civilians, the large majority of whom were indigenous people, during the civil conflict which convulsed Guatemala over a period of more than three decades. REMHI found the army responsible for some 79 per cent of the violations investigated, but also laid a number of past abuses against civilians at the door of the URNG.

The army denied involvement in Bishop Gerardi's murder and the government promised a full inquiry. However, a special joint commission, comprising representatives of both the government and the Archbishopric, soon virtually ceased to function. By the end of the year neither the circumstances nor the perpetrators of the killing had been established. However, local human rights groups believed that the timing of the murder, coupled with irregularities in the investigation process and the government's failure to pursue leads indicating a political motive, strongly suggested that Bishop Gerardi had been extrajudicially executed as a warning to those seeking to identify perpetrators of past abuses. In November a former attorney general who had been contracted by the Church to assess the official inquiries into Bishop Gerardi's murder, concluded that the killing had all the hallmarks of an extrajudicial execution and that the priest arrested for the crime had been wrongly accused.

Public prosecutor Silvia Jérez Romero de Herrera was killed in a volley of gunfire in May while travelling in the countryside. It was believed that the security forces or those acting at their behest may have been responsible. Silvia Jérez Romero de Herrera had been involved in prosecuting the case of guerrilla leader Efraín Bámaca who "disappeared" after being taken into military custody in 1992 (see *Amnesty International Reports 1994 to 1996*), the case was also the subject of examination by the Inter-American Court of Human Rights. Silvia Jérez Romero de Herrera had also been handling a number of investigations into criminal offences, including kidnapping and drug-running, in which it was alleged that officials may have been involved.

In July prisoner of conscience Colonel Otto Noack began serving a 30-day prison sentence for "indiscipline" imposed on him for an interview with *Radio Netherlands* in which he said he believed the army should acknowledge and apologize to the Guatemalan people for atrocities committed during the civil conflict. When the Director of the CEH declared his support for Colonel Noack's stand and visited him in detention, he was criticized by government officials for exceeding his mandate and interfering in Guatemala's internal affairs.

One prisoner was executed; 37 others remained under sentence of death. In February Manuel Martínez Coronado, an indigenous peasant from eastern Guatemala, was executed by lethal injection – the first person to be executed by this method in Guatemala. He had been sentenced to death in 1995 for multiple homicide after a trial which fell short of international standards for fair trial. The victims were members of a family to whom he was related and with whom he had been contesting ownership of a small plot of land sufficient to sustain only one family (see *Amnesty International Report 1998*). The execution went ahead despite a request from the IACHR that the execution be suspended until the IACHR had had time to consider whether the trial proceedings had violated the American Convention on Human Rights. This was the second time that the Guatemalan authorities had ignored such a request from the IACHR. The government also threatened to withdraw from the Convention on the grounds that the requests for such cautionary measures were an interference in national sovereignty. Despite the government's contention that lethal injection would be a more acceptable method of execution because it would "take only 30 seconds" and be painless, Manuel Martínez Coronado took some 18 minutes to die. Following expressions of dismay and revulsion after the public broadcast of his painful and prolonged execution and of the sobbing of his wife and children in an adjoining room, the government announced its intention to introduce legislation to ban journalists from witnessing executions, and declared that henceforth executions would no longer be broadcast.

Victims of threats and harassment included human rights, trade union and indigenous activists, journalists, religious leaders and lawyers, as well as witnesses, relatives and others involved in trying to clarify past human rights abuses. Only moments after the end of Bishop Gerardi's funeral service, Archbishop Próspero Peñados, other members of the clergy, and local human rights activists received telephone death threats. One threatened foreign priest fled abroad, in fear of his life. In July renewed threats were made against ODHA and REMHI workers after delegates from both groups made declarations, during a visit to Europe, protesting at shortcomings in the inquiry into Bishop Gerardi's murder.

In June a colleague of Juan León, a founder member of *Defensoría Maya*, Mayan Defence, was approached by two armed men in the town of Sololá, Sololá department, who told him they intended to kill him, Juan León and several others from *Defensoría Maya*. It was believed that the threats may have been related to *Defensoría Maya*'s efforts to bring former military commissioners, now demobilized, to trial for human rights violations committed during the civil conflict.

Also in June, defence lawyer Víctor Hugo Cano Recinos received a series of threatening telephone calls warning him to withdraw as chief defence counsel for three former policemen sentenced to death in 1996 for murder and attempted murder (see *Amnesty International Report 1998*). The proceedings that led to their convictons fell short of international standards. The three remained under sentence of death at the end of the year.

180

In the same month, members of the women's organization *Mamá Maquín* were assaulted by several men armed with grenades, machetes and firearms as they returned from meeting a returned refugee community in Ixcán, El Quiché department. The same day, members of *Mamá Maquín* in Guatemala City received telephone threats that they would be killed if they did not give up their efforts to ensure the safe return of refugees and the internally displaced and respect for their human rights, as agreed under the Peace Accords. The government's failure to protect members of *Mamá Maquín* and other human rights defenders from attacks or to identify and bring to justice those responsible, violated its undertaking under the 1994 Global Human Rights Accord, to "... take measures to protect persons and institutions working in the field of human rights".

In November Ramiro Contreras, a former prosecutor with the Public Prosecutor's Office, went into exile after receiving death threats. In October he had been assigned to the inquiry into the 1995 Xamán massacre in which 11 returned refugees, including children, were killed by soldiers in Alta Verapaz department (see *Amnesty International Reports 1996* to *1998*). In a press conference prior to his departure, Ramiro Contreras stated that his efforts to advance the inquiry had received no support from the Public Ministry and that in fact he had been under pressure from top Ministry officials to manipulate evidence in the accused soldiers' favour. Witnesses, lawyers and other officials involved in the Xamán investigation have been subjected to continual threats and harassment; other witnesses have allegedly been bribed to change or withdraw their testimonies.

There was little progress in bringing those responsible for past human rights abuses to justice. The case of Juan José Cabrera ("Mincho"), the former opposition commander who "disappeared" after his arrest by the military in 1996 (see *Amnesty International Report 1998*), remained unresolved. Local human rights groups were critical of MINUGUA's announcement in late September that it was turning over investigation of the case to the Public Ministry. MINUGUA had itself stated in its June report that the Public Ministry's investigation of the case had up to that point been inefficient and unproductive.

However, in December, three civil patrollers were sentenced to death for their part in two massacres in 1982. Some 270 non-combatant indigenous peasants died in the massacres in Río Negro, Baja Verapaz department, and in Agua Fría, El Quiché department. This was the first time that anyone had been brought to justice for any of the estimated 400 to 500 massacres which took place in the late 1970s and early 1980s in Guatemala.

The fates of Gisela López and Carlos Ranferí Morales López, who relatives said had been killed in 1982 by the URNG in the context of an internal power struggle, also remained unclarified.

Amnesty International called on the government to ensure that the inquiry into Bishop Gerardi's murder was exhaustive, transparent and public and that its findings were made public. Amnesty International also urged the authorities to implement effective guarantees for the security of all of those involved in human rights defence and the historical clarification process. In June and July the organization co-sponsored a European tour organized by ODHA to present REMHI's findings and to ensure continued international pressure for Bishop Gerardi's killers to be brought to justice.

Amnesty International appealed on a number of occasions for commutation of the death sentence passed on Manuel Martínez Coronado, for medical personnel in Guatemala not to participate in any way in executions, and for the request of the IACHR for cautionary measures to be granted.

In October Amnesty International appealed to US officials to grant visas to two witnesses of the 1982 Dos Erres massacre in which some 350 people were killed – one of 168 cases of human rights violations in Guatemala pending before the IACHR – so that they could give their testimonies before the IACHR in Washington.

In May Amnesty International submitted information about its concerns in Guatemala to the UN Committee against Torture.

In the same month, the organization also launched a report, *Guatemala: All the truth, justice for all*, and a two-year worldwide action program to call attention to past human rights abuses which it felt needed to be addressed by the CEH and the Guatemalan authorities as a necessary step to building a firm and lasting peace in the country, as called for in the Peace Accord. Throughout the year Amnesty International submitted information to the CEH concerning cases which it considered merited the CEH's attention.

GUINEA

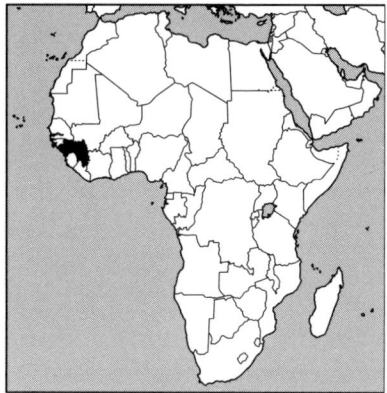

Hundreds of opposition party supporters were detained, some of whom were prisoners of conscience. Thirty-eight soldiers, including possible prisoners of conscience, were sentenced to prison terms after an unfair trial. Torture and ill-treatment continued to be widespread. Prison conditions were harsh. No death sentences or executions were reported.

In October El Hadj Biro Diallo, President of the National Assembly, was suspended from the *Parti de l'unité et du progrès* (PUP), Party of Unity and Progress, the party in power, for attacking the country's human rights record. He had publicly compared Guinea's detention centres with the Boiro camp, where scores of people "disappeared" when President Ahmed Sékou Touré was in power between the 1950s and 1980s. He had also condemned the use of torture and ill-treatment to extract confessions and exhorted President Lansanna Conté to take action to prevent such abuses.

General Conté, who seized power in 1984, was re-elected in the first round of the December presidential elections. Opposition parties accused the government of rigging the results by denying their supporters voting cards.

Scores of opposition party members and supporters were arrested in March and detained, some of whom were prisoners of conscience. The arrests took place following violent clashes between the security forces and residents in the town of Kaporo, north of the capital Conakry, during which at least 10 residents and one policeman were killed. Residents of Kaporo, an opposition stronghold, had refused to move out of a residential area which the authorities claimed they had illegally occupied. Among those arrested were three members of the National Assembly and of the opposition *Union pour la nouvelle République*, Union for the New Republic. They were the opposition party's President Ba Mamadou, Mamadou Barry and Thierno Ousmane. El-Hadj Alhassane Bah, imam of the Kaporo mosque, was also arrested.

Sixty of those detained and charged in connection with the clashes were tried in June before the court of first instance. During the trial, El-Hadj Alhassane Bah said that he had been tied up and tortured by members of the security forces. There was no investigation into the allegation. Fifty-eight of the defendants, including possible prisoners of conscience, were convicted of criminal offences, including violence and common assault, incitement to disobedience and racial hate. The three members of the National Assembly were sentenced to prison terms of between two and five months and a large fine; the others were sentenced to one year's imprisonment. In October all of them were released following a presidential pardon.

In April at least 20 people, including Momory Camara and Mamady Famory Condé – both members of the National Assembly and of the opposition *Rassemblement du peuple de Guinée* (RPG), Guinean People's Rally – were arrested in Beyla town following a political rally organized there by the RPG. The two members of the National Assembly were released after three days. The others, including Yasolo Camara and Mamady Sylla, were detained without charge or trial for a month; they were possible prisoners of conscience.

Hundreds of people were arrested during the presidential campaign and election. Some were released, but at the end of the year more than 100 people, including political leaders and members of the parliamentary opposition, continued to be

182

held without charge or trial. A candidate in the presidential election, Alpha Condé, President of the RPG, was accused by the authorities of wishing to leave Guinea illegally and of seeking to recruit troops to destabilize the country. Marcel Cros, President of the *Parti démocratique africain de Guinée*, African Democratic Party of Guinea, was accused of illegal possession of firearms. Together with other opposition activists, they were held in the detention centre at Conakry.

Opposition members of parliament and local government councillors, including Koumbafing Keita, Mamamdy Yo Kouyaté and Ramatoulaye Diallo as well as other elected officials of the RPG, were also detained without charge or trial. They were held in the civil prison in Kankan.

Foday Fofana, a Sierra Leonean journalist arrested in 1997 (see *Amnesty International Report 1998*), was released in January without charge. He was immediately expelled to Sierra Leone. Moussa Traoré, a supporter of the RPG and a possible prisoner of conscience who had been sentenced to three years' imprisonment in 1996 (see *Amnesty International Report 1998*), was released in September.

The trial of scores of soldiers accused of participation in a mutiny in 1996 (see *Amnesty International Report 1997*) began before the State Security Court in March. The trial failed to meet minimum international standards for fair trial. During the proceedings, some of the defendants stated that they had been forced to make confessions under torture (see below). Their allegations were not investigated. Others said they had spent nine months in prison without being presented before a judge. Thirty-eight soldiers, including possible prisoners of conscience, were sentenced to prison terms ranging from seven months to 15 years. Fifty-one defendants were acquitted.

Torture and ill-treatment continued to be widespread. In the June trial following the arrests in Kaporo, some defendants, whose wounds were still visible, said that the security forces had interrupted their prayers and then beaten them in front of the mosque at the time of arrest. During the trial of soldiers accused of participation in a mutiny (see above), some defendants who had been detained on Kasa islands said that they had been burned and "had endured the worst of humilia-

tions" by the security forces. One defendant said that he had been plunged into water with his hands and feet tied. He alleged that he was later put on a table and whipped. After the widespread arrests of opposition activists in December, members of the security forces held some detainees on the ground, stamped on their hands and feet, and beat them. Some of the detainees received up to 50 truncheon blows twice in the same day.

Prison conditions were harsh and often amounted to cruel, inhuman or degrading treatment.

In March Amnesty International sent a delegate to observe the trial of the soldiers accused of mutiny but he was refused admission to the courtroom. In July, near the end of the trial, the authorities wrote to Amnesty International reiterating their refusal to admit an Amnesty International observer. The letter stressed that since the arrival of the second republic in 1984, the rights of the defence had been effectively guaranteed.

GUINEA-BISSAU

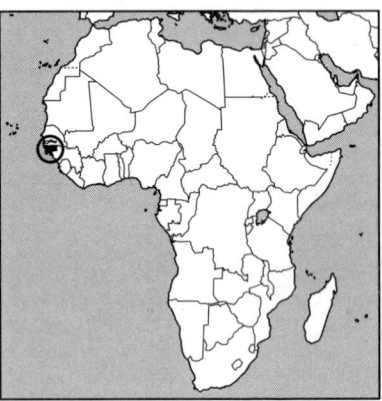

Prisoners of conscience detained during the year included six trade unionists, held briefly in January, and at least two political activists who were among many people arrested during armed conflict which engulfed the country following an army mutiny. Military and civilian detainees were frequently tortured. Women were reportedly raped by soldiers involved in the conflict. During the conflict security forces, as well as Senegalese and

Republic of Guinea soldiers supporting the government committed human rights violations. Rebel forces arrested civilians and reportedly beat them.

Under a security agreement between the government of President João Bernardo Vieira and Senegal, the army reinforced its presence on the border with Senegal in order to prevent rebels of the Senegalese *Mouvement des forces démocratiques de Casamance* (MFDC), Democratic Forces of Casamance Movement, from using Guinea-Bissau as a rear base. In January government troops reportedly killed 10 suspected MFDC rebels and arrested dozens of people, including Senegalese, accusing them of vehicle theft and gunrunning. In late January Brigadier Ansumane Mané, army Chief of Staff, was accused of negligence in connection with the arms trafficking and suspended from his post. He denied the allegations and publicly accused senior government and military officials of involvement in arms trafficking. He was dismissed on 6 June.

Brigadier Ansumane Mané's dismissal ignited a military revolt. Rebel soldiers laid an ambush on the road to the airport where President Vieira was due to pass and killed two officials. They seized military bases in Bissau, the capital, cutting it off from the rest of the country. Most of the 10,000-strong armed forces, embittered by long-standing grievances over poor conditions and low pay, joined the self-styled *Junta Militar* (military junta). Senegal and the Republic of Guinea acted immediately to support the government. Over the following weeks some 2,000 Senegalese and 400 Republic of Guinea troops arrived in the country. A Contact Group appointed by the *Comunidade de Paises de Lingua Portuguesa* (CPLP), Community of Portuguese-speaking Countries, negotiated a truce on 26 July. By then, *Junta Militar* troops controlled most of the northwest of the country. The fighting destroyed many buildings in Bissau and displaced about a third of the country's population of just over a million.

Throughout the conflict members of parliament and religious leaders inside the country, as well as individuals and human rights activists in exile, tried to promote peace talks. In August the Economic Community of West African States (ECOWAS) and the CPLP jointly brokered a reaffirmation of the cease-fire. However, the momentum of mediation slowed. In mid-October fighting flared again and, despite reinforcements of foreign troops supporting the government, the *Junta Militar* forces, reportedly joined by MFDC fighters, took control of most of the country. President Vieira then announced a unilateral cease-fire and, after further negotiations, a peace agreement was signed in November during an ECOWAS meeting of heads of state in Nigeria. Under the agreement, the Senegalese and Republic of Guinea forces were to be withdrawn and an ECOWAS monitoring force was to be deployed in Guinea-Bissau. Benin, Gambia, Niger and Togo agreed to contribute a total of 600 troops, but by the end of the year only 80 Togolese troops had arrived.

At the beginning of the year, six officials of the *Sindicato Nacional de Marinheiros* (SINAMAR), National Sailors' Syndicate, were arrested and held for several days: they were prisoners of conscience. Police held the wife of Cesar Vieira Có, SINAMAR's Vice-President, overnight as a hostage because her husband was not at home when they came to arrest him.

During the conflict security forces and Senegalese soldiers arrested civilians and soldiers suspected of supporting the *Junta Militar*. According to some reports, three detention centres in Bissau held over 200 prisoners. Some prisoners were detained solely on the suspicion of opposing government policies. They were prisoners of conscience. Among them was Ansumane Fati, a member of an opposition political party, *União para a Mudança*, Union for Change, who was arrested in early July. He had organized a petition for peace. Soldiers accused him of criticizing President Vieira and listening to the *Junta Militar* radio station. They beat him with military belts before releasing him.

Torture was frequently used during interrogation and as a punishment. Reports were received in February that about 20 people detained on suspicion of gunrunning were being tortured under interrogation in military custody. After initially being denied access, a parliamentary committee of inquiry and members of the *Liga Guineense de Direitos Humanos*, Guinea (Bissau) Human Rights League, visited the detainees and heard that they had been beaten with truncheons all over their bodies. As a result, four suffered temporary paralysis: Filipe Manga lost the use of his

184

left hand; three others, including Lamine Djata, a Senegalese man, could not walk.

After the conflict started, Samba Djaló, a soldier who had joined the *Junta Militar*, was arrested at Jugdul, 40 kilometres east of Bissau, in late June. He escaped from prison in July and told journalists that, at the time of his arrest, a Guinea-Bissau soldier had inserted sewing needles into the skin of his penis. There were many reports of prisoners being severely beaten by soldiers or security officials.

There were also reports of Senegalese soldiers beating civilians who refused to hand over money or other possessions, and some reports of other serious human rights violations. In late June Senegalese soldiers in a part of Bissau known as Little Moscow reportedly arrested a young man, beat him and then dripped over him a substance, possibly molten plastic, which burned his skin. Bystanders took him to a hospital. In July Senegalese troops reportedly intercepted a group of people who were trying to leave Bissau, selected 25 women, took them back to their barracks at the military headquarters, raped them and held them for two days. Capitão Quinhague sustained multiple fractures from a severe beating with gun butts and sticks in the Pluba II suburb of Bissau in July. Senegalese soldiers who beat him accused him of being a member of the *Junta Militar* forces. Despite his name of Capitão (captain), he was a civilian. Capitão Quinhague died a few days later, apparently as a result of internal bleeding.

A few days after the August cease-fire agreement was signed, security personnel arrested Braima Djassi, apparently because he was an official of the Union for Change, and reportedly beat him.

Soldiers arrested Armando Bion in September in Bissau on suspicion of spying for the *Junta Militar* and reportedly beat him severely with gun butts before taking him to the navy headquarters. There were several reports about life-threatening conditions in this prison where detainees were said to be held in overcrowded cells which flooded at high tide and had no toilets.

Six people arrested in Bafatá in late October were reportedly tortured by Republic of Guinea troops.

Soon after the conflict began the *Junta Militar* detained an estimated 200 foreign civilians, mostly from Senegal and some from other West African states. During interrogation they were reportedly tied up and beaten. By August, all had reportedly been released. Leopold Alfama "Duki Djarsi", a retired military officer, was arrested by the *Junta Militar* in June and held for over four months.

There were several reports that government and Senegalese soldiers extrajudicially executed unarmed civilians. According to an eyewitness, a group of five or six government security officials, one in police uniform, approached two youths who were standing chatting in the Reino area of Bissau in June. One official spoke to the youths, then reportedly fired his machine-gun, hitting one in the leg and the other in the stomach.

According to witnesses, in late June one of a group of Senegalese soldiers opened fire without warning on two unarmed security guards sitting at the gate of the US Embassy in Bissau. One of the guards was killed, the other injured.

Lai António Pereira was apparently extrajudicially executed in July by a security official who suspected him of theft.

Amnesty International expressed concern to the authorities about the torture of detainees. In *Guinea-Bissau: Human rights under fire*, published in July, Amnesty International appealed to all parties involved in the fighting to respect human rights. Before and after the peace agreement was signed in November, Amnesty International urged those involved in the peace negotiations to ensure that the agreement contained provisions to protect human rights.

GUYANA

At least one person was sentenced to death. About 22 people remained under sentence of death at the end of the year. There were no executions. There were further reports of ill-treatment and shootings in disputed circumstances by police.

An audit of the December 1997 presidential elections (see *Amnesty International Report 1998*) by the Caribbean Community and Common Market (CARICOM) team concluded that the result of the "recount varied only marginally from that of the final results". In July President Janet Jagan and Desmond Hoyte, leader of the People's National Congress Party, signed a "peace agreement" intended to end the succession of violent protests which erupted following the election.

In November parliament voted in favour of a motion proposed by the government to withdraw as a state party to the Optional Protocol to the International Covenant on Civil and Political Rights (ICCPR). It also voted to reaccede to the Optional Protocol to the ICCPR with a reservation purporting to preclude the UN Human Rights Committee from considering petitions brought by people under sentence of death claiming that their rights guaranteed by the ICCPR had been violated in the course of the capital proceedings against them.

At least one person was sentenced to death. There were approximately 22 people under sentence of death at the end of the year.

In March the UN Human Rights Committee issued its conclusions on petitions by two people under sentence of death – Abdool Saleem Yasseen and Noel Thomas (see *Amnesty International Reports 1997* and *1998*) – who alleged that their rights guaranteed under the ICCPR had been violated. The Committee concluded that both men had been deprived of a fair trial as their rights to a defence and to a trial without undue delay had been violated and that, therefore, sentencing them to death violated their right not to be arbitrarily deprived of their life, as guaranteed by Article 6 of the ICCPR. These conclusions were based, among other things, on the fact that the second trial went ahead despite the fact that Abdool Saleem Yasseen was not represented by counsel for the first four days of the proceedings. The Committee also concluded that the conditions in which they were held prior to trial and while under sentence of death violated their right to be treated with humanity and with respect for the inherent dignity of the human person. In August the government announced it would not follow the recommendations of the Committee to release Abdool Saleem Yasseen and Noel Thomas. Motions filed with the High Court in August by Abdool Saleem Yasseen and Noel Thomas seeking to have their death sentences commuted to life imprisonment were still pending at the end of the year.

Although no executions took place, in July warrants were issued for the executions of "Paulo" Rampersaud and Raymond Persaud (see *Amnesty International Report 1998*); their executions were stayed because they each had petitions pending before the UN Human Rights Committee. "Paulo" Rampersaud, however, died in prison in August.

Reports of ill-treatment and torture by police were received. In May Mark Brown was allegedly taken by police officers into an unoccupied room in a private house and held on the floor by an officer while other officers sprinkled acid on various parts of his body.

There were further reports of fatal shootings by law enforcement officials in disputed circumstances. In June, for example, Victor "Junior" Bourne, who was reportedly wanted by the police, was shot and killed by police officers in Rasville, Georgetown. Initial police reports allegedly indicated that he opened fire after being confronted by the police and was then shot. Witnesses, however, reported that he was still in bed when the police shot him. An investigation into his death was reportedly conducted by the police, but the findings had not been made public and no officer had been charged in connection with the killing by the end of the year.

In May Amnesty International called on the authorities to comply with the recommendations of the UN Human Rights Committee on the cases of Abdool Saleem Yasseen and Noel Thomas and asked what measures the government was taking to ensure that conditions of detention and imprisonment were consistent with international standards. In September Amnesty International expressed concern about

186

fatal shootings by police in disputed circumstances and requested information about the case of Victor "Junior" Bourne. In December the organization urged the government to submit Guyana's overdue reports to the UN Committee against Torture and Human Rights Committee and to reconsider the decision to withdraw as a state party to the Optional Protocol to the ICCPR. In December Amnesty International called on the authorities to investigate the alleged torture of Mark Brown and to bring those responsible to justice.

HAITI

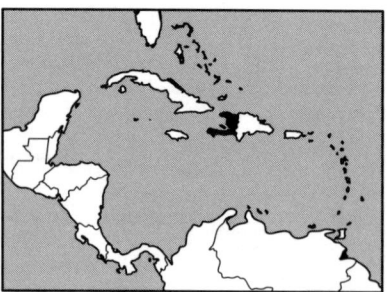

Little progress was made in bringing those responsible for human rights violations, past or present, to justice. Investigation and trial procedures continued to fall short of international standards and long delays in bringing detainees to trial continued. Some people remained in detention without trial despite judicial orders for their release. There were reports of ill-treatment and torture. At least three people died in custody. At least 24 people were shot dead by police in disputed circumstances.

In December parliament ratified Jacques Edouard Alexis as Prime Minister. It was the first time since June 1997 that President René Préval had been able to find a Prime Minister acceptable to parliament. By the end of the year, Jacques Edouard Alexis had not appointed his cabinet.

In April the UN Commission on Human Rights adopted a resolution welcoming the improvements in the human rights situation in Haiti since 1994 and noting the declarations by the authorities that human rights would be upheld. The Commission urged the government to bring to justice those identified by the *Commission*

nationale de vérité et de justice (CNVJ), National Commission for Truth and Justice, as responsible for human rights violations; to improve the justice system and prison conditions; and to continue training the police to carry out their duties with respect for human rights. It also extended for one year the mandate of the Independent Expert on Haiti.

In June the Inter-American Commission on Human Rights presented its annual report to the Organization of American States (OAS) General Assembly in which it reported on its visit to Haiti in 1997. Although the report stated that "there is no systematic pattern of violations attributed to the government", it identified "the unsatisfactory operation of the judicial branch" as a problem. It expressed concern about the number of people detained awaiting trial, prison conditions, killings by members of the *Police nationale d'Haïti* (PNH), Haitian National Police, and the continuing impunity of perpetrators of human rights violations carried out between 1991 and 1994 under the *de facto* military government of General Raoul Cédras. In July Haiti recognized the jurisdiction of the Inter-American Court of Human Rights.

In spite of some attempts to improve the human rights situation, the government failed to establish a strong legal framework, based on international human rights standards, which would guarantee access to justice for victims of human rights abuses, both past and present. In January the Director of the *Bureau de poursuites et suivi*, Proceedings and Follow-up Office, set up to oversee the implementation of the recommendations of the CNVJ (see *Amnesty International Report 1998*), announced that its work had begun and meetings had been held with victims of human rights violations under the military government. However, there were allegations that some funds destined for victims of human rights violations had been misspent and that little progress had been made by the Office.

The work of the *Bureau du protecteur du citoyen*, Citizens' Protection Office, established under the 1987 Constitution to protect individuals against abuse by state agents (see *Amnesty International Report 1998*), was hampered by lack of resources and delays in the appointment of a deputy and advisory board.

The judicial reform bill, introduced in 1996 (see *Amnesty International Reports 1997* and *1998*), was adopted by parliament in April and came into force in August. In July the *Unité de suivi et coordination pour la réforme du droit et de la justice*, Follow-up and Coordination Unit for the Reform of Law and Justice, (formerly the *Commission préparatoire à la réforme du droit et de la justice en Haïti*, Preparatory Commission for the Reform of Law and Justice in Haiti) (see *Amnesty International Report 1998*), presented a five-year strategic plan to the Minister of Justice. However, few concrete steps had been taken to implement the plan by the end of the year.

Legislative elections which should have taken place in November were postponed until 1999.

In June a *Bureau de contrôle de la détention préventive*, Preventive Detention Control Office, was set up at the *Pénitencier National*, National Penitentiary, to reduce the number of prisoners held in prolonged pre-trial detention. Lack of resources prevented it from being set up in other prisons.

In November the UN Security Council extended the mandate of the UN Civilian Police Mission in Haiti (MIPONUH) until November 1999. MIPONUH was to continue to assist the government by supporting and contributing to the training of the PNH. Under a separate bilateral agreement between the US and Haitian governments, a US Support Group, made up of some 500 US troops, was mandated to remain in Haiti until the end of December. In December the UN General Assembly mandated the joint OAS/UN International Civilian Mission in Haiti (MICIVIH) to remain in the country until December 1999.

Little progress was made in bringing those responsible for human rights violations, past and present, to justice. In February arrest warrants, issued in December 1997, for three of the 1991 coup leaders and seven other former military officers, were made public. Under these warrants, the government asked Panama, Honduras and the USA to extradite those named in connection with their alleged involvement in the 1994 massacre of some 50 people in Raboteau, Gonaïves (see *Amnesty International Reports 1995* to *1998*); the requests were unsuccessful. Eight people were arrested in connection with the massacre

during the year. By the end of the year, at least 27 people were detained on charges, including murder, in connection with the massacre. The trial of all those accused of involvement in the massacre was postponed until 1999. During the year several members of the judiciary involved in the case resigned, mainly because of problems with the justice system.

Several other people were arrested for human rights violations committed during the period of military government; others were still being sought. For example, in January and February, Rémy Lucas, Léonard Lucas and Jean Michel Richardson were arrested, accused of participating in the 1987 massacre at Jean-Rabel in which some 200 people were killed (see *Amnesty International Reports 1988* and *1996*). They remained in detention at the end of the year, despite judicial release orders.

Investigation and trial procedures for all detainees, including some suspected of politically motivated offences, fell short of international standards. Long delays in bringing detainees to trial resulted in severe prison overcrowding. MICIVIH reported that only 19 per cent of those in prison had been tried and sentenced.

Several people remained in detention without trial despite judicial orders for their release. For example, Osner Févry, a lawyer who was a State Secretary under former President Jean-Claude Duvalier and was alleged to have connections with former military coup leader General Raoul Cédras, was detained in March and remained in detention until December without being informed of the charges against him and despite a judicial order for his release. Evans François (see *Amnesty International Report 1998*) remained in detention despite a May 1997 order for his release. In July judicial release orders were issued for former General Claude Raymond, Claude Schneider and Phanuel Dieu (see *Amnesty International Report 1998*). The three men had been arrested in July 1996, allegedly for "terrorist actions intended to destabilize the government". The Court of Appeal upheld the order for their release in November. Claude Raymond was subsequently released and immediately served with a new arrest warrant and rearrested for "crimes against the Constitution, conspiracy, murder and complicity to murder".

188

There were several reports of torture and ill-treatment carried out by members of the PNH. According to reports, Gaston Pierre, who was arrested in May in connection with the killing earlier that month of Chenel Gracien, a member of an organization linked to land reform, was taken from prison to a private house where he was sprayed with tear gas, had water poured over him and was beaten.

According to reports, at least three people died in custody. Ludovic Difficile died in police custody in Fort-Liberté in July. A preliminary autopsy report gave the primary cause of death as strangulation. Three police officers were reportedly charged and detained in connection with the case. Hector Joanes also died in custody in July in Hinche, allegedly as a result of beatings.

At least 24 people were reportedly shot and killed by the PNH, or people working for the PNH, in circumstances suggesting excessive use of force.

Jean Paul Merisier, an unarmed passer-by, was shot dead by police trying to disperse a protest outside the police station in Mirebalais in February. There were conflicting reports as to whether the police fired into the air or directly at the 50-strong crowd. In reaction to the killing, the crowd, some of whom were armed with machetes and other weapons, stormed the police station and hacked the local police chief to death. They also set fire to vehicles and released 76 prisoners from the nearby prison. Special police units, called in to restore order, detained at least 30 people, several of whom reported being beaten during arrest or while detained in the police station. All but four were reportedly released without charge. Investigations were opened by both the Port-au-Prince judicial police and the local police. Both the Senate and the Permanent Human Rights Committee of the Chamber of Deputies sent commissions of inquiry to Mirebalais. However, it was not clear whether a specific investigation had been opened into police handling of the whole incident, including the police shootings and the allegations of ill-treatment. By the end of the year no one had been prosecuted in connection with the events.

In March a radio station guard was reportedly shot and injured by members of a specialist police unit who ransacked a radio station in Milot. The Minister of Justice subsequently ordered the radio station to be repaired and an investigation into the incident. A Senate Commission formed to investigate the incident reportedly condemned the behaviour of the police as "savage". The investigation was continuing at the end of the year.

Official investigations were opened by the police authorities into most reported cases of fatal shootings, but not into reported cases of torture or ill-treatment. In July the PNH declared that between January and June, 28 people had been suspended from duty for human rights violations. However, only a few were detained and charged or brought to trial.

Prison conditions were harsh. In April MICIVIH reported that the increased prison population had led to severe overcrowding, constraints on the provision of food and increased concerns for security. In some prisons, appalling sanitary conditions, insufficient out-of-cell time and severe deficiencies in the provision of medical treatment put prisoners' health at risk. Prison reform was hampered by lack of funds.

In July Amnesty International published *Haiti: Still crying out for justice* outlining recommendations to the authorities on issues including justice and impunity, policing and prisons. It urged principally that the authorities give the highest priority to the process of judicial reform in order to guarantee justice and the right to a fair, prompt and impartial trial for detainees, and expressed concern that insufficient efforts had been made to bring to justice the perpetrators of human rights violations, both past and present. It also called on international governmental and non-governmental organizations to continue to give the highest priority to assisting the government in this task. Amnesty International also requested that the legal situation of several prisoners be clarified and that they be brought to trial within a reasonable time in accordance with international fair trial norms. The organization further urged that investigations continue into several killings which had occurred since October 1994 and which may have been extrajudicial executions.

In February the organization expressed concern at reports that one man was killed and several detainees ill-treated in Mirebalais. It requested that the physical integrity of the detainees be guaranteed, that an independent and impartial investigation be carried out into the incident, and that those responsible be brought to justice.

HONDURAS

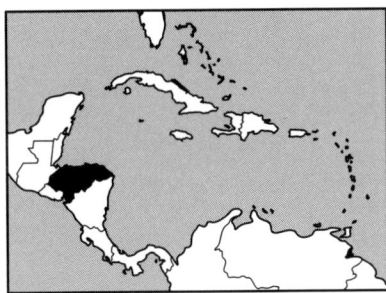

Human rights defenders were again victims of human rights violations. There were allegations of torture and ill-treatment, and deaths in police custody. Impunity for past human rights violations continued.

President Carlos Flores Facussé took office in January.

In July a new Police Law came into force which places the police under the civilian supervision of the newly created Ministry of Security. Elizabeth Chuiz Sierra was appointed as its head in September. In February the Law to Prevent, Punish and Eradicate Domestic Violence against Women came into force.

Human rights defenders were the victims of human rights violations, including threats, harassment and possible extra-judicial execution. In February Ernesto Sandoval Bustillo, regional coordinator of the *Comité de Defensa de Derechos Humanos en Honduras* (CODEH), Committee for the Defence of Human Rights in Honduras, was shot dead by unidentified men as he walked to the CODEH offices in Santa Rosa de Copán. He had been involved in investigating the killing of Cándido Amador Recinos (see below) and had reportedly received several death threats. In a statement issued in December 1997, a group calling itself *Los Justicieros de la Noche* (Avengers of the Night) had made death threats against 75 people and accused human rights defenders of causing an increase in crime by "protecting" criminals. Following the murder, the Attorney General reportedly said that there seemed

to be no doubt that death squads were resurfacing in Honduras. The *Dirección de Investigación Criminal* (DIC), Directorate of Criminal Investigation, opened an investigation. Three days after the murder there was a shoot-out between police and those suspected of the murder, members of an armed gang allegedly connected to military personnel. One gang member was killed and six were arrested. They were released 10 days later but a new arrest warrant was issued after ballistic evidence came to light linking a weapon seized from the leader of the gang to the one used to kill Ernesto Sandoval. The six were held awaiting trial at the end of the year. In August the UN Sub-Commission on Prevention of Discrimination and Protection of Minorities strongly condemned the murder.

Dr Ramón Custodio López, President of CODEH, and Bertha Oliva de Nativí, General Coordinator of the *Comité de Familiares de Detenidos Desaparecidos en Honduras*, Committee of Relatives of the Disappeared in Honduras, were among those who continued to receive threats or were subjected to harassment. In April the head of the Armed Forces in Honduras, General Mario Hung Pacheco, accused Ramón Custodio of forging documents linking General Hung with the "disappearance" of a student in 1988, and asked a court to order his arrest. By the end of the year the court had not acted on the request.

There were no investigations into threats and attacks against human rights defenders in 1997. No one was prosecuted for the attack in September 1997 on Benigno Ramírez García, a human rights defender working with the poor, in which his three-year-old son was killed (see *Amnesty International Report 1998*). No one was brought to justice for the killings of leaders and members of indigenous groups in previous years, including Cándido Amador Recinos, Ovidio Pérez, Jesús Álvarez Rochez and Jorge Manueles (see *Amnesty International Report 1998*). Investigations into the killings either made no progress or were never initiated.

Judicial proceedings in connection with past human rights violations continued. In February the First Criminal Court in Tegucigalpa, the capital, ruled in favour of applying amnesty laws to a member of the armed forces charged with human rights violations committed in the

190

1980s (see *Amnesty International Reports 1996* to *1998*). The Court found that the 1991 Amnesty Law had to be applied to Colonel Juan Blas Salazar, who was found guilty of the attempted murder, torture and unlawful detention of six students in 1982, and nine other army officers charged with the same offence, and that no penalties could be imposed. An appeal against the court's decision by the Attorney General's Office to the Court of Appeals was rejected on procedural grounds. A further appeal to the Supreme Court was still pending at the end of the year. In October procedures were initiated by the Honduran authorities for the extradition from Spain of retired Captain Billy Fernando Joya Améndola, also a defendant in the case, to stand trial for human rights violations.

In April arrest warrants were issued against Major Mario Asdrúbal Quiñónez and a former sergeant, Jaime Rosales, in connection with the extrajudicial executions of Miguel Angel Pavón Salazar and Moisés Landaverde in 1988 (see *Amnesty International Reports 1989*, *1990* and *1998*), allegedly carried out by members of a death squad. Miguel Angel Pavón, President of the San Pedro Sula chapter of CODEH, had given evidence highly critical of Honduran authorities to the Inter-American Court of Human Rights in October 1987 regarding three "disappearances" (see *Amnesty International Report 1989*). On his return to Honduras, Miguel Angel Pavón received several death threats. Moisés Landaverde, President of the Regional Committee of the Teachers' Union, had reportedly been under surveillance by unidentified men in the days before his death. Although an investigation was opened into the killings, it made no progress. It was reopened in 1994 by the Public Ministry's Special Prosecutor for Human Rights and in 1996 two investigators were appointed to work on the case. Major Asdrúbal, who was still on active duty, was taken into custody in April 1998. According to reports, he was provisionally released after six days for lack of evidence, and the main witness was imprisoned for giving false testimony. The arrest warrant could not be served on Sergeant Rosales who was resident in the USA.

There were reports of torture and ill-treatment, and deaths in police custody. In January, two teenage boys were reportedly driven away in a blue pick-up van by two men identified by witnesses as members of the DIC. The mutilated bodies of the two boys were found the next day in San Manuel, Cortes Department; they showed signs of torture. An investigation initiated by the Attorney General's office was continuing at the end of the year.

In January at least six demonstrators were injured, one requiring hospital treatment, when police attempted to disperse a group of people from the *Colonia Canaán* neighbourhood of Tegucigalpa. They were peacefully protesting outside the US embassy at the deportation of illegal Honduran immigrants from the USA. Officers belonging to a special police unit known as COBRAS, reportedly used excessive force against the demonstrators. No investigation was known to have been initiated into the incident.

Amnesty International appealed to the authorities to investigate the killing of Ernesto Sandoval Bustillo and urged that steps be taken to guarantee the safety of human rights defenders. It called on the authorities to take steps to end the impunity enjoyed by members of the military and security forces involved in human rights violations. The Director of the DIC replied in March informing Amnesty International about the steps that had been taken to investigate the killing.

In February Amnesty International expressed concern that the decision to apply amnesty laws in favour of a member of the armed forces involved in human rights violations was incompatible with Honduras' international obligations, and perpetuated impunity.

In April Amnesty International published *Honduras: Still waiting for justice*, which examined the lack of progress in investigations into "disappearances" and extrajudicial executions which took place in the 1980s.

HUNGARY

There were reports that detainees were ill-treated by police officers.

In November the UN Committee against Torture considered Hungary's third periodic report on its implementation of the UN Convention against Torture and Other Cruel, Inhuman or Degrading Treatment or

Punishment. The Committee was concerned that the provisions of Article 123 of the Criminal Code makes torture punishable only if the perpetrator was aware that the acts committed constitute a criminal offence. It was also concerned about "the persistent reports that an inordinately high proportion of detainees is roughly handled or treated cruelly before, during and after interrogation by the Police". The Committee recommended the implementation of all necessary measures, particularly prompt access to a defence counsel after arrest and improved training of the police, and urged the authorities to re-examine Article 123 and ensure that it is consistent with the terms and purposes of the Convention.

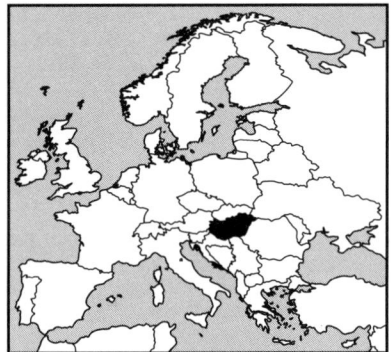

Ill-treatment by police was reported during the year. For example, in July, in the 13th District of Budapest, the capital, a police patrol stopped Martón Ill, Director of the *Magyar Emberi Jogvedo Kozpont*, Hungarian Centre for Defence of Human Rights, a local non-governmental organization. He was driving to Balassagymatra, accompanied by three men, to testify in a court hearing concerning an asylum application. After the police inspected the car, Martón Ill asked them for a statement that would explain to the court the reason for his delay, but this was refused by the officer in charge. When Martón Ill persisted with his request, the officer became abusive and was reported to have violently twisted Martón Ill's right arm behind his back and handcuffed his wrists. Martón Ill was then taken to the police car, where the same officer reportedly continued to verbally abuse him. The officer repeatedly punched him on the left side of his head, breaking his glasses, and all over the back, arms and abdomen. Martón Ill sustained

injuries to the mouth, lower back and wrists. His right foot was injured when he kicked and broke one of the police car's windows as he was being punched. He was taken to the 13th District Police Station where he asked to contact his lawyer and his relatives, but this was refused. Half an hour later an ambulance came and a doctor treated his injuries, but the police reportedly did not allow the ambulance to take him to hospital. Martón Ill's lawyer arrived at the police station later that afternoon and a statement was made about the ill-treatment.

In July Amnesty International urged the Chief Public Prosecutor to ensure that investigations into all incidents of ill-treatment were carried out promptly and impartially. In October the Chief Public Prosecutor replied that an officer had been charged with causing light physical injury to Mónika Gőgös in 1997 and that three officers had been charged with assault of a Russian national in a Budapest police station (see *Amnesty International Report 1998*). The investigation into the ill-treatment of László Máté (see *Amnesty International Report 1998*) was terminated because of insufficient evidence that a criminal offence had been committed. The complainant was reportedly unable to identify conclusively the person who had injured his left eye. The Budapest Public Prosecutor ordered an investigation into Martón Ill's complaint; it had not been completed by the end of the year.

INDIA

Thousands of political prisoners, including prisoners of conscience, were detained without charge or trial. Torture and ill-treatment continued to be widespread, and hundreds of people were reported to have died in custody. Conditions in many prisons amounted to cruel, inhuman or degrading treatment. "Disappearances" continued and hundreds of extrajudicial executions were reported. At least 35 people were sentenced to death; no executions were reported. Armed groups committed grave human rights abuses, including torture, hostage-taking and killings of civilians.

Following the fall of the United Front government in December 1997, general

192

elections were held in March 1998. The *Bharatiya Janata* Party (BJP), led by A.B. Vajpayee and backed by several regional parties, won a majority. The coalition remained in power at the end of the year.

In May a Prevention of Terrorist Activities Bill (1998) was passed in the Tamil Nadu state legislature. The legislation allows for detention without charge for up to a year, widens the scope of the death penalty and suspends other safeguards normally available under India's criminal law. In November the President of India returned the legislation to the state government, requesting it to reconsider several provisions. Other legislation that facilitates human rights violations continued to be used in parts of the country, including the Armed Forces (Special Powers) Act which gives the security forces powers to shoot to kill and grants them virtual immunity from prosecution.

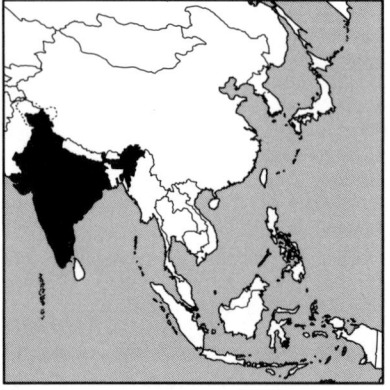

The National Human Rights Commission (NHRC) continued to monitor human rights abuses and make recommendations for the promotion and protection of human rights. During the year state human rights commissions were established in Kerala and Manipur. In June a high level Advisory Committee was appointed by the NHRC to look into provisions of the 1993 Protection of Human Rights Act under which the NHRC was established. Areas of consideration included Section 19 of the Act which restricts NHRC investigations of alleged human rights violations by members of the armed and paramilitary forces.

In September the Supreme Court dismissed a challenge by the central government to the NHRC's powers to investigate past human rights violations in Punjab. The Court ruled that the NHRC would be acting *"sui generis"* in such investigations and that provisions of the Protection of Human Rights Act which prevent the NHRC from investigating allegations of human rights violations which are more than a year old, therefore, did not apply. The Supreme Court had ordered the NHRC to investigate violations in Punjab in December 1996 after hearing allegations by human rights organizations that hundreds of bodies had been illegally cremated by Punjab police (see *Amnesty International Reports 1997* and *1998*). By the end of the year the NHRC had not begun investigations.

Armed conflict between government forces and armed groups continued in parts of the country, including Jammu and Kashmir, northeastern states and Andhra Pradesh. Civilians, including women and children, were often the victims of abuses by both sides.

Thousands of political prisoners, including prisoners of conscience, were detained without charge or trial. They included human rights defenders and people peacefully protesting against violations of civil, cultural, economic, political and social rights.

Thousands of people, most of them women, were arrested during the year in connection with peaceful protests against the Maheshwar Dam project in Madhya Pradesh. They were arrested under section 151 of the Code of Criminal Procedure which allows police to preventively detain people they suspect may commit a crime. Many of those arrested were reportedly beaten and some needed hospital treatment. Several women alleged that they were told they would be stripped naked if they protested again. Most of those arrested were released unconditionally within a few days following widespread protests at their arrest.

Many people were detained under the 1980 National Security Act (NSA), which permits administrative detention for up to one year on loosely defined grounds of national security. There were regular reports of arrests under the NSA in Tamil Nadu and Uttar Pradesh during the year. In Jammu and Kashmir, political leaders peacefully protesting against human rights violations were frequently detained without charge or trial under the 1978 Jammu and Kashmir Public Safety Act and the preventive detention provisions of the ordinary criminal law.

People defending their rights were also subjected to other forms of harassment or intimidation. In Orissa, those protesting against mining and other industrial projects in Rayagada district were attacked and had their property destroyed, reportedly by gangs acting in collusion with local authorities and police. In June several activists of Agragamee, a non-governmental organization working with tribal people in Rayagada district, were arrested on what appeared to be false charges.

In February residents of two colonies, one of bonded labourers and the other of a Scheduled Caste community, in the Kookal Panchayat area of Kodaikanal, Tamil Nadu, were attacked by police after they announced they would boycott local elections. More than 100 police officers, aided by supporters of the *Dravida Munnetra Kazhagam*, a political party standing in the elections, entered the colonies and beat men, women and children, and destroyed property. Sixteen women and nine men from the colonies were then arrested on charges of attempted murder and *dacoity* (criminal theft). A human rights activist, Henry Tiphagne, who supported the victims, was subsequently harassed by the authorities and in March charged with *dacoity*.

Several human rights defenders were arrested in Punjab. There were concerns that the arrests were connected with their involvement in the Punjab Committee for Coordination on Disappearances, a network of lawyers established in recent years to pursue the issue of redress for "disappearances". Among those arrested were Jaspal Singh Dhillon, Rajinder Singh Neeta and Daljit Singh Rajput, who were detained in July and accused of conspiring to secure the escape of prisoners. Jaspal Singh Dhillon, Chair of the Human Rights and Democracy Forum and closely involved with the Punjab Committee for Coordination on Disappearances, previously "disappeared" for a month in 1993 and was only released after an international campaign. All three men remained in judicial custody at the end of 1998.

Torture, including rape, and ill-treatment continued to be endemic throughout the country. Three employees of a society dealing with disadvantaged women and children in Rajasthan, which had been involved in state-wide protests about the treatment of rape victims, were reportedly tortured after their arrest in August. Abdul Sattar was taken to Bassi police station in August and reportedly stripped naked and beaten. For the next five days he said he was tortured, including with electric shocks to his hands, feet and genitals. Sita Ram and Satya Narain were repeatedly beaten by police. All three were threatened and reportedly forced to confess to serious crimes and to implicate other employees of the society. They were subsequently charged and were awaiting trial at the end of the year.

There were continuing reports of rape by members of the security forces in various parts of the country. In June Naorem Ongbi Thoinu Devi was reportedly raped by a soldier in her house in Kakching village in Manipur. An investigation was carried out by members of the armed forces under the Army Act which allows members of the armed forces to be tried by court martial rather than by a civil court. The outcome of the investigation was not known at the end of the year.

Hundreds of people were reported to have died in custody. The NHRC continued to monitor deaths in police and judicial custody and to call for reports from the authorities about steps taken to investigate such deaths and bring those responsible to justice.

Prison conditions amounted to cruel, inhuman or degrading treatment in many facilities, including juvenile homes. Severe overcrowding, lack of medical facilities, poor sanitation and ill-treatment by prison staff continued to be reported. NHRC recommendations issued in 1996 calling for reform of prison legislation had not been implemented by the end of the year (see *Amnesty International Report 1997*).

"Disappearances" continued to be reported during the year – predominantly in Jammu and Kashmir, Assam and Manipur. Legislation protecting members of the security forces from investigation and prosecution continued to prevent the determination of the fate of the "disappeared".

In Manipur, five separate inquiries were carried out into the "disappearance" of 15-year-old Yumlembam Sanamacha following his arrest by members of the 17th Rajputana Rifles in February from his home in Angtha village, Thoubal district,

194

Manipur. Two brothers – 15-year-old Bimol Singh and Inao Singh – who were arrested with him, said that they had last seen him shortly after arrest being tortured by army personnel at the side of the road. The authorities initially denied that Yumlembam Sanamacha had been arrested, then said that he had escaped from custody. Moves by the central government to prevent the state government from investigating the case meant that no members of the armed forces had been prosecuted for his "disappearance" by the end of the year.

In August Haleema Begum and her 14-year-old son, Shakeel Ahmed, were shot dead by unidentified gunmen in their home in Srinagar, Jammu and Kashmir. Since the "disappearance" of her son, Bilal Ahmad Bhat, following his arrest by the security forces in December 1992, Haleema Begum had campaigned to highlight the issue of "disappearances" in Jammu and Kashmir and the plight of relatives of the "disappeared", many of whom suffer severe economic disadvantage because of the loss of male members of their families. No investigation had been carried out into the deaths of Haleema Begum and her youngest son by the end of the year.

Hundreds of extrajudicial executions were reported in many states. In September, a judicial inquiry ordered by the Maharashtra High Court into three incidents among scores of so-called "encounter" killings of armed criminal suspects by the Mumbai (Bombay) police (see *Amnesty International Report 1998*) found that the police version of events was false and that there was evidence to suggest that the three men concerned were extrajudicially executed.

In September a 10-year-old boy was killed and several others were injured during a cordon-and-search operation in Nowpora village in Jammu and Kashmir. Parents were delivering their children to school when members of the Border Security Forces opened fire, reportedly indiscriminately. An investigation was reported to have been ordered, but had not been completed by the end of the year.

At least 35 people were sentenced to death. Among them were 26 men and women sentenced to death by a special court in Tamil Nadu in January after what

appeared to be an unfair trial. Most had been arrested in 1991 in connection with the assassination of former Prime Minister Rajiv Gandhi and were tried under the lapsed Terrorist and Disruptive Activities (Prevention) Act, which included provisions that contravened international fair trial standards. One of the women sentenced, A. Athirai, was reported to have been only 17 years old at the time of her arrest. Appeals against the sentences were still before the Supreme Court at the end of the year.

No executions were reported during the year but the Home Minister referred on several occasions to government plans to extend the use of the death penalty for crimes including rape, child rape and the carrying of explosives.

Two men under sentence of death in Andhra Pradesh (see *Amnesty International Report 1998*) had their sentences commuted to life imprisonment by the President in May.

There were increasing reports of attacks on religious minorities including Christians and Muslims, most notably in Gujarat state. Many of the attacks were reportedly carried out by members of militant Hindu groups. The National Commission for Minorities investigated reported incidents in Gujarat in August and expressed serious concern about the situation, pointing to violations of fundamental rights. Its recommendations included increased training of police in order to ensure respect for the rights of minorities.

In August, in response to public pressure, the state government of Maharashtra published the report of the Srikrishna Commission of Inquiry set up in 1993 to investigate the circumstances surrounding riots between members of the Hindu and Muslim communities in Mumbai in December 1992 and January 1993 following the destruction of the mosque at Ayodhya (see *Amnesty International Reports 1993* and *1994*). The report pointed to communalism within the police force which led to discrimination against members of the Muslim community during the riots and incitement to riot by members of the *Shiv Sena* political party. The government of Maharashtra, a *Shiv Sena*-BJP alliance, dismissed the majority of the recommendations which had been made in the report.

Armed groups continued to commit grave human rights abuses, including torture, hostage-taking and deliberate and arbitrary killings of civilians. In the north of Assam, violence between armed Bodo groups and non-Bodo tribal people escalated during September and October. More than 140 people were reported to have been killed between 1 September and 10 October. In December, 23 Muslims were shot dead by suspected members of an armed Bodo group in Kokrajhar district. In January unidentified gunmen shot dead 23 civilians, including four children, in the village of Vandhama, near the town of Ganderbal in Jammu and Kashmir, before setting fire to a Hindu temple. Similar incidents continued to occur throughout the year in Jammu and Kashmir.

Hostages abducted by armed groups in previous years remained held. The fate of Sanjay Ghosh, a social and environmental activist detained by the United Liberation Front of Assam in July 1997, remained unknown (see *Amnesty International Report 1998*). Hostage-taking by armed groups continued at an alarming rate in the state of Tripura.

Amnesty International published a number of reports, including *India: Manipur – the silencing of youth* in May and *India: A mockery of justice* in April. Amnesty International also raised concerns about the human rights of children in South Asia in a report, *Children in South Asia: Securing their rights*, in April.

In October Amnesty International submitted its comments on deficiencies in the 1993 Protection of Human Rights Act – under which the NHRC was established – to the Advisory Committee established by the NHRC in June to review the Act.

Amnesty International members took part in campaigns against sexual abuse of women and children by members of the security forces in Assam and Manipur and on a range of legal issues, including provisions of the ordinary criminal law which facilitate impunity for the police and security forces.

Throughout the year Amnesty International called on armed groups in Jammu and Kashmir and northeastern states to abide by the principles of international humanitarian law.

INDONESIA AND EAST TIMOR

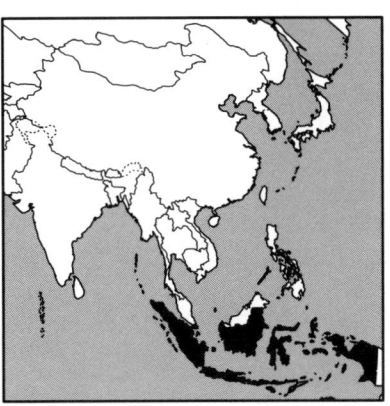

Although political reforms began, serious human rights violations continued. At least 358 prisoners of conscience were detained. Four were sentenced to prison terms and 19 others were on trial or awaiting trial at the end of the year. Hundreds of people were briefly detained without charge or trial. While at least 179 political prisoners, including prisoners of conscience, sentenced in previous years were released, at least 172 remained in custody. Torture and "disappearances" continued. Dozens of people were killed by the security forces in suspicious circumstances. Previous cases of "disappearances" and extrajudicial executions remained unresolved. At least 30 people remained under sentence of death. There were no executions.

In January deepening economic crisis caused widespread unemployment and financial hardship. In March President Suharto was re-elected for a seventh consecutive term after elections in which he was the only candidate. Widespread protest against the re-election and disquiet over the economic crisis culminated in demonstrations by thousands of students in the capital, Jakarta. In May, four university students were unlawfully killed by the military in Jakarta, prompting two days of rioting during which more than 1,000 people reportedly died. On 21 May President Suharto resigned and his deputy, B.J. Habibie, became President, promising political and economic reforms. In

196

November new laws covering elections, parliament and the formation of political parties were approved in principle and dates were set for parliamentary and presidential elections in 1999.

In April the Chairman of the UN Commission on Human Rights made a statement criticizing Indonesia's lack of implementation of recommendations contained in previous statements and resolutions from the Commission. The statement, which was accepted by the Commission's member states, also noted Indonesia's invitation to the UN Working Group on Arbitrary Detention to visit East Timor before the next session of the Commission.

In May the government ratified International Labour Organisation Convention No. 87 concerning Freedom of Association and Protection of the Right to Organise. In June the government announced a National Plan of Action on Human Rights, committing Indonesia to ratification of major human rights treaties over a five-year period.

In October Indonesia ratified the UN Convention against Torture and Other Cruel, Inhuman or Degrading Treatment or Punishment.

In August the government signed a Memorandum of Understanding with the UN High Commissioner for Human Rights (UNHCHR), providing the basis for a technical cooperation program, including human rights education and the strengthening of national institutions. The Memorandum envisaged the placement in Jakarta of a UNHCHR officer with access to East Timor, but regrettably excluded human rights monitoring.

In November the UN Special Rapporteur on violence against women conducted a mission to Indonesia and East Timor.

The National Commission on Human Rights (*Komnas HAM*) investigated land and labour disputes, allegations of unlawful killings, "disappearances" and torture. A *Komnas HAM* investigation into the riots in May was instrumental in establishing an independent inquiry into human rights violations during the riots. In August *Komnas HAM* released a report on human rights violations in Aceh over several years of counter-insurgency operations by the armed forces, concluding that at least 700 people had been unlawfully killed by the military. The *Komnas HAM* office in East Timor was not known to have con-ducted any investigations into human rights violations. *Komnas HAM* began operations in Irian Jaya.

At least 31 Indonesian prisoners of conscience remained in custody, including eight members of the People's Democratic Party or its affiliated organizations who were convicted in 1997. A ban on the organization was lifted during the year.

At least 358 prisoners of conscience were arrested during the year. At least 21 of them were threatened with charges or awaiting trial at the end of the year and two others were convicted. More than 330 people were arrested for peaceful political activities in connection with the March presidential election. Many had the charges against them dropped and the remaining prisoners were released after President Suharto resigned.

In September and October, six men were arrested in Irian Jaya for peaceful political activities, but were released pending trial. They were alleged to have arranged a meeting to discuss the political status of the province. A further 10 people were tried for their role in a flag-raising ceremony in Wamena, Irian Jaya. They were possible prisoners of conscience.

At least three East Timorese prisoners of conscience remained in prison; they were detained in connection with the 1991 Santa Cruz massacre (see previous *Amnesty International Reports*). Several East Timorese were arrested during the year for their peaceful activities in support of independence. In March Mateus Tilman and Manuel Gomes were sentenced to 18 months' imprisonment for insulting the President in leaflets they had distributed.

At least 179 Indonesian and East Timorese political prisoners, including prisoners of conscience, were released, had charges against them dropped or parole restrictions lifted in a program ordered by the new President. Many had only months to serve of their sentences and at least 47 had already been conditionally released. Independent labour leader Muchtar Pakpahan, serving a four-year prison sentence imposed in 1994, was among those released in May. Other subversion charges against him were dropped. Former member of parliament Sri Bintang Pamungkas, serving a 34-month prison sentence for insulting the President, was also released and additional subversion charges against him were dropped.

Three elderly men, in prison for over 30 years following their conviction for involvement in a coup attempt in 1965, were released. All three had been seriously ill for years and two required wheelchairs. A further 10 elderly men convicted after unfair trials in connection with the same events, four of whom were under sentence of death, remained in custody.

Hundreds of people were subjected to short-term arbitrary detention. In East Timor, at least 64 people were arbitrarily detained by the military in July for alleged links to armed opposition groups, despite the fact that the military has no legal authority to conduct arrests. Several others were held incommunicado by the military for months, including Rui Campus, an East Timorese man suspected of involvement with an armed opposition group, who was held without charge or trial from January.

Twenty men were tried unfairly on charges, including some brought under the Anti-subversion Law, relating to alleged activities in support of armed separatists in Aceh. Their trials had begun in 1997 and were completed in February. The men received prison sentences ranging from two and a half to 20 years. Many of the men were tortured, including by electric shocks, during long periods of incommunicado detention by the military. Information about their torture raised during the trials was not investigated or taken into account by the courts. Eight of them, who received lighter sentences, were released in August.

At least 14 East Timorese were sentenced to prison terms after unfair trials on charges of involvement in violent activities. Thirteen others were awaiting trial at the end of the year. In April Constancio dos Santos was sentenced to 20 years' imprisonment for possessing hand-made bombs. He said he had been tortured.

Torture and ill-treatment continued to be reported throughout Indonesia and East Timor. In March soldiers reportedly detained a village leader in Aceh, tied him to a wall, punched and kicked him and then held him under water. In the same area, soldiers reportedly tortured another man with electric shocks and then submerged him in sewage. In June soldiers reportedly arrested an East Timorese man named Samuel and poured boiling water on his upper body after accusing him of providing support to armed opposition groups.

In November a fact-finding team established by the government reported that 66 women, mostly ethnic Chinese, had been raped during violent disturbances in May which were partly provoked by members of the armed forces. The team recommended that those responsible be brought to justice, but by the end of the year no one had been charged. In East Timor, several women were raped by the security forces. Anastascia da Conceicao was reportedly raped and killed by the armed forces in Los Palos in September; there had been no investigation by the end of the year.

There were continuing reports of "disappearances". By the end of the year, the whereabouts of 13 political activists remained unknown. Five had "disappeared" in 1997, among them Yani Avri and Sony, who were arrested during the 1997 parliamentary election campaign. Eight "disappeared" during the political crisis in early 1998, including Suyat, Petrus Bima Anugerah and Herman Hendrawan, who were taken into military custody in February and March. A further nine men arrested and tortured by the military while being held incommunicado in Jakarta between February and April, who were subsequently released, confirmed that at least six of the missing activists were held in the same military facility. In August a military inquiry into the "disappearances" admitted that the nine released men had been abducted, but found no evidence of any military role in the "disappearance" of the other 13. The son-in-law of former President Suharto, Lieutenant General Prabowo, was discharged from the armed forces in connection with the abductions, purportedly for "misinterpreting" a military order. He later left the country. Two other senior military officers were relieved of their posts, but not discharged. It appeared that the three men would not face trial. Eleven lower ranking soldiers, however, were court-martialled in December for their role in the "disappearances".

In East Timor, at least eight people and possibly as many as 32 "disappeared" after being arrested by the security forces. In November Ernesto Gaspar, Domingos Soares and Julio Soares "disappeared" after they were arrested in Manufahi District.

In May, four unarmed university students were extrajudicially executed by the security forces during a demonstration in

198

Jakarta. Two policemen were convicted of disciplinary offences by a military court and sentenced to 10 and four months' imprisonment respectively in relation to the deaths, despite forensic evidence which indicated that the students were killed by weapons issued to the military, not the police. No one else was charged with ordering or carrying out the killings.

In Irian Jaya, several people were unlawfully killed in the context of pro-independence demonstrations. Six people were believed to have died after they were shot, wounded or ill-treated by soldiers during pro-independence demonstrations in different towns in July. Ruben Orboi was shot dead in Biak during a flag-raising demonstration. Although a few days earlier demonstrators had clashed with the security forces, on this occasion they were mostly sleeping when troops opened fire. In July *Komnas HAM* investigated his death, but the full results were not known by the end of the year.

In East Timor, several people were extrajudicially executed. In January Valente Bere-Mau, Simao Dau Mau, Lourenco Sorato and Jose Aru Biti were killed by members of the security forces and an armed paramilitary group in Coilima, Atabae, after they were detained on suspicion of links with armed opposition groups. Members of Indonesia's Human Rights Commission were believed to have investigated the killings, but the results were not publicly released and no one had been charged or arrested in connection with the killings by the end of the year.

At least 30 people remained under sentence of death at the end of the year. In April a husband and wife were sentenced to death in Medan for the murder of 42 women. The outcome of an appeal was not known by the end of the year. There were no executions.

There were claims by the armed forces, which were not independently confirmed, that armed opposition groups in East Timor, Aceh and Irian Jaya committed human rights abuses, including deliberate killings.

Amnesty International repeatedly appealed for the immediate and unconditional release of prisoners of conscience, the review of convictions of political prisoners, and an end to torture, "disappearances", extrajudicial executions and the death penalty.

Amnesty International released several reports, including in February, *Indonesia: Paying the price for stability*; in May, *Indonesia: An agenda for human rights reform*; and in June, *Indonesia and East Timor: Release prisoners of conscience now!* – a joint report with Human Rights Watch/Asia.

In a statement to the UN Commission on Human Rights in April, Amnesty International included reference to its concerns in both Indonesia and East Timor. In an oral statement to the UN Special Committee on Decolonization in July, Amnesty International called for a comprehensive human rights program in East Timor.

In September an Amnesty International delegation visited Indonesia and met representatives of the government and the armed forces.

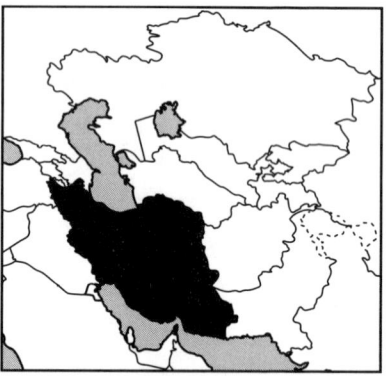

IRAN

Hundreds of political prisoners, including prisoners of conscience, were held. Some were detained without charge or trial; others continued to serve long prison sentences imposed after unfair trials. Reports of torture and ill-treatment continued to be received and judicial punishments of flogging and stoning continued to be imposed. Reports suggested that possible "disappearances" and extrajudicial executions had occurred. Scores of people were reportedly executed, including at least one prisoner of conscience; however, the true number may have been considerably higher. An unknown number of people remained under sentence of death, some after unfair trials. Armed opposition groups committed human rights abuses.

President Hojjatoleslam val Moslemin Sayed Mohammad Khatami proceeded cautiously with reforms in the face of opposition in the *majles* (parliament) and judiciary. Tensions increased on Iran's border with Afghanistan in September following the killing by Afghan *Taleban* forces of nine Iranian diplomats and a journalist.

The government continued to face armed opposition from the Iraq-based People's Mojahedin Organization of Iran (PMOI), as well as from the Kurdistan Democratic Party of Iran (KDPI), Arab separatist groups in Khuzestan, and Baluchi groups in Sistan-Baluchistan.

Civil unrest continued sporadically in various regions. In April clashes broke out after a demonstration in Tehran in support of former Tehran Mayor Gholam Hussain Karbaschi was attacked by members of *Ansar-e Hezbollah* (Helpers of Hezbollah), an informal group linked to elements in the Iranian government. A number of people were injured and others were arrested as security forces broke up the disturbances.

The UN Special Representative on the Islamic Republic of Iran continued to be denied access to the country during the year.

Prisoners of conscience continued to be detained. Four employees of the daily newspaper *Tous* – Mashallah Shamsolva'ezin, Hamid Reza Jalaipour, Mohammad Javadi Hessar and Rahim Nabavi – were arrested after *Tous* was banned in September. They were released conditionally in October. *Tous* had replaced the journal *Jameah*, banned in July for "publishing lies and disturbing public order", and maintained its editorial staff. Earlier in the year Mashallah Shamsolva'ezin, then editor of *Jameah*, had been attacked outside the journal's offices by members of *Ansar-e Hezbollah*.

Hojjatoleslam Sayed Mohsen Saidzadeh, an Islamic scholar, was arrested in June reportedly as a result of an article on the role of women in Islam. He was released in December.

In July Mohammad Reza Za'eri, editor of *Khaneh* magazine, was found guilty by the Press Court of publishing an article which allegedly insulted the late Ayatollah Ruhollah Khomeini. Mohammad Reza Za'eri was released from custody after issuing a public apology and paying a surety of 20 million rials (US$6,700).

Former Deputy Prime Minister 'Abbas Amir Entezam, who was released from detention in May 1997 (see *Amnesty International Report 1998*), was rearrested in September 1998 following a radio interview in which he reportedly criticized the human rights record of Assadollah Lajevardi, the former governor of Evin prison who was killed in August (see below). Despite recommendations by the presiding judge that 'Abbas Amir Entezam be released on bail, the authorities of Evin prison reportedly refused to release him at the end of September. A court hearing to answer charges of defamation brought against 'Abbas Amir Entezam was set initially for October. However, since 'Abbas Amir Entezam was reportedly prevented from attending the hearing by prison authorities, the hearing was postponed. 'Abbas Amir Entezam was reportedly still held in Evin prison at the end of the year.

Other prisoners of conscience who continued to be held after arrest in previous years included at least 20 members of the Baha'i religious minority, at least six of whom were under sentence of death. Among them were Sirous Zabihi Moqaddam and Hedayatollah Kashefi, arrested in 1997 and sentenced to death in Mashhad for their alleged role in the conversion of a Muslim woman to the Baha'i faith.

Grand Ayatollah Hossein 'Ali Montazeri, arrested in November 1997 after making a speech which apparently criticized the leadership of Iran, reportedly remained under house arrest in Qom (see *Amnesty International Report 1998*). Mass arrests of Grand Ayatollah Montazeri's supporters – including his son-in-law, Hadi Hashemi – took place prior to a planned demonstration in his home town of Najafabad in May. Some were reportedly ill-treated in detention.

Other Shi'a religious leaders opposed to aspects of government policy, as well as large numbers of their supporters, continued to be detained. Some or all were possible prisoners of conscience. Some were held without charge or trial, others following unfair trials. At least three Grand Ayatollahs were believed to remain under house arrest, including Grand Ayatollah Sayed Hassan Tabataba'i-Qomi, who was reportedly denied access to medical treatment for heart disease (see *Amnesty International Report 1998*). Several supporters of Grand Ayatollah Sayed Mohammad Shirazi also reportedly remained in detention.

Scores of people arrested following demonstrations in Tabriz and hundreds of others arrested on suspicion of offences such as espionage, "propagating pan-Turkism" or "counter-revolution", continued to be held without charge or trial (see previous *Amnesty International Reports*).

Faraj Sarkouhi, a magazine editor who had "disappeared" for seven weeks in 1996 and was rearrested in January 1997 (see *Amnesty International Reports 1997* and *1998*), was released from detention in January and subsequently left the country.

Political prisoners continued to receive unfair trials. Detainees were reportedly denied access either to any legal counsel or to a lawyer of their choice, despite legislation providing for the right to legal representation. Trials before special courts, such as the Special Court for the Clergy, continued to fall far short of international standards.

Gholam Hussain Karbaschi, former Mayor of Tehran and a close political ally of President Khatami, was arrested in April on charges of corruption and embezzlement. He was sentenced in July to five years' imprisonment, 60 lashes (subsequently set aside on appeal) and a heavy fine. He was also banned from public office for 20 years. Sixteen other Tehran district mayors were also arrested during the investigation, some of whom were sentenced to flogging. Trial proceedings in the case fell short of international standards for fair trial. For example, none of the Tehran municipality officials arrested during the investigation appeared to have had access to a lawyer during their detention. In December an appeal court reduced the custodial sentence against Gholam Hussain Karbaschi from five to two years. An appeal to the Supreme Court was pending at the end of the year.

Political prisoners serving long prison terms after unfair trials included: supporters of the PMOI; members of the *Mohajerin* movement (followers of Dr 'Ali Shari'ati); members of leftist organizations such as the *Tudeh* party, *Peykar* and factions of the Organization of the People's Fedaiyan of Iran; supporters of Kurdish groups such as *Komala* and the KDPI; and supporters of other groups representing ethnic minorities such as Baluchis and Arabs.

Torture and ill-treatment continued to be reported. Many of the Tehran municipality officials mentioned above claimed they were tortured to elicit confessions or to incriminate others: methods used reportedly included beatings with hands, feet and sticks; flogging with whips; sleep deprivation, at times combined with being forced to stand for long periods; exposure to loud noises; lack of food; and threats to relatives.

Judicial punishments amounting to torture or cruel, inhuman or degrading punishment continued to be reported. Flogging was reportedly imposed for a wide range of offences, at times in conjunction with the death penalty or a custodial sentence. Vahide Ghassemi, the co-accused of Helmut Hofer (see below), was reportedly sentenced to 100 lashes in October after she was convicted of illicit sexual relations. It was unknown whether the sentence was carried out. In November Khosrow Ebrahimi was acquitted after he escaped from the pit in which he had been buried to the waist in order to be stoned to death in the town of Lahijan. He had been sentenced to death for adultery. Mohammad 'Ali Ataei, originally sentenced to death by a military court in the city of Rasht in January on vaguely worded charges including robbery and "being against the people", reportedly received 300 lashes before being released in July.

A number of possible "disappearances" were reported. Pirouz Davani, a critic of the government who had spent four years in prison between 1990 and 1994, "disappeared" in August in Tehran. The authorities denied all knowledge of his whereabouts.

Reports of deaths in circumstances which suggested possible extrajudicial executions continued to be received. According to reports, Aman Naroui, a Sunni cleric from Zabol, Sistan-Baluchistan province, was killed by unidentified gunmen in July following his criticism of government policies in the region. To Amnesty International's knowledge the killing was not investigated.

The threat of extrajudicial execution continued to extend to Iranian nationals resident abroad, as well as to non-Iranians. In September President Khatami and other senior officials sought to distance themselves from the late Ayatollah Ruhollah Khomeini's 1989 *fatwa* calling for the death of author Salman Rushdie, a United Kingdom national, as well as from the US$2.5 million bounty offered for Salman Rushdie's life by the 15 Khordad Foundation (see previous *Amnesty International Reports*). However, several senior religious figures and members of parliament in Iran continued to support the *fatwa*, and in October the 15 Khordad Foundation increased to US$3 million the reward for killing Salman Rushdie.

In November Majid Sharif, a journalist and translator who had reportedly written articles advocating the separation of the state and religion, was found dead after he failed to return from a religious ceremony in the city of Mashhad. The circumstances of his death were suspicious. The same month Dariyush Foruhar, leader of the banned *Hezb-e Mellat-e Iran*, Iran Nation Party, and his wife, Parvaneh Foruhar, were killed at their home in Tehran. In December Mohammad Mokhtari and Mohammad Ja'far Puyandeh, both of whom had been questioned by the authorities in October in connection with their desire to establish an independent writers' association, were found dead. They had "disappeared" a few days earlier. Both had reportedly been strangled. An investigation was in progress at the end of the year.

The death penalty continued to be widely used, often imposed for vaguely worded offences – including political offences and those relating to freedom of belief – frequently after unfair trials. Scores of executions, including a number carried out in public, were reported, although the true figures may well have been considerably higher.

Morteza Firouzi, editor of the English-language daily *Iran News* who was held in unacknowledged detention for over 10 weeks in 1997 (see *Amnesty International Report 1998*), was reportedly sentenced to death in January on charges of "spying for a foreign country". In May the death sentence was upheld by the Supreme Court, but shortly afterwards the case was referred back to the Court of First Instance for reconsideration. There was no further news of Morteza Firouzi's fate.

Ruhollah Rowhani was executed in Mashhad in July after he was convicted of converting a Shi'a Muslim woman to the Baha'i faith. Two other Baha'is who were convicted in the same case remained in Mashhad prison under sentence of death.

Helmut Hofer, a German, was sentenced to death in January for having sexual relations with an Iranian Muslim woman, Vahide Ghassemi (see above). Following an appeal, the court of first hearing reinstated the death sentence in October. A second appeal was pending before the Supreme Court.

In August 'Abdollah Amini was reportedly given four death sentences on charges of KDPI membership and involvement in the killing of Iranian Revolutionary Guard prisoners while he was commandant of a KDPI internment camp during the 1980s. It was not known whether he was executed.

Hossein Dowlatkhah, a businessman reportedly convicted in 1997 of "corruption on earth" and other offences was hanged in Tehran in November.

In June the PMOI caused bomb explosions at three locations in Tehran, including the office of the Islamic Revolutionary Prosecutor, in which an unconfirmed number of people were killed, some or all of whom were civilians. The PMOI claimed responsibility for the killing in August of Assadollah Lajevardi, former governor of Evin prison, and two other people.

Amnesty International called for the unconditional and immediate release of all prisoners of conscience and a review of legislation which allows for the imprisonment of prisoners of conscience. Amnesty International urged the authorities to review the cases of political prisoners, so that those sentenced after an unfair trial could be promptly retried in accordance with international standards. Amnesty International also urged that those detained without charge or trial be charged with recognizably criminal offences and given fair trials, or released.

Amnesty International called on the government to ensure impartial and thorough investigations into allegations of torture, "disappearances" and extrajudicial executions, and to bring those responsible to justice. The organization also called for the commutation of death sentences and of judicial punishments amounting to torture or cruel, inhuman or degrading punishment.

Amnesty International received replies from the authorities clarifying some cases, but the replies did not address many of the organization's continuing human rights concerns.

Amnesty International continued to investigate the situation of detainees reportedly held by some armed opposition groups. It called on the PMOI to stop targeting civilians in armed attacks.

IRAQ

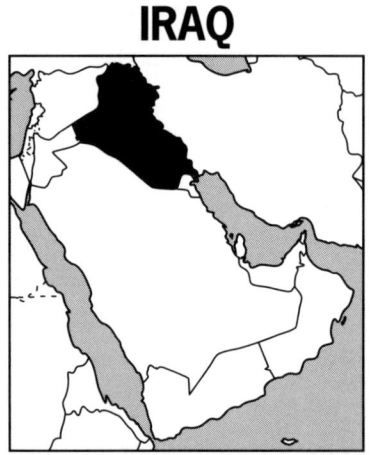

Suspected political opponents, including possible prisoners of conscience, continued to be arrested and tens of thousands of others arrested in previous years remained held. Scores of Kurdish families were forcibly expelled from their homes and members of targeted families detained. Torture and ill-treatment of prisoners and detainees were widely reported. According to reports, at least six people had their hands amputated as punishment. There was no further news on the fate of thousands of people who "disappeared" in previous years. Hundreds of people, including political prisoners, were reportedly executed; some may have been extrajudicially executed. Death sentences continued to be imposed, including for non-violent offences. Human rights abuses were reported in areas under Kurdish control.

Iraq remained under the economic sanctions imposed in 1990 by UN Security Council resolutions. Deaths of thousands of civilians, including many children, owing to malnutrition and lack of medicines as a result of the sanctions continued to be reported. In September, during consideration of the report on Iraq under the Convention on the Rights of the Child, the Committee on the Rights of the Child observed that children had been most affec-

ted by the sanctions. Two "air-exclusion zones" over northern and southern Iraq also remained in force.

In January the government barred some members of the UN Special Commission (UNSCOM) from inspecting suspected weapon sites, including eight presidential palaces. A US-government-led coalition threatened military action against Iraq unless full access to UNSCOM inspectors was allowed. In February Iraq signed a memorandum of understanding with the UN Security Council and agreed to allow unconditional and unrestricted access to all suspected weapon sites. However, in August Iraq suspended cooperation with UNSCOM, prompting the UN Security Council to adopt Resolution 1194 in September effectively maintaining UN sanctions on Iraq until it resumed cooperation with UN weapons inspectors. In October Iraq announced that it had ended all cooperation with UNSCOM. In November military strikes by US and United Kingdom (UK) government forces against Iraq were aborted after Iraq resumed full cooperation with UNSCOM. However, following an UNSCOM report which stated that Iraq had failed to cooperate fully with UN weapons inspectors, US and UK forces launched air strikes for four days against Iraq in December, during which civilians were reportedly killed.

In February the UN Security Council adopted a resolution authorizing Iraq to sell oil worth US$5.2 billion every six months and use the proceeds for humanitarian purposes. Iraq had previously been allowed to sell oil worth US$2 billion every six months.

Thousands of Turkish government forces remained deployed in parts of northern Iraq (see *Amnesty International Report 1998*) and made further incursions into the area in pursuit of members and fighters of the Turkish opposition Kurdish Workers' Party (PKK).

In September leaders of the Kurdistan Democratic Party (KDP) and Patriotic Union of Kurdistan (PUK) met in Washington, USA, and signed a peace agreement that included a commitment to elect a new parliament in 1999 for areas controlled by the two groups. Subsequent meetings took place in Iraqi Kurdistan and in Turkey to discuss implementation of the agreement. The two sides also exchanged prisoners.

In April the UN Commission on Human Rights condemned the "systematic, widespread and extremely grave violations of human rights and of international humanitarian law by the government of Iraq", and extended for a further year the mandate of the UN Special Rapporteur on Iraq.

Reports of arrests of suspected political opponents, including possible prisoners of conscience, continued throughout the year, although it was not possible to ascertain the number. Thousands of suspected political opponents and others arrested in previous years in connection with antigovernment protests remained held incommunicado.

Dawud al-Farhan, a well-known journalist and writer, was arrested and detained for at least two months after he was reportedly summoned to the Ministry of Information in the capital, Baghdad, apparently in connection with articles he had written in *al-Zawra'* newspaper which criticized government officials and the economic situation of Iraq. He was released in September reportedly after being pardoned by the President. A group of suspected government opponents from the southern city of al-Nassiriya were arrested; the date of arrest was not known. They were believed to have been held at *al-Amn al-'Am* (General Security Directorate) in Baghdad and reportedly sentenced to death. Details of trial procedures in their cases were not known. Those held included Sayyid 'Ubadi al-Batat, Yassin 'Ali al-Washah and Lieutenant-Colonel Muhammad Hardan al-Jubair. Their fate remained unknown at the end of the year.

In February President Saddam Hussein reportedly ordered the release of hundreds of Arab prisoners, including Palestinians, Lebanese, Syrians and Egyptians. More than 50 Jordanians had been released in January. All those freed were believed to have been held on criminal charges.

In January the authorities issued an order for the forcible expulsion of 1,468 Kurdish families resident in the Kirkuk province to provinces under KDP or PUK control, citing the "security and geographical importance" of the area as the reason for the expulsions. The order also stated that one person from each targeted family must be detained. By the end of June more than 100 families were said to have been expelled and further expulsions were subsequently reported. Members of the targeted families were detained as "hostages" until the expulsions of their respective families had been completed.

Torture and ill-treatment of prisoners and detainees were widely reported. Methods used included electric shocks to various parts of the body, long periods of suspension by the limbs accompanied by beating, *falaqa* (beating on the soles of the feet), cigarette burns and solitary confinement.

In August, six members of a group known as *Fida'yi Saddam* (Saddam's Fighters) reportedly had their hands amputated by order of 'Uday Saddam Hussain, the President's eldest son. They were reportedly accused of theft and extortion from travellers in the southern city of Basra.

There was no further news on the fate of thousands of people who "disappeared" in previous years (see previous *Amnesty International Reports*). Among the victims was Sayyid Muhammad Sadeq Muhammad Ridha al-Qazwini, a Shi'a Muslim cleric born in 1900, who was arrested in 1980 apparently to put pressure on his sons abroad to stop their anti-government political activities; and 'Aziz al-Sayyid Jassem, a well-known writer and journalist who was arrested in 1991. Unconfirmed reports suggested that 'Aziz al-Sayyid Jassem was still in detention in 1996 but his fate and whereabouts since then remained unknown.

Hundreds of people, including political prisoners, were reportedly executed; some may have been extrajudicially executed. Death sentences continued to be imposed, including for non-violent offences. The victims included suspected political opponents, members of opposition groups, military officers suspected of involvement in alleged coup attempts and other people convicted of criminal offences.

Around June Muhammad Haj Rashid Hussain al-Tamimi was executed and his body handed over to his family. He had been arrested at his home in Baghdad in December 1997 on suspicion of organizing opposition groups. His brother, Colonel Tariq Haj Rashid Hussain al-Tamimi, had been executed in 1988 for his involvement in a plot to overthrow the government. In April a senior Shi'a Muslim cleric, Ayatollah Shaikh Mortadha al-Borujerdi, aged 67, was shot dead, reportedly while walking home from early morning prayers in

204

the city of al-Najaf. He had reportedly survived two previous assassination attempts. In June another senior Shi'a Muslim cleric, Grand Ayatollah Shaikh Mirza 'Ali al-Gharawi, aged 68, his son-in-law Muhammad 'Ali al-Faqih and two other people were shot dead at night when the car in which they were travelling was stopped between Karbala' and al-Najaf. According to reports, their bodies were buried by the authorities immediately after the incident and their families were not allowed to hold a funeral ceremony. In November, eight people were said to have been arrested in connection with the killings of Ayatollah Shaikh Mortadha al-Borujerdi and Grand Ayatollah Shaikh Mirza 'Ali al-Gharawi. The authorities reportedly announced that robbery was the reason for the killings.

There were further reports of executions of prisoners, including political prisoners (see *Amnesty International Report 1998*). In June more than 60 prisoners were said to have been executed at Abu Ghraib Prison near Baghdad. Most had reportedly been arrested in the aftermath of the March 1991 uprising against the government. In September at least 100 political prisoners, including 21 women, were reportedly executed and their bodies buried in mass graves.

A number of people who were convicted of criminal offences were executed, including a group of 10 men who were convicted of smuggling and two others who were convicted of murder and theft. The executions reportedly took place in January and May respectively. No information was available about any trial procedures in the cases.

There was no further news about a group of five men and one woman who were sentenced to death in July 1997 on charges of organized prostitution and smuggling alcohol to Saudi Arabia (see *Amnesty International Report 1998*). However, Ghalib 'Ammar Shihab al-Din, a Jordanian national who was sentenced to death in December 1997 on charges of smuggling, was released in January and returned to Jordan after the death sentence against him had been commuted (see *Amnesty International Report 1998*).

In the areas under Kurdish control there was fighting between Turkish government forces and PKK forces. Thousands of civilians were said to have been forcibly

displaced as a result. Human rights abuses were also reported. In April, two members of the Iraqi Workers' Communist Party (IWCP) – Shapoor 'Abd al-Qadir and Kabil 'Adil – were shot dead, reportedly outside the unemployment union's office in Arbil by members of a group called the Islamic League. The incident was said to be connected with clashes that arose over a debate on women's rights on the occasion of International Women's Day between members of the IWCP and the Islamic League. Death threats, allegedly made by Islamist groups, against women members of women's organizations and members of communist groups were reported. In one such case, Nazanin 'Ali Sharif, a leading member of the Independent Women's Organization in Arbil, reportedly received death threats and escaped an assassination attempt in June. In July she fled abroad and sought asylum.

The fate of Ahmad Sharifi, an Iranian national who was arrested in Sulaimaniya in January 1997, reportedly by PUK security forces, and then "disappeared"; and of Bekir Dogan, a Turkish national and television reporter, who "disappeared" reportedly after KDP security forces entered the Mesopotamian Cultural Centre in Arbil in May 1997, remained unknown (see *Amnesty International Report 1998*).

Amnesty International called on the government to release any prisoners of conscience, to halt expulsions of Kurdish families and allow those families already expelled to return. It also urged the government to declare a moratorium on executions and review all outstanding death sentences with a view to commuting them.

Amnesty International sought clarification from the government of reports that hundreds of prisoners had been executed in late 1997 in Abu Ghraib and al-Radhwaniya prisons. A list of 288 alleged victims was enclosed. The organization also expressed concern that trial procedures in the case of four Jordanian nationals who were executed in December 1997 (see *Amnesty International Report 1998*) violated Iraq's obligations under the International Covenant on Civil and Political Rights, to which Iraq is a State Party. Clarification of the fate of the five men and one woman who were sentenced to death in 1997 (see above) was also sought. In June the government responded and accused Amnesty International of repeating the same allegations as in the organization's previous reports, and claimed that the list of people reportedly executed in late 1997 lacked details that would "facilitate finding the truth". However, the government failed to respond substantively to reports of mass executions and to Amnesty International's concerns about other human rights violations.

In April Amnesty International expressed concern at the expulsion of Kurdish families from Kirkuk province. In June it expressed concern about the killings in April and June of two senior Shi'a Muslim clerics (see above) and sought information about the circumstances of the killings as well as details of any judicial inquiries carried out. No response was received by the end of the year.

In April Amnesty International wrote to the KDP and raised concern at the killing in Arbil of two members of the IWCP (see above). The organization sought details of any inquiries carried out into the killings. In May the KDP responded that an investigation had been immediately launched and one person had been arrested, but the full results were not known by the end of the year.

In November and December Amnesty International called on the US, UK and Iraqi governments to ensure maximum protection of civilian lives in accordance with international humanitarian law. In its response the UK government indicated that in any military action by UK forces "everything possible will be done to avoid civilian casualties". No response was received from the US and Iraqi authorities.

IRELAND

One person was shot in disputed circumstances. Asylum-seekers were deported under procedures which do not guarantee a full and fair determination of asylum applications.

In April the government signed the Multi-Party Agreement concerning the future of Northern Ireland. The Agreement proposed the establishment of three interconnected bodies: one within Northern Ireland; one between Northern Ireland and the Republic of Ireland; and a third between the Irish Republic and the United Kingdom. The Agreement also contained proposals for mechanisms to promote and protect human rights, and included commitments to review emergency legislation provisions (see **United Kingdom** entry).

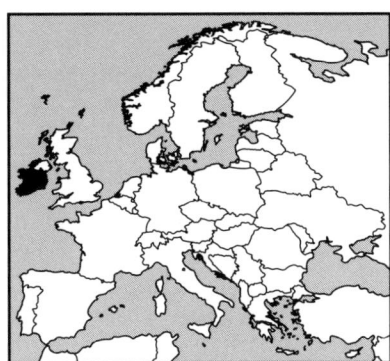

New emergency provisions passed in September violate international standards. The Offences Against the State (Amendment) Act 1998 was passed in the wake of a bomb-blast in Omagh, Northern Ireland, which resulted in the deaths of 29 people. In trials for certain offences, including membership of an unlawful organization, the new law permits courts to draw adverse inferences from a suspect's exercise of the right to remain silent during police questioning. The law also extends the period of detention without charge for certain offences and creates new offences, including collection or possession of information likely to be useful to members of illegal organizations, withholding information, and directing an illegal organization (see **United Kingdom** entry).

In May Rónán MacLochlainn was shot in disputed circumstances by officers from a special police unit while fleeing from the scene of an attempted armed robbery. Initial police statements reporting that he was killed during a shoot-out were subsequently retracted. The inquest into his death was pending at the end of the year.

Asylum-seekers were deported under procedures which were not independent, and which did not provide for a full and fair hearing of all asylum applications.

Amnesty International continued to urge the government to fully implement the 1996 Refugee Act and to ensure that all asylum-seekers, including those who arrived after travelling through other European Union countries, received full and fair hearings of their applications.

206

Amnesty International welcomed the repeated commitments to respect human rights in the Multi-Party Agreement, including proposals to establish a human rights commission for the Republic of Ireland; the commitment to consider incorporating the European Convention for the Protection of Human Rights and Fundamental Freedoms into domestic law; and the promise of a wide-ranging review of the Offences Against the State Act.

In September Amnesty International called on legislators not to adopt the Offences Against the State (Amendment) Bill 1998 which it believed violated international standards and was inconsistent with the government's commitment in the Multi-Party Agreement to the early removal of emergency powers.

Amnesty International urged the government to ensure that all killings in disputed circumstances, including those of Rónán MacLochlainn and John Morris, who was killed in similar circumstances in 1997, were promptly, thoroughly and impartially investigated. The organization urged that the families be kept informed of the progress of the investigations and that the results of investigations be published.

ISRAEL
(STATE OF)
AND THE OCCUPIED TERRITORIES

At least 1,200 Palestinians were arrested on security grounds and at least 270 administrative detention orders were served. Scores of administrative detainees were released early in the year. Eighty-three Palestinians remained held in administrative detention at the end of the year. Prisoners of conscience and possible prisoners of conscience included administrative detainees, conscientious objectors and sentenced prisoners. At least 40 Lebanese nationals were imprisoned in Israel; 22 of them were held without charge or trial or after expiry of their sentences. A further 140 Lebanese nationals were held without charge or trial in the part of South Lebanon occupied by Israel. Other political prisoners included more than 1,500 Palestinians sentenced after unfair trials in previous years. More than 70 Palestinian prisoners were released in the context of peace agreements. Hundreds of Palestinians were tried before military courts, whose procedures failed to comply with international fair trial standards. Torture and ill-treatment continued to be officially sanctioned and used systematically during interrogation of security detainees. Israeli security forces killed at least 20 Palestinian civilians in circumstances suggesting that they may have been extrajudicially executed or otherwise unlawfully killed. One house was destroyed as punishment.

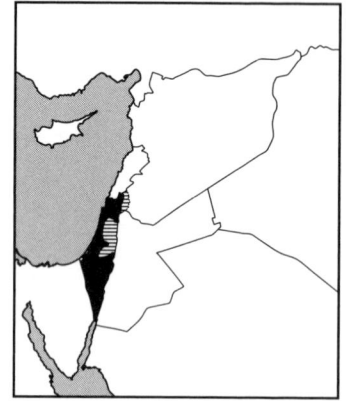

In October the Israeli government and the Palestine Liberation Organization (PLO) signed the Wye River Memorandum under which Israel agreed to withdraw its troops from a further 13 per cent of the West Bank, and the PLO agreed to "take all measures necessary" to protect Israel's security. The Israeli government maintained the border closures between Israel and the West Bank (excluding East Jerusalem), and between Israel and the Gaza Strip, restricting severely Palestinians' freedom of movement (see **Palestinian Authority** entry). The closure was strengthened in September after threats of attacks by the Islamist opposition group *Hamas* on Israeli civilians. Israeli security forces destroyed scores of Palestinian houses in the Occupied Territories claiming they had been built without permits.

Violent demonstrations occurred in many areas of the Occupied Territories, particularly in May (the 50th anniversary of the establishment of the State of Israel) and in December (calling for the release of political prisoners). During the year attacks continued to be carried out on Palestinians by armed Israeli settlers and on settlers by armed Palestinians. Armed opposition groups targeted civilians in attacks in Jerusalem and elsewhere.

A bill regulating the General Security Service (GSS) passed its first reading in the *Knesset* (parliament) in January; the law failed to outlaw the use of torture or ill-treatment. In July the government withdrew a draft law which would have invalidated the majority of compensation claims brought against the Israeli security forces for human rights violations committed in the Occupied Territories (see *Amnesty International Report 1998*).

In January the UN Special Rapporteur, appointed pursuant to Commission on Human Rights resolution 1993/2A "to investigate Israel's violations of the principles and bases of international law", visited areas under the Palestinian Authority's jurisdiction. Israel continued to refuse cooperation with the Special Rapporteur.

In May the UN Committee against Torture examined Israel's second periodic report. It stated that hooding, shackling in painful positions, sleep deprivation and shaking of detainees – interrogation methods which Israel admitted using – constituted torture as defined in Article 1 of the UN Convention against Torture and Other Cruel, Inhuman or Degrading Treatment or Punishment. The Committee also requested Israel to review the practice of administrative detention to ensure that it complied with Article 16 of the Convention. In May the UN Working Group on Arbitrary Detention declared that the detention of 21 Lebanese nationals (see below) by Israel was arbitrary. In July the UN Human Rights Committee's initial report on its implementation of the International Covenant on Civil and Political Rights (ICCPR) and affirmed the Covenant's applicability to territories occupied by Israel. It stated that interrogation methods used by Israel and the use of administrative detention violated the ICCPR and expressed concern about unlawful killings and demolition of Palestinian houses.

At least 270 administrative detention orders were served; 83 Palestinians remained in administrative detention at the end of the year. In early 1998 scores of ad-ministrative detainees, many of whom had been detained for years, were released. Wissam Rafidi, a prisoner of conscience, and 'Itaf 'Alyan were released in January (see *Amnesty International Report 1998*). Ahmad Qatamesh was released from administrative detention in April; he had been held for more than five years (see previous *Amnesty International Reports*). 'Usama Jamil Barham remained in administrative detention at the end of the year; he had been held since November 1993 except for 17 days in September 1994. He appealed twice against his detention; both appeals took place without him or his lawyer being able to examine evidence against him.

Prisoners of conscience and possible prisoners of conscience held during the year included administrative detainees, conscientious objectors and sentenced prisoners. For example, a military court sentenced Andrew Hare, a conscientious objector, to 28 days' imprisonment in June for refusing to serve in the Israeli Defence Forces (IDF). He was released in July. Charges brought against 'Ilham Abu Saleh in 1997 were dropped and she was released from house arrest (see *Amnesty International Report 1998*).

At the end of the year at least 40 Lebanese nationals were imprisoned in Israel. In addition, 140 Lebanese nationals – men, women and children – were held without charge or trial in Khiam Detention Centre in Israeli-occupied South Lebanon (see **Lebanon** entry). At least 21 of the imprisoned Lebanese nationals were held in administrative detention, including 10 held without charge or trial for up to 12 years. In March the Supreme Court authorized the publication of its November 1997 ruling concerning 10 of these detainees, who were detained administratively after the expiry of their prison sentences. The Supreme Court found it lawful to hold prisoners as "bargaining chips" for exchange with Israeli nationals killed or missing in Lebanon or information concerning them. In May 'Ali Ahmed Banjak, who had been abducted from Lebanon in 1996, was released after a military appeals court upheld his acquittal of charges of membership of an illegal organization and attacking Israel. In June, 10 prisoners held in Israel and 50 prisoners held in Khiam Detention Centre were released in exchange for the return to Israel

208

of three Israeli soldiers' body parts retained by the Lebanese armed opposition groups *Amal* and *Hizbullah.* Among those released was Husayn Mikdad, held in administrative detention in Israel since 1996 as a hostage (see *Amnesty International Report 1998*).

More than 1,500 Palestinians sentenced in previous years for political offences remained in prison following trials that failed to comply with international fair trial standards. Hundreds of Palestinians were tried before military courts for offences such as membership of illegal organizations and stone-throwing. Confessions extracted through torture frequently formed the main evidence against defendants.

In March Mordechai Vanunu, serving a 17-year prison sentence for treason, was allowed restricted association with other prisoners after spending more than 11 years in solitary confinement (see previous *Amnesty International Reports*). In May a parole board rejected his application for early release. In September a parole board released 80-year-old Avraham Klingberg to house arrest on health grounds. He had been held since 1983 on charges of spying. Amnesty International had expressed concern about his health (see previous *Amnesty International Reports*).

Torture and ill-treatment continued to be officially sanctioned and used systematically during interrogation of security detainees. Official secret guidelines allowed the GSS to use "moderate" physical and psychological pressure. The ministerial committee overseeing the GSS continued to extend, for three-month periods, authorization to use "increased physical pressure". GSS officers were allowed to use *tiltul* (violent shaking) after obtaining permission from the head of the GSS.

In January the High Court of Justice scheduled an unprecedented hearing by nine judges to review the legality of interrogation methods used by the GSS. The Court held two hearings and had not ruled on the petitions by the end of the year. However, the Court continued to reject petitions for injunctions to prevent the GSS from using physical force to interrogate named detainees. For example, the Court twice refused to grant an injunction to prevent the use of torture against 'Abd al-Rahman Ghanimat, who had been arrested in November 1997. During his interrogation,

which lasted for weeks, the GSS forced him for five-day periods to sit on a small slanting chair to which his hands and legs were shackled, with a thick sack over his head. Loud music was played and he was deprived of sleep. 'Abd al-Rahman Ghanimat complained of dizziness and pain throughout his body.

Palestinians were frequently beaten or otherwise ill-treated at check-points, during demonstrations or immediately after arrest. In September the Israeli police reportedly injured dozens of Palestinian Israelis by beating demonstrators and firing tear gas and rubber bullets as they broke up a sit-in near Umm al-Fahm protesting against government plans to use a plot of land as an IDF training ground. Security forces also beat and ill-treated Jewish protesters. In August the Israeli police reportedly beat ultra-Orthodox Jews repeatedly with clubs during a demonstration in East Jerusalem against a road construction project which the demonstrators claimed would desecrate Jewish graves. In October the Israeli police repeatedly beat student protesters with clubs during a demonstration in Tel Aviv.

Israeli security forces killed at least 20 Palestinian civilians in circumstances suggesting that they may have been extrajudicially executed or otherwise unlawfully killed. In many cases those killed posed no danger to the lives of the security officers. In September the IDF shot dead brothers 'Imad and 'Adel 'Awadallah, allegedly members of the *'Izz al-Din al-Qassam* brigades, the armed wing of *Hamas.* The killings appeared to be extrajudicial executions. The Israeli government refused to release their bodies and the High Court of Justice imposed restrictions on media reporting of the incident (see **Palestinian Authority** entry).

Members of the security forces who carried out extrajudicial executions or other unlawful killings almost invariably enjoyed total impunity. In March the Border Police shot dead Ghaleb Musa al-Rajub, 'Adnan Jibril Abu Zunayd and Muhammad Sharzi al-Sharawneh and injured six other Palestinian men as they approached a check-point in Hebron district. An IDF inquiry concluded that the Border Police officers had believed their lives were in danger, even though the victims were unarmed. The officers were not brought to trial.

In November the Israeli army carried out the punitive destruction of the house of 'Akram Maswadeh where the IDF killed 'Imad and 'Adel 'Awadallah (see above).

In May Amnesty International submitted its concerns on torture and administrative detention to the UN Committee against Torture. The organization also presented its concerns regarding the detention of prisoners of conscience, administrative detention, unfair trials, torture, extrajudicial executions and other unlawful killings to the UN Human Rights Committee in July.

In September Amnesty International published a report, *Israel/Occupied Territories and the Palestinian Authority: Five years after the Oslo Agreement – human rights sacrificed for "security"*.

During the year Amnesty International expressed concern to the Israeli authorities that the bill on the GSS would continue to legitimize Israel's systematic use of torture and grant impunity to perpetrators. The organization called for the immediate and unconditional release of all prisoners of conscience. Amnesty International also called for the release of all detainees held as hostages and for other administrative detainees to be released unless promptly charged with recognizably criminal offences and given fair trials in line with international standards. The organization also appealed for an end to extrajudicial executions and other unlawful killings, and recommended prompt and independent investigations into all cases of suspected unlawful killings, including deaths in custody, and for the results to be published.

In an oral statement to the UN Commission on Human Rights in March, Amnesty International stated that Israel had or was in the process of officially sanctioning human rights violations, such as extrajudicial execution of suspected "terrorists", hostage-taking, and the use of torture and ill-treatment, and was denying adequate compensation to victims of human rights abuses.

Amnesty International called on the armed opposition groups *Amal, Hamas, Hizbullah* and Islamic *Jihad* to refrain from the deliberate and arbitrary killing of civilians and to respect fundamental principles of humanitarian law.

ITALY

209

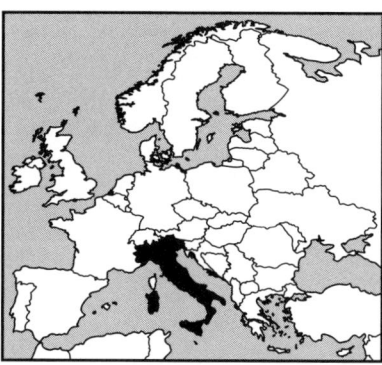

Several people were prosecuted for peacefully exercising their right to freedom of expression. Further cases of alleged torture and ill-treatment of Somalis by members of the Italian armed forces in Somalia in 1993 emerged. Criminal proceedings relating to alleged torture and ill-treatment of detainees by law enforcement and prison officers were often subject to long delays. Three political prisoners continued to serve prison sentences imposed in 1997 after possibly unfair trials.

In July the UN Human Rights Committee considered Italy's fourth periodic report on its implementation of the International Covenant on Civil and Political Rights (ICCPR). The Committee noted continued delay in introducing a criminal offence of torture, "as defined in international law". It remained concerned at "the inadequacy of sanctions" against law enforcement and prison officers "who abuse their powers" and recommended that "due vigilance be maintained over the outcome of complaints" made against such officers.

The Committee expressed concern that prison overcrowding remained "a serious problem" and recommended urgent remedial action. Although noting that the government had drawn attention to "steps taken to speed up both criminal and civil trials", the Committee was concerned that "so far, no result has become apparent". The Committee recommended that "further measures be taken to increase the efficiency and promptness of the entire system of justice".

210

A law replacing existing legislation governing conscientious objection to compulsory military service was promulgated in July. Reform of the legislation had been under consideration by successive legislatures for over a decade (see previous *Amnesty International Reports*). The new law broadened the grounds on which conscientious objector status and alternative civilian service might be granted but did not recognize the right to claim conscientious objector status during military service or within two years of applying for a job involving the use of arms.

In November the judicial authorities, acting on an international arrest warrant issued by Germany, detained Abdullah Öcalan, leader of the Kurdish Workers' Party (PKK), upon his arrival in Rome. Armed members of the PKK have committed hundreds of deliberate and arbitrary killings of civilians and prisoners in Turkey since the organization's foundation in 1978, and have reportedly attacked and killed its supposed enemies in various European countries, including Germany (see **Turkey** entry and previous *Amnesty International Reports*).

Abdullah Öcalan, who applied for political asylum on arrival, was first detained in hospital, then in private accommodation under a form of town arrest. An appeal court lifted the detention order in mid-December after Germany withdrew its arrest warrant and confirmed that, for reasons of internal security, it had decided against requesting the PKK leader's extradition to answer criminal charges.

Decisions on Abdullah Öcalan's asylum request and on a formal request for his extradition by Turkey had not been issued by the end of the year. However, in November the judicial and government authorities, in rejecting an international warrant for his arrest issued by Turkey, had already declared that he could not be returned to Turkey as he faced the death penalty there. Italian constitutional law precludes extradition of any person to a country where they could face the death penalty. The government also publicly opposed granting political asylum to Abdullah Öcalan and indicated that it was exploring the possibility of bringing him to trial before a national or international court. At the end of the year Abdullah Öcalan remained under police surveillance for security reasons but was free to leave the country.

Several criminal proceedings were under way against members of the secessionist parliamentary party *Lega Nord*, Northern League, for peacefully exercising their right to freedom of expression. They were accused of vilifying the Italian nation and the national flag, offences punishable by between one and three years' imprisonment. In court hearings held between January and April, Luca Paolini and Roberto Zaffini were tried on both charges on the basis of a placard displayed during a Northern League demonstration in November 1996 which read, "Italy is a sewer, thanks to thieves, friends, friends of friends and false enemies". Photographs of prominent Italian politicians appeared under each category. The Public Prosecutor's office accused them of thereby showing contempt for the Italian nation and for the colours of the Italian flag, because the words were written against the background of the Italian tricolour. Both men were acquitted in April after the Public Prosecutor's office, which in June 1997 had requested their committal for trial, asked the court to acquit them on the grounds that their actions did not constitute a crime.

In May a government Commission of Inquiry issued its second report on the conduct of Italian troops accused of the torture, ill-treatment and unlawful killing of Somalis while participating in a UN-authorized peace-keeping operation in Somalia in 1993 and 1994 (see *Amnesty International Report 1998*). The report indicated that the Commission had interviewed 11 Somalis flown to Italy in January but had failed to carry out on-site investigations in Somalia, as urged by Somali human rights monitors and Amnesty International in 1997. The Commission acknowledged that it had not had access to important documents forming the central body of the new evidence which had triggered the reopening of its investigations. These were already under investigation by the judicial authorities and so were subject to judicial secrecy, as was part of the testimony of several witnesses relevant to the Commission's investigations.

The Commission dismissed some new allegations of torture and unlawful killing as untrue and could not come to a definite conclusion on the credibility of others. However, the new allegations it considered credible included the attempted rape of a Somali girl with a pistol flare in August 1993 and the hooding and beating of three Somali men over a three-day period in July 1993. It considered the men's allegations possibly exaggerated, but indicated that members of the armed forces had presented false documentation to investigators to try to cover up their involvement.

The Commission confirmed some of the alleged abuses described in its first report, but failed to clarify exactly what had occurred in each incident. Thus, the Commission concluded that soldiers had raped a girl with a pistol flare in November 1993, as stated in its first report, but pointed out that a girl flown to Italy, claiming to be the victim, was not the one photographed at the time of the incident. It also identified a man photographed while being subjected to electric shocks by soldiers, but pointed out that he had failed to recognize his alleged torturers when brought face to face with them in Italy.

The Commission concluded that "episodes of violence were sporadic and localized, not widespread and general" and that ordinary soldiers in the ranks were responsible for the worst acts of abuse "with the active participation of, or in the complacent or amused presence of, young officers and non-commissioned officers". Some middle-ranking officers were blamed for not having known what men in their charge were doing. "At the highest level", which the Commission did not define, "there was an inability to foresee that certain events might occur and a failure to make checks which might have ensured that repeatedly given orders and instructions were properly applied".

The Commission recalled the recommendations made in its first report and emphasized the need for citizens to be better educated in ethics and democratic principles from the earliest age, as well as during training in military establishments. It advised that, in future, all similar overseas missions should include an adequate number of military police, experienced in investigative police work, and be accompanied by a magistrate to oversee relevant investigations.

Upon publication of the report, the Minister of Defence announced that 12 disciplinary proceedings, involving eight officers and five non-commissioned officers, had resulted in punishments apparently ranging from formal reprimands to suspensions and confinement to barracks. At the end of the year the military and civilian judicial authorities continued to carry out investigations into a number of specific allegations of human rights violations.

Judicial proceedings relating to alleged torture and ill-treatment of detainees by both law enforcement and prison officers were often subject to lengthy delays. Criminal proceedings against four of the Palermo police officers prosecuted in connection with the torture and death of Salvatore Marino in 1985 (see previous *Amnesty International Reports*) were apparently still continuing. The outcome of their retrial, ordered by the Supreme Court in February 1997, was not known.

The joint trial of two police officers charged with causing Grace Patrick Akpan serious injuries, insulting her, threatening her and abusing their powers in February 1996, and of Grace Patrick Akpan on charges of refusing to identify herself to them, and of insulting, resisting and injuring a police officer, which had been postponed since February 1997 (see *Amnesty International Reports 1997* and *1998*), did not open until December. However, after one day, the hearing was postponed until March 1999, apparently to allow the court to question further witnesses.

Trial proceedings against more than 60 prison officers in connection with the alleged systematic ill-treatment of inmates of Secondigliano in 1992 and 1993 (see previous *Amnesty International Reports*) had still not concluded by the end of the year.

The joint trial of an officer charged with causing Marcello Alessi bodily harm in San Michele prison in 1992 and of Marcello Alessi, charged for a second time with insulting the officer during the 1992 incident (see *Amnesty International Reports 1997* and *1998*), scheduled to take place in March, after being postponed from December 1997, was postponed until January 1999, after Marcello Alessi failed to appear in court.

Three leading members of the former extra-parliamentary left-wing group *Lotta Continua* (Continuous Struggle) – Adriano Sofri, Ovidio Bompressi and Giorgio Pietrostefani – continued to serve 22-year prison sentences for participation in the killing of Police Commissioner Luigi Calabresi in Milan in 1972 (see *Amnesty*

International Report 1998). In April Ovidio Bompressi was granted a temporary suspension of sentence on health grounds, converted into house arrest in August. In March the Fifth Section of Milan Appeal Court pronounced on the men's application, lodged in December 1997, for a judicial review of a sentence issued by the Third Section of Milan Appeal Court in 1995 which had resulted in their imprisonment in January 1997 after nine years of judicial proceedings and seven trials. The prisoners argued that the application contained new witness testimony and new technical and ballistic evidence and that therefore the proceedings qualified for review. However, the Court concluded that the application was based on information which had either been already examined, or was irrelevant, and was, therefore, inadmissible.

The prisoners then lodged an appeal with the Supreme Court. In October, in a highly critical analysis of the Appeal Court's reasoning, the Supreme Court annulled the Appeal Court's decision and referred the application back to another section of the Milan Appeal Court for re-examination and a decision on retrial. Following the introduction in November of new legislation preventing an application for judicial review from being examined twice by the same appeal court, the application was transferred to Brescia Appeal Court. The Court's decision was still awaited at the end of the year.

Throughout the year Amnesty International reiterated its concern about the excessive length and complexity of the proceedings and about several other aspects which raised serious doubts about their fairness.

The organization expressed concern about delays in judicial proceedings relating to alleged torture and ill-treatment by law enforcement and prison officers and sought information from the authorities on the progress and outcome of judicial and administrative investigations into such allegations, as well as into alleged human rights violations by Italian troops in Somalia.

Amnesty International welcomed several aspects of the new law on conscientious objection to military service. However, the organization reiterated its belief that conscientious objectors to military service should be able to seek conscientious objector status at whatever time they develop their objections.

In January Amnesty International expressed concern that the prosecution of Luca Paolini and Roberto Zaffini was inconsistent with Italy's obligations under Article 10 of the European Convention for the Protection of Human Rights and Fundamental Freedoms and Article 19 of the ICCPR, which guarantee the right to freedom of expression.

In December Amnesty International wrote to the Prime Minister, Massimo D'Alema, welcoming the government's decision not to extradite Abdullah Öcalan to Turkey where he would face the death penalty and possible risk of ill-treatment or torture. However, Amnesty International emphasized that it is essential that states uphold international humanitarian standards by seeking the means to bring to justice those who have directly violated those standards or ordered others to do so through a chain of command. The organization asked what steps the authorities were taking to ensure that Abdullah Öcalan would be tried for his part in the widespread human rights abuses committed by the PKK under his leadership.

JAMAICA

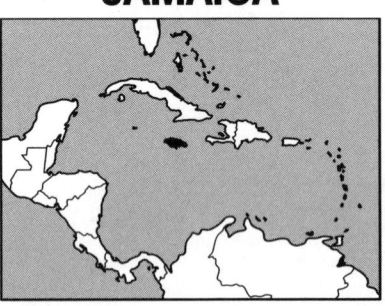

More than 45 people remained under sentence of death at the end of the year. Six people scheduled to be hanged had their executions stayed. Corporal punishment laws were ruled to have lapsed. Prison conditions were harsh. Many people were killed by police in disputed circumstances.

Local government elections, originally scheduled for 1993, took place in September. The governing People's National Party, led by Prime Minister P.J. Patterson, won a majority of seats in all parish councils and the Kingston and St Andrew Corporation.

In January Jamaica's withdrawal as a State Party to the Optional Protocol to the International Covenant on Civil and Political Rights (ICCPR) came into effect. This measure, which was taken to cut off an avenue of recourse for people sentenced to death, precludes all people claiming that Jamaican authorities have violated any of the rights guaranteed by the ICCPR from applying to the UN Human Rights Committee to seek redress.

In a series of cases submitted prior to January, the UN Human Rights Committee concluded that internationally protected rights of people who had been sentenced to death had not been respected. The Committee concluded that the failure to make legal counsel available during preliminary hearings to Clive Johnson and Conroy Levy, both of whom were charged with capital murder, violated their right to counsel. It also concluded that the death sentence imposed on Clive Johnson, who was 17 at the time of the murder, was void because of the prohibition on imposing a death sentence for crimes committed by someone under 18, and that his detention for more than seven years on death row violated his rights under the ICCPR. In a series of cases, the Committee also concluded that detaining people on death row in St Catherine's District Prison in cells for 23 hours per day without a mattress, bedding, furniture, natural light or plumbing, and in some cases failing to provide necessary medical treatment, violated the right of people deprived of their liberty to be treated with humanity and respect for the inherent dignity of the human person.

More than 45 people remained under sentence of death at the end of the year. During the year, six men – Neville Lewis, Peter Blaine, Milton Montique, Dalton Daly, Leroy Lamey and Kevin Mykoo – were moved to death cells adjacent to the gallows to await imminent execution, despite the fact that all had petitions pending before the Inter-American Commission on Human Rights (IACHR) alleging that their rights under the American Convention on Human Rights had been violated. All six received stays of execution from national courts pending the determination of constitutional motions which challenged, among other things, the validity of the time limits which the government pur-

ported to impose on the IACHR's consideration of cases filed by death row prisoners (see Amnesty International Report 1998). The constitutional motions and the IACHR's decisions on the petitions of the six men and on a challenge to the time limits, remained pending at the end of the year.

The death sentences of at least two men, Everton Morrison and Lansford James, were commuted to life imprisonment. Barrington Osborne, Samuel Lindsay and Henry McKoy had their death sentences quashed on appeal. Lansford James, Samuel Lindsay and Henry Mckoy had all been scheduled to hang in 1997 (see Amnesty International Report 1998).

In December in its decision on an appeal brought on behalf of Noel Samuda and Walford Ferguson, the Court of Appeal ruled that the corporal punishment laws had lapsed after the Second World War. Both men had been sentenced to be flogged with a tamarind switch in addition to terms of imprisonment.

Ill-treatment in prisons continued to be reported. For example, Michael Vincent, who reportedly witnessed an incident in which inmates in St Catherine's District Prison were killed and others were injured, was allegedly subjected to repeated assaults, threats and intimidation by prison guards.

In March the findings and conclusions were published of the Board of Enquiry into the August 1997 disturbances in St Catherine's District Prison and Kingston's General Penitentiary, during which 16 inmates were killed and at least 40 were injured (see Amnesty International Report 1998). The Board of Enquiry concluded that the initial cause which triggered the events was the interpretation by guards and inmates of an announcement by the Commission of Corrections of his intention to distribute condoms to guards and prisoners as part of an effort to control the spread of HIV/AIDS. A subsequent walk-out by warders, aggravations caused by privileges afforded to some inmates and "an end to tolerance of homosexual prisoners by heterosexuals" were identified as secondary causes. The Board of Enquiry's recommendations included the building of a new prison and a centre to house people detained on remand to alleviate overcrowding; the provision of training on issues such as riot control and conflict resolution for staff; and the creation of a

214

structure to ensure the airing of grievances without reprisals for inmates.

Conditions in some police lock-ups, places of detention and prisons were so severely overcrowded and insanitary that they amounted to cruel, inhuman or degrading treatment or punishment.

In October the mother of Agana Barrett was awarded compensation as constitutional redress for the inhuman and degrading treatment of her son who was one of three men who died in 1992, after being held for about two days in a 2.4m by 2.1m cell with 16 other people at the Constant Spring Police Station (see *Amnesty International Report 1993*). They had not been provided with food or water and some of the men drank their sweat or urine to alleviate their thirst. An Appeals Court judge who ruled on the case reportedly recommended that no more than three people be kept in a cell in police lock-ups. An appeal against the court's refusal to grant additional compensation for infringement of Agana Barrett's right to life was reportedly pending at the end of the year.

There were continued reports of fatal shootings by law enforcement officials in disputed circumstances. Bertland Morrison was shot by a police officer in August. Police reports allegedly claimed that he was shot after he attacked an officer who was walking by. Eyewitnesses, however, reportedly claimed that he was killed by an officer following an earlier argument and that a gun was planted on him. Murder charges were subsequently brought against the officer.

Proceedings continued against the officers charged in connection with the fatal shooting in 1997 of Rohan Fraser in Tivoli Gardens. In August an inquest jury found that no one was criminally responsible for the deaths of a six-year-old boy and three women who were shot during riots involving exchanges of fire with the security forces which followed Rohan Fraser's death (see *Amnesty International Report 1998*). Following the inquest, which heard evidence over a four-month period, many questions remained unanswered, including the identities of those who fired the fatal shots and who fired from the defence force helicopter.

Amnesty International urged the government to re-ratify the Optional Protocol to the ICCPR. It called on the government not to carry out the six scheduled execu-

tions and expressed concern that executing these men while their petitions to the IACHR were pending would contravene Jamaica's obligations as a State Party to the American Convention on Human Rights. The organization urged the government to repeal the instructions purporting to impose time limits on the IACHR's consideration of cases brought by people under sentence of death and to ensure that all people in Jamaica, including those sentenced to death, have full and effective recourse to petition the IACHR if they believe that their rights under the Convention have been violated.

JAPAN

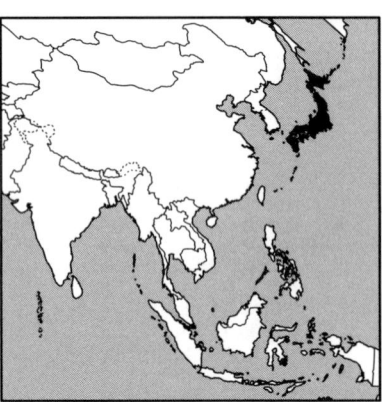

Reports persisted of detainees and prisoners being ill-treated in prisons, detention centres, immigration detention centres and police custody. Conditions of detention remained harsh, often amounting to cruel, inhuman or degrading treatment. Around 100 people remained under sentence of death; six were executed. Asylum-seekers continued to be detained on entry to Japan.

Japan was officially pronounced to be in economic recession, with the unemployment rate reaching a post-1945 record of over four per cent. The government announced a clamp-down on illegal foreign workers in June. The economic slump led to disastrous results for the ruling Liberal Democratic Party in Upper House elections in July, prompting the resignation of Prime Minister Hashimoto Ryutaro. His successor, Prime Minister Obuchi Keizo, vowed to tackle the economic problems beginning with reform of the banking sector.

In August the UN Special Rapporteur on systematic rape and sexual slavery during armed conflict of the UN Sub-Commission on Prevention of Discrimination and Protection of Minorities criticized Japan's initiative to provide compensation to former "comfort women" (women forced into prostitution by the Japanese army during the Second World War) through the establishment of unofficial, private "atonement" funds. She recommended that the government cooperate with the UN High Commissioner for Human Rights to establish a special panel to arrange for Japan to make official, monetary compensation to former "comfort women". Japan was also encouraged to seek out and prosecute all those responsible for establishing the "comfort stations" and to provide reports to the UN Secretary-General detailing the progress that had been made. In September the South Korean government called on Japan to stop offering private funds to former "comfort women" in South Korea. The Japanese government agreed to the request, but the wider issue of state compensation remained unresolved at the end of the year. In November the Tokyo District Court dismissed claims by former prisoners of war and civilian internees from five countries for compensation from the Japanese government for ill-treatment during the Second World War. The plaintiffs vowed to appeal against the decision.

In October the UN Human Rights Committee reviewed Japan's fourth periodic report under the International Covenant on Civil and Political Rights (ICCPR). Among its recommendations, the Committee urged the government to establish independent mechanisms for investigating complaints of human rights violations. It called on the government to conduct a review of immigration detention facilities with a view to bringing conditions into line with the ICCPR, take measures towards the abolition of the death penalty, improve the conditions of detention of death penalty prisoners, and institute immediate reforms to the pre-trial detention system. The Committee also registered "deep concern" about many aspects of the prison system.

Prisoners and detainees alleging ill-treatment continued to lodge claims in court for state compensation. Some claimed to have been subjected to arbitrary punishments which amounted to cruel, inhuman or degrading treatment. In July the Tokyo District Court came to a judgment in a state compensation case launched by Kobayashi Tatsuya after he had reportedly been assaulted by a prison guard and held in a leather body belt and metal handcuffs in a so-called "protection cell" in Fuchu Prison in the capital Tokyo. Kobayashi Tatsuya argued that, although he had spoken rudely to a prison guard, there was no reason to place him in such conditions since he had not behaved violently. He added that the body belt and handcuffs had caused him physical injury. The court rejected his claims and ruled that it was not a human rights violation to restrain him in this way. Kobayashi Tatsuya appealed against the court's decision, but the appeal had not been completed by the end of the year. The case was typical of a number of incidents where prisoners alleged that they had been punished for minor infractions of prison rules by detention in "protection cells". Commonly, prisoners held in such conditions were restrained in leather body belts and handcuffs, forced to wear trousers with an open crotch for defecation, and forced to eat without using their hands.

Saeid Pilhvar, an Iranian national, was transferred to Hachioji Medical Prison in July after staging a hunger strike to protest against his treatment in Kurobane Prison. He claimed that guards at Kurobane Prison had interrogated him for talking with another inmate and had refused to provide him with an interpreter during a meeting convened to decide his punishment. The prison authorities had reacted to his hunger strike by forcibly injecting a liquid into his leg. This reportedly caused severe swelling and paralysis necessitating the use of a wheelchair. Even after his transfer to Hachioji Prison, Saeid Pilhvar remained ill and underweight, and was reported to be suffering from anorexia. His lawyers applied for his provisional release for medical treatment outside the prison but the request had not been granted by the end of the year.

Police referred eight immigration officers to the Tokyo District Public Prosecutor's Office in February following an investigation into the death of Mousavi Abarbekouh Mir Hossein in Kita-ku Immigration Detention Centre in 1997 (see

Amnesty International Report 1998). They were suspected of causing bodily injuries resulting in death. However, prosecutors decided not to pursue the case. In October the victim's family launched a civil suit against the authorities to obtain state compensation for his death.

Conditions of detention in prisons remained harsh, often amounting to cruel, inhuman or degrading treatment. Internal rules governing almost every aspect of prisoners' lives remained confidential and secret, ostensibly on grounds of national security. Prison rules often prevent prisoners from making eye-contact with each other or talking to each other outside designated times. Prisoners may be forced to adopt a certain posture while sitting in their cells or to walk in a certain fashion when outside their cells. Some prison rules prevent prisoners from wearing gloves or extra clothing during the cold winter months and reports of frostbite among prisoners persisted. Minor infractions of prison rules continued to be punished with severe sanctions. For example, some prisoners were forced to kneel or sit in the same position in single cells every day for up to two months, with no form of exercise, mental stimulation or contact with other prisoners.

At the end of the year, around 100 prisoners remained under sentence of death and were held in conditions amounting to cruel, inhuman or degrading treatment. Three men were executed in June having spent more than 10 years in single cells with no contact with other prisoners and limited contact with the outside world. Muratake Masahiro, Takeyasu Yukihisa and Shimazu Shinji had been convicted in separate cases of robbery and murder. In November, three further executions were carried out just weeks after the UN Human Rights Committee had urged the government to take measures towards the abolition of the death penalty. The prisoners executed were Tsuda Akira, Ida Masamichi and Nishio Tatsuaki, who had all spent between 10 and 20 years under sentence of death. It was unclear why these six prisoners were selected for execution. In keeping with usual practice, no advance warning of the executions was given to the prisoners, their families or their lawyers.

In July a local court in Kochi imposed the death penalty on Sakamoto Haruno, a 71-year-old woman, for two cases of murder. In September the Supreme Court rejected an appeal by Miyazaki Tomoko against the death sentence imposed on her for the abduction and murder of two young women in 1980.

Asylum-seekers continued to be detained on entry to Japan. Li Xuemei, a pregnant woman from China, was arrested in February for attempting to enter Japan without valid travel documents. She was tried on criminal charges of illegal entry even though she had applied for refugee status. She was held in detention for five months throughout the investigation and trial. In July the local court in Matsue found her guilty, but exempted her from punishment on humanitarian grounds. Her application for asylum was rejected by the Ministry of Justice in October.

In January Amnesty International issued an appeal following a severe deterioration in the health of Saeid Pilhvar. The Ministry of Justice responded by denying that his life had been in danger. In June Amnesty International published a report, *Japan: Abusive punishments in Japanese prisons*, which summarized recent cases of ill-treatment through the punitive use of instruments of restraint, "protection cells" and solitary confinement. Amnesty International urged the government to publish all internal prison rules and carry out full, impartial and independent investigations into all deaths in custody and allegations of ill-treatment. The organization had not received any comments from the government on this report by the end of the year.

In November Amnesty International wrote to the authorities condemning the executions carried out that month. It urged the government to take steps to abolish the death penalty in line with the UN Human Rights Committee's recommendations.

JORDAN

At least 12 prisoners of conscience or possible prisoners of conscience remained in prison at the end of the year. At least 400 people, including possible prisoners of conscience, were arrested for political reasons. More than 60 people, including prisoners of conscience, were convicted after trials before State Security

Court which often fell short of international fair trial standards. There were some reports of torture or ill-treatment. At least nine people were executed and 14 were sentenced to death. There were reports that asylum-seekers were forcibly returned to countries where they were at risk of human rights violations.

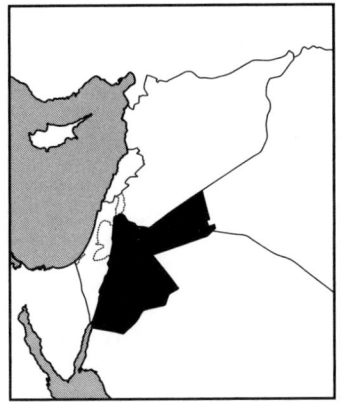

In July King Hussein bin Talal delegated Crown Prince Hassan as regent during his absence for cancer treatment. Crown Prince Hassan had a wide range of powers, including from August the power to dismiss and appoint governments. A new government headed by Prime Minister Fayez Tarawneh was formed in August after the resignation of Prime Minister 'Abd al-Salam Majali, partly triggered by a water crisis in the capital Amman.

The High Court of Justice declared the 1997 Press and Publications Law unconstitutional in January. A new Press and Publications Law, which includes many restrictions on freedom of expression, was promulgated in September. However, in October the government stated that it would not enforce punitive articles of the law.

Prisoners of conscience held at the end of 1997 were released during the year on expiry of their sentences (see previous *Amnesty International Reports*). However, one of them, 'Ata' Abu'l-Rushta (see *Amnesty International Report 1998*), spokesperson for the *Hizb al-Tahrir fi'l-'Urdun*, Liberation Party in Jordan (LPJ) – a party seeking to re-establish the Islamic Caliphate – was detained again and sentenced to one year's imprisonment on charges of membership of an illegal party.

Leith Shubeilat, a leading Islamist opponent of the government (see previous *Amnesty International Reports*), was arrested in February after addressing a meeting in Ma'an calling on people to defy an official ban on meetings and demonstrate their support for Iraq. He was charged with inciting an illegal gathering and sentenced to nine months' imprisonment by the State Security Court in May. King Hussein granted him an amnesty; however, he refused to leave prison saying that he would wait for the court to declare his innocence. In July the Court of Cassation confirmed the sentence. Leith Shubeilat was released on expiry of his sentence in October.

Other prisoners of conscience detained during the year included journalists arrested under the 1993 Press and Publications Law after the 1997 Press Law was declared unconstitutional. The chief editor and the managing editor of *Sawt al-Mar'a* (Woman's Voice) were detained for six days in March after they published an interview with a member of parliament critical of the Director of Intelligence. They were released without charge.

At least 400 people, including possible prisoners of conscience, were detained for political reasons. They included 250 people reportedly arrested during and after demonstrations in support of Iraq which took place in Ma'an after Leith Shubeilat's arrest in February. Demonstrations reportedly started peacefully, but turned into violent confrontations with the police that continued after a bystander, Muhammad 'Abdallah al-Kateb, was killed. Police arrested and charged Muhammad Salem 'Awad with manslaughter and inciting riots; he was acquitted by Amman Criminal Court, which concluded that confessions he made were extracted under "mental duress". All those arrested were pardoned by King Hussein in May.

More than 60 people, including prisoners of conscience, were convicted of political offences by the State Security Court after trials which often failed to meet international fair trial standards. More than 30 members of the LPJ, including 'Ata' Abu'l-Rushta, were arrested in July and August; some were released after a few days, but many were held incommunicado in the General Intelligence Department (GID) for up to three weeks. At least 25 were tried in September and October and

218

13 were sentenced to up to 18 months' imprisonment on charges of membership of an illegal association and distribution of leaflets. One such leaflet was said to have strongly criticized officials for negligence over the water crisis.

Scores of people were arrested in May and 10 were subsequently brought to trial before the State Security Court in September on charges of preparing bomb explosions in Amman. They had been held incommunicado in the GID for at least two months, where, they said, confessions were extracted from them under torture (see below). In October, after pressure from defence lawyers, medical examinations were ordered, which appeared to support their allegations. The trial was continuing at the end of the year.

The Court of Cassation in April overturned, because of "improper methods of investigation", the sentences of 15 years' imprisonment imposed by the State Security Court in 1997 on four alleged supporters of Islamist political groups. The four men had been charged with possessing explosives for illegal purposes. In September 'Isa Talaq al-Khalayeleh and Sa'ud al-Khalayeleh were sentenced by the State Security Court to 10 years' imprisonment; the two others were acquitted.

Some cases of torture or ill-treatment were reported. The 10 people detained in the Amman bombings case were allegedly subjected to beatings, *shabeh* (prolonged sleep-deprivation in painful positions), *falaqa* (beating on the soles of the feet), and prolonged suspension in contorted positions with nylon ropes. Relatives and lawyers who visited some of the detainees stated that during their visits marks of torture were visible, especially beatings on the feet. One detainee, 'Abd al-Nasser Shehadeh Salim, reportedly lost four toenails as a result of torture; another, 'Abd al-Nasser Sayyed Hassanayn, had one leg reportedly broken as a result of beatings.

Isma'il Suleiman al-Hamdan al-'Ajarmeh died in the GID in February. He had been arrested in September 1997, apparently in connection with an attack on employees of the Israeli embassy, and had no access to a lawyer during his detention. According to the authorities, Isma'il al-'Ajarmeh committed suicide by throwing himself down a stairwell and died instantly. The Interior Minister stated that the prisoner's death "happened shortly after an interrogation session and that the autopsy confirmed the cause of death". Amnesty International requested a copy of the autopsy report, but none was made available.

At least nine people were executed. They included Mustafa 'Abd al-Mustafa who was executed in October for murder. He had initially been sentenced to life imprisonment in 1997. However, the Court of Cassation reviewed the case and returned it to the Criminal Court, ordering a harsher penalty to be imposed; in March the Criminal Court sentenced him to death. In March the Court of Cassation returned to the Amman Criminal Court the case of eight members of a single family condemned to death in 1997 for killing two people in a quarrel (see *Amnesty International Report 1998*). The Criminal Court resentenced them to death in April, but in July the conviction was again overturned by the Court of Cassation, which decided that the case should be considered one of manslaughter and that not all eight could have caused the death. In September the Criminal Court sentenced them to life imprisonment.

Fourteen people were sentenced to death. They included Muhammad Mansur, sentenced in October by the Criminal Court for raping his 12-year-old niece. He had been acquitted by the Criminal Court in March, but the Court of Cassation sent the case back after genetic tests. His niece was sentenced to one year's imprisonment for the manslaughter of her new-born baby.

There were reports that asylum-seekers were forcibly returned to countries where they were at risk of human rights violations. They included an Iraqi army deserter who was reportedly returned to Iraq in August.

The government responded with detailed comments to reports issued by Amnesty International on the Middle East in 1997 on refugees and in 1998 on unfair trials. In June Amnesty International sent a memorandum to the government detailing the organization's concerns about the use of incommunicado detention, laws used to sentence prisoners of conscience, and reports of torture. No reply was received. In November Amnesty International issued *Jordan: An absence of safeguards*, which raised the same concerns.

KAZAKSTAN

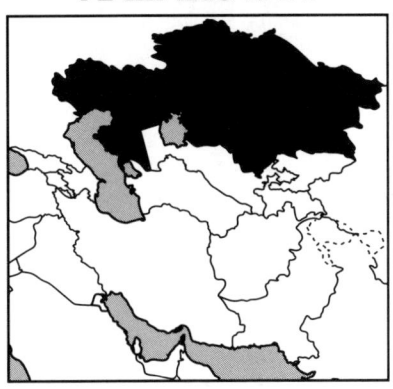

One prisoner of conscience was serving a one-year prison sentence for criminal libel. One possible prisoner of conscience was held incommunicado. There were further allegations of torture and ill-treatment in police custody and pre-trial detention. At least one death sentence was passed. No executions were reported.

In June President Nursultan Nazarbayev officially inaugurated the new capital, Astana, in the north of the country. In October the Kazak parliament adopted constitutional amendments prolonging the presidential term of office and removing restrictions on the president's age and eligibility to run for office more than twice. It also brought forward presidential elections from December 2000 to January 1999.

In August Kazakstan acceded to the UN Convention against Torture and Other Cruel, Inhuman or Degrading Treatment or Punishment and the UN Convention on the Elimination of All Forms of Discrimination against Women. Earlier in the year the Kazak parliament had also announced its intention to accede to the International Covenant on Civil and Political Rights and the International Covenant on Economic, Social and Cultural Rights.

In April Madel Ismailov, leader of the Workers' Movement opposition group, was sentenced to one year's imprisonment. He was a prisoner of conscience. He was convicted of "insulting the honour and dignity of the President" in connection with statements he allegedly made during a peaceful opposition demonstration in Almaty in November 1997. However, Madel Ismailov was not detained until February 1998, following a conference during which he had been elected deputy chairman of a new opposition coalition. His whereabouts were unknown until 5 March, when he was located in a central Almaty prison. There were allegations that Madel Ismailov had been beaten following his arrest. His appeal was rejected by the Almaty City Court in June. In 1997 Madel Ismailov had been detained for three and a half months on similar charges and allegedly ill-treated.

There were fears for the safety of Mikhail Vasilyenko, who was held incommunicado for three days in September before being released. He had been detained by police in Astana where he had gone to distribute draft amendments to the Constitution and to the law on elections, commissioned by Akezhan Kazhegeldin, the former Prime Minister, who subsequently announced his candidature for the presidency. Following a telephone call to his family to let them know what had happened to him, no one was able to establish Mikhail Vasilyenko's whereabouts. All police stations and directorates of internal affairs contacted denied that he had been detained. It was subsequently reported that he had been charged with hooliganism and summarily sentenced by a court in Astana to three days' administrative detention.

Petr Svoik, co-chairman of the opposition Azamat movement, and Mels Yeleusizov, leader of an environmental movement, were administratively detained for three days in October for holding an unauthorized meeting under the auspices of an organization called For Fair Elections in Kazakstan. Presidential candidate and former Prime Minister Akezhan Kazhegeldin was fined for participating in the meeting. This rendered him ineligible to run for the presidency.

There were further reports of torture and ill-treatment in police custody and pre-trial detention. Most of the complainants alleged that they were choked, or handcuffed to radiators, or had plastic bags or gas-masks placed over their heads to force them to divulge information. During the year criminal proceedings reportedly continued against officers involved in the ill-treatment of Natalya Zabolotnaya. She had been detained in February 1997 on suspicion of having murdered her mother and was reportedly kept in solitary confinement at the building of the Department of the State Investigation Committee of Ilyichovsk. It was alleged that drunken law enforcement officers forced her to confess her guilt by beating her with sticks on the back, heels, abdomen and head; twisting her fingers; and putting a cellophane bag over her head, restricting her air supply. They also allegedly demanded a bribe of US$10,000. Apparently, a forensic medical report supported the allegations that Natalya Zabolotnaya was ill-treated.

According to official records, in the first eight months of 1998 the cases of 24 people sentenced to death came before the presidential Clemency Commission; three received clemency. At least one death sentence was passed during the year. Vladimir Kardash, a policeman, was reportedly sentenced to death for the murder of three men, including a police officer, at the police station in the village of Auliekol in Kostanay region in April 1997. He denied the charges and alleged that his confession had been extracted by beatings and death threats from other police officers. He also alleged that a formal complaint against his ill-treatment, made to the procurator, received no response. In March the Supreme Court upheld the death sentence. A petition for clemency to the President was still pending at the end of the year. No executions were reported.

Amnesty International called for the immediate and unconditional release of Madel Ismailov. The organization urged the authorities to repeal Articles 318, 319 and 320 of the criminal code which allow for people to be prosecuted for the peaceful exercise of the fundamental right to freedom of expression.

In September Amnesty International expressed concern about the detention of Mikhail Vasilyenko. It urged that his whereabouts be immediately established and that he be protected from any form of ill-treatment.

Amnesty International expressed concern that the sentences handed out to opposition figures in October might be an attempt to punish them for their political opposition to the government and to dissuade them from campaigning in the forthcoming presidential elections.

In April the organization raised with the authorities 11 cases of alleged torture or ill-treatment in police custody and pre-

trial detention. Amnesty International called for full and comprehensive inquiries into allegations of torture by law enforcement officers, for the findings to be made public and for anyone responsible to be brought to justice in accordance with the norms of international law.

Amnesty International asked for assurances that three ethnic Uighurs from the Xinjiang Uighur Autonomous Region of China would not be returned to face possible torture and arbitrary detention.

Amnesty International continued to call for a moratorium on the death penalty and appealed for the commutation of all death sentences.

KENYA

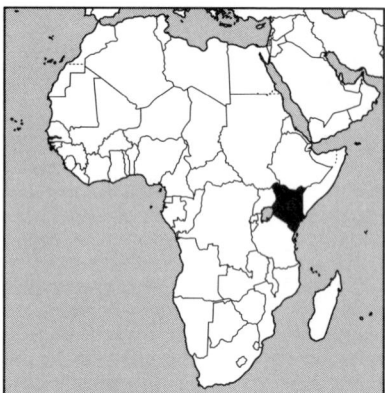

Government critics were detained, ill-treated and otherwise harassed. Among them were human rights activists, pro-democracy campaigners and journalists. All were released after a short time, but some were charged with criminal offences. If convicted, they would be prisoners of conscience. There were many reports of torture and ill-treatment of people in police custody and in prison. Prison conditions were extremely harsh and life-threatening; scores of prisoners reportedly died of infectious diseases. Excessive force was used by police on peaceful protesters. At least 168 people were sentenced to death; more than 900 people were under sentence of death at the end of the year. No executions were carried out. Asylum-seekers were threatened with forcible return to countries where they would face serious human rights violations.

Ethnic clashes in Rift Valley Province escalated in the first half of the year (see *Amnesty International Reports 1993* to *1998*). At least 127 people were killed and thousands displaced. The clashes started in Laikipia District and spread to Nakuru District, areas where large numbers had voted against the government of President Daniel arap Moi in the December 1997 general election. For the first time, members of the Kikuyu community retaliated to attacks in an organized fashion, justifying this by claiming that the government security forces had failed to act. In June a judicial commission of inquiry was set up into the causes of the ethnic clashes that had affected the country since 1992. The commission was due to report to the President in December, but this was later extended to April 1999.

Discussions continued throughout the year about the process for constitutional reforms. In August a consultative structure was agreed which will include members of parliament (MPs), district representatives, churches and non-governmental organizations (NGOs). It will look at all aspects of the judiciary, legislature and executive, and make recommendations on the functions and responsibilities of each. It will also consider different systems of governance in Kenya. The Constitutional Reform bill was enacted in December.

In August a bomb placed next to the US embassy exploded in central Nairobi killing 213 people and wounding more than 5,000. Two men were later arrested and charged in the USA with murder. It was not possible to establish how many others were in custody in Kenya at the end of the year in connection with the bombing.

In March, three human rights NGOs, including the Kenya Human Rights Commission (KHRC), were threatened with deregistration by President Moi. The threat followed their support for the National Convention Executive Council (NCEC), a loose alliance of political parties and NGOs that questioned the government's proposed process for constitutional reform. The NCEC's offices were searched by the police, documents removed and three staff members were held for several hours for questioning. In September, six Muslim NGOs were deregistered by the government without warning. The government cited "security" concerns in the wake of the US embassy bombing. A further 11 NGOs were threatened with deregistration. After substantial international and national pressure, the NGOs were allowed to challenge the bans in court. In October the High Court suspended the deregistrations pending appeal.

In July, three magazines had their licences rescinded after publishing stories about insecurity in the country. The newspapers were allowed to continue publishing after appealing to the High Court, which ruled that no infringements had been made to warrant the removal of licences.

Members of human rights and other non-governmental organizations, journalists, opposition politicians and other government critics continued to be harassed by the authorities. In May Njuguna Mutahi, publications officer of the KHRC, and a journalist were arrested and illegally held in incommunicado detention for four days before being charged with theft. They were then released on bail. It appeared that the charges were spurious; Njuguna Mutahi would be a prisoner of conscience if convicted. The case had not come to trial by the end of the year.

Many other government critics were detained for short periods or charged with criminal offences. Some of the charges were later dropped by the Attorney General. In January, for example, two members of the organization Release Political Prisoners were arrested and charged with unlawful assembly after a peaceful demonstration in Nairobi was violently broken up by the police. At a similar demonstration in February, seven men and women were charged with illegal assembly. Charges against them were later dropped. Also in February, three members of a human rights organization were detained while talking to inmates at Langata Women's Prison as part of a project. Their papers were confiscated and they were held for 24 hours before being released without charge. In October criminal charges against Juma Kiplenge, a human rights lawyer, were dropped after national and international pressure. The lay magistrate in charge of one of the cases brought against Juma Kiplenge had said that Juma Kiplenge would be convicted regardless of the evidence.

In January Professor Kivutha Kibwana, a leading member of the NCEC, was abducted by four armed men and threatened

222

with death. Confidential documents belonging to the NCEC were stolen. It was believed that the abductors were from Kenya's Special Branch. After Professor Kibwana's release, the police refused to investigate the case.

In May a meeting held by opposition and ruling party MPs in Kwanza, Trans Nzoia district, to discuss insecurity in the North Rift Valley, was declared illegal. The police beat politicians, journalists and others to prevent the meeting from continuing. A meeting organized three weeks later, in direct response to the first meeting, was attacked by 30 armed men. Two people were wounded by arrows and scores of others injured after a grenade was apparently thrown into the crowd. According to reports, the police did not intervene, leading to claims that the attackers were acting with official collusion or acquiescence.

Journalists continued to be detained and threatened because of reports they had written. In July Magayu K. Magayu, editor of *The Star* newspaper, was remanded in custody over an article about ethnic killings in the Rift Valley. The same day Tony Gachoka, editor of the *Post on Sunday*, locked himself in his office to avoid being arrested by police. He claimed there was no warrant for his arrest. Imanene Imathiu, a correspondent for the *Daily Nation*, was treated in hospital for injuries sustained when he was beaten by police. He had been investigating allegations of corruption in an Administration Police camp. He was among a team of journalists who had talked to local administration officials regarding the corruption allegations.

There were numerous reports of torture inflicted by the police to extract confessions. For example, John Chege Komu, from Thika town, was arrested in July and died reportedly as a result of torture while in detention. No steps were taken to investigate his death. Christopher Naza, a Roman Catholic aid worker in Nairobi, died after being beaten while in police custody. According to his father, policemen stormed into a bar at 10pm and arrested Christopher Naza and others who were drinking there, and took them away in a police car. The policemen hit Christopher Naza several times on the head. The police said they were investigating the death, but no findings were reported by the end of the year.

In March, after the killing of a policeman by bandits, 38 men and one woman were taken by police from Mbalambala village, 125 kilometres north of Garissa town in North Eastern Province, and then whipped and beaten. Some were tied upside down from trees with their arms tied behind their back. The woman was raped. Following the incident, 15 of them were taken to Garissa with flesh wounds, whip lacerations, genital injuries and limb paralysis. After pressure from local MPs and human rights groups, the police instituted an inquiry. The progress of this inquiry had not been made public, nor had those responsible been held to account, by the end of 1998.

In June an inquest ruled that Ali Hussein Ali had died as a result of torture while in police custody (see *Amnesty International Report 1998*) and that there was enough evidence to charge three named police officers in connection with his death. No charges had been brought against the accused by the end of the year.

Conditions were harsh in many prisons, and amounted to cruel, inhuman or degrading treatment. Scores of prisoners were reported to have died as a result of infectious diseases spread by severe overcrowding. In August, two High Court judges complained that prison officers had not taken prisoners for medical treatment despite receiving court orders to do so.

Scores of people were killed unlawfully by the police. In May, for example, six Administration Police officers shot and killed a 72-year-old woman, Wacera Muiruri, in a Nairobi suburb during a land dispute. A traditional chief had allegedly ordered the police to shoot into a crowd of unarmed protesters who posed no threat to the police. In the incident, four people were also injured, one seriously. In September a mentally handicapped man was shot dead by police through a window in his bedroom where he was hiding.

In August, three policemen from the Flying Squad were arrested after shooting dead a university student, James Odhiambo, in his car. He was suspected of having hijacked a car. The police apologized to the public, saying that the "slaying of the innocent student was a big embarrassment to the police force". In November Corporal Gideon Maino was jailed for five years for manslaughter after shooting dead Anthony Chege (see *Amnesty International Report 1998*).

At least 168 people were sentenced to death. More than 900 people were under sentence of death at the end of the year. No executions were reported.

Refugees and asylum-seekers continued to face forcible return to their countries. In August the government ordered all refugees and asylum-seekers to report to the Ministry of Immigration. Many had their registration documents confiscated and were issued with residence permits for two or four weeks. These refugees were threatened with forcible return to countries where they would be at risk of serious human rights violations. Others were ordered to reside in designated refugee camps where conditions were appalling. Following national and international appeals, most of the refugees were allowed to stay in Kenya.

In December at least 800 foreign nationals were detained following raids on a Nairobi housing estate. The police were accused by witnesses of raping women and stealing personal belongings; no investigation into the allegations was opened by the authorities. It was not clear whether any refugees were forcibly returned to their country of origin.

Amnesty International appealed to the Kenyan government to investigate the killing of Seth Sendashonga, and to use evidence gathered in connection with a previous assassination attempt in February 1996 in which a Rwandese diplomat in Kenya was detained but released without trial. Seth Sendashonga, a former Rwandese government minister, was shot dead with his driver in Kenya in May. The assassination was believed to be linked to his criticisms of the Rwandese government and his denunciation of human rights violations in Rwanda. Seth Sendashonga had been in exile in Kenya since 1995 and headed a Rwandese opposition party in exile. In June David Akiki Kiwanuka, a Rwandese man, and Charles Muhanji Wamuthoni and Christopher Lubanga Mlonda, both Ugandans, were charged with his murder. The men would face the death penalty if convicted.

Amnesty International appealed to the government to take urgent steps to protect the human rights of all communities in the context of escalating violence. The organization also appealed to the government to investigate fully allegations of unlawful killings, torture and ill-treatment, and to ensure that those responsible were brought to justice.

In March, at the UN Commission on Human Rights, Amnesty International raised its concerns about Kenya in a written statement. It also urged the government to fulfil its reporting obligations to the UN and to cooperate with the UN Special Rapporteur on torture and the Special Rapporteur on extrajudicial, summary or arbitrary executions.

Amnesty International delegates visited the country in April and met government officials and contacts. In June Amnesty International published a report, *Kenya: Political violence spirals.*

KOREA
(DEMOCRATIC PEOPLE'S REPUBLIC OF)

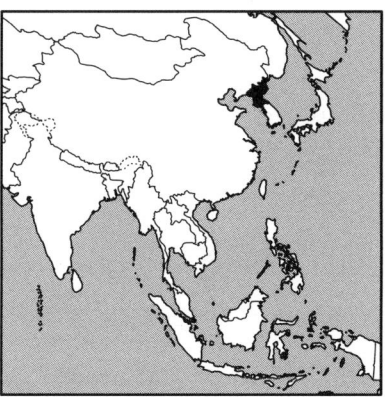

The human rights situation could not be adequately monitored by the international community because of government restrictions on access to the country, giving rise to concern that serious human rights violations remained hidden. Conditions for prisoners were likely to have deteriorated.

The country continued to suffer the effects of acute food shortages caused by a series of natural disasters and poor economic policies. Thousands of people were believed to have died of hunger and related illnesses, but aid agencies, which were denied access to large areas of the country, said they could not assess the real effects of the food shortages. Several independent aid agencies and non-governmental organizations reported that food was being distributed according to loyalty to the state and economic productivity, and that food aid was not reaching the most vulnerable groups within the population.

In September the aid agency *Médecins sans Frontières* announced its withdrawal from the country. The agency said it had been denied access to substantial parts of the population for monitoring purposes, including needy children. It criticized the government of the Democratic People's Republic of Korea (North Korea) for its lack of transparency and accountability with regard to the delivery of humanitarian aid.

In July the government announced that elections had taken place for representatives to the 10th Supreme People's Assembly (SPA), which had not met since the death of former President Kim Il Sung in 1994. The new SPA convened in September and adopted constitutional amendments which resulted in the abolition of the posts of President and Vice-President. The amended Constitution proclaimed the deceased Kim Il Sung to be the "eternal President". The SPA confirmed the leadership of his son, Kim Jong Il, by re-electing him as Chairman of the National Defence Commission, which became the highest post of state. Former Minister of Foreign Affairs Kim Yong Nam was appointed to a new position as President of the Presidium of the SPA. He was expected to assume many of the external functions of a head of state.

Government restrictions on access and information hampered the collection of independent and impartial information about the human rights situation. There was continued concern that human rights violations could not be adequately monitored by the international community and that the North Korea population therefore remained vulnerable to hidden human rights violations.

In August the UN Sub-Commission on Prevention of Discrimination and Protection of Minorities adopted a resolution calling on North Korea to cooperate fully with the procedures and services of the UN and urging the government to "facilitate inquiries by independent national and international human rights monitoring organizations concerning the current human rights situation within the country and to

allow the publication and distribution of all findings inside the Democratic People's Republic of Korea".

The North Korean government again failed to submit its overdue report to the UN Human Rights Committee, in accordance with its obligations under the International Covenant on Civil and Political Rights (ICCPR) and repeated its 1997 statement that it had "withdrawn" from the ICCPR (see *Amnesty International Report 1998*). In October government representatives told Amnesty International that North Korea had prepared its overdue report to the UN Human Rights Committee but would not submit it unless members of the UN Sub-Commission on Prevention of Discrimination and Protection of Minorities changed their "attitude" towards North Korea.

The government submitted its initial report to the UN Committee on the Rights of the Child and attended the examination of this report in May, reversing its 1997 decision to suspend reporting on its implementation of the UN Convention on the Rights of the Child (see *Amnesty International Report 1998*).

Some sources reported the continued detention of thousands of political prisoners, but these reports could not be confirmed. There was concern that economic hardship was likely to have led to a marked deterioration in conditions of detention and to have resulted in acute food shortages for prisoners. Several executions were reported to have been carried out, but independent confirmation was unavailable.

Hundreds of people are reported to have travelled to neighbouring countries in search of food, mostly to the People's Republic of China. Once there they risked being apprehended by the Chinese and North Korean public security authorities and sent back to North Korea where some were reportedly detained.

In September Amnesty International wrote to Kim Jong Il urging him to re-affirm North Korea's commitment to international human rights standards, in view of previous statements that the country had "withdrawn" from the ICCPR; to comply with its treaty obligations, including its reporting obligations under the ICCPR; to develop dialogue with UN human rights mechanisms; and to allow access to independent human rights monitors.

KOREA
(REPUBLIC OF)

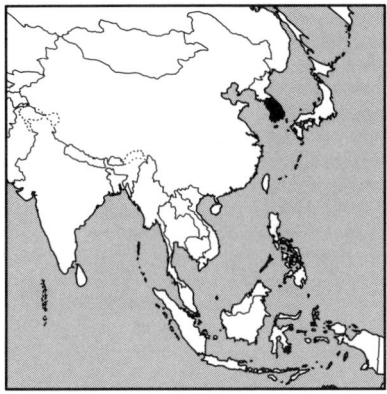

Over 150 political prisoners, including prisoners of conscience, were released in amnesties, but hundreds of others remained in prison. Almost 400 people were arrested under the National Security Law and hundreds of trade unionists were detained or had warrants issued against them; many were prisoners of conscience. There were reports of police ill-treatment and of prison conditions that did not conform to international standards. At least 37 people remained under sentence of death at the end of the year. There were no executions.

President Kim Dae-jung, himself a former political prisoner, took office in February. His commitments to human rights reforms included plans to establish a national human rights commission, improve human rights education, promote women's rights, and ensure that law and practice conformed with international human rights standards. He initiated a so-called "sunshine policy" towards the Democratic Republic of Korea (North Korea) which included increased civilian contacts with North Korea.

Thousands of workers in the Republic of Korea (South Korea) lost their jobs as a consequence of the severe economic crisis. Thousands of undocumented migrant workers, many of whom had not been paid for months, lost their jobs and were forced to leave the country. Women were often laid off before men. Public protests and strike action over job losses resulted in police crack-downs and arrests.

In February the National Assembly adopted amendments to labour legislation allowing mass redundancies for the first time. The government said that from 1999 it would permit teachers to form trade unions and civil servants to form a "consultative body".

In April the government announced that the Agency for National Security Planning would be renamed the National Intelligence Service and no longer used as a political tool or permitted to carry out human rights violations. However, the Agency did not appear to have been substantially reformed.

In July the Ministry of Justice announced that "conversion" statements renouncing communist or left-wing ideology would no longer be required from political prisoners as a condition of release. Certain categories of political prisoners who refused to sign a "conversion" statement had suffered discriminatory treatment and been denied early release. The government said that all political prisoners must sign instead a "law-abiding oath" to qualify for early release. Many prisoners refused, seeing this as a continued violation of their right to freedom of conscience and requiring them to respect laws which contravened international standards.

In September President Kim Dae-jung told Amnesty International delegates that "poisonous elements" of the National Security Law (see previous *Amnesty International Reports*) would be reviewed in the near future, but the review had not taken place by the end of the year.

A draft human rights act, aiming to establish a national human rights commission, was published in September. There was widespread concern that the draft law did not give the proposed commission independence, a wide mandate or sufficient powers to carry out its work.

Over 150 political prisoners were released in two presidential amnesties in March and August. Among them were Professor Park Chang-hee, Buddhist monk Jin Kwan, and long-term political prisoner Kang Hui-chol (see *Amnesty International Report 1998*). Prisoners released after the August amnesty were threatened with reimprisonment if they took part in certain political or anti-government activities.

Some 360 political prisoners, including many prisoners of conscience, were still held after the August amnesty. Those

226

denied release because they refused to sign a "law-abiding oath" included 17 elderly political prisoners arrested on spying charges under the National Security Law who had been held for between 28 and 40 years. Sentenced to life imprisonment, they had been denied release on parole because of their alleged communist views. Most were reported to be in poor health and held in isolation. Woo Yong-gak, aged 69, had been held for 40 years and suffered from muscular paralysis resulting from a stroke. Hong Myong-ki, aged 69 and held for 36 years, was reported to be suffering from heart disease. Other National Security Law prisoners who continued to be held included Cho Sang-nok and Kang Yong-ju, who had been convicted after unfair trials in 1978 and 1985 respectively.

Almost 400 people, including students, youth workers, publishers and workers, were arrested during the year under the National Security Law. Many were prisoners of conscience and sentenced to a short prison term or suspended sentence under Article 7 of the law which punishes the vaguely defined acts of "praising" and "benefiting" North Korea. They included Lee Sang-kwan, arrested in April for publishing two books about the lives of North Korean women and long-term political prisoners in South Korea, and released after trial; student Ha Young-joon, sentenced to one year's imprisonment in August for posting a socialist text on a computer bulletin board; and youth activist Kim Jong-bak, sentenced to two and a half years' imprisonment in October for leading the Anyang Democratic Young Federation, a community-based group with alleged left-wing principles.

Father Moon Kyu-hyun, a Roman Catholic priest, was arrested in August and accused of "praising" and "benefiting" North Korea during a government-approved visit to North Korea. The prosecution said he had violated the terms of his visit by attending a reunification rally and visiting the tomb of former North Korean President Kim Il Sung. The Reverend Kang Hee-nam, aged 78 (see *Amnesty International Report 1998*), who was released in the March amnesty, was rearrested in August for organizing a reunification festival at Seoul National University. They were prisoners of conscience. In October both of them were released on bail.

Hundreds of trade unionists, including many prisoners of conscience, were arrested or had warrants of arrest issued against them after a May Day rally and two general strikes in May and July which the authorities said were illegal. The strike action was led by the *Minju Nochong*, Korean Confederation of Trade Unions (KCTU), to protest against mass redundancies, inadequate social welfare provision, failure to prosecute employers for illegal lay-offs and related issues. Among those arrested were Koh Yong-ju, Secretary General of the KCTU, who was sentenced to 18 months in prison in October for calling an "illegal strike", and Dan Byung-ho, Vice President of the KCTU and President of the Korean Metal Workers Federation, who was arrested on the same charges in October and remained in prison awaiting trial at the end of the year. They were prisoners of conscience.

There were further reports that political and criminal suspects were deprived of sleep, threatened and beaten by law enforcement officials after arrest. At least two detainees died in custody after reported ill-treatment. Park Sun-jong, who was physically disabled, died in February in Songdong Detention Centre in Seoul, the capital. He was reported to have suffered three broken ribs and a brain haemorrhage which a pathologist said were likely to have been caused by external injury.

On several occasions police responded to large demonstrations with mass arrests and excessive force, resulting in injuries. In September, 2,400 workers were detained and dozens of people, including children, were reportedly injured when 10,000 riot police broke a strike at seven Mando Machinery factories. Television pictures of the raid showed policemen beating unarmed demonstrators.

There were reports that prisoners in several detention facilities had been held in handcuffs and chains, beaten and placed in solitary confinement for long periods as punishment for breaking rules. Long-term political prisoners and female political prisoners were among those held in prolonged solitary confinement. Migrant workers, detained pending deportation, were also reportedly ill-treated by immigration detention officials in Seoul. Medical provision throughout the prison system continued to be inadequate. Women were reported to suffer discrimination within the prison system.

At least 37 prisoners remained under sentence of death at the end of the year. In August the death sentences imposed on two Pakistan nationals convicted of murder after unfair trials, Mohammad Ajaz and Amir Jamil, were commuted to life imprisonment. In September President Kim Dae-jung told Amnesty International that he personally opposed the death penalty but needed more time to initiate public debate about abolition.

Asylum-seekers continued to experience problems claiming refugee status. As in previous years, there were no successful applications. Immigration officials reportedly discouraged applicants from making claims and rejected at least 10 claimants, including people who would be at risk of human rights violations if returned to their own countries.

Amnesty International delegates visited the country in February, June and September. During meetings with President Kim Dae-jung and Minister of Justice Park Sang-cheon in September, Amnesty International's Secretary General called for the release of remaining long-term political prisoners and withdrawal of the requirement to sign "law-abiding oaths"; a halt to high numbers of national security and trade union arrests; amendment of the National Security Law in accordance with international standards; and abolition of the death penalty. In October Amnesty International expressed concern to the government that the proposed law to establish a national human rights commission did not conform to international standards.

Amnesty International reports on South Korea issued during the year included: in May, *Proposed standards for the National Human Rights Commission*; in June, *Women's Rights in South Korea, a summary prepared for the Committee on the Elimination of Discrimination against Women*; and in September, *Summary of Amnesty International's concerns and recommendations to the Government* and *Foreign Policy and Human Rights*.

KUWAIT

Scores of political prisoners, including prisoners of conscience, remained in prison. Several political prisoners held after unfair trials since 1991 were released. The fate of more than 70 people who "disappeared" in 1991 remained unknown. At least three people were sentenced to death and six others were executed.

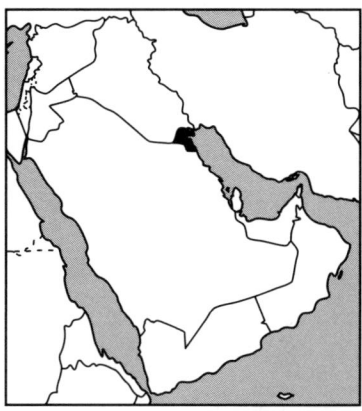

In May the UN Committee against Torture examined Kuwait's report and, while noting that Kuwait had confronted some incidents of torture and prosecuted those responsible, expressed concern that no crime of torture existed in law. The Committee recommended that such a crime be included in the criminal code and that Kuwait withdraw its reservation to Article 20 of the UN Convention against Torture and Other Cruel, Inhuman or Degrading Treatment or Punishment.

In June Mohammad Jassem al-Saqer, editor of the daily newspaper *al-Qabas*, was sentenced under provisions of the Press and Publications Law of 1961 to six months' imprisonment by the Court of First Instance for publishing a joke in January deemed offensive to Islam. Ibrahim Marzouq 'Aid, an Egyptian cartoonist, was sentenced to an equal term *in absentia*. Mohammad Jassem al-Saqer remained at liberty pending the outcome of his appeal, which had not been completed by the end of the year.

In December Fu'ad al-Hashem, a journalist for the newspaper *al-Watan*, was sentenced to three months' imprisonment for an article in which he had allegedly criticized the conduct of the Public Prosecutor. *Al-Watan* was also fined 100 dinars (US$300) in the same decision. An appeal was ongoing at the end of the year.

Scores of political prisoners, including prisoners of conscience, continued to be detained in Kuwait Central Prison following conviction on charges of "collaboration" during the occupation of Kuwait by Iraqi forces. The prisoners had been tried before the Martial Law Court and State Security Court since 1991 in trials which failed to conform to internationally recognized fair trial standards (see previous *Amnesty International Reports*). Those imprisoned included Intisar Rasan Khallati, an Iraqi national, and her sister Sabiha Rasan Khallati, a Kuwaiti citizen by marriage, both sentenced in 1991 to 15-year prison terms. Also still held was Hamda As'ad Yunis, an elderly woman, who was sentenced to life imprisonment in 1991. She was reported to be in poor health.

A group of 15 Bahraini nationals and two *Bidun* (stateless people) arrested in 1997 were tried by a criminal court on charges of straining relations with a friendly state (Bahrain) and possessing and distributing leaflets. Six Bahraini nationals were initially sentenced to three-year prison terms with hard labour, to be followed by deportation, including three tried *in absentia*. Eleven of the accused were initially acquitted, but two of them were subsequently sentenced to three years' imprisonment following an appeal by the Public Prosecutor. The Court of Cassation was reviewing the case at the end of the year. Those held at the end of the year were Hussein Mansur, Hussein al-Haiki, 'Adel al-Haiki, Mohammad Mirza and 'Abdallah Yunis.

A number of political prisoners held since 1991 were released following amnesties granted by the Amir, al-Shaikh Jaber al-Ahmad al-Sabah, during the year. Among them was Fatima Ramez Tafla, a Lebanese woman, held since 1991.

In June the Ministry of the Interior announced the closure of Talha detention centre, where conditions had caused concern (see *Amnesty International Report 1997*). It had housed foreign nationals suspected of violating national security laws, people without work permits, including *Bidun*, and individuals awaiting deportation after completing prison sentences.

The fate and whereabouts of more than 70 people who "disappeared" in custody in 1991 remained unknown (see previous *Amnesty International Reports*).

Six people were executed. In May, three men were reportedly executed by hanging in Kuwait City for murder. In July, two Iranian nationals, sentenced to death in 1997 on narcotics charges, were executed in Kuwait City's Central Prison. A Sri Lankan national was executed the same day for murder.

At least three people were sentenced to death. In January Saudi Arabian national Reda Saleh al-Shammari was sentenced to death *in absentia* for murder. In September a man was reportedly sentenced to death for the rape of a 14-year-old boy. In November a man was reportedly sentenced to death for killing two guards. Two death sentences were reportedly commuted on appeal during the year.

Amnesty International urged the government to release immediately and unconditionally all prisoners of conscience and to conduct a judicial review of the cases of people convicted by the Martial Law Court and the State Security Court.

KYRGYZSTAN

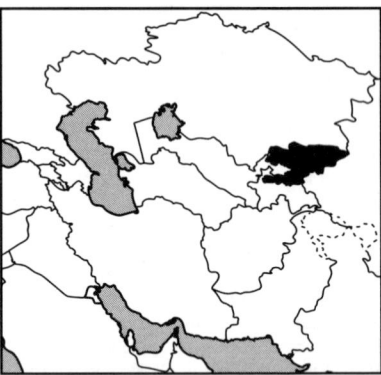

Four prisoners of conscience were administratively detained. One prisoner of conscience had his sentence reduced on appeal. At least 34 people were sentenced to death and at least four executions were carried out.

In March President Askar Akayev approved nominations to a new Presidential Human Rights Committee. At the end of September the non-governmental Kyrgyz Committee for Human Rights was informed in a letter from the Ministry of Justice that it had been deprived of its registration. Its appeal against the decision had not been heard by the end of the year.

In October a package of constitutional changes, including the privatization of land, changes to the structure of parliament, a reduction in parliamentary immunity, and the outlawing of state censorship were approved in a nationwide referendum.

In December a two-year moratorium on executions came into force.

Four human rights activists were detained in connection with a planned demonstration against the proposed referendum. Three activists from the regional branch of the Kyrgyz Committee for Human Rights were detained in the city of Jalal-Abad on 23 September. Albert Korgoldoev, the branch head, Tynybek Batyraliev and Abdunazar Mamatislamov were members of a committee which had sought permission to hold a peaceful demonstration in Jalal-Abad on 25 September. The committee was still awaiting a decision by the local authorities when the three were arrested. Albert Korgoldoev and Tynybek Batyraliev were reportedly charged with violating public order for inviting the public to attend the demonstration; according to some reports, they were found in possession of leaflets and posters. They were sentenced on the morning of 24 September by Jalal-Abad City Court to 15 days' administrative detention. Apparently they had not been given access to a lawyer. They were released on 7 October, but criminal proceedings were reportedly opened against Abdunazar Mamatislamov. Edgar Parpiev, a member of the regional human rights organization Justice, was administratively detained for 15 days in connection with the demonstration, which reportedly went ahead peacefully on 25 September.

In May the Supreme Court heard appeals by prisoner of conscience Topchubek Turgunaliyev (see *Amnesty International Report 1998*) against his sentences of 1996 and 1997. The Supreme Court upheld the sentence imposed in 1996 for libel, but decided to retroactively apply an amnesty of 1997, a step which was reported to be no more than a formality, since Topchubek Turgunaliyev had already completed the sentence. The appeal against a four-year sentence imposed in 1997 for "abuse of authority" was also rejected, but the Supreme Court reduced the sentence from four to three years. In November Topchubek Turgunaliyev was released before the end of his sentence. He had been serving the remainder of his sentence in Bishkek where he was allowed to live at home and to receive appropriate medical assistance.

Unofficial statistics on the application of the death penalty became available. In 1997 at least 40 death sentences had been passed, 31 people executed and three death sentences commuted. In 1998 at least 34 death sentences had been passed and four executions had taken place, prior to the moratorium on executions which came into force in December.

Amnesty International appealed for the immediate and unconditional release of Albert Korgoldoev, Tynybek Batyraliev and Abdunazar Mamatislamov. In a reply received in December, the government stated that the arrests of Albert Korgoldoev and Tynybek Batyraliev were in accordance with national legislation and that they had been released following repeal of this law on 1 October. Abdunazar Mamatislamov was released on 1 December when Susak Court sent his case back for further investigation.

Amnesty International asked for assurances that an ethnic Uighur from the Xinjiang Uighur Autonomous Region of China would not be returned to China, where he would be at risk of torture and arbitrary detention. It called for a moratorium on executions and appealed for commutation of all death sentences.

LAOS

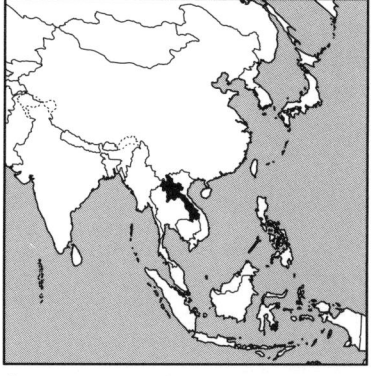

Three prisoners of conscience continued to be held throughout the year, one without trial. One prisoner of conscience died in custody. At least 45 prisoners of conscience were arrested for their religious

230

activities, 13 of whom were tried and sentenced and the remainder released without charge. Three political prisoners continued to serve prison sentences imposed after unfair trials, one of whom reportedly died in custody.

In February the National Assembly approved the appointment of Khamtay Siphandone as President and other ministerial changes in the cabinet.

Three prisoners of conscience continued to be held in Prison Camp 7 in a remote area of the northeastern province of Houa Phanh, one of whom died in detention. Latsami Khamphoui, Feng Sakchittaphong and Thongsouk Saysangkhi had been sentenced to 14 years' imprisonment in November 1992 after a grossly unfair trial. Despite the official charges against them, which included offences such as "preparations for a rebellion", it was believed that they were detained in 1990 for calling for peaceful political and economic change. Detained in extremely harsh conditions with no medical facilities, they continued to suffer from serious health problems requiring hospital treatment (see *Amnesty International Report 1997*). In January they appealed for help, describing the deterioration in their health and the refusal of the authorities to improve their situation. Thongsouk Saysangkhi died in mid-February reportedly from complications related to diabetes.

Information was received about the detention without trial since March 1996 of prisoner of conscience Khamtanh Phousy, an army captain and director of a military mapping company. Although initial charges against him were reportedly dropped in October 1997, he was not released. Khamtanh Phousy had converted to Christianity in 1992; it was believed that he was arrested because of official suspicion of his religious activities and because of contacts with foreign nationals through his work. He was transferred from C-156 Prison in the northern town of Xieng Khouang to Prison Camp 7 in December 1997 and detained under harsh conditions, including being chained and locked in wooden stocks for 20 days.

At least another 45 prisoners of conscience were arrested for the practice of their religious beliefs. In January, 44 people, including 39 Lao, three US, one French and one Thai national, were arrested at a Bible study meeting in the house of Sy Yilatchai in the capital, Vientiane, organized by the Church of Christ. Six Lao nationals were released within a few days, as well as the foreign nationals who were asked to leave the country. Twenty others were released in mid-February. The remaining 13 prisoners were tried on 25 March accused of organizing meetings to create disorder. They included six employees of *Partners in Progress*, a US humanitarian organization, affiliated to the Church of Christ, which was carrying out sanitation and health projects in Laos administered by the three arrested US nationals. Eight of those tried, including Sy Yilatchai and his two sons, were sentenced to three years' imprisonment; Sy Yilatchai's daughter and a farmer were sentenced to two years' imprisonment with one year suspended; three women were released after being given suspended sentences. The sentences were reportedly reduced on appeal by the Supreme Court in October to between 10 months and two and a half years' imprisonment, following which two of them were released in November.

Father Tito Banchong Thopayong, a Catholic priest, was arrested in January in Bokeo province after visiting Christian families in the area. He had been the assistant parish priest at the Catholic Cathedral in Vientiane for five years, and had reportedly spent several years in prison in the 1980s. The reported official reason for his arrest was teaching religion without permission. He was imprisoned and held under house arrest until June.

Political prisoners Pangtong Chokbengboun, Bounlu Nammathao and Sing Chanthakhoummane continued to be detained at Prison Camp 7. It was reported that Bounlu Nammathao died in detention in June or July. The three men had been sentenced to life imprisonment after an unfair trial in 1992 for a range of crimes allegedly committed prior to 1975. They had already been detained for "re-education" for 17 years without charge or trial (see *Amnesty International Report 1997*).

Amnesty International continued to call for Thongsouk Saysangkhi, Latsami Khamphoui and Feng Sakchittaphong to be immediately and unconditionally released and provided with urgently needed medical treatment while still in detention. In May it published *Lao People's Democratic Republic: Prisoners of conscience left to die*, which criticized the failure of the authorities to respond to concerns about their health.

In September Amnesty International published a report, *Lao People's Democratic Republic: Religious imprisonment*, which urged the authorities to release all prisoners of conscience detained for their religious beliefs. The organization continued to call for the fair trial or release of long-term political prisoners.

No response had been received from the authorities by the end of the year.

LEBANON

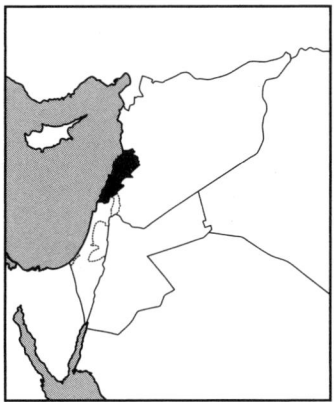

Dozens of political detainees were tried; some aspects of their trials fell short of international standards. There were reports of torture and ill-treatment of detainees which were not investigated. At least five people were sentenced to death and two others were executed. A militia allied to Israel continued to hold at least 140 prisoners in South Lebanon. Fifty former prisoners in South Lebanon and Israel were released in an exchange. At least 28 civilians were reportedly killed in the military conflict in South Lebanon, most in attacks which may have been indiscriminate. The fate of thousands of people abducted by armed groups in previous years remained unknown.

In October the Lebanese parliament elected General Emile Lahoud, head of the army since 1989, President. In May and June local elections were held in all provinces, for the first time in 35 years, with participation from all political forces in

the country. In June the Parliamentary Committee for Human Rights called on the government to ratify the UN Convention against Torture and Other Cruel, Inhuman or Degrading Treatment or Punishment. In December the new cabinet, formed under the premiership of Salim al-Hoss, decided to permit authorized demonstrations, banned since 1993, and to review the audio-visual media law of 1994, enforced in 1996 (see previous *Amnesty International Reports*).

In January the Lebanese army launched an attack on Sheikh Subhi al-Tufayli, former Secretary General of *Hizbullah* (Party of God), and a group of his followers in Ba'albek. In the violent clashes which ensued, scores of people were wounded and eight were killed, including a civilian woman and Khodr Tulays, a close aide to Sheikh Subhi al-Tufayli and a former member of parliament.

Conflict continued in South Lebanon in and around Israel's self-declared "security zone" mainly between the Israeli Defence Force (IDF) and Israel's proxy militia, the South Lebanon Army (SLA) on the one hand, and *Hizbullah* on the other. However, other groups such as the *Amal* Movement and the Lebanese National Resistance Movement were reported to have mounted operations against the IDF and SLA during the year. During the year military operations by all parties to the conflict threatened the safety of civilians.

In April the Israeli government offered to withdraw from South Lebanon, in accordance with UN Resolution 425 of 1978, if the Lebanese government undertook to stop *Hizbullah* attacks against Israel and to safeguard the security of Israel's northern border. The Lebanese government rejected the offer insisting that UN Resolution 425 required Israel to withdraw unconditionally. The International Monitoring Group met more than 30 times during the year to examine complaints lodged by Lebanon and Israel regarding violations of the 1996 "April Understanding" (see *Amnesty International Report 1997*).

With the agreement of the Lebanese government, Syrian forces remained deployed throughout most of the country.

In March, 121 Lebanese political prisoners were released from Syrian prisons, and handed over to the Lebanese authorities. Eighteen were remanded in custody in Lebanon; 103 were released. Among those detained was Kaytel al-Hayek, a former Lebanese army officer accused of involvement in the murder of former Prime Minister Rashid Karami (see below). Also detained was Zafer al-Muqadam who had been detained in Syria since 1996 for alleged links with the pro-Iraqi wing of the Arab Socialist *Ba'th* party (see *Amnesty International Reports 1997* and *1998*). Hani Shu'aib and Hassan Gharib, who were both detained in Syria for their suspected connection with pro-Iraqi wing of the Arab Socialist *Ba'th* party (see previous *Amnesty International Reports*), were among those released in March. Ahmad Hamad, a doctor who was arrested in Lebanon in 1997, was released from detention in Syria in June (see *Amnesty International Report 1998*). Scores of Lebanese nationals were still believed held in Syrian prisons (see **Syria** entry).

Dozens of political prisoners were tried during the year by the Military Court and the Justice Council, whose proceedings – such as summary proceedings in the Military Court and lack of judicial review for the verdicts of the Justice Council – fell short of international fair trial standards.

In July the Military Court sentenced journalist Pierre 'Attallah *in absentia* to three years' imprisonment on charges of "entry into enemy land [Israel] without permission and contempt of Lebanese security and judicial authorities" (see *Amnesty International Report 1997*).

The trial of those suspected of assassinating former Prime Minister Rashid Karami in 1987 continued throughout the year before the Justice Council. The defendants included Samir Gea'gea', head of the unauthorized Lebanese Forces (LF) organization, who was already serving three life sentences (see previous *Amnesty International Reports*); 12 other LF members, 10 of whom were being tried *in absentia*; army brigadier Khalil Matar; and Kaytel al-Hayek.

Kaytel al-Hayek also appeared before the Military Court in July accused of plotting to assassinate General Ghazi Kan'an, Head of Intelligence in the Syrian Forces operating in Lebanon, the same offence for which he had been tried *in absentia* in 1996 while held in Syria (see above). In August he was sentenced to three years' imprisonment, but the four years spent in Syrian custody were taken into consideration.

The retrial of Antoinette Chahin and others accused of the assassination of Father Sam'an al-Khoury (see *Amnesty International Report 1998*) began in June before the Criminal Court of Cassation and resumed, after recess, in October. During the trial two defendants, Rashid Daw and Sa'd Jubra'il, retracted their original testimonies, which constituted the sole basis for conviction in the previous trial, on the grounds that they had been extracted under torture. The trial was continuing at the end of the year.

There were reports of torture and ill-treatment of detainees during the year. In July, 11 people, mostly former LF members, were arrested and detained in the Ministry of Defence. The authorities stated that the detainees had confessed to crimes including plotting the assassinations of political figures and carrying out a number of violent attacks, such as the bombing of a Syrian minibus in Tabarjah in 1996 (see *Amnesty International Report 1997*). The detainees were reportedly tortured or ill-treated at the Ministry of Defence and confessed under duress. The 11 were charged with "forming a subversive network aimed at destabilizing order in the country". Their trial before the Military Court began in December and was continuing at the end of the year.

Criminal suspects were also reportedly tortured. Linda Sacbibit, a Philippine housekeeper, was arrested in August on suspicion of theft. Linda Sacbibit was allegedly beaten and otherwise tortured while being interrogated in police custody. No investigation into these allegations or other reports of torture was known to have been launched during the year by the authorities.

At least one warden and four inmates were wounded in clashes in April when a riot erupted in Rumieh Prison in northeast Beirut in protest against ill-treatment. The riot started after guards reportedly beat and burned a prisoner. Prisoners' complaints included severe overcrowding; cells designed for two prisoners were housing six. The incident sparked calls from local human rights organizations for urgent reform of prison conditions.

At least two people were executed. In May Hasan Nada Abu Jabal and Wisam Nayif 'Issa, were hanged in public in the central square of Tabarjah, north of Beirut. The bodies of the two men reportedly remained on display for an hour and the executions were broadcast by television stations in Lebanon and abroad. This was the first public hanging in Lebanon since the expansion of the scope of the death penalty in 1994. At least five others were sentenced to death, most convicted of murder. They included Yahya Muhammad al-Ayubi, who was sentenced to death for murder in January. Ahmad Rida Yasin, whose sentence was upheld by the Court of Cassation in 1997, remained under sentence of death (see *Amnesty International Report 1998*).

In South Lebanon at least 140 people were held without charge or trial in the Khiam Detention Centre run by the SLA in cooperation with the IDF (see **Israel and the Occupied Territories** entry). In June, 50 detainees held in Khiam and in Israel were released in the context of an exchange of prisoners and bodies between Israel and the two Lebanese armed groups, *Hizbullah* and *Amal*. The exchange was brokered by the International Committee of the Red Cross (ICRC) and the French government. Israel received the body of Itamar Ilya, an Israeli soldier who was killed in an Israeli operation in South Lebanon in September 1997. Israel gave back the bodies of 40 Lebanese killed in Lebanese operations against the IDF or SLA.

Other releases from Khiam unconnected with the exchange included those of Michel Nahra, 13-year-old Mazen 'Abdallah, and Suha Beshara (see *Amnesty International Report 1998*). Visits by the ICRC and by prisoners' families to Khiam resumed in July after about a 10-month suspension (see *Amnesty International Report 1998*).

During the year 28 Lebanese civilians were reportedly killed in the military conflict in South Lebanon, most as a result of attacks which may have been indiscriminate. For example, in December Nadwa 'Uthman and her six children were killed in their home when Israeli warplanes raided suspected *Hizbullah* targets near Ba'lbek in the Eastern Beqaa', outside the "security zone". *Hizbullah* retaliated by firing rockets into the towns of Kiryat Shemona and Nahariya in northern Israel, reportedly injuring 11 civilians.

The fate of thousands of people, including Palestinians, Lebanese and other nationals abducted in Lebanon by armed groups since 1975, remained unknown.

Throughout the year Amnesty International urged the authorities to guarantee fair trials for political prisoners, to investigate allegations of torture, and to commute death sentences. The organization expressed concern over the safety of civilians in South Lebanon and Israel to the Israeli authorities and to *Hizbullah*.

In August the Lebanese authorities wrote to Amnesty International regarding the death penalty, stating that the punishment for intentional murder had been strengthened since 1994 as a "temporary measure", that the penalty was not carried out "except against the criminal who deserves such a punishment as he constitutes a true menace to society", and stressing that conviction followed long and open trials where the accused were entitled to the right of defence. While welcoming the willingness of the Lebanese authorities to enter into dialogue with the organization on this matter, Amnesty International remained concerned about the increasing number of death sentences and executions since 1994.

LESOTHO

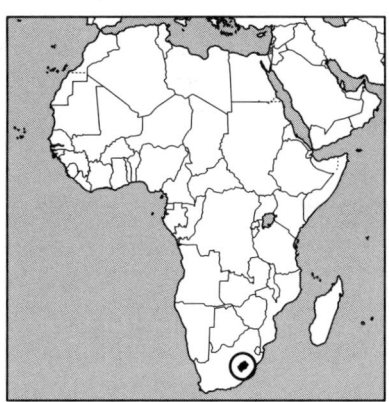

Security officials faced prolonged and unfair trial proceedings. Torture and ill-treatment by police were reported. Security forces used excessive force against striking workers and protesters.

The ruling Lesotho Congress for Democracy party won all but one seat in parliament in national elections held in May. Prime Minister Ntsu Mokhehle retired and was replaced by Pakalitha Mosisili. Opposition parties challenged the election

234

results through the courts and held protests outside the palace of King Letsie III in August and September. Their supporters, as well as government supporters, set up impromptu roadblocks, paralysing business. The police and army initially did not intervene. In August and September, however, there were sporadic armed clashes involving pro- and anti-government supporters, and sections of the police and army, as well as targeted attacks on members of both main political groupings. At least five people died and scores were injured.

A commission chaired by a South African constitutional court judge into the running of the elections concluded in its September report that, notwithstanding irregularities, the results were valid.

On 11 September junior army officers detained more than 20 of their senior officers and held some government ministers in their homes. The men were released after the intervention of South African negotiators.

On 16 September Prime Minister Mosisili made the first of several appeals to South Africa and the Southern African Development Community (SADC) for military assistance, stating that an army coup was imminent. On 22 September the South African National Defence Force (SANDF), and later the Botswana Defence Force (BDF), entered the country (see **South Africa** entry). They captured the Lesotho Defence Force (LDF) barracks in the capital Maseru and at Katse in the Lesotho Highlands Water Project dam area; at least 25 LDF soldiers and at least nine South African soldiers were killed. Some 150 LDF soldiers were kept prisoner by the SANDF but later released unconditionally after mediation by the International Committee of the Red Cross. About 1,000 SANDF and BDF soldiers were still in Lesotho at the end of the year.

A number of civilians died, some during the military conflict, others during the violence, looting and arson which erupted in Maseru and elsewhere in the following days. On 24 September a night curfew was imposed. Incidents of arbitrary killings, death threats and other politically motivated violence by opposition and government supporters against their opponents continued into October. There were also incidents of ill-treatment of civilians and arrested soldiers by the SANDF.

Journalists were subjected to death threats and other forms of harassment in the context of the conflict and the SANDF intervention.

Mediation talks chaired by South African government representatives ended with all political parties agreeing on draft legislation for the establishment of an Interim Political Authority (IPA), which was adopted by parliament on 3 November. The IPA provides for a body, composed of two representatives from the government and from each political party, to undertake reforms of the electoral system and to prepare for general elections within 18 months. The IPA must ensure free political activity prior to the elections.

There were concerns at prolonged and unfair trial proceedings, and ill-treatment of detainees. In October, 33 LDF soldiers were arrested in connection with the September mutiny and detained without charge at the Maximum Security Prison, Maseru. The 33 soldiers were held in cells which lacked adequate light, warmth, bedding and sanitation. At least six were interrogated at night by members of the military and police at various locations. At least one detainee had a gun pointed at him during interrogation. Relatives of some of the soldiers brought an application in the High Court for an order to allow the detainees access to their lawyer. In November the High Court ruled that the state had to charge the soldiers detained in the Maximum Security Prison within eight days or release them. In December the soldiers were charged with mutiny and allowed to consult their lawyers. Following some releases and further arrests, 50 soldiers were held at the end of the year.

The trial of 33 police officers in relation to the February 1997 mutiny (see *Amnesty International Report 1998*) began in February. Only a few witnesses had been heard prior to the destruction of the trial records and the chambers of the presiding judge during the looting and arson in Maseru in September. Fire also destroyed the record of the hearing on a third bail application on behalf of the accused. The trial resumed late in the year but was not concluded. Six of the accused, facing additional charges in relation to the 1995 Maseru Central Police Station shootings in which senior police officers were shot dead (see *Amnesty International Report*

1996), had still not been formally indicted by the end of the year.

In October police sergeant Thabo Tsukulu and army private Mokitimi Senekane, who together with Attorney Haae Phoofolo had been charged in 1997 with treason, were released on bail (see *Amnesty International Report 1998*). They had not been brought to trial by the end of the year.

Torture and ill-treatment by police were reported. At least four workers at a garment factory in Maseru, who were among 10 workers arrested in March during a labour dispute, were allegedly tortured in custody. Rekselisitsoe Nonyana said that he was denied food, hit with batons in the stomach, kicked and slapped, and tied to a tree before he was released without charge four days later. Five of those arrested were held beyond the legally allowed 48 hours before being brought to court and charged. None had been brought to trial by the end of the year.

In October a 16-year-old youth involved in protests at the palace was allegedly punched and kicked in the face and forced to do strenuous exercises by police at Maseru Central Police Station. He was released without charge and required medical treatment.

In September police administering the night curfew allegedly forced two women to lie down at the roadside and whipped them on their buttocks. The women were returning to their homes before the curfew hour and were too frightened to bring a charge against the police.

There were reports of killings and injuries as a result of police using lethal force in apparent violation of international standards. On 13 February police officers fired without warning into a crowd of workers in the compound of a garment factory in Ha-Thetsane, Maseru, killing a young woman, Libuseng Ramolata, and injuring dozens of others. One, Seabata Sehlabaka, died later from his injuries. According to the Commissioner of Police, one officer was charged with opening fire without orders. Other officers allegedly involved in the incident remained on duty.

On 17 August police fired on hundreds of protesters outside the palace. Although there were reports during August that a number of protesters were armed and that some police were injured, on 17 August police officers appeared to have used excessive force when they opened fire in response to protesters who were shouting abuse at them after the officers had allegedly beaten a protester. A 16-year-old girl died from a gunshot wound to her head; around 30 other people were injured. Another protester died later from his injuries.

In January a judicial commission of inquiry released its report into the 1996 shooting by police of construction workers at Butha-Buthe (see *Amnesty International Report 1997*). The commission found that the police contingent sent to clear the work camp had used "unreasonable force" inside the compound and "excessive force" in clearing workers from the surrounding area. The commission condemned police firing on an ambulance and the detention for three days without charge of the ambulance driver and workers assisting him. The commission also condemned worksite private security personnel for firing on the workers and the ambulance, and recommended that the Director of Public Prosecutions consider prosecuting those involved.

In January the death sentence imposed on Tahleho Letuka was commuted on appeal to a prison term. No new death sentences were reported.

Amnesty International expressed concern to the authorities about the detention and ill-treatment of trade unionists in March. In October an Amnesty International delegation visited Lesotho to conduct research and raise human rights concerns with the Lesotho and South African authorities. The delegates met officials, local human rights organizations and victims of human rights abuses and their relatives. They also visited 33 detained LDF soldiers at the Maximum Security Prison.

LIBERIA

At least 34 people were charged with treason, which carries a possible death sentence. There were reports of "disappearances" and extrajudicial executions. No one was held accountable for past or current human rights violations.

Human rights defenders continued to be threatened and harassed because of their human rights work. President Charles

G. Taylor publicly criticized the Justice and Peace Commission of Liberia in October when it called for an investigation into human rights abuses connected to renewed fighting in the capital, Monrovia, the previous month. The government claimed such calls damaged the country's image and denied reports that it had issued a warrant for the arrest of the Commission's director, Samuel Kofi Woods. Four staff members were summoned for questioning by senior government officials. In November President Taylor accused Liberian human rights organizations of telling lies in order to get more money from foreign donors.

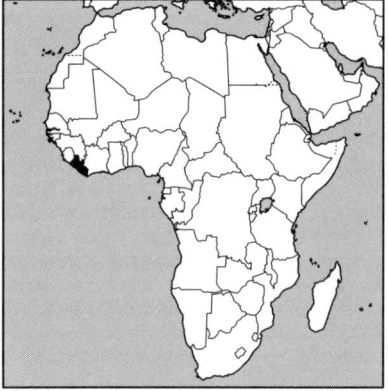

The fighting in Monrovia was a sign of the continuing tension between former armed factions and of the lack of accountability of the security forces. In early September President Taylor, himself a former faction leader, announced that the government had uncovered a coup plot by former faction leaders. Fighting began on 18 September when government security forces entered the Camp Johnson Road district – a stronghold of another former faction leader, Roosevelt Johnson, and his supporters, most of whom are members of the Krahn ethnic group. The government claimed that the purpose of the intervention was to restore law and order and to evict people from homes they were occupying illegally. The Camp Johnson Road district had been insecure for some weeks and many people had fled fearing that they would become the victims of rape, theft, or other attacks by supporters of Roosevelt Johnson, who were acting with apparent impunity. The Minister of Justice

stated that 52 people – two civilian women and 50 "combatants" loyal to Roosevelt Johnson – died during the intervention. The real figure was believed to be much higher and it seemed that some people may have been extrajudicially executed (see below).

The Economic Community of West African States (ECOWAS) Cease-fire Monitoring Group (ECOMOG) handed over responsibility for restructuring the army, a significant component of the peace agreement, to President Taylor. In December a committee set up by the President to analyse the reforms, recommended a restructuring based on countrywide recruitment to guard against ethnic imbalance in the future. The Status of Forces Agreement between ECOMOG and Liberia was agreed by the Senate in October, but was then put before the House of Representatives. This lack of clarity persisted at the end of the year.

Restrictions were imposed on the media. In March attempts to introduce legislation which demanded high registration fees for the press were thwarted. However, the media continued to be subjected to temporary restrictions in reaction to reports which were critical of the government. For a short while *Star Radio* was stopped from broadcasting its material on the Internet. Its transmission frequency was also changed in an apparent effort to reduce its influence. The restrictions on *Star Radio* were introduced in October and appeared to be an attempt to stifle comment on the recent fighting and associated human rights abuses.

The National Human Rights Commission, set up in 1997, experienced difficulties. In July the Senate approved, with some reservations, the modified legislation setting up the Commission. An outstanding point of contention was the right to subpoena witnesses. The Senate also rejected two of the nominees, including Kromah Bryemah who had apparently been flogged by the Police Director, Joe Tate. It seemed that a report into the incident was given to President Taylor, but its findings were not made public. After his official rejection Kromah Bryemah fled the country because of threats. In December the Commission's Chairman, Hall Badio, publicly stated that the Commission was weak because the government had failed to complete its establishment.

In July a national conference was held in Monrovia. It discussed a broad range of issues, including human rights.

The assisted voluntary return of refugees from West African countries continued at a slow pace. The delays were mostly for practical reasons, but among some communities there was a reluctance to return before the security situation could be guaranteed. Particularly fearful were the Krahn people (see above) and Mandingoes who appeared to be targeted for attack in Lofa County where six of their mosques were reported to have been burned. Despite efforts to mediate between the conflicting groups, the situation in Lofa County remained tense. In October, President Taylor ordered thousands of displaced people living in Monrovia to leave for their own areas saying they were becoming dependent on outside assistance. Many, mostly Krahns, had reportedly been forcibly evicted from their shelters during the fighting in September and the UN High Commissioner for Refugees reported that more than 4,000 Krahns had fled into Côte d'Ivoire in the weeks following the fighting.

At least 34 people were charged with treason, which carries a possible death sentence. At the end of the year, public hearings were continuing in the cases of 14 civilians accused of treason; five others became state witnesses. Another group of about 20 people was due to be tried by a Court Martial Board. However, the hearings were adjourned in December and the Board was still awaiting further instructions from the Ministry of Defence at the end of the year.

There were several reported "disappearances". In July Nowah Flomo, a market trader, was abducted. Several members of the Special Security Service were arrested in connection with the abduction, but later released. A police investigation was reportedly carried out after public pressure, but by the end of the year no one had been brought to justice for her "disappearance". Several members of the Krahn community were also feared to have "disappeared". After the fighting in September, the Minister of Justice issued a warning to the security forces not to arrest people and keep them in illegal detention centres. This followed widespread reports that the security forces were arbitrarily arresting people who were then "disappearing".

It appeared that some of those who died during the fighting in September may have been extrajudicially executed. Some of the bodies retrieved reportedly had their hands tied behind their backs and showed evidence of bullet wounds. It was also reported that others died when members of the security forces opened fire in one of two churches in the Camp Johnson Road area where people had sought refuge. Other victims were dragged out of ambulances despite appeals by the health personnel that they be allowed to receive the urgent medical attention they needed. It was difficult to estimate the number of people who may have been extrajudicially executed as the authorities refused to investigate alleged mass graves. By the end of the year no investigation had been held to establish how people died and who was responsible.

Others may have been extrajudicially executed in custody. In October a government spokesperson announced that 11 people had been killed on 22 September in what he described as a "shoot-out" between government soldiers and dissident troops trying to release their supporters from custody at the Post Stockade in Monrovia's Barclay Training Centre. The delay in making public this information and the refusal to return the bodies to the families, raised concerns that the 11 may have been extrajudicially executed.

In February the trial began of members of the security forces suspected of extrajudicially executing Samuel Dokie, a former minister and National Assembly official, and three of his relatives in 1997 (see *Amnesty International Report 1998*). Two members of the Special Security Services, who were the last people to be seen with the four victims, were charged with the murders. Three other officers who had been arrested were discharged and served as state witnesses. However, the two officers were acquitted as they claimed the four detainees had been handed over to the Regional Commander of the Special Security Services. A warrant was issued for the arrest of five other people, including the Regional Commander, who were believed to be in neighbouring Côte d'Ivoire.

In October Amnesty International publicly appealed to the government to investigate allegations of extrajudicial executions, "disappearances" and arbitrary

238

arrests in the context of the fighting in September. Amnesty International continued to call on the government to respect the right of human rights defenders and the media to continue their work without interference.

LIBYA

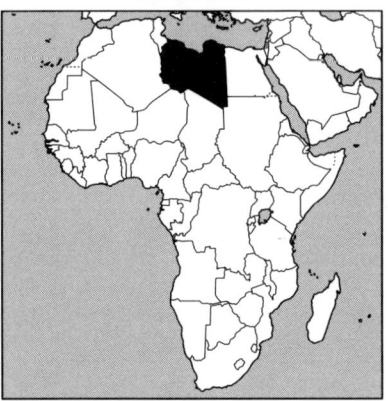

Five prisoners of conscience arrested in 1973 continued to serve life sentences. Scores of possible prisoners of conscience were arrested during the year in connection with their religious or political activities. Hundreds of political prisoners, including possible prisoners of conscience, remained in detention. Some were detained without charge or trial, others continued to be held despite acquittal by courts. Torture and ill-treatment were reported. At least three people were sentenced to death.

In August a draft resolution, put forward by the USA and the United Kingdom (UK), to try the two Libyan nationals suspected of involvement in the 1988 bombing of a US passenger airliner (see *Amnesty International Report 1995*) before Scottish judges at the Hague in the Netherlands was adopted unanimously by the UN Security Council. The resolution would suspend the UN sanctions on Libya, imposed since 1992, as soon as both suspects arrived in the Netherlands. At the end of the year the Libyan government was still seeking guarantees relating to the trial and possible imprisonment of the defendants.

The trial of five people accused of a bomb attack – two Palestinians, a former Libyan diplomat and two Germans – continued in Germany (see *Amnesty International Report 1998*). The prosecution claimed that the bombing of a West Berlin discotheque in 1986, apparently targeting US military personnel, had been carried out on direct orders from the Libyan intelligence service. In July a court in Berlin ruled that the confession of a former Libyan diplomat, Musbah 'Eter, was inadmissible because a prosecutor had wrongly given the impression that he would be spared a life prison sentence if he confessed to a role in the bombing. A few days later the prosecution challenged this ruling before an appeal court, which rejected the challenge saying that there was no reason to suspect the court (that made the July ruling) had been partial. In August the prosecution appealed again before a different chamber of the appeal court; at the end of the year no decision had been taken.

Five prisoners of conscience, who were arrested in 1973 and convicted of membership of the prohibited Islamic Liberation Party, continued to serve life sentences (see previous *Amnesty International Reports*).

Scores of possible prisoners of conscience were detained during the year in connection with their political or religious beliefs and were still held without charge or trial at the end of 1998. In June and July around 100 professionals, including engineers and university lecturers, were arrested on suspicion of supporting or sympathizing with *al-Jama'a al-Islamiya al-Libiya*, Libyan Islamic Group, an underground Islamist movement which was not known to have used or advocated violence. The arrests took place in a number of major cities, particularly Benghazi. Those arrested included Mohammad Faraj al-Qallal, an executive in a printing house in Benghazi, who was arrested in early June by plainclothes security men. He was given no reason for his arrest. Ahmad Jaballah al-Maghrebi was reportedly arrested near the Egypt-Libya border while trying to flee the country with his family. He was allegedly beaten in front of his family by the security men carrying out his arrest. At the end of the year the whereabouts of all those arrested in June and July remained unacknowledged. The detainees were reportedly held in Abu Salim and 'Ain Zara prisons, Tripoli, where they were allegedly at risk of torture and ill-treatment.

Hundreds of political prisoners arrested in previous years, including possible prisoners of conscience, remained held without charge or trial. Among them were Rashid 'Abd al-Hamid al-'Urfia and Muhammad Suleiman al-Qaid (see *Amnesty International Report 1998*), who remained in Abu Salim Prison in Tripoli. 'Omar al-Turbi, a dentist suspected of political opposition activities, continued to be held without charge or trial since his arrest in 1984. 'Omar al-Duffani, who had been arrested in 1995 because of his alleged Islamist opposition activities, also remained held without charge or trial. He was initially held in a detention centre in 'Ain Zara and was reportedly tortured. His family was not informed of his whereabouts, but in 1998 they heard unofficially that he was being detained in Abu Salim Prison.

Scores of other political detainees remained held despite having been tried and acquitted by courts. Others continued to serve prison sentences imposed in previous years after grossly unfair trials. Among them were the al-Fitouri family and others arrested and sentenced with them (see *Amnesty International Report 1998*).

At least 31 Libyan nationals – men, women and children – who had been detained in Saudi Arabia without charge or trial for more than two years following the November 1995 bombing of the Saudi Arabian National Guard training centre in Riyadh were forcibly returned to Libya in April or May (see **Saudi Arabia** entry). They were arrested following their arrival in Libya and their whereabouts at the end of the year were not known. Among them were 'Amer al-J'ayed, Khayri al-Fitouri Nasrat, Mahmoud al-Fitouri and 'Abd al-Karim al-Zawi.

A Libyan family – al-Sayyid Mohammad Shabou, his wife Manal Hussein, and their two children, Mohammad and Ahmad – were forcibly returned to Libya by Saudi Arabia in May or June allegedly because of al-Sayyid Mohammad Shabou's Islamist opposition activities (see **Saudi Arabia** entry). The family had been granted refugee status in the UK in November 1997 and travelled to Saudi Arabia in January for the pilgrimage. Manal Hussein and her children were released in Libya but al-Sayyid Mohammad Shabou continued to be held, reportedly without charge or trial, at the end of the year.

At least three people were known to have been sentenced to death during the year, but the total could have been much higher as information on death sentences and executions is rarely reported. Three men, all Ghanaian nationals, were sentenced to death after being found guilty of the murder in 1995 of a garage owner in Ghat, southwest Libya. All three reportedly denied the charges and appealed against the verdict. At the end of the year no details were available as to the outcome of the appeal.

Amnesty International continued to call for the immediate and unconditional release of all prisoners of conscience and for all other political prisoners to be granted fair and prompt trials or released. No information was made available as to whether the Egyptian government carried out a new inquiry into the 1993 "disappearance" in Egypt of Mansur Kikhiya, a former Libyan Foreign Affairs Minister and a human rights defender (see *Amnesty International Report 1998*). Mansur Kikhiya's wife, Baha al-'Emari, through her lawyer in Egypt, continued to use all legal avenues to obtain compensation from the Egyptian government, which she blamed for her husband's "disappearance".

In October the UN Human Rights Committee examined Libya's implementation of the International Covenant on Civil and Political Rights (ICCPR) and expressed concerns about allegations of extrajudicial, arbitrary or summary executions by state agents, the systematic use of torture, and the high incidence of arbitrary arrests and detention, including prolonged detention without trial. The Committee also expressed concern that in violation of Article 6(2) of the ICCPR, the death penalty was not being imposed solely for the most serious crimes and recommended that legal provisions be introduced that were compatible with this Article.

MACAO

Uncertainties remained about the adequacy of human rights protection in Macao in anticipation of the territory's return to Chinese control in December 1999.

Concerns grew over increased criminal activity in Macao. The Macaonese and Chinese authorities stepped up police cooperation on crime and border issues. There were fears that new offences incorporated into law in 1997 to combat gang-related crime could be used to curb freedom of association (see *Amnesty International Report 1998*). Reports of press censorship continued, particularly of coverage of human rights violations and dissident activity in China.

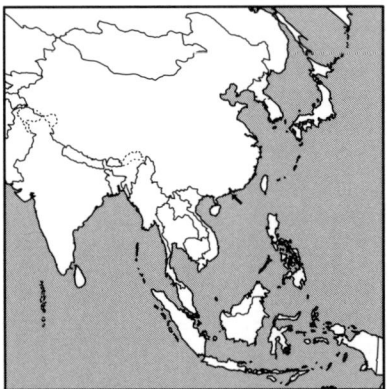

The Portuguese authorities made moves to incorporate further safeguards for human rights into Macaonese law before the handover to China, but many ambiguities remained. The Basic Law of the Macao Special Administrative Region (MSAR) of the People's Republic of China (PRC), which will govern Macao's affairs after 20 December 1999, fails to guarantee fully the rights enjoyed by Macao's citizens under the International Covenant on Civil and Political Rights (ICCPR) and other international human rights standards. The Basic Law and Macao's penal codes do not include adequate safeguards against torture and ill-treatment and for the independence of the judiciary and fair trials (see previous *Amnesty International Reports*).

In July the Portuguese President issued a series of decrees extending to Macao several international human rights standards, including the Convention on the Rights of the Child, the Convention on the Elimination of All Forms of Discrimination against Women, and the Convention relating to the Status of Refugees. The measures were suspended after the Legislative Assembly of Macao protested that it had not been consulted, but were subsequently reinstated in August.

Although China has signed the International Covenant on Economic, Social and Cultural Rights and the ICCPR, both of which had been extended to Macao by Portugal in 1992, there were no moves to incorporate these instruments in specific legislation for the MSAR. It was not clear whether China or the Macaonese authorities would continue reporting to the UN Human Rights Committee on their implementation of the ICCPR, as directed by the UN Human Rights Committee in 1997 (see *Amnesty International Report 1998*).

Ambiguities remained concerning the application of other international human rights treaties to Macao. Although the UN Convention against Torture and Other Cruel, Inhuman or Degrading Treatment or Punishment had been extended to Macao under Portuguese law, it was unclear whether China's failure to make a declaration under Article 22 of the Convention would prevent the UN Committee against Torture hearing individual complaints concerning Macao.

A new law regulating freedom of religion published by the Macao authorities in August contained important safeguards for religious practice. It was not clear, however, if provisions in the law dealing with conscientious objection would apply in all situations, such as the refusal by medical personnel to conduct forcible abortions.

Procedures to apply after December 1999 for the extradition of people wanted by jurisdictions in other parts of China remained unclear, giving rise to concerns that prisoners could be transferred to elsewhere in China in cases where they might face the death penalty. The rights of detainees of Chinese origin but with Portuguese nationality (who would be considered by the Chinese authorities to be nationals of the PRC) to consular assistance also remained unclear. Uncertainty continued about whether immigrants, including East Timorese and other refugees, would be authorized to remain in Macao after the handover.

The Chinese and Macaonese authorities gave no formal assurances that the death penalty would not be introduced into MSAR laws. Ambiguities concerning the respective jurisdictions of the PRC and Macaonese courts made it conceivable that PRC courts might apply the death penalty for offences committed in Macao.

Amnesty International representatives visited Macao several times during the year to discuss the organization's human rights concerns with members of the legal and human rights communities.

MACEDONIA
(THE FORMER YUGOSLAV REPUBLIC OF)

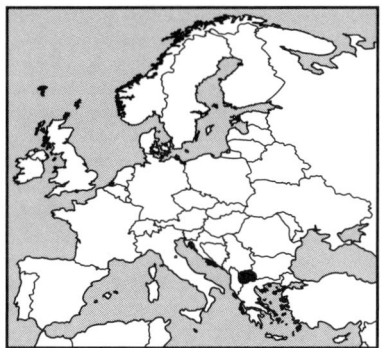

Two prisoners of conscience began serving prison sentences imposed in 1997. There were reports of torture or ill-treatment by police.

There were at least seven explosions outside public buildings; none caused casualties. Responsibility for some of the explosions was attributed to the *Ushtria Çlirimtare e Kosovës*, Kosovo Liberation Army, (see **Yugoslavia, Federal Republic of,** entry), an ethnic Albanian armed political group in Kosovo province of the neighbouring Federal Republic of Yugoslavia (FRY).

In March a parliamentary commission published a report on the events in Gostivar in July 1997, when police shot dead two men and beat hundreds of ethnic Albanian demonstrators, causing the death of one man (see *Amnesty International Report 1998*). The report concluded that police officers had "overstepped their authority". It called for investigations by the Ministry of Internal Affairs into the incidents; criminal investigations into the responsibility of individual officers; and reforms in the Ministry of Internal Affairs. No criminal or disciplinary actions were reported to have been initiated by the end of the year.

In July the mandate of the UN peacekeeping force UNPREDEP (UN Preventive

Deployment Force) was extended until January 1999 in response to concern about the situation in Kosovo province of the FRY. **241**

Parliamentary elections held in October gave the largest number of seats to a coalition of the former opposition party, the VMRO-DPMNE, and a recently formed party, *Demokratska Alternativa* (DA), Democratic Alternative. In November a new coalition government was formed, comprising ministers appointed by the VMRO-DPMNE, DA and the *Partia Demokratike e Shqiptarëve*, Democratic Party of Albanians.

In February the Court of Appeal in Skopje reduced the prison sentence of the Mayor of Gostivar, Rufi Osmani, from 13 years and eight months to seven years. He had been convicted in 1997 in connection with the July events in Gostivar after an unfair trial (see *Amnesty International Report 1998*). The sentence of the President of the Gostivar municipal council, Refik Dauti, who was convicted at the same trial, was reduced from three to two years' imprisonment. In May the prison sentences of the President of the neighbouring Tetovo municipal council, Bebi Bexheti, and the Mayor, Alajdin Demiri, were reduced on appeal from two and a half years to two years. All four men were ethnic Albanians and began serving their sentences during the year. Refik Dauti and Bebi Bexheti were prisoners of conscience. In September the sentence of Ičo Gavrilov, who had been convicted in 1997 for stamping on the national flag, was reduced on appeal from three to two years' imprisonment (see *Amnesty International Report 1998*). He reportedly remained free at the end of the year for medical reasons. In December parliament passed a law granting amnesty to the four ethnic Albanian political prisoners and other prisoners not sentenced on political grounds. The law had not been signed by the President by the end of the year.

In September, 17 ethnic Albanian men were arrested by police in several locations on suspicion of possessing arms or being responsible for explosions at public buildings. One man was killed near Kičevo in unclear circumstances in the course of a police operation to arrest the men. There was concern that the detainees were tortured or ill-treated during interrogation. For example, Shaban Arifi, from the Kumanovo area, alleged that he was beaten in Kumanovo police station before being taken to a town, which he presumed to be

Skopje, where he was further beaten during 24 hours' interrogation. He was released without charge. His son, Arif, who was also arrested and later charged with possessing arms, said that he was transferred from Kumanovo blindfolded in the boot of a car, then beaten during 30 hours' interrogation.

There were other reports of torture or ill-treatment by police. For example, in August a group of around five Roma were allegedly kicked and beaten with truncheons in the police station in Štip after arrest. In September police arresting journalist Marjan Gjurovski in Skopje late at night reportedly banged his head against a car deliberately, breaking his teeth. He stated that police then threatened him at a police station with further violence if he did not sign a confession. He was released the same night after the police claimed that it was a case of mistaken identity.

The police appeared to be more willing than previously to acknowledge human rights violations and to initiate investigations. For example, criminal charges were brought in November against a police officer in connection with the beating of Kristijan Ilievski in Skopje in October.

In December Amnesty International wrote to the authorities calling for independent, impartial and thorough investigations into a number of reports of ill-treatment by police.

MALAYSIA

At least 35 prisoners of conscience and possible prisoners of conscience were held. People suspected of posing a threat to national security, including opponents of government policy, Shi'a Muslims and peaceful demonstrators, were detained without charge or trial. Hundreds of nonviolent demonstrators were arrested; many were beaten by police during arrest and in detention. Detainees were at times ill-treated or degraded, or subjected to severe psychological and physical pressure in order to coerce confessions. Caning was inflicted for a range of crimes. At least six people were sentenced to death. Asylumseekers were among thousands of Indonesians forcibly returned to Indonesia.

Against a backdrop of severe economic recession, political tensions intensified,

contributing to the dismissal from office of Deputy Prime Minister Anwar Ibrahim in early September. Anwar Ibrahim's dismissal sparked mass demonstrations calling for wide-ranging political and social reform and for the resignation of Prime Minister Mahathir Mohamad.

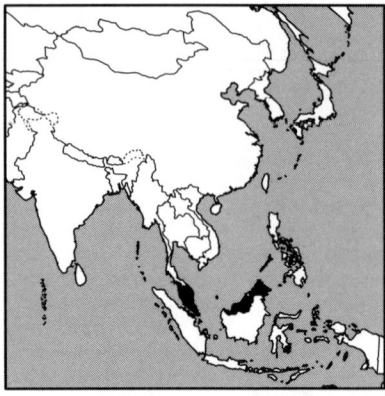

Anwar Ibrahim was arrested shortly after leading a 30,000-strong demonstration through the capital, Kuala Lumpur, in September (see below). Demonstrations in support of Anwar Ibrahim and calling for reform continued, despite a nationwide ban imposed in late September on all further "pro-reform" rallies.

At least 35 prisoners of conscience and possible prisoners of conscience, including human rights defenders and opposition politicians, were held.

Prisoner of conscience Lim Guan Eng, deputy leader of the opposition Democratic Action Party, had his sentence increased to 18 months' imprisonment by the Appeal Court in May. The prison sentence was upheld by the Federal Court, Malaysia's highest court, in August. In 1997 Lim Guan Eng had been sentenced to fines for sedition and "spreading false news" for criticizing the Attorney-General (see previous *Amnesty International Reports*).

Prime Minister Mahathir dismissed Anwar Ibrahim from his posts as Deputy Prime Minister and Finance Minister on 2 September. The next day the police announced publicly that Anwar Ibrahim was under criminal investigation and released detailed but unsubstantiated allegations of sexual misconduct, tampering with evidence, bribery, and threatening national security. Anwar Ibrahim's adopted brother,

Sukma Darmawan, and an academic associate, Munawar Ahmad Anees, were detained, held incommunicado and, on 19 September, pleaded guilty to unlawful sexual relations with Anwar Ibrahim. They were each sentenced to six months' imprisonment. In late September the two men retracted their confessions, saying that they were not given voluntarily (see below). They were prisoners of conscience.

Following his dismissal, rallies in support of Anwar Ibrahim gathered momentum and on 20 September Anwar Ibrahim was arrested under the Internal Security Act (ISA), which allows detention without charge or trial for up to two years, renewable indefinitely. Sixteen of his political associates, many of them influential within the ruling United Malays National Organization (UMNO), were also detained under the ISA. They included Ahmad Zahid Hamidi, head of UMNO Youth, Ahmad Azam Abdul Raham, President of the Muslim youth organization *Angkatan Belia Islam Malaysia*, and Professor Siddiq Baba of the International Islamic University. All 17 were prisoners of conscience; all except Anwar Ibrahim had been released by mid-November.

The authorities also issued a restriction order under the ISA in September against Wan Azizah, Anwar Ibrahim's wife, prohibiting her from speaking at public rallies or holding political gatherings at home.

Others arrested under the ISA included Shaari Sungip, President of *Jamaah Islah Malaysia*, an Islamic non-governmental organization, detained in October, and at least six other alleged "pro-reform" supporters detained between October and December.

The trial of Anwar Ibrahim on charges of sodomy and "corrupt practices" (allegedly misusing his ministerial office to interfere with a police investigation of witnesses linked to charges of sexual misconduct) began in November and was continuing at the end of the year.

The trial of Irene Fernandez, director of the non-governmental organization *Tenaganita*, Women's Force, had not been completed by the end of the year, becoming the longest trial in Malaysia's legal history. She was charged in 1995 with maliciously publishing "false news" in a report detailing allegations of ill-treatment, sexual abuse and denial of medical care in camps holding detained migrant

workers (see previous *Amnesty International Reports*). If imprisoned, she would be a prisoner of conscience.

Seven Shi'a Muslims arrested in 1997, including Lutpi Ibrahim, a university professor, were ordered to be detained without charge or trial for two years under the ISA (see *Amnesty International Report 1998*) for allegedly posing a threat to "national security and Muslim unity". In February they were sent to Kamunting Detention Centre, Perak state. Six of the detainees had been released by early December, reportedly after undergoing "Islamic faith rehabilitation courses". Two of those released remained subject to ISA restriction orders curtailing their freedom of association, expression and movement. Che Kamarulzaman Ismail remained in detention at the end of the year; he was a prisoner of conscience.

From September onwards hundreds of peaceful protesters were arrested. While in detention, their access to legal counsel was restricted. Most were charged with illegal assembly, which carries a maximum penalty of one year's imprisonment, and released on bail. Mass "pro-reform" demonstrations were forcibly broken up by police using tear gas and water cannon spray containing chemical irritants. In late October, protesters responded to police street clearance operations by throwing stones and violent clashes ensued. Sporadic small-scale peaceful protests continued for the rest of the year, along with the arrest and charging of scores of demonstrators.

Many of the protesters reported ill-treatment by police, including being beaten with fists and batons, kicked and slapped, during and after arrest. Tian Chua, Chairperson of the Coalition for People's Democracy, an alliance supportive of reform, lodged an official complaint stating that following a rally in September, he was beaten in a police truck with batons and later kicked and beaten while in detention.

Detainees arrested under the ISA or other legislation, who were held incommunicado at unknown locations, were also ill-treated. Anwar Ibrahim appeared in court in September after nine days' incommunicado detention with a swollen eye and visible bruising. Munawar Anees stated how he was ill-treated and degraded as he was stripped naked, insulted,

244

and shaved bald while being subjected to prolonged, aggressive and disorientating interrogation. Sukma Darmawan also alleged he suffered severe physical and psychological pressure as he was stripped naked in an extremely cold room, beaten and threatened with extended detention under the ISA.

Caning, a form of cruel, inhuman or degrading punishment, was imposed throughout the year as an additional punishment to imprisonment.

At least six people were sentenced to death during the year. The authorities revealed that 349 people had been executed between 1970 and 1996.

Asylum-seekers were among thousands of Indonesian undocumented migrant workers forcibly deported back to Indonesia. In March alone, more than 11,000 Indonesians were deported from immigration detention camps around the country. In one forcible repatriation operation in March, eight Indonesians were killed and scores injured. Those deported included people known to be at risk of human rights violations in Indonesia. About 500 of those deported were detained on their arrival in Indonesia and held incommunicado in Rancung Military Detention Centre, Aceh. In the past, detainees in Rancung have been tortured and ill-treated.

A group of 27 Acehnese asylum-seekers who sought protection in foreign embassies were arrested in April and forcibly repatriated later in the year. The UN High Commissioner for Refugees was denied access to them. At least 10 Acehnese with leave to remain in Malaysia, two of whom were members of the Acehnese Refugee Committee in Malaysia, were arrested during the year, including one who was ordered detained for two years under the ISA. Some were forcibly deported to Aceh.

In April Amnesty International published a report, *Malaysia: Asylum-seekers at risk in mass deportation of economic migrants*, calling for an investigation into deaths during deportation operations and urging the authorities to halt forcible deportations until they could guarantee that no refugees would be at risk of *refoulement* (forcible return) in the process.

Amnesty International delegates attended the trial hearings of Lim Guan Eng in March and August and the trial of Anwar Ibrahim in November. In October and November the organization published a

series of external briefings, including *Malaysia: The arrest of Anwar Ibrahim and his political associates*, calling for the immediate and unconditional release of all prisoners of conscience. Amnesty International also urged the government to respect the right of peaceful assembly, to ensure that the police did not use excessive force, and to amend the ISA to bring it into line with international standards.

MALDIVES

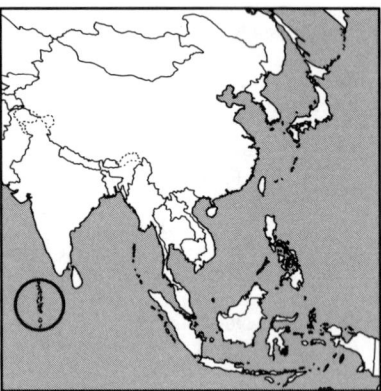

Dozens of prisoners of conscience and possible prisoners of conscience were held. Prisoners and detainees continued to be ill-treated.

A presidential election in October endorsed Maumoon Abdul Gayoom as President for the fifth term. As in previous years, political parties were not allowed to function.

At least 20 prisoners of conscience were detained in June, most of them in Dhoonidhoo detention centre, on suspicion of spreading Christian beliefs. They were held without trial until November when they were released. The government denied that they had been arrested for professing the Christian faith, but gave no other reason for their detention.

Wu Mei De, a Chinese national held since 1993 apparently as a result of official connivance in attempts by his business partner to prevent him from seeking judicial redress for business grievances (see *Amnesty International Report 1998*), remained in Gaamadhoo Prison without charge or trial.

The government provided no information about possible prisoners of conscience Hussain Shakir, Ibrahim Musthafa and Mohamed Rasheed (see *Amnesty International Report 1998*). Referring to their arrests in early 1996 in connection with a demonstration about a rise in electricity prices in Fuvahmulaku Island, the government said these "were for criminal offences of destroying and attempting to destroy properties. The offenders were arrested on criminal charges and dealt with in accordance with the law."

In February Ismail Saadiq (see *Amnesty International Report 1998*) was transferred from house arrest first to solitary confinement in police custody and then to Dhoonidhoo detention centre. On 15 December he was returned to house arrest. The government stated that he had been sentenced to six months' banishment on fraud charges and that two other fraud cases against him were pending before the courts. It gave no explanation about the date and the manner in which he had been tried or the reason why he was held in Dhoonidhoo detention centre for 10 months.

Prisoners continued to be ill-treated. Women detainees were reportedly held in small, hot and overcrowded cells without adequate sleeping space. Some prisoners of conscience were held continuously for several months in solitary confinement. A former detainee at Gaamadhoo Prison said that she had seen male and female prisoners handcuffed to coconut palms in front of prison cells trying to sleep. During her five-day detention there, she saw girls aged between 13 and 18 almost permanently handcuffed in their cells. Male soldiers jabbed the ribs of female prisoners with wooden batons to wake them for dawn prayers, pointing the batons in a humiliating way, especially at the girls' genitals.

It was learned that a girl had died in Gaamadhoo Prison in 1994 after she was gang-raped by guard soldiers. No further details were known.

Throughout the year Amnesty International sought information about prisoners, called for the immediate and unconditional release of prisoners of conscience, and expressed concern over reports of ill-treatment. The government responded with information on some cases and an assurance that it takes "human rights protection very seriously".

MALI

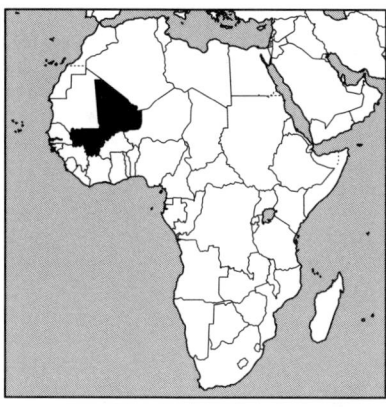

Seven prisoners of conscience were unfairly tried and imprisoned. Dozens of students and opposition party supporters, including prisoners of conscience and possible prisoners of conscience, were arrested. At least five people were sentenced to death. No executions were reported.

In October former President Moussa Traoré, his wife, Mariam, and three of his close associates were tried by the Assize Court on charges of embezzlement and other economic crimes. The trial was continuing at the end of the year.

Seven prisoners of conscience were sentenced to prison terms of 15 to 18 months in March. The seven – Mady Kamakoye Diallo, a minister in the government of former President Moussa Traoré and one of the leaders of the *Mouvement patriotique pour le renouveau*, Patriotic Movement for Renewal, and six soldiers, most of whom were members of a movement seeking to improve soldiers' living conditions – had been arrested in October and December 1996 (see previous *Amnesty International Reports*). Their trial before the Bamako Assize Court was grossly unfair. The only evidence produced against them consisted of statements apparently extracted under torture. Mady Diallo was reportedly deprived of sleep and threats were made against members of his family. Other defendants alleged in court that they had been regularly humiliated, beaten and tortured to force them to sign statements while in police custody. Despite the fact that some of the defendants bore visible injuries consistent with the allegations of torture, the court admitted the statements as evidence and made no effort to investigate the torture allegations. The seven defendants had been held in illegally prolonged incommunicado detention *(garde à vue)* and had had their access to families, lawyers and doctors restricted. An appeal with the Court of Cassation was pending at the end of the year.

Dozens of people, including opposition party supporters, students and a journalist, were arrested in Bamako, the capital, and in Ségou. Among them were prisoners of conscience Mrs Raiss, Tiemoko Sissoko and Chouaïdou Traoré, the publishing director of a privately owned newspaper, who were released without charge after a few days.

Several possible prisoners of conscience were sentenced to prison terms. In June, 83-year-old Madani Keita and 71-year-old Cheickna Camara were arrested following a demonstration organized by the opposition in Ségou. They were convicted on charges including obstructing a public highway and sentenced to one month's imprisonment by the Ségou tribunal.

Scores of students were arrested in Bamako and Ségou following protests in June and July. Most were released without charge, but 10, most of whom were leading members of the *Association des étudiants et élèves du Mali*, Association of Malian Students, were tried before the Bamako Assize Court on charges including arson, obstructing a public highway and manslaughter. At the trial witnesses for the prosecution stated that the students had not been present at the scene of the fire which destroyed school buildings and resulted in one death. One student was acquitted, but nine others, including possible prisoners of conscience, were sentenced to between three months' imprisonment and five years' hard labour.

Opposition supporters, including Adama Kouyate, Dacry Sine Sissoko, and Seydou Coulibaly, were arrested in June and remained in detention without charge or trial at the end of the year.

No independent or impartial investigations were known to have been initiated into allegations of torture made in 1997 (see *Amnesty International Report 1998*).

At least five people were sentenced to death. In February Bourama Konaté was convicted of murder and sentenced to death by the Assize Court. Four other people – Moussa Coulibaly, Emmanuel Johnson, Ibrahim Konte and Afousseyni Camara – were sentenced to death in October for offences including murder and armed robbery. No executions were reported. President Konaré stated that he was opposed to the death penalty and that all death sentences passed in previous years had been commuted to life imprisonment.

Amnesty International delegates visited Mali in March to attend the trial of Mady Diallo and the six soldiers, and to investigate allegations of torture. In October Amnesty International published a report, *Mali: An unfair trial and torture with impunity compromise the establishment of the rule of law*, which detailed the failure of the trial to comply with international standards of fair trial and the failure of the authorities to bring to justice those responsible for torture and ill-treatment in police stations throughout the country.

MAURITANIA

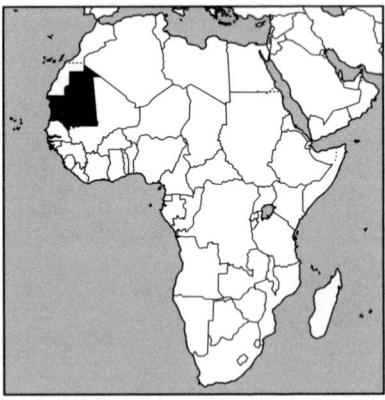

Five prisoners of conscience were sentenced to terms of imprisonment and at least five others had their movement restricted. Three other prisoners of conscience were put under house arrest. One prisoner of conscience was tried and acquitted. One person was sentenced to death.

In May an Assistant High Commissioner for Human Rights was appointed by the government. It was not clear what impact this new role would have on respect for human rights and the ability of human rights defenders to carry out their work without interference (see below).

Attacks on press freedom continued throughout the year. Individual editions of newspapers were seized when they covered issues the authorities did not wish to see publicized, and one newspaper, *Mauritanie nouvelles*, ceased publishing in January when it was issued with a further three-month ban just after a previous ban expired.

In late July and August at least 20 demonstrators were briefly detained after police intervened in a demonstration organized by maritime workers in Nouadhibou to protest against recruitment procedures. As a result of the use of firearms and tear gas, some 25 demonstrators and six police officers were injured. More than 20 people, including sailors, trade unionists and members of the political opposition, were reportedly arrested and held for about four days. One of those briefly held was believed to have been arrested following a complaint lodged by a police officer, which was later dropped, others were held without charge. A further demonstration calling for their release was dispersed by the security forces using excessive force which resulted in several demonstrators being injured.

Five prisoners of conscience, all human rights defenders, were sentenced to terms of imprisonment on account of their non-violent activities. In January, three human rights defenders – Boubacar Ould Messaoud, President of the non-governmental human rights organization *sos-Esclaves*, sos-Slaves; Maître Brahim Ould Ebetty, a prominent lawyer and member of sos-Slaves; and Professor Cheikh Saad Bouh Kamara, President of the *Association mauritanienne des droits de l'homme* (AMDH), Mauritanian Association for Human Rights – were arrested and were charged with running unauthorized associations. A fourth person was also charged *in absentia*. On 5 February, three days before their trial, an opposition party organized a demonstration to demand their release. Several demonstrators were arrested and at least five were then restricted without any charges being brought against them; they were sent into the interior of the country and required to report daily to the local authorities. On the same day, Maître Fatimata M'Baye, Vice-President of the AMDH, who was to have been one

of the defence lawyers in the trial, was also arrested. The arrests appeared to have been prompted by a television program on slavery broadcast on a French language cable channel, which featured an interview with Boubacar Ould Messaoud.

On 12 February the four people in custody and a fifth who was tried *in absentia* were sentenced to 13 months' imprisonment. The questioning by the court focused solely on issues related to freedom of expression and association. The four people in custody lodged an appeal with the Court of Appeal which confirmed their sentences in March. However, on the day the Appeal Court announced its verdict, the five were granted presidential clemency, and the remaining restrictions on their supporters were lifted. However, the organizations which they were accused of running remained unauthorized.

Three prisoners of conscience were placed under house arrest. In December, two opposition party activists and a human rights lawyer – Ahmed Ould Daddah, President of *Le Front des Partis d'Opposition* (FPO), Opposition Parties Front – an umbrella group of opposition parties – and Secretary General of *l'Union des Forces Démocratiques-Ere Nouvelle*, Union of Democratic Forces-New Era, another party activist, and Maître Mohameden Ould Ichiddou, a lawyer, were arrested for their non-violent political activities. They were moved to the remote town of Boumdeid and denied access to lawyers and their families. They were arrested following an FPO meeting where it was alleged that the government was planning to accept Israeli nuclear waste for dumping. No formal charges were brought and the three remained under house arrest at the end of the year.

Baba Ould Sidi Abdellah, High Commissioner of the *Organisation de la mise en valeur du fleuve Sénégal* (OMVS), Organization for the Development of the Senegal River, was arrested in January. He was charged with treason, apparently for agreeing to the loss of some jobs for Mauritanian officials. He appeared to be a prisoner of conscience, detained because of political rivalries with the government. He was held incommunicado for 10 days and then detained at the civil prison in the capital, Nouakchott, until August when he was acquitted by the criminal court and released.

248

Ahmed Ould Haimed was found guilty of murder in September by the Criminal Court in Nouakchott and sentenced to death.

Amnesty International appealed to the government of President Maaouya Ould Sid'Ahmed Taya for the immediate release of Maître Fatimata M'Baye and the three other human rights defenders and for the ending of restrictions on those who had demonstrated to demand their release. The organization also appealed for the release of the three activists held in Boumdeid and sought assurances that they were not being ill-treated while held incommunicado.

MEXICO

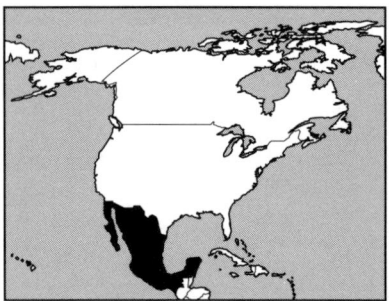

Prisoners of conscience detained in previous years continued to be held. Hundreds of people, including human rights defenders, were arbitrarily detained. Human rights defenders and workers for non-governmental organizations (NGOs) were the victims of death threats and other forms of harassment. Torture and ill-treatment by the army and police were widespread. Several "disappearances" and extrajudicial executions were reported.

There were continuing reports of human rights violations by the army and by paramilitary forces allegedly linked to the government in the context of law enforcement, anti-narcotics and counter-insurgency operations.

Peace negotiations between the armed opposition group *Ejército Zapatista de Liberación Nacional* (EZLN), Zapatista National Liberation Army, and the government remained suspended. Consequently, the *Comisión Nacional de Intermediación*, National Mediation Council, led by Bishop Samuel Ruiz, dissolved itself in

June. In November, however, there were talks between the EZLN and the *Comisión de Concordia Pacificación*, Concord and Pacification Commission, made up of federal deputies and senators.

In Guerrero and Oaxaca states, the armed opposition group *Ejército Popular Revolucionario* (EPR), Revolutionary Popular Army, allegedly carried out a number of attacks on the security forces. In March the *Ejército Revolucionario del Pueblo Insurgente* (ERPI), Insurgent People's Revolutionary Army, split from the EPR.

In the context of popular concern about public security and the perceived steep rise in violent crime, the Senate approved government proposals for measures to combat delinquency which significantly reduced judicial guarantees, particularly those relating to detention.

The arrest of an individual accused of more than 20 kidnappings in August led to a public debate on the death penalty. Although the Constitution allows for capital punishment, the death penalty had not been imposed in Mexico since 1937.

A draft law on "disappearances" was prepared by the *Comisión Nacional de Derechos Humanos*, National Human Rights Commission, in May. It had not been discussed by Congress by the end of the year.

In January the UN Special Rapporteur on torture concluded that "torture and similar ill-treatment are frequent occurrences in many parts of Mexico". The report followed his visit to Mexico in August 1997.

In August the UN Sub-Commission on Prevention of Discrimination and Protection of Minorities called on the government to ensure full respect for the international instruments to which Mexico was a party. In particular, the resolution urged the government to combat impunity for those who commit serious human rights abuses, particularly against members of indigenous populations, and to promote the work of human rights defenders and guarantee their safety.

In September the Inter-American Commission on Human Rights (IACHR) published a report on the human rights situation in Mexico. It urged the government, among other things, "to conduct meaningful, prompt and impartial investigations in all cases of disappearances" and punish those responsible; and to develop "strategies to effectively combat the proliferation of paramilitary groups" and measures to combat torture, including ending impunity for torturers. The government accepted the jurisdiction of the Inter-American Court of Human Rights in December but with the reservation referring to Article 33 of the Constitution which allows the Presidency to expel foreign nationals without a judicial hearing.

In October the government failed to attend an IACHR session which discussed the implementation of IACHR recommendations made previously on the cases of Brigadier General José Francisco Gallardo (see below); the killing of three peasant leaders from Morelia, Chiapas state, in 1994 (see *Amnesty International Report 1996*); and the massacre of 17 unarmed peasants in 1995 near the village of Aguas Blancas, Guerrero state (see *Amnesty International Reports 1996* and *1997*). The government failed to implement the recommendations, claiming that the cases were resolved.

In May the Ministry of the Interior introduced strict visa requirements for international human rights observers which jeopardized the confidentiality of victims, witnesses and relatives who provided testimonies on violations.

The government expelled dozens of foreign nationals who were on missions to monitor human rights in a clear attempt to reduce international observation of the deteriorating situation in Chiapas. Among those expelled was Father Michel Chanteau, a French priest who had been living and serving as a parish priest in Chiapas for 32 years and who was active in the defence of human rights. The expulsion of Thomas Hansen, former director of the US-based NGO Pastors for Peace, was successfully challenged in the courts and the ban on his returning to the country was lifted. A government appeal against the ruling was pending at the end of the year.

Prisoners of conscience detained in previous years continued to be held. Despite recommendations by the IACHR in 1996 that he be immediately released, in March and April Brigadier General Gallardo was condemned by military courts to two consecutive 14-year prison sentences on trumped-up charges. His right to receive visits was restricted and he suffered continual harassment by prison

guards. He had been arrested in 1993 for calling on the government to create the post of human rights ombudsman for the armed forces (see *Amnesty International Report 1997*).

Prisoners of conscience Benigno Guzmán and Bertoldo Ramírez Cruz (see *Amnesty International Report 1998*) remained in prison in Acapulco, Guerrero state, and were reportedly threatened by fellow prisoners, allegedly in collusion with the prison director. In October Benigno Guzmán was sentenced to more than 13 years' imprisonment following a trial which reportedly fell short of international fair trial standards.

In May prisoner of conscience Gerardo Demesa Padilla, a leader of the *Comité de Unidad de Tepoztlán*, Committee of Unity of Tepoztlán, was released after 29 months' imprisonment (see *Amnesty International Reports 1997* and *1998*).

More than 200 people, including human rights activists, were detained in five joint army and police operations in Chiapas state between April and June. Most were subsequently released without charge. However, the operations in Taniperla, Diez de Abril, Amparo Aguatinta, Nicolás Ruiz, and El Bosque appeared to be collective punishments against the communities, whom the authorities suspected of supporting the EZLN. In Nicolás Ruiz, for example, 167 people were detained on the basis of three individual arrest orders in an operation lasting six hours and involving hundreds of police officers and soldiers.

Human rights defenders and NGO workers, continued to suffer death threats and other forms of harassment. In March César Estrada Aguilar, a member of the *Centro de Derechos Indígenas*, Indigenous Rights Centre, in Chiapas state, was arbitrarily detained for some three hours by three members of the *Policía de Seguridad Pública* (PSP), Public Security Police, who threatened to kill him. In November Abel Barrera Hernández, President of the *Centro de Derechos Humanos de la Montaña Tlachinollan*, Centre for Human Rights of Tlachinollan, Guerrero state, received death threats.

Sister Consuelo Morales Elizondo of the organization *Ciudadanos en Apoyo a los Derechos Humanos*, Citizens for Human Rights, who publicly denounced the torture and ill-treatment of prisoners

250

in Nuevo León state, was subjected to intimidatory surveillance allegedly carried out by police. Members of other human rights organizations – including the *Comité de Derechos Humanos de Tabasco*, Human Rights Committee of Tabasco; several NGOs in Guerrero state; and the *Liga Mexicana por la Defensa de los Derechos Humanos*, Mexican League for the Defence of Human Rights, in Oaxaca state – were subjected to a widespread campaign by the authorities, clearly aimed at delegitimizing their work.

There were reports of torture and ill-treatment by the security forces, including the army. The victims were often denied medical treatment. Courts continued to accept confessions extracted under torture as evidence. Numerous cases of ill-treatment were reported in the prison at Apodaca, Nuevo León state. In March, José Luis Blanco Flores was reportedly detained by judicial police near the town of Atoyac de Alvarez, Guerrero state, and tortured while held in unacknowledged detention for three days. Efrén Cortés Chávez and Erika Zamora Pardo alleged that they were tortured by soldiers after being detained during an army operation in the village of El Charco, Ayutla, Guerrero state, in June in which 11 civilians, whom the authorities alleged were members of the ERPI, were killed. By the end of the year the circumstances surrounding the incident had not been clarified by the authorities.

In June the former director of the *Policía Judicial Federal*, Federal Judicial Police, was sentenced to four years' imprisonment for the torture of witnesses carried out in the context of the investigation into the murder of Francisco Ruiz Massieu, General Secretary of the ruling *Partido Revolucionario Institucional* (PRI), Institutional Revolutionary Party, in September 1994.

Several people "disappeared" and hundreds of "disappearances" from previous years remained unresolved. Juan Sosa Maldonado was detained in July while shopping with his wife in Oaxaca city. The authorities did not acknowledge his detention for a month. In August the State Attorney's Office announced that Juan Sosa Maldonado was in detention, accused of being an EPR quartermaster. Two people who had "disappeared" after being captured during military operations in April and June 1997, reappeared in mid-

1998. Both reported long periods of torture by their military captors to extract information and confessions.

Extrajudicial executions and deaths resulting from excessive use of force by the security forces continued to be reported. In January Guadalupe Méndez López was shot dead by members of the PSP in Ocosingo, Chiapas state, during a demonstration calling for justice for the victims of the 1997 Acteal massacre. Her three-year-old daughter Isabel Santís and 17-year-old Lázaro López Vázquez were wounded in the incident. Of the 22 police officers detained for the killing, 21 were released in June. By the end of the year no one had been charged.

In February José Tila López was shot dead when peasants returning from giving evidence to a human rights delegation were ambushed in northern Chiapas close to a PSP post. Survivors accused members of the so-called paramilitary group *Paz y Justicia* (Peace and Justice) of the shooting.

In March Magdaleno Correa and Carlos Ayala – two members of the *Partido de la Revolución Democrática* (PRD), Democratic Revolutionary Party – were shot dead in Guerrero state, allegedly by armed civilians linked to the PRI. The killings of several other PRD activists, allegedly by supporters of the PRI, in previous years had not been clarified by the end of the year.

At least 20 people were killed in two separate incidents in June involving the security forces at El Charco, Guerrero state, and El Bosque, Chiapas state. Some were reportedly extrajudicially executed. Official investigations had not clarified the circumstances, manner and cause of their deaths by the end of the year.

The judicial authorities failed to clarify a number of high-profile cases, such as the extrajudicial execution of six people in the Buenos Aires district of Mexico City in September 1997 (see *Amnesty International Report 1998*).

In April the Public Attorney's office appointed a Special Prosecutor to investigate the massacre of 45 indigenous peasants at Acteal in December 1997 (see *Amnesty International Report 1998*). In December, the Attorney General's Office published a report which failed to fully clarify the responsibility of state officials in the massacre. However, as details emerged of the circumstances surrounding the massacre, it became clear that state agents had facilitated the arming of those thought to be responsible and that the state authorities had failed to intervene promptly once the massacre had started.

In May Amnesty International published *Mexico: "Disappearances" – a black hole in the protection of human rights* which documented the growing number of "disappearances" between 1994 and 1997 and called on the government to take measures to prevent a return to systematic state-sponsored "disappearances" such as occurred in the 1970s and 1980s.

Amnesty International expressed concerns about the new visa regulations for human rights observers and the incidents at El Bosque and El Charco. The organization also reiterated its demand for the immediate and unconditional release of Brigadier General Gallardo.

Amnesty International delegates visited Mexico in September and held talks with government officials. The delegates were able to visit Brigadier General Gallardo, but only after a press campaign protesting at the previous denial of access to him. The Guerrero state authorities refused to allow the delegates to visit detainees in Acapulco prison, including Benigno Guzmán, Bertoldo Ramírez Cruz and two alleged ERPI members.

MOLDOVA

Conditions of detention amounted to cruel, inhuman or degrading treatment. At least four political prisoners remained imprisoned in the self-proclaimed Dnestr Moldavian Republic (DMR). Conscientious objectors to military service in the DMR continued to face imprisonment.

In fulfilment of Moldova's commitments on joining the Council of Europe, the European Convention for the Prevention of Torture and Inhuman or Degrading Treatment or Punishment, ratified by Moldova in October 1997, came into force in February. The Moldovan parliament said, however, that Moldova was unable to ensure the Convention's implementation in the self-proclaimed DMR. Experts of the European Committee for the Prevention of Torture and Inhuman or Degrading Treatment or Punishment, which monitors compliance with the Convention, con-

ducted their first monitoring visit to Moldova in October.

According to reports, little progress was made in legal and judicial reform. The parliament failed to adopt new criminal and criminal procedure codes and the norms of the old penal legislation continued to be applied, in some cases in violation of international standards. For example, under the provisions of the existing Criminal Code minor non-violent economic offences were still punishable by imprisonment. According to the Moldovan Helsinki Committee, a local human rights group, almost half of the detainees held in pre-trial detention centres had been charged with minor economic crimes, such as petty theft.

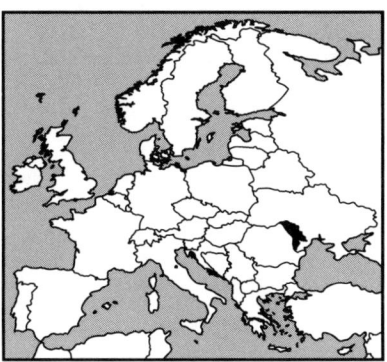

According to reports in April, the power to issue arrest warrants was finally transferred from the procurators to the courts, except in the DMR.

Prison conditions remained inadequate, with serious overcrowding. Conditions were especially harsh in pre-trial detention centres. The incidence of malnutrition and disease, especially tuberculosis, was high in all facilities.

There were reports of the continued use in the DMR of Presidential Decree No. 222 on the Introduction of a State of Emergency to detain political suspects. Under this decree, law enforcement officials can detain suspects for up to 30 days without charge and allegedly without access to a defence lawyer.

Ilie Ilaşcu, Alexandru Leşco, Andrei Ivanţoc and Tudor Petrov-Popa of the so-called "Tiraspol Six", convicted of murder in 1993 by a court in the DMR (see previous *Amnesty International Reports*), remained in prison. Their trial had apparently failed to meet international standards of fairness and the men had allegedly been prosecuted solely because of their membership of the Christian Democratic Popular Front, a Moldovan party that favours reunification with Romania.

Ilie Ilaşcu, Alexandru Leşco, and Andrei Ivanţoc were reported to be seriously ill and not receiving adequate medical care. The DMR authorities repeatedly refused to allow independent medical examination of the prisoners by outside experts, including representatives of the International Committee of the Red Cross. Tatyana Leşco, wife of Alexandru Leşco, reported that when she visited her husband in October 1997 he was so ill that she had to call the emergency services against the resistance of the prison authorities. Alexandru Leşco then had an emergency life-saving operation in hospital.

In March Ilie Ilaşcu was elected to Moldova's parliament for a second consecutive term, again from inside prison. According to his wife, Nina Ilaşcu, his conditions of detention remained very difficult and his health continued to deteriorate.

There were no provisions in the DMR for alternative service and conscientious objectors to military service continued to face imprisonment. According to reports, the DMR authorities repeatedly refused to register the Jehovah's Witnesses as a recognized religious confession, mainly on the grounds that their refusal to serve in the army, based on their religious beliefs, contradicted the law of the DMR for mandatory military service.

Amnesty International continued to call for a review of the case of Ilie Ilaşcu and his co-defendants, and for the four prisoners to receive appropriate medical care. The organization called on the DMR authorities to respect the right to conscientious objection to military service and to introduce an alternative civilian service.

MOROCCO AND WESTERN SAHARA

Twenty-eight political prisoners and prisoners of conscience were released under an amnesty, although more than 30 political prisoners imprisoned after unfair trials continued to be detained. At least five prisoners of conscience remained imprisoned and one remained under house arrest. Tens of possible prisoners of conscience were arrested and sentenced to terms of imprisonment during the year. Reports of torture and ill-treatment continued to be received, particularly of Sahrawi detainees. Hundreds of Sahrawis and some Moroccans who "disappeared" in previous decades remained unaccounted for, although the government confirmed the death of dozens of people who had "disappeared" in previous decades. A former prisoner of conscience forcibly exiled in 1991 remained unable to return to Morocco. At least 70 people reportedly remained under sentence of death at the end of the year. No executions were carried out.

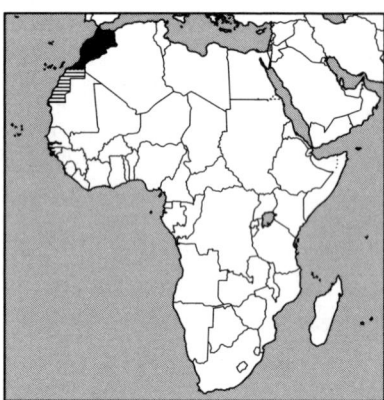

In February King Hassan II appointed Abderrahmane Youssoufi as Prime Minister. In March the Prime Minister formed a centre-left seven-party coalition government dominated by the *Union socialiste des forces populaires*, Socialist Union of Popular Forces, the *Istiqlal* (Independence) party and the *Rassemblement national des indépendants*, National Rally of Independents. He declared that his government's program would include resolving all outstanding human rights files and implementing judicial reforms.

The UN Secretary-General announced in September that the UN Mission in Western Sahara (MINURSO) had identified more than 147,000 applicants to vote in the planned referendum on the status of Western Sahara. The voter identification process was reportedly complete except for members of three disputed tribal groupings, numbering around 58,000 people, and some Sahrawis based elsewhere. The identification process had been repeatedly delayed due to differences between the Moroccan government and the *Frente Popular para la Liberación de Saguia el-Hamra y Rio de Oro*, Popular Front for the Liberation of Saguia el-Hamra and Rio de Oro (known as the Polisario Front). The UN Security Council extended the mandate of MINURSO several times during the year and the referendum was once again postponed and had not taken place by the end of the year.

The government released 28 political prisoners under an amnesty in October. All had been imprisoned after unfair trials, most in the 1970s and 1980s and two of them in the early 1990s. They had been convicted on charges including murder, arms trafficking, plotting against state security, disturbing public order, membership of illegal organizations and distributing leaflets. The majority had been convicted on the basis of confessions extracted under torture. They included four prisoners of conscience belonging to an unauthorized Islamist group – Ahmed Haou, 'Abdelkader Sfiri, Mustapha Marjaoui and Youssef Cherkaoui-Rbati; and two possible prisoners of conscience belonging to the *Union nationale des étudiants marocains*, National Union of Moroccan Students – Noureddine Jarir and Bensalem Aouniti (see previous *Amnesty International Reports*). The *Conseil consultatif des droits de l'homme* (CCDH), Consultative Human Rights Council, a body set up by King Hassan II in 1990, announced in October that it had examined 48 cases of possible political prisoners and that the cases of the 20 others who were not granted amnesty would be further studied.

More than 30 political prisoners and prisoners of conscience imprisoned after unfair trials in previous years continued to be detained. They included prisoner of conscience Mohamed Daddach, a Sahrawi who was arrested in 1979 and sentenced to life imprisonment for attempting to desert the Moroccan security forces into which he had reportedly been forcibly enlisted. At least four prisoners of conscience sentenced to up to five years' imprisonment for "insulting the royal family" remained in prison. They included Abderrahmane Elouadoudi, imprisoned since 1995.

Prisoner of conscience 'Abdessalem Yassine, the spiritual leader of a banned Islamist association, remained under administratively imposed house arrest for the eighth consecutive year.

Dozens of Islamist students were reportedly beaten by security forces and several were arrested during the year in various towns following demonstrations and protests on university campuses. Some were allegedly tortured in police custody. In October scores of people were injured, some seriously, and dozens arrested when police violently broke up a demonstration by hundreds of unemployed graduates. All those arrested were released later.

Following demonstrations in February in support of the independence of Western Sahara in Lemseyed, a town in Western Sahara, 20 Sahrawis were arrested. Eight were sentenced to two years' imprisonment and 12 were sentenced to three months' imprisonment and a fine. They were accused of arson, destruction of public buildings, breach of the peace and taking part in unauthorized demonstrations. They were possible prisoners of conscience. During their trial, the men allegedly showed signs of torture, including rope marks on their legs and cigarette burns. They claimed that torture had been used to make them sign police statements. The defence requested an independent medical examination, but this was rejected.

Torture and ill-treatment also continued to be reportedly used against detainees accused of common law offences. The authorities failed to investigate complaints of torture and ill-treatment of detainees during incommunicado detention in previous years (see previous *Amnesty International Reports*).

There were reports of deaths in suspicious circumstances, including several in places of detention which may have resulted from torture or ill-treatment. Many cases of death in custody and death in suspicious circumstances, both in 1998 and in previous years, had either not been investigated or had been waiting some years for the completion of the investigation process (see previous *Amnesty International Reports*).

Hundreds of Sahrawis and some Moroccans who "disappeared" after arrest in previous decades remained unaccounted

254

for (see previous *Amnesty International Reports*). They included 'Abdelhaq Rouissi, a trade unionist who "disappeared" in 1964 in Casablanca, and Mohamed-Salem Bueh-Barca and Tebker Ment Sidi-Mohamed Ould Khattari who "disappeared" in Laayoune in 1976.

In October the authorities officially acknowledged the deaths of 55 Moroccans and one Lebanese man who had "disappeared" at the hands of the security forces between the 1960s and 1980s and subsequently died in secret detention. However, the deaths of more than 30 of these 55 "disappeared" had already been officially acknowledged in previous years. Among the 55 was Houcine al-Manouzi, a trade unionist who "disappeared" in 1972. The name of 'Abdallah Cherrouk, a student who "disappeared" in 1981, was on a separate list of six people whom the authorities said had most probably died. The name of 'Abdelhaq Rouissi was on another list of 18 people whom the CCDH said had "disappeared" in unknown circumstances. No information was provided concerning the date, place and circumstances of the deaths of the 56 people or their place of burial. The government did not award any compensation to the families of the dead, nor did it hand over the bodies to them.

No steps were known to have been taken to investigate the "disappearance" of some 300 Sahrawis and more than 30 Moroccans who were released in 1984 and 1991 after up to 18 years in secret detention, or the deaths in secret detention of scores of others. The authorities continued to fail to account for the fate of more than 40 Sahrawi "disappeared" who died in secret detention centres in Agdz, Qal'at M'Gouna and Laayoune between 1975 and 1991. Neither those released in 1984 and 1991 nor the families of those who died in secret detention received any compensation.

Abraham Serfaty, a former prisoner of conscience who was forcibly expelled to France after his release in 1991 on the grounds that he was not Moroccan, remained unable to return to Morocco. In July the Supreme Court declared itself unable to rule on his nationality (see previous *Amnesty International Reports*).

Amnesty International welcomed the release of the 28 political prisoners and drew attention to the many cases on which concrete steps had been taken. It was concerned, however, that the relatively small number of "disappearances" which the government appeared to be addressing did not include any of the hundreds of Sahrawi "disappeared" who remained unaccounted for or any of the scores who died in secret detention. Amnesty International also highlighted the lack of investigations into past human rights abuses as well as the absence of measures taken to bring to justice those responsible.

An Amnesty International delegation visited Morocco in June and submitted a memorandum to the government welcoming the positive steps taken and stressing the need to address the outstanding human rights concerns in the country and to implement reforms to the administration of justice. In addition to senior government officials, including Prime Minister Youssoufi, the delegates met non-governmental organizations, former victims and families of victims, students and business community representatives.

MOZAMBIQUE

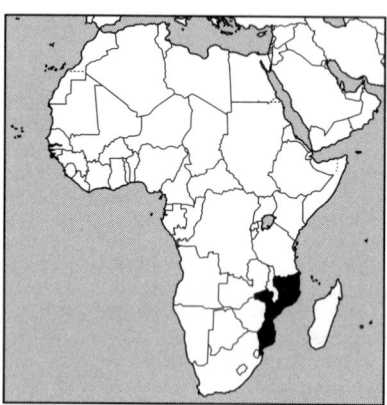

Scores of people were reportedly beaten by police. Investigations into allegations of torture or ill-treatment were slow or non-existent. Several people were shot and killed in circumstances that suggested excessive use of force or extrajudicial executions by the police.

Local elections were held in 33 municipalities in June, but opposition parties complained about the way they had been organized and refused to participate. Only 15 per cent of the electorate voted.

President Joaquim Chissano's party, the *Frente para a Libertaçao de Moçambique* (FRELIMO), Mozambique Liberation Front, won majorities in each municipal assembly.

Despite economic growth, Mozambique remained one of the poorest countries in the world. High unemployment and the availability of weapons contributed to high crime rates.

Under the terms of the project to restructure and retrain police agreed in 1997 (see *Amnesty International Report 1998*), members of the Spanish Civil Guard trained 66 police instructors who subsequently trained 1,210 selected trainees, including over 100 women. The syllabus included courses on police ethics and human rights. Originally, the whole police force, estimated at 18,766 officers, was to be retrained over a seven-year period. However, funding sufficient for only two years was available.

Progress was made in drafting legislation, including revisions of the penal and criminal procedure codes and new police statutes. A draft amendment to the Constitution, which contained substantially strengthened provision for human rights protection, was published in September. It was put forward for public debate and comment with a view to submitting the amendment to the National Assembly in 1999.

Other reforms included the appointment of magistrates to review and confirm detentions within 48 hours of arrest.

Robert McBride, a senior South African Foreign Ministry official and a prominent opponent of the previous apartheid government, was arrested in Mozambique in March and subsequently charged with espionage and gun-running. Six Mozambicans, including three military personnel, were arrested on related charges. All seven were held in excess of the 90-day period stipulated by law before being released on bail in September. Robert McBride said that he had been engaged in an investigation of arms trafficking between Mozambique and South Africa. By the end of 1998 none of the seven had been brought to trial.

The Special Rapporteur on prisons and conditions of detention of the African Commission on Human and Peoples' Rights, who visited Mozambique in December 1997, presented his report to the African Commission in April. It expressed concern about severe overcrowding and made recommendations for the improvement of prison conditions. On 10 December, the 50th anniversary of the Universal Declaration of Human Rights, the government announced that it was conducting an inquiry into prison conditions in order to ensure action to improve them. The government also said that from the year 2000, human rights would be part of the curriculum in all primary schools.

Scores of people were reportedly beaten by police. Reports of severe beatings or other forms of torture in police stations were not promptly and thoroughly investigated. In July, in the Hulene suburb of Maputo, Argentina Zacarias Valói was said to have been badly beaten by police officers searching for her stepson, who had been involved in a fight with another child and had fled when the police arrived. In September, also in Hulene, Chico Camabaco was reportedly beaten by two police officers as he tried to escape arrest. One of the officers then shot at his brother, Jaime Ernesto Camabaco, who was trying to stop the beating, and hit him in the foot. Chico Camabaco was taken to the Hulene police station. Five days later a police officer took him and another detainee to an isolated place outside the city and interrogated them about a case of arms trafficking. The two men were reportedly beaten with whips and truncheons studded with spikes. Chico Camabaco was released but later rearrested and remained in detention at the end of the year. No investigation was known to have been initiated into either incident.

Peter Mashaba, a Swazi businessman, and Edward Plaatjies, a South African, were brought before a judge in January. Despite allegations that they had been tortured at the time of their arrest in December 1997, the judge reportedly failed to order an investigation into the allegations. They were unconditionally released two weeks later and left the country.

In April, 12 people who had been arrested and allegedly tortured in August 1997 were tried in Pemba, Cabo Delgado Province, and sentenced to prison terms of between eight and 24 years. The prisoners claimed that they had been tortured in order to extract confessions and to implicate their co-defendants; several stated that they had been forced to stand and denied

256

food and water for prolonged periods. No official inquiry into the allegations was was known to have been initiated.

Several people were killed or injured by police using what appeared to be excessive force. Some may have been extrajudicially executed. In January police opened fire on 250 striking workers at a Maputo security firm. One striker was killed and four others were seriously injured. The results of an inquiry into the shootings had not been made public by the end of the year.

In January in Chonguene, Gaza Province, a police officer, who was allegedly drunk at the time, accosted 14-year-old Avelino Macuacua, accused him of setting off a firework and shot him. The bullet passed through Avelino Macuacua's stomach and killed a young girl. A second officer arrived and reportedly beat Avelino Macuacua, who was writhing on the ground in pain. According to reports, an investigation was initiated, but neither police officer was arrested.

Oscar Marrengula was shot dead by police from the 7th Police Station in Matola, Maputo Province, in May. He had been arrested on suspicion of armed robbery and the police claimed he was shot while trying to escape. Criminal investigation police said that they had taken Oscar Marrengula from the police station on the night of his arrest so that he could assist them to gather evidence. They reportedly did not use handcuffs or any other precaution against escape. The *Liga Moçambicana dos Direitos Humanos*, Mozambique Human Rights League, which followed the case, noted long delays in submitting the reports on the incident to the judicial authorities. The investigation into the killing had not concluded by the end of the year.

Amnesty International published a report, *Mozambique: Human rights and the police*, in April.

In June, an Amnesty International delegation, including a high-ranking Dutch police officer, visited Mozambique, principally to inquire into the project for restructuring and retraining the police. Amnesty International welcomed efforts to train police in the protection of human rights. It also expressed concern about the failure to conduct prompt and thorough investigations into reports of human rights violations.

MYANMAR

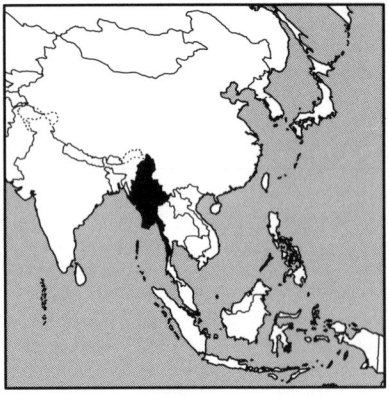

More than 1,200 political prisoners arrested in previous years, including 89 prisoners of conscience and hundreds of possible prisoners of conscience, remained in prison throughout the year. Hundreds of people were arrested for political reasons. Political prisoners were tortured and ill-treated, and held in conditions that amounted to cruel, inhuman or degrading treatment. Members of ethnic minorities continued to suffer human rights violations, including extrajudicial executions, torture, ill-treatment during forced portering, and other forms of forced labour and forcible relocations. Six political prisoners were sentenced to death. No executions were known to have taken place.

The State Peace and Development Council (SPDC), chaired by General Than Shwe, continued to rule by decree in the absence of a constitution. Martial law decrees severely restricting the rights to freedom of expression and assembly remained in force. Because of strict censorship and restrictions on freedom of expression, and lack of access to the country by independent human rights monitors and most journalists, information about human rights violations was limited.

The National Convention, which was convened by the State Law and Order Restoration Council (SLORC, the previous name of the military government) in 1993 to agree principles for a new constitution and was adjourned in March 1996, did not meet during the year. Throughout the year the National League for Democracy (NLD), the legal opposition party led by Daw Aung San Suu Kyi, appealed to the SPDC to enter into dialogue. In August the SPDC held a meeting with senior NLD leaders which Daw Aung San Suu Kyi did not attend.

In June the NLD resolved to demand that the SPDC convene in 60 days the parliament elected in May 1990 when the NLD won almost 82 per cent of the seats. In August the NLD declared that it would convene a parliament itself if the SPDC did not do so. In a pre-emptive move to block parliament from meeting, the SPDC arrested hundreds of NLD members between May and September, including NLD members-of-parliament-elect. The SPDC stated that more than 300 of them had subsequently been released; the NLD put the figure at less than 100. In September the NLD appointed a 10-member committee, which it said represented elected NLD members of parliament.

In July the SPDC refused to allow Daw Aung San Suu Kyi to visit NLD members outside Yangon, the capital. She remained in her car surrounded by security forces for several days before being forced to return home. On at least three other occasions she was prevented from travelling outside of Yangon.

The 10th anniversary of the August massive pro-democracy uprising and the subsequent military coup of September 1988 passed without major unrest. However, 18 foreign nationals who entered the country on tourist visas and handed out leaflets in Yangon expressing solidarity with the Burmese people on the 10th anniversary date, were arrested and detained for five days. They were then sentenced after a summary trial to five years' imprisonment with hard labour. Their sentences were suspended and they were all immediately deported.

There was no progress in cease-fire talks between the SPDC and the armed opposition groups the Karen National Union (KNU) and the Karenni National Progressive Party (KNPP). Skirmishes between government forces and the KNU, the KNPP and the Shan State Army (formerly the Shan United Revolutionary Army) continued throughout the year.

Some 21,800 Rohingyas (Burmese Muslims from the Rakhine State) remained in two refugee camps in Bangladesh. In February the UN High Commissioner for Refugees (UNHCR) and the Bangladesh government agreed a repatriation plan, despite continuing human rights violations in the Rakhine State. Repatriations under UNHCR supervision resumed in November after the SPDC agreed to take back 7,000 refugees. For the first time the Thai authorities allowed the UNHCR a permanent presence on the Thailand-Myanmar border to monitor the safety of over 100,000 Burmese refugees in camps.

In January the UN Special Rapporteur on Myanmar submitted his report to the UN Commission on Human Rights. In April the Commission adopted by consensus an extremely strong resolution, which extended the mandate of the UN Special Rapporteur for a further year. The resolution expressed its deep concern "at the absence of due process of law, including arbitrary arrest... inhuman treatment of prisoners... [and] violations of the rights of persons belonging to minorities..." A resolution was also adopted by consensus at the UN General Assembly in December. The UN Special Rapporteur was still refused access to Myanmar, but in January and October the Special Representative of the UN Secretary-General visited Myanmar. In August the SPDC refused entry to a Special Envoy of the UN Secretary-General in the midst of the ongoing confrontation between the NLD and SPDC. In July and October the UN High Commissioner for Human Rights called on the SPDC to respect human rights. The USA renewed sanctions banning new US investment in Myanmar, and in October the European Union (EU) extended its sanctions to include transit and tourist visas for members of Myanmar's military. The EU continued to block Myanmar from permanently joining the Asia Europe Meeting (ASEM), although Myanmar had been admitted as a member of the Association of South-East Asian Nations (ASEAN) in 1997.

In August the International Labour Organisation's (ILO's) Commission of Enquiry published a comprehensive report on Myanmar's failure to implement the provisions of ILO Convention No. 29 on forced labour, and stated that the SPDC was guilty of "an international crime that is also, if committed in a widespread or systematic manner, a crime against humanity".

More than 1,200 political prisoners arrested in previous years, including 89 prisoners of conscience and hundreds of

258

possible prisoners of conscience, remained in detention. They included prisoners of conscience Dr Aung Khin Sint, U Win Htein, U Aye Win, U Win Tin, Dr Than Aung, U Myo Khin and Cho Aung Than (see *Amnesty International Reports 1997* and *1998*). Ten long-term political prisoners were known to have been released during the year; it was not clear if others had also been released.

Hundreds of people were arrested for political reasons. Among them was 81-year-old prisoner of conscience U Ohn Myint, an unofficial NLD adviser who was arrested in February for helping to write and distribute a history of the student movement in Myanmar. He was sentenced in April to seven years' imprisonment. Prisoner of conscience U Myo Htun, a businessman who helped to write the history, was sentenced to 10 years' imprisonment in March. In April it became known that he had been severely beaten and was in poor health in Insein Prison. In September, 81-year-old prisoner of conscience Dr U Saw Mra Aung, an ethnic Arakan and NLD-appointed head of the NLD's People's Parliament, was arrested and held without charge or trial.

In March the SPDC named 40 people allegedly involved in plans to detonate bombs and assassinate government officials. Thirty-nine of them were arrested. They were sentenced in April, six of them to death, the first time for several years that the death penalty was known to have been imposed for political offences. In October the SPDC announced the arrest of 54 people for involvement in passing out leaflets supporting the NLD and the convening of parliament.

NLD sources claimed that more than 1,000 NLD members, including almost 200 members-of-parliament-elect, were arrested between May and September. Some of them, including 84-year-old Thakin Khin Nyunt, were released in September and October, but most remained in detention without trial. Student opposition sources said that more than 300 students were arrested between June and September, when students staged small demonstrations to protest against the poor quality of education and the human rights situation.

Political prisoners were tortured and ill-treated, and held in conditions that amounted to cruel, inhuman or degrading treatment. Prisoners suffered from beatings and prolonged shackling, lack of proper medical care and an inadequate diet. Extremely harsh conditions in prison labour camps continued to be reported.

NLD leader and writer U Thein Tin died in custody in February. Opposition sources said that he had been tortured; the SPDC reported that he had died of cancer. In May opposition sources said that a political prisoner, Aung Kyaw Moe, had been beaten to death during a hunger strike in Tharawaddy Prison, where conditions remained particularly harsh. In August NLD member-of-parliament-elect U Saw Win also died of unknown causes in Tharawaddy Prison. According to official sources, in October NLD member U Aung Min died in hospital of lymph cancer after he was sent there from detention by the authorities.

The military continued to commit widespread human rights violations against ethnic minorities, including extra-judicial executions, torture, ill-treatment during forced labour and portering, and forcible relocations. Nang Pang, for example, a Shan woman from Murngpan township, died in January: she had been reportedly raped and kicked in the chest by SPDC soldiers in October 1997.

Forcible relocations, apparently carried out solely because of ethnic origin or perceived political beliefs, continued, particularly in the Shan State. In May and June four massacres of 103 Shan civilians by SPDC troops were reported in the central Shan State. Villagers were said to have been forcibly relocated and were searching for food outside their relocation areas when they were killed by troops thought to be searching for members of Shan armed opposition groups. Thousands of Karen villagers were reported to have been forcibly relocated during June and July in Pa'an District, the Kayin (Karen) State. Mon, Karen, Shan and Karenni people continued to be subjected to forced portering and other forms of forced labour amounting to cruel, inhuman or degrading treatment. They were also detained solely on grounds of their ethnicity.

The Democratic Kayin Buddhist Organization (DKBO), a Karen armed opposition group allied with the SPDC, continued to attack refugees and Thai nationals in Thailand. In March the DKBO attacked three Karen refugee camps, killing five refugees and leaving thousands of them homeless.

Later that month the KNU, which was fighting against the SPDC and the DKBO, launched an attack against a cinema in DKBO-controlled territory in the Kayin State, killing many Karen civilians.

Throughout the year Amnesty International continued to call for the release of prisoners of conscience and for an end to extrajudicial executions, torture and ill-treatment. In April Amnesty International published a report, *Myanmar: Atrocities in the Shan State*, detailing extrajudicial executions and forcible relocation and forced labour of the Shan ethnic minority. In August the organization launched a campaign highlighting the human rights situation in the 10 years since the crackdown on the pro-democracy movement.

NEPAL

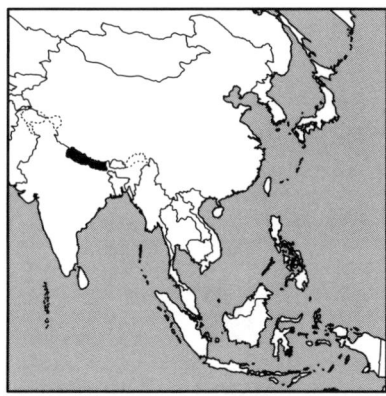

Approximately 1,800 people were arrested for political reasons, including scores of possible prisoners of conscience. Torture by police was widespread; at least one person reportedly died as a result. Five people were reported to have "disappeared". More than 200 people, including many civilians, were killed by police in disputed circumstances. An armed opposition group was responsible for human rights abuses, including deliberate killings of civilians.

Three different coalition governments held power during the year. Prime Minister Surya Bahadur Thapa, of the *Rastriya Prajatrantra Party*, National Democratic Party, resigned in April after losing the support of the Nepali Congress Party (NCP) and Nepal Sadbhavana Party (NSP). NCP

leader Girija Prasad Koirala was appointed Prime Minister in April. In August the government reached an agreement with nine leftist parties covering a number of issues such as law and order, the withdrawal of Indian troops from Kalapani in the Far-West Region, and review of the 1950 India-Nepal Friendship Treaty. On the strength of the agreement, the Prime Minister formed a new coalition with the support of the Communist Party of Nepal-Marxist Leninist (CPN-ML), a breakaway faction of the CPN-United Marxist Leninist (CPN-UML). In mid-December the CPN-ML pulled out of the government over failure in the implementation of the commitments in the August agreement. A new coalition between the NCP, CPN-UML and NSP was formed and parliamentary elections were scheduled for May 1999.

Armed conflict between the armed opposition group, Communist Party of Nepal (CPN) (Maoist), and the security forces, which began following the declaration of a "people's war" in 1996, continued to escalate and spread to at least 20 districts (see previous *Amnesty International Reports*). On 26 May the government launched an "intensified security mobilization" in the affected districts, involving the transfer of police units from the capital, Kathmandu. In July the Prime Minister offered a general amnesty to CPN (Maoist) members who agreed to give up arms. More than 1,400 of them reportedly surrendered to the police.

The government failed to institute any independent inquiries into serious human rights violations reported in the context of the "people's war". Despite repeated promises by Prime Minister Koirala to establish the National Human Rights Commission, enacted in January 1997, no move had been made to appoint the members by the end of the year. Twelve people initiated claims under the Torture Compensation Act 1996. Six people were reported to have withdrawn their claims because of intimidation or fear for their safety.

In March Nepal acceded to the Second Optional Protocol to the International Covenant on Civil and Political Rights, aiming at the abolition of the death penalty.

The International Committee of the Red Cross was invited to visit political detainees on a regular basis.

Approximately 1,800 people were arrested on suspicion of being members or sympathizers of the CPN (Maoist); scores were possible prisoners of conscience. At the end of the year, an estimated 400 remained in detention without trial. Many were arrested without warrant and kept in police custody without being brought before a judicial authority within 24 hours, in contravention of the Constitution. Scores of prisoners were also held for more than 25 days without being formally charged as required under the law. Many were not given access to lawyers or relatives.

Torture in police custody, particularly of political detainees, was widespread. A group of teachers arrested in Kailali District in the Far-West Region in August on suspicion of being involved in an attack by the CPN (Maoist) were tortured, including by *falanga* (beating on the soles of the feet) and beating on the buttocks and other parts of the body with a bamboo stick. Two young women from Bardiya District, arrested in August on suspicion of being involved in the murder of a local NCP member, were subjected to *falanga* and *belana* (rolling a weighted bamboo cane over the prisoner's thighs) while under interrogation by police in Banke District.

At least one person, Ganesh Rai, was reported to have died as a result of torture in Hanuman Dhoka police station in Kathmandu; he reportedly died on 14 October. A post-mortem recorded multiple contusions on his body.

Five people were reported to have "disappeared" after arrest. Among them were Mohan Prasad Oli, who "disappeared" after arrest in June by police at his home in Mahatepuri Village in Banke District.

More than 200 people, including many civilians, were killed during the "intensified security mobilization" operation by police. Among them were armed members of the CPN (Maoist) killed in what the authorities called "encounters" with the police; however, reports suggested that many of those killed were extrajudicially executed after being taken prisoner. In other instances, civilians suspected of being sympathizers of the CPN (Maoist) were alleged to have been extrajudicially executed. In one such incident in June in Sakla, Jajarkot District, nine villagers – two women and seven men – were killed by police during a festival and their bodies burned on the spot.

Members of the CPN (Maoist) were responsible for human rights abuses. Activ-

ists of mainstream political parties were reported to have been kidnapped, including one who was severely beaten as an apparent punishment for participating in local elections. At least 29 civilians were deliberately and arbitrarily killed. Among them was Govinda Poudel, an NCP member, who was hacked to death at Rambhapur, Bardiya District, on 9 August.

Amnesty International urged the government to establish independent investigations into all reports of human rights violations, including torture, alleged extrajudicial executions, and "disappearances", to make the findings public, and to bring to justice those responsible for violations.

An Amnesty International delegation visited the country in November to investigate reports of an escalation in human rights violations in the context of the "intensified security mobilization" operation, and raised its findings and concerns with government officials. The organization also expressed concern to representatives of the CPN (Maoist) about human rights abuses committed by the group.

NIGER

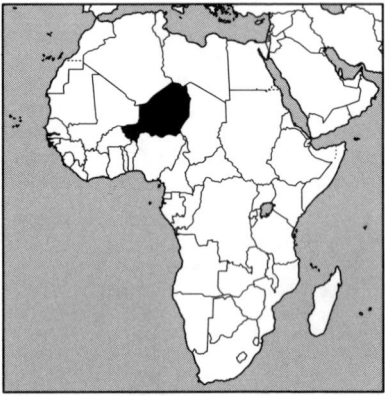

Dozens of opposition party supporters were detained; some were prisoners of conscience. Several journalists and a publisher were briefly detained. All appeared to be prisoners of conscience; some were ill-treated. Several people were killed by the security forces in circumstances suggesting they had been extrajudicially executed. An armed opposition group was responsible for deliberate and arbitrary killings.

In July an agreement between the government of President Ibrahim Baré Maïnassara and the opposition ended the political deadlock stemming from the 1996 military coup that overthrew the government of elected President Mahamane Ousmane. The opposition parties agreed to participate in local elections which were postponed until 1999.

Niger acceded to the UN Convention against Torture and Other Cruel, Inhuman or Degrading Treatment or Punishment in October.

In January, three political opponents – including former Prime Minister Hama Amadou, Secretary General of the *Mouvement national pour la société de développement*, National Movement for the Society of Development – were detained for several days, accused of plotting to assassinate President Baré Maïnassara. Hama Amadou was eventually charged with "creating a militia" but he was not rearrested.

In April several local officials belonging to opposition parties were arrested following demonstrations in Maradi and Zinder. The demonstrations were among several organized by the opposition *Front pour la restauration et la défense de la démocratie* (FRDD), Front for the Restoration and Defence of Democracy, some of which ended in violence. The demonstrations in Maradi and Zinder had been organized to prevent a meeting of the ruling *Rassemblement pour la démocratie et le progrès*, Rally for Democracy and Progress. Both demonstrators and police were injured during clashes. Later the same month the police banned demonstrations and arrested dozens of people in Niamey; some were prisoners of conscience. All were provisionally released in June.

Several journalists and a publisher were briefly detained; all appeared to be prisoners of conscience. Some were ill-treated. In April unidentified gunmen raided the offices of the most prominent pro-opposition publishing house and tried to set them on fire. The publishing house was owned by Maman Abou, the director of the weekly newspaper *Le Républicain*. In May Maman Abou was arrested, accused of attempted arson and insurance fraud. He was believed to have been arrested solely for his opposition to the military government and for his human rights activities. He was a prisoner of conscience. He was provisionally released after 18 days.

In April Saadou Assane, a journalist on *Le Républicain* was attacked by members of the security forces while he was covering an opposition demonstration in Maradi. In May Moussa Tchangari, publishing director of the independent weekly newspaper *L'Alternative*, was arrested at the premises of the independent radio station, *Radio Anfani*. He had read out on air a protest against censorship and threats against journalists. Moussa Tchangari was beaten by members of the security forces during his arrest. Elhadj Oumarou Oubandawaki, an FRDD member, who was with him at the time of his arrest, was also detained and beaten. Both men were released without charge some days later. The radio station was subsequently closed down.

In September Bory Seyni, the publisher of the newspaper *Le Démocrate*, was whipped by the Minister of the Interior himself, Souley Abdoulaye. Bory Seyni's shirt was torn and his spectacles were broken during the whipping. This attack followed the publication of an article linking the Minister to alleged corruption.

Several people were killed by the security forces in circumstances suggesting they may have been extrajudicially executed. Members of the Presidential Guard killed four unarmed people, none of whom appeared to pose any threat, in front of their barracks. Among the victims were Atta Harouna, a student, who was shot in January as he approached the gate; and Lompo Tchiangnagou and Lompo Oumbouni who were shot dead in February as they drove past the barracks. None of these apparent extrajudicial executions was investigated.

In July an armed Toubou opposition group, the *Front démocratique révolutionnaire*, Democratic Revolutionary Front, was reportedly responsible for killing 15 villagers in the area of N'Guigmi.

NIGERIA

More than 100 prisoners of conscience and possible prisoners of conscience were released, although at least 44 others remained imprisoned throughout the year. Early in the year, human rights activists

262

and journalists were arrested and beaten. Torture and ill-treatment of prisoners continued to be reported and at least two political prisoners died in prison in unexplained circumstances. At least 29 prisoners were sentenced to death and at least six were executed. Six death sentences imposed for political offences were commuted.

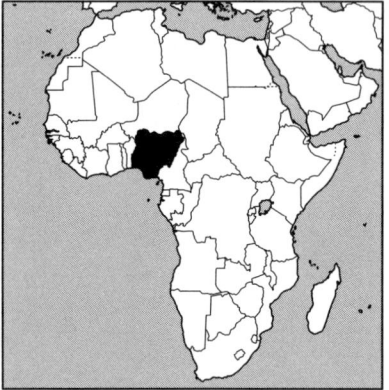

In April all five government-sponsored political parties – the only parties allowed to operate at that time – agreed to support General Sani Abacha, head of the military government, as presidential candidate. Political protests broke out and were suppressed: pro-democracy activists and human rights defenders were arrested and ill-treated, and 10 people were reportedly shot dead by police and others injured. In the first half of the year, private as well as public meetings involving human rights or democracy groups were forcibly broken up by the security police.

General Abacha died unexpectedly on 8 June and was replaced by General Abdulsalami Abubakar as head of the military government. Scores of prisoners of conscience and other political prisoners were subsequently released and six death sentences imposed for political offences were commuted.

General Abubakar promised that the military would step down in May 1999 under a new "transition to civil rule", but rejected calls by some pro-democracy groups for a sovereign national conference to agree a new constitution or for a government of national unity to supervise the transition. In August the government annulled earlier elections to local governments and to state and national legislatures conducted under the previous government's "transition to civil rule". It revoked decrees which had placed the Nigeria Labour Congress and the two main oil workers' unions under direct government control and had dissolved three university staff unions. However, it left in force decrees providing for arbitrary detention and the imprisonment of prisoners of conscience. In December local government elections were contested by nine new political parties.

There was increased hostage-taking of oil workers and attacks on oil installations by youths from Niger delta communities seeking a share of oil revenues, development assistance or compensation for environmental damage by oil companies. In May, two youths were shot dead in disputed circumstances when the military ended the occupation of an offshore oil platform by members of the Ilaje community. In December soldiers reportedly shot dead at least six demonstrators after a call by Ijaw groups for the military and the oil companies to leave Ijaw territories.

On 7 July prisoner of conscience Moshood Abiola, the reported winner of the 1993 presidential elections which were annulled by the military (see previous *Amnesty International Reports*), died in detention. Suspicions about the cause of his death led to unrest in the southwest of the country during which a number of people were killed.

In April the UN Commission on Human Rights extended the mandate of the Special Rapporteur on Nigeria, who was appointed in 1997, for a further year. In his report to the Commission, the Special Rapporteur highlighted the absence of the rule of law in Nigeria. In his September report to the UN General Assembly, he welcomed the releases of political prisoners and the commitments made by the new government but noted that the rule of law and constitutional rights had not been restored. In September the authorities invited him to visit Nigeria; he had previously been denied access to the country. He visited Nigeria in November and repeated his call for the revocation of decrees that provide for administrative detention and unfair trials by special courts. In March the International Labour Organisation established a commission of inquiry into persistent violations of trade union rights in Nigeria, including the detention of trade unionists, and in August sent a delegation to Nigeria. It had previously been denied access.

The government of General Abubakar and the courts ordered the release of more than 100 prisoners of conscience and possible prisoners of conscience. On 15 June the government announced the first nine releases. Among them were people who had been detained without charge or trial, including oil workers' leaders Frank Ovie Kokori and Milton G. Dabibi, held since 1994 and 1996 respectively, and lawyer and pro-democracy leader Chief Olabiyi Durojaiye, detained since 1996. Also released were retired General Olusegun Obasanjo, Head of State from 1976 to 1979; human rights and pro-democracy activist Dr Beko Ransome-Kuti; and a journalist, Christiana Anyanwu. They had been convicted of treason after secret and grossly unfair military trials in 1995. At least five political detainees were released in the following days, including human rights lawyer Ebun-Olu Adegboruwa, who had been detained without charge or trial since 1997.

On 25 June the government announced the release of 17 more political prisoners. Ten had been charged with treason in March 1997, including pro-democracy and human rights leaders Dr Frederick Fasehun and former government minister Olu Falae. Six had been detained without charge or trial following pro-democracy protests on 1 May in Ibadan, including lawyers and pro-democracy leaders Olisa Agbakoba (see below) and Ayo Opadokun, and human rights and pro-democracy activist Olusegun Maiyegun.

Also on 25 June the High Court discharged 33 of those arrested following pro-democracy protests in Ibadan and who were charged with riot and arson. They included former senator Alhaji Lam Adesina, trade union leader Alhaji Lateef Akinsola and newspaper editor Femi Adeoti, who had also been charged with subversion.

On 20 July the government announced that it had pardoned 10 civilians convicted of involvement in an alleged coup plot in 1995 and tried in secret by Special Military Tribunal. Among those released were Shehu Sani, Vice-Chairman of the Campaign for Democracy; and newspaper editors Kunle Ajibade, George Mbah and Ben Charles Obi. General Obasanjo, Dr Beko

Ransome-Kuti and Christiana Anyanwu had been released earlier (see above).

In September, 20 Ogoni prisoners who had been detained without trial, most of them since 1994, were released (see previous *Amnesty International Reports*). They had been ostensibly awaiting trial on the same murder charges that were brought against Ken Saro-Wiwa, head of the Movement for the Survival of the Ogoni People (MOSOP), and the eight other Ogoni men executed with him in November 1995 after unfair and politically motivated trials. Previous attempts to have the 20 prisoners released on bail or brought promptly to trial had been obstructed by government appeals against court rulings for their release on bail and by their lack of access to lawyers. For most of their detention, the 20 prisoners were detained incommunicado, denied access to their families and, for the first two years, their lawyers. They suffered serious illnesses as a result of insanitary prison conditions and lack of food and medical treatment.

In December Ibrahim Al-Zakzaky and three other leading members of the Muslim Brotherhood were released by the High Court in Kaduna, northern Nigeria, after charges of inciting public disaffection and sedition were withdrawn. They had been imprisoned since 1996.

In September General Abubakar confirmed that charges against political exiles, including writer and Nobel Prize laureate Wole Soyinka, had been withdrawn. Several of them subsequently returned to Nigeria.

At least 44 prisoners of conscience and possible prisoners of conscience remained held at the end of the year after being convicted of treason in unfair and secret trials by Special Military Tribunal. Following a coup attempt in April 1990 and a series of secret trials which resulted in the execution of 69 armed forces officers, 11 soldiers remained imprisoned despite pardons and court orders for their release. In July, one officer, David Mukoro, was reported to have died in detention from tuberculosis and medical neglect. In October a civilian unfairly convicted in the case, Turner Ochuko Ogburo, was released. A High Court order for his release in 1994 had previously been ignored.

Eighteen serving and retired armed forces officers were still held in connection with a series of treason trials in 1995 in which more than 40 defendants were convicted of involvement in an alleged coup attempt. Of the prisoners still held, Navy Commander L.M.O. Fabiyi, a lawyer, was sentenced to 15 years' imprisonment reportedly for passing a defendant's defence submission to others. Another lawyer, Colonel Roland N. Emokpae, sentenced to 25 years' imprisonment, was reported in June to be seriously ill with liver problems and to have been denied appropriate medical treatment in prison. There was no inquiry into reports of torture of some of the defendants, including Lieutenant-Colonel M.A. Igwe, who was sentenced to 25 years' imprisonment reportedly after he refused to implicate others.

In April a Special Military Tribunal convicted 10 armed forces officers, including former Deputy Head of State General Oladipo Diya, and six civilians of treason or related offences in connection with an alleged coup plot in December 1997. Their trials were grossly unfair, conducted in secret by a tribunal which denied them practically all rights of defence. In July the government announced the commutation of the death sentences imposed on General Diya and five others, including Adebola Adebanjo, an engineer. Long prison sentences passed on other detainees were reduced and one officer had his sentence reduced to dismissal from the army. In December, one of the six officers whose death sentences had been commuted, Lieutenant-Colonel Olu Akiode, died in unexplained circumstances in Makurdi prison. No investigation was conducted into the causes of his death. Eight officers and six civilians remained in prison at the end of the year.

Throughout the first half of the year human rights activists and journalists were arrested and beaten. In March human rights lawyer Femi Falana was held for six days. He was among a group of people detained without charge for attending a seminar in Ilorin, Kwara State. Also in March human rights lawyer Olisa Agbakoba (see above) was beaten and gunbutted in the face by police officers when he attempted to negotiate with them during a pro-democracy march in Lagos, the capital. He was detained for two days and charged with public order offences, with about 30 other people, for organizing the march.

Torture or ill-treatment of detainees by soldiers and police at the time of arrest and in order to induce them to make incriminating statements was routine. In January Batom Mitee, brother of Ledum Mitee, Acting President of MOSOP, and Tombari Gioro were among dozens of MOSOP supporters arrested by armed troops in Bori, the main town in Ogoniland, to stop them celebrating "Ogoni Day". They were reported to have been beaten with rifle butts and electric cables, and subsequently to have been denied food and medical attention for their injuries. They and other Ogoni detainees were detained without charge or trial until May. On several occasions, soldiers assaulted journalists carrying out their professional duties, including while they were reporting street protests.

At least 29 prisoners were sentenced to death for political and criminal offences and at least six people were executed. In February, six men convicted of armed robbery were executed by a firing squad in front of hundreds of people at Kirikiri prison, Lagos.

Hundreds of prisoners remained under sentence of death, some of them many years after their conviction. Most had been sentenced to death by Robbery and Firearms Tribunals, special courts which allow no right of appeal.

Amnesty International appealed for the release of prisoners of conscience, for the prompt and fair trial of all political prisoners, and for an end to torture and the death penalty. At the time of a visit to Nigeria by the Pope in March, Amnesty International protested at the arrests and beatings of human rights activists and journalists. In July it called for a full inquiry into the death of Moshood Abiola and into the cases of other prisoners of conscience who had died in detention in unexplained circumstances (see *Amnesty International Report 1998*).

Amnesty International welcomed the releases of prisoners of conscience and the commutation of six death sentences. It continued to appeal for the release of prisoners of conscience, the review of the conviction of unfairly tried political prisoners, and the repeal of military decrees which allow the imprisonment of prisoners of conscience and the suppression of the rule of law.

OMAN

Five possible prisoners of conscience were released after approximately eight months in detention, during which they were allegedly tortured or ill-treated. At least six people were executed and another was reportedly sentenced to death.

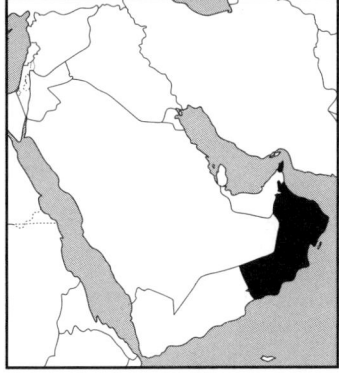

Five possible prisoners of conscience were released in April or May. They had been arrested in September 1997 as suspected Shi'a activists (see *Amnesty International Report 1998*). No information was available about the conditions of their release. However, they were reportedly placed under surveillance and their passports were confiscated. They had allegedly been tortured or ill-treated, including by beatings and threats of sexual assault.

At least six people, all foreign nationals, were executed for murder reportedly after unfair trials. They included four Pakistan nationals who were executed two days after they were sentenced to death in January and were reportedly denied any appeal. One person, an Indian national, was reportedly sentenced to death for murder.

Amnesty International expressed concern about the executions and appealed for commutation of outstanding death sentences. The Ambassador of Oman in London, United Kingdom, wrote to Amnesty International stating that, "Omani justice guarantees fair trial... as to the organization's [opposition to] the death penalty, [this] concerns Amnesty International alone and is not obligatory for others." He did not provide further details on the cases raised or on the trials of those executed.

PAKISTAN

Dozens of political prisoners, including prisoners of conscience, were detained, some without charge or trial. Torture and ill-treatment continued to be widespread, leading to at least 50 deaths in custody. Floggings continued to be carried out. At least 120 possible extrajudicial executions were reported. At least 428 people were sentenced to death and at least four were executed. State officials colluded in abuses by private individuals and religious groups. Armed opposition groups were responsible for deliberate and arbitrary killings of civilians.

The government of Prime Minister Nawaz Sharif declared a national emergency and suspended fundamental rights after conducting nuclear tests in May. In July the Supreme Court restored fundamental rights, declaring their suspension unjustified.

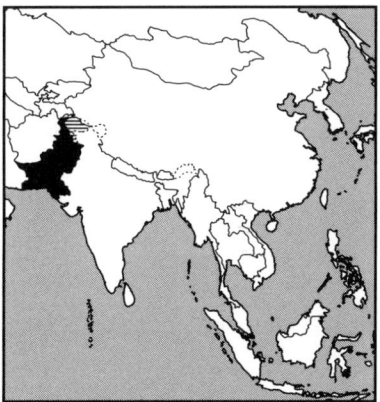

Law and order problems persisted as sectarian violence between the majority Sunni and the minority Shi'a communities, mainly in Punjab province, and fighting between different ethnic and religious groups in Karachi, led to more than 600 deaths. The government continued to resort to mass arbitrary arrests and detention, usually of short duration.

The Supreme Court ruled in May that 12 sections of the 1997 Anti-Terrorism Act were unconstitutional and therefore void. It directed the federal government to amend them "suitably", but held that cases concluded by special courts set up under the Act should not be reopened and

266

pending cases should be concluded. In October an ordinance was promulgated to amend the Act in accordance with Supreme Court directions.

The 15th constitutional amendment bill, passed by the National Assembly in September, was pending in the Senate at the end of the year. The amendment would make Islamic law supreme, authorizing the executive to issue directives "to prescribe what is good and to forbid what is wrong" irrespective of constitutional provisions or judicial precedent. Human rights groups warned that constitutionally secured fundamental rights, particularly those of women and minorities, would be at risk if the bill were passed.

In October the government of Sindh province was dismissed. In November the army was asked to assist police in law and order operations. Military courts were set up to try summarily civilians suspected of disturbing law and order.

In April the Supreme Court, responding to an appeal by the government of Sindh against the Sindh High Court judgment banning the use of bar fetters, allowed their use subject to police and judicial direction in each case.

Recommendations of the Commission of Inquiry for Women, which had submitted a report in 1997, were not implemented. The government announced its intention to establish a national human rights commission but no bill to that effect was produced.

At least 106 members of the Ahmadiyya community were charged with religious offences; of these, 28 were charged with blasphemy under Section 295-C of the Penal Code, which carries a mandatory death penalty. Twenty-three of the Ahmadis were prisoners of conscience.

In April an Ahmadi doctor from Badin, Sindh province, was sentenced to 10 years' imprisonment by an anti-terrorism court. He was convicted of falsely stating that 23 illiterate people whom he helped fill in census forms were Ahmadis. He was a prisoner of conscience.

Two Christians were charged with blasphemy for allegedly desecrating posters bearing Islamic words during demonstrations which followed the suicide of the Bishop of Faisalabad, John Joseph, in protest against the continued abuse of the blasphemy laws.

The trial resumed in February of Riaz Ahmed Chowdhury and three of his relatives from Mianwali, Punjab (see previous *Amnesty International Reports*), all Ahmadi men who had been detained on blasphemy charges since 1993. The Supreme Court had granted them bail in late December 1997.

Other prisoners of conscience included dozens of people arrested after instances of sectarian violence even though there appeared to be no evidence against them. Others were detained without charge or trial as hostages when relatives suspected of criminal offences could not be found, or to extract money from them. During mass opposition rallies, up to hundreds of participants were arrested; they were usually released within hours or days. Some opposition politicians were held without charge or trial. On 18 January Shaukat Ali Kashmiri, a lawyer and leader of the United Kashmir People's National Party, was abducted by armed men in Azad Jammu and Kashmir. Upon his release in August, he stated that he had been held in different detention centres by an intelligence agency.

Torture, including rape, in police custody and jails remained widespread, resulting in at least 50 deaths. Following his arrest on a robbery charge on 1 April in Multan, Gul Khan was allegedly tortured and denied food for 10 days; on 11 April he was taken to a health care centre which certified that he was in good health, reportedly under pressure from police. When he was admitted to hospital the same day he vomited blood. On 12 April a judicial magistrate signed Gul Khan's discharge certificate while ignoring his critical condition. He died on the same day. Criminal charges were filed against seven police officers and a judicial inquiry was set up. However, when police agreed to pay Gul Khan's family 800,000 rupees (US$16,000) compensation, his family dropped the charges and the inquiry was stopped. Impunity is facilitated in Pakistan by the law of *qisas* and *diyat*, which allows victims and their families to accept compensation and stop criminal prosecution.

Children were particularly at risk of torture and ill-treatment. In May an eight-year-old boy was allegedly raped by a constable inside a police station in Peshawar. After public protests, police officers registered a complaint against their colleague,

AMNESTY INTERNATIONAL REPORT 1999

but reportedly used sections of the criminal code likely to lessen the punishment.

Flogging sentences continued to be imposed for offences tried under Islamic law provisions. In July Saba Khan was administered 30 lashes in Shangla after serving two and a half years in prison for rape.

Perpetrators of abuses often faced only mild disciplinary action; no state official was convicted of human rights violations. In April a suspected thief, Shahzad Ali, suffered severe burn injuries when a police officer in Gujjarpura set his clothes on fire to make him confess. No action was taken against the officer, who claimed that the detainee had tried to immolate himself to avoid interrogation. A police officer who had severely beaten an elderly prayer leader in Gojra, Punjab province, in July had his service record reduced by two years.

Abuses against judicial officers increased. In March, two civil judges in Karampur, who had searched police premises and questioned the arbitrary detention of several people found there, were reportedly severely beaten by police. Several police officers were arrested, but the case remained pending. The judge of an anti-terrorism court in Sargodha who had convicted senior police officials of dereliction of duty, including falsifying evidence and torture, was held hostage in court by local police in January until the convicted officials had escaped.

Police often actively covered up abuses, particularly against the vulnerable and disadvantaged, and continued to deny women and girls equal protection of the law. In March a 14-year-old schoolgirl complained to police of gang-rape by four government officials in Peshawar. Police registered her complaint only after her father filed a petition in the provincial high court. The father was arrested and briefly detained when the main accused official claimed to have been threatened by him. In April, despite the provincial chief minister's reprimand that police were not investigating the case properly and in the face of the victim's complaint and medical evidence, the victim's father and the accused reached a compromise not to pursue the case against the main accused. They claimed that contradictions in the girl's initial statements indicated her unstable mental condition and unreliability as a complainant.

The whereabouts of people who "disappeared" in previous years remained unknown. No further steps were taken to trace four members of the Ansari family, who "disappeared" in May 1996 (see previous *Amnesty International Reports*). The senate committee investigating the fate of 28 members of the Muttahida Qaumi Movement (MQM), who "disappeared" around 1995, submitted its report to the Senate in April. In March the Interior Minister told the committee that 30 MQM workers had been arrested and killed near Islamabad under the previous government. The Chief Justice of the Sindh High Court in April asked the Interior Ministry for clarification, but no further steps were known to have been taken.

At least 120 possible extrajudicial executions were reported, mainly in Punjab province. Authorities claimed that the victims had died in exchanges of fire between police and "hardened criminals". In at least 30 of these supposed "encounter killings", the victims were reported to have been in police custody before being deliberately killed. In other cases, police shot dead criminal suspects rather than attempting to arrest them. In March police shot dead two men named Zahid and Umer in Lahore in what they claimed was a shoot-out. Relatives stated that Zahid had been arrested three days earlier on a robbery charge and had been seen in a police station at Shafiqabad.

Hearings in the case relating to the killing of Mir Murtaza Bhutto and seven associates in September 1996 resumed in May in Karachi Central Jail (see previous *Amnesty International Reports*). After charges had been brought against Senator Asif Zardari and 18 officials in July 1997, the case was transferred to an anti-terrorism court in October 1997, then to a district and sessions judge. However, several judges refused to preside, leading to long delays. Most of the accused remained in detention. By April only two of 223 witnesses had been heard.

At least 428 people were sentenced to death, including 113 sentenced by anti-terrorism courts and six by military courts following procedures which fell short of international standards for fair trial. Ayub Masih, a Christian man from Pakpattan, was sentenced to death for blasphemy by a sessions court in Sahiwal in April; observers believed that the charge was brought on the basis of a land dispute. An appeal was pending.

At least four people were executed. One of them, Maqsood Ahmad, had been sentenced to death in 1994 for the murder of a businessman in 1989; a police officer later declared that two other men had confessed to the murder. Despite appeals, the case was not reopened. Maqsood Ahmad was hanged in Lahore in March. Mehram Ali, sentenced for killing 26 people in a bomb attack on a Lahore court, was executed in August in Jang district jail.

In June the then Chief of Army staff commuted to life imprisonment the death sentence against an Indian national Roop Lal, who had been sentenced 25 years earlier by court martial and since then held in solitary confinement.

Among the 2,750 people who remained under sentence of death, around 50 were juveniles at the time of the alleged offence. In December a summary military court in Karachi sentenced to death a 13-year-old boy for murder; his appeal was due to be heard in January 1999.

Police continued to register criminal charges against women who married men of their choice without the consent of their male guardians, despite judgments of the higher judiciary that women have a right to do so. Police inadequately protected such couples against violent attacks by male relatives of the woman. In February a Pashtun *jirga* (tribal council) threatened to kill Riffat Afridi and Kunwar Ahsan who had not obtained Riffat Afridi's father's consent to marry. The father registered a complaint of abduction against Kunwar Ahsan and charges of *zina* (fornication) against both. The couple went into hiding, but were arrested within days. In late February Riffat Afridi was released, but in March Kunwar Ahsan was shot and critically injured in the court building by Riffat Afridi's relatives. Local human rights groups claim that police protection was inadequate.

Police did not apparently take any protective measures when religious groups in September and October issued *fatwas* offering rewards for anyone killing human rights activists, journalists and religious personalities, including the head of the Ahmadiyya community.

Armed opposition groups pursuing ethnic or religious causes continued to deliberately kill civilians. In January, 24 mourners gathered in a Shi'a graveyard in Lahore were killed and over 50 injured by sectarian opponents. A Sunni group, *Lashkar-e-Jhangvi* (Warriors of Jhangvi), claimed responsibility.

In January Amnesty International appealed to the authorities to reveal the whereabouts of Shaukat Ali Kashmiri following his "disappearance" after arrest. After the imposition of the emergency in May, Amnesty International called on the government to immediately restore fundamental rights.

In a report published in April, *Children in South Asia: Securing their rights*, Amnesty International documented human rights violations against children in Pakistan and other countries of the region and the failure of the government to fulfil its obligations under the UN Convention on the Rights of the Child. In September Amnesty International published *Pakistan: No progress on women's rights*, highlighting the government's failure to amend discriminatory laws and improve practices affecting women.

PALESTINIAN AUTHORITY
(AREAS UNDER THE JURISDICTION OF THE)

At least 450 people were arrested on political grounds; they included prisoners of conscience. More than 500 political detainees arrested in previous years, including prisoners of conscience, remained in detention without charge or trial. At least

two political prisoners were sentenced to prison terms after grossly unfair trials before the State Security Court. Torture and ill-treatment of detainees remained widespread. Three people died in custody in circumstances where torture or ill-treatment may have caused or hastened their deaths. Unlawful killings, including possible extrajudicial executions, were reported. Four people were sentenced to death; two people were executed and one death sentence was commuted.

In October the Palestine Liberation Organization (PLO) signed the Wye Memorandum which required it to "take all measures necessary" to protect Israel's security. In return Israel was to redeploy Israeli forces in three stages from 13 per cent of the West Bank; however only the first redeployment of one per cent had taken place by the end of the year.

The Israeli authorities repeatedly imposed border closures preventing those living in areas under the jurisdiction of the Palestinian Authority (PA) from visiting other parts of the West Bank, including Jerusalem. Palestinians from the West Bank or Gaza needed special authorization, rarely given, to enter Israel, and roads allowing free passage between areas in Gaza and the West Bank under the PA's jurisdiction had not been established by the end of the year.

The Basic Law had not been approved by President Yasser Arafat by the end of the year (see previous *Amnesty International Reports*).

Fayez Abu Rahma, who had been appointed Attorney General in 1997 (see *Amnesty International Report 1998*), resigned in April, stating that his work was obstructed. No new Attorney General had been appointed by the end of the year.

In August President Arafat reshuffled his cabinet, appointing 10 new ministers. Two ministers resigned in protest at what they saw as the failure of the reshuffle to address issues of corruption.

At least 450 people, including prisoners of conscience and possible prisoners of conscience, were arrested on political grounds during the year. They included people accused of criticizing the PA; suspected supporters of *Hamas* and Islamic *Jihad* – Islamist groups opposed to the peace process; and people suspected of "collaborating" with Israel. About 40 people were arrested in February for demonstrating or speaking against threatened military intervention in Iraq; they were prisoners of conscience. They were released without charge after a few hours or days. About 150 suspected supporters of *Hamas* and *Hizb al-Khalas* (Salvation Party) were arrested in the Gaza Strip after an attack in October on a bus carrying Israeli children from the Kfar Darom settlement in which a soldier and the suicide bomber were killed. Many of those arrested were released without charge after some weeks, but at least 50 remained in prison at the end of the year.

Prisoners of conscience detained during the year included Shaykh 'Abdallah al-Shami, a leader of Islamic *Jihad*, who was arrested in April and detained for three days apparently for criticizing the PA in a sermon. He was rearrested in August by the criminal investigation department and interrogated about an article published in the newspaper *al-Istiqlal* criticizing the cabinet reshuffle. He was then placed in solitary confinement for 41 days. He was released in September without charge or trial. Muhammad Muqbel, General Director of the Ministry of Youth and Sports, was arrested in September the day after participating in a protest in Ramallah against the deaths of the 'Awadallah brothers (see **Israel and the Occupied Territories** entry). He was released the following day, after protests from the Legislative Council.

According to a letter from the Minister of Justice, charges against Fathi Subuh (see *Amnesty International Report 1998*) were dropped. However, following recommendations from the Preventive Security Service (PSS), he was not allowed to return to work at al-Azhar University.

More than 500 people, including possible prisoners of conscience, continued to be held without charge or trial. Faruq Abu Hassan, detained incommunicado by military intelligence (*istikhbarat*) in a special wing of *al-Saraya* (the PA security forces' headquarters) since November 1994 (see *Amnesty International Report 1998*), was allowed access to his family in January but continued to be held without charge or trial. Karima Hamad, arrested by the PSS in June 1996, was reportedly tortured for 28 days in 1996 in Tel al-Hawa Prison to force her to confess to hiding Yahya 'Ayyash, an engineer and member of *Hamas* accused of fabricating suicide bombs. She and her family stated that she had no knowledge of his presence in the family house. At the end of the year she remained in Gaza Central Prison and her brother, 'Usama Hamad, arrested in March 1996, remained detained by the *istikhbarat*. Neither had been charged or tried.

At least two political prisoners were sentenced after grossly unfair trials before the State Security Court. In January Nasser Abu Rus and Jasser Samaru received a half-hour trial seven days after their arrest on charges of setting up a bomb factory in Nablus. The trial was closed, the defendants were represented by state-appointed military lawyers and lawyers offering to represent the accused were allowed into the Court only to hear the sentence of 15 years' imprisonment with hard labour.

There were frequent reports of torture and ill-treatment at the hands of the security services, especially the PSS, the Intelligence (*mukhabarat*), and the *istikhbarat*. For instance, most of the 35 *Hamas* activists arrested in Ramallah after the death of *Hamas* leader Muhi al-Din al-Sherif in March said they were tortured by the PSS or by the *mukhabarat*. 'Imad 'Awadallah, who was arrested in April and taken to Jericho, described being tortured for more than 30 days by PSS officers to make him confess to the killing of Muhi al-Din al-Sherif. He said he was beaten while hooded and forced to stand or to hang from a window for prolonged periods. He was then held in solitary confinement by the *mukhabarat* for 34 days before being handed back to the PSS who held him for a further 30 days, forcing him to remain in painful positions while standing or suspended for 20 hours a day. In July he went on hunger strike for 16 days and was finally allowed to see his family after 100 days' incommunicado detention. In August he escaped. His family in Ramallah was placed under house arrest for 12 days. Demonstrators opposed to the treatment of his family, including members of the Legislative Council, were beaten by police officers. In September 'Imad 'Awadallah and his brother, 'Adel, a leader of the military wing of *Hamas*, were killed by Israeli security forces in apparent extrajudicial executions (see **Israel and the Occupied Territories** entry).

Three people died in custody in circumstances where torture or ill-treatment appeared to have caused or hastened their deaths. In August Walid Mahmud Qawasmeh died in Jericho apparently as a result of torture. He had been arrested in Hebron in July and was held incommunicado for 12 days. His family stated that when they saw him, in the presence of guards, he had bruises on his head and neck. He died three days later. Palestinian security officials said that Walid Qawasmeh died of heat stroke, but the autopsy showed that death occurred as a result of a fractured skull followed by a brain haemorrhage. In November a military court sentenced two members of the security services to six months' imprisonment and one other *in absentia* to seven years' imprisonment after a summary trial for causing the death by negligence.

The findings of investigations into human rights abuses were not made public and court decisions were often ignored. More than 50 petitions for the release of those detained without charge or trial were submitted to the Palestinian High Court. Shaykh Mahmud Muslah, a *Hamas* activist arrested in September 1997 whose release had been ordered by the High Court in November 1997, remained in detention (see *Amnesty International Report 1998*). In March, nine men from al-Khader village were acquitted by the Ramallah District Court and released. They had been arrested in 1996 and had confessed to murders after they were tortured by the *istikhbarat*. In October, two members of the security services were charged in connection with the kidnapping and beating of the General Secretary of the Palestinian Popular Force in June.

Four appellants, including the Legislative Council's human rights committee, brought a petition for habeas corpus before the Palestinian High Court of Justice on behalf of Shafiq Muhammad Hassan 'Abd al-Wahhab, who "disappeared" after his arrest by the *istikhbarat* in July 1997 (see *Amnesty International Report 1998*). The Court had not ruled on the case by the end of the year.

Unlawful killings, including possible extrajudicial executions, continued to be reported. Muhammad 'Anqawi, who had previously been detained in 1996 on suspicion of "collaborating" with Israel, was found dead in April half an hour after telling a friend he was going to the *mukhabarat*. His body had nine bullet holes in it and his car was outside the *mukhabarat* office. No investigation was held into his death.

Four people were sentenced to death and two were executed, the first executions under the PA. Ra'ed, Muhammad and Fares Abu Sultan, three members of the *istikhbarat*, were brought to trial before a military court in Gaza in August on charges of killing two members of another family during an armed confrontation. The trial, which was unannounced, was held the day after the murders. A journalist who tried to enter the court was reportedly beaten by police. The death sentence was handed down the next day and the following day, three days after the murder, Ra'ed and Muhammad Abu Sultan were executed by firing squad. The death sentence on Fares Abu Sultan was commuted.

Amnesty International delegates visited areas under the jurisdiction of the PA on several occasions, meeting President Arafat and other officials, and raising concerns about prolonged detention without charge or trial, unfair trials and torture. Officials said *Hamas* and Islamic *Jihad* supporters were detained without charge or trial for fear of further suicide bombings.

In September Amnesty International published a report, *Israel and the Occupied Territories and the Palestinian Authority: Five years after the Oslo Agreement – human rights sacrificed for 'security'*. The organization made frequent appeals to Israel and to the USA not to put pressure on the PA to detain opponents of the peace process without charge or trial or after unfair trials.

PAPUA NEW GUINEA

Ill-treatment by members of the security forces continued to be reported. Prison conditions amounting to cruel, inhuman or degrading punishment were highlighted after rioting and mass escapes by prisoners. There were reports that at least five people were shot dead by police in disputed circumstances.

Significant progress was made towards resolving the armed conflict on the island of Bougainville, where the October 1997 truce appeared to be holding (see *Amnesty International Report 1998*). In January the Papua New Guinea government, the Bougainville Transitional Government, the Bougainville Resistance Forces, the Bougainville Interim Government, community leaders and the Bougainville Revolutionary Army jointly announced the "Lincoln Agreement" in New Zealand, which formalized steps towards peace on Bougainville, including a formal cease-fire signed in April. The agreement included plans for the gradual withdrawal of Papua New Guinea Defence Force (PNGDF) personnel from Bougainville during the restoration of civil authority, a return to civilian policing, and democratic elections for a provincial Bougainville Reconciliation Government. Parties to the meeting also agreed "to renounce the use of armed forces and violence" and to respect "human rights and the rule of law".

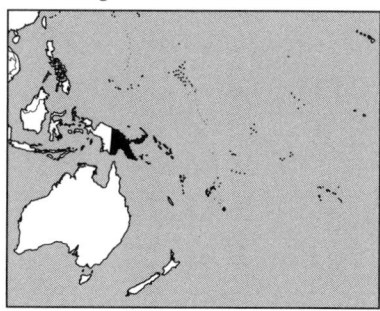

In April the UN Security Council issued a Presidential Statement supporting the "Lincoln Agreement" and the development of a UN peace monitoring mission as requested in the agreement. A UN office was established in Bougainville. In June the government announced the withdrawal of PNGDF forces from the capital of Bougainville, Arawa, and other parts of the island, and the restoration of the national and village court system. In December, however, parliament twice failed to pass legislation necessary for the holding of provincial elections in Bougainville.

In a move linked to the peace process in Bougainville, an advisory "Committee on the Power of Mercy" was reportedly re-established in September. The Committee was to investigate and make recommendations on appeals from prisoners to be released or to have their sentences reduced.

There was no substantial progress in the establishment of a National Commission on Human Rights announced by the

272

government in 1997 (see *Amnesty International Report 1998*).

Charges of sedition against the PNGDF Commander, Brigadier-General Jerry Singirok, dismissed in 1997 for his role in preventing the planned use of foreign mercenaries in the Bougainville conflict and for calling on former Prime Minister Sir Julius Chan to step down, were suspended during judicial inquiries into the affair (see *Amnesty International Report 1998*). The second of two judicial inquiries found in October that he had not tried to overthrow the previous government, but had acted unlawfully in seeking to expel the mercenaries. Brigadier-General Singirok was reappointed as Commander, but the sedition charges were reinstated in November.

Ill-treatment by the security forces continued to be reported. In June at least 20 people were reportedly injured and some ill-treated when approximately 100 armed police officers fired tear gas at students to break up non-violent demonstrations at the University of Papua New Guinea Waigani Campus. Police defended their action by saying they could not wait for more than an hour until students removed a roadblock to prevent access to the campus.

In May a group of women publicly expressed concern about police use of force during arrests, alleging that officers in Port Moresby had used a sledgehammer to hit the leg of a suspect they had already arrested. In August Louis Mark and Andrew Aubu alleged they were beaten by police and whipped with a bamboo branch after officers stopped them for questioning. In September there were reports that several people had lodged formal complaints of police ill-treatment during the police's "Operation Sweep" in Manus island, ahead of an international sports competition there.

Severe and prolonged shortages of food contributed to rioting and mass escapes of prisoners, including at Bomana Prison near the capital, Port Moresby, and at Kerevat Jail in East New Britain province. An official investigation was opened.

Reports in August cited complaints about the killing of five criminal suspects in disputed circumstances by police officers at Tabubil and Laloki. At least one of them was reportedly shot in the back by police who claimed they were pursuing armed suspects shooting at officers. One

police officer was suspended from duty when investigations began into the death of a villager who died in September after police reportedly fired three shots to disperse men who were fighting in Kagua, Southern Highlands Province.

Amnesty International continued to monitor developments in Bougainville and reports of human rights violations by police in other provinces.

PARAGUAY

Landless peasant farmers were arrested and intimidated in the context of land disputes; three were shot dead. Criminal suspects were tortured and ill-treated by police and there were continued reports of ill-treatment, "disappearance" and deaths in unclear circumstances of armed forces recruits, including minors. Prosecutions for past human rights violations continued, although little progress was made in investigating more recent abuses.

A prolonged political crisis led to continued instability throughout the year. In March former army commander and presidential candidate Lino Oviedo was sentenced to 10 years' imprisonment by an extraordinary military tribunal for an attempted coup against President Juan Carlos Wasmosy in 1996 (see previous *Amnesty International Reports*). The sentence was confirmed by the Supreme Court of Justice in April. Former General Oviedo was also given a dishonourable discharge and barred from running for elective office. His vice-presidential running mate, Raúl Cubas Grau, took his place as the ruling Colorado Party's candidate and won the presidential elections in May.

Three days after his inauguration in August, President Cubas issued Decree Law 117 which reduced General Oviedo's 10-year prison sentence to three months and ordered his immediate release on the grounds that he had already served the sentence. In December the Supreme Court ruled Decree Law 117 unconstitutional and ordered that General Oviedo return to jail to serve his full prison term. The institutional and political crisis deepened when President Cubas refused to comply. General Oviedo remained at liberty at the end of the year.

A new penal code, making torture, genocide and enforced disappearance criminal offences punishable by minimum five-year prison sentences, came into force in November.

Against the backdrop of the long-running political crisis there was a deterioration in respect for human rights. Reports of harassment, intimidation and attacks on peasant farmers in the context of land disputes increased. Peasant farmer Cristino Romero Vera was reportedly shot dead by police agents in the locality of Maciel in August. An investigation was opened. In a growing number of cases, those responsible for attacks against landless peasants were civilian gunmen – allegedly hired by landowners – who acted with the complicity of the police or judicial authorities. More than 500 families legally settled on 226,000 hectares of land in Amambay and Concepción departments were repeatedly threatened and harassed by a group of gunmen composed of police, retired army officers and civilians believed to be acting on behalf of the former owner of the land. The land, known as Antebi-cué, was expropriated by Congress in 1996 in favour of landless peasant families. Despite repeated complaints of harassment lodged on behalf of the families before judicial authorities, no action was taken to investigate and bring to justice those responsible. In November unidentified gunmen shot dead Gumercindo Pavón Díaz, a peasant farmer resident on the disputed land, and tortured his friend, Víctor Ramón Fernández.

There were renewed reports of torture and ill-treatment in police custody. Criminal suspects, including minors, were routinely ill-treated by police. In January brothers Narciso and Emilio Fernández were arrested by police and accused of theft. They were taken to the 3rd police station in the capital, Asunción, and allegedly tortured and threatened in order to extract confessions. A formal criminal complaint was filed by their parents on their release.

There were numerous reports of enforced recruitment and ill-treatment – in some cases resulting in death – of military conscripts, many of whom were minors. Fourteen-year-old Cristian Ariel Núñez Lugo and 15-year-old Marcelino Gómez Paredes "disappeared" in January while carrying out their military service in the army's General Colmán detachment based in the western Chaco region bordering Bolivia. Military authorities claimed the two conscripts were alive in Bolivia. However, the investigating judge charged an army second lieutenant in connection with their "disappearance". Their whereabouts remained unknown. Military authorities continued to forcibly and arbitrarily recruit youths, including minors, in contravention of national legislation and international standards. In January, 15-year-old Rubén Viera Martínez was reported missing after he failed to arrive in Asunción from his home in Yegros, department of Caazapá. Forty days later, after a petition of habeas corpus had been presented on his behalf to judicial authorities, he was located in a military barracks in Pedro Juan Caballero, Amambay department, where he had been posted after being seized and forcibly recruited by military personnel. He was returned to his family.

Judicial proceedings into human rights violations by state agents during the administration of General Alfredo Stroessner (1954 to 1989) continued. At least 20 cases of torture, "disappearance" and death in custody were pending before the courts (see previous *Amnesty International Reports*). In September the Supreme Court of Justice confirmed a prison sentence of 12 and a half years imposed on Agustín Belotto, a member of the Police Investigations Department, for his responsibility in the torture and death in custody of Amílcar Oviedo in 1975. However, efforts to bring former President Stroessner and former Interior Minister Sabino Augusto Montanaro to justice were unsuccessful and they continued to live in exile.

Paraguayan national Ángel Francisco Breard was judicially executed in the USA in May. The case caused controversy in Paraguay after the execution was allowed to proceed in defiance of an explicit order from the International Court of Justice which required the USA to halt the proceedings (see USA entry).

PERU

At least 600 prisoners of conscience and possible prisoners of conscience accused of terrorism-related crimes remained in prison. Some 4,000 people charged with these offences were in prison under procedures which fell short of international fair trial standards. Death threats and other acts of intimidation were directed at critics of the government. Reports of torture and ill-treatment continued. Prison conditions amounted to cruel, inhuman or degrading treatment. Armed opposition groups continued to commit human rights abuses.

The amnesty laws, which sanctioned impunity surrounding thousands of cases of human rights violations committed in the context of counter-insurgency operations between 1980 and 1995, remained on the statute books. Despite several UN human rights bodies recommending that the authorities repeal the amnesty laws, in July President Alberto Fujimori stated publicly that the laws were approved because Peru was a sovereign state.

Armed operations by the clandestine *Partido Comunista del Perú (Sendero Luminoso)* (PCP), Communist Party of Peru (Shining Path), and *Movimiento Revolucionario Túpac Amaru* (MRTA), Túpac Amaru Revolutionary Movement, re-

mained confined to isolated regions of Peru's rainforest. By the end of the year 20 per cent of the population remained under a state of emergency covering 16 per cent of the national territory.

No judges were nominated by Congress to replace the three judges dismissed from the Constitutional Tribunal in May 1997 (see *Amnesty International Report 1998*). As a result the Constitutional Tribunal was unable to exercise its full functions in upholding the Constitution, including the protection of human rights. In keeping with requirements enshrined in the Constitution, sufficient signatures from the public were obtained to hold a referendum on whether President Fujimori should be allowed to stand for a third term of office. However, in September Congress rejected the referendum as a result of a law, passed during the collection of signatures, stating that referendums could only be held with the additional approval of Congress.

In May, following Congress' approval of a law curtailing the functions of the National Council of the Magistracy, a constitutional body responsible for the appointment and removal of judges and attorneys, the Council protested that the law undermined its independence and its members resigned *en bloc*. This concern was echoed by opposition parliamentarians, jurists, and many sectors of civil society. Steps taken to reinstate the functions of the Council were deemed by these critics to be purely cosmetic. The Attorney General publicly stated that his autonomy and independence also remained curtailed, blaming the situation on the ongoing reform of Peru's judicial system. Intergovernmental organizations and critics of the government expressed concern that the rule of law, the independence of the judiciary, and the protection of human rights were being undermined.

The mandate of the *Ad Hoc* Commission charged with recommending a presidential pardon for prisoners falsely accused of terrorism was further extended to December 1999 (see *Amnesty International Reports 1997* and *1998*). In November a law came into effect which made provision for judges to immediately quash the criminal records and outstanding judicial procedures of these prisoners. Since the Commission started its work in 1996, 444 prisoners had been pardoned and released. Scores of other prisoners falsely accused of terrorism-related crimes were acquitted by the courts and released.

In June the executive passed a set of Decree Laws which defined certain serious common crimes as "aggravated terrorism". Under this legislation those accused can be held incommunicado for up to 10 days and tried by military courts. The Decree Laws, widely regarded as being modelled on Peru's 1992 anti-terrorism legislation, were severely criticized by jurists and human rights organizations.

In February Congress approved a law on crimes against humanity in which the crimes of genocide, enforced disappearance and torture were incorporated into Peru's Criminal Code and were punishable by at least 20, 15 and five years' imprisonment respectively. The law also stipulated that these crimes would be dealt with by the civilian courts.

In January a civilian and six members of the army, who had confessed to involvement in a 1996 bomb attack in the city of Puno on a television station which was critical of the authorities, were acquitted of terrorism charges. The court ruled that acts of terrorism could only be attributed to members of the PCP and MRTA and not to members of the security forces on active service.

The long-standing border dispute between Peru and Ecuador, which in 1995 spilled over into an armed conflict, was brought to an end in November with the signing of a new border treaty. During the armed conflict civilians from both countries suffered human rights violations (see *Amnesty International Report 1996*).

The UN Special Rapporteur on the independence of judges and lawyers and the UN Committee against Torture published statements on Peru's human rights situation in February and May respectively. Both welcomed the ending of the use of "faceless judges", but expressed concern at the continued use of military courts to try civilians accused of terrorism and at the passing of legislation curtailing the functions of the National Council of the Magistracy which undermined the independence of the judiciary. The Committee against Torture also expressed concern about "frequent and numerous allegations of torture".

The government continued to ignore the recommendations of the Inter-American system for the protection of human rights that compensation be paid to victims of human rights violations and their relatives. María Elena Loayza Tamayo, a victim of torture and unfair trial; the relatives of Ernesto Castillo Páez, who "disappeared" in 1991; and the 21 victims of the 1990 Chumbivilcas massacre, did not receive compensation. However, compensation was paid to the relatives of the three El Frontón prisoners who "disappeared" in 1986 (see *Amnesty International Report 1998*). At the conclusion of a visit to the country in November, the Inter-American Commission on Human Rights publicly recognized important advances in the protection of human rights since the Commission last visited Peru in 1993, including that no complaints of "disappearances" or extrajudicial executions had been filed before the Commission since 1995. However, the Commission expressed concern at the lack of independence of the judiciary, at the failure to fully observe the rule of law and fair trial standards, and at the use of military courts to investigate human rights cases and try civilians. The Commission urged the authorities to repeal the 1995 amnesty laws and to establish the truth surrounding human rights violations in the past.

By the end of the year, at least 600 prisoners of conscience and possible prisoners of conscience accused of terrorism-related crimes remained in prison. Prisoner of conscience Carlos Ortega López had initially been detained in May 1993 and falsely charged with terrorism-related offences. He was acquitted and released seven months later. However, in November 1996 he was again detained, following a ruling by the Supreme Court of Justice that he be retried. He was subsequently sentenced to 20 years' imprisonment. Other prisoners of conscience still detained at the end of the year included Marco Antonio Ambrosio Concha, Carlos Florentino Molero Coca and Marco Antonio Monge Hoyos (see *Amnesty International Report 1998*) and former Congressman Yehude Simon Munaro.

Seven prisoners of conscience, including Zacarías Merma Farfán (see *Amnesty International Report 1998*), and 77 possible prisoners of conscience falsely accused of terrorism benefited from presidential pardons and were released during the year.

276

Some 4,000 people were serving sentences or awaiting trial under anti-terrorism legislation which fell short of international fair trial standards. Despite positive but piecemeal reforms to this legislation in previous years (see *Amnesty International Reports 1993* to *1998*), civilians accused of treason continued to be tried by military courts, defence lawyers were still prohibited from cross-examining members of the security forces involved in arrests and interrogations, and trials were not heard in public.

Death threats and other acts of intimidation directed at critics of the government persisted. Opposition parliamentarians Jorge del Castillo, Javier Diez Canseco and Gustavo Mohme Llona; human rights defenders Sofía Macher, Francisco Soberón and Heriberto Benítez Rivas; and journalists César Hilderbrandt and Luis Ibérico, were among those who received intimidatory telephone calls or faxes, most threatening them with death. Several had received death threats in previous years (see *Amnesty International Report 1998*). In October papers and files relating to women's rights were stolen during a break-in at the home of Giulia Tamayo León, an activist campaigning against the forced sterilization of women. She subsequently received intimidatory telephone calls.

Reports of torture and ill-treatment continued. In September, Charly Soto Ríos, a recruit based at a police training school in the Vargas Guerra military camp in the city of Iquitos, was shot dead, reportedly as a result of a stray bullet. However, film broadcast on television showed heavy bruising on his thorax and the soles of his feet, suggesting that Charly Soto may have been severely beaten prior to his death. The victim's body was apparently buried without forensic examination and an investigation into the death appeared to ignore the extensive bruising on his body.

An investigation by the Public Ministry into the death in unclear circumstances of intelligence agent Mariela Lucy Barreto Riofano in 1997 was provisionally shelved on the grounds that it had not been possible to identify those responsible (see *Amnesty International Report 1998*).

Prison conditions continued to be harsh and in some circumstances amounted to cruel, inhuman and degrading punishment. For example, under special penitentiary regulations introduced in 1992, prisoners accused of terrorism-related offences could receive one 30-minute family visit per month. Under 1997 reforms to the regulations, prisoners could receive weekly one-hour family visits, but direct contact with their visitors remained prohibited during the first two years of detention. The reforms progressively allowed for prisoners with more than two years' detention to receive two and then four-hourly family visits per week, including direct contact with their relatives, and to have access to workshops and educational classes and longer periods out of their cells. However, these benefits were only granted following a favourable official evaluation of the prisoner's behaviour. During prison visits by Amnesty International delegates in September, several PCP and MRTA prisoners informed the organization that they were denied these benefits because they refused to renounce their "revolutionary ideas".

The conditions endured by prisoners accused of terrorism in Yanamayo Prison and in the prison in the Callao Naval Base near the capital, Lima, continued to be particularly harsh (see *Amnesty International Report 1998*). In several prisons inmates were reported to be suffering from illnesses for which they did not receive adequate medical attention. They included wheelchair-bound prisoners Florencio Arturo Varillas Tizón, Manuel Mendoza Chiara and Juan Francisco Tulich Morales held in Yanamayo Prison.

Conditions were also harsh in the Lurigancho Prison in Lima where some 6,300 inmates convicted of criminal offences were held in an establishment designed to hold 1,200 prisoners. Despite calls on the authorities to review the decision to bring the Challapalca Prison into operation (see *Amnesty International Report 1998*), prisoners accused of common crimes continued to be transferred there. The prison's location in an isolated region of the Andean highlands at least 4,600 metres above sea level, made regular visits by relatives, defence lawyers and pastoral visitors virtually impossible.

Human rights abuses by armed opposition groups continued to be reported. In May members of the PCP stormed the villages of Cachicoto and Puente Pacae, Huánuco department. They gathered the inhabitants together and then shot dead five peasants accused of passing information to the authorities. In September Rolando Amancio Enríquez and Juan Nalvarte Chuquillanqui were shot dead in the village of San Francisco, near Uchiza, San Martín department, for refusing to shout slogans in support of the PCP.

Amnesty International repeatedly appealed to the authorities to immediately and unconditionally release all prisoners of conscience. In February the organization appealed to the authorities to review the conditions prevailing in Challapalca Prison, including the effects of its location on prisoners' health and their right to maintain effective contact with relatives, lawyers and pastoral visitors. In June Amnesty International wrote to the authorities reiterating previous appeals for the antiterrorism laws to be brought into line with international fair trial standards.

In August Amnesty International appealed to the authorities to transfer the three wheelchair-bound prisoners from Yanamayo Prison to a hospital where they could be given adequate medical care. In November the three prisoners were transferred to Socabaya Prison near the city of Arequipa, but it was not known if they received the treatment they required. In September an Amnesty International delegation visiting the country was granted access to prisoners accused of terrorism in Castro Castro and Chorrillos Prisons, but was refused access to them in Yanamayo Prison. Permission was also granted to visit Lurigancho Prison but access to Challapalca Prison was denied.

Throughout the year the organization appealed to the authorities to ensure the safety of numerous individuals threatened with death and called on President Fujimori to publicly condemn these and other forms of intimidation directed at critics of his government. In several of the cases the authorities indicated that measures were taken to protect the victims but failed to bring those responsible to justice.

PHILIPPINES

At least 145 political prisoners, including possible prisoners of conscience, remained in detention. Detainees continued to be tortured and ill-treated during interrogation. The incidence of human rights violations in the context of counterinsurgency continued to decline, but at least four possible "disappearances" were reported and at least nine people were alleged to have been extrajudicially executed. More than 400 people were sentenced to death. Armed opposition groups were responsible for human rights abuses.

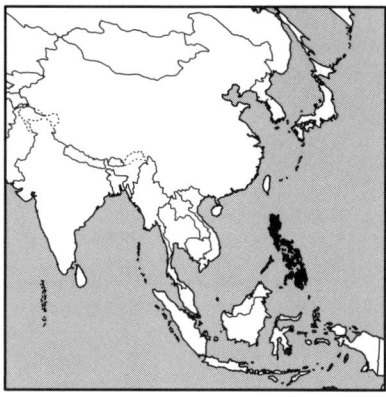

In June President Joseph Estrada took office after elections in May. He identified as his government's priorities law and order and the improvement of conditions for the poor.

In March the government and the National Democratic Front, representing the Communist Party of the Philippines (CPP) and its armed wing, the New People's Army (NPA), initialled a draft accord on human rights, the first of a four-stage agenda designed to lead to a comprehensive peace agreement. President Estrada approved the accord in August, but disagreements over its implementation and the proposed release of political prisoners delayed further peace negotiations. Local cease-fire agreements between the government and the Moro Islamic Liberation Front (MILF) on the southern island of Mindanao broke down for periods throughout the year. Recurrent fighting impeded intermittent peace talks, and the two sides made limited progress towards a general peace agreement.

At least 145 political prisoners, including possible prisoners of conscience, remained in detention at the end of the year. Most of the political detainees were held on criminal charges, particularly illegal possession of firearms, robbery and murder, which had allegedly occurred within

278

the context of the CPP-NPA insurgency. The majority had not been convicted by the end of the year. In December President Estrada approved a new amnesty proclamation, subject to congressional approval, which extended until March 1997 the period in which crimes committed by communist or Muslim secessionist rebels could be considered "politically motivated" and therefore eligible for consideration by the National Amnesty Commission (NAC). In December the NAC announced that it had granted nearly 11,000 amnesty applications since 1994, including those put forward by former communist, Muslim and rightist military rebels.

Torture and ill-treatment of people detained for alleged involvement in insurgency continued. In February, two farmers, Eric Carculan and Pepito Carculan, belonging to the Mangyan indigenous community in Occidental Mindoro province, were accused by the Armed Forces of the Philippines (AFP) Scout Rangers of being NPA members. The soldiers allegedly beat the two men repeatedly, tied plastic bags over their heads to restrict their breathing, and submerged them in a stream to coerce them to reveal the location of an NPA camp. Ordinary criminal suspects were also ill-treated or tortured in order to coerce confessions or implicate other alleged accomplices, particularly while held in Philippine National Police (PNP) cells during the initial interrogation period. Methods reported included beating with fists and gun butts, and the placing of plastic bags over the head to restrict breathing.

Levels of grave human rights violations occurring within the context of counter-insurgency operations continued a gradual decline, but at least four possible "disappearances" and at least nine possible extrajudicial executions allegedly carried out by members of the security forces were reported. For example, in December Danilo Caisip and Jayson Nieva were taken into custody by district officials in Batangas province on suspicion of being NPA members. They were reportedly handed over to a PNP Mobile Force Company in Nasugbu town, but PNP officers subsequently denied any knowledge of the arrest. The two men's whereabouts remained unknown. In a possible extrajudicial execution, Roberto Bornales was shot dead in an alleged armed encounter with

AFP Marines in Palawan province in October. Roberto Bornales' companion, Abe Sungit, who claimed the shooting was unprovoked, was reportedly beaten after his arrest.

Human rights abuses in the context of land disputes and the demolition of poor residential areas included deliberate and arbitrary killings, harassment and ill-treatment. They were carried out throughout the year by unidentified armed men and private security guards, at times with the apparent connivance and collusion of local officials and members of the security forces. In February and March respectively farmers Marcelito Cacal and Arnulfo Banares went missing and were later found dead in San Francisco district, Quezon province. Local residents claimed the killings were linked to a land dispute and that the murders involved the collusion of AFP members.

More than 400 people were sentenced to death. The date for the first execution since 1976, that of house painter Leo Pilo Echegaray, was set for early 1999. Since the death penalty was restored in December 1993 at least 850 people have been sentenced to death for a range of crimes. Reports of the continued use of torture and ill-treatment to coerce confessions from some suspects accused of capital crimes heightened concern over the risk of judicial error in death penalty cases.

Armed opposition groups were responsible for human rights abuses. Members of Muslim armed groups, including the MILF, *Abu Sayyaf* and renegade members of the Moro National Liberation Front, continued to take civilians hostage and to carry out deliberate and arbitrary killings. In July the MILF reportedly executed by firing squad a man convicted of murder by the group's *Shari'a* courts.

In March an Amnesty International delegation, accompanied by four relatives of crime victims and the parents of a death-row inmate from the USA, visited the Philippines to participate in a campaign by local anti-death penalty groups against a resumption of executions. During the year Amnesty International called on President Estrada to exercise clemency for prisoners whose death sentences had been confirmed by the Supreme Court, including a deaf-mute prisoner who appeared not to have understood his trial's proceedings. It also called on the government to abolish the death penalty and to launch an independent inquiry into allegations of ill-treatment and torture of criminal suspects by police. In May Amnesty International expressed concern for the safety of a lawyer who had received death threats related to his involvement in the prosecution of PNP officers linked to the extrajudicial execution of 11 bank robbers (see *Amnesty International Report 1998*). In December it called on the authorities to act immediately to guarantee the safety of two men who had reportedly "disappeared".

PORTUGAL

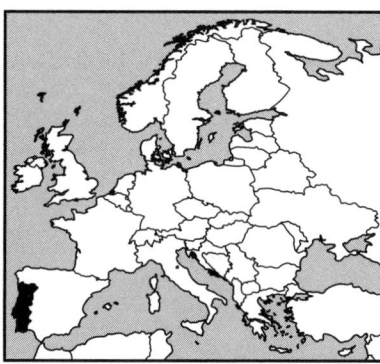

There were new reports of ill-treatment and excessive use of force by law enforcement officers and prison guards. Judicial inquiries continued into allegations of ill-treatment and deaths in police custody from previous years. Law enforcement officers accused of ill-treatment were tried, in some cases after delays of many years.

In January President Jorge Sampaio described the situation in Portuguese prisons as a "real national scandal", referring among other things to serious overcrowding and lengthy pre-trial detention. In January the European Committee for the Prevention of Torture and Inhuman or Degrading Treatment or Punishment (CPT) published a report critical of ill-treatment and insanitary conditions in Oporto prison, which it last visited in 1996. The CPT report referred to a large number of allegations of physical ill-treatment of inmates by custodial staff, such as blows with batons, punches and kicks, and night-time beatings. The CPT also ex-

pressed concern at inter-prisoner intimidation and violence, and at the devolution of many tasks to a small number of privileged prisoners known as *"faxinas"* – a practice that could reinforce exploitation of fellow inmates. In its published reply, the government stated that abuse of prisoners by prison staff was a "permanent concern" and referred to measures being taken to reduce overcrowding and inter-prisoner intimidation.

There were new allegations of ill-treatment by law enforcement officers. Seventeen-year-old Rui Pedro and his elder brother, José Pedro Batista dos Santos Mecha, alleged that in February they were severely beaten by Public Security Police (PSP) officers in Moita. Both said that they were repeatedly kicked and beaten on the head, back and all over the body with batons, and dragged along the ground by the hair to a patrol car. José Mecha said that the beatings continued after he was handcuffed. Both were taken to the PSP station at Moita, then to hospital. Rui Mecha said he suffered severe head pains, dizziness, vomiting and bleeding from the ears. José Mecha described injuries to the left leg and back, and temporary partial facial paralysis. Both remained in hospital for four days. They lodged judicial complaints against the police officers in July.

In September the Ombudsman for Justice and the General Inspectorate of Internal Administration (IGAI) both opened inquiries into the conduct of an officer of the National Republican Guard (GNR) during a farmers' demonstration near Ourique, Alentejo. Portuguese television transmitted pictures of people already under arrest being beaten while they appeared to be offering no resistance. The Ombudsman reportedly expressed concern that on two occasions an officer had used "unnecessary and disproportionate force". IGAI, which concluded that police action at Ourique was, in general, correct, found that one officer had made "inappropriate and non-proportional" use of his baton on two demonstrators and initiated disciplinary proceedings against him.

Allegations of serious ill-treatment by custodial staff, as well as cruel, inhuman and degrading prison conditions, were widespread. Augusto da Conceição Mata, imprisoned at Vale de Judeus, Alcoentre, stated that in January he was beaten unconscious by several prison guards and

280

did not receive prompt medical assistance. He lodged a judicial complaint with the Cartaxo court and with the Ombudsman for Justice. Alberico A. Lopes Correia alleged that he was beaten and trampled, and had his nose fractured, by prison staff at the same prison in January. He was made to take a cold bath and racially insulted. He lost consciousness and was left to lie, bleeding from the nose, on a concrete floor. He reported that he did not receive prompt medical assistance and that although a subsequent medical report confirmed the fracture of the nose, he had still not received the required surgery three months later.

In July Dionísio Alberto Oriola, imprisoned at Coimbra prison, was found hanging in a punishment cell after allegedly attacking a guard. Prison sources reported he had been "violently beaten by prison guards hours before committing suicide". He had staged a rooftop protest at Sintra prison earlier in the year, apparently about prison conditions. Administrative inquiries were opened into the circumstances surrounding his death.

In July Fernando Azevedo, reportedly known to the police as a petty criminal, was shot dead in Oporto in the course of a routine operation of the PSP's Transit Division. After he was stopped by police on suspicion of car theft, Fernando Azevedo attempted to escape arrest by driving away while an officer was still holding on to the door. He then tried to shake the officer off by bumping into other cars. A second officer apparently fired first at the tyres, then through one of the car's windows. Fernando Azevedo was hit in the back. It was not clear whether the officer had fired in "legitimate defence". An inquiry was opened.

A number of inquiries relating to alleged ill-treatment and deaths in custody in previous years remained open or were concluded, in some cases after many years. In January, almost six years after the assault on Francisco Carretas and another man in Charneca da Caparica, the appeal of five GNR officers against conviction for unnecessary violence was rejected by the Constitutional Court; they were committed to the military prison of Santarém. Their sentences, ranging from 12 to 14 months' imprisonment, had been reduced by the Supreme Military Tribunal in 1995. Persistent delays had dogged the judicial proceedings (see *Amnesty International Reports 1994* and *1995*).

In January the prosecutor closed an inquiry that had been reopened in November 1997 into the death of Vítor Manuel Santos, without being able to clarify the exact circumstances surrounding his death (see *Amnesty International Report 1998*).

In March the Interior Minister ordered the resignation from the PSP of an officer who, in 1994, shot dead Romão Monteiro, a Rom, while he was handcuffed and under interrogation at Matosinhos police station. A three-year suspended prison sentence passed on the officer for manslaughter had been reduced by two months in 1996 by the Supreme Court which had also ordered the reopening of an internal disciplinary inquiry. The officer remained on active but unarmed duty at an airport. He appealed to the Supreme Administrative Tribunal against the Minister's decision.

In July the Justice Ministry informed Amnesty International that a prison guard had been charged with a breach of discipline, punishable with exclusion from the prison service, in connection with the use of disproportionate force against prisoner Belmiro Santana in 1997 (see *Amnesty International Report 1998*). Administrative and judicial inquiries were continuing.

In December a PSP officer was sentenced to a fine for the manslaughter of Carlos Araújo (see *Amnesty International Report 1998*). During the trial, the officer, who claimed he had fired in the air, could not explain how he had shot Carlos Araújo, and questions were raised about the inadequacy of firearms training. Carlos Araújo's companions, Luis Correia and 16-year-old Sérgio Nogueira, were sentenced in February to two years' imprisonment for theft by a juvenile court in Évora. They were appealing against the sentence. IGAI had brought disciplinary charges against another officer for beating them and Carlos Araújo while they were in custody "without any of them having done anything to justify" the beating.

Amnesty International wrote to the Justice Minister about five specific cases of alleged ill-treatment of prisoners by custodial staff, including two fatalities, and raised with the Interior Minister cases of alleged ill-treatment and the use of excessive force by law enforcement officers.

It urged the authorities to ensure full and prompt investigations into all such allegations and sought information from the authorities on the progress of inquiries already opened.

The Director-General of the Prison Service, attached to the Ministry of Justice, subsequently informed Amnesty International that internal inquiries into the cases of Augusto da Conceiça Mata and Alberico A. Lopes Correia had been closed because there was no evidence that custodial staff had acted improperly against the prisoners. The Director-General added that, in the latter case, a fracture of the nose had not been confirmed. While admitting that prison guards had used force against Alberico Correia, he said that it had been "necessary and proportional", and that Alberico Correia faced criminal charges of violent resistance against prison guards.

In November Amnesty International representatives attended an international seminar, "Human Rights and Police Efficiency", organized by IGAI, which is responsible for monitoring and improving the quality of law enforcement. The seminar was attended by numerous officers from police forces in Portugal.

QATAR

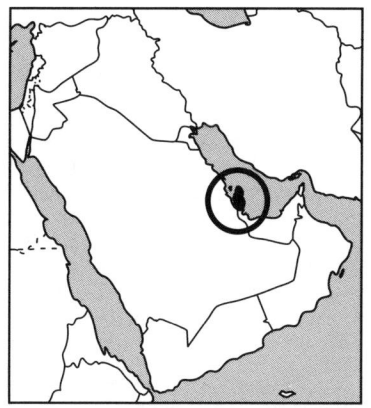

Up to a dozen political opponents of the government were detained. Three political trials took place which may not have met international standards of fairness. Allegations of torture were made.

In July the Amir, al-Shaikh Hamad Ibn Khalifa Al-Thani, enacted a law stipulating

the establishment, for the first time, of a municipal council to be elected by universal suffrage. The law provides for the right for both men and women to stand for election as well as to vote. The government stated that the municipal elections were expected to take place in March 1999. In November the Amir announced that parliamentary elections would take place following the drawing up of a new constitution. The Amir stated that the parliament would also be elected by universal suffrage.

Up to a dozen political opponents of the government were detained during the year. Most were held in connection with the failed coup attempt of February 1996. Many of them were arrested after being forcibly returned from the United Arab Emirates (UAE) and Yemen (see **United Arab Emirates** and **Yemen** entries). They included Mubarak 'Abdullah Jassim Al-Malki and deputy head of the intelligence service Fahd 'Abdullah Jassim Al-Malki, who were forcibly returned from the UAE and Yemen respectively. Their cases were joined to a case already being tried (see below).

The trial of more than 100 people accused in connection with the February 1996 coup attempt (see previous *Amnesty International Reports*) was continuing before a criminal court in the capital Doha at the end of the year. Most of those arrested during the year had been charged *in absentia* and appeared before the High Court following their arrest. Many of the defendants in the trial stated in court that their confessions had been obtained as a result of torture.

Two political trials concluded. The first, concluded in February, involved seven people charged with forming an illegal organization and divulging military secrets. Three defendants were convicted of divulging military secrets and sentenced to prison terms; four were acquitted. In June the Court of Appeal found six of the defendants not guilty and reduced the sentence of the seventh defendant from 10 to three years' imprisonment. The second trial involved seven people charged with planting a bomb at the Passport Office in Doha in 1996. In November, five of them were sentenced to 10 years' imprisonment, one received three years' imprisonment and one was acquitted. The defence claimed that at least some of the

282

defendants were convicted on the basis of testimonies obtained under torture. No ruling on the issue of torture was known to have been made as the appeal proceedings had not been concluded by the end of the year.

Allegations of torture of detainees arrested during the year as well as of those held from previous years were received. In most cases torture was alleged to have occurred immediately following arrest and during interrogation, while the detainees were held in incommunicado detention. Reported methods of torture included beating with truncheons, particularly on the genitals; suspension of the detainees upside down for long periods so that they were compelled to urinate while suspended; dragging of the detainees on the floor; threats of rape or of killings of relatives; and electric shocks. The lawyer of 'Abd al-Hadi Jaber Hadi al-Rakib stated that his client's "confession" presented by the prosecution was obtained as a result of beatings and of the detention of his client's son in order to force the father to "confess".

An Amnesty International delegation visited Qatar in April. It attended sessions of two political trials and met government officials as well as members of the judiciary. Amnesty International was aware that in some individual cases, judges had ordered investigations into allegations of torture. However, Amnesty International urged the government to carry out independent investigations into all such allegations. It also called for the courts to exclude evidence which had been given under duress. Amnesty International recommended that pre-trial procedures at the military camp and at the *Mukhabarat* (the secret intelligence unit) in Doha, where most detainees said they had been tortured, should be reviewed in order to limit pre-trial incommunicado detention and the attendant risks of torture and ill-treatment. In response the government pointed out that Qatar's laws and procedures contained safeguards against torture, but did not specify whether any of the allegations of torture brought to its attention were actually investigated.

Amnesty International urged the government to ratify the International Covenant on Civil and Political Rights and the International Covenant on Economic, Social and Cultural Rights. Neither treaty had been ratified by the end of the year.

ROMANIA

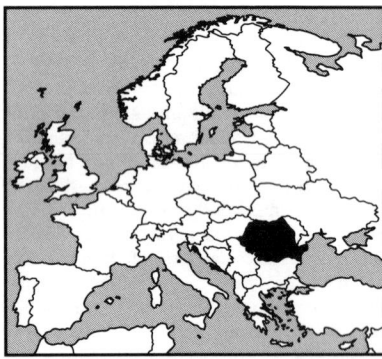

At least two prisoners of conscience were held. There were numerous reports of torture and ill-treatment, in at least one case resulting in death. Shootings by police officers in disputed circumstances resulted in at least one death. Some of the victims were Roma.

In February the government authorized the publication of the report of the European Committee for the Prevention of Torture and Inhuman or Degrading Treatment or Punishment on its visit to places of detention in Romania in September and October 1995. The Committee stated that "persons detained on suspicion of committing a crime, at the time of arrest and/or in the course of interrogation, face a not inconsiderable risk of being subjected by the police to ill-treatment, which is sometimes severe ill-treatment, even torture". Conditions of detention in the municipal police stations visited by the Committee in Bucharest, Cluj-Napoca and Timişoara were described as "at best mediocre, but often deplorable... [and] could justifiably be designated as inhuman and degrading". The Committee recommended that high priority should be given to human rights training of police officials at all levels, and to improving conditions, particularly overcrowding, in penitentiaries. The Committee issued extensive recommendations concerning the rights of all detainees. The government responded that the recommendations would be taken into consideration and steps taken to incorporate them into law. However, the government had failed to revise the Law Concerning the Execution of

Sanctions, which was last amended in 1973, by the end of the year.

In April the governing coalition elected Radu Vasile to be the new Prime Minister.

In May the government introduced in parliament a draft Penal Code and Penal Procedure Code, proposing to abolish Article 200, which criminalizes homosexual relations between consenting adults in private, and the first paragraphs of Articles 238 and 239, concerning defamation of public officials. The draft also proposed to reduce the sanctions for Articles 205 and 206, which make insult and libel criminal offences. In June, in recognition of this legislative proposal, the Parliamentary Assembly of the Council of Europe decided to end the procedure for monitoring Romania's compliance with the obligations and commitments accepted on admission to the Council of Europe (see *Amnesty International Report 1998*). Five days later, the Chamber of Deputies of Romania's parliament rejected the government's proposal to abolish Article 200 and the debate on the draft as a whole was closed.

Mariana Cetiner, a prisoner of conscience who had been arrested in October 1995 and sentenced to three years' imprisonment under Article 200, paragraph 5, of the Penal Code for attempting to seduce another woman, was released in March following a pardon by President Emil Constantinescu. The draft law abolishing Article 200 noted that all convictions under paragraphs 1 and 5 of the law would be officially re-examined by the courts responsible for the execution of the sentence. After the draft law was rejected by parliament, the authorities did not disclose the number of detainees still held under this law.

In August Cornel Sabou, a journalist, was arrested in Baia Mare. He had reported allegations made by some farmers that the judge used forged documents to take possession of their property. He was convicted of libelling a local judge and sentenced to 10 months' imprisonment, but was temporarily released in October after his sentence was suspended for three months. Cornel Sabou was a prisoner of conscience. In July Ovidiu Scutelnicu and Dragoș Sfîntu, journalists from Iași, were sentenced to one year's imprisonment for an article which the court found to be libellous of a judge. In their article the journalists speculated that a police colonel, who was in charge of investigating corruption cases, would be dismissed and stated that his wife, who is a judge, had tried some of the corruption cases. The colonel was reportedly suspended from duty on the same day that the article was published. The two journalists were at liberty pending an appeal.

Reports of torture and ill-treatment were numerous. Relatively few victims filed complaints and investigations in most cases appeared not to have been carried out promptly and impartially. The Minister of the Interior and police authorities repeatedly claimed that such incidents were rare. Nevertheless, information received from the office of the General Prosecutor indicated that a significant number of officers had been brought to justice for ill-treatment of detainees in their custody. In 1997 military prosecutors had indicted 48 law enforcement officials for the offence of "abusive conduct", 17 for "abusive investigations" and two for torture. In the first six months of 1998, 21 officers were indicted for "abusive conduct" and two officers for "abusive investigations".

One man died in suspicious circumstances, apparently as a result of ill-treatment. In August Elinoiu Toader was punched and kicked by a police officer in front of a store in Nereju, Vrancea county. The officer then reportedly instructed the owner of the store to take Elinoiu Toader behind the building and to beat him all over the body. The following morning Elinoiu Toader died in his sister's house. In the course of an investigation, a witness was allegedly beaten with a truncheon on the palms by another officer to induce him to sign a statement that Elinoiu Toader had died as a result of alcohol abuse. At least two other witnesses were also threatened by local police. A day before the autopsy was carried out, the police inspectorate issued a statement that Elinoiu Toader had died as a result of consumption of surgical spirit and that the body of the deceased did not bear any signs of violence. However, photographs of the body showed injuries that were consistent with the alleged beating, and the autopsy reportedly established that Elinoiu Toader had suffered three fractured ribs.

In September in Poiana Lacului, Argeș county, four boys were questioned by the police about a theft of a bicycle. One

284

13-year-old boy was allegedly beaten with a truncheon on the palms to make him confess to the theft. Another boy was hit on the head. Three police officers then arrested 23-year-old Nicolae Cazacu and questioned him for four or five hours. He was reportedly punched in the face and kicked. After refusing to sign a statement confessing to the theft, he was reportedly forced to lie on a table with his face down and severely beaten with a truncheon on the back until he fainted. He was then splashed with water and beaten with a truncheon on the palms. Following his release, Nicolae Cazacu was photographed and examined by a forensic medical expert who described in a certificate multiple injuries on the nose, both palms and the back, which were consistent with his allegations of torture. The three officers suspected of torture were still on duty in Poiana Lacului at the end of October.

Some of the victims of police beatings were members of the Romani community. In June in Săruleşti, Călăraşi county, dozens of police officers broke into Romani homes and were reported to have indiscriminately beaten men, women and children. Three officers reportedly beat Gabriel Mihai who then ran outside his house. One officer shot him in the back and the leg, seriously injuring him. Margareta Mihai was reportedly kicked in the back and then, while attempting to help her husband, hit with the butt of a gun in the face. Seven or eight officers who entered the home of Mihai Cristache punched and kicked him. They then handcuffed him to another Rom and pushed them into a van. The 10 detained Roma, who were held at the local police station for around five hours, were subsequently released without charge.

There were other reports of shootings by police officers in disputed circumstances. In May, following a fight in a discotheque in Codlea, 16-year-old Marian Ciulei, who was running to catch a train, was ordered by the police to stop. He was then shot in the back and later taken to hospital where he was treated for injuries to the lung, kidney and liver. His family reportedly did not file a complaint. The results of an official investigation, obligatory when the police use firearms, had not been made public by the end of the year.

In August in Oprişor a police officer came to arrest Constantin Stan to serve 108 days' imprisonment for disturbing the peace and public order. Constantin Stan reportedly attempted to flee and the police officer, after ordering him to stop, fired once into the air. He then shot him in the back, in the region of the right kidney. Constantin Stan died on the way to hospital. The results of an investigation into the shooting had not been made public by the end of the year.

In January the Ministry of the Interior published a report on cases Amnesty International had raised with the authorities in 1997.

In February Amnesty International wrote to the then Prime Minister, Victor Ciorbea, expressing concern about investigations into allegations of police torture and ill-treatment, noting what appeared to be a pattern of evasive responses by the authorities to communications from Amnesty International.

In March Amnesty International published a report, *Romania: A summary of human rights concerns*, which included extensive recommendations regarding legislative reforms and the prompt and thorough investigation of allegations of torture and ill-treatment by law enforcement officers. In June the authorities published a reply to this report, which outlined the government's proposal to revise the Penal Code and the Penal Procedure Code. However, it failed to provide Amnesty International with requested information concerning specific cases of police shootings, torture and ill-treatment.

RUSSIAN FEDERATION

At least one prisoner of conscience, a conscientious objector, was held. Torture and ill-treatment by law enforcement officers and within the armed forces continued. Conditions in penitentiaries and pre-trial detention centres amounted to cruel, inhuman or degrading treatment. One possible extrajudicial execution was reported.

About 900 prisoners remained under sentence of death. Legal provisions for asylum-seekers remained inadequate. In the Chechen Republic (Chechnya), at least one person was executed and up to 30 people faced imminent execution.

President Boris Yeltsin dismissed Prime Minister Viktor Chernomyrdin and his cabinet in March. The President's nominee for Prime Minister, Sergey Kirienko, was approved by parliament in April and formed a new cabinet. In August a financial crisis brought another change in government and Victor Chernomyrdin became Acting Prime Minister. A new Prime Minister, Evgeny Primakov, was appointed and a new government formed in September.

In October President Aslan Maskhadov dismissed the entire government of the Chechen Republic. A new government was approved in December and the parliament was suspended by the Supreme *Shari'a* Court, which ruled that it contravened Islamic law.

A presidential order issued in April outlined government undertakings for 1998 – proclaimed by President Yeltsin as "the year of human rights in the Russian Federation". The order included a list of federal laws concerning human rights, among them the law on alternative civilian service and the Code on Criminal Procedure, which were to be adopted. It also contained a list of international standards that were to be ratified. However, there was no reference to ratification of the Second Optional Protocol to the International Covenant on Civil and Political Rights, aiming at the abolition of the death penalty, or of Protocol No. 6 to the European Convention for the Protection of Human Rights and Fundamental Freedoms (European Convention on Human Rights) concerning the abolition of the death penalty.

In May the Russian Federation ratified the European Convention on Human Rights and the European Convention for the Prevention of Torture and Inhuman or Degrading Treatment or Punishment. In August the government pledged to abolish the death penalty by April 1999, although senior officials later spoke in favour of capital punishment. In September the Ministry of Justice took over the penitentiary system from the Interior Ministry; the transfer was one of the Russian Federa-

tion's commitments when it joined the Council of Europe in 1996.

By the end of 1998 no law introducing alternative civilian service had been adopted. Furthermore, under the 1997 law on freedom of conscience and religion, young men who claimed conscientious objection to military service based on their religious beliefs were often not considered as legitimate conscientious objectors by the courts.

One prisoner of conscience, Vitaliy Gushchin, a Jehovah's Witness from Kurchatovo, Kursk Region, was released in July pending further investigation of his case. He had served eight months of an 18-month prison sentence for refusing to carry out military service because of his religious beliefs. The Kursk Regional Court had ruled in December 1997 that Vitaliy Gushchin was a member of a "sect" and that his claims to religious beliefs were "groundless". Two other conscientious objectors, Vasiliy Bazhenov and Vsevolod Sukhanov, were awaiting trial.

Other prisoners of conscience continued to be detained pending trial. Oleg Pazyura, a human rights defender and retired naval officer arrested in 1997 and charged with "slander of a person or a public official" and "a threat or violent actions against a procurator, investigator, interrogator or other officials" (see *Amnesty International Report 1998*), was convicted in January, but immediately released under an amnesty.

Aleksandr Nikitin, a former prisoner of conscience, appeared before St Petersburg City Court in October on charges of treason and exposing state secrets (see *Amnesty International Reports 1997* and *1998*). After two weeks of hearings, the Court referred the case back to the Office of the Procurator for additional investigation. Aleksandr Nikitin continued to be under orders not to leave the city.

Torture and ill-treatment by law enforcement officers, including cases from previous years, were reported. In February the Supreme Court of the Republic of Mordovia convicted seven police officers of torturing criminal suspects and sentenced them to prison terms ranging from three to nine and a half years. The case was brought after a series of incidents, including the death in 1995 of Oleg Igonin, who was arrested on suspicion of burglary and tortured by several police officers. He was

286

asphyxiated when officers put a gas mask on him and cut off the air supply, a method known as "elephant" torture.

Mikhail Yurochko, who was arrested in 1993 in Arkhangelsk and charged with murder, had reportedly been tortured and ill-treated in order to extract a confession. He had only been allowed to see his lawyer three weeks after arrest. He was reported to have been severely beaten and deprived of food, raped by cell mates with the complicity of the prison authorities, and told that he would be driven to suicide. Two co-defendants, Yevgeny Mednikov and Dmitry Elsakov, alleged they were similarly tortured. Although all three reportedly had alibis, Mikhail Yurochko and Yevgeny Mednikov were sentenced to death. Dmitry Elsakov was sentenced to 15 years' imprisonment. In 1995 the Supreme Court of the Russian Federation overturned the death sentences and sent back the case to the court of first instance for additional investigation. Mikhail Yurochko and Dmitry Elsakov were released in July when the legal terms of their pre-trial detention expired; Yevgeny Mednikov remained in prison for a separate conviction. In December the investigation concluded. However, the case had not been sent to court by the end of the year because the Office of the Procurator General intervened and decided to review the case because the confessions had allegedly been extracted under torture and to consider transferring the investigation to another regional procurator.

In December 1997 Larisa Kharchenko was released from pre-trial detention where she had been held incommunicado and reportedly denied medical treatment (see *Amnesty International Report 1998*).

Reports of torture in the armed forces continued to be received. In May it was reported that a young soldier serving in the Russian army, stationed in the town of Budyonnovsk, Stavropol Territory, had been beaten to death by an older soldier for refusing to mend his shoe. He was reportedly the 14th soldier killed by *dedovshchina* (the practice of bullying and humiliating new recruits) in the 205th Brigade in 18 months. During this period over 350 soldiers reportedly complained of torture and ill-treatment to the Budyonnovsk and Stavropol committees of Soldiers' Mothers. In October the Office of the Procurator General stated that it was con-

cerned about the abuses. No investigation was known to have been set up into the allegations of torture.

Viktor Fyodorovich Andreyev remained in a pre-trial detention centre in Moscow where, according to his lawyer, he was deliberately denied medical treatment despite being near death from tuberculosis. He had been arrested in 1995, while serving in the Russian army in Chechnya, for the murder of his commanding officer, who had allegedly tortured him and other conscripts. According to his lawyer, the military justice authorities wanted to avoid bringing the case to court to avert a precedent-setting verdict of manslaughter in self-defence, rather than murder.

In September the Chief Military Procurator stated that 25 investigations into compliance with legislation aimed at protecting servicemen since August 1997 had revealed 605 crimes, of which 270 qualified as *dedovshchina*.

Conditions in penitentiaries and pre-trial detention centres that hold up to a million people continued to amount to cruel, inhuman or degrading treatment. Prisons were grossly overcrowded. Thousands of detainees had to sleep in shifts, often without bedding. Many cells were filthy and pest-ridden, with inadequate light and ventilation. Food and medical supplies were frequently inadequate. Diseases and mental illness were widespread. A new amnesty law for detainees announced in October, reportedly aimed at easing overcrowding, was expected to lead to the release of up to 115,000 people from pre-trial detention centres. Under the December 1997 amnesty law, only 14,290 people were released, according to official figures, even though the law applied to at least 267,000 people.

One possible extrajudicial execution was reported. The body of Larisa Yudina, a journalist and editor of the opposition newspaper *Sovetskaya Kalmykia* in the Republic of Kalmykia, was found in June in a pond near the city of Elista with a fractured skull and multiple stab wounds. She had been repeatedly warned to stop her critical reporting on Kalmykian President Kirsan Ilyumzhinov, whom she accused of corruption. On the night she was killed, a man reportedly telephoned her, offering documents relating to her investigation of corruption. She reportedly went to meet the man and never returned. A criminal investigation into her killing was opened and three men were reportedly detained as suspects.

Galina Starovoitova, a member of parliament and co-Chairperson of the Democratic Russia Party, was killed in St Petersburg in November. She was an outspoken critic of corruption among the political elite, an opponent of the communists and nationalists in parliament, and an active human rights defender. According to police, a man and a woman shot Galina Starovoitova and one of her aides, Ruslan Linkov, in the stairwell of her apartment. Galina Starovoitova died instantly; her aide suffered serious head wounds. Two days before her murder, eight officers of the Russian Federal Security Services (FSB) alleged at a press conference that the FSB had been involved in extortion, terrorism, hostage-taking and contract killing.

In April the government stated that 894 prisoners remained under sentence of death. However, in October the Minister of Justice said the figure was 839. No executions had been reported since August 1996. One execution was reported in Chechnya in 1998 (see below).

Legal provisions for asylum-seekers remained inadequate. Many people remained at risk of return to countries where they would be in danger of human rights violations. Guram Absandze, Minister of Finance in the Georgian government of former President Zviad Gamsakhurdia and Vice-President of the "Georgian Government in Exile", was arrested in the Russian Federation in March, allegedly at the request of the Georgian authorities. He was forcibly returned to Georgia later that month and was immediately detained pending trial. It was feared that he might be ill-treated.

In February the Russian Constitutional Court ruled again to abolish the need for residence permits, known as the *propiska* system. The government at federal and local level had failed to inform law enforcement officials that the system was abolished, or that federal laws and the Constitution overrode local regulations. People continued to be detained by police for not having a permit, particularly people from ethnic minorities.

In the Chechen Republic, at least one person was executed and up to 30 others were facing imminent execution. Salan Bakharchiyev was sentenced to death by the Chechen Supreme *Shari'a* Court for murder. He was executed in June. Assa Larsanova again faced imminent execution after giving birth in prison in Grozny, the capital (see *Amnesty International Report 1998*). In June the scope of the death penalty in Chechnya was widened to include blood feud murders.

Continuing abductions of journalists, media employees, humanitarian aid workers and Russian political representatives in Chechnya led to questions about the ability of both the Russian and Chechen authorities to guarantee the safety of civilians and to allegations of acquiescence by Chechen officials in such abuses. Among those taken hostage were Valentin Vlasov, the Russian President's plenipotentiary representative in Chechnya, who was abducted in May and released in November. In October the body of Akmal Saidov, a departmental head at the Russian Federation mission in Chechnya, was found near the border between Chechnya and Ingushetia a few days after he was kidnapped. A note attached to the body was allegedly signed "the wolves of Islam". In October, three United Kingdom nationals and one New Zealander working in Chechnya were abducted in Grozny; their bodies were recovered in December. The Chechen government responded by introducing a state of emergency and initiating a crackdown on crime. In December French aid worker Vincent Cochetel, who had been kidnapped in January, was released.

Amnesty International continued to urge the authorities to release prisoners of conscience immediately and unconditionally, and to enact legislation creating alternative civilian service of non-punitive length.

In May an Amnesty International delegation visited the Russian Federation and met official bodies, victims of human rights abuses, human rights defenders, and women's groups. Amnesty International urged the government to introduce an effective system of independent inspections and public control of all places of detention. Amnesty International's delegation was refused access to pre-trial detention centres.

In response to the authorities' invitation to contribute to the drafting of a federal program for the protection of human

288

rights and fundamental freedoms, Amnesty International presented a "Working Document" setting out 51 recommendations to improve human rights protection in line with international standards. Senior officials responded, stating that lack of financial resources, the transition to the market economy and the high level of crime were the main obstacles to adequate protection of human rights.

In June Amnesty International received assurances from the Russian Minister of Internal Affairs that all steps would be taken to stop torture and ill-treatment of suspects in custody by law enforcement officials and that all such allegations would be promptly investigated and the perpetrators brought to justice.

In March Amnesty International urged Chechen President Aslan Maskhadov to grant clemency to all prisoners under sentence of death. The organization also called for revision of the provisions of the Chechen *Shari'a* Criminal Code, which provide for the death penalty and corporal punishments, with a view to abolishing the death penalty and all acts which constitute cruel, inhuman or degrading punishments.

RWANDA

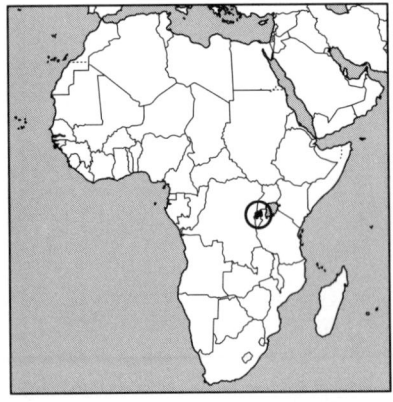

Thousands of unarmed civilians were killed by the security forces and armed opposition groups. There was a sharp increase in "disappearances". More than 130,000 people were detained, many for prolonged periods without charge or trial, most of them accused of involvement in the 1994 genocide. Conditions in many detention centres amounted to cruel, inhuman or degrading treatment. Ill-treatment of detainees was reported. At least 800 people were tried on charges of participation in the genocide, some in unfair trials. At least 74 people were sentenced to death for participation in the 1994 genocide and 22 were executed. At least 12 other people were sentenced to death. At least two people were summarily executed without trial. Hundreds of Burundian refugees returned to Burundi, many apparently under duress.

Armed conflict continued, mostly in the northwest of the country, between the Rwandese Patriotic Army (RPA) and insurgent groups that included members of the *Forces armées rwandaises*, (the former Rwandese army), known as ex-FAR, and *interahamwe* militia who participated in the 1994 genocide. Both the RPA and the armed opposition carried out widespread, deliberate killings of civilians. The conflict caused large-scale population displacement. In the second half of the year, hundreds of thousands of people were living in camps in Gisenyi and Ruhengeri, in very poor conditions; some had reportedly been moved there by force.

In August fighting broke out in the Democratic Republic of the Congo (DRC – see DRC entry) between Congolese armed groups and government forces of DRC President Laurent-Désiré Kabila. RPA troops were present in eastern DRC, backing the armed opposition. There were also reports of members of the ex-FAR and *interahamwe* militia fighting alongside DRC government forces.

In July the UN Human Rights Field Operation for Rwanda (UNHRFOR) withdrew from Rwanda after the government and the UN High Commissioner for Human Rights failed to agree on a review of its mandate. Its activities had been suspended in May. The government had insisted that monitoring and reporting on the human rights situation be dropped from UNHRFOR's mandate, claiming that national organizations, including the newly established but not yet functional National Human Rights Commission, could take on these functions.

In April the UN Security Council adopted a resolution to reactivate the commission of inquiry set up in 1995 to investigate transfers of arms and equipment to the ex-FAR (see previous *Amnesty*

International Reports). The commission's final report, issued in November, described the presence and activities of the ex-FAR in a number of countries, and stated that the free flow of small arms was a major cause of insecurity and instability in the region. The report asked the Security Council to reaffirm its arms embargo on the ex-FAR and proposed broader measures to address uncontrolled arms flows and to ensure respect for arms embargoes. However, it included no reference to grave human rights violations carried out by parties other than the ex-FAR and their allies, and did not mention killings of thousands of civilians by Rwandese security forces.

The government did not report on measures to investigate and bring to justice members of its security forces responsible for massacres committed in the DRC in 1996 and 1997, as requested by the UN Security Council (see **DRC** entry).

The Special Representative of the UN Commission on Human Rights visited Rwanda three times. His report to the UN General Assembly included recommendations to ensure that the National Human Rights Commission could be fully established and function effectively and independently.

Thousands of people, including many vulnerable people such as the elderly and young children, were unlawfully killed by members of the security forces, the majority in the context of military operations in the northwest. In some cases, soldiers were arrested for their alleged participation in such killings. However, in the majority of cases, no action was known to have been taken to bring the perpetrators to justice. Hundreds of people were killed in Mukingo, Ruhengeri, in January and February. They included more than 200 people reportedly killed by RPA soldiers in Shingiro and Muhingo on 21 January, around half of whom were young children and babies. The victims also included around 50 young men whose arms were reportedly tied behind their backs before they were shot dead. More than 120 people were reportedly killed by RPA soldiers assisted by armed Tutsi civilians in Nyabirehe, Mukingo, on 24 January. Some were killed with bayonets and knives, some had their heads crushed with large stones or rocks, and some, mainly women and children, were reportedly burned alive in their homes.

Also in January more than 300 unarmed civilians were killed by RPA soldiers in Rubavu, Gisenyi, including more than 200 killed at Keya, Muhira. The victims included Emmanuel Rutikanga, a judicial official, his wife Thérèse Mujawayezu, a primary-school teacher, and their four children. On 12 May around 150 civilians were reportedly killed by RPA soldiers in Birembo, in Giciye, Gisenyi. The victims included elderly people such as Rubyeyi, aged 84, and children such as Uwamahoro, aged nine. In mid-July around 250 civilians were reportedly killed by RPA soldiers at Nanga, Nkuli, Ruhengeri. The victims included entire families who happened to live in the area; the RPA soldiers reportedly accused them of supporting the armed groups. Some of the victims' bodies were thrown into nearby latrines.

Seth Sendashonga, former Minister of the Interior in Rwanda and leader of a Rwandese opposition party in exile, was shot dead in Kenya in May. The assassination was believed to be linked to his criticisms of the Rwandese government and his denunciation of human rights violations in Rwanda (see **Kenya** entry).

Armed opposition groups carried out many deliberate and arbitrary killings of unarmed civilians. On 19 January around 40 people were killed in an attack on a bus carrying workers of a brewery in Gisenyi. Many of the passengers were trapped and burned alive after petrol was poured over the bus and set alight. Others were shot dead as they tried to escape. On 5 February more than 40 civilians were killed by an armed opposition group in Jenda, Nkuli, Ruhengeri; the victims included Sebahutu, Mucocori, Nzabarinda and Gaudence. The following night, up to 60 people were killed with machetes, bayonets and knives at a settlement of displaced persons at Byahi, Gisenyi. In June at least 25 people were killed at Nkamira, Gisenyi, at another settlement of internally displaced persons.

People perceived as collaborators with the authorities were also among those targeted by armed opposition groups. Charles Komeza and his wife Laurence Nyirampundu, both in their seventies, were among nine people killed in Nyabikenke, Gitarama, in March. Both their bodies were reportedly found decapitated.

There were reports of hostage-taking by armed opposition groups. On 19 September,

290

after an unsuccessful attack on a military position, an armed group reportedly abducted several people in Birembo, in Giciye, Gisenyi, and killed at least one of them, Mavugabandi.

There were many cases of killings of civilians where the identity of the perpetrators remained unknown or where there were contradictory reports about who was responsible. On 16 August, 14 people were killed by unidentified perpetrators in Nyamagana, near Ruhango, Gitarama. The victims included the wife and children of Emmanuel Gasana – an Anglican pastor who had recently been released from prison – and Joseph Karamage, another pastor and a school official. On 12 July at least 34 people were killed in an inn at Tare, in Rural Kigali, where people had gathered to watch a football match. Some were shot dead, others were stabbed or burned to death. The attack was widely reported as having been carried out by an armed opposition group. However, several eyewitnesses claimed that the assailants were RPA soldiers.

The number of "disappearances" rose sharply during the year. Many of the "disappeared" were presumed dead. Others were believed to be held in detention centres to which access was denied. In the vast majority of cases, no conclusive investigation was known to have been carried out. Ladislas Mutabazi, prosecutor of Gisenyi, was reportedly last seen on 18 January with an RPA soldier at Base, near Ruhengeri, where he was visiting relatives. Investigations were launched by the Ministry of Justice and the gendarmerie, but their results were not known. Onesphore Byampiliye, a businessman, was led away by RPA soldiers in Rubavu, Gisenyi, on 28 June. He was never seen again. His wife, Immaculée Twagiramariya, was reportedly killed by soldiers the following day.

Scores of people "disappeared" in Umutara in the east in late December 1997 and January 1998. The victims were mostly former refugees in Tanzania who had returned to Rwanda in late 1996. They were reportedly rounded up from various locations and taken away by RPA soldiers assisted by local Tutsi civilians. The victims included Abraham Ndumviriye, aged around 80, his two sons, Joseph Tegeri and Seth Rwamirera, and their wives and children.

More than 130,000 people were detained in civilian prisons and detention centres across Rwanda, most of them awaiting trial on accusations of participation in the 1994 genocide. In addition, an unknown number were detained in military detention centres to which access to families and other visitors was denied. In October the Minister of Justice announced that around 10,000 detainees who did not have a case file would be released; a few hundred had been released by the end of the year. Several thousand detainees indicated their willingness to confess under the plea-bargaining system.

In many detention centres, conditions amounting to cruel, inhuman or degrading treatment continued to cause serious health problems and led to deaths of detainees.

Cases of torture or ill-treatment were reported, usually at the time of arrest and interrogation, and during detention in the *cachots communaux* (local detention centres) and military detention centres. Tharcisse Rusagara, director of a primary school in Bicumbi, Rural Kigali, was reportedly beaten on the arm and back by soldiers with rifle butts after his arrest in February. Another man testified that he was badly beaten all over his body in a local detention centre in Kicukiro in Kigali town after his arrest in January; he was initially denied access to medical treatment for injuries caused by the beatings.

At least 800 people were tried on charges of participation in the 1994 genocide. Although certain aspects of the trials were better than earlier trials (see previous *Amnesty International Reports*), most defendants continued to be denied a trial within a reasonable time. More witnesses testified during trials than before, but securing the presence of witnesses remained difficult, especially for the defence. More defendants had access to lawyers than in 1997, but this access mostly remained limited to trial and post-trial phases. Most trials taking place in areas of armed conflict proceeded without lawyers, who would generally not risk travelling there. Legislation establishing a compensation fund for the victims of the genocide was adopted, although victims still awaited compensation. The work of the Court of Cassation became paralysed after the suspension of several judges, including the Court's President, who subsequently resigned.

The International Criminal Tribunal for Rwanda (ICTR) based in Arusha, Tanzania, announced its first judgments. Among those sentenced was Jean Kambanda, former Prime Minister in the interim government at the time of the genocide, who received life imprisonment after pleading guilty to six charges including genocide and crimes against humanity. Jean-Paul Akayesu, a former local official, was also sentenced to life imprisonment. By the end of the year, 32 people were held in Arusha.

At least 74 people were sentenced to death by the national courts for their role in the genocide. On 24 April, 22 people were executed in public, the first executions of people found guilty of participation in the genocide. Several of them had received an unfair trial, including Silas Munyagishali, former assistant prosecutor of Kigali, whose arrest may have been politically motivated and in whose trial defence witnesses had been threatened and effectively prevented from testifying. Déogratias Bizimana and Egide Gatanazi, two of those executed, had no access to a defence lawyer (see previous *Amnesty International Reports*).

Four RPA soldiers were sentenced to death in January by a military court of appeal in connection with the assassination of Captain Théoneste Hategekimana in 1997; they had initially been sentenced to life imprisonment (see *Amnesty International Report 1998*). The same month two RPA soldiers accused of murder, Gaspard Mutabazi and Emmanuel Rutayisire, were summarily executed in public in Ruhengeri and Gisenyi without a trial. In November a military court confirmed the death sentences of RPA Captain Godfrey Ntukayagemo and Corporal John Simbaburanga, convicted of the murder of two women in August.

In May, six people were sentenced to death in Cyangugu in connection with the killing of five members of UNHRFOR in 1997 (see *Amnesty International Report 1998*).

Hundreds of Burundian refugees returned home from Rwanda. Many appeared to have been coerced into returning to Burundi despite widespread human rights abuses there. It appeared that many refugees' decision to return was motivated primarily by unfavourable factors in Rwanda, including ill-treatment and threats by the security forces and harsh conditions in the refugee camps.

Amnesty International raised its concerns with the authorities throughout the year. In June it published a report, *Rwanda: The hidden violence – "disappearances" and killings continue*, based in part on the findings of an Amnesty International visit to Rwanda in February. During the visit, Amnesty International delegates discussed human rights concerns with senior government and military officials.

In April Amnesty International published *International Criminal Tribunal for Rwanda: Trials and tribulations*, which expressed concern about several aspects of the ICTR's work, including a weak witness protection scheme. In September Amnesty International welcomed the first judgments of the ICTR, but regretted that it had taken the ICTR so long to issue them.

Amnesty International campaigned for the UNHRFOR to be allowed to remain in Rwanda and for monitoring and reporting to remain in its mandate.

Amnesty International welcomed the resumption of the work of the UN commission of inquiry into arms transfers to the ex-FAR and recommended that the commission's mandate be broadened to cover arms transfers to other armed groups as well as to security forces in the Great Lakes region, in recognition of the fact that grave human rights abuses were being carried out by all parties.

SAUDI ARABIA

Scores of people were arrested as suspected political or religious opponents of the government, including possible prisoners of conscience. Many were held in secret detention. Political prisoners, believed to number in the hundreds, including possible prisoners of conscience, arrested in previous years remained held without trial and possibly without charge. At least one possible prisoner of conscience continued to serve a prison sentence imposed after a grossly unfair trial. There were continued allegations of torture and ill-treatment. Two people were reported to have died in custody in circumstances which suggested that torture was a contributory factor. The cruel judicial punishments of amputation and flogging continued to be imposed. An

292 unknown number of people were sentenced to death and at least 29 people were executed after trials which fell far short of international standards. At least 37 foreign nationals were forcibly returned to their country where they were at risk of serious human rights violations.

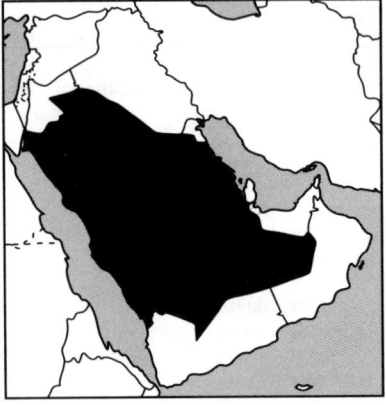

The government of King Fahd bin 'Abdul-'Aziz continued to enforce a ban on political parties and trade unions. Press censorship also continued to be strictly enforced. Information on human rights violations remained severely limited. The government continued to impose restrictions on access to the country by international human rights organizations.

Scores of people were arrested as suspected political or religious opponents of the government or on political or religious grounds, including possible prisoners of conscience. They included tens of Christians who were apparently detained solely for their religious beliefs. They also reportedly included scores of so-called Arab Afghan veterans – people who had taken part in armed conflicts in Afghanistan and Bosnia – who were arrested in the first few months of the year. Some of those arrested were understood to have been subsequently released.

Suha al-Mas'ari was arrested in Jeddah in November, upon arrival from the United Kingdom (UK). She was reportedly taken to al-Ha'ir prison in Riyadh. The reasons for her arrest were not clear, but were reportedly connected to her kinship to the exiled Muhammad al-Mas'ari, in which case she would have been a prisoner of conscience. She was released without charge in December.

Up to 30 Christian migrant workers were arrested in Riyadh in June, reportedly after a copy of the Bible was found outside a house. They were arrested purely for their religious beliefs and were prisoners of conscience. Among those arrested were Ariel Ordona, Angelito Sison, Juanito Manalili and Ruban Aguire, all Philippine nationals, and Wim Den Hartog, a Dutch national. They were reportedly held in incommunicado detention. Yolanda Aguilar, a Philippine national, who was heavily pregnant at the time of the June arrests, was interrogated in hospital shortly after giving birth. She was ordered to remain under house arrest until her husband returned from the Philippines to be questioned about his religious activities. All of those arrested were reported to have been released without charge in July and deported.

Political prisoners believed to number hundreds, including possible prisoners of conscience, arrested in previous years continued to be held without trial. At least several others arrested with them were released during the year. Those still held included so-called Arab Afghan veterans as well as Shi'a and Sunni Muslim critics or opponents of the government. Among the latter were Sheikh Salman bin Fahd al-'Awda and Sheikh Safr 'Abd al-Rahman al-Hawali, both arrested in 1994, and Dr Nasser al-'Umr, arrested in 1995. All three remained held in al-Ha'ir Prison throughout 1998 (see *Amnesty International Report 1997*). Bander Fahd al-Shihri, who was arrested on political grounds in 1997 after he was forcibly returned to Saudi Arabia from Canada, also remained detained without trial (see *Amnesty International Report 1998*). Scores of prisoners, including possible prisoners of conscience and political prisoners, detained in the wake of the 1996 bombing of the US military complex of al-Khobar, remained held without trial and possibly without charge.

Also held without charge or trial were Farzana Kauzar, a Pakistan national, and her three children – Muhammad Assad Ijaz, aged three, Fakeyha Ijaz, aged six, and Muhammad Sa'ad, aged nine. Arrested in October 1997, they were held under house arrest until their release in July. At times they were also held in secret detention and the children were separated from their mother and from each other during interrogation. The family was believed to have been held in order to force the children's father, Ahmed Muhammad Ijaz, to return to Saudi Arabia. He was apparently sought by the authorities as a possible witness to a business dispute. Farzana Kauzar and her three children were prisoners of conscience held solely because of their relationship to Ahmed Muhammad Ijaz.

At least one possible prisoner of conscience continued to serve a prison sentence imposed after a grossly unfair trial. 'Ali al-'Utaybi was sentenced in 1996 to three years in prison on charges reportedly including having contact with the Committee for the Defence of Legitimate Rights (CDLR), an illegal organization based abroad.

Among the political prisoners released during the year were Muhsen Hussain al-'Awaji, Ibrahim 'Abd al-Rahman al-Hudayf, Muhammad 'Abd al-Rahman al-Hudayf, Naser Ibrahim al-Barak, Salih Mansur al-Barak, Khalid 'Abdallah Salih al-Yahya, Sultan 'Abd al-'Aziz al-Suwaylem and Sultan 'Abd al-Muhsen al-Khamis. All eight were arrested in 1994 on charges relating to an alleged attack against a security officer and for having links with the CDLR (see *Amnesty International Report 1996*). They were sentenced in 1995 to prison terms ranging from three to 18 years after trials which fell far short of international standards for fair trial. Ibrahim 'Abd al-Rahman al-Hudayf was sentenced to 300 lashes in addition to 18 years' imprisonment. A number of leading Shi'a clerics, arrested in 1996 in the wake of the al-Khobar bombing, were also released. They included Sheikh Ja'far 'Ali al-Mubarak, Sheikh 'Abd al-Karim al-Hobail, Sayyed Hashim al-Shekuss and Sheikh Hussain al-'Abbas (see *Amnesty International Report 1997*).

There were allegations of torture and ill-treatment. Dr Omran Muhammad, a Kuwaiti national visiting Saudi Arabia for the *Hajj* pilgrimage, was reportedly detained in April, apparently in connection with his political views, and held in the *al-Mabahith al-'Amma* (General Intelligence) headquarters in the city of al-Madina and then in deportation prisons in al-Madina and Jeddah. During his detention he was allegedly beaten, kicked and suspended upside down with chains for periods of several hours. He was allegedly denied contact with the Kuwaiti embassy and his family. He was released without charge and deported to Kuwait at the end of April.

There were reports that two prisoners died in custody in circumstances which suggested that torture may have been a contributory factor. Muhammad al-Hayek was reported to have died in June in the *al-Mabahith al-'Amma* headquarters in al-Dammam. He had been detained for more than two years without charge or trial. He was reportedly held incommunicado and there was no known official investigation into the cause of death.

Ahmad bin Ahmad al-Mubalbil, a prayer leader from al-Jufer village in al-Ihsa, died reportedly in November while in the custody of members of the *Hay'at al-Amr bil Ma'ruf Wan-Nahi 'an al-Munkar*, Committee for the Propagation of Virtue and Prevention of Vice. His relatives were said to have refused to collect his body and were reported to have lodged a complaint with the Ministry of the Interior. The exact reasons for the arrest of Ahmad bin Ahmad al-Mubalbil were not known, but they were believed to be connected to his religious practices.

Cruel judicial punishments continued to be imposed, although information about court cases and the carrying out of such punishments was limited. In October Nasser bin Khamis bin 'Abdullah al-Malluhi, a Saudi Arabian, and Sa'id bin 'Abd Al-Razak Sayyed Madkur, an Egyptian, both reportedly had a hand amputated after being found guilty of theft. The judicial punishment of flogging also continued to be imposed routinely.

At least 29 people were executed after grossly unfair trials conducted in secret and without legal assistance; all were convicted of murder or rape. Most of those executed were Saudi Arabian; others were migrant workers from Egypt, India, Pakistan and the Philippines. Two executions were carried out on the same day in July: one was of Yolando Isanan from the Philippines, who had been found guilty of murdering four people; the other was of Mud'ij bin Musib bin Nasir al-Subay'i, a Saudi Arabian, who had been convicted of murder. No details of court proceedings were made public. In the cases of Yolando Isanan and other foreign nationals executed in Saudi Arabia, neither the families nor the relevant embassies were believed to have been informed of the executions until after they had been carried out.

294

The exact number of prisoners who remained under sentence of death at the end of the year was not known as the government continued to keep such information secret. Those arrested in connection with capital offences during 1998 included Eugenio Catapang, Reynaldo Dela Cruz and Taha Pagayocan, all Philippine nationals, who were arrested in February on drug-related charges. Joel Blaza, also from the Philippines, was arrested in April on charges relating to possession of drugs and firearms. Dozens of people arrested on capital offences in previous years remained at risk of execution. They included four Pakistani men, arrested in 1997 in connection with drug trafficking. Ten Pakistani women arrested with them were reportedly released and deported to Pakistan. Sarah Dematera, a Philippine national who was convicted of murdering her employer in 1992, also remained under sentence of death (see *Amnesty International Report 1997*). However, Deborah Parry, a nurse and UK national, who had reportedly been convicted of murder, was released from prison in May after being pardoned by King Fahd bin 'Abdul-'Aziz. The verdict and sentence were never officially announced. Her colleague, Lucille McLauchlan, also a UK national, was also pardoned and released in May. She had been found guilty of being an accessory to murder and was sentenced to eight years in prison and 500 lashes (see *Amnesty International Report 1998*).

At least 35 Libyans, including three children, and two Egyptians were forcibly returned to their countries where they were at risk of torture. Among them were 31 Libyans, including Hamida al-Wa'ir and her son Youssef, aged about 19 months, who were forcibly returned to Libya in April or May (see **Libya** entry). The Libyans were among scores of foreign and Saudi Arabian nationals arrested in the wake of the November 1995 bombing of the Saudi Arabian National Guard training centre in Riyadh, the capital. They had been held without trial in al-Ruwais prison in Jeddah since their arrest in December 1995. The forcible return coincided with the signing of a security agreement in April by Arab Ministers of the Interior and Justice. Among other things, the agreement encourages extradition of suspected "terrorists". A family of four Libyans, including Mohammad

Shabou, aged five, and Ahmad Shabou, aged four, who were arrested in January, were also forcibly returned to Libya where all four were detained. The family had been granted refugee status in the UK in November 1997. They were arrested in Saudi Arabia, reportedly after overstaying a two-week visa which allowed them to go on pilgrimage to Mecca. Al-Sayyid Mohammad Shabou, the father, remained in custody in Libya at the end of the year where he was believed to be at risk of torture.

In communications to the Saudi Arabian government Amnesty International requested clarification of the reasons for the arrest and detention of political detainees and called for the immediate and unconditional release of all prisoners of conscience and for fair trials in accordance with international standards for all others held on political grounds. The organization also called for reports of torture to be investigated, for anyone found responsible to be brought to justice, and for the commutation of all sentences of flogging, amputation and death. No response was received from the government.

In April Amnesty International updated its previous submissions on Saudi Arabia for review by the UN Commission on Human Rights under a procedure established by UN Economic and Social Council Resolutions 728F/1503, for confidential consideration of communications about human rights violations. Amnesty International deplored the Commission's decision to discontinue its consideration of Saudi Arabia under the 1503 procedure despite the persistent pattern of gross human rights violations in the country.

SENEGAL

More than 160 alleged supporters of an armed separatist organization in the Casamance region, some of them arrested in previous years, remained detained without trial; most appeared to be prisoners of conscience. Trade unionists and human rights defenders, including prisoners of conscience, were arrested during the year. There were reports of torture and ill-treatment. The army was responsible for "disappearances" and extrajudicial executions in Casamance. Armed

separatists in Casamance also committed human rights abuses, including deliberate and arbitrary killings of civilians.

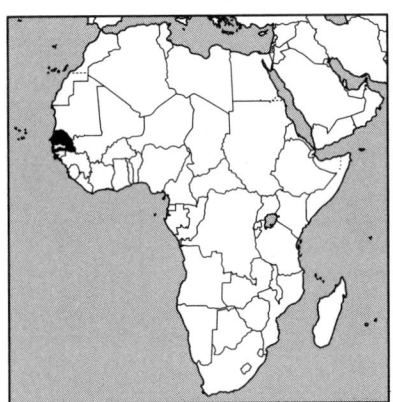

In January Father Diamacoune Senghor, Secretary General of the *Mouvement des Forces Démocratiques de Casamance* (MFDC), Democratic Forces of Casamance Movement, made a new call for a negotiated settlement in Casamance. He asked the MFDC to stop laying anti-personnel landmines, killing civilians and destroying property. He also said for the first time that the MFDC was ready to give up its demand for Casamance's independence. Despite his call, tension continued in the region, notably after the intervention of Senegalese troops in neighbouring Guinea-Bissau (see **Guinea-Bissau** entry).

In May, despite claims of fraud made by the opposition parties, the general elections passed off peacefully. The ruling *Parti Socialiste*, Socialist Party, won a majority in the national assembly.

More than 160 suspected MFDC sympathizers remained in prison without trial throughout the year. About 90 had been arrested in 1995 and at least 60 since September 1997. Most appeared to be prisoners of conscience, arrested because they were members of the Diola community. They were charged with "threatening state security", but no evidence was produced of their individual responsibility for acts of violence (see previous *Amnesty International Reports*).

In July, following a strike by electricity workers, 26 trade unionists were detained, including Mademba Sock, leader of SUT-ELEC, the electricity workers' union. They were charged with sabotage, but appeared to have been detained because they opposed the privatization of the state-owned electricity company. All had been released by the end of the year, except Mademba Sock and another trade unionist who were sentenced to six months' imprisonment in December.

Human rights defenders were also targeted. In April Professor Cheikh Saad Bouh Kamara, President of the *Association mauritanienne des droits de l'homme*, Mauritanian Human Rights Association, was detained in Dakar as he was about to attend a meeting on human rights and expelled to Mauritania. In October Anquiling Diabone, the Casamance regional representative of the Senegalese human rights organization, *Rencontre africaine pour la défense des droits de l'homme*, African Conference for the Defence of Human Rights, was arrested at a military checkpoint 40 kilometres from Ziguinchor, the main city in Casamance. He was held for four hours and severely beaten by soldiers.

Many Casamance civilians arrested by the security forces were reportedly tortured or ill-treated while held incommunicado for up to 10 days before being presented before an examining judge. A number of them were allegedly burned with petrol-filled plastic bottles set alight. None of these allegations were investigated.

Despite official promises, no steps were taken to end the impunity enjoyed by members of the security forces. None of the nine police officers and gendarmes charged in 1995 and 1996 with acts of torture had been tried by the end of the year (see *Amnesty International Report 1998*). Following protests by a human rights organization, an inquiry was opened into the beating to death of Moussa Ndom by police officers in February in Dakar.

In May security forces fired live ammunition to break up a student demonstration in Saint-Louis, Senegal's second city. Nine students and one policeman were hurt in these clashes. The university was subsequently closed.

The army was responsible for "disappearances" and extrajudicial executions in Casamance. In April Djoumondong Bassène, Louis Bassène, Babao Manga and Lamine Tendeng were detained in Djiromaïte. They were reportedly asked to dig their own graves and then shot. Adrien

296

Sambou "disappeared" after being arrested by soldiers in Kabrousse in July. In November soldiers broke into Djifangor Banjal, a neighbourhood near Ziguinchor, and killed some 30 civilians in a door-to-door search for MFDC rebels. The fate of those who "disappeared" in previous years remained unknown (see previous *Amnesty International Reports*).

The MFDC was also responsible for human rights abuses, including deliberate and arbitrary killings of civilians, some of whom were targeted because of their ethnic origin. In February suspected MFDC members killed seven fishermen in Saloulou. The same month, six people suspected of supporting the Senegalese authorities were killed in Singuere.

In February Amnesty International published a report, *Senegal: Terror in Casamance,* in which it called for the immediate and unconditional release of anyone detained in the context of the conflict in Casamance where there was no evidence of their direct participation in a recognizably criminal offence. The report also denounced human rights abuses committed by both sides against civilians. President Abdou Diouf dismissed the report as a "web of untruths and lies". In April the Senegalese authorities published a white paper about the Casamance crisis, but this failed to answer Amnesty International's questions, notably concerning extrajudicial executions and "disappearances".

SIERRA LEONE

The Armed Forces Revolutionary Council (AFRC) continued to detain prisoners of conscience without charge or trial and was responsible for torture and extrajudicial executions. After their removal from power in February, the AFRC and the armed opposition Revolutionary United Front (RUF) killed and mutilated thousands of unarmed civilians. A civilian militia supporting the government of President Ahmad Tejan Kabbah, the Civil Defence Forces (CDF), was also responsible for extrajudicial executions and torture, although on a significantly smaller scale. Hundreds of people alleged to have collaborated with the AFRC and RUF were detained without charge by the reinstated government. Thirty-four soldiers were

sentenced to death by a court martial which did not meet international standards for fair trial; 24 were executed. Forty-two civilians and the leader of the RUF were also sentenced to death.

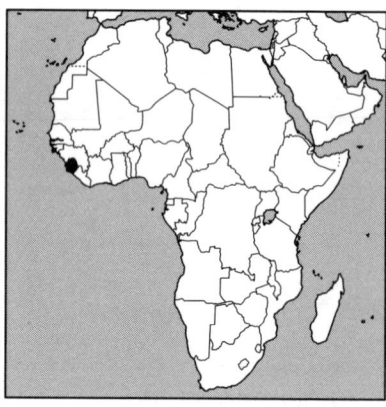

The elected government of President Kabbah was reinstated after the AFRC was forced from power in February by West African forces deployed in Sierra Leone – the Economic Community of West African States (ECOWAS) Cease-fire Monitoring Group (ECOMOG). The AFRC had seized power in a military coup in May 1997 and was joined by the RUF (see *Amnesty International Report 1998*).

During the ECOMOG offensive on Freetown, the capital, in February, AFRC and RUF forces deliberately and arbitrarily killed many civilians. Several hundred others were injured or killed as a result of shelling by both sides, which in some cases appeared to be indiscriminate.

Following their removal from power and throughout the rest of the year, AFRC and RUF forces embarked on a systematic campaign of killing, rape, mutilation, abduction and destruction in the east and north of the country. By December rebel forces had advanced towards Freetown and an attack on Freetown appeared imminent. The government of Liberia was widely reported to be providing combatants, arms and ammunition to rebel forces.

In late April President Kabbah announced that the CDF, composed of traditional hunters such as the *kamajors*, had been placed under the command of ECOMOG.

On 10 March President Kabbah proclaimed a state of emergency, subsequently ratified by parliament, which included provisions for indefinite detention without charge or trial. Some 2,000 soldiers and civilians suspected of collaboration with the AFRC and RUF were detained following the ECOMOG intervention. Many were suspected of human rights abuses.

In May the government established an independent committee of investigation to review the cases of several hundred detainees and recommend whether they should be charged or released.

Implementation of a comprehensive plan for disarmament, demobilization and reintegration of former combatants, including an estimated 5,000 child soldiers, from the RUF, CDF and national army, was limited because of continuing conflict.

The UN and other intergovernmental organizations repeatedly condemned as gross breaches of international humanitarian law the atrocities committed against civilians by rebel forces. The Special Representative of the UN Secretary-General for Children and Armed Conflict, following a visit to Sierra Leone in May, called for a more vigorous and concerted response by the international community to the needs of children affected by the conflict.

In July the UN Security Council established a peace-keeping operation, the UN Observer Mission in Sierra Leone (UNOMSIL). UNOMSIL human rights officers consistently investigated and reported human rights abuses, monitored treason trials and undertook several other important initiatives which contributed to the protection of human rights.

On 30 July the UN Secretary-General convened a special conference in New York, USA, attended by representatives of the government of Sierra Leone, intergovernmental organizations including the UN, the Organization of African Unity, ECOWAS, the European Union and the Commonwealth, and humanitarian organizations. The conference agreed to establish an international contact group to coordinate support for efforts to restore peace, stability, democracy and human rights in Sierra Leone. It first met in November.

While in power, the AFRC and RUF committed widespread human rights violations, including detention without charge or trial, torture and extrajudicial executions. Among prisoners of conscience detained by the AFRC were Sylvanus Kanyako, a journalist on the *Herald Guardian*, and David Kamara, its proprietor, who were arrested in January, held without charge for three weeks, and tortured.

In mid-January in Kenema, Eastern Province, the RUF detained several community leaders accused of supporting the *kamajors*. They were repeatedly beaten and one died as a result. Some were released, but several others remained held, including B.S. Massaquoi, Chairman of the town council. He was killed by RUF forces in February, and his mutilated body was reported to have been found with 35 others in a mass grave near Kenema the following month.

After they were removed from power, AFRC and RUF forces killed thousands of unarmed civilians, including many women and children, in the east and north of the country. The exact number of those killed remained unknown. The town of Koidu, in Kono District, Eastern Province, was virtually destroyed by rebel forces in April, and more than 650 bodies were reported to have been found there. More than 200 unarmed civilians were killed during an attack on Yifin, a village in Koinadugu District, Northern Province, in late April.

As many as 4,000 men, women and children suffered mutilation, crude amputations of their hands, arms, legs, lips or ears; others suffered lacerations and gunshot wounds. Survivors of attacks recounted that many others from their villages had been killed or had fled into the bush where many died of their injuries. They reported that villagers had been rounded up and locked in houses which were then set alight. Women and girls were systematically raped or subjected to other forms of sexual assault. Men who refused to rape members of their own families had their limbs amputated as punishment. Children were ripped from their mothers' backs and killed with machetes. Among the victims who were evacuated to Freetown was a 15-year-old schoolboy from Koidu who had severe lacerations to his right ankle after an attempted amputation; about 50 people with him were killed when they were attacked on 1 May.

Reports of atrocities declined significantly during July, but from August onwards, atrocities by rebel forces in Northern and Eastern Provinces escalated. In early September, for example, at least 40 civilians, including children, were reported to have been killed in Kamalu, Bombali District, Northern Province. Some of those killed had first been tortured and sexually assaulted and others were burned alive. Some 50 civilians were reported to have been abducted in Kamalu.

Hundreds of civilians, in particular children and young men and women, were abducted during attacks by rebel forces. They were forced to fight and used as forced labour; women and girls were forced into sexual slavery. All those abducted were at risk of ill-treatment and deliberate and arbitrary killing. As many as 10,000 civilians in rebel-controlled areas, in particular in Kailahun District, Eastern Province, were effectively held captive.

An estimated 570,000 civilians fled to neighbouring countries to escape the violence or became internally displaced. Many remained at risk of killing, mutilation and abduction. In September rebel forces attacked a refugee camp at Tomandu in Guinea, killing at least seven women refugees and three Guineans and forcing others to carry looted goods across the border. In November, 20 refugees in Tomandu who crossed the border in search of food had their hands cut off by rebel forces. The UN High Commissioner for Refugees subsequently moved thousands of refugees from Tomandu to camps further inside Guinea.

In mid-February several foreign humanitarian aid workers were captured and held hostage for two weeks by RUF forces who demanded the release of their leader, Foday Sankoh, who had been detained in Nigeria since March 1997. An Italian priest abducted in Kamalu by rebel forces in November remained held hostage at the end of the year.

The CDF were responsible for extrajudicial executions and torture and ill-treatment of captured combatants and real or suspected supporters of the AFRC and RUF. AFRC soldiers were summarily executed by *kamajors* in Koidu in February; some were decapitated, others were doused with petrol or had tyres placed around them and were burned alive. At least 50 people were extrajudicially executed in Kenema in February. Human rights violations by the CDF decreased significantly after June, apparently following intervention by the government and ECOMOG.

There were some reports that ECOMOG forces were responsible for illegal detention of civilians and torture and ill-treatment of combatants during surrender or capture. Reports also suggested that ECOMOG forces handed over some captured rebels to the CDF who then summarily executed them. UNOMSIL also expressed concern that ECOMOG forces did not consistently respect international humanitarian law in relation to the protection of non-combatants in areas affected by conflict.

Hundreds of people alleged to have collaborated with the AFRC and RUF were held without charge under legislation allowing indefinite detention without charge or trial. By December about 100 detainees had been released unconditionally and others were released either on bail or pending further investigation after their cases were reviewed by the independent committee of investigation; in other cases the committee concluded that there was evidence of criminal offences.

In April, 59 civilian prisoners, one of whom later died in detention, were charged with treason and some also with murder and arson. Three separate trials began the following month before the High Court in Freetown. Sixteen defendants were convicted and sentenced to death in August, 11 in October and 15 in November. Seven were sentenced to terms of imprisonment and the others were acquitted. Appeals against conviction and sentence had not been heard by the end of the year. Another 22 civilians were charged with treason in December.

RUF leader Foday Sankoh was returned to Sierra Leone from Nigeria in July and in September brought to trial for treason and other offences. Efforts by the government to obtain legal representation for Foday Sankoh were unsuccessful because lawyers feared reprisals. In October he was convicted and sentenced to death. His appeal against conviction and sentence, during which he was to be represented by lawyers from abroad, had not commenced by the end of the year.

A court martial of 37 soldiers, including prominent AFRC members, charged with treason and other offences began in late July. In October, 34 were convicted and sentenced to death; the others were acquitted. Despite a 1975 Appeal Court ruling that the death penalty for treason was discretionary, the court martial refused to accept arguments that the death penalty was not mandatory for these offences. The court martial allowed no right of appeal to a higher jurisdiction, contrary to international standards for fair trial. The convicted soldiers appealed to a special committee for the prerogative of mercy, chaired by the President. Despite calls for clemency by the international community and submissions on behalf of 18 of those convicted to the UN Human Rights Committee under the Optional Protocol to the International Covenant on Civil and Political Rights, 24 were publicly executed a week later. The others had their sentences commuted to life imprisonment.

In December, two journalists, Winston Ojukutu-Macaulay and Sylvester Rogers, both *British Broadcasting Corporation* correspondents, were arrested. Winston Ojukutu-Macaulay was charged with publication of false news for allegedly publishing false information about hostilities and failing to check his stories with ECOMOG, and released on bail. A third journalist was also sought.

Prisoners and detainees were held in conditions which in some cases amounted to cruel, inhuman and degrading treatment. Following large-scale detentions after February, the Central Prison, Pademba Road, in Freetown was severely overcrowded. Conditions were particularly harsh in prisons outside the capital and at the headquarters of the police Criminal Investigation Department and the Central Police Station in Freetown.

Before the AFRC and RUF were removed from power, Amnesty International repeatedly appealed for the release of prisoners of conscience and an end to detention without charge or trial, torture and ill-treatment, and extrajudicial executions.

In late February Amnesty International requested that those detained for alleged collaboration with the AFRC and RUF be charged and brought to trial in accordance with international standards with a minimum of delay and that those not to be charged be released. The Minister of Justice and Attorney General responded that detainees included prisoners of war and those who had surrendered for their own safety and that criminal investigations were proceeding.

In early May Amnesty International publicized escalating atrocities by rebel forces. It called for an end to human rights abuses against civilians and for the urgent establishment of an independent human rights presence in the country.

An Amnesty International delegation visited Sierra Leone in May and met government officials and members of the military, the legal profession and non-governmental organizations, as well as victims of human rights abuses.

Amnesty International addressed a report to the UN special conference in July – *The United Nations special conference on Sierra Leone: The protection of human rights must be a priority for the international community.* The report called for an end to impunity as a prerequisite for lasting peace and recommended: that UNOMSIL be given the necessary resources to monitor violations of international humanitarian and human rights law; that particular attention be given to the needs of children affected by the conflict; and that assistance be provided to create effective institutions for the protection and respect of human rights.

An Amnesty International representative observed the early stages of the court martial of AFRC members in late July. Amnesty International repeatedly urged the government to allow a judicial appeal procedure from the court martial.

Amnesty International appealed to President Kabbah to commute all death sentences and in October condemned the execution of the 24 soldiers.

In November Amnesty International published *Sierra Leone: 1998 – a year of atrocities against civilians*, which documented in particular the gross human rights abuses committed by rebel forces and made specific recommendations to the government, rebel forces and the international community for ending human rights abuses and ensuring the protection of human rights in the future.

SINGAPORE

An opposition party leader continued to face civil defamation suits brought by government leaders, in apparent violation of his right to freedom of expression. At least 36 prisoners of conscience were held throughout the year for their conscientious objection to military service. A former prisoner of conscience continued to have his rights to freedom of expression and

300

association restricted. **Criminal offenders continued to be sentenced to caning. At least five people were sentenced to death and at least 28 executions were reported.**

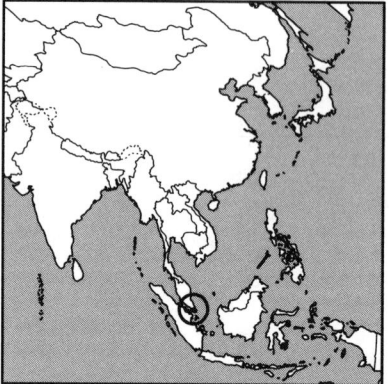

There was continued concern that civil defamation suits were being misused by government leaders to curb the right to freedom of expression and the right to participate freely in public life of their political opponents. In late 1997 Prime Minister Goh Chok Tong had appealed against the level of damages awarded against J.B. Jeyaretnam, leader of the opposition Workers' Party. The damages had been awarded in a civil defamation suit brought by the Prime Minister against J.B. Jeyaretnam for referring at a public election rally in January 1997 to reports filed with the police alleging that the Prime Minister and other members of the ruling People's Action Party (PAP) had made false statements about Tang Liang Hong, a Workers' Party candidate, and thereby incited religious groups against him (see *Amnesty International Report 1998*). In July the Court of Appeal increased the damages from US$13,000 to US$59,000 and ordered J.B. Jeyaretnam to pay full costs. In August the Prime Minister issued a statutory demand for full payment of damages within 21 days, but later agreed to accept payment in five equal instalments and to adjourn bankruptcy proceedings against J.B. Jeyaretnam. The issue of the costs of the Prime Minister's suit and the hearing of seven related civil defamation suits brought against J.B. Jeyaretnam by other members of the PAP were pending at the end of the year. J.B. Jeyaretnam continued to face possible bankruptcy and the subsequent loss of his parliamentary seat.

At least 36 conscientious objectors to military service were imprisoned during the year. They were prisoners of conscience. All were members of the Jehovah's Witnesses, a religious group which has been banned in Singapore since 1972. All refused to perform military service on religious grounds. There is no alternative civilian service for conscientious objectors to military service in Singapore (see *Amnesty International Reports 1996 to 1998*).

Chia Thye Poh, a former opposition member of parliament and prisoner of conscience who had been detained without trial between 1966 and 1989 under the Internal Security Act (ISA), continued to have his freedom of expression and association restricted by government orders issued under the ISA (see *Amnesty International Report 1998*). The orders prohibited him from participating in any organization or making public statements without official permission, and from freely associating or communicating with detainees formerly held under security legislation. In November the restriction orders expired and were not renewed. The government stated that if Chia Thye Poh "reinvolved" himself in activities which they regarded as prejudicial to Singapore's security, he would be "dealt with firmly under the law".

Caning, which constitutes cruel, inhuman or degrading punishment, remained mandatory for some 30 crimes, including attempted murder, rape, armed robbery, drug trafficking, illegal immigration and vandalism. It can also be imposed for a number of other crimes, including extortion, kidnapping and causing grievous injury. In June the anti-drug laws were amended to stipulate a mandatory prison sentence of between five and seven years and between three and six strokes of the cane for drug abusers who had been admitted at least twice to drug rehabilitation centres. Subsequent offences may carry longer prison sentences and a larger number of strokes of the cane. In September, ostensibly in an attempt to curb an influx of undocumented migrant workers from neighbouring countries, the authorities increased the penalties for immigration offences to longer prison sentences plus caning. In October Paramasivan Patti Thevar, a Malaysian national, was sentenced to four years in prison and 18 strokes of the cane for smuggling six illegal immigrants into the country. It was not known how many sentences of caning were carried out during the year.

At least five death sentences were reported to have been passed during the year for murder or drug offences. The true figure was almost certainly higher.

At least 28 executions by hanging were reported to have been carried out, the majority for drug-related offences. In a rare move in May, President Ong Teng Cheong granted clemency to Mathavakannan Kalimuthu who had been sentenced to death for murder. His sentence was commuted to life imprisonment. His alleged accomplices, Asogan Ramesh and Selva Kumar, were executed the same month. In June the scope of the death penalty was expanded to include a mandatory death sentence for those convicted of trafficking, manufacturing or importing more than 250 grams of the drug crystal methamphetamine, also known as "ice".

An Amnesty International observer attended the appeal hearing in the case of J.B. Jeyaretnam in July. The organization criticized the use of civil defamation suits by the ruling PAP as politically motivated and aimed primarily at curbing dissenting voices and deterring their participation in public life.

Amnesty International continued to urge the government of Prime Minister Goh Chok Tong to release all prisoners of conscience. In November the organization noted the lifting of restriction orders against Chia Thye Poh, expressed the belief that the move was long overdue, and again called for the ISA to be amended so that it no longer allowed for the arrest and detention without trial of those who peacefully express political or religious beliefs. The organization also urged the authorities to end the punishment of caning, to commute all death sentences and to publish statistics on the use of the death penalty.

SLOVAKIA

One conscientious objector to military service was imprisoned. He was a prisoner of conscience. There were reports that detainees were ill-treated by police officers.

In January the three parties supporting Prime Minister Vladimír Mečiar's government prevented a parliamentary discussion about the reinstatement of two deputies who had been stripped of their mandate in violation of Constitutional Court rulings. In February and March, by abstaining in the parliamentary vote for a new president, the ruling coalition blocked presidential elections and prevented the organization of a referendum on whether the president should be elected by a popular vote. When President Michal Kováč's mandate expired in March, the government assumed some presidential powers. Parliamentary elections in September were won by a broad coalition of parties which were opposed to Prime Minister Mečiar. In October Mikuláš Dzurinda was appointed Prime Minister.

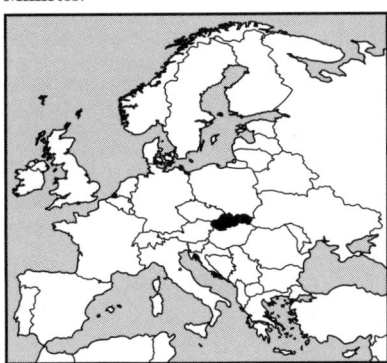

Slovakia signed in September the Second Optional Protocol to the International Covenant on Civil and Political Rights, aiming at the abolition of the death penalty.

In March Prime Minister Mečiar declared an amnesty in connection with the abduction of former President Kováč's son in 1995, in which agents of the Slovak Secret Service had allegedly been involved. However, in December the new Prime Minister revoked this amnesty.

In April Miroslav Albert, a conscientious objector to military service, was released from prison. He had been imprisoned in September 1997 for refusing to perform military service (see Amnesty International Report 1998). At least three other conscientious objectors who failed to apply for alternative service within 30 days of being declared fit for service, as required by the Law on Civilian

Service, were prosecuted and faced possible imprisonment.

In March, in Bratislava, Viera O. was asked by two police officers to remove posters she was putting up about a peaceful demonstration organized by the Ecological Party. Although she explained that the demonstration had been approved by the authorities one officer reportedly grabbed the last poster from her hand. When she tried to take it back, the officers reportedly twisted her arms, pushed her face against a fence and held her in this position for approximately 20 minutes. They also reportedly used abusive language. She was then taken to Račianska street police station where she was questioned concerning her alleged assault on police officers. Viera O. was medically examined that same evening and issued with a certificate which described contusions and haematoma on her left arm and shoulder. An investigation conducted by the Ministry of the Interior established that Viera O. had insulted a police officer, a minor offence for which she had been fined. However, the report of the investigation made no reference to allegations of ill-treatment or to possible causes of Viera O.'s physical injuries.

Amnesty International appealed to the authorities to release Miroslav Albert and to bring the Law on Civilian Service into line with internationally recognized principles. The organization also urged the authorities to promptly and impartially investigate the reported ill-treatment of Viera O.

SOMALIA

Dozens of deliberate and arbitrary killings of unarmed civilians were carried out by militias of clan-based factions. Human rights abuses by clan militias included hostage-taking and rape. Some prisoners of conscience were held in Somaliland. Islamic and clan courts condemned to death several prisoners who were subsequently executed.

A national reconciliation conference planned in 1997 (see *Amnesty International Report 1998*) was repeatedly postponed on account of disagreements between political factions and had not taken place by the end of the year. There

was no further progress towards establishing a central transitional government. Mediation efforts by the UN, the Inter-Governmental Authority for Development, governments in the region and the European Union, were also unsuccessful. The Somaliland Republic in the northwest continued to seek international recognition, and in July a new "Puntland State" was declared in the northeast by the ruling political group there, the Democratic Front for the Salvation of Somalia. Its Charter said that it would be an integral part of a future federal Somalia and would respect human rights.

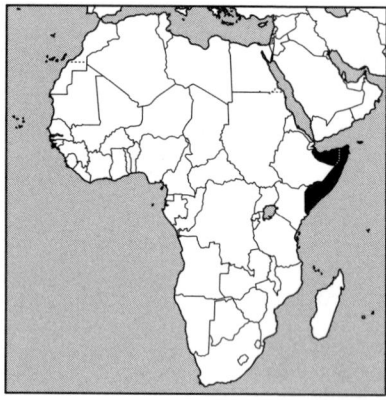

In August the two main political factions in Mogadishu, led by Ali Mahdi and by Hussein Aideed, formed a joint committee for the surrounding Benadir region and established a locally funded police force. However, they were opposed by three other factions and consequently the port and airport had not been reopened by the end of the year. Faction fighting broke out sporadically in Mogadishu throughout the year, but in and around Kismayu port in the south there was sustained fighting between the Majarten clan militias of the Somali Patriotic Movement and the Marehan clan militias of the Somali National Front (SNF). In the central Bay and Bakol regions there was fighting throughout the year between Hussein Aideed's Somali National Alliance militias, which had captured Baidoa town in 1995, and the Rahenweyn Resistance Army. In August an uneasy peace was made between the SNF and the *Al-Itihad al-Islam* force in Gedo region, but all other regions in the south experienced flare-ups of fighting during the year.

In February the UN Independent Expert on human rights in Somalia issued her report to the UN Commission on Human Rights. She called on all the warring factions to respect human rights and humanitarian law. Her recommendations included a program of technical cooperation to support human rights advocacy groups and establish the rule of law, the appointment of a human rights field officer, and the integration of human rights into UN programs. In April the Commission endorsed these proposals.

The conduct of UN peace-keeping troops in Somalia in 1993 and 1994 continued to be the subject of government investigations. In Italy in May the second report of a commission of inquiry was published, and in September a Canadian commission of inquiry published a 10-volume report. In Belgium criminal proceedings continued during the year (see **Belgium** and **Italy** entries).

Human rights abuses by faction militias were committed with impunity. There were hundreds of killings of unarmed civilians. Journalists and human rights activists were targeted. One person, Ahmed Mohamed Ibrahim, was shot dead at a peace rally in Mogadishu in July. Two Islamic court officials were assassinated in August. Members of vulnerable minority communities, such as Bantu agriculturalists and artisan "castes", and of the wealthier Benadiri business community, continued to be at risk of arbitrary killing, looting and rape.

There were many incidents of hostage-taking. Ten International Committee of the Red Cross (ICRC) staff in Mogadishu were kidnapped in April by gunmen who threatened to kill them. The kidnapping, ostensibly for ransom, seemed to have a political motivation too, and some connection to clan militias. All 10 hostages were released unharmed after two weeks. A Somaliland opposition leader, Suleiman Mohamed Aden (also known as "Gal"), was kidnapped by gunmen in May in an inter-clan dispute and held for two weeks. There were attacks on UN staff and workers for non-governmental organizations (NGOs); some were killed, others were abducted for short periods. In October a new Islamic court in south Mogadishu sentenced six gunmen to one-year prison terms for kidnapping an Italian nun. In general, there was no rule of law or consistent application of justice in most parts of the collapsed state.

Prisoners of conscience held in Somaliland included media workers who were arrested on several occasions on account of published articles. The chief editor of *Jamhuriya*, Hassan Said Yusuf, was arrested on four occasions between May and September for publishing articles criticizing President Mohamed Ibrahim Egal's government. He was held for a total of six weeks without charge. Yasin Mohamed Ismail, editor of *The Republican*, *Jamhuriya*'s English language publication, was also arrested and held for several days without charge. Iid Jama Mohamed, a journalist on the *Himilo* newspaper, was detained in Berbera in October, accused of publishing false information. He was released after some weeks without charge.

Prisoner of conscience Ahmed Farah Jirreh, a businessman in Hargeisa, the Somaliland capital, was detained in September by the Somaliland security authorities who claimed that a community road building project he had initiated was subversive. The Regional Security Committee (RSC) in Hargeisa, consisting of the mayor and the police and prison commanders, imposed a one-year prison sentence on him, although he was never charged or tried. The RSC had also detained 20 youths and children, including three sisters aged between 10 and 13 years who were released after a week, and imposed one-year prison sentences on them without any trial process, for alleged offences against public order. Ahmed Farah Jirreh was released in November but other RSC detainees were reportedly still held at the end of the year.

Several people were executed after being condemned to death by Islamic or clan courts in trials which fell short of international standards. In Beletweyn in October, Tofay Abdullah Ahmed was arrested immediately after the murder of her husband, sentenced to death by an Islamic court and executed, all on the same day.

During the year Amnesty International condemned human rights abuses by faction militias and called on them to respect human rights. In October Amnesty International representatives held a workshop for NGO workers in Somaliland on human rights awareness and action. The representatives also met members of the Somaliland authorities to discuss human rights

304 | issues. They appealed for the release of prisoners of conscience and called for an immediate end to administrative detention by the RSC.

SOUTH AFRICA

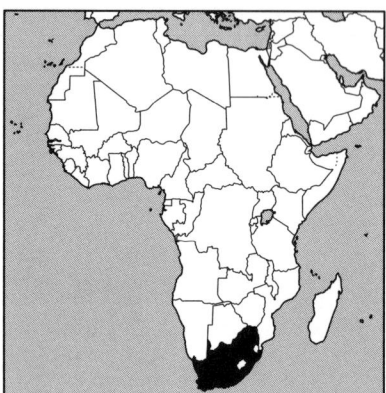

There were frequent reports of deaths in custody, some of which resulted from torture or ill-treatment of detainees and prisoners by police, the military or prison warders. A number of people shot dead by police may have been extrajudicially executed, and some political killings were carried out apparently with the complicity of security forces.

On 22 September the South African National Defence Force (SANDF) intervened in Lesotho at the request of the Lesotho government who feared a coup by members of the Lesotho Defence Force (LDF). At least nine South African and 25 LDF soldiers died in the following days. About 1,000 SANDF and Botswana Defence Force soldiers were still in Lesotho at the end of the year (see **Lesotho** entry).

In October the Truth and Reconciliation Commission (TRC) submitted a report to President Nelson Mandela. Officials from the ruling African National Congress (ANC) unsuccessfully attempted to delay its publication by court action. However, former President F.W. De Klerk obtained agreement from the TRC to remove findings against him from the report, pending a further court hearing in March 1999.

The TRC's report concluded that most gross human rights violations between 1960 and May 1994 had been committed by "the former state through its security and law enforcement agencies... and in collusion with certain other political groupings, most notably the Inkatha Freedom Party (IFP)", whom the TRC identified as "a major perpetrator of gross human rights violations from 1983". The TRC found that from the late 1970s, the former state "knowingly planned, undertook, condoned and covered up the commission of unlawful acts, including the extrajudicial killings of political opponents and others, inside and outside South Africa". The TRC also concluded that opposition organizations, including the ANC and Pan Africanist Congress, although fighting a "just war" against a system condemned internationally as a crime against humanity, breached international humanitarian law and committed gross human rights violations. The TRC found both organizations responsible for violations against dissident members in their camps abroad.

In an interim report, the TRC's Amnesty Committee named 171 people who had been granted amnesty for specific crimes. The Committee continued hearings on hundreds of remaining amnesty applications. The TRC recommended that prosecutions should be considered in cases where evidence existed against individuals who had failed to apply for amnesty or had been denied amnesty.

The TRC noted that a number of political organizations and former officials had failed to cooperate with it. However, only former President P.W. Botha was prosecuted for refusing to obey a subpoena from the TRC. He was sentenced to a fine or alternatively 12 months in prison; an appeal was pending at the end of the year.

In December South Africa ratified the International Covenant on Civil and Political Rights and the UN Convention against Torture and Other Cruel, Inhuman or Degrading Treatment or Punishment.

In April a judicial commission of inquiry, the Mahomed Commission, reported that it found no substance to Military Intelligence (MI) allegations of a "left-wing plot" against President Mandela's government. The MI report appeared to implicate Lieutenant-General Siphiwe Nyanda, Department of Foreign Affairs official Robert McBride and others in the plot. In March Robert McBride was arrested in Mozambique in connection with alleged arms trafficking, along with a man who had known links to former police and intelligence covert operations. Robert McBride was released in September and returned to South Africa pending the outcome of judicial investigations in Mozambique.

In May parliament approved the Regulation of Foreign Military Assistance Bill which obliges South Africans and permanent residents to obtain the approval of the National Conventional Arms Control Committee to offer military related services abroad.

In June an Inspecting Judge of the Judicial Inspectorate was appointed "to facilitate the inspection of prisons in order to report on the treatment of prisoners and conditions in prisons". In July the first National Director of Public Prosecution (NDPP) was appointed under new legislation. By November the NDPP had established two Investigating Directorates: one in Cape Town to investigate and bring prosecutions in connection with organized crime and killings, the other in Pietermaritzburg focusing on political violence in KwaZulu Natal (see below).

In October the Constitutional Court ruled that laws criminalizing sodomy (referring to consensual sex between men) were discriminatory and unconstitutional. In November Section 49 of the Criminal Procedure Act was amended to curtail police discretion to use force when arresting criminal suspects. The same month the Refugees Act was passed to bring national law and practice into line with international law. However, the Act's provisions for detention of asylum-seekers fall short of international standards.

Statutory and non-governmental human rights monitoring organizations continued to receive and investigate numerous reports of torture, ill-treatment and suspected unlawful killings by members of the security forces. In March the Minister of Safety and Security stated that more than 5,300 complaints of assault during 1997 had been lodged against the police. The statutory Independent Complaints Directorate (ICD) received 607 reports of deaths in police custody in the first 10 months of 1998, the majority in Gauteng and KwaZulu Natal provinces. It also received 13 complaints of torture in police custody and 103 complaints against the police of assault or attempted murder, the majority in Gauteng province. The ICD was still investigating these cases at the end of the year.

In June journalist Thabo Mabaso was beaten so severely at Gugulethu police station where he had gone to report a traffic accident that he required hospital treatment for his injuries, including loss of sight in his left eye. In July, nine police officers were suspended from duty after obstructing the ICD's investigations into the incident and were subsequently brought to trial for the assault.

In September Zweli Kenneth Ndlozi died in police custody, two days after allegedly being assaulted at his home in Soweto by military police looking for weapons. His family searched but failed to find him at local police stations. On 7 September police informed them that Zweli Kenneth Ndlozi had been found hanging in his cell at Germiston police station. A post-mortem examination had already been conducted by a doctor who apparently concluded that the cause of death was hanging. However, another post-mortem by an independent forensic pathologist revealed that there were extensive abrasions on Zweli Kenneth Ndlozi's legs, arms, shoulders, back, chest and head, as well as lesions probably caused by cigarette burns. No inquest had been held by the end of the year.

There were reports of torture by SANDF members deployed in KwaZulu Natal and Lesotho. An independent post-mortem examination revealed that Bongenseni Zondi, an IFP supporter, suffered multiple fractures and other injuries to his head and body prior to his death in May in New Hanover, KwaZulu Natal, while in the custody of the SANDF.

On 20 October Monaheng Kala, a self-employed builder and opposition party supporter in Lesotho, was arrested at his home in Maseru by members of the SANDF and Lesotho police. He was allegedly taken by the SANDF across the border into South Africa to a military camp near Ladybrand, where he was tortured with electric shocks, partially suffocated with rubber tubing, and beaten while being interrogated. Four days later he was taken back to Maseru and released without charge. He required extensive medical treatment for bone fractures and other injuries. No effective investigation was instituted by the end of the year.

In September the Empangeni magistrate's court convicted six members of the Umfolozi Public Order Policing Unit in

KwaZulu Natal of assault with intent to do grievous bodily harm and of common assault in connection with the arrest and torture in 1996 of environmental activist Kevin Kunene and four other community activists (see *Amnesty International Report 1998*). The court sentenced them to two years' imprisonment, and a further two years suspended for five years. Two defendants were acquitted for lack of evidence. The convicted officers were released on bail pending appeal.

There were reports of ill-treatment of prisoners awaiting trial or serving sentences. In August the South African Human Rights Commission (SAHRC) expressed concern at serious overcrowding and the resulting breakdown of standards within the prison system. The SAHRC found that a number of prisons failed to provide hot water, electricity, ventilation, beds or bedding, proper sanitation or lighting. From its inspections, the SAHRC concluded that "prisoners were assaulted indiscriminately, in many prisons on a daily basis, and... no action was taken against offending [staff] members".

The Minister of Correctional Services suspended from duty the head of Ingwavuma prison in KwaZulu Natal pending an inquiry into the death in May of a prisoner, Mduduzi Tembe, who was allegedly assaulted by the prison head and denied medical care.

The ICD and non-governmental organizations expressed concern about the high number of criminal suspects killed by police. In November the ICD stated that it was investigating the cases of 187 suspects allegedly shot dead by police during arrest in the first nine months of the year. For example, Josias "Fingers" Rabotapi was shot dead by police, allegedly in self-defence when the suspect drew a gun on them as they searched his house. Post-mortem and ballistics findings indicated that he was assaulted before being shot in the back and that he had not fired his gun.

On 7 October Sheikh Abdurahmaan Gasieldien, a prominent religious leader involved in the peace movement, was shot in the head and critically injured at his home in Cape Town by unidentified gunmen. None of those responsible for hundreds of violent incidents in the greater Cape Town area was successfully prosecuted. In March the statutory Office of the Public Protector reported that senior Cape

Town police were effectively shielding notorious gang members from investigations into serious crimes.

Politically motivated killings and other violence continued in KwaZulu Natal. In Richmond area, for example, a new wave of politically motivated killings occurred after the acquittal on murder charges and release in May of United Democratic Movement leader Sifiso Nkabinde. Forty people were killed in July alone. On 3 July, eight people were shot dead in a tavern, including the ANC-aligned Deputy Mayor Percy Thompson, who was killed as he lay injured on the floor. On 28 July, nine members of the Shezi family, including four children, were shot dead while sleeping in their home in the ANC-supporting area of Esimozomeni, Richmond. The killings forced hundreds of families to flee their homes. The national government ordered increased deployments of soldiers and police to the area. Members of the Richmond police station, including officers accused of complicity in the killings, were transferred out of the area. However, despite new investigations ordered by national and provincial police authorities, the perpetrators were still at large in November when the Investigating Directorate began its work (see above).

In March the Moerane Commission of Inquiry, set up by the national Minister of Safety and Security, began hearing evidence on alleged police complicity in the December 1995 Shobashobane massacre (see *Amnesty International Report 1996*). One officer admitted that he knew who had masterminded the attack, but was too afraid to name them. Other police witnesses established that senior regional and local police authorities had prior notice of the impending attack, but said that on the day all police and military resources based in the area had been withdrawn. The hearings were expected to continue until February 1999.

In July a police officer and another person were acquitted by Mtubatuba magistrate's court of murder and attempted murder in connection with the 1997 death of Fikhani Reginald Manana, from Mkhuze, KwaZulu Natal. He had been dragged behind a vehicle together with another man, Mr Msibi, who survived the incident. Mr Msibi later died as a consequence of ill-treatment in prison while held on apparently false charges brought against him by the police officer investigating Fikhani Manana's death. Following complaints about the acquittals, the NDPP instituted inquiries into the conduct of the investigation and prosecution.

In January an inquest court found three police officers criminally liable for the death in 1995 of African Municipal Workers' Union official Josias Mogolla during a strike in Pietersburg, Northern Province. The court criticized the police for using live ammunition without warning or justification. The court records were transferred to the Attorney-General for a decision on prosecution. However, the Attorney-General declined to prosecute anyone.

In June a former agent of the covert Civil Cooperation Bureau, Ferdie Barnard, was convicted and sentenced to life terms of imprisonment for two murders, including the 1989 murder of human rights activist and academic David Webster.

Independent investigators were threatened with death and legally harassed. Civil rights lawyer Jenny Wild, who had researched police and military involvement in organized crime, was subjected to death threats, illegal searches of her office and home, attacks on her property and a suspected arson attack on her home in August. In November, after a protracted five-year legal battle, the KwaZulu Natal Attorney-General withdrew criminal charges which had been pending against Jenny Wild since 1993. The ICD confirmed allegations of police fabrication of evidence and interference with witnesses in criminal cases brought against the poet Mzwakhe Mbuli, who remained in custody at Pretoria Local Prison after three failed bail applications. His trial on one remaining criminal charge was due to resume early in 1999. Prior to his arrest in October 1997 he was investigating allegations of police and official involvement in organized crime and an attempt had been made on his life.

Amnesty International representatives visited South Africa twice to research human rights concerns. In July Amnesty International co-organized a workshop on forensic medicine and the investigation of human rights violations. The same month an Amnesty representative attended a session of the Moerane Commission of Inquiry. In October Amnesty International representatives met officials from the

Department of Foreign Affairs and officers from the SANDF in Pretoria and Maseru in connection with investigations into allegations of human rights abuses by SANDF members deployed in Lesotho.

Amnesty International appealed to the authorities for prompt and effective investigations into allegations of torture and ill-treatment in custody and for preventive measures to be taken for communities or individuals at risk of extrajudicial execution or other deliberate and arbitrary killings. It also sought assurances that no arms transfers were being made to parties to the conflict in the Democratic Republic of the Congo (DRC) and that respect for human rights should be central to any negotiated solution to the conflicts in the DRC and Lesotho.

SPAIN

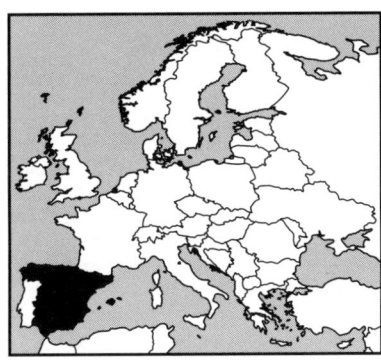

Judicial inquiries continued into the "dirty war" of the 1980s, waged against the Basque armed group *Euskadi Ta Askatasuna* (ETA), Basque Homeland and Freedom, by the *Grupos Antiterroristas de Liberación* (GAL), Anti-terrorist Liberation Groups. Two former senior government officials were among those convicted and imprisoned after the first trial relating to GAL crimes. There were new reports of torture and ill-treatment by law enforcement and prison officers. Law enforcement officers charged with torture were tried and sentenced, often after lengthy delays; sentences were frequently nominal. ETA continued to commit human rights abuses, including deliberate killings of political representatives, before declaring an indefinite cease-fire.

308

In March the Disciplinary Committee of the *Consejo General del Poder Judicial* (CGPJ), the governing body of the judiciary, agreed that about 40 specific complaints of ill-treatment of prisoners between 1996 and 1997, many of which had been closed, should be examined by its inspection service to determine whether the judges involved in the relevant inquiries had performed their tasks competently. The complaints were submitted to the CGPJ by prisoners' relatives and a number of non-governmental organizations in Spain.

In May, in his annual report to parliament, the Ombudsman criticized the prison department for failing to take sufficiently rigorous disciplinary measures against prison officers under investigation in some cases where prisoners had died or been ill-treated.

In May the UN Committee against Torture found that in the case of Encarnación Blanco Abad, the Spanish authorities had violated the internationally recognized right of an individual to a prompt and impartial investigation where there were reasonable grounds to believe that an act of torture had been committed, or where the individual had alleged torture. Encarnación Blanco, whose allegations of torture by the Civil Guards in 1992 had been rejected as unfounded by Spanish courts, had exhausted all internal judicial remedies by 1996. The Committee found that evidence in a number of medical reports should have been deemed sufficient to open a prompt inquiry, and that the failure to examine the officers of the Civil Guards reportedly involved, as well as the failure to hear other witnesses, showed lack of diligence.

In June parliament gave final approval to a law reforming legislation in force since 1985 on conscientious objection to military service and alternative civilian service. However, the new law, like the previous legislation, made no provision for conscientious objection developed during military service. Since 1985 over a dozen conscripts have been imprisoned for their refusal to complete military service on grounds of conscience, developed after joining the armed forces.

In September ETA declared an indefinite cease-fire. This unprecedented action followed the signing of the Declaration of Lizarra by 23 Basque and other political parties, trades unions and organizations.

The Declaration resolved to open unlimited dialogue to resolve the "Basque conflict" so long as no acts of violence were committed.

In October Chile's former Head of State, Augusto Pinochet, was arrested in London, the United Kingdom (UK), on the basis of a commission rogatory filed by a National Court judge in Madrid on charges of attempted murder, torture, conspiracy to torture, hostage-taking and conspiracy to take hostages. In his committal for trial order, the National Court judge listed 16 Spanish citizens among the thousands of people who "disappeared" or were tortured or killed when General Pinochet was Head of State (see **Chile** and UK entries).

The first trial in connection with crimes committed by GAL in the 1980s opened in May before the Supreme Court. In July former Interior Minister José Barrionuevo and former Secretary of State Security Rafael Vera were sentenced to 10 years' imprisonment for illegal detention and misappropriation of public funds in connection with the kidnapping of French businessman Segundo Marey who, in 1983, had been held hostage for 10 days. According to medical reports, Segundo Marey was still suffering severely from the mental effects of the kidnapping. Ten other defendants, including the former civil governor of Vizcaya and a number of senior police officers, were sentenced to terms of imprisonment ranging from 10 years to two years, four months and one day. In December, however, on the recommendation of the Second Chamber of the Supreme Court, the Council of Ministers granted 10 of the 12 convicted, including José Barrionuevo and Rafael Vera, a partial pardon of two thirds of their sentences. The remaining parts of the sentences were subsequently suspended by the Constitutional Court pending consideration of their appeals to the court. The prisoners were released, but remained barred from public office.

Judicial inquiries continued into the kidnapping, torture and murder by GAL of two ETA members, José Antonio Lasa and José Ignacio Zabala, and into the killing of a presumed ETA member, Ramón Oñederra, in the 1980s.

There were new claims by suspected ETA members or supporters that they had been tortured during incommunicado detention. The allegations made consistent references to the practice of partial asphyxiation with plastic bags, known as "*la bolsa*". David Gramont, arrested near Seville in March by national police and handed over to the Civil Guards, alleged that his head had been pushed repeatedly into a bath of water, a torture method known as "*la bañera*".

José Ignacio Armendariz Izaguirre alleged that he was tortured by Civil Guards after arrest in Pamplona in March and while being held incommunicado in Madrid. He said a plastic bag was placed over his head and that he was repeatedly beaten on the head and body and forced to repeatedly bend up and down. On arrival in Madrid he was taken to see a doctor, who ordered X-rays, blood tests and treatment for his knees. However, José Ignacio Armendariz Izaguirre alleged that when returned to his cell, blindfolded and manacled, he was beaten on the head, body and testicles, hooded and partially asphyxiated by insertion of fingers in his nose and mouth.

Maite Pedrosa Barrenetxea, arrested in March, alleged that she was raped at the Civil Guard headquarters in Madrid and that Civil Guards placed fingers, hands and a cold object, which they said was a pistol, in her anus and vagina. Cristina Gete, arrested in May, alleged that she was beaten, partially asphyxiated with a hood, sexually humiliated, fondled and threatened with rape. All the above-mentioned victims lodged judicial complaints.

Racially motivated assaults by law enforcement officers, including police officers of the autonomous regions, were also reported. Moroccan national Driss Zraidi lodged a judicial complaint stating that he had been assaulted in August by two officers of the Catalonian autonomous police force, the *Mossos de Esquadra*, in San Pedro Pescador. Driss Zraidi alleged that after he had been asked for his papers, he was pushed against a wall and beaten. One of his teeth was broken, his glasses were smashed, and his gold chain was seized and deliberately pulled apart. At the police station he was repeatedly beaten, trampled on and racially abused. Four of his ribs were broken and, after his release, he needed hospital treatment for 10 days. Eight officers were reportedly charged with involvement in the assault and were suspended from duty.

There were also reports about systematic beatings and prolonged isolation, in some cases for up to three years, in certain high security prison sections under a special regime for surveillance of detainees known as FIES. The regime was set up in 1991 by government circular and incorporated in the penitentiary regulations in 1996. Several prisoner support organizations alleged that many prisoners were frightened to make complaints about ill-treatment or that, if they did, these were filed, while prison officers often made counter-complaints that were pursued through the courts.

A number of trials relating to ill-treatment and torture took place, some of which highlighted lengthy delays and effective impunity. In January the trial opened in Bilbao, 14 years after the crime was committed, of five national police officers accused of torturing two suspected members of a Basque armed group, *Iraultza* (Revolution). Three officers were sentenced to a total of five months' detention suspended for two years and eight months for the torture of José Ramón Quintana and José Pedro Otero. However, the court decided that two other officers could not be tried because more than five years had elapsed between the alleged acts of torture and the opening of proceedings against them. An appeal against this decision was lodged.

In February, two national police officers were sentenced by a Barcelona court to six months' imprisonment for torturing a detainee by beating him, forcing him to his knees, and pushing his head into a lavatory bowl and repeatedly pulling the chain.

In February reports were received that one of three Civil Guards convicted to more than four years' imprisonment for the illegal detention and torture of Kepa Urra Guridi (see *Amnesty International Report 1998*) had been selected for a promotional course while his appeal against the sentence was still pending. In October the Supreme Court reduced by three years the original sentence passed on the Civil Guards, while maintaining the sentence of six years' disqualification from public service.

In March the trial of two municipal police officers for ill-treatment of Moroccan national Sallam Essabah (see *Amnesty International Report 1997*) was suspended because of a technical error in the judicial proceedings. The trial of four municipal police officers for the ill-treatment of Senegalese national Mamadou Kane (see *Amnesty International Report 1998*) was also suspended, owing to the failure to appear of witnesses for the prosecution and defence.

In April ETA member Fernando Elejalde Tapia was sentenced by the National Court to 37 years' imprisonment for the killing of prison psychologist Francisco Gómez Elósegui (see *Amnesty International Report 1998*). After consulting medical reports, the Court concluded there was no evidence that injuries sustained by Fernando Elejalde, who said he had been tortured in detention, occurred after his arrest.

In April, 10 Civil Guards from the Colmenar Viejo barracks, near Madrid, were sentenced to between eight and two months' imprisonment for multiple acts of torture, ill-treatment and threats, after arresting three young men in a bar in 1994. Three officers were acquitted. One received a non-custodial sentence (see *Amnesty International Report 1997*).

Before ETA's declaration of a cease-fire, it pursued its campaign of killings, predominantly of local councillors and allies of the ruling Popular Party. In January José Ignacio Iruretagoyena was killed in a car bomb explosion in the Basque area of Zarautz, and Alberto Jiménez Becerill and his wife Asunción García Ortíz were shot dead in Seville. In May Pamplona councillor Tomás Caballero was shot dead in Pamplona. In June councillor Manuel Zamarreño was killed in an explosion in Rentería. He had recently replaced José Luis Caso, shot dead in December 1997.

In March Amnesty International delegates held talks with a large number of national and autonomous government and opposition leaders in Catalonia, the Basque Country and Madrid. They met, among others, the Minister of the Interior of the Spanish government and the *lehendakari* (the President of the Basque government). During the talks, Amnesty International expressed its concerns, including torture and ill-treatment during incommunicado detention and a perceptible increase in racially motivated assaults by law enforcement officers.

Amnesty International sought information from the authorities on new allega-

tions of torture and ill-treatment and urged them to ensure that all such allegations were thoroughly and impartially investigated. It repeatedly condemned abuses by armed groups and called for a halt to ETA's killings of political representatives.

In June Amnesty International wrote to the Senate Constitutional Commission prior to its examination of the draft law on conscientious objection to military service and final parliamentary approval. The organization expressed concern that the text made no provisions for conscientious objection developed during military service and reiterated its belief that people should have the right to seek conscientious objector status whenever they developed their objections. It called on the Commission to do everything in its power to ensure that the law was amended to incorporate this right, as urged by the UN Human Rights Committee in 1996 (see *Amnesty International Report 1997*).

SRI LANKA

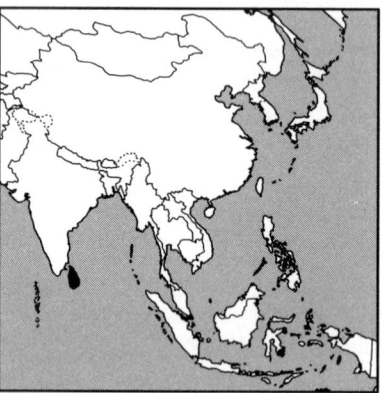

Thousands of people were arrested, including scores of possible prisoners of conscience. Torture and ill-treatment were widespread and four prisoners were reported to have died as a result. At least 14 people reportedly "disappeared". There were several reports of extrajudicial executions. An armed opposition group was responsible for grave human rights abuses.

Armed conflict continued between the armed opposition Liberation Tigers of Tamil Eelam (LTTE) and the government of President Chandrika Bandaranaike

Kumaratunga. Thousands of combatants died in heavy fighting in the "Vanni", an area largely under LTTE control.

The state of emergency, which had been in force in parts of the country (see *Amnesty International Report 1998*), was extended to the whole country in August. In February emergency regulations (ERs) banning the LTTE were promulgated. Emergency powers were also used to impose censorship in June and postpone provincial council elections in August. The censorship remained in force at the end of the year.

In May the UN Committee against Torture examined Sri Lanka's initial report. The government delegation acknowledged that torture was a problem. The Committee recommended firmer action to bring perpetrators to justice and that Sri Lanka's Convention against Torture Act 1994, ERs and Prevention of Terrorism Act (PTA) be reviewed to ensure compliance with the UN Convention against Torture and Other Cruel, Inhuman or Degrading Treatment or Punishment.

The Special Representative of the UN Secretary-General on Children and Armed Conflict visited Sri Lanka and held talks with government officials and LTTE leaders in May. According to UN press releases, the LTTE undertook to stop immediately the recruitment of children under the age of 17 and their deployment in combat under the age of 18.

The final and interim reports of three presidential commissions of inquiry established in 1994 to investigate past human rights violations, particularly "disappearances" (see *Amnesty International Reports 1995* to *1998*), were made public in January. A new commission was set up in May to look into complaints which the three commissions had not been able to investigate before their term ended. The Board of Investigation which inquired into more than 700 "disappearances" that had been reported in Jaffna between 1995 and 1997 submitted its report to the President in April. It reportedly found that 16 of the 765 reported "disappeared" were killed and recommended further investigations with a view to prosecution in 25 cases. It also reportedly traced 201 of the 765 people reported as "disappeared".

A Committee to Inquire into Undue Arrest and Harassment, comprising five ministers and three members of parliament,

was appointed in July. It received 154 complaints, including 10 which related to non-implementation of presidential directives and 47 which related to torture or illtreatment (see *Amnesty International Reports 1996* to *1998*).

There were several incidents of harassment of and threats to journalists. On 12 February air force personnel attempted to abduct Iqbal Athas, a military reporter, from his home and threatened his family. In the same month, Pradeep Dharmaratne, a provincial reporter who had exposed trade in illicit liquor, was taken in for questioning by police and reportedly tortured. In June the home of Lasantha Wickrematunge, editor of the *Sunday Leader*, was fired on. He also reportedly received anonymous telephone threats warning him against criticizing the government.

Thousands of Tamil people, including scores of possible prisoners of conscience, were arrested in the north and east of the country and in the capital, Colombo. Safeguards for the welfare of detainees were not fully implemented in many cases. Unauthorized places of detention were used, including by Tamil armed groups cooperating with the security forces. In Vavuniya, evidence emerged of three unofficial detention places run by the People's Liberation Organization of Tamil Eelam after a prisoner escaped.

Torture and ill-treatment were widespread. Reported methods of torture included being hung upside down by the ankles or being hung by the thumbs, beatings with cricket bats, whipping with chains, near-suffocation with plastic bags filled with petrol and chillies, and rape of female detainees. Thambirajah Kamalathasan, a Tamil man from Chunnakam, Jaffna, was reportedly tortured for several days following his arrest by police from Pettah police station, Colombo, on 15 July. He alleged that chilli powder was rubbed into his eyes and that his genitals were squeezed. Two witnesses said they saw him being assaulted with a rod. Thambirajah Kamalathasan was one of 192 Sri Lankan asylum-seekers who had been returned to Sri Lanka from Senegal in February. On return, they were all arrested and detained for several weeks.

The Supreme Court awarded compensation to Kumaru Selvaratnam who had been tortured in Colombo in 1997 (see *Amnesty International Report 1998*) and

312

whose testicles had to be removed as a result.

Four prisoners were reported to have died in custody as a result of torture. Among them was 18-year-old Sathasivam Sanjeevan, who was arrested by police in Amparai district in October. Although an initial post-mortem failed to identify signs of torture and confirmed the police version that he had been killed by being shot, a second post-mortem, carried out after the body was exhumed, confirmed that the body showed signs of "injuries by blunt weapon" inflicted before the shooting. A magisterial inquiry continued at the end of the year.

At least 14 Tamil civilians reportedly "disappeared" after arrest by the army or armed Tamil groups working alongside it. In Vavuniya, Kathirgamathamby Sentilkumar remained unaccounted for after he was seen being taken into custody on 23 January from Poonthoddam camp for internally displaced people by a group of armed men, three of whom reportedly wore army uniform.

There were several reports of alleged extrajudicial executions. On 1 February, eight Tamil civilians were deliberately shot at close range by police and home guards in Tampalakamam, Trincomalee district. Among them were six people attending a party in a house near the police post. Around 20 police and home guards who appeared drunk reportedly took the victims, including two brothers aged 13 and 17, inside the police post and shot them in the compound. Corroboration of other reports of alleged extrajudicial executions was often difficult to obtain, partly because of pressure exerted by the security forces on relatives and witnesses. In several instances, the latter were forced to sign statements saying that those killed were members of the LTTE or had been killed by the LTTE.

Further evidence emerged about approximately 600 "disappearances" reported in Jaffna in 1996. In a landmark judgment, five members of the security forces were found guilty by the Colombo High Court of the abduction, rape and murder of Krishanthy Kumarasamy and the abduction and murder of her mother, brother and a neighbour in September 1996 (see *Amnesty International Report 1997*). They were sentenced to death. Two of the convicted soldiers told the court

that there were 300 to 400 bodies at Chemmani, where the bodies of Krishanthy Kumarasamy and the others had been discovered. Statements about the alleged mass graves at Chemmani were taken from the five convicted men by the Criminal Investigation Department and the Human Rights Commission. The latter requested assistance of forensic experts from the UN. However, by the end of the year, exhumations had not yet commenced.

Investigations into other past human rights violations, including cases recommended for further investigation by the three presidential commissions of inquiry (see above), continued. According to the Attorney General's department, investigations into 485 of the 3,861 such cases had been completed by mid-October and 150 alleged perpetrators had been charged in the High Court.

The trial of a school principal and eight army personnel charged in connection with the "disappearance" of a group of young people at Embilipitiya in late 1989 and early 1990 continued throughout the year (see *Amnesty International Reports 1995* to *1998*). Investigations into the abduction and killing of Richard de Zoysa, a journalist, in 1990 (see *Amnesty International Reports 1991* and *1992*) were reopened.

The report of the presidential commission of inquiry investigating the killing of three detainees at Kalutara prison in December 1997 (see *Amnesty International Report 1998*) had not been made public by the end of the year.

The LTTE was responsible for grave human rights abuses, including the deliberate killing of two mayors of Jaffna town. Sarojini Yogeswaran, a member of the Tamil United Liberation Front, was killed at her home on 17 May. On 11 September, her successor, Ponnuthurai Sivapalan, was among five civilians killed by a mine which exploded during a meeting at a municipal building. In February the LTTE was held responsible for killing 10 civilians during an attack on the Temple of the Tooth in Kandy. Thirty-four civilians were unlawfully killed in March when an otherwise empty bus believed to be driven by an LTTE member exploded in their midst at Maradana junction, Colombo.

People who refused to cooperate with the LTTE were taken prisoner and sometimes killed; others were unaccounted for.

In July and August, four members of the Socialist Equality Party, a left-wing revolutionary party, were taken prisoner by the LTTE and held for several weeks at an unknown location thought to be in Killinochchi district. They were not given access to the International Committee of the Red Cross (ICRC). One Tamil member and three Sinhalese members of the seven crew of the passenger ferry *Misen* taken prisoner in July 1997 (see *Amnesty International Report 1998*) were released in July and October respectively. In October, two Sinhalese crew members of another ferry who had been held since 1995 and six members of the security forces were also released. Five other crew members, four Sinhalese and one Muslim, apparently held solely on the basis of their ethnicity, had not been released by the end of the year. They were, however, allowed regular access to the ICRC and to communicate with their relatives after March.

Scores of children were reported to have been forcibly recruited by the LTTE in October, particularly in Batticaloa district and parts of the Vanni.

In September/October, an Amnesty International delegation visited the country. In talks with government officials, it focused on measures for the prevention and investigation of torture.

In February Amnesty International published *Sri Lanka: Implementation of the Recommendations of the UN Working Group on Enforced or Involuntary Disappearances* [WGEID] *following their visits to Sri Lanka in 1991 and 1992.* Throughout the year, Amnesty International appealed for the full implementation of the recommendations of the three presidential commissions and WGEID, and for the review of ERs, the PTA and the remedy of habeas corpus. It also called for proper investigations into the alleged mass graves at Chemmani, and for international forensic experts to be invited to assist local experts with the exhumations.

Amnesty International repeatedly appealed to the leadership of the LTTE to adhere to international humanitarian law. In a meeting with an LTTE representative in October, Amnesty International expressed concern about the LTTE's apparent breaches of commitments to the UN Special Representative (see above).

Amnesty International sought clarification from the government and the LTTE after an attack apparently carried out by the LTTE on a Lionair airplane in which 55 civilians were killed, and about measures taken by both parties to protect civilian lives. It also urged the government and the LTTE to agree to a UN proposal for the decommissioning of anti-personnel mines.

SUDAN

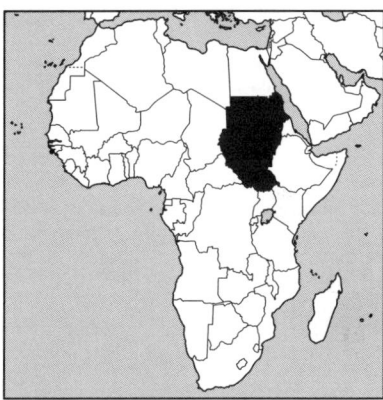

Scores of suspected government opponents, including prisoners of conscience, were detained without charge or trial for periods ranging from a few weeks to several months. At least 40 political prisoners received unfair trials. Torture and ill-treatment in detention centres and offices of the security services were common; at least one man died under torture. Courts imposed cruel, inhuman and degrading punishments. Hundreds of civilians were extrajudicially executed by soldiers and militia. Scores of women and children were abducted by soldiers and militia; the fate of hundreds abducted in previous years remained unknown. At least nine prisoners were sentenced to death; there was at least one execution. Armed opposition groups were responsible for human rights abuses.

A new Constitution was promulgated in June on the ninth anniversary of the military coup that brought the government of President Omar Hassan Ahmad al-Bashir to power. This followed a referendum widely assumed to have been rigged – the electoral commission claimed a turnout of 91.9 per cent but other observers reported a low turnout. Bombs

314

exploded in Khartoum on 30 June, the day the constitution came into force.

The referendum was not held in areas contested by armed opposition organizations, grouped under the umbrella of the National Democratic Alliance. Large swathes of southern Sudan, Blue Nile state and parts of South Kordofan were under the control of the Sudan People's Liberation Army (SPLA), led by John Garang de Mabior; areas along the Ethiopian and Eritrean borders were contested by the Sudan Alliance Forces (SAF), led by Abdel Aziz Khalid, the Beja Congress and other armed groups. Over 100,000 people were displaced by fighting in the east during the year, especially in Kassala, Gedaref and Blue Nile states. The government accused the Eritrean government of sending troops into Sudan to support Sudanese opposition forces.

In southern Sudan the government militia calling itself SPLA Bahr al-Ghazal, led by Kerubino Kuanyin Bol, switched sides to join the SPLA in January and attacked the garrison town of Wau. More than 100,000 people fled the area. The government quickly regained control of Wau town but fighting continued in rural areas for the next four months, displacing tens of thousands more people. Years of raiding by SPLA Bahr al-Ghazal, the government's Popular Defence Forces (PDF) and other militia groups had already displaced hundreds of thousands; the additional disruption caused the rural economy to collapse and a famine followed in which thousands of people died.

Both the government and the SPLA declared cease-fires in Bahr al-Ghazal in July and extended them in October. The cease-fires did not apply to other parts of southern Sudan. In September the SPLA, supported by Ugandan troops, attacked government garrisons in Eastern Equatoria. The government closed the universities and declared a general mobilization. The SPLA were pushed back; tens of thousands of people were displaced.

In October approximately 40,000 Sudanese refugees in the Democratic Republic of the Congo (DRC) were forced back into Sudan by the SPLA. At the end of the year an estimated 4.5 million people were displaced inside Sudan.

Peace talks mediated by the Inter-Governmental Authority on Development countries (Eritrea, Ethiopia, Kenya and Uganda) in May and August adjourned without progress.

The Sudanese authorities continued to support Ugandan armed opposition movements responsible for gross human rights abuses, supplying arms and allowing them to use bases inside Sudan (see **Uganda** entry). In March the Sudanese government allowed the UN to relocate 17 Ugandans who had been abducted by the Ugandan armed opposition group the Lord's Resistance Army (LRA) back to Uganda. In October the Sudanese authorities deployed troops, some of whom were from Ugandan armed opposition movements, in the DRC in support of President Laurent-Désiré Kabila.

In August one man died when the USA bombed a pharmaceutical factory in Khartoum North in retaliation for the bombing of the US embassies in Nairobi, Kenya, and Dar es Salaam, Tanzania. The US government claimed the plant was manufacturing precursors for chemical weapons and had a connection with Usama bin Laden, the alleged mastermind behind the bombings in East Africa.

In January the UN Special Rapporteur on Sudan reported that the authorities, security forces and militia were all responsible for a broad range of human rights violations. In April the UN Commission on Human Rights again expressed deep concern at continued serious human rights violations. For the fourth year running, the Commission recommended deploying human rights field officers to monitor human rights. Yet again they were not in place by the end of the year.

Scores of suspected opponents of the government, including prisoners of conscience, were arrested during the year and detained without charge or trial for periods ranging from a few weeks to several months. In Khartoum most prisoners were held in a section of Kober Prison run by the security services. However, the security headquarters and secret detention centres were also used. Some political detainees were held in Dabak Prison outside Khartoum and there were reports of political prisoners detained in Port Sudan and other regional centres. Many suspected political opponents had to report daily to security offices where they were made to wait until sunset.

Among those detained without charge or trial were five imams from Islamist groups. Mudathir Mohamed Ismail and

Mohamed Abdel Karim of the group *Safar al-Hawamil*, and Ali Sayyid, Rifa'at and Khalil of the *Hizb al-Tahrir Islami*, Islamic Liberation Party, were reportedly arrested in 1997 and in October were still in detention without charge in the security-run section of Kober Prison. They were reported to have cast doubt on the religious credentials of Hassan al-Turabi, Secretary General of the National Congress and ideological mentor of the government.

The authorities arrested dozens of suspected political activists in May, June and July after opposition calls for a boycott on the constitutional referendum. In May Hashim Tulub, a former member of the banned Sudan Communist Party (SCP), Abdel Wahab Ahmad al-Mustapha, a trade unionist, and Khalid Omar al-Sadiq, a lawyer and member of the opposition National Alliance for the Restoration of Democracy, were among more than 30 prisoners of conscience detained for two weeks in a secret detention centre in Khartoum North. After their release the men were made to report each day to security offices.

In late June at least 20 senior political figures were questioned after they announced in a challenge to the new Constitution that they intended to re-establish banned political parties. The majority were released within 48 hours. However, al-Haj Abdelrahman Abdalla Nugdullah, a member of the banned Umma Party and a former Minister of Religious Affairs, and Suleiman Khedir, a businessman, remained in incommunicado detention.

Scores more political opponents were arrested after the bomb explosions in Khartoum in June, reportedly on suspicion of involvement in the bombings. Mahjoub al-Zubeir, Siddig Yahya and other prominent trade unionists were briefly detained. Baha al-Din Hassan Osman, an electrical engineer, and at least three other men working at the bombed Burri power station, were beaten in a secret detention centre before being transferred to Kober prison and from there to Dabak. They were released without charge in mid-August.

In early July the authorities announced they had evidence that members of banned political parties including the SCP and the Umma Party were behind the explosions. Abdelmahmud Abbo, Secretary General of the *Ansar* Affairs Commission

(close to the Umma Party), and al-Haj Abdelrahman Abdalla Nugdullah, who had been arrested before the explosions, were named in particular. However, neither man was charged. They were eventually released in October.

Four leaders of the *Ansar* order of Islam, including Adam Ahmad Yousuf, imam of the 'Abd al-Rahman mosque, were arrested after a speech at Friday prayers protesting at the detention of the *Ansar* leaders. They were accused of undermining public security and released on bail after two weeks in prison. Although acquitted at a trial in August, they were detained as a "precautionary measure" until November.

At least 40 political prisoners received unfair trials. For example, in August, 10 men arrested in 1997 and accused of being members of the SAF, including retired military personnel, a student and a doctor, were sentenced to prison terms ranging from five to 10 years on charges including inciting war against the state; five men were acquitted. The men had been tortured and threatened to secure confessions, and allowed to see defence lawyers only three times. In October the trial of 25 civilians and one soldier (six *in absentia*), accused of being members of the SPLA, opened in a specially convened military court in Khartoum. The defendants, who included Hillary Boma and Lino Sebit, both Roman Catholic priests, were arrested in July and August, ill-treated and tortured and then charged with the June bomb explosions in Khartoum. Defence lawyers did not have access to them until the trial began. There was no right of appeal. The trial had not concluded by the end of the year.

Torture and ill-treatment by security officials remained common; detainees held in security offices on suspicion of plotting against the government were particularly at risk. During February John Dur Manok, a southern Sudanese returned from Ethiopia, was beaten daily in a cell in the security-run section of Kober Prison. As in previous years, anti-government demonstrators were frequently beaten on arrest and on arrival at security offices. In August, three students at Khartoum University were beaten by security personnel following violent demonstrations against rises in student fees. Mohamed Abdelsalaam Babiker, a law student and demo-

316

cracy activist, died after being beaten about the head. In October students from Omdurman Ahlia University arrested during violent demonstrations against the general mobilization of students for military service were also beaten by security personnel.

Courts imposed cruel, inhuman and degrading punishments for theft and offences against "public order" or "public decency". For example, in August a student convicted of participating in the demonstrations at Khartoum University was sentenced to 20 lashes.

Hundreds of civilians were extrajudicially executed by soldiers, PDF troops and other militia. Most incidents were in the war zones of eastern and southern Sudan but in April scores of student conscripts died as hundreds of youths broke out of a military training camp at al-Ayfun near Khartoum. The authorities announced that more than 50 deserters had drowned trying to cross the Blue Nile. However, other reports said that over 100 were killed, many of whom had been shot and others beaten to death.

In January soldiers, PDF and militia drawn from the Fertit community launched a 12-day reprisal attack on civilians, the majority of them Dinka and Jur, after Kerubino Kuanyin Bol's assault on Wau. At least 300 civilians were killed, among them government officials and internally displaced people fleeing camps around the town. Armed men entered Wau hospital and killed patients unable to flee. The government, which did not set up an independent or impartial inquiry, said that 60 civilians were killed in "ethnic fighting" between the Dinka and Fertit.

In the months that followed, government forces, including regular soldiers, PDF and irregular militia, raided the countryside in Bahr al-Ghazal. In addition to killings, scores of women and children were abducted. For example, in April and May dozens of villagers were captured and killed and scores of women and children abducted in raids on villages west of Aweil. In May more than 40 civilians were killed by PDF troops who looted the market of Abindau, north of Gogrial; scores of women and children were taken captive. Hundreds of women and children abducted from Bahr al-Ghazal in previous years and allegedly held as domestic slaves remained unaccounted for.

At least nine men convicted of criminal offences were sentenced to death. A member of the Islamist group al-Takfir Walhijra was executed in March for murdering two worshippers at a mosque in 1997.

Armed opposition groups were responsible for human rights abuses, including torture and deliberate and arbitrary killings. For example, in May SPLA forces raiding Rizeiqat cattle camps in Southern Darfur were reported to have shot dead at least 19 civilians in retaliation for raids by militia forces in Bahr al-Ghazal.

Amnesty International urged both government and armed opposition groups to end human rights abuses. The organization called on the authorities to release prisoners of conscience, to end detention without charge or trial and torture, and to commute death sentences. In June Amnesty International renewed its appeals to the government to end its supply of weapons, bases and other support to the LRA and to intervene to free abducted children (see **Uganda** entry). Although the government assured the Special Representative of the UN Secretary-General for Children and Armed Conflict that it would assist in further repatriations of abducted children, it took no really decisive action. In October the government admitted for the first time that it was working with the LRA and other Ugandan armed groups.

In August Amnesty International expressed concern at the bombing of a pharmaceutical plant in Khartoum by the USA. In September the organization wrote to the UN Secretary-General urging him to investigate whether the attack constituted a breach of international humanitarian law.

In December the organization issued a report, *Sudan: Justice? The military trial of Father Hillary Boma and 25 others*, documenting concern about the unfair trial of 26 men charged with planting bombs in Khartoum in June.

SWAZILAND

Government opponents were detained, prosecuted or harassed solely because of their non-violent political activities. Law enforcement officers ill-treated detainees and unarmed demonstrators. At least eight prisoners remained under sentence of death.

Political activity continued to be banned and the rights of freedom of assembly and expression restricted under the terms of the King's Proclamation of 1973. A number of demonstrations took place in protest at these restrictions. Opposition organizations petitioned the King in August and in October to repeal the proclamation, dismantle the Constitutional Review Commission (CRC) and suspend national elections scheduled for October. The CRC, appointed by King Mswati III in 1996 for two years, had still not concluded its work by the end of the year. Parliamentary elections were held in October; about 30 per cent of those eligible voted and a new cabinet of ministers was sworn in during November.

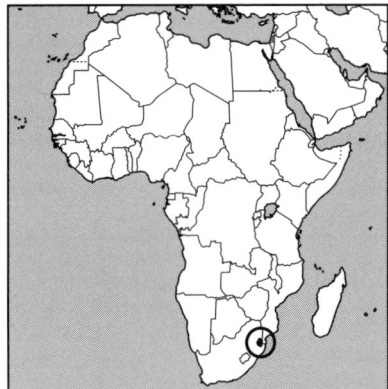

On 20 November a security guard was killed and seven others injured when a bomb exploded at the office of the Deputy Prime Minister. The governments of the USA and South Africa sent experts to investigate the cause of the explosion.

Two days before the elections, soldiers and armed police raided the homes of officials of the opposition Swaziland Democratic Alliance, searching for materials calling for a boycott of the elections. Those harassed included the President of the People's United Democratic Union (PUDEMO), Mario Masuku, the President of the Swaziland Youth Congress (SWAYOCO), Bongani Masuku, and a senior official of the Swaziland Federation of Trade Unions (SFTU), Zodwa Mkhonta.

In November there were further raids on the homes and offices of officials from SWAYOCO, PUDEMO and the SFTU, and the home of Simon Noge, the treasurer of the Human Rights Association of Swaziland.

In the same month many of the same individuals, including the SFTU Secretary General, Jan Sithole, were arrested and interrogated before being released without charge. One SFTU official, Themba Motsa, who was arrested in late November, alleged that police had threatened him with death and assaulted him while interrogating him about the 20 November bomb explosion.

During the October elections, the security forces mounted patrols and roadblocks in urban areas and allegedly ill-treated unarmed youths and others suspected of opposing the elections. In one incident on the night of 16 October police dispersed a group of protesters in Msunduza township, Mbabane. Later police and soldiers arrested members of the group, took them to Mbabane police station where they allegedly beat and kicked them and made them do strenuous exercises. The detainees were released without charge. At least nine required medical treatment. At least three lodged complaints against the police. David Langwenya, a civil servant, was himself severely assaulted when he intervened to try and stop the security forces from beating one of the arrested protesters.

Opposition protests against the elections led in some cases to the prosecution of arrested activists. In October Sandile Phakathi and Bhekani Simelane, members of SWAYOCO, were convicted in the Manzini Magistrate's Court of offences under the Public Order Act in connection with anti-election protests in August and sentenced to two years' imprisonment or a fine. When they appeared in court two days after their arrest they had bruises on their faces, allegedly as a result of beatings by the police, and were denied bail. There were allegations that police interference during the course of the trial undermined the impartiality of the court proceedings. The two men could not pay the fine within the stipulated period, but police did not rearrest them and they remained at liberty at the end of the year.

Eight prisoners remained under sentence of death. At least one new sentence of death was imposed. The Minister of Justice announced in February that he was seeking the appointment of an executioner. The last judicial execution took place in 1983. In September and October, the Appeal Court, composed of South

African judges, set aside three death sentences on the grounds that the trial courts had imposed the sentences wrongly.

Amnesty International delegates visited Swaziland in October to investigate reports of ill-treatment in police custody and other concerns. The organization expressed concern to the authorities about the ill-treatment of government opponents by the security forces, and the use of restrictive laws to detain and harass them for political reasons.

SWEDEN

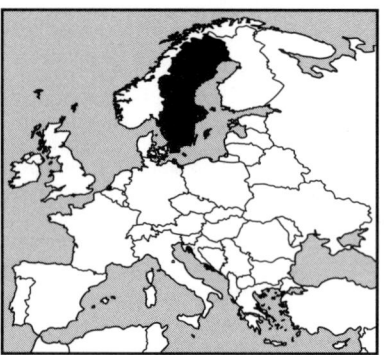

There were further developments in investigations into a death in custody and ill-treatment.

Investigations continued into the 1995 death in police custody of Osmo Vallo (see *Amnesty International Report 1998*). A further post-mortem on the body of Osmo Vallo was performed in February. The post-mortem report concluded that the main cause of death was the violence of the arresting police officers and, in particular, the forceful pressure caused by an officer stamping on his back. This pressure fractured ribs and resulted in impaired breathing and heart failure. As a consequence of these findings the Prosecutor General was considering whether to bring additional charges against police involved in the arrest and ill-treatment of Osmo Vallo. In view of disagreement about the findings of this post-mortem examination, the Prosecutor General requested the opinion of the National Board of Health and Welfare.

In November the government published the findings and recommendations of the Chancellor of Justice's inquiry into the procedures for handling cases of deaths in custody. The Chancellor stated that in the course of the inquiry he found examples of cases in which police conduct towards detainees was unacceptable. He recommended a wide range of measures to be taken by the police and government bodies including: improved training; continuing assessments of existing and proposed restraint techniques; better communication of the risks involved in the use of various restraint techniques; and procedures to guarantee that police vehicles were equipped with functioning life-saving equipment.

He also recommended changes in the process for investigation by police of deaths and serious injury in police custody in order to strengthen public confidence in such inquiries. These included creation of special regional police investigation units, ensuring that prosecutors lead such inquiries and promulgation of regulations requiring all relevant police reports to be handed over to forensic pathologists conducting post-mortem examinations.

In February the European Committee for the Prevention of Torture and Inhuman or Degrading Treatment or Punishment carried out its second periodic visit to police establishments and prisons in Sweden. Its findings and recommendations had not been made public by the end of the year.

In March a prosecutor closed the investigation into the alleged ill-treatment by police in 1997 of three men of ethnic minority origin (see *Amnesty International Report 1998*). She concluded that there was insufficient evidence of wrongful conduct by the police.

Upon examination of petitions brought by Iranian, Iraqi and Turkish nationals who had been refused asylum in Sweden, the UN Committee against Torture concluded that the decisions of the Swedish authorities in their cases violated the government's obligation under the UN Convention against Torture and Other Cruel, Inhuman or Degrading Treatment or Punishment not to expel or return a person to another state where there are substantial grounds for believing that they would be in danger of being subjected to torture or of being expelled to another state where they might face such a risk. Subsequently the authorities allowed one of the four to remain in Sweden; decisions on the other three were still pending at the end of the year.

SWITZERLAND

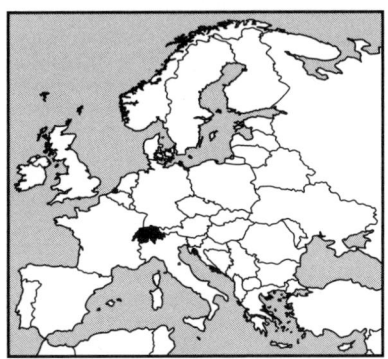

Police officers were the subject of fresh allegations of ill-treatment. A prisoner claimed his tetraplegia was the result of ill-treatment by a prison guard.

In February a committee of experts appointed by the Federal Office of Justice published the findings of a preliminary study identifying the possible characteristics of a future code unifying all 26 cantonal codes of penal procedure. In the context of their concern about alleged police ill-treatment, both the UN Human Rights Committee and the UN Committee against Torture had recommended in 1996 and 1997 respectively (see *Amnesty International Reports 1997* and *1998*) that Switzerland intensify efforts to harmonize the cantonal codes, particularly with regard to the granting of fundamental guarantees to detainees in police custody, including the introduction of a legal right for all detainees to inform relatives or a third party of their arrest and to have access to a lawyer from the moment of arrest. The study indicated support for the introduction of the former but not the latter. It was expected that the text of a draft code would be prepared by 2000.

In March the UN Committee on the Elimination of Racial Discrimination, following its consideration of Switzerland's first periodic report, expressed concern about "serious incidents of police brutality in dealing with persons of foreign ethnic

or national origin" and recommended more intensive training programs for law enforcement officials.

The text of a new Federal Constitution was adopted by parliament in December. It updated the 1874 Constitution, introducing reforms in the justice system and enhancing civil rights. The text, which included specific prohibitions on torture and all other cruel, inhuman or degrading treatment or punishment and on the return of any individual to a state where they would risk such treatment, was due to be put to a national referendum in April 1999.

Allegations of police ill-treatment came from several cantons and often concerned foreign nationals.

Judicial and administrative investigations were carried out into allegations made by Mamadou Sidibé, a national of Côte d'Ivoire, following his detention by Bern Municipal Police in December 1997 while on a holiday visit to relatives. In a criminal complaint lodged against the police at the end of that month he claimed that, while sightseeing in the city centre, two plainclothes police officers detained him on the street, without explanation, used unnecessary force to handcuff him, and racially abused him. He said that at the police station, when he asked for the reason for his arrest, the officers said it was because he was "black" and a "drug dealer", subjected him to further racial abuse, made him strip naked for a body search, slapped and repeatedly kicked and punched him, and threatened him with imprisonment and deportation as a drug dealer. His request to telephone his relatives was refused. He was released without charge the next day. According to a press statement issued by Bern Police four days later, the officers involved had been questioned and had made written statements and on the basis of these Mamadou Sidibé's allegations of ill-treatment and racial abuse could not be confirmed in any way at that time. He had been stopped in an area where the police were carrying out a check on African and Albanian drug dealers and taken to the police station for an identity check. Discrepancies had been found in his travel documents and he had been detained because of the need for further inquiries. The Bern authorities subsequently stated that the judicial investigation into Mamadou Sidibé's allegations

320

had not found grounds for any criminal or disciplinary action against the police.

In January the Geneva Prosecutor General dismissed a criminal complaint which Clement Nwankwo, a prominent Nigerian lawyer, had lodged against Geneva police (see *Amnesty International Report 1998*). He accused the police of assaulting him on the street and subjecting him to degrading treatment in a police station following his arrest in April 1997. The Prosecutor General acknowledged that, after being strip-searched, Clement Nwankwo had been "prevented – for almost an hour – from getting dressed again" and that this might be considered a criminal offence of abuse of authority. However, he concluded that disciplinary sanctions imposed on three officers following an administrative inquiry carried out in 1997 appeared to be sufficient punishment. The cantonal authorities had rejected Clement Nwankwo's allegations of physical assault, but had apologized for "the conditions" of his detention in the police station and promised sanctions against the officers concerned.

In his 1998 annual report, the UN Special Rapporteur on torture observed that "the facts in the Nwankwo case, where there was overwhelming evidence of abuse leading finally to some welcome disciplinary action against the law enforcement officials involved, suggest a judicial disposition precipitately and prematurely to believe the police and to disbelieve the foreign accused/complainant, as well as a reluctance to fully rectify the original wrong". The UN Special Rapporteur on the independence of judges and lawyers, in his 1998 annual report, expressed concern about several aspects of the case and recommended that Clement Nwankwo be offered "adequate compensation" for the incorrect treatment already acknowledged by the authorities. In April the federal authorities informed the Special Rapporteur that in March the Supreme Court had rejected Clement Nwankwo's final appeal against his conviction for resisting the police at the time of arrest and that, as this had put an end to all judicial proceedings, the Geneva authorities would be able to examine the question of compensation as soon as possible. No compensation had been paid by the end of the year. In October Clement Nwankwo learned from press reports that

the disciplinary sanctions against the three police officers had been annulled following appeals proceedings. The Geneva authorities had not informed him of the decision or of the reasoning behind it by the end of the year.

In October Clement Nwankwo lodged a petition against Switzerland with the European Commission of Human Rights claiming violation of two articles of the European Convention for the Protection of Human Rights and Fundamental Freedoms.

In November the Ticino cantonal authorities stated that criminal investigations opened into the formal complaint lodged against police officers by two Turkish Kurds in 1994 (see *Amnesty International Report 1998*) had been definitively closed by the Public Prosecutor in November 1997. The Prosecutor had concluded that there was no concrete evidence to support the men's claims that they had been beaten by Lugano police or to prove completely, or to render it highly probable, that the injuries recorded in medical reports accompanying their complaint were the result of blows inflicted by the police. The injuries included a perforated ear-drum in one case and multiple contusions, bruising and the loss of two teeth in the other.

In November the Public Prosecutor confirmed that A.S., an asylum-seeker from the Kosovo province of Yugoslavia, was not directly questioned about his allegations of ill-treatment by Lugano police or given an opportunity to identify his alleged aggressors during the investigation of the formal complaint he had lodged following his detention in December 1995 (see *Amnesty International Report 1998*). A.S. had sought the prosecution of unidentified officers on charges of serious bodily harm, failure to provide medical assistance and abuse of authority. In July 1997 the Prosecutor had stated that, after investigation, there was no reason to doubt the veracity of the police version of events rejecting A.S.'s allegations. In November the Ticino Prosecutor General ruled that there were no grounds to pursue criminal proceedings as a result of A.S.'s complaint. He concluded that there was insufficient evidence of abuse of authority and, although recognizing that A.S. had sustained injuries and had received no medical assistance, found no proof of deliberate failure to provide assistance. He said that A.S.'s injuries, which police claimed had been incurred during an escape attempt, did not qualify as serious bodily harm under the penal code, but as mere bodily harm. Unlike the former offence, which could be pursued on the Prosecutor's own authority, the latter required the alleged victim to seek prosecution. However, in March A.S. had withdrawn from the prosecution and this alleged offence could not now be considered for prosecution.

In November the Ticino judicial authorities also reported that they had informed the Federal Office of Police that a request in A.S.'s name, withdrawing his asylum application, had been made during his police interrogation when he had no access to an interpreter, lawyer or magistrate. A.S. claimed police coerced him into signing the document, whose contents he had not understood.

In June Felipe Lourenço, a Brazilian national, lodged a criminal complaint against a guard at Champ-Dollon prison, Geneva, accusing the guard of causing him grievous bodily harm on the day of his admission to prison. Felipe Lourenço said that when the guard escorted him to a small cell, he began to feel claustrophobic and resisted the guard's efforts to make him enter, eventually going down on all fours. He alleged that the guard then threw him with force against a wall. After falling to the ground he realized that his arms and legs were paralyzed and asked the guard for help. He claimed that the guard then tried to force him into a sitting position and hit him, accusing him of faking injury, and that there was a delay of around two hours before he received any medical assistance.

He was transferred to a local hospital where he underwent an operation but hospital doctors reportedly stated that he had suffered irreversible damage to the spine, meaning that, at best, he might eventually recover the use of his arms: his breathing difficulties were due to a perforated lung.

In the following days the prison authorities stated that, according to the guard in question, Felipe Lourenço had incurred his injuries by suddenly throwing himself head first against a closed door, and that there was no undue delay in providing medical assistance. The judicial investiga-

tion into the case was still under way at the end of the year.

Amnesty International expressed concern about allegations of ill-treatment and sought information from the authorities on the progress and outcome of judicial and administrative investigations. Replies were received regarding the status of inquiries and court proceedings.

SYRIA

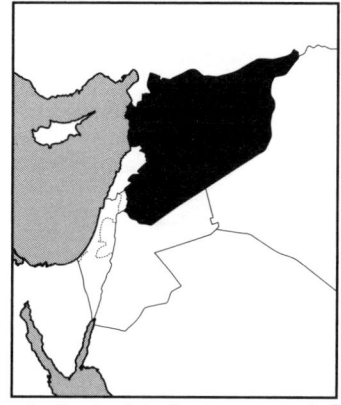

Hundreds of political prisoners, including prisoners of conscience, were released. Dozens of people were arrested on political grounds and hundreds of political prisoners, including prisoners of conscience, continued to serve prison sentences imposed after unfair trials. At least four prisoners of conscience continued to be held beyond the expiry of their sentences. Torture and ill-treatment continued to be routine in some prisons. Political prisoners faced harsh prison conditions and denial of adequate medical care. The fate of scores of prisoners who "disappeared" in previous years remained unknown. At least one person was sentenced to death and executed.

Following a decree by President Hafez al-Assad, parliamentary elections for the People's Assembly were held in November and December. The National Progressive Front, led by the ruling Arab Socialist Ba'th party, won the majority of seats; the rest were allocated to "independents".

Hundreds of political prisoners, including prisoners of conscience, were released following presidential amnesties. Among those freed were prisoners of conscience

Riad al-Turk, a lawyer detained without charge or trial since 1980; Aktham Nu'asa, a human rights defender and lawyer who was serving a nine-year prison sentence imposed by the Supreme State Security Court (SSSC) after an unfair trial; and Khalil Brayez, a former army officer and a writer who was held for nearly 28 years, including 13 years beyond the expiry of his sentence (see previous *Amnesty International Reports*). All were released in May. In March, 121 Lebanese political prisoners were released. They had been detained in Syria since the 1980s mostly without charge or trial (see **Lebanon** entry).

Others released included 'Umar 'Abd al-Mutallab Sarsur, a Jordanian who was freed in January. He had reportedly been detained for four months on charges of spying for Iraq after he delivered a letter from a Syrian prisoner in Iraq to his family in Latakia. Zubayda Muqabel, who was arrested in July 1997 (see *Amnesty International Report 1998*), was released in March or April. Most of the Syrian Kurds who were arrested in 1997 (see *Amnesty International Report 1998*) were also reportedly released.

Dozens of people were arrested on political grounds. They included Musa 'Aliqa, a Syrian Kurd who had lived in Germany as a political refugee for several years. He was arrested in July by military intelligence upon his return to Syria. Ra'fat 'Issa al-Balbul, a Jordanian, was also arrested in July while on a visit to Syria on suspicion of working for the Jordanian intelligence services. He was held in Sednaya prison and had not been tried by the end of the year.

Two Iraqi nationals – Fa'iq Ibrahim al-Yasseri, Director of the Damascus-based Iraqi Centre for Humanitarian Activities (ICHA), and Khalil Ibrahim Hussain, a former Iraqi army officer – were arrested in November reportedly after an article by Khalil Ibrahim Hussain was published in the ICHA's journal *Al-Karama*. Both were reportedly still held incommunicado at the end of the year.

Ma'ruf al-Jarrah, a poet, was also arrested in November for his suspected links with the unauthorized opposition groups *Hizb al-'Ummal al-Thawri al-'Arabi*, Arab Workers' Revolutionary Party, and *al-Tajmu' al-Watani al-Demoqrati*, National Democratic Alliance. He was reportedly arrested by the Military Intelligence in the capital, Damascus, and remained held at the end of the year.

Hundreds of political prisoners, including prisoners of conscience, remained held mostly serving prison sentences imposed after grossly unfair trials.

At least 70 prisoners of conscience remained held in connection with suspected membership of the unauthorized *Hizb al-'Amal al-Shuy'i*, Party for Communist Action (PCA). They included 'Abbas Mahmud 'Abbas, who was arrested in 1987 and sentenced in 1994 to 15 years' imprisonment by the SSSC. 'Abd al-'Aziz al-Khayyir, who was sentenced by the SSSC to 22 years' imprisonment in 1995, the longest term known to have been passed by the SSSC, remained in detention (see previous *Amnesty International Reports*). Doha 'Ashur al-'Askari, who was serving a six-year prison sentence (see *Amnesty International Report 1998*), was reportedly transferred to 'Adra civil prison. At least 20 prisoners of conscience, mostly detained since the 1980s and sentenced by the SSSC to various terms of imprisonment in connection with the PCA, were released. They included Khadija As'ad Dib, al-Hareth al-Nabhan and Safwan 'Akkash.

At least seven prisoners of conscience continued to serve prison sentences for alleged activities in connection with *al-Hizb al-Shuyu'i al-Maktab al-Siyassi*, Communist Party-Political Bureau (CPPB). They included Aram Karabayt, who was arrested in 1987 and sentenced to 12 years' imprisonment by the SSSC; and Ibrahim al-Khouri, who was reportedly arrested in al-Qamishli in 1996 and remained in detention at the end of the year. It was unclear whether Ibrahim al-Khouri, who had apparently been sought by the authorities since 1988, was tried or continued to be held without charge or trial.

Five prisoners of conscience held in connection with the unauthorized Committees for the Defence of Democratic Freedoms and Human Rights in Syria (CDF) since 1992 continued to serve prison sentences of up to 10 years imposed by the SSSC. They were Nizar Nayyuf, Muhammad 'Ali Habib, 'Afif Muzhir, Bassam al-Sheikh and Thabit Murad.

At least four prisoners of conscience remained in custody despite having completed their prison sentences. They included Fateh Jamus and Isam Dimashqi, both detained since 1982 for their alleged links with the PCA and sentenced to 15 years' imprisonment in 1994 by the SSSC. Both remained detained in Far' Falastin prison at the end of the year. Prisoners of conscience Bassam Budur, Taisir Hassoun and 'Adib al-Jani, who had been held for three years beyond the expiry of their sentences (see *Amnesty International Report 1998*), were released.

At least 13 Kurdish political prisoners, most arrested between 1995 and 1996 for distribution of leaflets, remained in detention. They included Muhammad Ma'sum Dawud, held in 'Adra, and Faris Muhammad Khalil, held in Sednaya, both detained since 1995. They were reportedly each sentenced by the SSSC to four years' imprisonment.

Scores of political prisoners held in connection with the unauthorized *al-Ikhwan al-Muslimun* (Muslim Brotherhood) were released. However, several hundred remained in detention, mostly held in incommunicado detention since the 1970s or early 1980s without charge or trial or after summary and secret trials (see previous *Amnesty International Reports*). They included Sarih Fawzi 'Amin, a medical student arrested in 1980 and reportedly held in Tadmur military prison, and 'Ihssan Murad, a medical doctor who was reportedly arrested in 1992. It was not known whether they had been charged or tried.

Hundreds of Palestinians and Jordanians arrested for political reasons since the 1980s in Lebanon, Syria or at the Syrian border with Jordan continued to be held, mostly in incommunicado detention (see previous *Amnesty International Reports*). They included Mustafa Dib Khalil (known as Abu Ta'an), a Palestinian in his sixties who was arrested in 1983 in Tripoli, north Lebanon, by a breakaway Palestinian group and subsequently handed to Syrian authorities; and Sa'id al-Hatamleh, a Jordanian who was arrested in Syria in 1985 in connection with the unauthorized Jordanian Revolutionary Party and reportedly sentenced to 10 years' imprisonment. Mustafa Dib Khalil was held for eight years in solitary confinement and had been held incommunicado apparently without charge or trial for most of the past 15 years. Both were apparently held in Sednaya prison at the end of the year.

Scores of Lebanese political prisoners continued to be held in Syria either without charge or trial, or after grossly unfair trials. They were either captured or abducted in Lebanon during the civil war there from 1975 to 1990, or were arrested by Syrian forces operating in Lebanon and taken to Syria after 1990. Among the prisoners were Najib Yusuf Jarmani, who was arrested in January 1997 from his house in Ba'bdat, Lebanon, and apparently transferred a few days later to Syria; and Samir 'Ali Hassan, who was arrested by Syrian intelligence forces in connection with *Harakat al-Tawhid al-Islami*, Islamic Unification Movement, in 1989. Both were reportedly still held in Sednaya prison at the end of the year. Bashir al-Khatib, who had been detained in Syria since 1996 (see *Amnesty International Report 1998*), was among the 121 Lebanese released in March.

Torture continued to be routine in some prisons. At least four prisoners of conscience – Jurays al-Talli, Nu'man 'Abdu, Salama George Kayla and Mahmud 'Issa – serving sentences of up to 15 years' imprisonment for their alleged links with the PCA, were transferred in July to Tadmur military prison, where torture is routine, apparently as a form of punishment. After their transfer, they were mostly held incommunicado and denied access to their families, adding to fears that they were tortured and ill-treated.

Three police officers were sentenced to 10 years' imprisonment with hard labour by the First Criminal Court in Aleppo on charges of inflicting grievous bodily harm and the killing of Ahmad Farwati during interrogation. Ahmad Farwati, who had been arrested for his alleged involvement in drug dealing, was reportedly tortured to death in Bab al-Nayrab police station in Aleppo. No investigation into allegations of torture of political detainees in previous years was known to have been initiated.

The health of a number of prisoners of conscience and other political prisoners gave cause for concern because of lack of adequate medical treatment or harsh prison conditions. Three of the prisoners of conscience transferred to Tadmur (see above) were suffering from ailments requiring specialist medical care, and there were fears that their health deteriorated further as a result of their transfer to Tadmur. Other prisoners with illnesses who were denied adequate medical treatment included Nizar Nayyuf, who reportedly has Hodgkin's disease, a form of cancer; 'Abdalla Qabbara, aged 60, who has chronic diabetes; and 'Abd al-Majid Zagh-mout, who has heart problems and high blood pressure. 'Abd al-Majid Zaghmout, a Palestinian detained for 32 years (including nine years after his release was ordered by the Minister of Defence), went on hunger strike to protest against his continued detention.

No information was available about the fate and whereabouts of scores of people who "disappeared" in previous years. The victims included Dani Mansurati, a Lebanese man who "disappeared" following his arrest in 'Arnus Square in al-Sha'lan area of Damascus in 1992; and Muhammad Zahed Derqal, who was reportedly arrested at the Abu-Khair Mosque in Damascus in 1980 apparently for his suspected links with the Muslim Brotherhood.

At least one person was sentenced to death and executed. Bilal Suleiman Khuzam, who had been convicted of murder and rape, was hanged in 'Adra prison in February.

Throughout the year Amnesty International urged the government to release prisoners of conscience, review cases of long-term political prisoners, provide adequate medical care to prisoners and investigate allegations of torture and ill-treatment. The government responded to some of Amnesty International's communications and provided information on some political prisoners.

TAIWAN

There were continuing reports of police ill-treatment, despite legislative amendments strengthening human rights protection of detainees. There were at least 32 executions, continuing a trend of increased use of the death penalty.

In December the ruling *Kuomintang*, led by President Lee Teng-hui, won a majority of seats in elections to the Legislative *Yuan* (the main law-making body).

A major revision to the code of criminal procedure adopted in late December 1997 took effect in 1998. The new code strengthened human rights protection by obliging prosecutors and police to release suspects within 24 hours unless a warrant is obtained from a court. It also stipulated that suspects be informed of their right to remain silent and that lawyers may be present during interrogation. Overnight interrogation is prohibited, except in certain circumstances. In January the Council of Grand Justices (CGJ) – a constitutional tribunal – ruled unconstitutional articles in the Assembly and Parade Law which ban advocacy of independence or communism.

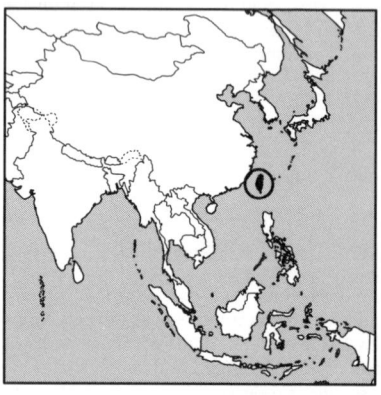

In June Cheng Chung-mo was appointed Minister of Justice. The new Minister said he would take a "pragmatic" approach to the death penalty. He also stated that he did not support the doctrine of "severe punishments under strict laws" which calls for longer prison sentences, increased use of the death penalty and a reduction in the rights of suspects and defendants. The previous Minister of Justice had dropped earlier plans to reintroduce whipping as a punishment for certain criminal offences committed by juveniles (see *Amnesty International Report 1998*).

In September the government announced that it was planning to introduce a civilian alternative to compulsory military service, but by the end of the year legislation and regulations regarding compulsory military service remained unchanged.

The government drew up draft proposals for amendments to the law governing military tribunals, following the 1997 ruling by the CGJ that several aspects of the law were unconstitutional (see *Amnesty International Report 1998*). There were concerns that the draft amendments would fall short of the constitutional criteria set down by the CGJ.

In a ruling in September the Supreme Court awarded 10 million New Taiwan dollars (around US$300,000) compensation to seven people who had been wrongfully imprisoned on sedition charges in the early 1950s, overturning a previous government decision. The victims, including Chen Tsu-hung and Lu Tung-po, had been held for up to one year for alleged activities to overthrow the government. The government had refused their claim on the grounds that official documents about their cases had been misplaced.

Human rights groups continued to record instances of police ill-treatment, mostly in local police stations when interrogations were not recorded and lawyers were not present. Conditions of detention in some police stations were reported to be below minimum international standards. Two foreign nationals held in police detention for two weeks in March said they had been handcuffed and chained together and refused permission to go to the toilet during the first night of detention. Thereafter, they were reportedly held in dirty, cramped cells and refused permission to make a telephone call.

At least 32 people were executed. The executions continued the trend of increased use of the death penalty, apparently in response to public concern about crime rates. The death penalty is mandatory for 65 offences and optional for a further 95 offences. The criminal code allows for executions by shooting or lethal injection, although no lethal injection execution has been carried out to date. The practice of continuously shackling the hands and feet of prisoners sentenced to death continued.

Su Chien-ho, Liu Bin-lang and Chuang Lin-hsuing, who were sentenced to death in 1991 for murder despite strong indications that they were innocent, remained at imminent threat of execution having exhausted all avenues of appeal (see *Amnesty International Reports 1996 to 1998*).

The authorities were reported to have continued an informal policy of transferring refugees to third countries: Taiwan has no law or set of procedures under which non-citizens may apply for political asylum. Those awaiting "deportation" were generally detained, sometimes for long periods. Illegal immigrants from the People's Republic of China continued to be regularly detained in immigration detention centres before deportation, sometimes for many months in conditions that were often overcrowded.

In June an Amnesty International delegate visited Taiwan to discuss human rights concerns with President Lee Teng-hui and senior government ministers. The same month Amnesty International published a report, *Death sentences based on unfair convictions: three men face execution*, which called for a full and impartial investigation into the convictions of Su Chien-ho, Liu Bin-lang and Chuang Lin-hsuing and for their death sentences to be commuted. Amnesty International continued to call for the abolition of the death penalty and urged the government to establish a national human rights commission.

TAJIKISTAN

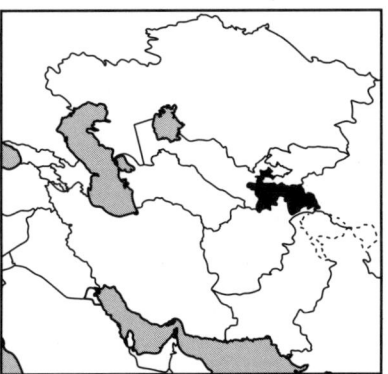

Several political prisoners were allegedly tortured in pre-trial detention and six were sentenced to death after an unfair trial. One of them, who was critically ill, was denied appropriate medical treatment. At least 18 other people were sentenced to death. No executions were reported.

In January President Imomali Rakhmonov signed a decree granting an amnesty to all opposition leaders, including Sayed Abdullo Nuri, leader of the United Tajik Opposition (UTO) and chairman of the National Reconciliation Commission (NRC). The same month an agreement was reached on which government posts would be given to UTO members, but progress in sharing out cabinet posts was slow.

In April the NRC announced that it would investigate reports that five mass graves containing the bodies of an estimated 2,600 victims of the 1992-1993 civil war had been discovered close to the capital, Dushanbe.

In May, following international protests, parliament amended a controversial draft law which would have banned religious political parties, thereby outlawing the UTO.

In July President Rakhmonov rejected a new law on the protection of the honour and dignity of the President of Tajikistan, which provided for punishments including terms of imprisonment of up to six years for making public statements critical of the President. The provisions of the law were, however, incorporated into the new criminal code which came into force in September. The new criminal code also decriminalized consenting homosexual acts between adult males and reduced to 15 the number of articles carrying a possible death sentence. It also stipulated that on commutation death sentences should be replaced with 25 years' imprisonment.

In March, six men were sentenced to death by the Supreme Court for treason, banditry and terrorism, apparently without right of appeal. Among them was Abdulkhafiz Abdullayev, the younger brother of Abdumalik Abdullojonov, a former prime minister and the head of the opposition National Revival Bloc. Abdulkhafiz Abdullayev, Firdavs Dustboboyev, Ilkhom Dodojonov, Buriboi Akbarov, Jumaboy Juraev and Rustam Shaykhitdinov were found guilty of planning and carrying out an assassination attempt on President Rakhmonov in Khujand in April 1997 (see Amnesty International Report 1998). Nine other co-defendants received prison sentences ranging from one to 14 years. Supporters of Abdulkhafiz Abdullayev claimed that the motive for his inclusion in this criminal case and for the charges against him was to intimidate the Khujand-based opposition, which had been excluded from the peace process.

There were allegations that during the investigation and even during the trial his co-defendants had been forced under duress to incriminate Abdulkhafiz Abdullayev. According to one report, Firdavs Dustboboyev, Buriboi Akbarov

and Ilkhom Dodojonov were tortured after they had denied in court that Abdulkhafiz Abdullayev had been involved in the assassination attempt. They were reportedly subjected to electric shocks and beaten with sticks at the Ministry of Security. Firdavs Dustboboyev allegedly had two of his ribs broken, one hand severely injured, and lost his sight in one eye.

Abdulkhafiz Abdullayev was tried and sentenced to death despite medical evidence that he was critically ill with cancer and was unfit to stand trial. He was reportedly still not receiving appropriate medical attention a month after being sentenced, despite a further recommendation by a medical panel that he be transferred to a specialist oncological unit. He was reportedly denied chemotherapy treatment and remained on death row, where his condition was said to be steadily deteriorating. He was reportedly unable to walk unaided.

Petitions for clemency by the six men sentenced to death were submitted to President Rakhmonov who reportedly rejected them at the end of December.

At least 18 other people were sentenced to death. No executions were reported during the year.

Amnesty International expressed grave concern at reports that Abdulkhafiz Abdullayev was denied appropriate medical treatment and urged that he be moved to a specialist hospital. The organization also called on the authorities to investigate swiftly and impartially allegations that several of Abdulkhafiz Abdullayev's co-defendants were beaten or otherwise tortured in order to extract confessions.

Amnesty International expressed concern that the law on protecting the honour and dignity of the President of Tajikistan proposed by parliament could be applied in ways which violated the right to freedom of expression as set out in Article 19 of the International Covenant on Civil and Political Rights.

Amnesty International welcomed the reduction in the number of offences punishable by death in the new criminal code. It continued to appeal for the commutation of death sentences and to call for the total abolition of the death penalty.

TANZANIA

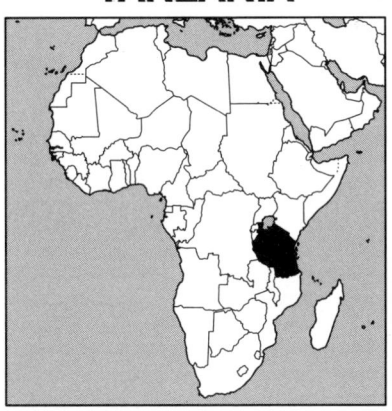

Eighteen prisoners of conscience, including three arrested during the year, were facing trial for treason on the island of Zanzibar, an offence that carries the death penalty. Scores of other opposition supporters in Zanzibar were imprisoned for short periods; some were possible prisoners of conscience. More than 300 demonstrators arrested on the mainland in the capital Dar es Salaam were held for several weeks and reportedly tortured. Conditions in some prisons were harsh. Several death sentences were imposed. There were no executions.

Tanzania was host to more than 300,000 refugees from the continuing crisis in the Great Lakes region, including new arrivals. Refugees included 5,500 Rwandans remaining after the forced repatriations of 1997, as well as at least 260,000 Burundians and 47,000 people from the Democratic Republic of the Congo.

Throughout the year Commonwealth officials sought to mediate in the political crisis in Zanzibar between the government and ruling *Chama cha Mapinduzi* (CCM), Party of the Revolution, and the opposition Civic United Front (CUF), which was boycotting the Zanzibar parliament in protest against allegedly rigged presidential elections in 1995.

In July the Tanzanian government instituted public and parliamentary consultations on constitutional reform. The Law Reform Commission was studying the Preventive Detention Act (not used for several years), the Corporal Punishment Ordinance, and laws restricting press freedom. However, press freedom continued to be restricted: two newspapers were banned on the mainland and two in Zanzibar, and several journalists were interrogated on account of articles critical of the government. The reform process, welcomed by human rights groups and non-governmental organizations, was resisted by the government in Zanzibar, which has a separate semi-autonomous constitution and legal system.

A bomb attack on the US embassy on 7 August killed 11 people and injured more than 70. Over 30 people were arrested, most of them foreign nationals of Middle Eastern origin. All but two, who were charged with murder, were released within a week.

Tanzania submitted its third periodic report in July to the UN Human Rights Committee on its observance of the International Covenant on Civil and Political Rights. Although the Committee raised questions, several human rights issues, particularly those concerning Zanzibar, were not addressed.

Three CUF members were arrested in Zanzibar: Hamad Rashid Mohamed, a member of the House of Representatives (Zanzibar's parliament) and former Tanzanian Deputy Finance Minister, who was arrested in January; and Zeina Juma Mohamed, a housewife, and Juma Duni Haji, a member of the House of Representatives and formerly CUF's candidate for the Tanzanian vice-presidency, both of whom were arrested in May. They were charged with treason along with the 15 other CUF members who had been arrested in 1997 (see *Amnesty International Report 1998*). By the end of the year the prosecution had not demonstrated any evidence to substantiate the charge and the start of the trial was repeatedly delayed. All 18 were prisoners of conscience imprisoned for their peaceful opinions and non-violent political activity. Many of them fell ill because they were denied access to hospital or to treatment by medical doctors of their choice. One of the women prisoners, Zulekha Ahmed Mohamed, suffered a suspected femoral hernia, diabetes and high blood pressure, for which proper treatment was refused.

Scores of other CUF supporters were arrested by police or by CCM militias and held for days or for weeks. Others were

328

imprisoned for months after unfair and politically motivated trials on fabricated criminal charges: they appeared to be prisoners of conscience.

Torture and ill-treatment by police were reported. On 12 February soldiers entered the Mwembechai mosque in Dar es Salaam and beat worshippers, accusing them of blaspheming against Christianity, spreading "Islamic fundamentalism" and preaching against the government. Demonstrations in the following two days led to attacks on government vehicles and the arrest of 320 people. Three people were shot dead by police. Those arrested, who included men, women and children, were reportedly beaten and otherwise tortured. Women were stripped naked in front of guards and prisoners of both sexes, and searched internally, purportedly for weapons. Many of those detained were held without charge for weeks before being released. Charges against most of the remaining 140 prisoners were withdrawn by the end of March. A further 15 people were arrested on 29 March during a demonstration at Mwembechai mosque. By May all those held in connection with these two incidents had been released without charge.

Harsh conditions in some prisons amounted to cruel, inhuman and degrading treatment. In Mbeya prison in western Tanzania, such conditions led to the deaths of 47 prisoners in the first half of the year.

Several people were sentenced to death for homicide. No figures were available for the total number of people sentenced to death. There were no executions.

Amnesty International delegates visited Tanzania in March to obtain information about the treatment and reasons for flight of refugees from Burundi. In November Amnesty International wrote to the government expressing concern about restrictive articles in the new Refugee Act passed by parliament, but not ratified by the President during the year, which were inconsistent with international standards for refugee protection. In May Amnesty International delegates visited the country to investigate conflicting accounts of the alleged deaths of gold-miners in Bulyankulu, western Tanzania, in 1996 (see *Amnesty International Reports 1997* and *1998*). Amnesty International's memorandum to the government in December recommended the establishment of an independent commission of inquiry into the incident.

Delegates also visited Zanzibar in June to investigate the trial and treatment of 18 CUF prisoners of conscience. Amnesty International appealed for their release.

THAILAND

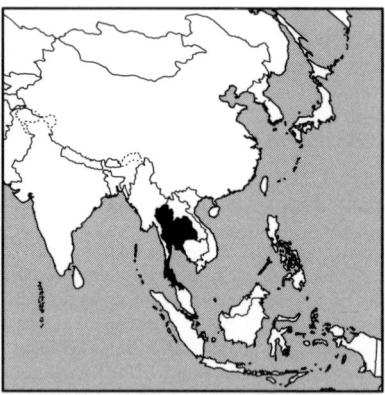

Although Thailand gave refuge to thousands of refugees from neighbouring Cambodia and Myanmar, thousands more Burmese asylum-seekers were denied access. Burmese asylum-seekers and refugees continued to be arrested for "illegal immigration". One Karen refugee was beaten to death by security forces. The security forces ill-treated demonstrators and detainees. Conditions in places of detention amounted to cruel, inhuman or degrading treatment. Thirteen people were sentenced to death; one person was executed.

The coalition government of Prime Minister Chuan Leekpai remained in power amid a severe economic downturn, which necessitated a substantial loan from the International Monetary Fund. Legislation establishing a National Human Rights Commission, provided for in the 1997 Constitution, had been drafted but not adopted by the end of the year.

Thailand's report to the UN Human Rights Committee on its implementation of the International Covenant on Civil and Political Rights was due in January, but the report had not been submitted by the end of the year.

AMNESTY INTERNATIONAL REPORT 1999

Throughout the year asylum-seekers from the Karen, Karenni and Shan ethnic minorities fled Myanmar into Thailand. In March and April the Democratic Kayin Buddhist Organization, an armed ethnic minority group allied to the Burmese army, attacked three Karen refugee camps in Tak Province, killing five people and leaving thousands homeless. The Ninth Infantry Division of the First Army continued to prevent thousands of Karen asylum-seekers from entering Thailand, who remained at risk of human rights violations in Myanmar. Some 3,000 Karen asylum-seekers at Htee Wah Do village in Myanmar were still denied permission to cross the border into Thailand after almost two years. The government permitted the UN High Commissioner for Refugees (UNHCR) to establish a permanent presence on the Thai-Myanmar border to monitor more than 100,000 refugees on the Thai side. By the end of the year the government had agreed five areas of work for UNHCR: to witness the process of refugee admission; to assist the authorities in registration; to assist and advise the authorities on camp relocation; and to assist refugees on their safe return.

Immigration officials and police continued to arrest asylum-seekers and refugees from Myanmar and other countries for "illegal immigration". Detained asylum-seekers were not given an opportunity to challenge the legality of their detention as required by international standards. In January, nine Burmese asylum-seekers, all members of groups opposed to the Myanmar government, were arrested in Sangklaburi, Kanchanaburi Province, and detained for two weeks before being taken to the Myanmar side of the border. In August, 30 Burmese refugees and asylum-seekers were arrested during a prolonged peaceful protest in front of the Myanmar embassy in the capital Bangkok, held in the immigration detention centre for two weeks, and transferred to the Special Detention Centre at Bankhen Police Academy, where they were believed to be still detained without trial at the end of the year. Throughout the year immigration officials and police arrested and sent to the border tens of thousands of Burmese migrant workers, some of whom were asylum-seekers. There continued to be no legal mechanism in Thailand for seeking asylum.

Some asylum-seekers were ill-treated. In January around 20 Karen refugees, including two women aged over 65, were reportedly beaten and kicked by soldiers when they returned to Mae La camp, Tak Province, after foraging for food. In March Nyan Lin, a Karen refugee, was beaten to death by soldiers because he returned to his camp after curfew. No investigation was known to have taken place, although his widow received financial compensation from the security forces.

The security forces also ill-treated demonstrators and detainees. In January police beat and kicked demonstrators who had given themselves up during a violent workers' demonstration in Samut Prakhan Province near Bangkok. Also in January, three Muslims belonging to the Patani United Liberation Organization, an armed ethnic Malay separatist group in southern Thailand, were reportedly severely beaten while handcuffed and bound by security forces during 10 days of interrogation after their arrest. They were still detained and their trial on charges of treason, murder and possession of weapons was continuing at the end of the year.

The case brought by the families of six suspected drug traffickers shot dead by police in November 1996 was brought to Suphan Buri court in October (see *Amnesty International Report 1998*), and was still being heard at the end of the year.

Conditions in police lock-ups, immigration detention centres and prisons amounted to cruel, inhuman or degrading treatment. Prisoners were shackled continuously for months at a time, held in solitary confinement for extended periods, or held in extremely overcrowded conditions. Adequate medical care, sanitation, food and water were lacking in many places of detention. In Bombat Piset Prison, where people convicted of drugs offences were imprisoned, there was severe overcrowding and routine beatings. In Bangkwang Prison, prisoners were continuously kept for months in shackles weighing between seven and 15 kilograms welded to the ankles. Prisoners in Chonburi Prison were also kept in heavy shackles for prolonged periods and severely beaten.

In October Supoj Pengklai, a policeman who had been convicted of murder in 1996, was executed by firing squad. Thirteen people were sentenced to death for

330

rape, rape and murder, and amphetamine trafficking. At least 52 others were believed to be under sentence of death at the end of the year.

In January and February Amnesty International delegates visited Thailand to research its human rights concerns and hold discussions with government officials. Throughout the year Amnesty International appealed to the government not to forcibly return asylum-seekers to Myanmar. In November the organization condemned the execution of Supoj Pengklai and urged the authorities not to carry out any further executions.

TOGO

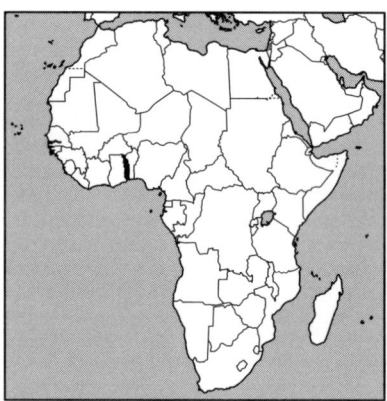

Hundreds of people were extrajudicially executed by the security forces. Scores of people, including refugees extradited from Ghana, opposition supporters, students and journalists were detained without charge or trial. Torture and ill-treatment continued to be widespread. Harsh prison conditions amounted to cruel, inhuman or degrading treatment. One person "disappeared".

In October a law forbidding female genital mutilation was passed by the National Assembly.

President Gnassingbe Eyadéma, leader of the *Rassemblement du peuple togolais* (RPT), Assembly of the Togolese People, faced five challengers in presidential elections held in June. President Eyadéma, in power since 1967, was re-elected for another five years, but there were serious doubts over the fairness of the elections. European Union observers criticized the

outcome. The run-up to the elections was marked by arrests and intimidation of supporters of the main opposition parties by the security forces.

Hundreds of people – both unarmed civilians and soldiers – were extrajudicially executed by the security forces before and after the presidential elections. Bodies of victims, some handcuffed, were found in the sea and on beaches in both Togo and Benin, reportedly after being dropped from aeroplanes and helicopters. At least three victims were reportedly beaten to death by soldiers and their bodies left on the streets of Lomé, the capital.

Armed RPT supporters, acting with the security forces, were responsible for terrorizing and harassing members of opposition political parties, particularly in Afagnan, the Yoto and Atakpamé. In the Yoto, Mathieu Kegbe Koffi, a representative of the opposition *Comité d'action pour le renouveau* (CAR), Action Committee for Renewal, was killed in September in front of his family by an armed group, including RPT supporters and men in uniform.

Scores of people, including Togolese refugees extradited from Ghana, opposition party supporters, students and journalists were detained without charge or trial during the year. They included prisoners of conscience.

In January, nine refugees, including Kove Sossouvi Komlan and Seke Akouete, were handed over by the Ghanaian authorities to the Togolese authorities who accused them of theft. One, Nutsukpi Attiso, died in custody as a result of lack of medical care. At the end of the year, the others were still held without charge in Kara prison. An asylum-seeker sent back to Togo from Germany was arrested on his arrival in January and held in a secret detention centre, from where he escaped in September.

In January police arrested at least 11 students and seriously injured several after a protest demonstration. After more than 10 days' detention, the students were released without charge on the instructions of President Eyadéma.

Scores of people were arrested before and after the June elections. Two representatives of the CAR, Adjiba Kossi and Okouta Biayeva Antoine, were arrested in Atakpamé and held without charge until mid-July. Oladokou Olabode, who was arrested at about the same time, remained in detention without charge or trial at the end of the year. One week after the elections, three members of the opposition *Parti pour la démocratie et le renouveau* (PDR) Party for Democratic Renewal, including Boukary Seydou, were arrested at Badou, Wawa district. They were taken to Lomé, then released after interrogation.

In July scores of opposition party supporters were arrested after a protest march and leaflet distribution by the *Union des forces de changement* (UFC), Union of the Forces for Change. Some were released without charge or trial after a few days, others were tried and sentenced to prison terms, and others were still held without charge at the end of the year. Kodjo Gbadogbe, a UFC supporter, was sentenced to six months' imprisonment. Two others, Atsu Abaya and Attiogbe Sassou, were charged with distributing leaflets. They were prisoners of conscience. They were released in December, but a few days later they were summoned by the tribunal. They were in hiding at the end of the year.

In August Kouni Kodjo, a painter, and Edoh Komlan, a student, were arrested in Adidogomé, near the border with Ghana. At the end of the year, they were still held without charge or trial and had been denied family visits. They were possible prisoners of conscience.

Two army officers – Dr Abony Koffi and Lieutenant Gnassenou – were arrested in August and November respectively and accused of supporting the opposition. They were still held without charge in the gendarmerie at the end of the year.

In September at least 11 prisoners of conscience including Gaï Yao, a student, and Badjagbo Adjovi, were arrested by the security forces in Afagnan and later transferred to Aného prison. They were held without charge for two weeks.

In October, three prisoners of conscience, including Masseme Kodjo and Adoyi Komlan, arrested in October 1997 were sentenced to one year's imprisonment, then released as they had already spent one year in detention.

Numerous journalists and newspaper editors were arrested during the year. In August Pamphile Gnimassou, editor-in-chief of *Abito*, and Augustin Assiogbo and Elias Hounkali of *Tingo-Tingo* were arrested for "attacking the honour" of the presidential couple. In November Edoh Amenouhou, a journalist at *Le Nouveau* *Combat* was arrested in connection with the same case. Augustin Assiogbo and Pamphile Gnimassou were released without charge or trial after a few days but the other journalists were still in detention at the end of the year. Appolinaire Mewenemesse, editor-in-chief of *La Dépêche*, was detained without charge from October to December following a defamation complaint lodged by the Minister of Defence.

In November new information came to light about detainees, including possible prisoners of conscience, arrested in previous years. Alowou Kokou and Marc Atidépé, arrested in 1993 on suspicion of being rebels, were still held without charge in Lomé civil prison and Kara prison. Paul and Pierre Hooper, two trade unionists arrested in 1995 and sentenced to prison terms were still detained in Lomé civil prison; they were prisoners of conscience. Dr. Gandi, a human rights activist, and several people arrested with him in 1997 were still awaiting trial.

The security forces ill-treated people who peacefully protested against the results of the presidential elections in different parts of the country, notably in Afagnan, Notsè and the capital. In August the security forces attacked and burned the homes of some opposition leaders. In the course of these attacks, civilians including women and children were severely beaten with rifle butts, batons and military belts; some were seriously injured.

Torture and ill-treatment of both political detainees and criminal suspects by the security forces remained routine. Detainees were frequently stripped, handcuffed and beaten. Many were held in overcrowded cells, provided with insufficient food and denied sanitary facilities. All nine refugees handed over by Ghana to the Togolese authorities were tortured in Lomé civil prison and severely beaten when they arrived at Kara prison. Nyableji John, also known as Django, was reportedly compelled to eat sand in Lomé civil prison. Political activists arrested after the presidential election were beaten on the head, buttocks and feet. Detainees were reportedly tied on a table and were beaten with sticks, cables and military belts by members of the security forces. Relatives stated that some prisoners were covered with scars and that some had swollen faces.

Prison conditions throughout the country, and particularly in Lomé civil prison,

332

remained extremely harsh and amounted to cruel, inhuman or degrading treatment. Severe deficiencies in food, sanitation, and medical care resulted in a high mortality rate. Seriously ill prisoners were denied medical treatment. Adossi Kokouvi, who was arrested in January, died in April as a result of medical neglect.

In August Djiewone Adjisse Essie "disappeared" from the gendarmerie where he was detained after his arrest at Yokoe.

Amnesty International delegates visited Togo and met government ministers, judicial and security officials. The delegates also met leaders of the opposition, human rights activists and representatives of international organizations. In talks with the authorities, Amnesty International raised concerns about extrajudicial executions and "disappearances", the detention of prisoners of conscience, widespread torture and impunity. One minister acknowledged that a "rebel" had been extrajudicially executed, but the authorities denied the other concerns, particularly arbitrary arrests of prisoners of conscience followed by torture. In a meeting with the Minister of Defence, his French military adviser denied the possibility that aeroplanes and helicopters of the Togolese armed forces had been used to drop bodies into the sea.

TRINIDAD AND TOBAGO

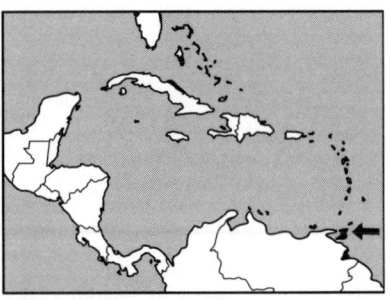

About 80 people remained under sentence of death. Twenty men were scheduled to be hanged, some in defiance of international court orders. No executions took place. One person was reportedly subjected to corporal punishment while his appeal was pending. Conditions of detention and imprisonment were reported to be cruel, inhuman or degrading.

In order to facilitate executions, the government, led by Prime Minister Basdeo Panday, took unprecedented steps to cut off recourse to international bodies for redress of violations of human rights. On 26 May it informed the Secretary-General of the Organization of American States of Trinidad and Tobago's withdrawal as a state party to the American Convention on Human Rights. Unless rescinded, the withdrawal will take effect on 26 May 1999. Calling this a "serious step backwards in the hemispheric attempt to strengthen the Inter-American human rights system", the Inter-American Commission on Human Rights (IACHR) called on the government to reconsider its decision. This message was echoed by the General Assembly of the Organization of American States.

The government also took measures to preclude the UN Human Rights Committee from considering petitions brought by people sentenced to death who claim that their rights under the International Covenant on Civil and Political Rights (ICCPR) have been violated in connection with capital proceedings against them or any matter related to the carrying out of the death sentence. To this end, the government notified the UN Secretary-General on 26 May that Trinidad and Tobago was withdrawing as a state party to the Optional Protocol to the ICCPR, and on the same day submitted an instrument to rejoin the treaty as a state party, but with a reservation that seeks to prevent the Human Rights Committee from examining claims submitted by people sentenced to death.

About 80 men and women remained under sentence of death under laws which make the death penalty mandatory for murder. Among them was Indravani Pamela Ramjattan, a battered woman who was convicted in 1995 of involvement in the murder of her abusive common-law husband. The UN Special Rapporteur on extrajudicial, summary or arbitrary executions raised concern that the beatings she sustained, threats to shoot her and repeated rapes were not considered by the investigating authorities or courts to constitute mitigating circumstances. Considering the death penalty to be "too harsh a punishment for a crime committed in such situations", the Special Rapporteur urged the government to commute her death sentence and to respect the *de facto* moratorium on the execution of women in Trinidad and Tobago. She also expressed concern about the time limits placed by the government on international human rights bodies' scrutiny of death penalty cases.

The government scheduled the executions of 20 men, relying on instructions issued by the government in October 1997, which purport to set strict time limits for the IACHR's consideration of petitions brought by people under sentence of death (see *Amnesty International Report 1998*). Ten of the men were scheduled to be hanged despite the fact that the IACHR had not completed consideration of their petitions which claimed that their rights under the American Convention on Human Rights had been violated. Execution dates for five of the 10 men – Denny Baptiste, Anthony Briggs, Anthony Garcia, Wenceslaus James and Anderson Noel – were set even though the Inter-American Court of Human Rights had ordered the government to preserve their lives while their cases were pending in the Inter-American system.

In August the Inter-American Court of Human Rights noted that executing people while their petitions to the IACHR were pending would: "create an irremediable situation incompatible with the object and purpose of the [American] Convention and would amount to a disavowal of the authority of the [Inter-American] Commission and would adversely affect the very essence of the Inter-American system". The IACHR stated that in accordance with international law, the government could not invoke provisions of national law to justify its failure to comply with an international treaty.

No executions took place as all 20 men received stays of execution, almost all pending determination of constitutional challenges in the national courts.

The death sentences of more than 20 people, several of whom had spent more than five years on death row, were commuted to terms of imprisonment.

It was unclear whether at least three people, who were sentenced during the year to corporal punishment in addition to terms of imprisonment, had been whipped. The Court of Appeal reportedly described as "monstrous" the fact that Edward Boucher received 15 lashes in August while the appeal of his conviction and sentence was pending.

Despite requests, Amnesty International received no information from the authorities about developments in investigations into criminal proceedings brought in cases of fatal shootings by police in previous years (see *Amnesty International Report 1998*).

Reports gave rise to concern that conditions in places of detention continued to be so insanitary as to constitute cruel, inhuman or degrading treatment or punishment. Complaints about conditions of confinement on death row were pending before national courts and the IACHR.

Amnesty International expressed dismay at Trinidad and Tobago's withdrawal as a state party to the American Convention on Human Rights and urged the government to reconsider the decision. Amnesty International expressed deep regret about Trinidad and Tobago's reservation on reaccession to the Optional Protocol to the ICCPR. The organization also expressed regret that these measures were taken to enable executions to proceed without international scrutiny of whether the internationally protected rights of people sentenced to death had been upheld. Amnesty International urged the UN High Commissioner for Human Rights and the IACHR to take appropriate action in order that Trinidad and Tobago withdraw the instructions purporting to set time limits for the consideration by international human rights bodies of petitions brought by people under sentence of death. The organization also urged the government not to carry out executions, to commute the sentences of all people currently under sentence of death and, among other things, to propose and support legislation to create alternative punishments for murder.

TUNISIA

Hundreds of people, including many prisoners of conscience, were detained because of their alleged links with unauthorized political opposition groups or their non-violent activities. Among them were human rights defenders. Up to 2,000 political prisoners, most of them

334

prisoners of conscience, remained in prison. Political trials continued to violate international fair trial standards. Torture and ill-treatment, especially during incommunicado detention, continued. At least one person died in custody possibly as a result of torture or ill-treatment. Several people remained under sentence of death. No executions were reported during the year.

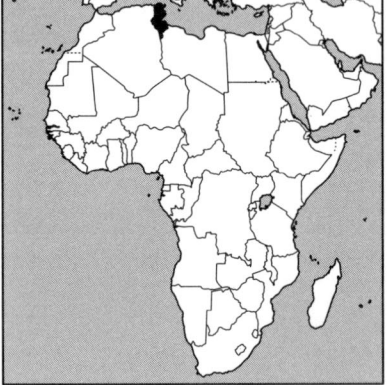

The government of President Zine el 'Abidine Ben 'Ali increased restrictions on freedom of expression. In May a law on postal services was passed banning any mail considered to "undermine public order and security" and allowing the confiscation of such mail. A draft amendment to the law on the external security of the state, which proposed making contacts with agents of foreign or international organizations a crime (see *Amnesty International Report 1998*), was withdrawn. Access to numerous Internet sites, including some of Amnesty International's websites, carrying information about human rights in Tunisia was blocked.

In November the UN Committee against Torture examined Tunisia's report and called on the government to put an end to the practice of torture and to eliminate the gap between the law and its implementation. The Committee concluded that the government was granting immunity to those responsible for torture by constantly denying all allegations of torture. It urged the government to reduce the police custody period to a maximum of 48 hours and to ensure strict enforcement of the provisions of law and procedures of arrest and police custody.

The UN Special Rapporteur on the independence of judges and lawyers and the UN Special Rapporteur on the promotion and protection of the right to freedom of opinion and expression, who had asked the government for permission to undertake a joint mission, were not allowed access to the country.

The authorities continued to target human rights defenders and suppress their activities. In February prisoner of conscience Khemais Ksila, Vice-President of the *Ligue tunisienne des droits de l'homme* (LTDH), Tunisian League for Human Rights, who was arrested in September 1997 (see *Amnesty International Report 1998*), was sentenced to three years' imprisonment for "outrage to public order". The sentence was upheld in April by the Appeal Court and confirmed in May by the Cassation Court. In August the UN Sub-Commission on Prevention of Discrimination and Protection of Minorities requested the UN High Commissioner for Human Rights to inquire about the situation of Khemais Ksila.

Human rights lawyer Radhia Nasraoui and her two daughters suffered increasing harassment by the security services. In February her office was ransacked. In March, as she was observing a trial for Amnesty International in Mali, she was charged *in absentia* with "links to a criminal and terrorist gang, holding unauthorized meetings and inciting rebellion". On her return, she was granted bail but forbidden to leave Tunis. No date had been set for her trial by the end of the year.

Lawyer Najet Yaqoubi and her children were under constant police surveillance from June. Lawyer Anouar Kousri was also under heavy surveillance throughout the year. Human rights lawyer Najib Hosni and LTDH former President Moncef Marzouki continued to be subjected to harassment and restrictions (see *Amnesty International Report 1998*).

Scores of prisoners of conscience suspected of having links with unauthorized left-wing groups or the Islamist group *al-Nahda* (Renaissance) were among hundreds of people arrested for political reasons. At least 10 were released without charge or trial, but most remained in detention or were tried and sentenced to prison terms. Dozens of female relatives of imprisoned or exiled supporters of *al-Nahda* were detained; they were prisoners of conscience. Among them was Radhia 'Aouididi; she was sentenced in May to three and a half years in prison on charges of links with a criminal gang and holding a false passport (see *Amnesty International Report 1998*). In October Radhia 'Aouididi and four of her relatives were charged with "belonging to a criminal gang" on the grounds that her family had received money from her brother and her fiancé exiled in Europe.

In May Nizar Cha'ari, a Tunisian studying in France, was arrested at Tunis airport after visiting his family. He was reportedly tortured during incommunicado detention, which was prolonged well beyond the maximum stipulated by Tunisian law. He was charged with "links with an unauthorized association (*al-Nahda*) and criminal gang". At the end of the year he remained in detention awaiting trial.

In July, two women, Salwa Dimassi and Ahlam Garat-'Ali, both prisoners of conscience arrested in May 1996 and charged with links with "a criminal gang" (see *Amnesty International Report 1997*) were brought to trial, but the trial had not concluded by the end of the year.

In May Samir and 'Abdessatar Gasmi, two brothers exiled in Libya, were arrested by the Libyan authorities. They were handed to the Tunisian authorities in August, who detained them. Samir Gasmi was released a week after his forcible return; 'Abdessatar Gasmi was kept in detention, allegedly tortured and transferred in August to 9 Avril prison in Tunis.

Families of exiled supporters of *al-Nahda* suffered increasing harassment and were prevented from leaving the country. Hayat Hammi and her three children, for example, were prevented from leaving Tunisia to be reunited with her husband, Samir Ben 'Arfa, a refugee in Switzerland.

Up to 2,000 political prisoners arrested in previous years, most of them prisoners of conscience, remained in detention. They included Sou'ad Charbati, sentenced to seven years' imprisonment in 1997, and Mohamed Habib Hemissi, sentenced to 10 years' imprisonment in 1997 (see *Amnesty International Report 1998*). Jalel Ma'alej (see *Amnesty International Report 1995*) was released in January but subjected to administrative control. 'Imed 'Ebdelli was released and fled abroad; 'Ali Hafdi, released in 1997, was authorized to leave the country; and 'Abdelmoumen Belanes

was released after completing his sentence (see *Amnesty International Report 1998*). Lazhar No'man, who had been released on expiry of his sentence in late 1997, was subjected to administrative surveillance (see *Amnesty International Report 1998*).

Political trials continued to violate international standards for fair trial. The courts did not investigate allegations of torture and ill-treatment, and sometimes failed to call witnesses for cross examination. In August Tareq Soussi, a former prisoner of conscience suffering from poliomyelitis, a physically debilitating disease, was charged with "physical assault" and "blasphemy" after he stopped reporting to the police station. He was sentenced in September by the Bizerte Court to five months' imprisonment. The court refused to summon the plaintiff and the witnesses for cross-examination. Tareq Soussi's sentence was reduced to three months on appeal in November and he was released. In November Lazhar Belgacem (see *Amnesty International Report 1998*) was sentenced to three years' imprisonment on charges of "links with a criminal gang". He was never allowed to see the police report that allegedly contained his confession and no evidence was brought against him.

Torture and ill-treatment continued to be reported, especially in the premises of the Ministry of the Interior. In February and March, following student strikes and meetings calling for improved studying conditions, scores of students and young people were arrested in the capital Tunis and other cities. Some were released within days or weeks, but 16 of them remained in prison at the end of the year. Lotfi Hammami, a student, was reportedly tortured during incommunicado detention by having his genitals tied and pulled with a rope. He was denied specialized medical care until September. Another student, Najib Baccouchi, was also reportedly tortured. In June 'Imen Derouiche was beaten so badly in prison that she needed hospital treatment for several days. No investigations into these cases were carried out, nor were trial dates set.

At least one person died in custody possibly as a result of torture or ill-treatment. Tijani Dridi, a former political prisoner sentenced in 1992 by a military court to five years' imprisonment, had been under administrative control since his release. In August he went to report to Ariana police station in the suburbs of Tunis but never returned. The police informed his family that he had been injured in a traffic accident but forbade them to go to the hospital. Seven days later Tijani Dridi's body was buried under heavy police surveillance. His family was not allowed to see the body. No investigation into this and other cases of deaths in custody reported in previous years took place.

Several people remained under sentence of death, convicted of non-political crimes. No executions were reported.

Amnesty International attended the trial of Khemais Ksila. In November Amnesty International issued a report, *Tunisia: Human rights defenders in the line of fire*, highlighting the increasing intimidation and harassment of human rights defenders. An Amnesty International researcher continued to be banned from Tunisia.

TURKEY

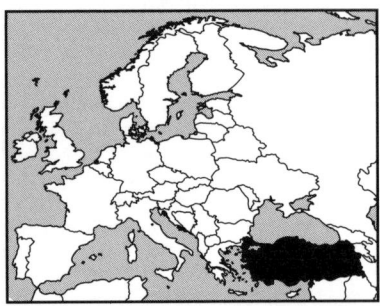

Hundreds of people were detained because of their non-violent political activities; most were released after a short period of police detention but others were sentenced to terms of imprisonment. Torture was commonplace, although there was evidence that the pattern of routine torture of people detained under the Anti-Terror Law had been disrupted. There were at least 10 reported deaths in custody apparently as a result of torture. Five people reportedly "disappeared" and at least 15 people were killed in circumstances suggesting that they had been extrajudicially executed. There were no judicial executions, although courts continued to pass death sentences. Armed opposition groups committed at least 39 deliberate and arbitrary killings of prisoners and civilians.

A coalition government was headed by the Motherland Party leader Mesut Yılmaz. Other partners were the Democratic Left Party and the Democratic Turkey Party. State of emergency legislation remained in force in six provinces of the southeast, where the 14-year conflict between government forces and armed members of the Kurdish Workers' Party (PKK) claimed 2,000 lives, including civilians, during the year.

The European Court of Human Rights (ECHR) upheld a number of complaints against Turkey. In several cases it ruled that the Turkish authorities had not properly investigated allegations of extrajudicial execution, including official complaints by Eşref Yaşa that state agents were involved in an armed attack on him and a fatal attack on his brother Haşim Yaşa in 1993. The ECHR also found that Salih Tekin, a journalist, had been blindfolded, threatened with death and beaten by gendarmerie officers in 1993 at Derinsu Gendarme Station in Mardin province.

Demonstrators, including human rights defenders, students and Islamists, were frequently taken into custody from peaceful public meetings or their organization's offices, and held for hours or days in police detention solely because of their non-violent political activities.

Prison sentences were imposed on many people who had non-violently criticized the government's policies towards the Kurdish minority. Charges were mainly brought under Article 8 of the Anti-Terror Law which outlaws any advocacy of "separatism", and Article 312 of the Turkish Penal Code (TPC) which deals with "incitement to hatred". In July, while still recovering from an attempted assassination (see below), Akın Birdal, President of the Human Rights Association (HRA), was sentenced to one year's imprisonment under Article 312 for a speech he had made on World Peace Day in 1996. The sentence was confirmed in October, but postponed for some months. Zeynep Baran, President of the Foundation for Solidarity with Kurdish Women, was sentenced to two years' imprisonment under Article 312 because of a pamphlet she published introducing the organization. The sentence was confirmed by the Appeal Court in November.

Article 312 was also used against people who criticized the government from a religious point of view. In April Recep Tayyip Erdoğan, Mayor of Istanbul, was sentenced to 10 months' imprisonment for a speech he had delivered in December 1997. The indictment referred specifically to four lines, a rallying call to Islam, quoted by Recep Tayyip Erdoğan from a poem by Ziya Gökalp. The lines, which did not advocate violence, appear in a book recommended by the Ministry of Education. The sentence was confirmed at appeal in September. One consequence of the sentence was a ban from politics; it appeared that this may have been the principal motivation for the prosecution. Recep Tayyip Erdoğan had been considered a serious candidate for the leadership of the Islamist *Fazilet* (Virtue) party.

Writer and biologist Edip Polat was imprisoned in April to serve a 10-month sentence under Article 159 of the TPC for "insulting the organs of state". He was released in August after serving his sentence with remission. Lawyer Eşber Yağmurdereli was imprisoned in June to serve the remainder of a 10-month sentence under Article 8 of the Anti-Terror Law for a speech he made in 1991. As a consequence of this conviction he also lost remission on the remainder – 16 years – of a previous life sentence imposed after an unfair trial.

In June journalist Ragıp Duran began serving a 10-month prison sentence imposed in December 1995 for a 1994 interview with the leader of the PKK.

Turkey continued not to recognize the right of conscientious objection to military service. Conscientious objector Osman Murat Ülke, Chairperson of the Izmir War Resisters' Association, remained in custody throughout the year, serving sentences for "alienating the public from the institution of military service", "persistent insubordination" and "desertion".

As a result of the revised detention procedures which were introduced for people detained under the Anti-Terror Law, detainees were generally held for shorter periods than in previous years. In law, such detainees are permitted access to their lawyers, a vital safeguard against torture, only after the fourth day of detention. In practice, this access continued frequently to be denied or so limited as to be virtually meaningless.

The reduction in the overall number of reports of torture noted in 1997 appeared to have been sustained. Nevertheless, well-documented reports of torture by police and gendarmes (soldiers carrying out police duties, mainly in rural areas) were very common. Male and female detainees frequently complained that they were sexually assaulted. Victims of torture again included children.

Cengiz Süslü, who had absconded from military service, was detained in Istanbul in May. After seven days' incommunicado interrogation he was taken to hospital and had to be fitted with a colostomy bag because his bowel had been perforated by a hard object inserted into his anus. When he spoke to a lawyer – after he had been denied access to a lawyer for more than two weeks – he reported that electric shocks had been administered to his genitals during interrogation and that a truncheon had been forced into his anus.

Relatives of victims of "disappearance" who continued to hold a vigil every Saturday in the Galatasaray district of Istanbul were repeatedly harassed, detained and ill-treated by police. Hanım Tosun, whose husband Fehmi Tosun "disappeared" in Istanbul in October 1995, reported that she was beaten with a truncheon, punched and kicked when she was detained during a vigil in September. She was put by police with others in a vehicle. Video footage showed police spraying pepper gas into the vehicle and shutting the door, a potentially lethal action. Hanım Tosun and 30 other detainees needed hospital treatment after the incident.

There were at least 10 deaths in custody apparently as a result of torture. For example, in March, 18-year-old Mehmet Yavuz died after interrogation at Adana Police Headquarters in connection with a theft. Police authorities initially stated that he had died of a heart attack, but the autopsy indicated that the cause of death was "stomach trauma caused by a blow". Eleven police officers were detained and charged with torturing and killing Mehmet Yavuz. Their trial continued at Adana Criminal Court at the end of the year.

There were at least five "disappearances". They included a woman, Neslihan Uslu, and three men, Hasan Aydoğan, Metin Andaç and Mehmet Mandal, who were last seen in Izmir in March. All four were known to the police and had reportedly been threatened with death and "disappearance". Neslihan Uslu and Hasan Aydoğan were both wanted by the police after the Court of Appeal confirmed prison sentences against them for membership of an illegal armed organization. Mehmet Mazaca "disappeared" in October in Elazığ. He was still suffering from the after-effects of torture inflicted in 1993 and was reportedly seen in custody in Elazığ Police Headquarters.

In May Akın Birdal, President of the HRA, was shot by two gunmen at the association's headquarters in Ankara. Akın Birdal nearly died after being hit by six bullets. The attack followed publication by the authorities of spurious allegations about Akın Birdal, contained in confessions purported to have been made by a former military commander of the PKK and illegally leaked from the prosecutor's office. While Akın Birdal was still close to death, Prime Minister Yılmaz described the attack as an "internal dispute". In fact, seven men close to right-wing political groups – one of them a gendarmerie officer – were shortly afterwards arrested and charged with planning and carrying out the attempted killing.

At least 15 people were allegedly victims of extrajudicial executions. In May Ömer Dusak was taken from his home in Eyyübiye, Şanlıurfa province, by people thought to be gendarmerie officers. The abduction was witnessed by the women of the house. Seven days later his body was found near Pınarbaşı, Kayseri, with five bullet wounds in the head and body.

For the 14th consecutive year there were no judicial executions, although death sentences continued to be imposed.

Armed separatist and leftist organizations, including the PKK, the Turkish Workers and Peasants' Liberation Army (TIKKO) and the Revolutionary People's Liberation Party-Front (DHKP-C), were responsible for at least 39 deliberate and arbitrary killings of civilians and prisoners. Tacettin Aşçı, treasurer of the Bursa branch of the HRA, and another man, Ahmet Aydın, were abducted in May by the Marxist-Leninist Communist Party (MLKP). The organization later announced that the two had been "executed" as police informers. The HRA condemned the killing. Those who killed Tacettin Aşçı and Ahmet Aydın did not hand over the bodies or reveal their whereabouts and it was feared that they may have died under torture. Amnesty International condemned these grave abuses and publicly called on armed opposition groups to ensure that their members are instructed to respect basic international humanitarian law standards.

Throughout the year Amnesty International appealed for the release of prisoners of conscience and urged the government to initiate prompt and independent investigations into allegations of torture, extrajudicial executions and "disappearances". Amnesty International reports published on Turkey during the year included, *"Birds or earthworms" – the Güçlükonak massacre, its alleged cover-up and the prosecution of independent investigators* in June, and *Listen to the Saturday Mothers* in November.

Amnesty International delegates observed several trial hearings, including the final hearing in the trial of a number of HRA officials at Ankara State Security Court who were accused of making separatist statements. The HRA officials were acquitted. Amnesty International delegates also attended the May hearing of a retrial at Izmir State Security Court of a group of high-school students convicted and sentenced to long terms of imprisonment on the basis of evidence extracted under torture (see *Amnesty International Reports 1997* and *1998*); the May and August hearings of a retrial of eight student campaigners found guilty of membership of an illegal armed organization and sentenced to 18 years' imprisonment after conducting a peaceful campaign for students' rights; and the October hearing in the trial of Hüzni Almaz, an asylum-seeker forcibly returned from Germany.

TURKMENISTAN

At least two prisoners of conscience were imprisoned for their conscientious objection to military service. One prisoner of conscience was released. At least three possible prisoners of conscience continued to serve long prison sentences and one was briefly detained. Six political prisoners were released; at least two others continued to serve long prison sentences. One political prisoner died, allegedly as a result of ill-treatment. One

government opponent was briefly detained. At least 16 people were sentenced to death, including eight women.

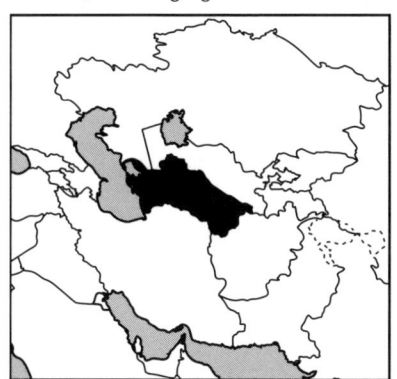

In April President Saparmurad Niyazov made his first official visit to the USA. In September, following a mutiny by a military unit in which several people were killed, he replaced several high-ranking officials from the Committee for National Security (KNB), as well as the Ministers of Defence and Internal Affairs.

In December the authorities announced their intention to institute a moratorium on executions.

In March Turkmenistan acceded to the UN Convention relating to the Status of Refugees and its 1967 Protocol.

At least two prisoners of conscience were imprisoned for their conscientious objection to military service; both were Jehovah's Witnesses. Roman Sidelnikov was sentenced to two years' imprisonment in June for "evading regular call-up to active military service". Oleg Voronin declared his conscientious objection to military service to the military enlistment commission in the city of Chardzhev in May. He was reportedly severely beaten and taken to a military prison in the closed city of Gushgi. In September it was reported that Oleg Voronin had been sentenced by a military court to five and a half years' imprisonment for desertion. According to reports no one had been granted access to him by the end of the year.

Prisoner of conscience Durdymurad Khodzha-Mukhammed, who had been confined in a psychiatric hospital for political reasons since February 1996, was released in April (see *Amnesty International Report 1997*). Following his release, he resumed his political opposition activities and gave interviews critical of the Turkmen authorities. In September, as Durdymurad Khodzha-Mukhammed was returning from a meeting at the United Kingdom embassy in Ashgabat, the capital, he was forced into a car by three unidentified men, driven to the outskirts of the city, beaten and kicked until he lost consciousness, and abandoned. It was alleged that the assault was intended to frighten Durdymurad Khodzha-Mukhammed into stopping his political opposition activities.

In December possible prisoners of conscience Mukhametkuli Aymuradov and Khoshali Garayev, serving 15- and 12-year sentences respectively in a maximum security prison (see previous *Amnesty International Reports*), received additional sentences of 18 years' imprisonment. There was strong evidence to suggest that they were innocent of the additional charge of an alleged escape attempt, and of the anti-state crimes of which they were convicted in 1995, and that the case against them was fabricated, solely to punish them for their association with exiled government opponents, such as Abdy Kuliyev (see below). Possible prisoner of conscience Ashirgeldy Syadiyev (see *Amnesty International Report 1998*) continued to serve a long prison sentence on allegedly politically motivated, fabricated charges.

Abdy Kuliyev, a former minister of foreign affairs and leader of the Turkmen opposition, was arrested at Ashgabat airport on 17 April on his return to Turkmenistan after five years in exile. He was initially detained at the investigation-isolation prison of the KNB, but later released and placed under house arrest, before being returned to Russia on 24 April. He had reportedly been charged with trying to overthrow the government of Turkmenistan, organizing an anti-government demonstration and extortion. It was not clear whether these charges had been dropped.

In April, under pressure over his country's human rights record, President Niyazov announced at a press conference in the USA that the political prisoners known as the "Ashgabat Eight" had been released from detention. They had been serving long prison sentences for criminal offences, some involving violence, arising from their participation in an anti-government protest in Ashgabat in July 1995 (see

340 *Amnesty International Report 1998*). Concerns for the safety of one of the men, Khudayberdi Amandurdyyev, were heightened when one of his co-defendants, Charymyrat Gurov, died in prison at the beginning of January, reportedly after repeated beatings. Khudayberdi Amandurdyyev, Amanmyrat Amandurdyyev, Charymyrat Amandurdyyev and Kakamyrat Nazarov were released from detention in April. It emerged that two others, Begmyrat Khojayev and Batyr Sakhetliyev, had been released earlier. Gulgeldi Annanyyazov, remained in detention, allegedly because he was viewed by the authorities as one of the organizers of the 1995 protest. He had received the longest sentence – 15 years' imprisonment. There were reports that Gulgeldi Annanyyazov's health was failing. In June information emerged that a ninth man, Gurbanmurat Mammetnazarov, was serving a prison sentence for participating in the 1995 protest. In May, while serving the last year of his sentence, he was convicted on reportedly fabricated drugs-related charges and sentenced to a further four years' imprisonment.

Durdymukhammed Gurbanov, a former presidential press spokesperson, was arrested in Ashgabat in September on corruption charges relating to his time in office. There were allegations that the charges against him had been fabricated in order to punish him for a radio interview in June which was critical of President Niyazov. He was detained for several days in the investigation-isolation prison of the KNB before being released without charge.

At least 16 people, including eight women, were sentenced to death, many for drug-related offences. All were at the last stage of the appeals process and faced imminent execution. No official statistics on death sentences and executions were published and the total number of death sentences was believed to be much higher. According to unofficial sources, as many as 50 people were awaiting execution in Chardzhev alone. Andrey Voronin and Kamal Nepesov, sentenced to death in April for murder, claimed that their confessions had been extracted under torture. They alleged that their toes were crushed with pliers, that electric shocks were applied to the anus, and that threats were made against their families. They did not gain access to a lawyer until one month after their arrest.

Amnesty International called on the authorities to immediately and unconditionally release Roman Sidelnikov and Oleg Voronin and to introduce a civilian alternative to military service. It also called for a comprehensive and independent investigation into the allegations that Oleg Voronin was beaten. Amnesty International welcomed the release of Durdymurad Khodzha-Mukhammed. It urged the authorities to launch an immediate investigation into the attack on him.

In April Amnesty International expressed concern that Abdy Kuliyev might have been charged with serious anti-state crimes simply to punish him for his peaceful opposition to President Niyazov's government and reiterated that there was strong evidence to suggest that Mukhametkuli Aymuradov and Khoshali Garayev were innocent of the anti-state crimes of which they had been convicted. The organization also expressed concern at the new charges brought against them.

In April Amnesty International welcomed the release of six of the "Ashgabat Eight" but expressed concern that at least one remained in detention. In January the organization had called for a full and comprehensive inquiry into the allegations that beatings and ill-treatment may have caused the death of Charymyrat Gurov. In a meeting with Amnesty International, representatives of the Turkmen government disputed the allegations of ill-treatment and claimed that Charymyrat Gurov had died of tuberculosis.

The organization urged the authorities to ensure that Khudayberdi Amandurdyyev was not subjected to ill-treatment.

In September Amnesty International expressed concern about the detention of Durdymukhammed Gurbanov. The organization continued its calls for a moratorium on the death penalty and appealed for the commutation of every death sentence that came to its attention.

UGANDA

Prisoners of conscience were among hundreds of political prisoners arrested during the year, scores of whom were detained incommunicado in unofficial places of detention. Serious charges that preclude bail for statutory periods were

used to hold more than 200 prisoners without trial. Hundreds of political and criminal prisoners were tortured. Soldiers were allegedly responsible for dozens of rapes. Courts imposed the cruel, inhuman and degrading punishment of caning. Four men apparently wanted by neighbouring states "disappeared". Soldiers and police were responsible for more than 40 possible extrajudicial executions, including of children. At least 21 prisoners were sentenced to death. Armed opposition groups were responsible for gross human rights abuses, including child abduction, beatings, rape and deliberate and arbitrary killings.

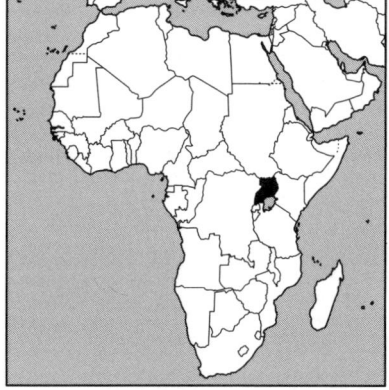

Bomb attacks in March, April and July in and around Kampala marked the extension to the capital of wars involving armed opposition movements operating out of the Democratic Republic of the Congo (DRC) with the support of the Sudanese government. In August President Yoweri Museveni ordered troops into the DRC in support of a rebellion by the Congolese armed opposition group, the *Rassemblement Congolais pour la démocratie* (RCD), the Congolese Rally for Democracy. In response, the Sudanese government airlifted soldiers from Ugandan armed opposition groups based in Sudan to the DRC as part of a troop deployment in support of DRC President Laurent-Désiré Kabila. Also in August there were bomb threats against the US Embassy and other targets in Kampala immediately after the bombing of the US Embassies in the Kenyan capital Nairobi and the Tanzanian capital Dar es Salaam. The

authorities blamed some of the threats on Ugandan armed opposition movements. Before the end of the month three buses leaving Kampala were bombed, killing 28 people. In this tense political climate, intensified activity by security agencies often breached international human rights standards and Ugandan constitutional provisions.

Fighting in the west, north and northwest between the government's Uganda People's Defence Forces (UPDF) and armed opposition groups continued throughout the year. In the west the Allied Democratic Front (ADF) was active in districts bordering the Rwenzori mountains on the frontier with the DRC. In the north, fighting between the UPDF and the armed opposition Lord's Resistance Army (LRA) displaced approximately 30,000 people in Kitgum District early in the year. The LRA extended its operations to Lira District and, briefly, as far east as Soroti; over 15,000 people were displaced in Lira. LRA bases in Sudan were overrun by the Sudan People's Liberation Army (SPLA) supported by UPDF troops in September. However, within a few weeks the Sudanese army had dislodged the SPLA and UPDF, and in November an LRA unit crossed into Uganda from Sudan and renewed military operations in Kitgum. Armed opposition groups in northwest Uganda regrouped after defeats in early 1997; the Uganda National Rescue Front II (UNRF-II) renewed activity in March 1998 and the West Nile Bank Front (WNBF) began incursions from bases in the DRC in June.

Over 400,000 people remained internally displaced in Gulu and Kitgum Districts in the north. Many expressed the wish to return to their villages but were not allowed to by the UPDF. In western Uganda at least 15,000 people were displaced in April, but tens of thousands who fled their homes in 1997 were able to return home.

In April the UN Commission on Human Rights adopted a resolution condemning the abduction of children by the LRA and calling on member states, international organizations, humanitarian bodies and others to exert pressure on the armed group to release children.

In July the Uganda Human Rights Commission published its first annual report, covering 1997. It identified human rights violations by the state and reported that

342

despite the Commission's constitutional status, on some occasions state institutions had failed to cooperate fully with it.

Prisoners of conscience were among hundreds of political prisoners arrested during the year, scores of whom were detained incommunicado in secret detention centres. Muslims were particularly targeted. Prisoners of conscience included members of the Ugandan Somali community detained outside the law in September. Omer Ahmed Mandela, treasurer of the popular Kampala football club S.C. Villa, Sheikh Abdul Weli Abdullai, imam of the Tawheed mosque, and 27 men and boys were arrested by security officials and by agents from the US Federal Bureau of Investigation. Questioned about the bombing of the US Embassy in Nairobi and alleged plans to bomb US targets in Uganda, they were held incommunicado in a secret place of detention. Most were released without charge after two weeks. However, Abdul Kadir Ali, a 15-year-old school student, and three men were not released until mid-October, again without charge.

Over 100 Muslim political prisoners, the majority from the Islamist *Jumaiyat Da'awa Salafiyya* sect, were arrested in Kampala and other places in south and west Uganda on suspicion of involvement with the ADF and other armed opposition movements. For example, 40 men detained in Kampala in May, including Sheikh Abdul Karim Sentamu, a senior imam of the sect, were held incommunicado at unknown locations – they effectively "disappeared". In June the Uganda Human Rights Commission publicly ordered their release because their detention was illegal. One of the men arrested in May was known to be among 50 men charged with treason in June. However, most remained in incommunicado detention without charge or trial. There were further detentions of Muslims in July and August. Although some were released, at least 14 and possibly many more were still detained at the end of the year.

The authorities continued to use serious charges that preclude the granting of bail for statutory periods as a way of holding political prisoners without trial. On several occasions prisoners who were granted bail at the end of a statutory remand period were rearrested on new serious charges as they left the court. In March, 87 alleged members of the WNBF were rearrested and charged with murder after they were granted bail at the end of a mandatory 360-day remand period on treason charges. In July treason charges were withdrawn against 110 other prisoners held since 1995. They were released but were almost immediately rearrested on new treason charges.

Torture and cruel, inhuman and degrading treatment remained endemic in police stations and was common when soldiers and security officials detained security suspects. At least five prisoners died reportedly after being tortured. In June more than 100 uncharged detainees suspected of collaborating with the ADF were freed from military barracks in Kasese; the newly deployed UPDF commander said that many had been tortured by being beaten and burned with molten plastic. Security suspects held incommunicado in Kampala were also brutally treated. In August detainees held in an illegal secret location by the Directorate of Military Intelligence on suspicion of involvement with the bombing of the US Embassy in Nairobi or of links with the ADF were reportedly beaten and tortured with electric shocks.

Soldiers deployed in rural areas in northern and eastern Uganda were said to have been responsible for dozens of rapes. In July soldiers deployed north of Mbale detained and allegedly raped a number of women, including two who were pregnant. After protests by local councillors an officer and several soldiers were arrested.

Courts imposed the cruel, inhuman and degrading punishment of caning, often for sexual offences. In March, for example, a man convicted of rape was sentenced to 12 strokes and 12 years in jail.

In February, four men – two Rwandese, a Congolese and a Ugandan of Rwandese origin – apparently wanted by neighbouring states "disappeared" after being arrested, continuing a pattern established in previous years. Their fate remained unknown at the end of the year. The Uganda Human Rights Commission said that it believed police officers and officials in the Office of the President were responsible for the "disappearances".

Soldiers and police were responsible for at least 40 killings that appeared to be extrajudicial executions. For example, in

January, three prisoners in Luwero were shot dead by police officers who had taken them into the countryside, ostensibly to recover abandoned arms. In May, three alleged armed robbers were shot dead in Gulu. In both cases the police claimed that the prisoners were trying to escape. In March at least 30 children recently abducted by the LRA and bound together were killed by soldiers in circumstances that amounted to an extrajudicial execution at Wang Alur swamp in Kitgum District. In May, soldiers killed Oyet David after he left a camp for the internally displaced near Gulu and returned to his village. Captured by UPDF soldiers, he was reportedly made to lie face down and shot through the head.

The High Court sentenced at least 21 people to death. The sentences against five others were confirmed by the Supreme Court. In the condemned section of Luzira Prison in May there were 112 civilian prisoners whose appeals against the death penalty had been dismissed in previous years and 60 UPDF soldiers who had not been able to appeal because a military appeal court had not been convened. There were no executions.

Armed opposition movements were responsible for gross human rights abuses, including the abduction of children, beatings, rape, sexual slavery and deliberate and arbitrary killings. The LRA abducted hundreds of boys and girls to become soldiers and sexual slaves in Gulu, Kitgum and neighbouring districts such as Soroti. According to escaped children, new captives were beaten or made to kill others. In July, 30 exhausted child captives unable to keep up with an LRA unit heading towards bases in Sudan were reportedly clubbed to death in the Agoro hills in Kitgum. Camps for the internally displaced were attacked to force people to move out of them. Scores of civilians, many of them relatives of local councillors or government officials, were captured and then killed.

Other armed opposition groups also abducted villagers as a method of forced conscription. For example, in June the UNRF-II abducted more than 100 adults and children in Aringa County in the northwest; over 60 escaped or were freed by the UPDF. In August the WNBF abducted over 200 villagers in raids on Koboko and Aringa; 50 escaped.

In western Uganda the ADF abducted several hundred adults and children and unlawfully killed scores of villagers. In February, five civilians were beheaded after their car was stopped at an impromptu ADF roadblock. In June over 70 students were reported to have been deliberately burned alive at Kichwamba Technical College. More than 80 others were abducted and taken to bases inside the DRC.

Amnesty International expressed grave concern at the detention without charge or trial of political prisoners. In May an Amnesty International delegation visited northern Uganda to research human rights abuses in the context of the armed conflict in the north. In meetings with civilian and military officials, the organization raised concerns about the failure to complete legal action against soldiers arrested for alleged human rights violations. In June the organization called on LRA leaders to end their policy of abducting children. In an address in July to the *Kacoke Madit*, a gathering of Acholi from inside and outside Uganda that brought together government ministers, local officials and government opponents, Amnesty International said that establishing respect for human rights was part of the process of creating the conditions for peace. The organization called on all parties in the northern war to ensure accountability for human rights abuses.

UKRAINE

At least 345 prisoners remained under sentence of death at the end of the year; at least 81 of them were reportedly sentenced to death in the first six months of 1998. Torture and ill-treatment in detention continued to be reported.

In January the Parliamentary Assembly of the Council of Europe adopted its third successive resolution strongly condemning Ukraine for continuing to carry out executions. The Parliamentary Assembly stated that unless it received formal notification that all executions had been halted, it would consider revoking the credentials of the Ukrainian delegation. Ukraine had made a commitment to impose a moratorium on executions, and to abolish the death penalty in law and practice by

344

November 1998, when it entered the Council of Europe in November 1995 (see *Amnesty International Reports 1996* to *1998*). However, between November 1995 and March 1997, when executions were unofficially halted two months after the second Council of Europe resolution, Ukraine executed at least 212 people. A further execution was reportedly carried out in 1997 after May, when Ukraine signed Protocol No. 6 to the European Convention for the Protection of Human Rights and Fundamental Freedoms concerning the abolition of the death penalty.

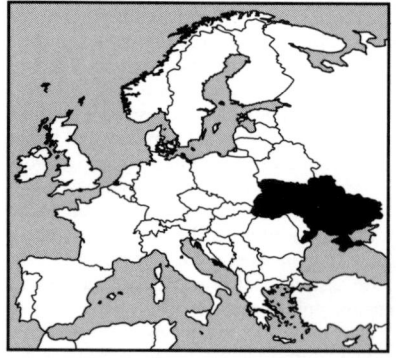

The Council of Europe resolution in January also called on Ukraine to put an end to the secrecy surrounding executions. In March the government reported that, under instruction from Ukrainian President Leonid Kuchma and Prime Minister Valery Pustovoitenko, it had lifted the secrecy on data and information on the death penalty. By the end of the year the government had failed to incorporate these steps into national law.

In September a draft new criminal code was passed on first reading by the Ukrainian parliament, which contained no articles providing for the death penalty and introduced life imprisonment as an alternative punishment. However, also in September the chairman of the Ukrainian parliament, Oleksandr Tkachenko, reportedly told a delegation from the Parliamentary Assembly of the Council of Europe that it was too early to speak about full abolition of the death penalty in Ukraine.

The government failed to abolish the death penalty by the Council of Europe's November 1998 deadline. In November the Committee on the Honouring of Obligations and Commitments by Member States

of the Council of Europe adopted a draft resolution to be considered at the January 1999 session of the Parliamentary Assembly, which stated that the Ukrainian delegation's credentials would be annulled at the Assembly's June 1999 session if the country's commitment to abolish the death penalty had not been honoured.

Also in November President Kuchma made a public statement which put at risk the existence of the moratorium on executions. Commenting on the trial of Anatoly Onuprienko, accused of murdering 52 people, he reportedly said: "As a human being I cannot see any punishment for him other than death." In connection with this case, there were reports that Yury Mozola, who had been arrested in 1996 in Lviv on suspicion of murders later attributed to Anatoly Onuprienko, had been tortured to death while being interrogated about the murders. He died in custody four days after his arrest. Another man arrested in Lviv and sentenced to death in connection with other murders subsequently attributed to Anatoly Onuprienko, was reportedly released following Anatoly Onuprienko's arrest.

Amnesty International received reports that 91 people were sentenced to death during the first six months of 1998. Ten of them were later granted clemency. Among those who remained under sentence of death were two women. The Ukrainian government, however, reportedly told the Parliamentary Assembly of the Council of Europe in September that 73 people had been sentenced to death in Ukraine between January and September 1998. No executions were reported during the year.

In January the Supreme Court of Ukraine upheld the death sentence on Yuriy Vladimirovich Bubyr, who was sentenced to death by Donetsk Regional Court in July 1997. Yuriy Bubyr was allegedly convicted on the basis of evidence extracted under duress. He was held incommunicado after his arrest, and a defence lawyer was granted access to him only after five days.

Cases of torture and ill-treatment continued to be reported. Sergey Mikhailovich Voronok, a deputy of the Supreme Soviet of Crimea, and Aleksandr Vitalyvich Kovalenko, a deputy of the Yalta City Council, were arrested in February and allegedly tortured and ill-treated while held in incommunicado detention.

Law enforcement officials in the city of Uzhgorod reportedly tortured Yaroslav Mysyak with electric shocks after his arrest in May on charges of premeditated murder. It was reported that no investigation of these allegations of torture was carried out by the authorities and Yaroslav Mysyak remained in detention at the end of the year.

In January information was received about the case of Dmytro Volodymyrovich Vazhnenko, an artist who was allegedly tortured in detention by Kiev police. He was apprehended in June 1997 following the murder of a police officer and was taken to the Leningrad District Department of the Ministry of Internal Affairs. He was severely beaten during interrogation and lost consciousness at least three times. His treatment reportedly included having his head banged on a table and being beaten on the spine with a stick. He was reportedly also threatened with being shot or buried alive. Both Dmytro Vazhnenko and his girlfriend Oksana Konovalova were reportedly forced to sign statements testifying that he had killed the police officer, Oksana Konovalova under the threat of rape. The District Procurator was allegedly present for some of the time Dmytro Vazhnenko was being beaten.

Dmytro Vazhnenko was allegedly beaten again by prison officers with clubs on arrival at Lukianivsky prison in Kiev in 1997. In January 1998 he was released pending trial. Further death threats were reportedly made against him and his lawyer by officers of the Leningrad District Department of the Ministry of Internal Affairs.

Amnesty International urged the President to grant clemency to all death row prisoners, to observe the moratorium on executions and to ratify Protocol No. 6 to the European Convention (see above). The organization was also concerned about the apparent discrepancies in official government statistics regarding the number of people under sentence of death.

Amnesty International urged the authorities to stop torture and ill-treatment in detention. It called for full and comprehensive inquiries into the allegations of torture or ill-treatment, with the findings made public, and for anyone responsible for such acts to be brought to justice in accordance with the norms of international law.

UNITED ARAB EMIRATES

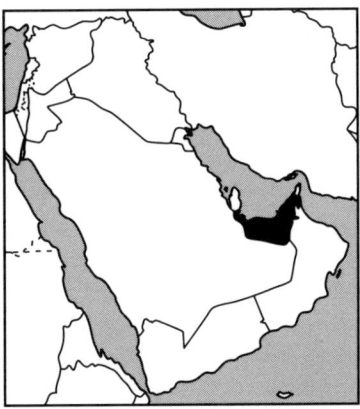

Three possible prisoners of conscience were released. There were reports of ill-treatment as well as of the imposition of cruel judicial punishments. At least six people were sentenced to death and one person was executed. Three Qatar nationals were forcibly returned to Qatar.

Three possible prisoners of conscience – brothers Jassim and Yassir 'Issa al-Yassi and Ahmad 'Abdullah Makki – were released in January (see Amnesty International Reports 1997 and 1998). They had been held without charge or trial, reportedly in solitary confinement, since their arrest in Dubai in June 1996. Ill-treatment of detainees continued to be reported.

Cruel, inhuman or degrading punishments, including flogging and amputation, were reportedly imposed. In January an Indian and a Bangladeshi were reportedly sentenced by a Shari'a (Islamic) court in Ras al-Khaimah to 90 lashes each in connection with a sexual offence involving a Sri Lankan woman. It was reported in June that three Omani nationals who had reportedly confessed to robbery had been sentenced by a court in Fujairah to amputation of their right hands. It was not known if the reported sentences of flogging and amputation were carried out. Reports received during the year suggested that the sentence of flogging imposed on Elie Dib Ghalib, a Lebanese national, was not carried out (see Amnesty International Reports 1997 and 1998).

346

At least six people were sentenced to death, the majority for drug offences. Among them was Qamar 'Ali Khan, a Pakistani, who was sentenced to death in April in Dubai for drug trafficking. In June an appeal court upheld the sentence.

At least six other death sentences were upheld on appeal. In June the Supreme Court in Dubai upheld the death sentence against Touran Ibrahim 'Abbas, an Iranian national. She had been sentenced to death in December 1997 for drug trafficking. The sentence was awaiting ratification by the President, Al-Sheikh Zayed bin Sultan Al-Nahyan, at the end of the year.

In June the Supreme Court in Dubai referred the cases of Rabi' Ghassan Taraf, a Lebanese national, and Ryan Dominic Mahoney, a Canadian, back to the appeal courts for a retrial. They had been sentenced to death in November 1997 for drug trafficking. In December an appeal court in 'Ajman postponed the appeal of three Russian men, Anton Samoilenkov, Ruslan Gerbekov and Ivan Tziberkine, who had been sentenced to death in June 1997 by a *Shari'a* court in 'Ajman in connection with the murder of another Russian national.

A further five people sentenced in previous years were believed to remain under sentence of death. The Supreme Court in Abu Dhabi again allowed the lawyers of John Aquino, a Philippine national under sentence of death for murder (see *Amnesty International Reports 1996* to *1998*), more time to seek clemency from the victim's family.

There was no further news of other people sentenced to death in 1997, including Ahmad Mohammad Amin Bada'u, Mohammad 'Abdullah 'Abdul 'Aziz and Nur Ibrahim (see *Amnesty International Report 1998*), or of people sentenced in previous years, such as Mashal Badr al-Hamati, a Yemeni national, and Zad Khan Shah, a Pakistani (see previous *Amnesty International Reports*).

'Atallah Khair Mohammad, a Pakistani, was executed by firing squad in Dubai in June. He had been sentenced to death with two other Pakistanis and a Sri Lankan in April 1997 for a murder committed in 1993. It was not known whether the death sentences against the three other men had been upheld or commuted.

In June, three Qatar nationals were forcibly returned to Qatar. Fawaz al-Mahdi, 'Abd al-Hadi Jaber Hadi al-Rakib and Mubarak 'Abdullah Jassim al-Malki were subsequently arrested by the Qatar authorities in connection with a failed coup in Qatar in 1996 (see **Qatar** entry). 'Abd al-Hadi Jaber Hadi al-Rakib was allegedly tortured in Qatar, and if found guilty, all three would face the death penalty.

During the year Amnesty International called for the commutation of all death sentences. No response was received from the authorities.

UNITED KINGDOM

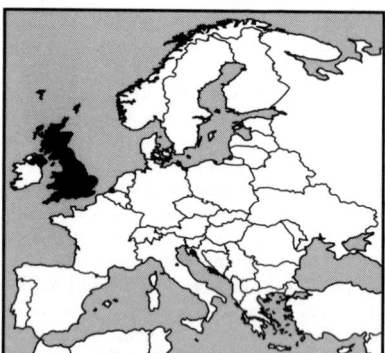

Reports of human rights abuses continued, including killings in disputed circumstances, deaths in custody and ill-treatment by police and in prisons, and detention in cruel, inhuman or degrading conditions. Many asylum-seekers were detained. Armed political groups committed human rights abuses.

Referendums in Northern Ireland and the Republic of Ireland in May approved a Multi-Party Agreement concerning the future of Northern Ireland. It proposed the establishment of three interconnected bodies: a Northern Ireland Assembly, which was elected in June; a North-South Ministerial Council, and a Council of the Isles. The Agreement also proposed initiatives to enhance human rights promotion and protection, including the establishment of a Northern Ireland Human Rights Commission. The Commission is empowered to review laws and practice relating to human rights, to conduct research and to promote human rights awareness. Although it may carry out investigations, the Commission is not empowered to compel information.

Under the Multi-Party Agreement, an Independent Commission on Policing for Northern Ireland was established to recommend reforms to ensure fair, impartial and accountable policing. The Commission accepted written submissions and held public meetings throughout Northern Ireland. A criminal justice review was also launched. Appointed commissioners approved the release of about 230 people sentenced under emergency legislation in Northern Ireland, who were associated with armed political groups which maintained cease-fires.

Violence continued in Northern Ireland before and after the Multi-Party Agreement. In July violence erupted during protests by the Protestant Orange Order and other groups, over the Parades Commission's decision to re-route a Protestant march in Portadown away from a predominantly Catholic neighbourhood. Three brothers, aged eight, nine, and 10, were killed when their home in Ballymoney was fire-bombed, allegedly by Loyalists, although no group claimed responsibility. Protests continued in Portadown, erupting sporadically into violence. In August "the Real IRA", an armed Republican group opposed to the Multi-Party Agreement, claimed responsibility for a bomb in Omagh which killed 29 people and injured hundreds. Following strong public condemnation, "the Real IRA" announced a cessation of military activity.

Following the Omagh bombing, the government rushed to introduce additional emergency powers. The Criminal Justice (Terrorism and Conspiracy) Act 1998, passed in September, contained measures which even the government called "draconian". They included relaxing the rules of evidence to allow opinions of senior police officers to form the basis of prosecutions for membership of proscribed organizations (see **Ireland** entry). This law also created a new offence of conspiracy to commit offences outside the United Kingdom (UK).

In October former Chilean General Augusto Pinochet was arrested in England following a request from Spain, where charges against him for crimes against humanity, torture and hostage-taking were pending. Claiming immunity, he challenged the legality of his arrest and detention for extradition. In November the House of Lords rejected his claim of immunity as a former head of state but, after a successful challenge to the composition of the judicial panel, a new panel of the House of Lords was scheduled to reconsider the claim of immunity in 1999 (see **Chile** and **Spain** entries).

In November, following its examination of the government's third periodic report, the UN Committee against Torture recommended measures to improve implementation of provisions of the UN Convention against Torture and Other Cruel, Inhuman or Degrading Treatment or Punishment.

In November the Human Rights Act was enacted, incorporating most of the provisions of the European Convention for the Protection of Human Rights and Fundamental Freedoms into UK law. It also abolished the death penalty, except for acts committed in time of war or imminent threat of war. The Act, which does not provide for a human rights commission, was not due to come into force for over a year.

In March a judicial inquiry began into the Metropolitan Police investigation of the killing of Stephen Lawrence in an unprovoked racist attack in south London in 1993. The inquiry heard evidence about police failure to carry out an impartial and thorough investigation into the killing. A second part of the inquiry – which looked into issues relating to policing, including racism – was continuing at the end of the year.

The Police Complaints Authority began an inquiry into serious mistakes made during the Metropolitan Police's investigation of the death of black musician Michael Menson, after an inquest concluded in September that he had been unlawfully killed by white youths. The Racial and Violent Crime Task Force, created by the Metropolitan Police in response to the Stephen Lawrence inquiry, reopened investigations into his death and that of Ricky Reel.

In January, seven men were convicted on charges relating to their consensual homosexual activities in private, under laws which place discriminatory restrictions on sexual behaviour between men. If imprisoned Amnesty International would consider them prisoners of conscience. An appeal was pending at the end of the year.

There were reports of killings by law enforcement officials in disputed circumstances and developments in cases from

348

previous years. In January James Ashley was shot and killed by police in disputed circumstances in Hastings. Five officers were suspended and investigations were pending at the end of the year.

In January the government announced the establishment of a new inquiry into the killing of 13 unarmed people in Northern Ireland on "Bloody Sunday" (see *Amnesty International Report 1998*). Hearings were scheduled to begin in 1999.

In September the family of Fergal Caraher, who was killed by soldiers in Northern Ireland in 1990, was awarded compensation (see *Amnesty International Reports 1991* and *1994*).

In November it was announced that two soldiers, who had been released in September from their life sentences for killing Peter McBride in Northern Ireland in 1992, would not be dismissed from the army (see *Amnesty International Reports 1993* and *1996*).

In November the retrial began of Lee Clegg, a British soldier convicted of murdering Karen Reilly in 1990 (see *Amnesty International Reports 1992*, *1994* and *1996*), after hearing new forensic evidence. The retrial had not been completed by the end of the year.

Deaths in custody were reported. In April Christopher Alder died in police custody in Hull. It was reported that, after being restrained, he was dragged from a police van and left lying motionless for about 10 minutes, face down, before officers attempted to give assistance. Five officers were suspended, although no decisions to prosecute had been made by the end of the year. In July Nathan Delahunty died, reportedly after being restrained by police officers.

Courts refused to order new inquests into the unrelated deaths in police custody in 1995 of Brian Douglas and Wayne Douglas (see *Amnesty International Reports 1996* and *1997*).

The Director of Public Prosecutions completed reviews of decisions not to prosecute police officers involved in arresting Richard O'Brien, Shiji Lapite, and Ibrahima Sey, whose deaths in previous years each involved postural asphyxia after being restrained. In separate inquests, juries found that each had been unlawfully killed. Three police officers were charged in connection with Richard O'Brien's death. Decisions were made not

to prosecute officers involved in the arrest or restraint of the other two (see *Amnesty International Reports 1996* to *1998*).

In March an inquest jury ruled that Alton Manning, who died in 1995 in Blakenhurst prison (see *Amnesty International Report 1996*), had been unlawfully killed. Although seven officers were suspended from the prison, no charges had been brought by the end of the year.

In November the UN Committee against Torture expressed concern about the number of deaths in police custody and the apparent failure of the state to provide effective investigative mechanisms to deal with allegations of police and prison authorities' abuse. The report of an inquiry into the prosecution authorities' handling of deaths in custody had been completed, but not published, by the end of the year.

Ill-treatment by police continued to be reported and compensation was awarded in cases from previous years. In February the High Court in Belfast found that most of the injuries inflicted on David Adams during arrest and at Castlereagh Holding Centre in 1994 were "more likely the result of direct, deliberate blows" and awarded him compensation. An investigation was carried out by Scottish police, but no decision on whether to prosecute had been taken by the end of the year.

In the report of his 1997 fact-finding mission, the UN Special Rapporteur on the independence of judges and lawyers concluded that police officers in Northern Ireland engaged in "activities which constitute intimidation, harassment and hindrance" of lawyers. He recommended an inquiry into such practices and a judicial inquiry into the 1989 killing of Patrick Finucane, a lawyer who had been a target of such practices by the security forces. Metropolitan Police officers were appointed to inquire into complaints of harassment by police in Northern Ireland of another lawyer, Rosemary Nelson.

Concerns continued about the use of plastic bullets by security forces in Northern Ireland (see *Amnesty International Report 1998*). The number of people who suffered head and upper body injuries after being shot with plastic bullets by the security forces during the parade season indicated that guidelines requiring shots to be aimed below the waist had not been consistently followed. In November the UN

Committee against Torture recommended that the government abolish the use of plastic bullets.

Police inquiries were launched after allegations emerged in March that prisoners at Wormwood Scrubs prison in London had been subjected to wide-ranging and systematic abuse by prison officers.

Róisín McAliskey was released in March after the Home Secretary declined to extradite her to Germany (see *Amnesty International Reports 1997* and *1998*).

People continued to be detained in small-group isolation in a special unit within Belmarsh Prison, in conditions similar to those in Special Security Units which had been closed in 1997 following reports that they caused mental and physical deterioration of prisoners (see *Amnesty International Report 1998*).

Courts quashed the convictions of Derek Bentley, who was hanged in 1953, and Danny McNamee, who was sentenced to 25 years' imprisonment in 1987 on the basis of subsequently discredited forensic evidence (see *Amnesty International Report 1998*).

In December the Crown Prosecution Service decided not to charge any of the seven police officers alleged to have fabricated evidence which led to the miscarriage of justice in the case of the Bridgewater Four (see *Amnesty International Report 1998*).

Many asylum-seekers, including children, were detained pending the outcome of their claims. The prosecution for destruction of property by refugees, who took part in a demonstration at the Campsfield House detention centre in 1997, collapsed after videotapes of the incident showed that evidence provided by staff during the investigation and trial was inconsistent.

Fifty-five people were killed by members of armed political groups in Northern Ireland; a third of the killings were attributed to Loyalists and two-thirds to members of Republican groups. In March Damian Trainor, a Catholic, and Philip Allen, a Protestant, were shot and killed in Poyntzpass by armed men believed by the authorities to belong to the Loyalist Volunteer Force (LVF). The LVF subsequently called a cease-fire.

In March retired police officer Cyril Stewart was shot dead as he left a supermarket in Armagh; the Irish National Liberation Army (INLA) reportedly claimed responsibility for his death. The INLA subsequently called a cease-fire.

Members of armed groups in Northern Ireland carried out more than 200 "punishment" beatings or shootings. Andrew Kearney was dragged from his flat, allegedly by IRA gunmen, and shot in both legs. He bled to death. The IRA admitted responsibility for killing Jean McConville, a Belfast widow and mother of 10, in 1972 and secretly burying her body. In March David Keys, a Loyalist prisoner held in the LVF-wing of the Maze prison, was reportedly tortured before being killed by other prisoners. David Keys was one of four former soldiers facing charges connected with the murders of Philip Allen and Damian Trainor (see above).

Amnesty International welcomed the commitments within the Multi-Party Agreement to respect human rights. Throughout the year it pressed for a review of emergency legislation, called for full implementation of measures to protect human rights and condemned human rights abuses by members of armed political groups in Northern Ireland.

In an oral statement at the UN Commission on Human Rights in April, Amnesty International welcomed the report of the UN Special Rapporteur on the independence of judges and lawyers, which criticized emergency law practices in Northern Ireland, and published *United Kingdom: UN report criticizes emergency law practices*.

Amnesty International sent an observer to Northern Ireland during the parade season in July in the light of concerns about policing.

In November the organization published its *Submission to the Independent Commission on Policing for Northern Ireland* and in December, an Amnesty International delegate discussed concerns about policing in Northern Ireland with the Commission.

Amnesty International published *United Kingdom: Briefing for the Committee against Torture* highlighting deaths in custody, cruel, inhuman or degrading prison conditions, ill-treatment in prisons and refugee detention centres, and discriminatory policing. Amnesty International also expressed concern about emergency legislation provisions in Northern Ireland.

350

In May the organization published *United Kingdom: Time to repeal anti-gay criminal laws*, urging the government to equalize the age of consent for sexual activity and bring legislation into compliance with its obligations under international law.

In November, appearing as a third party intervenor in the proceedings before the House of Lords relating to former General Pinochet, Amnesty International submitted that no person was immune from prosecution for alleged crimes against humanity and torture.

Amnesty International welcomed government proposals for a limited backlog clearance program for asylum applications, but expressed concern about proposals relating to asylum-seekers, including the imposition of additional pre-entry controls, withdrawal of statutory welfare, curbing access to legal aid and detaining all rejected asylum applicants. The organization reiterated its concerns about the policy and practice of detaining asylum-seekers.

In view of the UK government's agreement to participate with the USA in air strikes against Iraq, Amnesty International called on the UK government to ensure maximum protection of civilian lives in accordance with international humanitarian law. In December the government replied stating that "everything possible would be done to avoid civilian casualties."

UNITED STATES OF AMERICA

Sixty-eight prisoners, including three juvenile offenders, were executed in 18 states. More than 3,500 people remained on death row. There were continuing reports of torture and ill-treatment by police and prison officers, and of shootings by police in disputed circumstances.

In January the UN Special Rapporteur on extrajudicial, summary or arbitrary executions issued a report on his 1997 visit to the USA. The report called for a moratorium on executions and concluded that "race, ethnic origin and economic status appear to be key determinants of who will, and who will not, receive a death sentence." In February the UN Special Rapporteur on religious intolerance visited the USA. In August the UN Special Rapporteur on violence against women visited prisons and immigration detention facilities in New York, New Jersey, Connecticut, Georgia, California and Minnesota. The state authorities refused her entry to three Michigan prisons where it was alleged that female inmates had been sexually abused by guards.

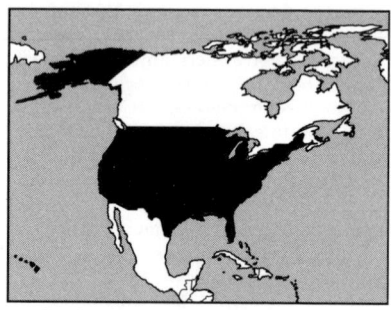

The death penalty continued to be used extensively. Sixty-eight people were executed, bringing the total number executed since the end of the moratorium on the death penalty in 1977 to 500.

Three juvenile offenders were executed, the first in the USA since 1993. All three had serious mental health problems and were put to death for crimes committed when they were 17 and emerging from abusive, poverty-stricken childhoods. Joseph Cannon and Robert Carter were executed in Texas in April and May respectively. Dwayne Wright was executed in October in Virginia. At Joseph Cannon's execution, the needle delivering the chemicals into his arm "blew out". Witnesses were removed while the needle was reinserted. Joseph Cannon's mother collapsed and needed hospital treatment after seeing her son killed.

Paraguayan citizen Ángel Francisco Breard was executed in April, despite an International Court of Justice (ICJ) order that his execution be suspended. Under the UN Vienna Convention on Consular Relations, to which the USA is a party, Ángel Breard had the right to assistance from Paraguayan consular officials. Paraguay took the case to the ICJ on the grounds that he had been denied this assistance, in breach of the Convention. Five days after the ICJ ordered the execution to be suspended until it had considered the case, Ángel Breard was executed. In November the US government issued an apology to the government and people of Paraguay for the violation of Ángel Breard's rights under the Convention. Seventy-three foreign nationals remained under sentence of death in the USA; almost all had been denied their rights under the Convention.

Eleven death-row prisoners were executed after abandoning their appeals and "consenting" to their execution. Jeremy Sagastegui was executed in Washington State in October. At his trial, Jeremy Sagastegui represented himself, refusing the assistance of an attorney, entered a guilty plea and requested that the jury sentence him to death. He had been diagnosed as suicidal three months before the crime for which he was condemned and had previously been diagnosed as a manic depressive and schizophrenic.

There were new reports of police shootings in disputed circumstances and of torture or ill-treatment of people by police and prison officers. Several unarmed teenagers were shot by police following car chases. They included 14-year-old black teenager Jenni Hightower, who was killed in March in New Jersey after police officers fired 20 shots into the stolen car in which she was a passenger. In April, three young black and latino men received multiple gunshot wounds when police fired into a car stopped for alleged speeding on the New Jersey Turnpike. The incident reinforced accusations that police officers along the New Jersey Turnpike stopped black and Latino drivers solely on the basis of race. Such arrests for "driving while black" were allegedly common in several states. In June the Maryland branch of the American Civil Liberties Union filed a class-action lawsuit alleging racial bias in traffic stops.

In October sheriff's deputies in Humboldt County, California, applied OC (pepper) spray-soaked pads to the eyes of four female anti-logging protesters who had chained themselves together. Later that month, a federal judge dismissed a lawsuit brought by protesters who had received similar treatment in 1997 (see *Amnesty International Report 1998*) on the grounds that the procedure caused only "transient pain" and did not amount to excessive force. Amnesty International had condemned the treatment as torture in that instance and called for the use of OC spray against non-violent demonstrators to be banned (see *Amnesty International Report 1998*).

In July a police Use of Force Review Board report concluded that police in Eugene, Oregon, had acted within policy when they sprayed demonstrators with OC spray during a non-violent protest in June 1997 (see *Amnesty International Report 1998*); however, the report was critical of some aspects of the operation.

In October a former New York City Police Department (NYPD) officer was sentenced to seven and a half years in prison by a federal judge for violating the civil rights of Anthony Baez who died after a confrontation with officers in 1994 (see *Amnesty International Reports 1996* to *1998*). An appeal by the officer was pending at the end of the year.

The trial of four NYPD officers for the 1997 assault on Abner Louima was still pending at the end of the year (see *Amnesty International Report 1998*). In December, two other NYPD officers were arrested and charged with lying to federal investigators in the case.

There were reports of abusive use of restraints and of electro-shock weapons, and allegations of sexual and physical abuse in several prisons and jails. A prisoner in the El Paso Criminal Justice Center in Colorado died in May after being strapped for hours to a restraint board. Other prisoners in the Center alleged in a lawsuit filed in May that they had been strapped to the board for up to 12 hours during which time they had had difficulty breathing, were forced to urinate and defecate in their clothing, and were taunted by guards. Use of the board was suspended in the prison following the death, and a review of the jail's restraint policies was undertaken.

In July the Immigration and Naturalization Service (INS) removed 34 detainees from Jackson County Jail in Florida following allegations that they had been tortured with electro-shock shields while held in four-point restraints, and subjected to beatings and excessive periods of punitive solitary confinement. The case was still under investigation by the Justice Department at the end of the year.

There were allegations of sexual abuse of women prisoners in states including California, Michigan and New York. There were allegations that prison staff in Michigan had threatened or harassed inmates and staff who reported complaints. In March a federal court agreed to pay three women US$500,000 to settle a lawsuit in which they claimed that they had been beaten, raped and sold for sex to male inmates by guards at the Federal Detention Center in Pleasanton, California.

In February, eight guards were indicted on federal charges for staging fights between rival inmates in Corcoran State Prison in California, between 1988 and 1994, during which seven inmates were fatally shot by guards (see *Amnesty International Report 1997*). In October, five guards at the prison were indicted on state charges for arranging and covering up the rape of an inmate by another prisoner in 1993. In October state legislative hearings on systematic brutality in the prison ended with recommendations for a series of policy changes, including tighter guidelines controlling the use of lethal force and more training for prison guards.

In February inmates beaten and injured by guards at Hays State Prison in Georgia in 1996 received US$283,000 in damages to settle a federal lawsuit against the authorities (see *Amnesty International Reports 1997* and *1998*).

An appeal lodged by the State of California against a 1997 ruling by a lower court that Geronimo ji Jaga (Pratt) should be granted a retrial (see *Amnesty International Report 1998*) was heard by the California Court of Appeals in December. No ruling had been given by the end of the year.

Amnesty International launched a worldwide campaign against human rights violations in the USA with the publication in October of a 150-page report, *USA: Rights for All*. The report focused on police brutality, ill-treatment in prisons and jails, the treatment of detained asylum-seekers, the death penalty, the US government's failure to abide by international standards, and concerns surrounding US arms trading. Amnesty International made over 40 recommendations for changes to bring US policies and practice into line with international standards at the federal, state and local level. It recommended, among other things, establishing independent monitoring bodies to investigate allegations of police brutality and abuses in jails and prisons; a ban on electro-shock stun belts and other dangerous restraint procedures as well as on the routine shackling of pregnant women; restrictions on interactions between male staff and female inmates to prevent rape and sexual

abuse in jails and prisons; a ban on the death penalty for juvenile offenders and a moratorium on executions as a first step toward total abolition; the adoption of a binding code of conduct covering transfers of military, security and police equipment, services and expertise; and ratification, without reservation, of the UN Conventions on the Rights of the Child and on the Elimination of All Forms of Discrimination against Women.

Amnesty International had not received a direct response from the government to its report by the end of the year.

During the year, the organization published several other reports. In May it issued *USA: Human rights concerns in the border region with Mexico*, on ill-treatment by Border Patrol INS officers. In October Amnesty International delegates met senior INS officials in Washington DC to discuss the organization's concerns.

Amnesty International published *USA: The death penalty in Texas, lethal injustice* in April, and *On the wrong side of history: children and the death penalty in the USA*, highlighting the cases of juvenile offenders on death row, in October. In November Amnesty International launched *USA: Fatal flaws – innocence and the death penalty* at a major conference in Chicago attended by nearly half the 75 wrongfully convicted prisoners released from US death rows since 1973.

Also in November, Amnesty International released *USA: Betraying the young – human rights violations against children in the US justice system* which described ill-treatment of children in both the juvenile justice and the general criminal justice systems.

During the year Amnesty International wrote to numerous federal, state and local authorities about issues including the death penalty; police shootings and brutality; ill-treatment in prisons, jails and juvenile detention centres; and the cruel use of restraints and stun weapons. It called for a ban on the use of OC spray against non-violent demonstrators. It raised concern about the shackling of pregnant women and called for an independent, comprehensive inquiry into the Maine Youth Center, in Portland, Maine, following reports of ill-treatment.

In March Amnesty International wrote to the Federal Bureau of Prisons expressing concern about the alleged punitive conditions under which Oscar López Rivera, a supporter of Puerto Rican independence imprisoned on criminal charges, was held at Marion Federal Prison; he was subsequently transferred to another facility where conditions improved.

In July Amnesty International submitted an *amicus curiae* brief to the California Appeals Court concerning the case of Geronimo ji Jaga (Pratt), arguing that the failure to disclose crucial information about a key prosecution witness to the defence should result in a final reversal of his conviction.

Amnesty International wrote to the Los Angeles court authorities and the Los Angeles Sheriff's Department calling on them to ban the use of remote control electro-shock stun belts after a defendant Ronnie Hawkins was stunned with the belt on the order of a judge during a Los Angeles court hearing in June; the order was given after he had repeatedly verbally interrupted the proceedings. Amnesty International said that use of stun belts constituted inherently cruel, inhuman or degrading treatment and that, in Ronnie Hawkins' case, the deliberate infliction of pain as punishment, by or at the instigation of a public official, fell within the definition of torture under international standards. The organization reiterated its concerns in October in an *amicus curiae* brief to a federal district court, which heard a lawsuit filed on behalf of Ronnie Hawkins and others, seeking, among other things, a preliminary injunction to prevent the use of the stun belt in Los Angeles county and municipal courtrooms. A ruling on the case was pending at the end of the year. In November Amnesty International raised concern with the authorities about the use of stun belts on low security HIV-positive inmates in New Orleans Parish Jail in Louisiana, while they were being transported to hospital and awaiting treatment.

In September Amnesty International wrote to the US government about the air strikes in Afghanistan and Sudan, seeking clarification on the measures taken to protect civilian lives. Amnesty International also wrote to the UN Secretary-General asking for an investigation into the bombing of Sudan. In December the organization called on the US government to ensure maximum protection of civilian lives in accordance with international humanitarian law in its air strikes against Iraq after UN weapons inspectors reported non-cooperation by the Iraqi authorities.

URUGUAY

Two possible extrajudicial executions were reported. HIV-positive detainees were ill-treated because of their medical condition. Human rights violations committed in past years remained unclarified.

In April the UN Human Rights Committee urged the authorities to adopt legislation correcting the effects of the 1986 Expiry Law which grants immunity to all military and police personnel responsible for human rights violations committed between 1973 and 1985 (see previous *Amnesty International Reports*). The Committee also expressed concern at the failure to incorporate the crime of torture into the penal code and at the practice of pre-trial detention.

Human rights organizations expressed outrage at the appointment as adviser to the Commander-in-Chief of the Armed Forces in March of a military official alleged to have committed serious human rights violations during past military governments, including the torture of scores of women at the former Punta Rieles Prison in Montevideo, the capital.

The asylum bill proposed by President Julio María Sanguinetti and other members of the executive in 1997 did not come into effect. Concerns remained that the bill weakened the right to asylum and contravened international standards (see *Amnesty International Report 1998*).

Two men were killed in circumstances suggesting that they were extrajudicially executed. In June Roberto Sandro Cardozo, a civilian prisoner, was shot dead by

354

a military guard patrolling the Santiago Vázquez Prison in the department of Montevideo, reportedly as he was trying to escape. The Commander-in-Chief of the Armed Forces justified the action arguing that the prison was in a "military zone" and that the guard "had acted under military regulations". He informed the judge in charge of the investigation that this was a matter for military justice and that those involved in the incident would not appear before a civilian court. The Minister of the Interior stated that the incident would serve as a warning to all "criminals" that the authorities were "serious" about combating crime. The Supreme Court of Justice had not ruled on whether the case should be heard before a civilian or military court by the end of the year.

Also in June, Héctor Mauro Valente Gómez, a taxi driver, was shot dead by a policeman. According to Héctor Valente's father, who was with him at the time, their car was stopped by the police, but Héctor Valente drove off because he was not wearing his seat-belt. However, police officers intercepted them again a few kilometres further on and shot at the car. Héctor Valente reportedly stopped and got out of the car with his hands raised above his head and was shot in the head. A police officer was under investigation, but the case remained open at the end of the year.

Two men were reportedly ill-treated by police officers during detention because they were HIV-positive. In July a man detained by the police in connection with a fight in a bar in Montevideo was beaten after informing officers that he was HIV-positive. He was released without charge the following day. In September another man detained by the police was subjected to death threats and verbal abuse when he informed them of his medical condition. Both incidents were reported to the authorities. However, by the end of the year those responsible had not been brought to justice.

In February the Supreme Court of Justice rejected the case brought by Sara Méndez challenging the adoption of a boy she believed to be her "disappeared" son, Simón Riquelo (see *Amnesty International Report 1996*).

In November the case of Eugenio Berríos, a former Chilean military agent who "disappeared" in 1992, was provisionally shelved, subject to new evidence

coming to light (see previous *Amnesty International Reports*).

Members of the security forces accused of human rights violations committed during past military governments were not brought to justice (see previous *Amnesty International Reports*).

In May Amnesty International reiterated calls on the authorities to ensure full and independent investigations into human rights violations committed under past military governments and to bring those responsible to justice.

UZBEKISTAN

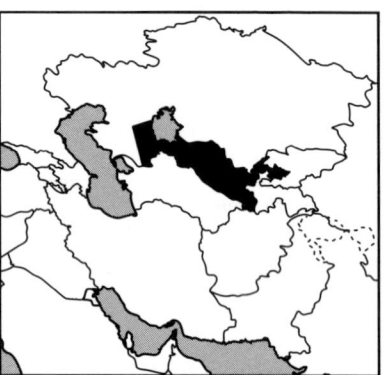

One prisoner of conscience was sentenced to 11 years' imprisonment. At least three possible prisoners of conscience were sentenced to long terms of imprisonment. At least one human rights activist was detained and there was concern for the safety of another. One political prisoner was sentenced to death. Scores of others may have received unfair trials. Death sentences were believed to have been passed and carried out.

During the year President Islam Karimov repeatedly condemned the perceived spread of "Wahhabism", a strict Islamic sect, in Uzbekistan. On 1 May he endorsed tough measures against "those who are trying by any means to introduce political Islam, religious extremism and fanaticism" and told parliament that "fundamentalists should be shot". The same day parliament adopted a revised version of the 1991 law on freedom of conscience and religious organizations. The new law raises the number of citizens required to form a religious organization from 10, under the 1991 law, to 100. All religious groups must be registered, and activities by unregistered religious organizations are illegal. According to new articles in the criminal code, which also entered into force in May, anyone organizing an unregistered religious group could face up to five years in prison. The law punishes private religious teaching or missionary activity with three-year prison terms.

In June Syrdarya Regional Court sentenced 62-year-old journalist Shadi Mardiyev to 11 years' imprisonment for criminal libel and extortion. In August the Supreme Court upheld the verdict. According to reports, Shadi Mardiyev was arrested in November 1997 and charged with defamation and extortion following a radio broadcast which satirized alleged corrupt practices of a local procurator. A co-defendant was reportedly sentenced to 12 years in prison on allegedly fabricated charges of bribery. Shadi Mardiyev was said to have suffered a heart attack in detention.

Arbitrary arrests of alleged "Wahhabists" following a spate of murders of police officers and regional officials in the Fergana Valley in November and December 1997 continued throughout the year (see *Amnesty International Report 1998*). Some human rights monitors estimated the number of those detained to be over a thousand. There were reports that weapons or narcotics were planted on many of them in order to fabricate a criminal case against them. Allegations persisted that a large number of those detained were threatened, beaten and otherwise ill-treated in police custody. In March brothers Abdulkhai and Murod Egamberdiyev were sentenced to four years' imprisonment by Andijan Regional Court for illegal possession of narcotics and weapons. Both were possible prisoners of conscience. They said that the charges against them were fabricated and that they were prosecuted solely for refusing to shave their beards. The brothers had reportedly been arrested in Andijan in January by plainclothes police officers two weeks after they had been ordered by their local police station to shave off their beards. The police allegedly beat them and planted a small quantity of narcotics and 10 bullets in their pockets during the arrest.

On 29 April Fergana Regional Court sentenced Abdumalik Nazarov, the youngest brother of independent Islamic leader Obidkhon Nazarov, to nine years' imprisonment for illegal possession of narcotics and forgery of official documents. He was a possible prisoner of conscience. Abdumalik Nazarov had been detained in December 1997 with his father and an older brother at the Uzbek-Kyrgyz border (see *Amnesty International Report 1998*). It was alleged that the charge against Abdumalik Nazarov was fabricated because of his relationship to Obidkhon Nazarov. On 5 March Uzbek security forces had surrounded the house of Obidkhon Nazarov in Tashkent, allegedly in an attempt to take him and another imam, Tulkin Ergashev, to the Procurator General's office to answer questions about their activities. Neither man was present. There were reports that arrest warrants had been issued against the two men for promoting "Wahhabism", preaching illegally and trying to set up an Islamic state. An Islamic student, Ikromiddin Yusupov, claimed that he had been detained by officers of the Ministry of Internal Affairs in February and forced under duress to incriminate Obidkhon Nazarov and Tulkin Ergashev in anti-state activities.

In August possible prisoner of conscience Rakhmat Otakulov, a religious teacher, was released from prison after his term of imprisonment was commuted to a non-custodial sentence (see *Amnesty International Report 1998*).

There was concern for the safety of Zafarmirza Iskhakov, a human rights activist and former political detainee, who went into hiding after he received death threats from the Committee for National Security (KNB) in April. Zafarmirza Iskhakov had been monitoring the human rights situation in the Fergana Valley and had passed information of arrests and ill-treatment of alleged "Wahhabists" to international human rights organizations. Following his contacts in March with international human rights monitors and foreign journalists, KNB officers reportedly came to question him about his human rights monitoring activities, warning him that "something could happen" to him or his children if he did not stop. Zafarmirza Iskhakov had previously been detained on a number of occasions as a result of his activities as deputy chairman of the

356

outlawed non-violent opposition "Birlik" group and as a member of the banned independent Human Rights Organization of Uzbekistan in Andijan.

Shovruk Ruzimuradov, a former prisoner of conscience and head of the Kashkadarya branch of the Human Rights Society of Uzbekistan, was arrested at his home in Kashkadarya Region in southern Uzbekistan in April on charges of illegal possession of 12 firearms cartridges. He was held for 10 days. Human rights activists believed the cartridges were planted by law enforcement officers during a reportedly unsanctioned search of his house. He had reportedly been asked repeatedly by the authorities to stop engaging in human rights activities and to resign from the Human Rights Society.

In January Abdulfattakh Mannapov, an Uzbek human rights activist and member of the Moscow-based Society for Monitoring the Observance of Human Rights in Central Asia, was severely beaten in a street in Moscow, the Russian Federation, by two unknown men who also set their dog on him. He was admitted to hospital with multiple fractures and dog bites. Nothing was stolen during the attack, which led human rights monitors to believe the unprovoked attack was politically motivated. Abdulfattakh Mannapov had been approached in Moscow in 1997 by three unknown men, at least one of whom he recognized as an Uzbek, who threatened to harm him and his family if he did not stop his "treacherous activities" against Uzbekistan.

Scores of men were sentenced to long terms of imprisonment in at least five separate trials in connection with the 1997 murders in Namangan and the Fergana Valley (see above). In May Namangan Regional Court sentenced eight men to prison terms of between five and eight years for "terrorism", attempting to overthrow the constitutional order, and creation of a criminal group. The men were also accused of seeking to promote "Wahhabism". In a separate trial in May, Namangan Regional Court sentenced a further six men to similar terms of imprisonment for attempting to undermine the country's Constitution and forming an illegal criminal group. In June the Supreme Court sentenced seven men to prison sentences of between six and 10 years for attempting to destabilize the country and

establish an Islamist state. In all the trials there were allegations that the defendants had been beaten and otherwise ill-treated in detention and forced under duress to confess. There was also concern that these men may have been imprisoned solely for their alleged affiliation to independent Islamic congregations.

In July the Supreme Court sentenced Talib Mamadzhanov to death for the murder of eight people. Seven co-defendants, one of them a minor, received prison sentences ranging from three to 10 years. Talib Mamadzhanov reportedly confessed to a series of murders between 1994 and 1997, including the murders of five police officers in the Fergana Valley which sparked the wave of arrests of alleged "Wahhabists" that began in December 1997. Talib Mamadzhanov was quoted as saying that the murders were religiously motivated. There were reports that the defendants had been beaten and otherwise ill-treated in pre-trial detention and that at least three defendants claimed to have been tortured and forced under duress to give false evidence. Nosir Yusupov was said to have had a plastic bag placed over his head and to have been tortured with electric shocks. His 16-year-old son, Dzhamaliddin, told the court that he too had been tortured. Co-defendant Isroil Parpiboyev stated in court that he was tortured with electric shocks, and that he was taken naked to the prison yard after cold water had been poured over him. It was winter. He also alleged that a bottle was inserted into his anus and that vodka was poured onto his wounds. International observers at the trial noted that Talib Mamadzhanov appeared to be ill and lost consciousness during one hearing.

In October a further 15 men, all said to have been followers of independent Islamic leader Abduvali Mirzoyev who "disappeared" in 1995 (see *Amnesty International Reports 1996* to *1998*), went on trial before the Supreme Court for their alleged participation in the 1997 Namangan murders. In December they received prison sentences ranging from five to 16 years.

At least 10 men were sentenced to death. Other death sentences were believed to have been passed and carried out, but no official information was available. In August parliament removed the death penalty as a possible punishment under five articles of the criminal code. It remained in force for eight crimes.

Amnesty International expressed concern that the restrictions and penalties imposed on religious groups by the new law on freedom of conscience and religious organizations might lead to persecution of their members and possibly the imprisonment of prisoners of conscience.

Amnesty International called for the immediate and unconditional release of Shadi Mardiyev. The organization urged the authorities to repeal Articles 139 and 140 of the criminal code to prevent further prosecutions for peaceful exercise of the right to freedom of expression.

Amnesty International was concerned that the prosecutions of the Egamberdiyev brothers and Abdumalik Nazarov were part of a clampdown against Islamic leaders, including Obidkhon Nazarov, and congregations not affiliated to the state-regulated Muslim Spiritual Directorate.

The organization was gravely concerned that the trials of political prisoners might have been influenced by negative statements made by President Karimov against Islamic activists and called for full and impartial inquiries into allegations of torture, beatings and other ill-treatment made during the trials.

Amnesty International called on the President to commute the death sentence of Talib Mamadzhanov and all other death sentences that came before him, and to abolish the death penalty.

VANUATU

Dozens of people were ill-treated by police and military officers during mass arrests under a four-week state of emergency. Conditions in some prisons amounted to ill-treatment.

A four-week state of emergency, suspending most constitutional human rights guarantees, was declared in January following widespread rioting and looting in the capital, Port Vila. Protests were prompted by a report on official corruption by the Ombudsman. Former opposition leader Donald Kalpokas became Prime Minister after elections in March, called to restore political stability.

In June the new government pledged to introduce a new Ombudsman's Act which

would include provisions for human rights monitoring. The Ombudsman's Act had been repealed in November 1997 by the former government after a failed attempt to remove the Ombudsman from office. In November the Ombudsman criticized provisions in the proposed legislation which would limit her independence by allowing government interference. A new Leadership Code law to make politicians more accountable came into effect in September.

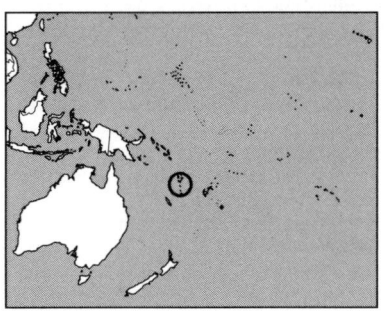

Dozens of people reported that they were kicked and beaten by military and police officers during the arrest of some 500 criminal suspects under the state of emergency. At least 200 of them were held for up to three days in conditions amounting to cruel, inhuman or degrading treatment. Some were denied medical attention and investigators from the office of the Ombudsman were refused permission to visit prisons. More than 20 people sought medical treatment after their release, and three were admitted to hospital.

The police started to investigate 16 complaints of ill-treatment after a man nearly died from internal injuries inflicted by military officers while he was in custody. However, no officer was suspended from active duty.

As a result of police investigations, 18 police officers were charged with "intentional assault" of prisoners; all pleaded not guilty. By the end of the year, none had been convicted.

Most people arrested under the state of emergency were held in conditions described in a government report as "extremely poor" and "dangerous" as a result of earthquake damage, with "considerable overcrowding" and a lack of adequate facilities for women. Most prison cells were decaying and frequently wet during rain and had no lighting and poor ventilation.

358

Food and prison medical services were inadequate.

In June all male prisoners in Port Vila Central Prison were transferred to an alternative prison, known as "the former British prison", because of concerns about the structural safety of the building. However, two female prisoners, who also asked to be evacuated, continued to be held there.

As a result of the evacuation, most of Vanuatu's male prisoners were held in inhuman and often overcrowded conditions. Convicted prisoners were held with those awaiting trial and there were no facilities to separate juveniles from adults. Despite improvised repairs to cells, conditions remained extremely poor; for example, prisoners were unable to sleep because rain leaked onto their beds.

An Amnesty International delegate visited the Port Vila area in February to investigate prison conditions and reports of ill-treatment. Its report issued in September, *Vanuatu: No safe place for prisoners*, recommended urgent measures to improve prison conditions and police and prison complaints mechanisms. It urged the government to seek assistance from the international community. A joint statement by the Vanuatu government and police welcomed Amnesty International's report and pledged to implement its recommendations.

VENEZUELA

Human rights defenders and community activists were threatened and harassed. Reports of ill-treatment and torture by the police and army were frequent. Prison conditions often amounted to cruel, inhuman or degrading treatment. Dozens of people were killed by the security forces in circumstances suggesting excessive use of force or extrajudicial execution. An asylum-seeker was extradited to Peru.

The deep economic crisis and rumours of a possible coup seemed to threaten stability for several months prior to the December presidential election. The election, which passed off peacefully, was won by Hugo Chávez Frías who, as an army colonel, led a failed coup attempt in 1992.

The new penal code was approved in January and was due to be fully intro-

duced in July 1999. Among other reforms, it established clear regulations concerning the use of force at the time of arrest. However, local human rights organizations expressed concern that despite some reform of the Code of Military Justice, the President continued to enjoy considerable powers to intervene in the military justice system, retaining the legal power to decide not to open proceedings or to close those already in progress when he or she "considers it to be in the national interest".

A number of constitutional guarantees, including the right not to be arrested without a warrant, continued to be suspended in areas bordering Colombia. The military authorities in these areas continued to be allowed to hold people for up to 20 days in preventive detention.

Following the annulment at the end of 1997 of the *Ley de Vagos y Maleantes*, Law of Vagrants and Crooks, which permitted administrative detention by the police without judicial review, over 500 detainees were released and there were no reports of continued detention under the law. However, thousands of arbitrary detentions were reported, apparently in attempts at social cleansing targeted at the poorest and most vulnerable sectors of society.

Human rights defenders were increasingly subjected to death threats, defamation and intimidatory surveillance. Following the alleged extrajudicial execution in June of three criminal suspects by the *Policía Técnica Judicial*, Criminal Investigation Police, in Maracaibo, Zulia state, three members of the nongovernmental human rights organization *Red de Apoyo por la Justicia y la Paz*, Support Network for Justice and Peace, were followed and received several anonymous death threats. The following month, Sergio Salvador, a volunteer with the network, was approached by two strangers outside the organization's offices who warned him to stop working on the case or he would be killed; a third man in a nearby car pointed a gun at him.

In October Juan Bautista Moreno of the *Comité para la Defensa de los Derechos Humanos*, Committee for the Defence of Human Rights, based in Guasdualito, near the Colombian border, was threatened with "disappearance" by the commander of military operations in the area. Juan Bautista Moreno had been arbitrarily detained in 1996 (see *Amnesty International Report 1997*). Wilfredo Alvarado Baldaggio, a community activist, was threatened by members of the *Guardia Nacional*, National Guard, to make him withdraw his allegation that they had tortured him in 1997 (see *Amnesty International Report 1998*).

Torture and ill-treatment by the police and army continued to be frequently reported. Methods included beatings, use of electric shocks and mock executions. Victims included Roberto Cabrera Márquez, a Jehovah's Witness and conscientious objector, who was allegedly beaten in the air force base in Maracay by soldiers who then placed him in a cupboard and let off tear-gas grenades.

Hundreds of detainees complained of ill-treatment by prison warders and Ministry of Justice employees. In March more than 100 relatives of detainees in Los Llanos prison, Portuguesa state, carried out a four-day protest inside the prison in support of their demand for the removal of the local head of the *Guardia Nacional* accused of responsibility for the ill-treatment of prisoners.

Prison conditions continued to amount to cruel, inhuman or degrading treatment. During the year, the Ministry of Justice implemented a number of measures, such as the creation of a new *Cuerpo de Seguridad Penitenciaria*, Prison Security Force, and the redistribution of prisoners according to their legal status. Despite these measures, which could lead to improvements in the future, violence in prisons remained endemic. According to reports, more than 300 prisoners and detainees were killed and over 1,000 wounded, the overwhelming majority by other prisoners. Acute overcrowding and the failure of the

authorities to ensure the security of those in their custody were contributing factors to the problem. Poor standards of food provoked at least one hunger strike by prisoners and sanitary conditions continued to be inadequate.

Dozens of people were killed by the security forces in circumstances suggesting excessive use of force or, in some cases, extrajudicial execution. According to reports, in July in the municipality of Sucre, Miranda state, municipal police shot dead Freddy Díaz after chasing his 14-year-old cousin, Ali Eduardo Sojo, into the family home. The family and witnesses to the shooting were threatened by the police to discourage them from pursuing the case.

The judicial system failed to bring to justice those responsible for the massacre of 14 fishermen in El Amparo in 1988 (see previous *Amnesty International Reports*). In October the Supreme Court upheld the previous decision of the *ad hoc* military tribunal which absolved 15 soldiers accused of involvement in the massacre of all charges. The ruling did not include four other soldiers who were also implicated; they remained at large at the end of the year.

In July asylum-seeker Cecilia Rosana Núñez Chipana, a Peruvian citizen and alleged member of the *Partido Comunista del Perú (Sendero Luminoso)*, Communist Party of Peru (Shining Path), was extradited to Peru where it was feared she could be at risk of torture, despite a request by the UN Committee against Torture that the extradition procedures be suspended until it had had an opportunity to reach a decision. There were a number of irregularities in the proceedings, including the hampering of the work of the defence counsel, which put into question the independence of the judiciary. The Foreign Relations Ministry informed the Committee that Cecilia Rosana Núñez Chipana had already been extradited three days before she actually was, suggesting that a political agreement had been reached prior to the legal ruling. In November the Committee ruled that Venezuela had failed to meet its obligation not to proceed with the extradition and had therefore breached the UN Convention against Torture and Other Cruel, Inhuman or Degrading Treatment or Punishment.

Amnesty International continued to call on the authorities to take all necessary

360

measures to guarantee the safety of human rights defenders, to end the intimidation of victims' relatives and witnesses of human rights violations and to curb the excessive use of force by the security forces. Amnesty International also urged the government to respect the recommendations of the UN Committee against Torture in the case of Cecilia Rosana Núñez Chipana.

VIET NAM

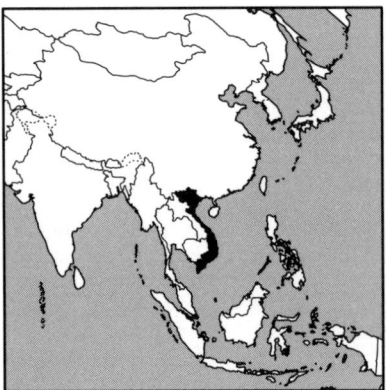

At least 56 prisoners of conscience and possible prisoners of conscience continued to be held throughout the year. At least 15 prisoners of conscience were released. At least a further 10 possible prisoners of conscience were arrested, tried and sentenced. A further 40 people were imprisoned for political offences following unfair trials. Fifty-three new death sentences and 18 executions were reported, but the actual numbers were believed to be much higher.

The government announced that revisions to the criminal code would be introduced; no details were given. Some senior members of the Vietnamese Communist Party publicly issued letters critical of the party's policies and calling for reform. Social unrest in Dong Nai province, prompted in November 1997 by local anger against perceived official corruption and land disputes, continued in January. President Tran Duc Luong approved two major prisoner amnesties in September and October, which included some political prisoners.

In October the UN Special Rapporteur on religious intolerance visited the country. He was prevented from meeting most religious dissidents. Viet Nam became an official member of the Asia-Pacific Economic Co-operation in November.

Lack of official information and restrictions on freedom of expression made obtaining details of human rights violations difficult.

At least 56 prisoners of conscience and possible prisoners of conscience arrested in previous years and known to Amnesty International continued to be detained. During the year, it was learned that 17 members of the People's Action Party (PAP) who were expelled from Cambodia to Viet Nam in December 1996 (see *Amnesty International Report 1997*), remained in detention without charge or trial in Ho Chi Minh City. Two others expelled at the same time were quickly released. It was also learned that four other members of the PAP who visited Viet Nam from Cambodia had been arrested in 1997 and were still detained. All were possible prisoners of conscience. The trial of newspaper editor Nguyen Hoang Linh, a prisoner of conscience who was arrested in October 1997 (see *Amnesty International Report 1998*), took place in October. He was found guilty of "taking advantage of democratic freedoms to damage the interests of the state, social organizations and the public" and sentenced to one year and 13 days in prison. He was released after the trial, having served his sentence in pre-trial detention.

Nguyen Dinh Huy, a former professor of English and history serving a 15-year prison sentence for his leadership of the Movement to Unite the People and Build Democracy (MUPBD – see *Amnesty International Reports 1996* and *1998*), remained in prison throughout the year, as did 78-year-old Nguyen Ngoc Tan, a fellow MUPBD member. Other elderly prisoners of conscience serving sentences for their peaceful political activities included Do Van Hung and his brother Do Van Thac, members of the Greater Viet Nam People's Party.

Prisoners of conscience remained in detention for their religious beliefs. Among them were the Supreme Patriarch of the unofficial Unified Buddhist Church of Viet Nam (UBCV) Thich Huyen Quang, held without charge or trial for almost 14 years; and four members of the Catholic Congregation of the Mother Co-Redemptrix, including Brother Mai Duc Chuong (Nghi), who was serving a prison sentence of 16 and a half years for holding training courses and distributing religious books without permission. The government denied that it held any political prisoners.

At least 15 prisoners of conscience were among more than 7,000 prisoners who were released in two amnesties in September and October. They included Dr Nguyen Dan Que, an endocrinologist serving a 20-year prison sentence for founding the High Tide of Humanism Movement which called for peaceful political and economic change (see *Amnesty International Reports 1991* and *1997*). Membership of Amnesty International was the basis for one of the charges against him at his trial.

Doan Viet Hoat, a former English professor serving a 15-year prison sentence for his involvement in the *Freedom Forum* newsletter, was released and forcibly exiled to the USA.

Nguyen Van Thuan, a writer and former teacher imprisoned for his involvement in both the High Tide of Humanism Movement and the *Freedom Forum*, and who suffered serious health problems in prison, was released.

UBCV monks Thich Tri Sieu and Thich Tue Sy, who had been in detention since 1984 and were convicted in 1988 of "conducting activities to overthrow the people's administration", were released in the September amnesty. Thich Quang Do, Secretary General of the UBCV, and Thich Nhat Ban, both of whom were convicted in 1995 of involvement in an unofficial charitable mission to flood victims in 1994, were also released. So too were Brother Nguyen Chau Dat and Reverend Dinh Viet Hieu (Thuc) from the Catholic Congregation of the Mother Co-Redemptrix, who were both serving long sentences for holding training courses and distributing religious books without permission.

Ten followers of a Taiwan-based religious group were sentenced to prison terms of between 10 months and two years by a court in Bac Lieu province for "engaging in heretical propaganda and taking advantage of the people's rights to freedom and democracy to transgress state and public interests". They were possible prisoners of conscience.

At least 40 people were sentenced to prison terms of up to 11 years after unfair trials for offences relating to social unrest in Thai Binh province in 1997 (see *Amnesty International Report 1998*). The group – believed to include some public officials – was charged with disrupting public order, abuse of power while carrying out a public mission, and illegal arrest. It was believed that some of the defendants were involved in protests against local officials, some of which were violent. Information on the trial was limited. However, trials in Viet Nam, especially those relating to political offences, are routinely unfair, with defendants denied the right to call and question witnesses, and defence lawyers permitted only to plead for clemency.

Fifty-three death sentences and 18 executions were reported, but the actual numbers were believed to be much higher. Among those sentenced to death were four people convicted in June of drug trafficking in a continued crack-down by the authorities on so-called "social evils". One death sentence was commuted to life imprisonment. Among those executed were three men convicted of corruption in 1997. The executions by firing squad took place in public, with the victims blindfolded and gagged with a lemon in their mouth. Six men and one woman were executed in March following conviction for drugs offences in 1997. Witnesses reported that the woman fainted three times before the execution.

Amnesty International continued to call for the release of all prisoners of conscience, for fair trials of political prisoners, for the commutation of death sentences and for an end to the use of the death penalty. The organization wrote to President Tran Duc Luong welcoming the amnesties which led to the release of prisoners of conscience. In a report published in December, *Socialist Republic of Viet Nam: A step forward for human rights?*, Amnesty International appealed to the authorities to release all remaining prisoners of conscience and ensure that proposed law reforms meet international human rights standards.

361

YEMEN

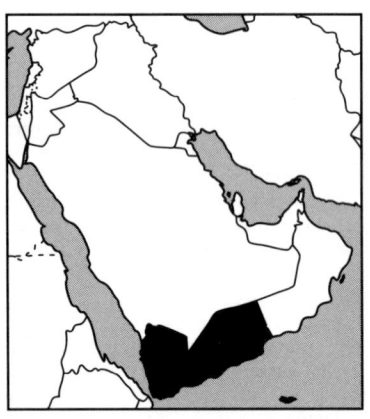

Dozens of people, including prisoners of conscience, were arrested on political grounds. Many were detained for short periods without charge or trial, and then released. One prisoner of conscience under sentence of death was released. At least 33 political prisoners received unfair trials; four were sentenced to death. At least 13 political prisoners, most of them sentenced to death in previous years, remained in prison. There were continued allegations of torture. One person reportedly died in circumstances which suggested that torture was a contributory factor. Cruel judicial punishments, including flogging, continued to be imposed. The fate of hundreds of people who "disappeared" in previous years remained unknown. Two people were killed by government forces in circumstances which suggested that they were victims of excessive use of force. At least 17 people were executed; hundreds of others were believed to be under sentence of death. At least one person was forcibly returned to a country where he was at risk of torture and execution.

In August President 'Ali 'Abdullah Saleh issued a decree extending the scope of the death penalty to include kidnapping and looting public or private property.

In January the government established the National Supreme Committee for Human Rights, responsible for liaison with international human rights organizations and for monitoring the implementation of human rights treaties. The President also established the Human Rights, Liberties and Non-Governmental Organizations Committee, which, as part of the Consultative Council, advises the President.

Dozens of suspected opponents of the government, including prisoners of conscience, were detained during the year on political grounds. Among them was prisoner of conscience Dr al-Murtada bin Zayd al-Muhatwari, imam of the Badr mosque in Sana'a, who was arrested in September by members of the political security and the Republican Guard, without a judicial warrant. He was held solely for his public criticism of the government and was released in November without charge.

Dozens of other people, including possible prisoners of conscience, were briefly detained in connection with demonstrations against cuts in food subsidies and against government plans to administratively divide the province of Hadramout. They were reportedly released without charge or trial.

Dozens of possible political prisoners were arrested during the year in connection with explosions in Lahj, Abyan and Aden. It was unclear at the end of the year whether they were still detained. In December a number of political prisoners, including four United Kingdom (UK) nationals and one man with dual Yemeni and UK nationality, were arrested in connection with possession of explosives and plans to carry out attacks.

Mansur Rajih, a prisoner of conscience, was released in February after more than 14 years under sentence of death (see *Amnesty International Reports 1997* and *1998*).

Four political prisoners were sentenced to death and at least 29 others received prison sentences of up to 12 years after trials which fell short of international standards for fair trial. Defendants were denied access to lawyers during the initial period of their detention and many were tortured in order to obtain confessions. In October, three men – Bajash 'Ali Mohammad 'Abid al-Aghbari, Sa'eed Suleiman Sa'ad bin Nilah and Mohammad Ahmed Saleh Haidara – were sentenced to death and nine others were sentenced to prison terms for involvement in an armed group in the governorate of al-Mahrah and having links with government opponents abroad. The group's access to legal assistance was reportedly severely restricted.

In two separate trials for bombings in Aden in 1997 (see *Amnesty International Report 1998*), one man – Nabil Kanakli Kasaybati, a Spanish national of Syrian origin – was sentenced to death and at least 20 others were sentenced to prison terms of up to 12 years. A further four were sentenced *in absentia*. In both cases defendants alleged that they were held in incommunicado detention and tortured to force them to confess. Torture included beatings all over the body, *falaqa* (beatings on the soles of the feet), suspension while tied up for prolonged periods of time, and electric shocks. In all three cases defence lawyers were expected to appeal against the sentences.

At least 13 political prisoners, suspected members of the former opposition organization *al-Jabha al-Wataniya al-Dimuqratiya*, National Democratic Front, in the former Yemen Arab Republic, remained in prison. Most of them had been sentenced to death in 1986 (see *Amnesty International Report 1998*).

There were further reports of torture and ill-treatment. Methods included beatings, prolonged suspension upside down, electric shocks and the prolonged use of shackles. At least one person reportedly died in circumstances which suggested that torture may have been a contributory factor. Ahmed Qa'id 'Abd Rabeh Muthanna, a teacher, was arrested by *al-Najda* (Rescue) police officers after a criminal complaint was lodged against him. According to official records he was taken to hospital in Dhamar by *al-Najda* officers on 22 March and died two days later. A medical report stated that injuries to his head and bleeding were major contributory factors in his death. The public prosecutor in Dhamar repeatedly ordered that the four men suspected of being responsible for his death be brought to him for questioning. However, there was no evidence of further investigation.

New information came to light concerning the death in custody in 1997 of Wadi' al-Sheibani, who had been arrested in connection with bombings in Aden (see above and *Amnesty International Report 1998*). According to an official medical report Wadi' al-Sheibani died from head injuries. The public prosecutor informed Wadi' al-Sheibani's family that he had committed suicide. However, the victim's family, who believed that he died as a result of torture, refused to collect Wadi' al-Sheibani's body until a thorough investigation into his death had been carried out and anyone responsible brought to justice. The government offered financial assistance to the family but stressed that this was not compensation. The government did not initiate an independent investigation.

The judicial punishment of flogging was widely imposed and often carried out immediately after sentencing. Defendants were denied a real opportunity to appeal as those who did so faced a lengthy period in prison while the appeal was pending. It was not clear whether any sentences of amputation were passed during the year, nor whether sentences passed in previous years were carried out (see *Amnesty International Report 1998*).

The fate and whereabouts of hundreds of people who "disappeared" in previous years remained unknown. Undertakings made by the government to investigate the cases of those who had "disappeared" since 1994 were apparently not implemented (see previous *Amnesty International Reports*).

At least two people were killed by government forces in circumstances which suggested excessive use of force. In April residents of the town of Al-Mukalla held a march to protest against government plans to administratively divide the province of Hadramout. Soldiers fired at protesters, who apparently presented no threat to their security. Ahmad 'Omar Barjash and Faraj Murjan Ben Hammam were killed. Subsequently the parliamentary Committee for General Freedoms and Human Rights carried out an investigation which recommended that the local criminal investigation unit and the public prosecutor should seek to bring to justice those members of the security forces who fired guns during the protest. It was not clear at the end of the year whether the recommendations had been acted upon. Other clashes between government troops and demonstrators reportedly resulted in dozens of deaths. However, no details of the circumstances of these deaths were available by the end of the year.

At least 17 people were executed, often following trials which fell short of international norms for fair trial. Nasser Saleh

364

Nasser Zuba'a was executed in October – just two days after the murder of which he was convicted. The speed with which he was executed indicated that he was not given adequate opportunity to prepare a defence or appeal against the verdict or sentence.

Information came to light that Muhammad Hussein 'Ali al-Zandani was executed at the end of 1997. He had been sentenced to death in 1995 for a murder reportedly committed when he was 16 years old (see *Amnesty International Report 1998*). He was reportedly executed without his family or lawyer having been informed. Jalal 'Abdullah al-Rada'i and 'Abdullah 'Ali Idris al-Rada'i, sentenced to death and crucifixion in August 1997, were executed at the end of 1997 (see *Amnesty International Report 1998*). Their bodies were publicly displayed on crosses. Both men were reported to have been denied access to legal assistance during their trial. The death sentence for adultery imposed on Sabah al-Difani in 1995 was overturned. However, a sentence of 100 lashes was upheld and she was released after the flogging had been carried out (see *Amnesty International Report 1997*).

Hundreds of prisoners were believed to be under sentence of death at the end of the year, although the exact number was not known.

In August the government forcibly returned Fahd 'Abdullah Jassim al-Malki to Qatar, where he was allegedly tortured and where he faced capital charges for alleged involvement in an attempted coup in 1996 (see **Qatar** entry).

Amnesty International called for the immediate and unconditional release of prisoners of conscience and for prompt and fair trials for all political prisoners. The organization also called for an end to the arbitrary arrest and detention of political suspects and urged that all allegations of torture, deaths in custody, "disappearances" and use of excessive lethal force be investigated.

Amnesty International expressed concern at the widening of the scope of the death penalty and urged that all sentences of death, amputation and flogging be commuted.

In response to the kidnapping in December of 16 tourists and the subsequent killing of four of the tourists and, reportedly, three kidnappers, Amnesty International urged the government to carry out an impartial and independent investigation into all the killings. The organization called for the findings of such an investigation to be made public and for anyone found to be responsible for any of the killings to be brought to justice. Amnesty International called on the government to ensure that legal proceedings against those arrested in connection with the kidnapping met international standards for fair trial in capital cases. The organization also urged the government to exercise clemency and commute any death sentences passed.

In September an Amnesty International delegation met the Attorney General and the Chief Co-ordinator of the National Supreme Council for Human Rights. The delegates sought clarification from the Attorney General concerning, among other things, undertakings made by the government during Amnesty International's visit to Yemen in 1996 (see *Amnesty International Reports 1997* and *1998*), which included the establishment of a unit within the Attorney General's office to investigate allegations of torture. The Attorney General said that his office already had the power to undertake such investigations and that a specific unit was not necessary. The former attorney general had informed Amnesty International in 1997 that such a unit had been established (see *Amnesty International Report 1998*).

YUGOSLAVIA
(FEDERAL REPUBLIC OF)

Hundreds of ethnic Albanians and smaller numbers of Serbs or Montenegrins were killed in armed conflict in Kosovo. Many of them were extrajudicially executed by police or deliberately and arbitrarily killed by armed ethnic Albanians. Hundreds of people, all of them ethnic Albanians, "disappeared" at the hands of security forces. More than 250,000 people, the vast majority of them ethnic Albanians, were displaced, many of them forcibly, by police, soldiers or opposition ethnic Albanian forces. Armed opposition forces were responsible for human rights abuses, including the abduction of dozens of people, many of

whom remained unaccounted for. There were numerous reports of ill-treatment, torture and excessive use of force. At least five people died in police custody. At least 1,000 ethnic Albanians were detained and placed under investigation on charges of "terrorism" and "armed rebellion". Many were reportedly tortured or ill-treated during interrogation. Many were convicted after unfair trials; some were possible prisoners of conscience. At least one conscientious objector was imprisoned. Four students were detained for a short period; they were prisoners of conscience. At least two people were sentenced to death.

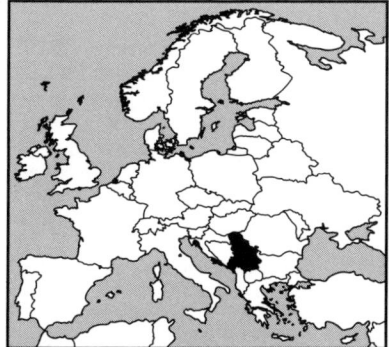

Ethnic Albanians, who form the majority in Kosovo province, continued to demand independence from the Federal Republic of Yugoslavia (FRY). From March the police, and later the Yugoslav Army, deployed large forces in response to small-scale attacks by the *Ushtria Çlirimtare e Kosovës* (UÇK), Kosovo Liberation Army, which seeks independence by violent means. Since 1996 the UÇK had attacked Serbian police, civilians and ethnic Albanians it regarded as "loyal" to the Serbian authorities. From March onwards confrontations increased. Many ethnic Albanians joined the UÇK and by July it effectively controlled a large area in western Kosovo. However, the police and army launched a major offensive in July and by September they had retaken control of most of the territory.

In October, following two UN Security Council resolutions and the threat of military intervention by the North Atlantic Treaty Organization (NATO), the President of the FRY, Slobodan Milošević, agreed to the withdrawal of forces and the deployment of a 2,000-strong Verification Mission assembled by the Organization for Security and Co-operation in Europe. The Mission was not operational by the end of the year. However, from October, following the withdrawal of the police and army and a cease-fire which was largely effective, the UÇK regained control of a large area of territory.

Federal and Serbian authorities failed to cooperate with the International Criminal Tribunal for the former Yugoslavia, despite a UN Security Council resolution in November condemning the FRY for its failure to execute the Tribunal's arrest warrants.

In June the trial opened in Prijepolje of Nebojša Ranisavljević who was accused of being one of the perpetrators of the abduction and killing of 20 people at the Štrpci railway station in Bosnia-Herzegovina in 1993 (see *Amnesty International Report 1994*). The trial had not been concluded by the end of the year.

The Serbian authorities applied pressure on the independent media. A government decree and new media law resulted in the temporary or indefinite closure of five newspapers. Independent radio stations complained of a restrictive licensing policy and the closure of stations.

More than 1,500 people, predominantly ethnic Albanians, were reported to have been killed in the armed conflict by the end of the year. Evidence suggested that many of the killings were extrajudicial executions by the police, army or civilians armed by the authorities. In February police killed 26 ethnic Albanians in the villages of Likošane and Ćirez in the Drenica region of Kosovo. Police had been deployed after UÇK members reportedly fired at a school near Glogovac housing ethnic Serb refugees. Four police officers were killed in the subsequent fighting around Likošane and Ćirez. It appeared that most or all of the ethnic Albanian civilian victims had been extrajudicially executed by police after UÇK members had withdrawn. The victims included Rukije Nebiu from Ćirez who was pregnant; photographs of her corpse indicated that she had been shot in the head. Ten male members of the Ahmeti family were reportedly separated from the women and children in a house in Likošane and taken away by police. Two days later their bodies were discovered in the morgue in Priština. Evidence indicated that they had been extrajudicially executed.

In early March there was a large-scale police operation in Donji Prekaz, another village in Drenica. Armed men, apparently associated with the UÇK, were present in the village. Police asserted that they had been attacked on the morning they began their operation, although this claim did not appear credible. At least 54 ethnic Albanians were killed in Donji Prekaz, some of whom were armed men. However, at least 12 of the bodies that were identified were women and 11 were children aged under 17. It appeared that many of the victims had been extrajudicially executed. Witness testimony, supported by the conclusions of an independent forensic pathologist, indicated that some of the male victims may not have been carrying arms or had surrendered at the time they were killed. For example, the body of one victim, Nazmi Jashari, showed evidence of beating and gunshots fired at point-blank range. The authorities failed to ensure that autopsies and independent and impartial investigations were carried out into the killings in Donji Prekaz.

There were many other reports of extrajudicial executions or other unlawful killings in the armed conflict which followed.

Hundreds of ethnic Albanians were reported missing by the end of the year. There was evidence that many of them had "disappeared" as a result of action by the police. For example, in April Hafir Shala, an ethnic Albanian doctor, was detained and taken to a police station in Priština. Although others detained with him were quickly released, Hafir Shala was not seen again and the authorities neither acknowledged his detention nor provided information on his whereabouts. In May, eight ethnic Albanian men "disappeared" in Novi Poklek. Police attacked the village and detained the men after separating them from women and children. No substantive reply was received from the authorities to a request for an investigation from lawyers representing the families of the "disappeared" men.

Between March and September more than 250,000 people, predominantly ethnic Albanians, were estimated to have been displaced, many of them forcibly as a result of deliberate actions by the police such as extrajudicial executions and targeting of civilians. The police also set on fire, damaged or destroyed thousands of houses of ethnic Albanians and killed or destroyed livestock or crops. By September, tens of thousands of people were reported to be living without shelter. They were only able to find shelter or return to their homes, many of which were destroyed or badly damaged, after the October cease-fire.

There were numerous reports that the UÇK and other armed ethnic Albanians perpetrated human rights abuses, particularly forcible displacement, ill-treatment, abduction or detention of non-combatants of Serbian, Montenegrin, Albanian or Romani ethnicity. Many of those abducted remained "missing" at the end of the year. For example, in June, three elderly Serbs – Miloslav, Sultana and Aleksandra Smigić – and Aleksandra's son Radomir went missing in the village of Leočina. Armed UÇK men entered Leočina, beat Miloslav Smigić and tried to set fire to his house. Later, a larger group of UÇK men came and shots and screams were heard from the house of Radomir and Aleksandra Smigić. No trace of them was subsequently found. They had been the last Serbs left in Leočina after other Serb villagers had fled in May following threats by armed ethnic Albanians.

Also in June, nine Serbian workers were abducted by the UÇK in the vicinity of the Belaćevac mine. In August, two Serbian journalists went missing; they were believed to have been abducted by the UÇK. Two other journalists were detained for 40 days in October and November. Some 100 people, predominantly Serbs and Montenegrins, who went missing in UÇK-controlled areas or who were detained by the UÇK remained unaccounted for at the end of the year. The UÇK refused to acknowledge that it held detainees other than those it released.

Numerous reports of ill-treatment or torture by police or soldiers were received, not all of these connected to the armed conflict. Hundreds of ethnic Albanians were beaten by police during demonstrations against police violence in towns throughout Kosovo in March. For example, around 100 people were injured in Peć during and following a demonstration. At least six unarmed ethnic Albanian demonstrators were reportedly shot by police during the incident, one of whom died of his injuries. The victims of the beatings included a 16-year-old schoolgirl who was beaten by police in a house where she was hiding. Her head and legs were injured by blows from truncheons. In May and June police beat Serbian students and others who were protesting in Belgrade against a new law which they claimed restricted the independence of universities.

Ill-treatment or torture often took place during interrogation in police stations, most frequently in Kosovo province. For example, Besa Arllati, an activist in the Djakovica branch of the *Lidhja Demokratike e Kosovës*, Democratic League of Kosovo (the main ethnic Albanian political party), was detained for several days in the local police station. She reported being held in a cell fouled with urine and faeces and being severely beaten during interrogation. She was told that she must help secure the release of police officers believed to have been kidnapped by the UÇK. In July Destan Rukiqi, a lawyer and human rights activist, was charged with insulting a judge who refused to give him access to a client in July. He was sentenced to 60 days' imprisonment. After six days he was transferred to hospital with kidney injuries sustained as a result of beatings in police custody.

Five people died in custody apparently as a result of torture or ill-treatment, all of them in Kosovo province. For example, Rexhep Bislimi, a human rights activist, was arrested in July and transferred two weeks later to hospital with heavy bruising, several broken ribs and internal bleeding allegedly as a result of beating by police. He died in hospital three days later.

Many of those interrogated by police were kept in custody. By the end of the year, more than 1,000 ethnic Albanians had been remanded in custody. Many were tried and convicted of "terrorism", "armed rebellion" or similar charges. The trials frequently did not meet international standards of fair trial; the accused were denied access to consult with defence lawyers in private, and statements extracted from defendants under torture were reportedly accepted as evidence. The evidence did not in all cases support charges of using or advocating violence; some of the detainees were possible prisoners of conscience.

In February Pavle Božić was sentenced to one year's imprisonment for refusing to perform military service. His request to perform alternative service had been granted, but he was nevertheless called up to serve in the army. In November, four students were imprisoned for 10 days for spraying anti-government slogans in Belgrade. They were prisoners of conscience.

Dejan Andjelković and Zlatan Zakić were sentenced to death in March for premeditated murder. No judicial executions were carried out.

Amnesty International appealed repeatedly to the authorities and to the UÇK to respect international humanitarian law and to prevent human rights abuses in Kosovo. The organization also called on the authorities to initiate thorough, independent and impartial investigations into allegations of extrajudicial executions and other unlawful killings, "disappearances", forcible displacement, torture and ill-treatment. It appealed for political prisoners to receive prompt and fair trials. Amnesty International also called for displaced persons to be enabled to return to their homes in safety and dignity. During the year the organization issued a series of reports under the title, *A human rights crisis in Kosovo province*, which documented human rights violations and abuses.

ZAMBIA

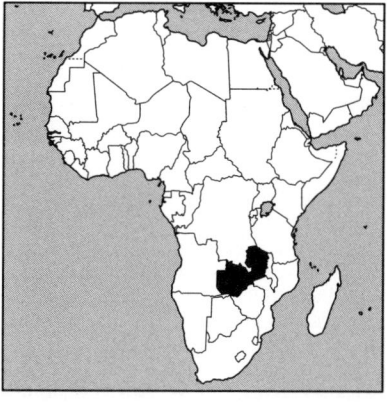

More than 100 people, including possible prisoners of conscience, were detained in connection with a 1997 coup attempt. They were held in conditions amounting to cruel, inhuman and degrading treatment; at least one detainee died in custody. Journalists and human rights defenders

368

continued to face imprisonment for exercising their right to freedom of expression. **Torture and ill-treatment, shootings and unlawful killings by police were widespread. More than 20 people were sentenced to death and more than 150 remained on death row at the end of the year. No executions were reported.**

The state of emergency, which suspended many fundamental rights, was renewed in February for another three months but lifted in mid-March (see *Amnesty International Report 1998*).

Zambia acceded to the UN Convention against Torture and Other Cruel, Inhuman or Degrading Treatment or Punishment in October, but it did not recognize the competence of the Committee against Torture to receive individual complaints.

In May a donors' consultative group meeting convened by the International Bank for Reconstruction and Development (World Bank), pledged US$530 million in aid on condition that the Zambian government initiate further economic reforms and "swift and decisive action on alleged human rights violations".

In September, following demands by a newly formed gay and lesbian organization for formal registration, Vice-President Lieutenant-General Christon Tembo told parliament that homosexuals and homosexual rights activists would be arrested. He also banned the publication of information about "gay activities". Amnesty International would consider anyone imprisoned solely for their homosexuality, or for non-violent advocacy of gay and lesbian rights, a prisoner of conscience.

Further arrests in early 1998 brought the total number of people detained in connection with the 1997 coup attempt to more than 100 (see *Amnesty International Report 1998*). Those detained included Kenneth Kaunda, former President and leader of the United National Independence Party (UNIP); Moyce Kaulung'ombe, his security chief; Dean Mung'omba, leader of the opposition Zambian Democratic Congress (ZDC); and Princess Nakatindi Wina, Women Affairs Chairperson of the ruling Movement for Multiparty Democracy. Despite High Court rulings in 1997 and in January that some apparently politically motivated detentions were unlawful, presidential detention orders issued under the state of emergency blocked the release of those unlawfully detained.

In April independent observers were granted access to Kenneth Kaunda, who had spent four months under house arrest with strict limitations on communication and access to visitors.

Also in April, 82 suspects detained in connection with the coup attempt were finally charged. In June, 79 defendants pleaded not guilty to treason, which is punishable by death. Kenneth Kaunda and Moyce Kaulung'ombe were released in June after charges of concealing knowledge of treason were withdrawn. In December Dean Mung'omba and Princess Nakatindi Wina were released for lack of evidence.

In March the government's Permanent Human Rights Commission concluded in a report that at least nine of the detainees held in connection with the 1997 coup attempt had been tortured, and identified some 12 police officers as responsible. However, it recommended that the alleged perpetrators not be criminally prosecuted but rather disciplined and retired. In May the government announced that it would establish an impartial inquiry into the allegations of torture and develop a comprehensive human rights training program for law enforcement officials. In August High Court Judge Japhet Banda was appointed to head a commission to investigate the allegations of torture. His appointment meant the investigation was further delayed because he was also the presiding judge at the trial of those charged in connection with the coup attempt, which was set to continue into 1999.

The detainees suffered serious health problems as a result of overcrowding, poor sanitation, inadequate diet and lack of medical facilities. Their trial was adjourned several times during the year because defendants were too ill to appear. Investigations by the Permanent Human Rights Commission, the Parliamentary Committee on Social Services and the presiding High Court judge all concurred that prison overcrowding and general conditions put prisoners' health and lives at serious risk. One detainee, Private John Nalilungwe Akapelwa, died in June. More than 10 detainees were hospitalized for illnesses including tuberculosis, malaria and chest infections. Some detainees continued to suffer from ill health, including partial blindness and deafness, caused by their torture at the hands of police in

1997. The health of Major Musonda Kangwa, who was tortured in 1997, deteriorated when he was sent back to a prison cell just days after undergoing surgery in March.

Some of those arrested in connection with the coup attempt appeared to be prisoners of conscience. At the end of February Frederick Mwanza, a journalist, and Priscilla Chisala Chimba, a secretary to Dean Mung'omba, were released without being tried after almost four months of detention. In April journalist Dickson Jere was detained briefly in connection with his interview with Kenneth Kaunda shortly before the coup. In June, police detained businessman Rajan Mahtani for 41 days on charges of treason; the charges were withdrawn.

Journalists continued to be threatened with arrest for exercising their right to freedom of expression. In January members of parliament demanded the arrest of Fred M'membe, editor of *The Post* newspaper, for describing parliament as "useless" in an editorial. In May staff at *The Post* were acquitted of contravening the State Security Act by publishing details of a cabinet plan to hold a referendum (see *Amnesty International Report 1998*). At the end of the year Masautso Phiri, former *The Post* editor, was still being tried for "conduct likely to cause a breach of the peace". He had been arrested in August 1997 at a political rally in Kabwe for photographing police ill-treating opposition party members (see *Amnesty International Report 1998*). By the end of the year, there were up to 20 cases outstanding in which government-sponsored charges had been brought against journalists.

Opposition politicians and human rights defenders also risked imprisonment for carrying out their legitimate, peaceful activities. In May police arrested ZDC politician Ruth Emelio for allegedly conducting herself in a manner likely to cause a breach of the peace. The arrest appeared to be politically motivated. Her trial had not started by the end of the year.

Police also routinely and arbitrarily detained criminal suspects' relatives to force the wanted person to surrender. In August police in Kasama city detained Joyce Musonda, the wife of a civil servant suspected of stealing money. She and her one-and-a-half-year-old child were held for three nights in a police station.

Torture and ill-treatment by police officers remained widespread. There was an increase in the number of police officers prosecuted for torture, but in scores of cases those responsible for torture were not brought to justice. Between June 1997 and May 1998 the Permanent Human Rights Commission received information about 73 cases of torture, ill-treatment and unlawful detention, including 17 deaths apparently at the hands of the police. In June, seven police officers were arrested for allegedly torturing to death Steward Mwantende. A Commission investigation had found that he died from beatings and burns they inflicted. The trial had not begun by the end of the year. In February, police shot and killed Milupi Sitwala and wounded another man during an apparent altercation with a police constable in Limalunga village, near Mongu city in the Western Province. Police responded with indiscriminate beatings when angry villagers vandalized the police station. A dozen people were detained, including Masiye Lowendo and Sinaali Siseho who were allegedly beaten with a spanner, an axe, a metal gear shaft and batons. All 12 were held incommunicado and denied food and medical treatment for four days. By August, one police constable involved was arrested on charges of murder. His trial started in October and was continuing at the end of the year. The allegations of torture were apparently not investigated.

Dozens of bystanders and unarmed criminal suspects were shot and killed by police. In February police reportedly shot and killed Theo Mijoni and Felix and Sydney Chitama as they stood unarmed beside a broken-down vehicle in the capital Lusaka. One officer was charged in September and the trial was continuing at the end of the year. In November police shot and killed eight men suspected of involvement in the murder of former Finance Minister Ronald Penza. Among the victims were Jordan Kapomba, Ackim Mumba, White Daka and Chanda Chayafya, who was tortured and killed by police after being taken into custody. By the end of the year only one officer had been charged with the killings and no commanding officer had been disciplined or charged.

Investigations into apparently unlawful shootings by police were flawed or nonexistent. In October the Permanent Human

370

Rights Commission suspended investigations into the August 1997 police shooting that injured Kenneth Kaunda and Rodger Chongwe, Chairman of the Liberal Progressive Front, as they attempted to drive away from a rally in Kabwe city which was broken up by police (see *Amnesty International Report 1998*).

More than 20 people were sentenced to death, including two police officers, for murder or aggravated robbery. More than 150 prisoners remained on death row at the end of the year. An estimated 73 prisoners had their death sentences confirmed by the Supreme Court of Zambia, while another 79 were awaiting the outcome of their appeals.

In March Amnesty International released a report, *Zambia: Misrule of law – human rights in a state of emergency*, describing the allegations of torture of those detained in connection with the 1997 coup attempt. It made a series of recommendations, including the suspension of police officers alleged to have been involved in the torture of detainees, pending a thorough, impartial investigation that resulted in those responsible being brought to justice; the condemnation of torture by President Frederick Chiluba and other senior officials; and legal reforms to break what appeared to be a pattern of torture. The organization also called for the powers of the Permanent Human Rights Commission to be strengthened. In May Amnesty International wrote to the authorities, welcoming the government's concern about torture and ill-treatment but stating that more training for police officers was not enough.

In September the organization expressed concern that arrests solely for advocating equal rights for lesbians and gays would be in contravention of international human rights standards.

In October Amnesty International brought a complaint to the African Commission on Human and Peoples' Rights on behalf of William Banda, an opposition politican who had been forcibly exiled to Malawi in 1994 (see *Amnesty International Report 1998*).

Throughout the year Amnesty International called on the authorities to drop government-initiated criminal charges against journalists that appeared designed to imprison journalists for exercising their right to freedom of expression.

AMNESTY INTERNATIONAL REPORT 1999

ZIMBABWE

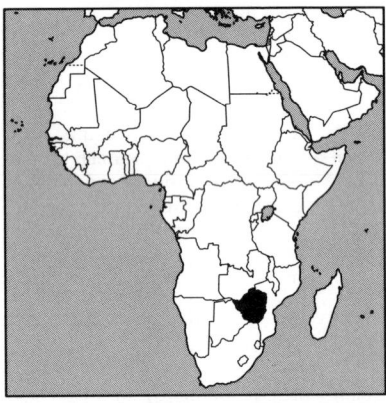

A gay rights activist was arrested because of his human rights work. The security forces ill-treated citizens, killing at least 10 people during and after demonstrations and rioting. Two prisoners were executed and more than five were sentenced to death. Police assaulted at least 50 refugees.

In January there were demonstrations and riots over food price rises, and civic society groups launched a forum to discuss constitutional reform. In March trade unions organized a nationwide strike against tax and price rises for staple foods. The authorities declared the action illegal, threatened reprisals and ordered state-run news media not to report on union activities. There were further strikes in November. A temporary ban was decreed in November to prevent trade unions and employees' organizations from inciting or participating in mass strikes against government policies. By the end of the year, human rights organizations and trade unions had challenged the constitutionality of the ban in court.

Student demonstrations against corruption and for greater state assistance began in March and led to clashes on and off campus. The University of Zimbabwe and Harare Polytechnic were closed indefinitely in June. Student protests continued nationwide in July and August.

In February members of the ruling Zimbabwe African National Union–Patriotic Front (ZANU-PF) party threw a petrol bomb at opposition member of parliament Margaret Dongo, who escaped injury. Police failed to investigate immediately, but later arrested four ZANU-PF supporters. It emerged in April that two police officers who failed to intervene in the June 1997 assault by ZANU-PF supporters against Fidelis Mhashu, an opposition mayoral candidate, had been suspended.

In March, the UN Human Rights Committee expressed concern about Zimbabwe's discrimination against homosexuals and reports of the excessive use of force by the security forces during the January food riots. In April President Robert Mugabe attacked the World Council of Churches for allowing homosexuals to attend their general assembly in Harare, and in May he said that the Constitution guaranteed freedom, "except for gays".

The government sent 10,000 Zimbabwean troops to the Democratic Republic of the Congo (DRC) to assist President Laurent-Désiré Kabila from April onwards. Zimbabwean warplanes reportedly bombed civilian targets and Zimbabwean troops killed civilians during indiscriminate shelling in an intervention that faced growing opposition inside Zimbabwe. (See DRC entry.) In October, a police sergeant was reportedly arrested for criticizing Zimbabwe's involvement in the DRC.

Gay rights activist Keith Goddard of Gays and Lesbians of Zimbabwe was arrested in June and charged with committing forcible sodomy at gunpoint, apparently to curb his legitimate human rights activities. He faced up to seven years' imprisonment if convicted. He remained at liberty, pending appeal. In July a Catholic priest in Bulawayo was sentenced to 10 months' imprisonment, half of which was suspended, after being convicted of consensual sodomy. He was a prisoner of conscience.

At least 20 people were shot by the police and army and at least nine fatally injured, after demonstrations that began on 19 January in Harare developed into rioting and spread across the country. On 20 January the army was deployed with orders to shoot to kill. Afterwards, the army with police support assaulted residents of townships around Harare and threw tear gas into homes. Almost 1,000 people were detained without bail, creating dangerous overcrowding in jails and remand centres. Some detainees were beaten and ill-treated in custody. During protests in the eastern city of Mutare in November, police shot dead bystander Clever Gunda in what appeared to be an extrajudicial execution.

Riot police blocked student demonstrations using tear gas and batons, despite a court order allowing a demonstration to take place. In April police shot and injured student More-Memories Chawira during a non-violent demonstration at the University of Zimbabwe. Police authorities admitted that the police officer had overreacted and said that he faced criminal prosecution.

Two men – Nyenyai Mudenge and George Chikwamure – were executed in April for murder. More than five people were sentenced to death during the year for murder and at least seven people had their death sentences confirmed by the Supreme Court.

In August police beat at least 50 refugees who staged a sit-in protest for several days at the Harare offices of the UN High Commissioner for Refugees (UNHCR). Many, including young children, were injured and required hospital treatment. Two of the refugees, whose grievances included lack of assistance and harassment by security agents, were reportedly arrested by the police, although the authorities denied this. No investigation into this incident was reported.

In January Amnesty International condemned a statement by the Minister of Home Affairs that the army would shoot looters or "troublemakers", and appealed to President Mugabe to ensure that human rights were not violated while the army and police restored order. In March Amnesty International and local human rights groups informed the UN Human Rights Committee of concerns in Zimbabwe. In July Amnesty International asked the authorities to drop the charges against Keith Goddard.

In September Amnesty International called upon President Mugabe, as chair of the Southern African Development Community (SADC) Organ on Politics, Defence and Security, to ensure that SADC member states involved in the conflict in the DRC adhered to international humanitarian standards. Amnesty International called on the SADC to halt any transfers of military, security or police equipment to the conflicting parties that might contribute to further human rights violations.

APPENDICES

AMNESTY INTERNATIONAL VISITS 1998

DATE	COUNTRY/TERRITORY	PURPOSE
January	Tunisia	Legal proceedings
January/February	Thailand	Research on region
February	Albania	Research
February/March	Turkey	Research
February/March	Bangladesh	Research
February/March	Pacific States	Research
February/March	Rwanda	Research/Talks with government
February/March	South Korea	Talks with government
February/March	Japan	Talks with government
February/March	Philippines	Research on region
February/March	Iran	Intergovernmental meeting
February/March	Israel/Occupied Territories	Research
February/March	Palestinian Authority	Research
March	Australia	Research
March	Guinea	Legal proceedings
March	Cambodia	Research
March	Federal Republic of Yugoslavia	Research
March	Philippines	Campaigning
March	Mali	Talks with government/Legal proceedings
March	Egypt	Research
March	Spain	Talks with government
March	Tanzania	Research/Talks with government
March/April	Brazil	Research/Talks with government
March/April	Malaysia	Research
March/April	USA	Research on region
March/April	Kenya	Research
March/April	Pakistan	Research
March/April	Lebanon	Research/Legal proceedings
March/April	Zimbabwe	Research
March/April	Namibia	Research
March/April	Romania	Research
April	Zambia	Research
April	Tunisia	Legal proceedings
April	Canada	Research on region
April	Qatar	Research/Talks with government/Legal proceedings
April/May	Burundi	Research/Talks with government/Legal proceedings
April/May	Singapore	Legal proceedings
April/May	France	Research on region
April/May	Israel/Occupied Territories	Research/Talks with government
April/May	Palestinian Authority	Research/Talks with government
April/May	Argentina	Research/Talks with government
May	Chile	Research
May	Turkey	Legal proceedings

DATE	COUNTRY/TERRITORY	PURPOSE
May	Spain	Talks with government
May	USA	Research
May	Georgia	Research/Talks with government
May	Morocco	Research
May	Germany	Research
May	Croatia	Research
May	Kenya	Research on region
May	Uganda	Research
May	Sierra Leone	Research/Talks with government
May/June	Equatorial Guinea	Research/Talks with government
May/June	Morocco	Talks with government
May/June	USA	Research
May/June	Russian Federation	Talks with government
May/June	Tanzania	Research
May/June	Mozambique	Research/Talks with government
June	Chad	Research/Legal proceedings
June	Israel/Occupied Territories	Research
June	Palestinian Authority	Research
June	Hungary	Research
June	Bangladesh	Research
June	South Korea	Research/Talks with government
June	Yugoslavia	Research
June	Macedonia	Research
June	Taiwan	Talks with government
June	Finland	Talks with government
June/July	Japan	Research
June/July	Russian Federation	Research/Campaigning
June/July	United Kingdom	Legal proceedings
July	United Kingdom	Research
July	Colombia	Research
July	South Africa	Research/Legal proceedings
July	Portugal	Research on region
July	Philippines	Intergovernmental meeting
July/August	Thailand	Research on region
July/August	Cambodia	Research
July/August	Republic of the Congo	Research/Talks with government
July/August	Sierra Leone	Legal proceedings
July/August	USA	Research
July/August	Côte d'Ivoire	Research on region
August	Brazil	Legal proceedings
August	Croatia	Campaigning
August	Côte d'Ivoire	Research on region
August	Egypt	Research
August	Malaysia	Legal proceedings
August	Turkey	Research/Legal proceedings
September	Kyrgyzstan	Research
September	Kazakstan	Research

DATE	COUNTRY/TERRITORY	PURPOSE
September	Hungary	Research/Talks with government
September	Romania	Research/Talks with government
September	Mexico	Research
September	Zambia	Research
September	Indonesia	Research/Talks with government
September	South Korea	Talks with government
September/October	Sri Lanka	Research/Talks with government
September/October	Turkey	Research/Legal proceedings
September/October	France	Research
September/October	Yemen	Research
September/October	Peru	Research
September/October	USA	Research
October	Turkey	Research on region
October	Somaliland	Research/Talks with government
October	Djibouti	Research
October	USA	Talks with government/Campaign
October	Netherlands	Research on region
October	Colombia	Research
October	Ghana	Research
October	Russian Federation	Legal proceedings
October	Ethiopia	Research/Talks with government
October	France	Research on region
October	United Kingdom	Research on region
October	China	Intergovernmental meeting
October	Morocco	Research
October	Lesotho	Research/Talks with government
October	South Africa	Research/Talks with government
October/November	Malaysia	Research/Legal proceedings
October/November	Swaziland	Research
November	USA	Research/Talks with government
November	Brazil	Legal proceedings
November	Jordan	Research on region
November	Senegal	Research on region
November	Nepal	Research/Talks with government
November	Malaysia	Research/Legal proceedings
November/December	Brazil	Research/Talks with government
November/December	Azerbaijan	Research
November/December	Federal Republic of Yugoslavia	Research
November/December	Bhutan	Research/Talks with government
November/December	Lebanon	Research/Legal proceedings
November/December	Togo	Research/Talks with government
November/December	Ghana	Research on region
December	Macedonia	Research
December	Jordan	Research on region
December	France	Research on region
December	Zimbabwe	Research
December	Russian Federation	Research

378

DATE	COUNTRY/TERRITORY	PURPOSE
December	France	Legal proceedings
December	India	Research on region
December	Nepal	Research on region
December	Philippines	Research

APPENDIX II

STATUTE OF AMNESTY INTERNATIONAL

As amended by the 23rd International Council, meeting in Cape Town, South Africa, 12 to 19 December 1997

Articles 1 and 2

Object and Mandate

1. The object of AMNESTY INTERNATIONAL is to contribute to the observance throughout the world of human rights as set out in the Universal Declaration of Human Rights.

In pursuance of this object, and recognizing the obligation on each person to extend to others rights and freedoms equal to his or her own, AMNESTY INTERNATIONAL adopts as its mandate:

To promote awareness of and adherence to the Universal Declaration of Human Rights and other internationally recognized human rights instruments, the values enshrined in them, and the indivisibility and interdependence of all human rights and freedoms;

To oppose grave violations of the rights of every person freely to hold and to express his or her convictions and to be free from discrimination, and of the right of every person to physical and mental integrity, and, in particular, to oppose by all appropriate means irrespective of political considerations:

a) the imprisonment, detention or other physical restrictions imposed on any person by reason of his or her political, religious or other conscientiously held beliefs or by reason of his or her ethnic origin, sex, colour, language, national or social origin, economic status, birth or other status, provided that he or she has not used or advocated violence (hereinafter referred to as 'prisoners of conscience'; AMNESTY INTERNATIONAL shall work towards the release of and shall provide assistance to prisoners of conscience);

b) the detention of any political prisoner without fair trial within a reasonable time or any trial procedures relating to such prisoners that do not conform to internationally recognized norms;

c) the death penalty, and the torture or other cruel, inhuman or degrading treatment or punishment of prisoners or other detained or restricted persons, whether or not the persons affected have used or advocated violence;

d) the extrajudicial execution of persons whether or not imprisoned, detained or restricted, and "disappearances", whether or not the persons affected have used or advocated violence.

Methods

2. In order to achieve the aforesaid object and mandate, AMNESTY INTERNATIONAL shall:

a) at all times make clear its impartiality as regards countries adhering to the different world political ideologies and groupings;

b) promote as appears appropriate the adoption of constitutions, conventions, treaties and other measures which guarantee the rights contained in the provisions referred to in Article 1 hereof;

c) support and publicize the activities of and cooperate with international organizations and agencies which work for the implementation of the aforesaid provisions;

d) take all necessary steps to establish an effective organization of sections, affiliated groups and individual members;

e) secure the adoption by groups of members or supporters of individual prisoners of conscience or entrust to such groups other tasks in support of the object and mandate set out in Article 1;

f) provide financial and other relief to prisoners of conscience and their dependants and to persons who have lately been prisoners of conscience or who might reasonably be expected to be prisoners of conscience or to become prisoners of conscience if convicted or if they were to return to their own countries, to the dependants of such persons and to victims of torture in need of medical care as a direct result thereof;

g) provide legal aid, where necessary and possible, to prisoners of conscience and to persons who might reasonably be expected to be prisoners of conscience or to become prisoners of conscience if convicted or if they were to return to their own countries, and, where desirable, send observers to attend the trials of such persons;

h) publicize the cases of prisoners of conscience or persons who have otherwise been subjected to disabilities in violation of the aforesaid provisions;

i) investigate and publicize the disappearance of persons where there is reason to believe that they may be victims of violations of the rights set out in Article 1 hereof;

j) oppose the sending of persons from one country to another where they can reasonably be expected to become prisoners of conscience or to face torture or the death penalty;

k) send investigators, where appropriate, to investigate allegations that the rights of individuals under the aforesaid provisions have been violated or threatened;

l) make representations to international organizations and to governments whenever it appears that an individual is a prisoner of conscience or has otherwise been subjected to disabilities in violation of the aforesaid provisions;

m) promote and support the granting of general amnesties of which the beneficiaries will include prisoners of conscience;

n) adopt any other appropriate methods for the securing of its object and mandate.

The full text of the Statute of Amnesty International is available free upon request from: Amnesty International, International Secretariat, 1 Easton Street, London WC1X 8DJ, United Kingdom.

AMNESTY INTERNATIONAL AROUND THE WORLD

In 1998 there were more than 7,500 Amnesty International groups, including local groups, youth or student groups and professional groups, in more than 90 countries and territories throughout the world. In 55 countries and territories these groups are coordinated by sections, whose addresses are given below. There are individual members, supporters and recipients of Amnesty International information (such as the bimonthly *Amnesty International News*) in over 140 countries and territories. Amnesty International information is also available on the Internet on more than 250 websites worldwide.

SECTION ADDRESSES

Algeria:
Amnesty International,
Section Algérienne,
BP 377 Alger,
RP 16004

Argentina:
Amnistía Internacional,
Sección Argentina,
Av. Rivadavia 2206 - P4 A,
1034 Ciudad de Buenos Aires

Australia:
Amnesty International,
Australian Section,
Private Bag 23, Broadway,
New South Wales 2007

Austria:
Amnesty International,
Austrian Section,
Moeringstrasse 10/1 Stock,
A-1150, Wien

Bangladesh:
Amnesty International,
Bangladesh Section,
28 Kabi Jasimuddin Road, 1st Floor
Kamalapur,
Dhaka - 1217

Belgium:
Amnesty International,
Belgian Section (AI Vlaanderen),
Kerkstraat 156,
2060 Antwerpen

Amnesty International,
Section belge (francophone),
Rue Berckmans 9,
1060 Bruxelles

Benin:
Amnesty International,
BP 01-3536,
Cotonou

Bermuda:
Amnesty International,
Bermuda Section,
PO Box HM 2136,
Hamilton HM JX

Brazil:
Anistia Internacional,
Rua Jacinto Gomes 573,
CEP 90040-270,
Porto Alegre - RS

Canada:
Amnesty International,
Canadian Section,
    (*English-speaking branch*),
214 Montreal Rd, 4th Floor,
Vanier, Ontario, K1L 1A4

Amnistie Internationale,
Section canadienne francophone,
6250 boulevard Monk,
Montréal,
Québec H4E 3H7

Chile:
Señores,
Casilla 4062,
Santiago

Costa Rica:
Amnistía Internacional,
De la Casa Italia,
100 Sur, 300 Este,
50 Sur, Yoses Sur,
San José

Côte d'Ivoire:
Amnesty International,
Section ivoirienne,
04 BP 895,
Abidjan

Denmark:
Amnesty International,
Danish Section,
Dyrkoeb 3,
1166 Copenhagen K

Ecuador:
Amnistía Internacional,
Sección Ecuatoriana,
Casilla 17-15-240-C,
Quito

Faroe Islands:
Amnesty International,
Faroe Islands Section,
PO Box 1075, FR-110,
Tórshavn

Finland:
Amnesty International,
Finnish Section,
Ruoholahdenkatu 24 D,
00180 Helsinki

France:
Amnesty International,
Section française,
4, rue de la Pierre Levée,
75553 Paris, Cedex 11

Germany:
Amnesty International,
German Section,
53108 Bonn

Ghana:
Amnesty International,
Ghanaian Section,
Private Mail Bag,
Kokomlemle,
Accra - North

Greece:
Amnesty International,
Greek Section,
30 Sina Street,
106 72 Athens

Guyana:
Amnesty International,
Guyana Section,
c/o PO Box 10720,
Palm Court Building,
35 Main Street,
Georgetown

Hong Kong:
Amnesty International,
Hong Kong Section,
Unit C 3/F,
   Best-O-Best Commercial Centre,
32-36 Ferry Street,
Kowloon

Iceland:
Amnesty International,
Icelandic Section,
PO Box 618,
121 Reykjavík

Ireland:
Amnesty International,
Irish Section,
Sean MacBride House,
48 Fleet Street,
Dublin 2

Israel:
Amnesty International,
Israel Section,
PO Box 14179,
Tel Aviv 61141

Italy:
Amnesty International,
Italian Section,
Via Giovanni Battista De Rossi 10,
00161 Roma

Japan:
Amnesty International,
Japanese Section,
Sky Esta 2f,
2-18-23 Nishi Waseda,
Shinjuku-ku,
Tokyo 169

Korea (Republic of):
Amnesty International,
Kyeong Buk RCO Box 36,
706-600 Daegu

Luxembourg:
Amnesty International,
Luxembourg Section,
Boîte Postale 1914,
1019 Luxembourg

Mauritius:
Amnesty International,
Mauritius Section,
BP 69 Rose-Hill

382

Mexico:
Sección Mexicana
    de Amnistía Internacional,
Calle Patricio Sanz No. 1104 Depto. 8,
Col. del Valle,
CP 03100,
México DF

Nepal:
Amnesty International,
Nepalese Section,
PO Box 135, Bagbazar,
Kathmandu

Netherlands:
Amnesty International,
Dutch Section,
Keizersgracht 620,
1017 ER Amsterdam

New Zealand:
Amnesty International,
New Zealand Section,
PO Box 793,
Wellington

Nigeria:
Amnesty International,
Nigerian Section,
PMB 3061, Suru-Lere,
Lagos

Norway:
Amnesty International,
Norwegian Section,
PO Box 702 Sentrum,
0106 Oslo

Peru:
Señores,
Casilla 659,
Lima 18

Philippines:
Amnesty International,
Philippines Section,
PO Box 286, Sta Mesa Post Office,
1008 Sta Mesa,
Manila

Portugal:
Amnistia Internacional,
Secção Portuguesa,
Rua Fialho de Almeida, Nº 13, 1º,
1070 Lisboa

Puerto Rico:
Amnistía Internacional,
Sección de Puerto Rico,
Calle El Roble Nº 54-Altos,
Oficina 11, Río Piedras,
Puerto Rico 00925

Senegal:
Amnesty International,
Section Sénégalaise,
BP 21910,
Dakar

Sierra Leone:
Amnesty International,
Sierra Leone Section,
PMB 1021,
Freetown

Slovenia:
Amnesty International,
Komenskega 7,
1000 Ljubljana

Spain:
Amnesty International,
Sección Española,
PO Box 50318,
28080, Madrid

Sweden:
Amnesty International,
Swedish Section,
PO Box 23400,
S-104 35 Stockholm

Switzerland:
Amnesty International,
Swiss Section,
Postfach,
CH-3001, Bern

Taiwan:
Amnesty International,
Room 525, Nº 2, Section 1,
Chung-shan North Road,
100 Taipei

Tanzania:
Amnesty International,
Tanzanian Section,
PO Box 4331,
Dar es Salaam

Togo:
Amnesty International,
Togo Section,
CCNP,
BP 20013,
Lomé

Tunisia:
Amnesty International,
Section Tunisienne,
67 rue Oum Kalthoum,
3ème étage, Escalier B,
1000 Tunis

United Kingdom:
Amnesty International,
United Kingdom Section,
99-119 Rosebery Avenue,
London EC1R 4RE

United States of America:
Amnesty International of the USA
   (AIUSA),
322 8th Ave,
New York, NY 10001

Uruguay:
Amnistía Internacional,
Sección Uruguaya,
Tristan Narvaja 1624, Apto 1,
CP 11200 Montevideo

Venezuela:
Amnistía Internacional,
Sección Venezolana,
Apartado Postal 5110,
Carmelitas 1010-A,
Caracas

COUNTRIES AND TERRITORIES WITHOUT SECTIONS BUT WHERE LOCAL AMNESTY INTERNATIONAL GROUPS EXIST OR ARE BEING FORMED

Albania
Aruba
Azerbaijan
Bahamas
Barbados
Belarus
Bolivia
Botswana
Burkina Faso
Cameroon
Chad
Croatia
Curaçao
Cyprus
Czech Republic
Dominican Republic

Egypt
Gambia
Grenada
Hungary
Jamaica
Jordan
Kazakstan
Kuwait
Macao
Malaysia
Mali
Malta
Moldova
Mongolia
Morocco
Pakistan

Palestinian Authority/
   Israeli Occupied
   Territories
Paraguay
Poland
Romania
Russian Federation
Slovakia
South Africa
Thailand
Turkey
Ukraine
Yemen
Zambia
Zimbabwe

INTERNATIONAL EXECUTIVE COMMITTEE

Colm Ó Cuanacháin/Ireland
Mary Gray/United States of America
Habiba Hasan/Pakistan
Menno Kamminga/Netherlands
Robin Rickard/United Kingdom
Mahmoud Ben Romdhane/Tunisia
Cristina Sganga/International Secretariat
Susan Waltz/United States of America
Samuel Zan Akologo/Ghana

SELECTED INTERNATIONAL HUMAN RIGHTS TREATIES

States which have ratified or acceded to a convention are party to the treaty and are bound to observe its provisions. States which have signed but not yet ratified have expressed their intention to become a party at some future date; meanwhile they are obliged to refrain from acts which would defeat the object and purpose of the treaty.

(AT 31 DECEMBER 1998)

	International Covenant on Civil and Political Rights (ICCPR)	Optional Protocol to the ICCPR	Second Optional Protocol to the ICCPR, aiming at the abolition of the death penalty	International Covenant on Economic, Social and Cultural Rights	Convention against Torture and Other Cruel, Inhuman or Degrading Treatment or Punishment	Convention relating to the Status of Refugees (1951)	Protocol relating to the Status of Refugees (1967)	Convention on the Elimination of All Forms of Discrimination against Women
Afghanistan	x			x	x(28)			s
Albania	x			x	x	x	x	x
Algeria	x	x		x	x(22)	x	x	x
Andorra								x
Angola	x	x		x		x	x	x
Antigua and Barbuda					x	x	x	x
Argentina	x	x		x	x(22)	x	x	x
Armenia	x	x		x	x	x	x	x
Australia	x	x	x	x	x(22)	x	x	x
Austria	x	x	x	x	x(22)	x	x	x
Azerbaijan	x			x	x	x	x	x
Bahamas						x	x	x
Bahrain					x*			
Bangladesh				x*	x*			x
Barbados	x	x		x				x

	International Covenant on Civil and Political Rights (ICCPR)	Optional Protocol to the ICCPR	Second Optional Protocol to the ICCPR, aiming at the abolition of the death penalty	International Covenant on Economic, Social and Cultural Rights	Convention against Torture and Other Cruel, Inhuman or Degrading Treatment or Punishment	Convention relating to the Status of Refugees (1951)	Protocol relating to the Status of Refugees (1967)	Convention on the Elimination of All Forms of Discrimination against Women
Belarus	x	x		x	x(28)			x
Belgium	x	x	x*	x	s	x	x	x
Belize	x				x	x	x	x
Benin	x	x		x	x	x	x	x
Bhutan								x
Bolivia	x	x		x	s	x	x	x
Bosnia and Herzegovina	x	x		x	x	x	x	x
Botswana						x	x	x
Brazil	x			x	x	x	x	x
Brunei Darussalam								
Bulgaria	x	x		x	x(22)(28)	x	x	x
Burkina Faso				x	x	x	x	x
Burundi	x			x	x	x	x	x
Cambodia	x			x	x	x	x	x
Cameroon	x	x		x	x	x	x	x
Canada	x	x		x	x(22)	x	x	x
Cape Verde	x			x	x			x
Central African Republic	x	x		x		x	x	x
Chad	x	x		x	x	x	x	x
Chile	x	x		x	x	x	x	x
China	s*			s	x(28)	x	x	x
Colombia	x	x	x	x	x	x	x	x
Comoros								x
Congo (Democratic Republic of the)	x	x		x	x	x	x	x

	International Covenant on Civil and Political Rights (ICCPR)	Optional Protocol to the ICCPR	Second Optional Protocol to the ICCPR, aiming at the abolition of the death penalty	International Covenant on Economic, Social and Cultural Rights	Convention against Torture and Other Cruel, Inhuman or Degrading Treatment or Punishment	Convention relating to the Status of Refugees (1951)	Protocol relating to the Status of Refugees (1967)	Convention on the Elimination of All Forms of Discrimination against Women
Congo (Republic of the)	x	x		x		x	x	x
Costa Rica	x	x	x*	x	x	x	x	x
Côte d'Ivoire	x	x		x		x	x	x
Croatia	x	x	x	x	x(22)	x	x	x
Cuba					x			x
Cyprus	x	x		x	x(22)	x	x	x
Czech Republic	x	x		x	x(22)	x	x	x
Denmark	x	x	x	x	x(22)	x	x	x
Djibouti						x	x	x*
Dominica	x			x		x	x	x
Dominican Republic	x	x		x	s	x	x	x
Ecuador	x	x	x	x	x(22)	x	x	x
Egypt	x			x	x	x	x	x
El Salvador	x	x		x	x	x	x	x
Equatorial Guinea	x	x		x		x	x	x
Eritrea								x
Estonia	x	x		x	x	x	x	x
Ethiopia	x			x	x			x
Fiji						x	x	x
Finland	x	x	x	x	x(22)	x	x	x
France	x	x		x	x(22)	x	x	x
Gabon	x			x	s	x	x	x
Gambia	x	x		x	s	x	x	x
Georgia	x	x		x	x			x

	International Covenant on Civil and Political Rights (ICCPR)	Optional Protocol to the ICCPR	Second Optional Protocol to the ICCPR, aiming at the abolition of the death penalty	International Covenant on Economic, Social and Cultural Rights	Convention against Torture and Other Cruel, Inhuman or Degrading Treatment or Punishment	Convention relating to the Status of Refugees (1951)	Protocol relating to the Status of Refugees (1967)	Convention on the Elimination of All Forms of Discrimination against Women
Germany	x	x	x	x	x	x	x	x
Ghana						x	x	x
Greece	x	x	x	x	x(22)	x	x	x
Grenada	x			x				x
Guatemala	x			x	x	x	x	x
Guinea	x	x		x	x	x	x	x
Guinea-Bissau				x		x	x	x
Guyana	x	x		x	x			x
Haiti	x					x	x	x
Holy See						x	x	
Honduras	x	s	s	x	x	x	x	x
Hungary	x	x	x	x	x(22)	x	x	x
Iceland	x	x	x	x	x(22)	x	x	x
India	x			x	s			x
Indonesia					x*			x
Iran (Islamic Republic of)	x			x		x	x	
Iraq	x			x				x
Ireland	x	x	x	x	s	x	x	x
Israel	x			x	x(28)	x	x	x
Italy	x	x	x	x	x(22)	x	x	x
Jamaica	x	x		x		x	x	x
Japan	x			x		x	x	x
Jordan	x			x	x			x
Kazakstan					x*			x*

	International Covenant on Civil and Political Rights (ICCPR)	Optional Protocol to the ICCPR	Second Optional Protocol to the ICCPR, aiming at the abolition of the death penalty	International Covenant on Economic, Social and Cultural Rights	Convention against Torture and Other Cruel, Inhuman or Degrading Treatment or Punishment	Convention relating to the Status of Refugees (1951)	Protocol relating to the Status of Refugees (1967)	Convention on the Elimination of All Forms of Discrimination against Women
Kenya	x			x	x	x	x	x
Kiribati								
Korea (Democratic People's Republic of)	x			x				x
Korea (Republic of)	x	x		x	x	x	x	x
Kuwait	x			x	x			x
Kyrgyzstan	x	x		x	x	x	x	x
Lao People's Democratic Republic								
Latvia	x	x		x	x	x		x
Lebanon	x			x				x
Lesotho	x			x		x	x	x
Liberia	s			s		x	x	x
Libyan Arab Jamahiriya	x	x		x	x			x
Liechtenstein	x*	x*	x*	x*	x(22)	x	x	x
Lithuania	x	x		x	x	x	x	x
Luxembourg	x	x	x	x	x(22)	x	x	x
Macedonia (former Yugoslav Republic of)	x	x	x	x	x	x	x	x
Madagascar	x	x		x	x	x	x	x
Malawi	x	x		x	x	x	x	x
Maldives								x
Mali	x			x	x(22)	x	x	x
Malta	x	x	x	x	x	x	x	x
Marshall Islands								
Mauritania						x	x	

	International Covenant on Civil and Political Rights (ICCPR)	Optional Protocol to the ICCPR	Second Optional Protocol to the ICCPR, aiming at the abolition of the death penalty	International Covenant on Economic, Social and Cultural Rights	Convention against Torture and Other Cruel, Inhuman or Degrading Treatment or Punishment	Convention relating to the Status of Refugees (1951)	Protocol relating to the Status of Refugees (1967)	Convention on the Elimination of All Forms of Discrimination against Women
Mauritius	x	x		x	x			x
Mexico	x			x	x			x
Micronesia (Federated States of)								
Moldova	x			x	x			x
Monaco	x			x	x(22)	x		
Mongolia	x	x		x				x
Morocco	x			x	x(28)	x	x	x
Mozambique	x		x			x	x	x
Myanmar								x
Namibia	x	x	x	x	x	x		x
Nauru								
Nepal	x	x	x*	x	x			x
Netherlands	x	x	x	x	x(22)	x	x	x
New Zealand	x	x	x	x	x(22)	x	x	x
Nicaragua	x	x	s	x	s	x	x	x
Niger	x	x		x	x*	x	x	
Nigeria	x			x	s	x	x	x
Norway	x	x	x	x	x(22)	x	x	x
Oman								
Pakistan								x
Palau								
Panama	x	x	x	x	x	x	x	x
Papua New Guinea						x	x	x
Paraguay	x	x		x	x	x	x	x

	International Covenant on Civil and Political Rights (ICCPR)	Optional Protocol to the ICCPR	Second Optional Protocol to the ICCPR, aiming at the abolition of the death penalty	International Covenant on Economic, Social and Cultural Rights	Convention against Torture and Other Cruel, Inhuman or Degrading Treatment or Punishment	Convention relating to the Status of Refugees (1951)	Protocol relating to the Status of Refugees (1967)	Convention on the Elimination of All Forms of Discrimination against Women
Peru	x	x		x	x	x	x	x
Philippines	x	x		x	x	x	x	x
Poland	x	x		x	x(22)	x	x	x
Portugal	x	x	x	x	x(22)	x	x	x
Qatar								
Romania	x	x	x	x	x	x	x	x
Russian Federation	x	x		x	x(22)	x	x	x
Rwanda	x			x		x	x	x
Saint Kitts and Nevis								x
Saint Lucia								x
Saint Vincent and the Grenadines	x	x		x		x		x
Samoa						x	x	x
San Marino	x	x		x				
Sao Tome and Principe	s			s		x	x	x
Saudi Arabia					x			
Senegal	x	x		x	x(22)	x	x	x
Seychelles	x	x	x	x	x	x	x	x
Sierra Leone	x	x		x	s	x	x	x
Singapore								x
Slovakia	x	x	s*	x	x(22)	x	x	x
Slovenia	x	x	x	x	x(22)	x	x	x
Solomon Islands				x		x	x	
Somalia	x	x		x	x	x	x	
South Africa	x*			s	x*(22)	x	x	x

	International Covenant on Civil and Political Rights (ICCPR)	Optional Protocol to the ICCPR	Second Optional Protocol to the ICCPR, aiming at the abolition of the death penalty	International Covenant on Economic, Social and Cultural Rights	Convention against Torture and Other Cruel, Inhuman or Degrading Treatment or Punishment	Convention relating to the Status of Refugees (1951)	Protocol relating to the Status of Refugees (1967)	Convention on the Elimination of All Forms of Discrimination against Women
Spain	x	x	x	x	x(22)	x	x	x
Sri Lanka	x	x		x	x			x
Sudan	x			x	s	x	x	
Suriname	x	x		x		x	x	x
Swaziland						x	x	
Sweden	x	x	x	x	x(22)	x	x	x
Switzerland	x		x	x	x(22)	x	x	x
Syrian Arab Republic	x			x				
Tajikistan	x	x			x	x	x	x
Tanzania	x			x		x	x	x
Thailand	x							x
Togo	x	x		x	x(22)	x	x	x
Tonga								
Trinidad and Tobago	x	x		x				x
Tunisia	x			x	x(22)	x	x	x
Turkey					x(22)	x	x	x
Turkmenistan	x	x		x		x*	x*	x
Tuvalu						x	x	
Uganda	x	x		x	x	x	x	x
Ukraine	x	x		x	x(28)			x
United Arab Emirates								
United Kingdom	x			x	x	x	x	x
United States of America	x			s	x	x	x	s
Uruguay	x	x	x	x	x(22)	x	x	x

	International Covenant on Civil and Political Rights (ICCPR)	Optional Protocol to the ICCPR	Second Optional Protocol to the ICCPR, aiming at the abolition of the death penalty	International Covenant on Economic, Social and Cultural Rights	Convention against Torture and Other Cruel, Inhuman or Degrading Treatment or Punishment	Convention relating to the Status of Refugees (1951)	Protocol relating to the Status of Refugees (1967)	Convention on the Elimination of All Forms of Discrimination against Women
Uzbekistan	x	x		x	x			x
Vanuatu								x
Venezuela	x	x	x	x	x(22)		x	x
Viet Nam	x			x				x
Yemen	x			x	x	x	x	x
Yugoslavia (Federal Republic of)	x	s		x	x(22)	x	x	x
Zambia	x	x		x	x*	x	x	x
Zimbabwe	x			x		x	x	x

s — denotes that country has signed but not yet ratified

x — denotes that country is a party, either through ratification, accession or succession

* — denotes that country either signed or became a party in 1998

(22) denotes Declaration under Article 22 recognizing the competence of the Committee against Torture to consider individual complaints of violations of the Convention

(28) denotes that country has made a reservation under Article 28 that it does not recognize the competence of the Committee against Torture to examine reliable information which appears to indicate that torture is being systematically practised, and to undertake a confidential inquiry if warranted

SELECTED REGIONAL HUMAN RIGHTS TREATIES

(AT 31 DECEMBER 1998)

ORGANIZATION OF AFRICAN UNITY (OAU)
African Charter on Human and Peoples' Rights (1981)

Algeria	x	Libya	x
Angola	x	Madagascar	x
Benin	x	Malawi	x
Botswana	x	Mali	x
Burkina Faso	x	Mauritania	x
Burundi	x	Mauritius	x
Cameroon	x	Mozambique	x
Cape Verde	x	Namibia	x
Central African Republic	x	Niger	x
Chad	x	Nigeria	x
Comoros	x	Rwanda	x
Congo (Democratic Republic of the)	x	Saharawi Arab Democratic Republic	x
Congo (Republic of the)	x	Sao Tome and Principe	x
Côte d'Ivoire	x	Senegal	x
Djibouti	x	Seychelles	x
Egypt	x	Sierra Leone	x
Equatorial Guinea	x	Somalia	x
Eritrea		South Africa	x
Ethiopia	x	Sudan	x
Gabon	x	Swaziland	x
Gambia	x	Tanzania	x
Ghana	x	Togo	x
Guinea	x	Tunisia	x
Guinea-Bissau	x	Uganda	x
Kenya	x	Zambia	x
Lesotho	x	Zimbabwe	x
Liberia	x		

x denotes that country is a party, either through ratification or accession

This chart lists countries which were members of the OAU at the end of 1998.

ORGANIZATION OF AMERICAN STATES (OAS)

	American Convention on Human Rights (1969)	Protocol to the American Convention on Human Rights to Abolish the Death Penalty (1990)	Inter-American Convention to Prevent and Punish Torture (1985)	Inter-American Convention on Forced Disappearance of Persons (1994)
Antigua and Barbuda				
Argentina	x (62)		x	x
Bahamas				
Barbados	x			
Belize				
Bolivia	x (62)		s	s
Brazil	x (62)	x	x	s
Canada				
Chile	x (62)		x	s
Colombia	x (62)		s	s
Costa Rica	x (62)	x	s	x
Cuba				
Dominica	x			
Dominican Republic	x		x	
Ecuador	x (62)	x	s	
El Salvador	x (62)		x	
Grenada	x			
Guatemala	x (62)		x	s
Guyana				
Haiti	x		s	
Honduras	x (62)		s	s
Jamaica	x			
Mexico	x (62)		x	
Nicaragua	x (62)	s	s	s
Panama	x (62)	x	x	x
Paraguay	x (62)		x	x
Peru	x (62)		x	
Saint Kitts and Nevis				
Saint Lucia				
Saint Vincent and the Grenadines				
Suriname	x (62)		x	
Trinidad and Tobago				
United States of America	s			
Uruguay	x (62)	x	x	x
Venezuela	x (62)	x	x	s

s   denotes that country has signed but not yet ratified
x   denotes that country is a party, either through ratification or accession
(62) denotes Declaration under Article 62 recognizing as binding the jurisdiction of the Inter-American Court of Human Rights (on all matters relating to the interpretation or application of the American Convention)
This chart lists countries which were members of the OAS at the end of 1998.

COUNCIL OF EUROPE

	European Convention for the Protection of Human Rights and Fundamental Freedoms (1950)	Article 25	Article 46	Protocol No. 6*	European Convention for the Prevention of Torture and Inhuman or Degrading Treatment or Punishment (1987)
Albania	x	x	x		x
Andorra	x	x	x	x	x
Austria	x	x	x	x	x
Belgium	x	x	x	x	x
Bulgaria	x	x	x		x
Croatia	x	x	x	x	x
Cyprus	x	x	x		x
Czech Republic	x	x	x	x	x
Denmark	x	x	x	x	x
Estonia	x	x	x	x	x
Finland	x	x	x	x	x
France	x	x	x	x	x
Germany	x	x	x	x	x
Greece	x	x	x	x	x
Hungary	x	x	x	x	x
Iceland	x	x	x	x	x
Ireland	x	x	x	x	x
Italy	x	x	x	x	x
Latvia	x	x	x	s	x
Liechtenstein	x	x	x	x	x
Lithuania	x	x	x		x
Luxembourg	x	x	x	x	x
Macedonia	x	x	x	x	x
Malta	x	x	x	x	x
Moldova	x	x	x	x	x
Netherlands	x	x	x	x	x
Norway	x	x	x	x	x
Poland	x	x	x		
Portugal	x	x	x	x	x
Romania	x	x	x	x	x
Russian Federation	x	x	x	s	x
San Marino	x	x	x	x	x
Slovakia	x	x	x	x	x
Slovenia	x	x	x	x	x
Spain	x	x	x	x	x
Sweden	x	x	x	x	x
Switzerland	x	x	x	x	x
Turkey	x	x	x		x
Ukraine	x	x	x	s	x
United Kingdom	x	x	x		x

s   denotes that country has signed but not yet ratified
x   denotes that country is a party, either through ratification or accession
Article 25   denotes Declaration under Article 25 of the European Convention for the Protection of Human Rights and Fundamental Freedoms, recognizing the competence of the European Commission of Human Rights to consider individual complaints of violations of the Convention
Article 46   denotes Declaration under Article 46 of the European Convention for the Protection of Human Rights and Fundamental Freedoms, recognizing as compulsory the jurisdiction of the European Court of Human Rights in all matters concerning interpretation and application of the European Convention
* Protocol No. 6 to the European Convention for the Protection of Human Rights and Fundamental Freedoms concerning the abolition of the death penalty (1983)

This chart lists countries which were members of the Council of Europe at the end of 1998.

United Nations
Declaration on the Right and Responsibility of Individuals, Groups and Organs of Society to Promote and Protect Universally Recognized Human Rights and Fundamental Freedoms

The Declaration on the Right and Responsibility of Individuals, Groups and Organs of Society to Promote and Protect Universally Recognized Human Rights and Fundamental Freedoms (also known as Declaration on Human Rights Defenders) was adopted by the UN General Assembly in December 1998. It took 13 years of painstaking negotiations to agree the rights of human rights defenders; the Declaration represents the minimum acceptable standard. The next step is to build on the Declaration and ensure its effective implementation.

The General Assembly,

Reaffirming the importance of the observance of the purposes and principles of the Charter of the United Nations for the promotion and protection of all human rights and fundamental freedoms for all persons in all countries of the world,

Reaffirming also the importance of the Universal Declaration of Human Rights and the International Covenants on Human Rights as basic elements of international efforts to promote universal respect for and observance of human rights and fundamental freedoms and the importance of other human rights instruments adopted within the United Nations system, as well as those at the regional level,

Stressing that all members of the international community shall fulfil, jointly and separately, their solemn obligation to promote and encourage respect for human rights and fundamental freedoms for all without distinction of any kind, including distinctions based on race, colour, sex, language, religion, political or other opinion, national or social origin, property, birth or other status, and reaffirming the particular importance of achieving international cooperation to fulfil this obligation according to the Charter of the United Nations,

Acknowledging the important role of international cooperation for and the valuable work of individuals, groups and associations in contributing to the effective elimination of all violations of human rights and fundamental freedoms of peoples and individuals, including in relation to mass, flagrant or systematic violations such as those resulting from apartheid, all forms of racial discrimination, colonialism, foreign domination or occupation, aggression or threats to national sovereignty, national unity or territorial integrity, and from the refusal to recognize the right of peoples to self-determination and the right of every people to exercise full sovereignty over its wealth and natural resources,

Recognizing the relationship between international peace and security and the enjoyment of human rights and fundamental freedoms, and mindful that the absence of international peace and security does not excuse non-compliance,

Reiterating that all human rights and fundamental freedoms are universal, indivisible and interdependent and interrelated, and should be promoted and implemented in a fair and equitable manner, without prejudice to the implementation of each of those rights and freedoms,

Stressing that the primary responsibility and duty to promote and protect human rights and fundamental freedoms lie with the State,

Recognizing the right and the responsibility of individuals, groups and associations to promote respect for, and foster knowledge of, human rights and fundamental freedoms at the national and international levels,

Declares:

Article 1
Everyone has the right, individually and in association with others, to promote and to strive for the protection and realization of human rights and fundamental freedoms at the national and international levels.

Article 2
1. Each State has a prime responsibility and duty to protect, promote and implement all human rights and fundamental freedoms, *inter alia*, by adopting such steps as may be necessary to create all conditions necessary in the social, economic and political as well as other fields and the legal guarantees required to ensure that all persons under its jurisdiction, individually and in association with others, are able to enjoy all those rights and freedoms in practice.

2. Each State shall adopt such legislative, administrative and other steps as may be necessary to ensure that the rights and freedoms referred to in the present Declaration are effectively guaranteed.

Article 3
Domestic law consistent with the Charter of the United Nations and other international obligations of the State in the field of human rights and fundamental freedoms is the juridical framework within which human rights and fundamental freedoms should be implemented and enjoyed, and within which all activities referred to in the present Declaration for the promotion, protection and effective realization of those rights and freedoms should be conducted.

Article 4
Nothing in the present Declaration shall be construed as impairing or contradicting the purposes and principles of the Charter of the United Nations or as restricting or derogating from the provisions of the Universal Declaration of Human Rights, the International Covenants on Human Rights and other international instruments and commitments applicable in this field.

Article 5
For the purpose of promoting and protecting human rights and fundamental freedoms, everyone has the right, individually and in association with others, at the national and international levels:

   (a) To meet or assemble peacefully;

   (b) To form, join and participate in non-governmental organizations, associations or groups;

   (c) To communicate with non-governmental or intergovernmental organizations.

Article 6
Everyone has the right, individually and in association with others:

   (a) To know, seek, obtain, receive and hold information about all human rights and fundamental freedoms, including having access to information as to how those rights and freedoms are given effect in domestic legislative, judicial or administrative systems;

   (b) As provided in human rights and other applicable international instruments, freely to publish, impart or disseminate to others views, information and knowledge of all human rights and fundamental freedoms;

   (c) To study, discuss, form and hold opinions on the observance, both in law and in practice, of all human rights and fundamental freedoms and, through these and other appropriate means, to draw public attention to those matters.

Article 7
Everyone has the right, individually and in association with others, to develop and discuss new human rights ideas and principles, and to advocate their acceptance.

Article 8
1. Everyone has the right, individually and in association with others, to have effective access, on a non-

discriminatory basis, to participation in the government of his or her country and in the conduct of public affairs.

2. This includes, *inter alia*, the right, individually and in association with others, to submit to governmental bodies and agencies and organizations concerned with public affairs, criticism and proposals for improving their functioning and to draw attention to any aspect of their work that may hinder or impede the promotion, protection and realization of human rights and fundamental freedoms.

Article 9

1. In the exercise of human rights and fundamental freedoms, including the promotion and protection of human rights as referred to in the present Declaration, everyone has the right, individually and in association with others, to benefit from an effective remedy and to be protected in the event of the violation of those rights.

2. To this end, everyone whose rights or freedoms are allegedly violated has the right, either in person or through legally authorized representation, to complain to and have that complaint promptly reviewed in a public hearing before an independent, impartial and competent judicial or other authority established by law, and to obtain from such an authority a decision, in accordance with law, providing redress, including any compensation due, where there has been a violation of that person's rights or freedoms, as well as enforcement of the eventual decision and award, all without undue delay.

3. To the same end, everyone has the right, individually and in association with others, *inter alia*:

   (a) To complain about the policies and actions of individual officials and governmental bodies with regard to violations of human rights and fundamental freedoms by petition or other appropriate means to competent domestic judicial, administrative or legislative authorities or any other competent authority provided for by the legal system of the State, which should render their decision on the complaint without undue delay;

   (b) To attend public hearings, proceedings and trials, so as to form an opinion on their compliance with national law and applicable international obligations and commitments;

   (c) To offer and provide professionally qualified legal assistance or other relevant advice and assistance in defending human rights and fundamental freedoms.

4. To the same end, and in accordance with applicable international instruments and procedures, everyone has the right, individually and in association with others, to unhindered access to and communication with international bodies with general or special competence to receive and consider communications on matters of human rights and fundamental freedoms.

5. The State shall conduct a prompt and impartial investigation or ensure that an inquiry takes place whenever there is reasonable ground to believe that a violation of human rights and fundamental freedoms has occurred in any territory under its jurisdiction.

Article 10

No one shall participate, by act or failure to act where required, in violating human rights and fundamental freedoms, and no one shall be subjected to punishment or adverse action of any kind for refusing to do so.

Article 11

Everyone has the right, individually and in association with others, to the lawful exercise of his or her occupation or profession. Everyone who, as a result of his or her profession, can affect the human dignity, human rights and fundamental freedoms of others should respect those rights and freedoms and comply with relevant national and international standards of occupational and professional conduct or ethics.

Article 12

1. Everyone has the right, individually and in association with others, to participate in peaceful activities against violations of human rights and fundamental freedoms.

2. The State shall take all necessary measures to ensure the protection by the competent authorities of everyone, individually and in association with others, against any violence, threats, retaliation, *de facto* or *de jure* adverse discrimination, pressure or any other arbitrary action as a consequence of his or her legitimate exercise of the rights referred to in the present Declaration.

3. In this connection, everyone is entitled, individually and in association with others, to be effectively protected under national law in reacting against or opposing, through peaceful means, activities and acts, including those by omission, attributable to States that result in violations of human rights and fundamental freedoms, as well as acts of violence perpetrated by groups or individuals that affect the enjoyment of human rights and fundamental freedoms.

Article 13

Everyone has the right, individually and in association with others, to solicit, receive and utilize resources for the express purpose of promoting and protecting human rights and fundamental freedoms, through peaceful means, in accordance with article 3 of the present Declaration.

Article 14

1. The State has the responsibility to take legislative, judicial, administrative or other appropriate measures to promote the understanding by all persons under its jurisdiction of their civil, political, economic, social and cultural rights.

2. Such measures shall include, *inter alia*:

   (a) The publication and widespread availability of national laws and regulations and of applicable basic international human rights instruments;

   (b) Full and equal access to international documents in the field of human rights, including the State's periodic reports to the bodies established by the international human rights treaties to which it is a party, as well as the summary records of discussions and the official reports of these bodies.

3. The State shall ensure and support, where appropriate, the creation and development of further independent national institutions for the promotion and protection of human rights and fundamental freedoms in all territory under its jurisdiction, whether they be ombudsmen, human rights commissions or any other form of national institution.

Article 15

The State has the responsibility to promote and facilitate the teaching of human rights and fundamental freedoms at all levels of education, and to ensure that all those responsible for training lawyers, law enforcement officers, the personnel of the armed forces and public officials include appropriate elements of human rights teaching in their training programme.

Article 16

Individuals, non-governmental organizations and relevant institutions have an important role to play in contributing to making the public more aware of questions relating to all human rights and fundamental freedoms through activities such as education, training and research in these areas to strengthen further, *inter alia*, understanding, tolerance, peace and friendly relations among nations and among all racial and religious groups, bearing in mind the various backgrounds of the societies and communities in which they carry out their activities.

Article 17

In the exercise of the rights and freedoms referred to in the present Declaration, everyone, acting individually and in association with others, shall be subject only to such limitations as are in accordance with applicable international obligations and are determined by law solely for the purpose of securing due recognition and respect for the rights and freedoms of others and of meeting the just requirements of morality, public order and the general welfare in a democratic society.

Article 18
1. Everyone has duties towards and within the community in which alone the free and full development of his or her personality is possible.

2. Individuals, groups, institutions and non-governmental organizations have an important role to play and a responsibility in safeguarding democracy, promoting human rights and fundamental freedoms and contributing to the promotion and advancement of democratic societies, institutions and processes.

3. Likewise, they have an important role and a responsibility in contributing, as appropriate, to the promotion of the right of everyone to a social and international order in which the rights and freedoms set forth in the Universal Declaration of Human Rights and other human rights instruments can be fully realized.

Article 19
Nothing in the present Declaration shall be interpreted as implying for any individual, group or organ of society or any State the right to engage in any activity or to perform any act aimed at the destruction of the rights and freedoms referred to in the present Declaration.

Article 20
Nothing in the present Declaration shall be interpreted as permitting States to support and promote activities of individuals, groups of individuals, institutions or non-governmental organizations contrary to the provisions of the Charter of the United Nations.

Paris Declaration

by the Human Rights Defenders Summit, 10 December 1998

The Paris Declaration was adopted by the Human Rights Defenders Summit on 10 December 1998, the 50th anniversary of the Universal Declaration of Human Rights. The Summit, held in Paris at the Palais de Chaillot, was organized jointly by four non-governmental organizations – Amnesty International, the *Fédération Internationale des Ligues des Droits de l'Homme* (International Federation of Human Rights Leagues), *France Libertés* and ATD *Quart-Monde* – and brought together 350 human rights defenders from over 100 countries.

We, human rights defenders,

1. **Are gathered** as a World Summit of human rights defenders on the occasion of the fiftieth anniversary of the Universal Declaration of Human Rights at the Palais de Chaillot, a place of symbolic importance where this Declaration was adopted on 10 December 1948 by the Member States of the United Nations;

2. **We are committed** in our daily lives to make a reality of the high aspirations of the Universal Declaration of Human Rights for all people throughout the world of all the rights guaranteed by the international and regional instruments for the protection of human rights;

3. **We insist** that human rights are universal, indivisible and inalienable and represent the birthright of all men, women and children and the common legacy of humanity which binds us and future generations;

4. **We welcome** the fact that, in the last fifty years, the increasing number of organizations and individuals who defend human rights has opened up new possibilities for action and considerably strengthened the influence of human rights defenders at national and international levels;

5. **We believe** that the Universal Declaration of Human Rights represents "a common standard of achievement for all peoples and all nations", and establishes, for the present and the future, principles essential for living in society with respect for human dignity; and that, as such, the Universal Declaration constitutes an indisputable moral and legal reference;

6. **We are witnesses** to the fact that in the fifty years since the adoption of the Universal Declaration of Human Rights, "disregard and contempt for human rights" remain the everyday reality in which many people continue to live and that human rights violations take on increasingly varied and complex forms, involving a growing number of actors, particularly economic actors, in the context of globalization;

7. **We affirm that**:

7.1 it is the responsibility of States to ensure the realization of all human rights enshrined in the Universal Declaration of Human Rights and other international and regional human rights instruments,

7.2 human rights are the concern of the international community as recognized in the Vienna Declaration and Plan of Action and it is the responsibility of all in that community, intergovernmental organizations, financial institutions, multinational corporations and private business, to contribute to their realization,

7.3 it is the right of any individual to protect and promote the human rights enshrined in the Universal Declaration of Human Rights and other international and regional human rights instruments, in conformity with them;

8. **We denounce** the growing disparity between the often dramatic reality of human rights violations in many countries and the rhetorical speeches made by those same States to support their international image;

9. **We denounce** the attempts by certain States to justify or excuse human rights violations in the name of cultural, religious or historical specificity, or of particular or national security interests; and by misleadingly setting civil and political rights against economic, social and cultural rights and the right to development; or, on the contrary, by denying the value of the latter;

10. **We denounce** economic and social insecurity, which in its most serious and persistent forms leads to extreme poverty and exclusion, and constitutes a violation of human rights; we stress that those who are subject to conditions of extreme poverty are among the principal victims of the full range of human rights abuses and that the efforts they expend in their daily struggle to stay alive place them among human rights defenders;

11. **We denounce** the failure of states to address impunity which constitutes one of the main obstacle to the full respect of human rights and which continues to obstruct the work of human rights defenders; we welcome the creation of the International Criminal Court and call upon States to ratify its Statute immediately and to ensure that it functions efficiently and effectively;

In this spirit,

12. **We affirm** that the realization of all human rights remains today as yesterday, the common aim for which we live, work and act and that we are resolute in our belief that until

human rights are respected for all, the peace and security for which we all strive will remain unattainable;

13. **We invite** all people, individually or collectively, to contribute to the realization of the rights guaranteed by the Universal Declaration of Human Rights and other international and regional instruments, as proclaimed in particular in the Declaration for the protection of human rights defenders adopted by the United Nations;

14. **We deplore** the fact that the increase in the number and influence of human rights defenders in the world has been accompanied by a development and systematisation of repressive measures and practices used against them;

15. **We deplore** the fact that in some countries, those systematic measures of repression are such that women and men have no means of promoting and protecting human rights and fundamental freedoms at a national level;

16. **We denounce** in particular the fact that human rights defenders are a target of those whose regimes and practices they condemn; and that, because of their commitment, they are among the victims of summary executions, enforced disappearances, torture, arbitrary detention, violations of the right to a fair trial, freedom of opinion, expression, association, assembly, demonstration, movement, the right to privacy, the right to employment and employment rights, the right to housing, health, education and culture and that they are increasingly forced into exile or enforced displacement, or to live in inhuman or degrading conditions;

17. **We condemn** the proliferation of systematic measures and practices used by States to prevent or impede the legitimate work of human rights defenders, including censorship and seizure of publications, defamation, administrative and police

harassment, intimidation, implication in criminal cases, their identification with 'terrorist' groups, restrictions imposed on the creation or registration of associations, the legal and administrative obstacles to the right of access to and dissemination of information, the surveillance and control of access to funding and the use made of such funds, the creation by the authorities of State-controlled non-governmental organizations, reliance on a state of emergency or public order requirements, impunity for the perpetrators of such acts against human rights defenders;

18. **We express** our solidarity with those whose rights are violated without any recourse to mechanisms for the protection of human rights because of the systematic repression of their rights;

19. **We call upon** States to fulfill their obligations under international human rights law and to respect, and enforce respect for, the right to freedom of action for human rights defenders, and to this end:

19.1 to fulfill their obligation, in accordance with the Universal Declaration of Human Rights and other international or regional instruments, to which they have freely subscribed, not to impede the free and effective exercise of the right to protect and promote human rights;

19.2 to adopt the necessary measures to guarantee this right and protect those exercising it; in particular by ensuring that their national laws are in conformity with the Universal Declaration of Human Rights and other international and regional human rights instruments;

19.3 and to provide such protection against acts or omissions of the State, as well as against acts of violence and affronts to human dignity perpetrated by armed groups, private groups or individuals;

20. **We call upon** intergovernmental organizations, international or regional, to protect human rights defenders and to this end, to set up the necessary instruments and mechanisms to guarantee effectively the freedom of action of human rights defenders, and to protect them against all forms of repression; and, in this respect:

20.1 welcome the United Nations General Assembly's adoption finally on 10 December 1998, of the Declaration for the protection of human rights defenders[1] which has been in preparation for thirteen years;

20.2 call upon States to immediately take the necessary measures at national and international levels to ensure the effective implementation of the rights enunciated in that Declaration;

21. **We reaffirm** the fact that the realization of all the rights enshrined in the Universal Declaration of Human Rights is the responsibility of everyone, and we call upon private business, multinational companies and international financial institutions to ensure that their strategies and projects contribute to the implementation of civil, cultural, economic, political and social rights, and do not obstruct the freedom of action of human rights defenders;

22. **Finally, we urge** men and women of all ages and all organs of society to engage in their daily lives in their communities to respect and promote all rights for all people everywhere, and to join us to make of the high aspirations proclaimed by the Universal Declaration of Human Rights a reality for present and future generations.

---

[1] Declaration on the Right and Responsibility of Individuals, Groups and Organs of Society to Promote and Protect Universally Recognized Human Rights and Fundamental Freedoms.

SELECTED STATISTICS

AMNESTY INTERNATIONAL MEMBERSHIP

In 1998 there were more than 1,000,000 Amnesty International members and supporters in over 140 countries and territories. There were more than 4,200 local Amnesty International groups, registered with the International Secretariat, plus around 3,200 youth and student groups and professional groups, in more than 90 countries and territories throughout the world. In addition, there were many hundreds of other coordinators, groups, specialized networks, individual members, subscribers and supporters.

LONG-TERM GROUP WORK

Amnesty International local groups worked on behalf of more than 5,000 named individuals, including prisoners of conscience and victims of other human rights violations, whose cases had been assigned to them as long-term Action Files, or as medium-term actions through a Regional Action Network (RAN). There are 23 RANs, involving around 1,800 groups, which cover human rights abuses in every country of the world.

During the year, groups worked on more than 2,100 Action Files and RAN actions, of which 330 had been launched during the year, on behalf of victims of human rights violations in 86 countries and territories. During 1998 Amnesty International was able to close more than 200 group assignments on the detention of prisoners of conscience and possible prisoners of conscience.

Amnesty International sections maintain networks of over 1,000 country and RAN coordinators – individual activists with specialist knowledge of particular countries or regions, to support the work of the wider membership, including local groups.

URGENT ACTION APPEALS

During 1998 Amnesty International initiated 425 actions which required urgent appeals from the Urgent Action network. There were also 272 calls for further appeals on actions already issued. Members of the Urgent Action network were therefore asked to send appeals on 697 occasions. These actions were issued on behalf of people in 94 countries and territories.

The 425 new actions were issued on behalf of people who were either at risk or had been victims of the following human rights violations: torture or ill-treatment – 131 cases; "disappearance" – 50 cases; judicial execution – 107 cases; political killings and death threats – 60 cases; and legal concerns – 49 cases. (These categories are not mutually exclusive; more than one concern may have been featured in an action.) Other concerns included ill health (31 cases), deaths in custody (two cases) and *refoulement* (forcible repatriation) of asylum-seekers (21 cases).

AMNESTY INTERNATIONAL FUNDING

The international budget adopted by Amnesty International for the financial year April 1998 to March 1999 was £17,673,000. This sum represents approximately one quarter of the estimated income likely to be raised during the year by the movement's national sections to finance their campaigning and other activities. Amnesty International's national sections and local volunteer groups are primarily responsible for funding the movement. An international fundraising program is being developed. No funds are sought or accepted from governments for Amnesty International's work investigating and campaigning against human rights violations. The donations that sustain this work come from the organization's members and the public.

RELIEF

During the financial year April 1998 to March 1999, the International Secretariat of Amnesty International distributed an estimated £220,000 in relief (financial assistance) to victims of human rights violations such as prisoners of conscience and recently released prisoners of conscience and their dependants, and for the medical treatment of torture victims. In addition, the organization's sections and groups distributed a further substantial amount, much of it in the form of modest payments by local groups to their adopted prisoners of conscience and dependent families.

Amnesty International's ultimate goal is to end human rights violations, but so long as they continue it tries to provide practical help to the victims. Relief is an important aspect of this work. Sometimes Amnesty International provides financial assistance directly to individuals. At other times, it works through local bodies such as local and national human rights organizations so as to ensure that resources are used as effectively as possible for those in most need. When Amnesty International asks an intermediary to distribute relief payments on its behalf, it stipulates precisely the intended purpose and beneficiaries, and requires the intermediary to report back fully on the expenditure of the funds.